Systems Auditability & Control Study

EXECUTIVE REPORT

Prepared for:
THE INSTITUTE OF INTERNAL AUDITORS, INC.
Altamonte Springs, Florida

Researched by:
STANFORD RESEARCH INSTITUTE
Malin E. See
Tom S. Eason

Under a grant from:
INTERNATIONAL BUSINESS MACHINES CORPORATION

ABOUT SAC PROJECT ADMINISTRATION

This project was administered by The Institute of Internal Auditors (IIA), an international, nonprofit organization devoted to the advancement of the auditing profession. IIA utilized its resources, over 14,000 members in 64 lands and a 51-member staff, to administer the project and publish the three reports which resulted from the study. For many years, The Institute of Internal Auditors has been concerned with the problem of system auditability and control. For this reason, a grant was sought and obtained from International Business Machines Corporation for the purpose of compiling the best known systems control and audit practices in use today. The grant of $500,000 from IBM permitted IIA to contract the services of the Stanford Research Institute (SRI). SRI's independent study produced three reports: Executive, Data Processing Control Practices, and Data Processing Audit Practices. To assure wide dissemination of the reports, The Institute distributed over 4,000 sets of the reports at no cost to the chief executive officer of organizations represented by its members. In addition, each IIA member received a complimentary copy of the Data Processing Audit Practices report. The Institute of Internal Auditors is pleased to have been of service to the auditing profession, to the business community and to government organizations by administering this unique project.

ISBN 0-89413-050-1

CONTENTS

FIGURES

Figure No.		Page No.

TABLES

Table No.		Page No.

FOREWORD

It is commonly accepted that the function of auditing and controlling data processing systems in many organizations is lagging behind the data processing capabilities. Expanding the use of the computer, discovering new applications, and putting these applications to use in processing and decision-making operations have appeared to be more important than simultaneously considering the development and implementation of adequate controls over these new applications.

This Systems Auditability and Control (SAC) research project was founded on the belief that audit and control techniques have been developed by many of the larger organizations. In concert with The Institute of Internal Auditors' motto "Progress Through Sharing," it was felt that there would be considerable value in providing a compendium of these proven controls and techniques to the auditing and data processing communities. These project reports are designed to provide practitioners with practical solutions to the known current problems associated with computer audit and control.

The Institute believes this is the first definitive step in providing a current comprehensive framework for the auditability of computer system applications. The Institute is indebted to the organizations that participated in the fieldwork. Their experience should provide internal auditors and computer system analysts with an insight into the various methods with which practitioners approach their responsibilities in designing, controlling, and auditing the total information processing system.

The Institute of Internal Auditors expresses its appreciation to the IBM Corporation, which provided the funding for this project. The Institute expresses its appreciation to all those who contributed to the completion of this project, including the Stanford Research Institute which undertook the fieldwork, and the Advisory Committee whose interest, advice, and direction contributed a great deal to the successful completion of this project.

The Institute extends a special recognition to the project team headed by Mr. William E. Perry, director of EDP and research for The IIA and to the SAC Steering Committee who were so helpful to him, including: Mr. Edward T. Johnson of the IBM Corporation, Mr. Frederick B. Palmer of the Colgate-Palmolive Company, and Mr. Frank F. George of the Norton Company.

Stanley C. Gross, CIA
International President

ACKNOWLEDGMENTS

SRI appreciates and acknowledges the participation, assistance, and general cooperation of the people contacted during this study. The willing participation of firms visited by SRI has been essential in compiling much of the information upon which these reports are based. Similarly, the interest and response of firms included in the mail survey phase of the research have been essential in identifying broad trends in both internal audit and controls in the data processing environment.

SRI is particularly grateful to the advisory and steering committees formed by The Institute of Internal Auditors to review project progress and direction. Consultation with the research staff of The Institute of Internal Auditors has been important to the successful completion of this work. Their contribution is also gratefully acknowledged.

Systems Auditability and Control Steering Committee

Frank F. George, CIA
Chief Auditor
Norton Company

Edward T. Johnson
Program Manager
Information Systems Control & Auditability
IBM Corporation

Frederick B. Palmer, CIA
Project Manager — MIS Quality Assurance
Colgate-Palmolive Company

William E. Perry, CIA, CPA
Director of EDP and Research
The Institute of Internal Auditors

Project Coordinator

H. C. Warner, CIA
Assistant Director EDP and Research
The Institute of Internal Auditors

Systems Auditability and Control Advisory Committee

Donald L. Adams
Managing Director,
Administrative Services
AICPA

F. Andrew Best
Computer Audit Specialist
Advanced Techniques Consultants, Inc.
Affiliation: Former Director of
Advanced Techniques
Department of Agriculture

L. C. Bethards
Manager, Systems Auditing
Federal Reserve Bank of Kansas City
Affiliation: SHARE, Inc.

Richard C. Bluestine
Hurdman & Cranstoun

Wayne S. Boutell
Professor of Business Administration
University of California

J. D. Bradt
General Auditor
Imperial Oil Ltd.
Affiliation: Past President,
The Institute of Internal Auditors

Charles L. Brown
Divisional V. P. &
Director of Auditing
J. C. Penney Co., Inc.

John C. Burton
Deputy Mayor for Finance
The City of New York
Affiliation: Former Chief Accountant,
Securities and Exchange Commission

Benjamin Conway
Manager, Information System Audits
International Business
Machines Corporation

Garland Cupp
Director of Business Systems Services
McDonnell Douglas Corporation
Past President, GUIDE International

Gordon B. Davis
Professor
University of Minnesota

Ruth M. Davis
Director, Institute for Computer
Sciences and Technology
National Bureau of Standards

William J. Duane, Jr.
General Auditor
Manufacturers Hanover Trust Co.

David V. Dunbar
Director of Personnel & Administration
Comptrollers & Finance Departments
Bell Canada

J. R. Ellison
Manager Computer Security & Privacy
The National Computing Centre
Manchester, UK

Arthur Fields
Second Vice-President
The Chase Manhattan Bank N.A.

John C. Gambles
Partner
Deloitte, Haskins & Sells
Affiliation: Canadian Institute of
Chartered Accountants

George Glaser
Consultant
Affiliation: Past President, American
Federation of Information Processing
Societies

Richard J. Guiltinan
Partner
Arthur Andersen & Co.

Vico E. Henriques
Vice President
Computer and Business Equipment
Manufacturers Association

William W. Higgins
V. P. for Automated Systems
Advanced Technological Services, Inc.
Affiliation: Former Director for Data
Automation Department of Defense

Stephen Landekich
Research Director
National Association of Accountants

H. Clifford Lazarine
Manager Information Systems
Texas Instruments, Inc.

David H. Li
Associate Director
Cost Accounting Standards Board

William C. Mair
Partner
Touche Ross & Co.

Benjamin R. Makela
Research Director
Financial Executives
Research Foundation

Lynn J. McKell
Associate Professor
Institute of Professional Accountancy
Brigham Young University
Affiliation: American Accounting
Association

Mort Nelson
Director of Education
Society of Industrial Accountants
of Canada

Frederick L. Neumann
Professor of Accountancy
University of Illinois at
Urbana-Champaign

John Nuxall
Partner
Peat, Marwick, Mitchell & Co.

Robert W. Olsen
President
Computer Services Corporation
Affiliation: Past President ADAPSO

Robert W. Parker
V. P., Director of Corporate Systems
Merrill Lynch, Pierce, Fenner & Smith

E. Read Peirce
General Auditor
Burroughs Corporation

Charles R. Perkett
Assistant to the Financial Vice President
Norton Company

Ken Pollock, CPA
Assistant Director for ADP Policy
U.S. General Accounting Office

Shirley F. Prutch
Director, Advanced Systems
Martin Marietta Corporation
Affiliation: Past President SHARE, Inc.

James H. Reber
Manufacturing Control
Systems Administrator
Sperry-New Holland, European Division
Former member SAC Steering Committee

Richard A. Ress
Manager, Audit & Internal Control
Shell Oil Co.

Arnold Schneidman
Partner
Seymour Schneidman & Associates
Affiliation: ACUTE

Ilario Simonette
Principal
Peat, Marwick, Mitchell & Co.
Affiliation: GUIDE International

Harry Steele
Director of Services
Society for Worldwide Interbank
Financial Telecommunication S. C.
Brussels, Belgium

Berny L. Thurman, Jr.
Assistant Comptroller
U.S. Steel Corporation

George R. Troost
General Auditor
General Motors Corporation

Norman L. Vincent
Vice President — Data Processing
State Farm Mutual Automobile
Insurance Company

Joseph J. Wasserman
Consultant
Past President, Computer Audit
Systems, Inc.

Frederick Weingarten
Program Director — Special Projects
National Science Foundation

Harold Weiss
President
Automation Training Center

EXECUTIVE SUMMARY
INTRODUCTION

During the past few years, some spectacular losses have befallen companies that had not installed adequate controls and audit provisions in their electronic data processing systems. Among these were highly publicized — and embarrassing — cases of erroneous payment, miscalculations of sales or inventories, misuses of information obtained from computer files, and outright fraud.

While by no means widespread, these incidents quite naturally aroused concern among managers in business and government, who had come to rely more and more on computer-generated information as a basis for decision making and on computer files for storage of vital information. If the accuracy, completeness, and security of such data could not reasonably be assured, then the integrity of the organization might be in jeopardy.

Top management, as well as regulatory agencies and the general public, have tended to rely increasingly on the internal audit community to protect organizations against the hazards of inadequate control in electronic data processing (EDP) systems. However, preliminary investigations into the problem revealed a dangerous gap; auditing and control procedures for EDP systems have failed to keep pace with the introduction of new technology and new concepts in EDP system design. Though techniques for EDP auditing and control have been developed in some organizations, these have not been widely communicated or extended for general application to potential problem situations.

It was these conditions that provided the impetus for this study — believed to be the first definitive evaluation of the subject of data processing system audit and control. The project was conceived and organized in 1975 by The Institute of Internal Auditors, with the objectives of:

- Obtaining a comprehensive survey of the present status of EDP system audit and control, including an identification of current trends and a documentation of what specific audit and control techniques now in use have proven to be of practical value.

- Increasing management's awareness of changes in the data processing environment as they affect internal audit and the controls governing data processing.

- Placing the auditability and control of computer-based information systems in a proper perspective within the total system environment.

The research was funded by International Business Machines Corporation and performed by Stanford Research Institute (SRI). The scope of the study was international, covering the United States, Canada, the major Western European countries, and Japan.

THE GENESIS OF THE PROBLEM

A number of forces have interacted to heighten the importance of EDP audit and control:

Management's Information Needs — Managers at all levels have become increasingly dependent on data processing for the information they need to plan, evaluate, and control the activities of their organizations. As businesses have expanded geographically — both within countries and across national borders — their need for communication of data has intensified. Similarly, acquisitions, consolidations, and diversifications made in attempts to expand markets and product lines have created a need for data interchange among previously unrelated management information systems. These factors, in conjunction with the complexity of doing business internationally, have made accurate and complete management information a critical need.

This demand for information exists among leaders of government and noncommercial organizations as well. The motivations to increase cost effectiveness in operations and to improve service to their constituencies have inevitably led government and social institutions to rely more on data processing.

Government and Association Requirements — Federal, state, and local regulations, along with their associated reporting requirements, have caused an enormous increase in the amount and kinds of information that organizations must collect, process, and retain. Occupational health and safety programs, affirmative action, pension plan reporting, and consumer protection laws are but a few of the government activities that are having repercussions for organizations' data processing systems. Companies frequently find it necessary to modify and expand existing systems in order to satisfy reporting requirements, and to avoid the penalties that may be exacted for inadequate or inaccurate reporting.

In a similar way, new accounting standards and guidelines promulgated by professional groups impose substantial new requirements on computer-based information systems. Organizations active in this area include the American Institute of Certified Public Accountants, the Financial Accounting Standards Board, the Cost Accounting Standards Board — all in the United States — and their counterparts in other countries.

AUDITABILITY VERSUS CONTROL

The title of the study — Systems Auditability and Control — reflects the interrelationship between internal audit and control. The *auditability* of computer-based information systems refers to the features and characteristics needed to *verify* the adequacy of controls as well as to verify the accuracy and completeness of data processing results. Systems *control* pertains to the mechanisms within the total system environment that *ensure* the accuracy and completeness of the computer-based information system and its output. Thus, the scope of this study includes both internal audit and internal control, two separate but closely related subjects.

This division is reflected in the two technical reports that serve as companions to this Executive Report. They are intended as reference works to aid managers in charge of data processing systems and managers concerned with the audit of EDP systems in evaluating and establishing adequate, complementary audit and control procedures.

The Data Processing Audit Practices Report presents information relating to auditing in the computer-based information systems environment. Current data processing audit methodology, tools, and techniques are presented. The analysis is written primarily for internal auditors and presumes that the reader has some auditing background. It will, however, be of interest to systems designers and data processing managers who work with internal auditors or are concerned with improving auditability of computer-based information systems.

The Data Processing Control Practices Report presents information relating to control techniques applicable to computer-based information systems, computer service center operations, and the system development process. It provides an overview of data processing control practices and describes specific controls and techniques of practical value. The Data Processing Control Practices Report complements the audit information presented in the Data Processing Audit Practices Report and is written for systems analysts, computer programmers, data processing users, auditors, and others concerned with effective auditability and control in an increasingly complex data processing environment.

Advancing EDP Technology — Changes in data processing technology have occurred concurrently with the expansion of management's information needs and government requirements. Not only has the number of computer systems installed multiplied — from about 25,000 general purpose computers in the U.S. in 1966 to over 70,000 in 1975 — but new capabilities and user applications have continually been developed and refined. These advances have had a number of implications for auditing and control procedures.

The growth in the use of data communications to connect processing facilities at many locations is one example of how new technology has complicated auditing and control. The number of data communications terminals installed was less than 250,000 in 1970, but by the end of 1975, the figure was almost a million. A further jump to three million terminals is expected by 1980, thus multiplying the number of locations subject to control and audit.

Moreover, new concepts in the organization of computer-based information systems have resulted in a trend toward integration of related systems. The result is greater efficiency and a reduced need for manual intervention at the interfaces. A corollary outcome is substantially increased difficulty of auditing the integrated systems and a correspondingly greater exposure to loss. In these circumstances, many traditional control and audit techniques are outmoded.

Figure 1 shows how the forces of management's information needs, government and association requirements and advancing EDP technology interact to strain the organization's EDP auditing and control mechanisms. The consequence of improper safeguards is the vulnerability of the organization to a variety of potentially costly hazards, as outlined in the next section.

Figure 1

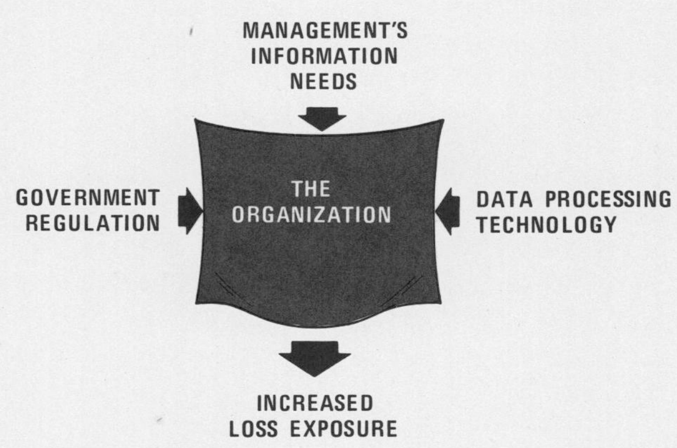

FORCES AFFECTING COMPUTER-BASED INFORMATION SYSTEMS

THE HAZARDS OF INADEQUATE AUDIT AND CONTROL

The potential for loss associated with the use of data processing is increasing as procedures once performed manually are automated. Today, computer programs rather than human beings perform many of the checks and verifications necessary to ensure accuracy and completeness of data and records. This development has exposed information systems to the possibility of loss from several sources.

The principal potentials for loss cited by respondents to the mail survey conducted as part of this study, in order of frequency, were:

- Errors and omissions
- Improper controls
- Inadequate system design
- Fraud and defalcation
- Failure to comply with standards or procedures.

The consequences of lapses such as those listed were highlighted in responses to questionnaires from executives whose companies are considered to be in the forefront of EDP auditing and control. A number of those interviewed indicated that although the number of errors generally does not increase as a result of the transition from a manual to a computer-based information system, the effects of any one error are potentially much greater now than in the past. Moreover, tracing an error has been found to be considerably more difficult.

Despite a growing awareness of the potential for loss, most top executives interviewed by SRI seemed confident that actual losses are minimal. Yet while some of them maintained that they have not experienced losses related to data processing, they simultaneously admitted that they had no formal procedures to identify and report incidents of this sort. In fact, no organization contacted during the study felt it had a satisfactory method of measuring overall loss or loss potential.

THE CONCLUSIONS IN BRIEF

The results of this study show that, although data processing systems and internal audit techniques have been evolving, there has been little coordination between the two disciplines. From the standpoint of those managing the EDP facility, the internal auditors' mandate and their scope of activities are not clear. At the same time, internal auditors are faced with the task of investigating an environment in which most of them have only limited experience, knowledge, and tools. Compounding these conditions is the fact that top management in many organizations has not been sufficiently informed to give adequate attention to the potential repercussions of inadequate EDP audit and control procedures.

In addition to the above general findings, eight specific conclusions were drawn from the results of the study:

1. The primary responsibility for overall internal control resides with top management, while the operational responsibility for the accuracy and completeness of computer-base information systems should reside with users.

2. There is a need for improved controls because inadequate attention has been given to the importance of internal controls in the data processing environment.

3. Internal auditors must participate in the system development process to ensure that appropriate audit and control features are designed into new computer-based information systems.

4. Verification of controls must occur both before and after installation of computer-based information systems.

5. As a result of the growth in complexity and use of computer-based information systems, needs exist for greater internal audit involvement relative to auditing in the data processing environment.

6. An important need exists for EDP audit staff development because few internal audit staffs have enough data processing knowledge and experience to audit effectively in the data processing environment.

7. Few current EDP audit tools and techniques are adequate to the needs of the EDP auditors as they approach the task of verifying the accuracy and completeness of data processing activities and results. New tools and techniques are needed.

8. Many organizations are not adequately evaluating their audit and control functions in the data processing environment. Top management should initiate a periodic assessment of its audit and control programs.

The section of this report entitled "Discussion of Conclusions" provides support for each of the findings presented above. That discussion is a distillation of the analyses reported in the two technical reports that accompany this volume.

Table 1 INDICATED MANAGEMENT ACTIONS

One outcome of this study was the identification of a series of management actions designed to reasonably assure that computer-based information systems are developed with adequate controls, are auditable, and operate in a reliable manner. While it was not within the scope of the study to fix specific responsibility for these various management activities, the following list is indicative of the management concerns and the probable location of primary (P) and supporting (S) responsibility for each:

	Responsibility		
Action	Executive Management	Audit Management	Data Processing Management
Ensure that all management realize the importance of internal audit in data processing.	P	S	S
Issue a clearly defined internal audit mandate that specifies the responsibility of internal audit as it relates to all phases of data processing.	P	S	S
Clearly define the working relationship among users, internal auditors, and the data processing department for the development and maintenance of computer-based information systems.	P	S	S
Encourage the development of new data processing control techniques and internal audit approaches to ensure the reliability of computer-based information systems.	P	S	S
Require the development of control guidelines.	P	S	S
Ensure that internal audit participates in the system development process.	P	S	S
Ensure adequate preinstallation testing of computer-based information systems.	S	S	P
Ensure that periodic postinstallation verification takes place.	S	P	S
When auditing computer-based information systems, computer service center operations, and system development, ensure that there are reviews of controls, test to verify the controls, and tests to verify the data.	S	P	S
Encourage data processing and internal audit to work together to achieve improved system audit and control capabilities.	P	S	S
Ensure that training programs are developed to provide the needed skills to audit data processing, and also to reflect the internal audit discipline.	S	P	S
Upgrade the quality and quantity of EDP auditors. As a starting point, use individuals from the internal audit staff with a specific interest in data processing.	S	P	S
Add data processing personnel to the EDP audit staff for specialized data processing assistance.	S	P	S
Ensure that data processing, internal audit, and external audit work together to develop required EDP audit tools and techniques.	P	S	S
Ensure that assessments of the internal audit function are performed jointly by internal audit and data processing.	P	S	S

PROJECT METHODOLOGY

Two complementary objectives guided the formulation of the research methodology for this project. The first objective was to identify and document specific audit and control techniques of proven value. The second objective was to identify practices and trends in internal audit in data processing for broad segments of business and government, both domestic and international. The two major approaches used to achieve these objectives were field interviews and a mail survey.

Members of the research team visited 45 selected business and government organizations in the United States, Canada, Europe, and Japan. These companies were believed to be leaders in either their approach to data processing or internal auditing in the data processing environment. The interviews yielded valuable management perspectives on trends and expertise in EDP audit and control, as well as much detail on the specific audit and control techniques currently in use.

The mail survey was designed to identify practices and trends in internal audit in data processing for broad segments of business and government. For the survey, SRI developed three separate questionnaires — one each for executive management, internal audit management, and data processing management. A total of 4,725 questionnaires were sent out. Replies numbered 1,852: 631 from executive management, 606 from internal audit management, and 615 from data processing management — yielding an unusually high response (39%) for this type of study. Complete sets of questionnaires were received from 482 organizations.

Seven different sampling frames for use in the mail survey were designed by SRI and approved by The Institute of Internal Auditors. From these sampling frames, organizations were selected for the mail survey in each geographic area. In view of the differences in management and audit practices in Canada, Europe, and Japan, it is difficult to make direct comparisons with the United States. Therefore, the Primary U.S. Mail Survey was the only survey intended to provide statistically supportable generalizations.

The methodology for this research was established by SRI in conjunction with the Steering Committee and the Advisory Committee of The Institute of Internal Auditors. For a complete description of the research methodology, see the appendix to the Data Processing Audit Practices Report or the Data Processing Control Practices Report.

DISCUSSION OF CONCLUSIONS

MANAGEMENT RESPONSIBILITIES

As part of its overall responsibilities, the top management of any organization must be concerned with the internal controls and provisions for auditing data processing systems. Evidence gathered during the survey for this project indicates that in many organizations there is not yet a clear delineation of the responsibilities among top management, data processing, internal audit, and the users of EDP systems for the control of such systems.

The responsibility problem has three aspects. Ultimately, it is the users of a computer-based information system who bear the main burden of ensuring the accuracy and completeness of inputs and the eventual reports. However, users typically are not technically competent to judge which controls will yield the degree of reliability they expect. For this, they tend to rely on specialists in data processing.

While the data processing specialists are expected to provide whatever controls are needed in an EDP system, they do not have the complete perspective required to make actual decision on which controls should be used for what purpose, since the latter decisions affect both reliability and cost – again, the responsibility of the users.

Internal auditors must be in a position to verify that the controls are adequate and are properly used, yet the auditors must also maintain their objectivity and independence from other departments. The internal auditor frequently has come in only after a system was developed, when it may be difficult to review and verify the controls.

Since the design of a computer-based information system is extremely complicated, top management too often has tended to leave its development to the "experts," without clarifying the responsibilities to ensure that proper controls and audit capabilities are built in. Top management must now ensure that clear lines of responsibility exist for the control of data processing systems.

NEED FOR IMPROVED CONTROLS

Management relies on internal controls to ensure the reliability of information it gets from data processing systems. These internal controls govern the recording and processing of an organization's transactions and the resultant reports. Internal controls include the practices and procedures to ensure that manual and automated transactions are handled properly, and that errors are avoided or detected and corrected.

SRI believes that inadequate attention is being given to the importance of internal controls in developing computer-based information systems and in establishing data processing operations. This conclusion applies not only to individual organizations, but to the data processing industry in general. The reason is that each stage in the evolution of EDP systems brings new control problems which require new solutions.

The importance of controls for computer-based information systems has been recognized as a result of the losses arising from errors, omissions, and frauds reported in the media. Improvements are being made, but several years may be required to incorporate needed controls in existing computer-based information systems, particularly in organizations with a large number of such systems.

The scope of internal control in the data processing environment includes computer-based information systems, computer service centers, and the process of systems development. Because of the different control objectives and techniques that are applicable to these three areas, it is useful to consider the requirements of each separately. The areas are, however, interdependent because they all affect the accuracy and completeness of data processing. Accordingly, it is important that control objectives and alternative control techniques be evaluated within the context of the total management information and data processing environment (see Figure 2).

Figure 2

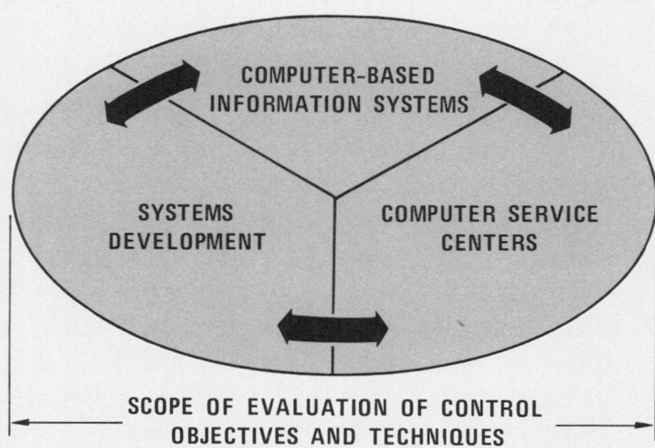

TOTAL MANAGEMENT INFORMATION AND DATA PROCESSING ENVIRONMENT

Computer-Based Information Systems Controls – These controls are important because they directly govern the flow of transactions, the maintenance of records, and the preparation of reports used by management. They include both manual and automated procedures that are unique to the requirements of individual computer-based information systems.

Computer Service Center Controls – Internal controls required within the computer service center are independent of, and in addition to, those built into computer-based information systems. The accuracy and completeness of data processing depends upon the controls governing the computer service center operations as well as controls within computer-based information systems. Important control functions within the computer service center include input-output control; production scheduling; media library facilities and procedures; equipment malfunction reporting and preventive maintenance; physical security and environmental control; separation of duties; and disaster recovery procedures.

Systems Development Controls – Formal procedures are needed to govern the systems development process and ensure that the systems are methodically designed, tested, and installed. With careful control of the systems development process, it is possible to achieve higher levels of dependability in development and maintenance of systems. This is achieved by many data processing organizations through the use of standard procedures governing computer program structure and coding, testing and user acceptance, documentation, and program change authorization and control.

Little progress has been made in developing comprehensive control guidelines for use in system development. System designers rely primarily on their prior experience to evaluate and select appropriate controls. The lack of control guidelines and standards also affects the work of internal auditors who, in the absence of guidelines, have few standards against which to evaluate the adequacy of control techniques and procedures.

In addition, control guidelines need to be developed jointly by data processing user groups, professional associations, the National Bureau of Standards, regulatory agencies, and equipment and software vendors. Coordination should be sought with similar groups in other countries, to stimulate international compatibility in the requirements for and application of EDP controls. A compendium of control guidelines would be of great benefit in promoting adequate control within individual business and governmental organizations. Management should support such broad efforts to establish effective control guidelines.

PARTICIPATION BY INTERNAL AUDIT IN SYSTEM DEVELOPMENT

Many organizations report some internal audit involvement during the development of computer-based information systems. However, most such participation is superficial. Two divergent viewpoints are offered on the desirability of internal audit participation in system development.

Some internal auditors believe that they should review systems only after the development process is completed. They believe independence and objectivity are lost if they actively participate in system development. This viewpoint, frequently encountered in interviews, seems now to be giving way to that of the internal auditors who believe that their early participation is the key to ensuring that controls are given proper consideration in the design of a system. They argue that it is too expensive to modify application systems once they are completed, and thus, that internal auditors have little opportunity to affect the adequacy of controls unless they participate in development. The fear of a loss of objectivity is overcome by placing the operational responsibility for internal controls where it belongs, with data processing users; the internal auditor's responsibility is limited to making recommendations for appropriate audit and control techniques that should be included in computer-based systems.

Results of the Primary U.S. Mail Survey presented in Figure 3 indicate that internal audit involvement with computer-based information systems development has not measured up to management's expectations.

Survey questions distinguished degrees of internal auditor involvement, as perceived by the different types of management, from "none" to "heavy." Figure 3 shows the small percentages of heavy involvement, especially in the system development stages. It also shows that internal auditors believe that their involvement is greater than do data processing managers. These results indicate that better understanding and closer cooperation is needed between internal auditors, top management, and data processing management regarding the scope and content of EDP audit activities. Figure 3 indicates that heavy internal auditor involvement progressively increases in subsequent stages of computer-based information systems development from about 2% at the development requirements stage, to 20% to 25% after installation. Several leading organizations interviewed by SRI have internal audit programs that include heavy involvement during system development. The practices of these organizations are not, however, representative of the majority of organizations contacted, particularly smaller organizations with internal auditors who have little, if any, involvement in the system development process.

SRI believes that effective involvement in system development is possible when:

- Top management clarifies the responsibility for controls and the scope of the internal audit mandate as it relates to all phases of data processing, particularly the system development phase.
- Data processing accepts the expanded mandate and role of internal audit regarding data processing activities.
- Internal auditors are able to articulate their audit objectives in terms understandable to data processing personnel.
- Audit tools and techniques are developed as an integral part of the design and implementation of computer-based information systems.

Figure 3

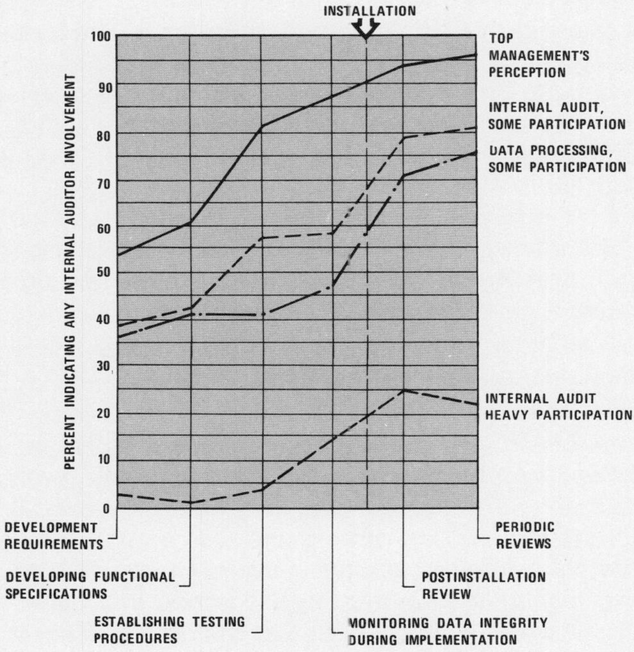

INTERNAL AUDIT INVOLVEMENT WITH COMPUTER-BASED INFORMATION SYSTEMS – PRIMARY U.S. MAIL SURVEY

Percentages are based on actual responses weighted to reflect the probable response distribution of all organizations with internal auditors in the sampling frame. See project background and methodology section for further description of weighting procedures.

VERIFICATION OF CONTROLS

The verification of computer-based information system controls must occur both before and after the installation of computer-based information systems. In this regard, it is important that:

- Adequate preinstallation testing is performed and not compromised in order to achieve system development and installation schedules.
- Effective, periodic, postinstallation verifications are performed by internal auditors, including the verification of controls as well as processing results such as records and reports.

The verification of these controls, although a new task to many internal auditors, is important to complement more traditional data verification techniques. It is, therefore, important that management recognize the value of, and ensure the performance of both pre- and post-installation audits.

Once a system has been installed and the controls verified, it is important to be sure that any modification of the system does not have the effect of defeating the controls or impairing its auditability. For this reason, internal audit should be notified whenever a system change may affect its provisions for audit.

NEED FOR IMPROVED INTERNAL AUDIT INVOLVEMENT

The role of the internal auditor with regard to data processing is changing and taking on new importance, as more functions within the organization are automated. Top management looks to internal audit to verify the effectiveness of internal controls and the reliability of data processing results. This expanded role is a logical extension of internal auditing's traditional responsibility.

Internal audit has traditionally placed emphasis on the verification of records and controls to ensure the accuracy and completeness of records and reports. The verification of records was performed manually from ledgers and other written documents. In the early years of data processing, internal auditors could still verify processing results without reviewing controls internal to data processing or tracing transactions through data processing. This internal audit approach is often described as "auditing around the computer." Little specialized EDP knowledge, tools, or techniques were required by internal auditors.

Computer-based information systems currently in use and under development present new problems for internal auditors. Changes in system design concepts and structure are taking place in both large and small organizations:

- Input transactions are being entered for immediate, on-line, processing from remote terminal locations, in contrast to single entry point, batch input, typical of earlier years.
- Single-purpose systems are being tied together so that one input transaction performs multiple functions.
- Audit trails are less visible and "hard copy" is being eliminated.

Internal auditors working in this environment report they can no longer audit around the computer and still satisfy the mandate of their management. This is because so many of the controls that ensure the accuracy and completeness of data processing are now automated and can no longer be viewed and verified through direct observation.

The general recognition of the need for an EDP audit function is a relatively recent phenomenon. Results from the Primary U.S. Mail Survey indicate that although 78% of the respondents have an internal audit function, only 62% of the respondents have an EDP audit function. Table 2 shows the growth of EDP audit functions among organizations surveyed that currently have EDP auditors. Note that 70% of the organizations that now have EDP audit functions founded that function since 1970. The development of an EDP audit function in organizations reflects greater reliance on data processing, increasingly complex management information systems, and greater reliance upon internal audit to verify the accuracy and completeness of data processing results.

Table 2

YEAR OF ESTABLISHMENT OF EDP AUDIT FUNCTION

Year Established	Percentage* Established
Before 1950	0.7%
1950-1959	3.2
1960-1964	10.8
1965-1969	15.1
1970-1974	42.0
1975-1976	28.1

Total respondents to this question = 172.

*Percentages are based on actual responses weighted to reflect the probable response distribution of all organizations in the sampling frame.

EDP AUDIT STAFF DEVELOPMENT

With the growing dependence on internal auditors to evaluate and verify important data processing control functions, the quality and quantity of the staff responsible for these activities are becoming important concerns. Most organizations that are large users of data processing need not only more but better trained EDP auditors on their internal audit staff. At the same time, there are not enough auditors with the necessary credentials to meet the demand.

Based on results of field interviews, SRI believes it is preferable to select individuals from the internal audit staff who have a specific interest and desire to work with data processing and to train them to form a cadre of internal auditors with a strong data processing orientation. Once such a nucleus is formed, this group can support other internal auditors and encourage them in their greater involvement with data processing. The activities of such an EDP audit staff may include providing technical support to the entire audit staff as well as performing specialized audits of computerized application systems within the data processing department. It may be appropriate, as involvement with data processing increases, to add data processing personnel to the EDP audit staff to provide specialized assistance in areas such as data communications.

Just as internal audit practice has not kept pace with the growing use of data processing and the introduction of new technology and application design concepts, EDP audit training programs have not kept pace with the expanding responsibilities of internal auditors. Programs designed to meet the needs of data processing professionals are not entirely satisfactory. Rather, training programs for EDP auditors must bring together information from both disciplines — data processing and internal audit.

Despite the need for more emphasis on the training of EDP auditors, results of the Primary U.S. Mail Survey indicate that about half the respondents with internal auditors have no budget at all for EDP audit training. Almost 90% of those organizations that do set aside funds for this purpose allocate to it less than 5% of their total internal audit budget. SRI believes that a greater allocation is appropriate and is justified once formalized training programs are structured.

Top management emphasis and direction is necessary to ensure that EDP auditor training is a continuing process. Because data processing technology will continue to change and grow, internal auditors will be required to keep up with the changes and anticipate new requirements. They will consequently need training on a regular, expanding basis.

NEED FOR IMPROVED EDP AUDIT TOOLS AND TECHNIQUES

SRI has identified and documented 28 tools and techniques* used by internal auditors for auditing computer-based information systems, computer service center operation, and the systems development process. However, most of these have been used as after-the-fact checks, rather than being built into the system. Few are adequate to the current or future needs of the EDP auditor. Unless greater emphasis is placed on development of such tools and techniques, the gap between the sophistication of the computer-based information systems and the capability to audit them will continue to widen.

At present, the most frequently used tool or technique is generalized audit software, a tool most suitable for verification of data. (Of respondents to the Primary U.S. Mail Survey, 33% reported employing this approach.) Use of tools and techniques designed to evaluate and verify controls is reported less often.

Efforts to develop more effective EDP audit tools and techniques can be accelerated in two ways. First, development programs within organizations should be based on cooperation among internal audit, data processing personnel, and users. Cooperation between the first two parties, though, has been insufficient in the past because of a lack of understanding between internal audit and data processing personnel of internal audit's responsibilities, goals, and approach to auditing in the data processing environment. Close interaction during system development is particularly important, since integration of audit tools and techniques into the design of systems seems to hold the most promise for effective EDP audit in the future.

Second, as in the case of control guidelines, the development work that takes place within individual organizations needs to be complemented by coordinated, industry-wide efforts involving data processing user groups, professional groups such as The Institute of Internal Auditors, The American Institute of Certified Public Accountants, and equipment and software vendors. Although useful tools and techniques can be developed within individual organizations, it seems unlikely that improvements on a broad scale can be achieved without bringing together interest groups that broadly represent the accounting and auditing professions, the data processing profession, equipment and software designers, and regulatory agencies.

Internal audit management, data processing management, and top management can encourage progress in both these areas. A first step is for management to clarify the role of internal audit in relation to the computer-based information system and data processing. A second step is internal audit to identify and define audit objectives relating to the data processing environment. A third step is to acquaint users with the need for and availability of audit tools and techniques, so they can better understand the requirements for controls in the systems they use. Once these steps are taken and the role of the EDP auditor in system development is clarified, serious efforts can get under way to close the gap between EDP audit capability and rapidly advancing data processing technology.

---

*Chapters 6 and 10 through 33 of the Data Processing Audit Practices Report deal with these tools and techniques.

NEED FOR AUDIT AND CONTROL ASSESSMENT

Top management concerned about the adequacy of systems auditability and control in their organizations should initiate periodic assessments that include three objectives:

- An evaluation of current audit and control practice and of the range of data processing skills within the internal audit staff.
- An identification of likely future trends in the development of computer-based information systems and data processing technology.
- A review of existing, and the formulation of new, programs to improve capabilities in both the audit and control areas within the data processing environment. Specific program plans, based on the organization's overall information systems plan, are needed to develop new information systems and data processing technology.

These assessments must be performed jointly by internal audit and data processing management. Appropriate action plans should then be prepared with related economic justification when possible.

In reviewing the recommendations offered after such assessments, top management must realize that it may take some time after plans are approved to achieve audit and control program objectives. Additional expenditures may be necessary or at least a reallocation of existing resouces. Such expenditures are an investment in the continuing accuracy and completeness of computer-based information system results.

COST IMPLICATIONS OF SYSTEMS AUDITABILITY AND CONTROL

Although an attempt was made during this study to identify costs associated with auditing computer-based information systems and with the implementation of necessary internal controls, little quantitative information was available to reflect either present levels of expenditure or anticipated trends. Few organizations separately budget EDP audit activities, and the costs of developing or implementing specific audit tools and techniques are typically not separately recorded. In addition, little information regarding the cost of internal control in the data processing environment is available, because few data processing organizations recognize internal control as a separate objective in systems development.

Data processing managers and internal audit managers interviewed by SRI frequently reported that they expect intensifying top management concern about potential loss exposure to result in greater emphasis on, and consequently more spending for, the development of audit and control tools and techniques. Many of these managers report that they believe higher levels of expenditure are justified.

The cost of detecting and correcting errors in computer-based information systems increases markedly at each successive stage of development and operation. Recent studies* indicate that it appears cost effective to spend more during earlier stages of the development process in an attempt to identify potential latent error conditions. The studies confirm that such effort is more than compensated by a consequent reduction in cost associated with identification and correction of errors during the operation of such systems. Similar factors affect the costs and benefits of controls and audit provisions to prevent or detect misuse of EDP systems by fraud or defalcation.

Information compiled by SRI indicates that expenditures for internal auditing will increase during the period ahead. The extension anticipated is a result of the following factors:

- Necessary investment in EDP audit training.
- Rising salaries as a result of the general demand for competent EDP auditors.
- Increasing numbers of EDP auditors as more business functions are automated.
- Greater use of data processing for audit purposes.
- Expanded participation in systems development.
- Increasingly rigorous regulatory requirements.
- Research and development of new audit tools and techniques.

Concurrently, data processing cost can also be expected to increase as a result of the following factors:

- The formation and application of control guidelines and standards for developing computer-based information systems.
- The inclusion of both audit and control objectives in system design documents.
- The inclusion of audit features and capabilities in computer-based information systems.
- More methodical systems development, including improved planning, design reviews, and preproduction testing to verify processing logic and controls.

---

*For example, *Software Reliability — Measurement and Management,* conducted at TRW Systems Group by Dr. Barry W. Boehm.

These factors represent an extension of the current practice in some well-managed organizations. The need for increased expenditures in these organizations to establish or improve data processing controls will probably have a limited impact in terms of total EDP expenditures. Organizations that have not paid adequate attention to these factors until now should expect that improvements may add significantly to the present data processing cost.

In contrast, internal audit costs can be expected to increase sharply in the near term, if internal auditors are to fulfill the role described for them in this report. Cost is not, however, the primary constraint on the development of an adequate EDP audit capability. Rather, the development of such a capability is constrained by the time required to recruit and train internal auditors in order for them to audit effectively in the data processing environment and to participate constructively in the systems development process.

SRI believes that top management interest and direction are the keys to overcoming the inertia that has prevented the development and acceptance of effective EDP audit programs. The direction of top management is needed to ensure that an appropriate internal audit mandate is established for data processing and that specific programs are established in which data processing and internal audit work together effectively.

THE INSTITUTE OF INTERNAL AUDITORS, INC.
249 Maitland Avenue, Altamonte Springs, Florida 32701

Reorder Number G320-5791

ISBN 0-89413-050-1

Systems Auditability & Control Study

DATA PROCESSING CONTROL PRACTICES REPORT

Prepared for:
THE INSTITUTE OF INTERNAL AUDITORS, INC.
Altamonte Springs, Florida

Researched by:
STANFORD RESEARCH INSTITUTE
SUSAN HIGLEY RUSSELL
TOM S. EASON J. M. FITZGERALD

Under a grant from:
INTERNATIONAL BUSINESS MACHINES CORPORATION

ABOUT SAC PROJECT ADMINISTRATION . . .

This project was administered by The Institute of Internal Auditors (IIA), an international, nonprofit organization devoted to the advancement of the auditing profession. IIA utilized its resources, over 14,000 members in 64 lands and a 51-member staff, to administer the project and publish the three reports which resulted from the study. For many years, The Institute of Internal Auditors has been concerned with the problem of system auditability and control. For this reason, a grant was sought and obtained from International Business Machines Corporation for the purpose of compiling the best known systems control and audit practices in use today. The grant of $500,000 from IBM permitted IIA to contract the services of the Stanford Research Institute (SRI). SRI's independent study produced three reports: Executive, Data Processing Control Practices, and Data Processing Audit Practices. To assure wide dissemination of the reports, The Institute distributed over 4,000 sets of the reports at no cost to the chief executive officer of organizations represented by its members. In addition, each IIA member received a complimentary copy of the Data Processing Audit Practices report. The Institute of Internal Auditors is pleased to have been of service to the auditing profession, to the business community and to government organizations by administering this unique project.

ISBN 0-89413-051-X

CONTENTS

FIGURES

TABLES

FOREWORD

It is commonly accepted that the function of auditing and controlling data processing systems in many organizations is lagging behind the data processing capabilities. Expanding the use of the computer, discovering new applications, and putting these applications to use in processing and decision-making operations have appeared to be more important than simultaneously considering the development and implementation of adequate controls over these new applications.

This Systems Auditability and Control (SAC) research project was founded on the belief that audit and control techniques have been developed by many of the larger organizations. In concert with The Institute of Internal Auditors motto "Progress Through Sharing," it was felt that there would be considerable value in providing a compendium of these proven controls and techniques to the auditing and data processing communities. These project reports are designed to provide practitioners with practical solutions to the known current problems associated with computer audit and control.

The Institute believes this is the first definitive step in providing a current comprehensive framework for the auditability of computer system applications. The Institute is indebted to the organizations who participated in the fieldwork. Their experience should provide internal auditors and computer system analysts with an insight into the various methods with which practitioners approach their responsibilities in designing, controlling, and auditing the total information processing system.

The Institute of Internal Auditors expresses its appreciation to the IBM Corporation, which provided the funding for this project. The Institute expresses its appreciation to all those who contributed to the completion of this project, including the Stanford Research Institute who undertook the fieldwork, and the Advisory Committee whose interest, advice, and direction contributed a great deal to the successful completion of this project.

The Institute extends a special recognition to the project team headed by Mr. William E. Perry, director of EDP and research for The IIA and to the SAC Steering Committee who were so helpful to him, including: Mr. Edward T. Johnson of the IBM Corporation, Mr. Frederick B. Palmer of Colgate-Palmolive Company, and Mr. Frank F. George of Norton Company.

S. Gross

Stanley C. Gross, CIA
International President

PREFACE

PROJECT BACKGROUND

The internal audit community has for some time recognized that advances in data processing are causing important changes in both the internal controls governing data processing and associated internal audit requirements. It is believed that the adequacy of internal control practices in the data processing environment has not kept pace with the expansion of data processing and the introduction of new technology and new information system design concepts. It is also believed that progress has been made in developing new techniques for audit and control in the data processing environment, but that these development efforts have occurred within a variety of organizations and on an isolated basis. As a result, although many useful solutions to specific data processing audit and control problems have been developed, they have not been widely communicated or adopted. This study was conceived in an attempt to determine current internal audit and control problems, and to document solutions that have been successfully applied. The Institute of Internal Auditors conceived and organized this study to survey the state of the art in the audit and control of computer-based information systems and data processing.

STUDY OBJECTIVES

SRI was commissioned in 1975 by The Institute of Internal Auditors to research data processing audit and control practices on an international basis. This research was funded by the IBM Corporation. Study objectives that have guided the conduct of the research and the preparation of resulting reports are threefold:

- To survey the state of the art in the audit and control of computer-based information systems and data processing to identify current trends in audit and control and to document specific audit and control techniques now in use that have been demonstrated to be of practical value.
- To increase management's awareness of the changing data processing environment as it affects internal audit and the controls governing data processing, and the need to build appropriate controls and audit procedures into computer-based information systems.
- To place internal audit and control of computer-based information systems and data processing in a proper perspective within the total information system environment.

TERMINOLOGY AND REPORTS

The name of the study, Systems Auditability and Control Study, reflects the interrelationship between internal audit and control, and the scope of the research. Systems auditability pertains to the features and characteristics of information systems needed to verify the accuracy and completeness of data processing results. Systems control pertains to the internal controls governing information systems in the data processing environment that assure the accuracy and completeness of processing results, the security of the environment in which data processing is effected, and the effectiveness of computer system design and operations. Thus, the scope of this study includes both internal audit and internal control, two separate but closely related subjects. Because considerable research has been conducted on data security and computer fraud, these areas were excluded from the study.

Audit and control in the data processing environment need to be considered together because they are two sides of the same coin. Internal control in the data processing environment covers transaction processing, record keeping, and reporting. Internal audit is the evaluation and verification of these controls and the results of data processing. Thus, internal controls, records, and reports produced by data processing are the object of internal audit. Because of this interrelationship, to consider internal audit it is necessary to consider internal control. Similarly, a comprehensive examination of the subject of internal control requires consideration of internal audit as it relates to the evaluation and verification of controls. To deal with this interrelationship, two volumes, the Data Processing Audit Practices Report and the Data Processing Control Practices Report have been prepared. They are intended as reference works to aid in evaluating and establishing audit and control procedures.

The Data Processing Audit Practices Report presents information relating to auditing in the data processing environment. Current data processing audit methodology, tools, and techniques are presented. The report is written primarily for internal auditors and presumes that the reader has some auditing background. It will, however, be of interest to system designers and data processing managers who work with internal auditors or are concerned with improving auditability of computer application systems. Chapters 5-9 of the report provide a general description of auditing in the data processing environment. Chapters 6 and 10-33 present information on audit tools and techniques applicable to auditing in the data processing environment.

The Data Processing Control Practices Report presents information relating to control techniques applicable to computer-based information systems, computer service center operations, and the information system development process. It provides an overview of data processing control practices and describes, in Chapters 5-16, specific controls and techniques of practical value. The Data Processing Control Practices Report complements the audit information presented in the Data Processing Audit Practices Report and is written for system analysts, computer programmers, data processing users and auditors, and others concerned with effective auditability and control. The first four chapters in each of these reports are identical, with the exception of a few pages at the end of Chapter 4.

A third document, the Executive Report, provides a high-level overview of the study and presents the principal findings and conclusions.

SCOPE OF STUDY

The scope of SRI's research included visits to 45 organizations in Canada, the United States, Europe, and Japan. These organizations represent a variety of industry groups and government. In addition, over 1,500 organizations were contacted as part of SRI's mail survey program. The scope of the mail survey activities included Canadian, European, Japanese, and U.S. organizations in representative industry and government groupings. As a result of this fact-finding and of subsequent analysis, these reports have been prepared. Audit and control tools and techniques included in these reports are representative of the thought and experience of larger business and governmental organizations with internal audit programs that are more advanced than most. SRI findings are, however, not based exclusively on larger organizations. For more detailed information on the research methodology, see the appendix.

ACKNOWLEDGMENTS

SRI appreciates and acknowledges the participation, assistance, and general cooperation of the people contacted during this study. The willing participation of firms visited by SRI has been essential in compiling much of the information upon which these reports are based. Similarly, the interest and response of firms included in the mail survey phase of the research have been essential in identifying broad trends in both internal audit and controls in the data processing environment.

SRI is particularly grateful to the advisory and steering committees formed by The Institute of Internal Auditors to review project progress and direction. Consultation with the research staff of The Institute of Internal Auditors has been important to the successful completion of this work. Their contribution is also gratefully acknowledged.

Systems Auditability and Control Steering Committee

Frank F. George, CIA
Chief Auditor
Norton Company

Edward T. Johnson
Program Manager
Information Systems Control & Auditability
IBM Corporation

Frederick B. Palmer, CIA
Project Manager — MIS Quality Assurance
Colgate-Palmolive Company

William E. Perry, CIA, CPA
Director of EDP and Research
The Institute of Internal Auditors

Project Coordinator

H. C. Warner, CIA
Assistant Director EDP and Research
The Institute of Internal Auditors

SYSTEMS AUDITABILITY AND CONTROL ADVISORY COMMITTEE

Donald L. Adams
Managing Director,
Administrative Services
AICPA

F. Andrew Best
Computer Audit Specialist
Advanced Techniques Consultants, Inc.
Affiliation: Former Director of
Advanced Techniques
Department of Agriculture

L. C. Bethards
Manager, Systems Auditing
Federal Reserve Bank of Kansas City
Affiliation: SHARE, Inc.

Richard C. Bluestine
Hurdman & Cranstoun

Wayne S. Boutell
Professor of Business Administration
University of California

J. D. Bradt
General Auditor
Imperial Oil Ltd.
Affiliation: Past President,
The Institute of Internal Auditors

Charles L. Brown
Divisional V. P. &
Director of Auditing
J. C. Penney Co., Inc.

John C. Burton
Deputy Mayor for Finance
The City of New York
Affiliation: Former Chief Accountant,
Securities and Exchange Commission

Benjamin Conway
Manager, Information System Audits
International Business
Machines Corporation

Garland Cupp
Director of Business Systems Services
McDonnell Douglas Corporation
Past President, GUIDE International

Gordon B. Davis
Professor
University of Minnesota

Ruth M. Davis
Director, Institute for Computer
Sciences and Technology
National Bureau of Standards

William J. Duane, Jr.
General Auditor
Manufacturers Hanover Trust Co.

David V. Dunbar
Director of Personnel & Administration
Comptrollers & Finance Departments
Bell Canada

J. R. Ellison
Manager Computer Security & Privacy
The National Computing Centre
Manchester, UK

Arthur Fields
Second Vice-President
The Chase Manhattan Bank N.A.

John C. Gambles
Partner
Deloitte, Haskins & Sells
Affiliation: Canadian Institute of
Chartered Accountants

George Glaser
Consultant
Affiliation: Past President, American
Federation of Information Processing
Societies

Richard J. Guiltinan
Partner
Arthur Andersen & Co.

Vico E. Henriques
Vice President
Computer and Business Equipment
Manufacturers Association

William W. Higgins
V. P. for Automated Systems
Advanced Technological Services, Inc.
Affiliation: Former Director for Data
Automation Department of Defense

Stephen Landekich
Research Director
National Association of Accountants

H. Clifford Lazarine
Manager Information Systems
Texas Instruments, Inc.

David H. Li
Associate Director
Cost Accounting Standards Board

William C. Mair
Partner
Touche Ross & Co.

Benjamin R. Makela
Research Director
Financial Executives
Research Foundation

Lynn J. McKell
Associate Professor
Institute of Professional Accountancy
Brigham Young University
Affiliation: American Accounting
Association

Mort Nelson
Director of Education
Society of Industrial Accountants
of Canada

Frederick L. Neumann
Professor of Accountancy
University of Illinois at
Urbana-Champaign

John Nuxall
Partner
Peat, Marwick, Mitchell & Co.

Robert W. Olsen
President
Computer Services Corporation
Affiliation: Past President ADAPSO

Robert W. Parker
V. P., Director of Corporate Systems
Merrill Lynch, Pierce, Fenner & Smith

E. Read Peirce
General Auditor
Burroughs Corporation

Charles R. Perkett
Assistant to the Financial Vice President
Norton Company

Ken Pollock, CPA
Assistant Director for ADP Policy
U.S. General Accounting Office

Shirley F. Prutch
Director, Advanced Systems
Martin Marietta Corporation
Affiliation: Past President SHARE, Inc.

James H. Reber
Manufacturing Control
Systems Administrator
Sperry-New Holland, European Division
Former member SAC Steering Committee

Richard A. Ress
Manager, Audit & Internal Control
Shell Oil Co.

Arnold Schneidman
Partner
Seymour Schneidman & Associates
Affiliation: ACUTE

Ilario Simonette
Principal
Peat, Marwick, Mitchell & Co.
Affiliation: GUIDE International

Harry Steele
Director of Services
Society for Worldwide Interbank
Financial Telecommunication S. C.
Brussels, Belgium

Berny L. Thurman, Jr.
Assistant Comptroller
U.S. Steel Corporation

George R. Troost
General Auditor
General Motors Corporation

Norman L. Vincent
Vice President — Data Processing
State Farm Mutual Automobile
Insurance Company

Joseph J. Wasserman
Consultant
Past President, Computer Audit
Systems, Inc.

Frederick Weingarten
Program Director — Special Projects
National Science Foundation

Harold Weiss
President
Automation Training Center

HOW TO USE THE CONTROL PRACTICES REPORT

The Data Processing Control Practices Report presents information relating to control techniques applicable to computer-based information systems, computer service center operations, and the system development process. It provides an overview of data processing control practices and describes specific controls and techniques identified during the study. This report is written for system analysts, computer programmers, data processing users, internal auditors, and others concerned with effective auditability and control in the data processing environment. This report complements the information presented in the Data Processing Audit Practices Report.

The report is designed to meet three needs:

- To provide information to computer system analysts responsible for designing new computer-based information systems. This information can assist them in developing control programs.
- To provide an array of controls and associated terminology that can serve as a basis for communications between computer system analysts, users, and internal auditors.
- To provide information to internal auditors that can be of assistance to them in reviewing and evaluating computer-based information systems.

In this volume, computer information systems are presented in six phases: transaction origination, data processing transaction entry, data communication controls, computer processing, data storage and retrieval, and output processing. Each phase is further subdivided into control areas and the control types that SRI found in use in organizations visited. The controls listed are not all-inclusive but, rather, are representative of the types of controls currently implemented in data processing operations.

Part I of the report discusses the state of the art of EDP auditing and the importance of the EDP audit function and outlines a comprehensive role for internal audit in the data processing environment.

Part II describes specific controls for computer-based information systems. Controls are presented for each of the six control phases listed above.

Part III describes general controls applicable to the computer service center and application systems development. Internal auditors or data processing management can use this part of the report to review the general controls in their computer service centers and systems development procedures.

Part IV concludes the volume with four illustrative case studies documented by SRI during their fieldwork. They are presented not as ideal models of control but, rather, as representative computer-based information systems in existence in large organizations. The reader can use this part of the report to understand how some organizations have implemented some of the controls discussed in this report.

Part I

STATE OF THE ART

Chapter 1

MANAGEMENT SUMMARY

*Important changes in recent years have affected management's need for information to plan, evaluate, and control the operations of business and government. Increasingly, management requires more comprehensive information in order to make timely decisions. This growth in the need for management information has been paralleled by the growth of data processing. Management at all levels has become increasingly dependent on data processing and, consequently, more concerned about the continuing accuracy and completeness of data processing results. With the introduction of new technology and with this greater dependence on data processing, new audit and control techniques and procedures are required and are being developed. However, developments in audit and control have not kept pace with the growth of data processing. This chapter summarizes important SRI findings and conclusions relative to the improvements needed in audit and control in the data processing environment. Findings and conclusions are based on extensive field interviews and a large international mail survey.**

BACKGROUND

Economic growth in the private sector, widespread operational diversification, and growth in government activities have resulted in increasingly complex requirements for management information systems. As data processing technology has been successfully applied to meet these information needs, management at all levels has become increasingly reliant on data processing to effectively plan, evaluate, and control organizational activities. The growth in the number of computer systems installed is one measure of management's increasing reliance on data processing. In 1966, more than 25,000 general-purpose computer systems were installed in the United States. In 1975, over 70,000 general-purpose computer systems were installed.

Changes in data processing technology have occurred concurrent with the expansion of management's information needs. Data communications is one example of this growth in new technology. Only 25% of the general-purpose computers installed in 1970 were equipped with data communications terminals. By 1975, 54% had terminals. As a result of the introduction and use of this and other new technology and new computer-based system design concepts, traditional control techniques and procedures are becoming obsolete. Thus, new audit and control techniques are needed to meet the changing requirements and to ensure the integrity of data processing.

The changes in data processing have caused changes in the traditional role of the internal auditor. To understand this changing role, one must understand the changes occurring in internal control that are being brought about by increasing automation and new data processing technology. In addition, audit and control must be considered together, rather than separately, because they are completely interrelated. Internal controls in the data processing environment govern transaction processing, record keeping, reporting, and environmental security; internal auditing is the evaluation and verification of these controls and the results of data processing. Thus, internal controls and the records and reports produced by data processing are the objects of internal audit. Because of this interrelationship, one cannot consider internal audit without considering internal control.

The reports produced as a result of this study reflect both control and audit practices. Chapters 5-16 of the Data Processing Control Practices Report present information on control techniques applicable to computer-based information systems, computer service center operations, and system development. Chapters 6 and 10-33 of the Data Processing Audit Practices Report present information on audit tools and techniques applicable to auditing in the data processing environment. The first four chapters in each of these reports are identical, with the exception of a few pages at the end of Chapter 4. Chapters 5-9 of the Data Processing Audit Practices Report provide a general description of auditing in the data processing environment. A third document, the Executive Report, provides a high-level overview and the findings and conclusions of the study.

*Details of the research methodology and characteristics of the mail survey can be found in the appendix to this report.

PRINCIPAL SRI CONCLUSIONS

Following are SRI's principal study conclusions, based on the results of field interviews and the mail survey. Each of these conclusions is briefly discussed in this chapter; later chapters provide more detail.

1. The primary responsibility for overall internal control resides with top management, while the operational responsibility for the accuracy and completeness of computer-based information systems should reside with users.
2. There is a need for improved controls because inadequate attention has been given to the importance of internal controls in the data processing environment.
3. Internal auditors must participate in the system development process to ensure that appropriate audit and control features are designed into new computer-based information systems.
4. Verification of controls must occur both before and after installation of computer-based information systems.
5. As a result of the growth in complexity and use of computer-based information systems, needs exist for greater internal audit involvement relative to auditing in the data processing environment.
6. An important need exists for EDP audit staff development because few internal audit staffs have enough data processing knowledge and experience to audit effectively in the data processing environment.
7. Few current EDP audit tools and techniques are adequate to the needs of the EDP auditors as they approach the task of verifying the accuracy and completeness of data processing activities and results. New tools and techniques are needed.
8. Many organizations are not adequately evaluating their audit and control functions in the data processing environment. Top management should initiate a periodic assessment of its audit and control programs.

The above conclusions indicate needs for the attention of top management and needs for investments of money, staff, and management time to ensure the adequacy of the audit and control functions for each data processing system.

Following is a brief discussion of each principal conclusion:

Top Management Responsibility for Internal Controls (Conclusion 1)

The primary responsibility for overall internal control resides with top management. The responsibility for internal controls relative to specific computer-based information systems resides with those organizational elements to whom management assigns the functional responsibility (i.e., users such as payroll or accounts payable). However, the current practice in many organizations is to distribute this responsibility between users and data processing. Because computer-based information systems and associated controls are developed to meet user needs, the operational responsibility for accuracy and completeness should reside with users. When data processing builds in adequate controls, users are in the best position to evaluate and verify the accuracy and completeness of data processing records and reports. It is improper to hold the internal auditor responsible for internal control and processing accuracy except within the context of periodic reviews and verifications. The relationships among users, internal auditors, and the data processing department should be clearly established by top management.

Need for Improved Controls (Conclusion 2)

The adequacy of internal controls in the data processing environment has not kept pace with the expansion of data processing and the introduction of new technology. In the past, inadequate attention has been given to the importance of internal controls in developing computer-based information systems and in establishing data processing operations. More emphasis is needed on internal controls governing computer-based information systems and data processing if such controls are to catch up and keep pace with the anticipated growth of data processing. Control guidelines must be developed, based on cooperation among data processing, users, internal auditors, and external auditors; these efforts should emphasize the development of more effective controls within the context of total information processing systems.

SRI believes that the following are among the elements that characterize effective internal control programs:

- Control objectives are identified during the system development process and are recognized as separate development requirements.
- Control objectives for computer-based information systems, computer service center operations, and system development are considered within this context of the total management information processing system.
- Before new data processing technology or system design concepts are introduced within an organization, they are evaluated in terms of associated control requirements, capabilities, and procedures.
- Design review programs that include an evaluation of the adequacy of planned controls are established as part of the information system development process.
- Control features are built into information systems to allow the organization using data processing to evaluate and verify the accuracy and completeness of data processing records and reports.
- The operational responsibility for internal control resides with data processing users.

■ Clear statements of responsibility for controls are established to define the relationship among data processing users, the data processing department, and the internal audit function.

■ Data processing users, internal auditors, and data processing personnel work together to develop appropriate guidelines and standards for controls governing data processing.

■ System designers consider human factors affecting the reliability of computer-based information systems and data processing operations.

■ Preinstallation testing is not compromised in order to achieve system development and installation schedules.

■ Effective preinstallation evaluations are performed by internal auditors who also perform periodic post-installation verification of controls and of processing results such as records and reports.

More detailed information on internal control in the data processing environment is included in Chapter 3.

Participation by Internal Audit in the System Development Process (Conclusion 3)

Internal auditors must participate in the systems development process to ensure that necessary audit and control features are built into new computer-based information systems. An evaluation of the adequacy of controls after a system is installed determines weakness too late in the development process. The cost and time for modifying the system after installation can cause operational delays and may be used to argue against the inclusion of desired controls.

Some internal auditors argue that objectivity is lost as a result of such participation. This objection is overcome by placing the responsibility for internal controls with data processing users and by limiting internal audit participation to reviews of controls that result in recommendations to data processing and its users regarding audit and control techniques appropriate for inclusion.

SRI concludes that effective involvement in computer-based information system development is possible when:

■ Internal auditors participate in the development process to ensure that appropriate audit and control features are included in the computer-based information systems being developed.

■ Audit tools and techniques are developed as an integral part of the design of computer-based information systems.

■ Data processing accepts the expanded mandate and role of internal audit regarding data processing activities.

■ Internal auditors are able to articulate their audit objectives in terms understandable to data processing personnel.

More detailed information regarding internal audit involvement in systems development is presented in Chapter 4, and in Chapter 12 of the Data Processing Control Practices Report.

Verification of Controls Before and After Installation (Conclusion 4)

Verification of controls must occur both before and after installation of computer-based information systems. It is important that adequate preinstallation testing be performed and not compromised in order to achieve system development or to satisfy installation schedules. In addition, effective, periodic, postinstallation reviews should be performed by internal auditors. Such reviews include the verification of controls and of processing results. The verification of controls, although a new task to many internal auditors, is important as a complement to more traditional data verification techniques. It is therefore important that management recognize the value of, and ensure the performance of, both pre- and post-installation reviews.

Need to Improve Internal Audit Involvement (Conclusion 5)

Based on the successful experience of leading organizations visited during the study, SRI concludes that greater involvement by the internal audit functions in all phases of data processing is necessary and proper in today's increasingly complex data processing environment.

As management has become more dependent on data processing, data processing responsibilities have become more diffused throughout each organization. Previously, a department such as payroll or purchasing was responsible for its files and processing. That responsibility is now shared with a separate service facility, data processing, and frequently with other departments that use integrated systems as sources of information or as users. This brings about an upward shift in the lowest level of common responsibility or line management control. As a result, management increasingly looks to internal audit as the logical group to evaluate and verify the effectiveness of internal controls across the entire organization.

Formalized programs for progressively increasing internal audit involvement in the various phases of data processing and a parallel effort to develop the EDP audit skills and capabilities are needed. The evaluation/verification of controls is an important function that complements more traditional data verification techniques. The expansion of internal audit activities into computer-based information systems, computer service center operations, and systems development is a logical and desirable extension of internal audit's traditional mandate. Expanded EDP audit programs are based on two premises. First, an evaluation and verification of data processing controls are as important as the more traditional verification of data processing results; second, internal controls must be evaluated in the context of the total information handling process, rather than as individual control procedures.

As internal audit programs expand into data processing, a new type of internal auditor, called the EDP auditor, is coming into existence. EDP auditing is a specialized activity within the internal audit organization. Results of SRI's Primary U.S. Mail Survey indicate that currently about 60% of the large U.S. corporations have EDP audit functions. However, of those that have an EDP audit function, more than two-thirds were established since 1970, which indicates that the EDP audit specialty is a relatively recent phenomenon.

SRI believes that effective EDP audit programs are characterized by elements such as the following:

- Management's mandate to internal audit reflects an expanded scope of audit activities to include computer-based information systems, computer service center operations, and information system development.
- Formalized programs are maintained within the internal audit function to develop needed skills and knowledge through appropriate recruiting and/or training.
- Close cooperation is maintained between data processing and internal audit to coordinate programs that improve internal controls in the data processing environment.
- Internal audit plans and objectives are periodically updated to reflect the expanded scope of audit in the data processing environment as needed skills and knowledge are acquired.

More detailed information on internal audit involvement with data processing is presented in Chapter 4.

Need for EDP Audit Staff Development (Conclusion 6)

Few internal audit staffs have sufficient data processing knowledge and experience to effectively audit data processing. Thus, plans must be established to upgrade existing staff capabilities. Organizations have tried different approaches to acquire needed EDP audit expertise. The range of alternatives includes:

- Establishing a separate staff of data processing professionals trained in audit.
- Training existing internal auditors in data processing concepts and practices, and in the use of computer audit tools and techniques.
- Training existing internal auditors and supplementing this staff with a few data processing specialists.

It is preferable to develop required EDP audit capabilities by training existing internal auditors who have an interest in and desire to work in data processing, or to recruit experienced EDP auditors. Hiring or transferring data processing professionals to supplement the internal audit staff has met with only mixed success. Attracting and retaining qualified data processing professionals on the internal audit staff can prove to be difficult because they are not auditors by background and will be removed from the mainstream of their professional interest. In addition, data processing professionals generally lack the audit perspective necessary to work effectively with other internal auditors. However, it may be appropriate, as involvement with data processing increases, to add data processing personnel to the EDP audit staff to provide specialized assistance in areas such as data communications or data base software.

Elements that SRI believes characterize effective programs to train internal auditors in data processing include the following:

- Courses in the fundamentals of data processing are required for internal auditors with no prior data processing experience. It is appropriate that such courses emphasize system design concepts and data processing capabilities rather than computer program coding.
- Internal auditors involved in EDP audit work are required to acquire additional professional training in auditing in the data processing environment. Such training is offered through private organizations, public accounting firms, and professional associations.
- Internal auditors involved in advanced aspects of data processing, such as data communications or data base, are encouraged to attend data processing technical courses in relevant subject areas. Such courses are offered by private institutions, professional associations, and computer hardware and software suppliers.
- Internal auditors involved in EDP audit work are encouraged to attend seminars and conferences wherein recent experience with advanced EDP audit tools and techniques is discussed.

More detailed information on internal audit staff development and training is presented in Chapter 5 of the Data Processing Audit Practices Report.

Need for New EDP Audit Tools and Techniques (Conclusion 7)

New EDP audit tools and techniques are needed as computer-based information systems become logically and technologically more complex. Despite the number and variety of tools and techniques available, SRI concludes that few are adequate to the needs of the EDP auditor. Efforts to develop tools and techniques within individual organizations need to be complemented by more broadly based cooperative efforts among such groups as data processing user organizations, professional associations, and hardware and software suppliers. Emphasis in these efforts should be placed on audit techniques designed to be an integral part of computer-based information systems, such as integrated test facilities (ITFs), rather than on after-the-fact techniques independently developed by internal auditors. SRI has identified and documented 28 EDP audit tools and techniques used by internal auditors in auditing computer-based information systems, computer service center operations, and the system development process.

Although an increasing number of internal auditors are using the computer, many are still only auditing around data processing. Auditing around data processing may efficiently verify historical results, but, if used exclusively, it overlooks the possibility that the programs and the programming process itself may not be properly controlled.

Even though the internal auditor may use the computer to perform data verification, two important audit objectives are not realized, namely, the evaluation of and verification of application program controls. A thorough data verification, complemented by selective functional testing, is an effective EDP audit approach to evaluating and verifying computer-based information system and program controls. The combination of generalized audit software for data verification and functional test methods, such as the use of test decks or ITFs, offers an approach to EDP audit that satisfies all basic audit objectives.

SRI believes that efforts to develop more effective EDP audit tools and techniques can be accelerated if:

- Development programs within organizations are based on cooperation between internal auditors and data processing personnel.
- The role of the internal audit function in the computer-based information system development process is defined as described elsewhere in this chapter.
- Audit objectives relating to the data processing environment are well-defined.
- Particular EDP audit techniques are based on the appropriateness of the technique to accomplish the audit objective.
- Representatives from the organization's public accounting firm are used to relate their experience in use and development of similar EDP audit approaches, tools, and techniques.

For more information regarding EDP audit tools and techniques, refer to Chapters 6 and 10-33 of the Data Processing Audit Practices Report.

Need for Audit and Control Assessment (Conclusion 8)

Top management should initiate a periodic assessment of the audit and control programs pertaining to the data processing environment. This review should ensure that the responsibility for control is clearly established and that the internal audit mandate includes appropriate data processing involvement. This review and evaluation should be performed jointly by internal audit and data processing management. Both perspectives are required in evaluating audit and control needs and capabilities. Such a review and evaluation should consider audit and control objectives, the adequacy of control guidelines, the scope of internal audit, internal audit involvement within data processing, the inclusion of control guidelines in design reviews performed for new information systems, internal auditor training, and the need for loss investigation reporting programs.

SRI concludes that an assessment of the audit and control function should include the following three objectives:

- An evaluation of current audit and control practices and an assessment of data processing capabilities within the internal audit staff.
- An identification of likely future trends in the development of computer-based information systems and data processing technology.
- Formulation of programs to improve both the audit and the control capabilities in the data processing environment.

Appropriate action plans should be prepared with related economic justification when possible. In reviewing the results of such a review, top management should realize that it may take some time to achieve audit and control program objectives after recommendations are accepted. Additional expenditures, or at least a reallocation of resources, may be necessary. Such expenditures are an investment in the continuing accuracy and reliability of data processing.

INDICATED MANAGEMENT ACTIONS

SRI has identified a number of areas of management responsibility for ensuring that computer-based information systems are developed with adequate controls, are auditable, and operate in a reliable manner. Top management, internal audit management, and data processing system management must work together to make sure that their actions are coordinated and complementary.

While it is not within the scope of the study to fix responsibility for the various management activities related to data processing control and audit, the following list is offered as indicative of the management concerns and the probable location of primary (P) and supporting (S) responsibility for each:

Action	Responsibility: Executive Management	Responsibility: Audit Management	Responsibility: Data Processing Management
Ensure that all management realize the importance of internal audit in data processing.	P	S	S
Issue a clearly defined internal audit mandate that specifies the responsibility of internal audit as it relates to all phases of data processing.	P	S	S
Clearly define the working relationship among users, internal auditors, and the data processing department for the development and maintenance of computer-based information systems.	P	S	S
Encourage the development of new data processing control techniques and internal audit approaches to ensure the reliability of computer-based information systems.	P	S	S
Require the development of control guidelines.	P	S	S
Ensure that internal audit participates in the system development process.	P	S	S
Ensure adequate preinstallation testing of computer-based information systems.	S	S	P
Ensure that periodic postinstallation verification takes place.	S	P	S
When auditing computer-based information systems, computer service center operations, and system development, ensure that there are reviews of controls, tests to verify the controls, and tests to verify the data.	S	P	S
Encourage data processing and internal audit to work together to achieve improved system audit and control capabilities.	P	S	S
Ensure that training programs are developed to provide the needed skills to audit data processing, and also to reflect the internal audit discipline.	S	P	S
Upgrade the quality and quantity of EDP auditors. As a starting point, use individuals from the internal audit staff with a specific interest in data processing.	S	P	S
Add data processing personnel to the EDP audit staff for specialized data processing assistance.	S	P	S
Ensure that data processing, internal audit, and external audit work together to develop required EDP audit tools and techniques.	P	S	S
Ensure that assessments of the internal audit function are performed jointly by internal audit and data processing.	P	S	S

OUTLOOK FOR THE FUTURE

Although data processing and internal auditing have each been changing in recent years, there has been little coordination in the areas where the two disciplines interface. Due to the rapidly changing data processing environment, the internal auditors' mandate and the scope of internal audit activities are not clear to most internal audit and data processing managers. Internal audit management is being faced with increasing emphasis from top management to audit in the data processing environment, an environment in which it has only limited experience, knowledge, skills, or tools and techniques. The need for internal auditors to completely audit data processing functions is becoming recognized. However, most organizations still have to establish effective, comprehensive EDP audit programs.

Top management interest and direction are the keys to overcoming the inertia that has prevented the development and acceptance of effective EDP audit programs. The direction of top management is needed to ensure that an appropriate internal audit mandate is established for data processing and that specific programs are established in which data processing and internal audit work together effectively.

Chapter 2

THE CHANGING MANAGEMENT INFORMATION SYSTEMS ENVIRONMENT

Management's information needs have changed dramatically during the last 20 years as a result of the growth and diversification of business activities. Government regulation and regulatory reporting requirements have increased concurrently. These trends have resulted in the need for more comprehensive and sophisticated computer-based information systems. During this same period and particularly since the early 1960s, new data processing technology and concepts have been applied to satisfy management's information needs. As new technology is successively introduced and applied, computer application systems and controls have become more complex. For example, data communication capabilities bring data processing users closer to the computer, and thus allow faster access to needed data. The implementation of such technology has, however, resulted in fundamental changes in the structure of computer application systems and controls. As a result, audit and control techniques appropriate to earlier business operations have, to some extent, become outmoded. In addition, with increasing reliance upon data processing, management is increasingly concerned about insufficient controls and the complexity of data processing. These concerns are translated to data processing management's increasing concerns about losses arising from errors and improper controls that may occur and remain undetected. In this environment, the audit and control of computer application systems and supporting data processing activities are becoming more important to management.*

CHANGES IN MANAGEMENT'S INFORMATION NEEDS

The information needs of both business and government have increased dramatically in recent years. The private sectors of the economies in Canada, Western Europe, Japan, and the United States grew rapidly during the 1960s and early 1970s, until the slowdown was experienced. With economic recovery now under way in most areas, there is no reason to believe management's information needs will not continue to grow in the years ahead.

Economic growth has occurred as a result of an expansion of existing markets and products. Business activity has also expanded geographically within countries and across national borders. The latter is exemplified by the multinational corporation phenomenon, which became prominent during the mid and late 1960s. The geographic spread of business increases the need for communication facilities to allow the exchange of information between business locations. In response to this need, communication and digital computer technologies have been joined to provide the high-speed data communication capabilities now used by many businesses. Multinational business operations share the need for data communications capabilities, but also have other requirements that increase the complexity of management information needs. For example, multinational corporations must accommodate currency conversion, additional regulatory reporting, and variations in practices in developing computer-based information systems.

Expanding markets and product lines have involved acquisitions for many businesses. This has led to consolidation of operations in some situations and diversification in others. Consolidation is often accompanied by increased transaction volumes and an expansion of existing information systems. Diversification through acquisition has, in contrast, often required an information exchange between previously unrelated management information systems. In some situations, diversification has resulted in a significant expansion of data processing capabilities in order to provide necessary management information on a consolidated basis.

The rapid growth of the private sector of the economy has been paralleled by increasing government activities. Legislation and governmental regulation to control business increased significantly during the 1960s and early 1970s. Such regulation and associated regulatory reporting have caused an increase in the amount and complexity of information that must be captured and processed. Top management, data

*Definitions of selected data processing and internal audit terms are included in the Glossary.

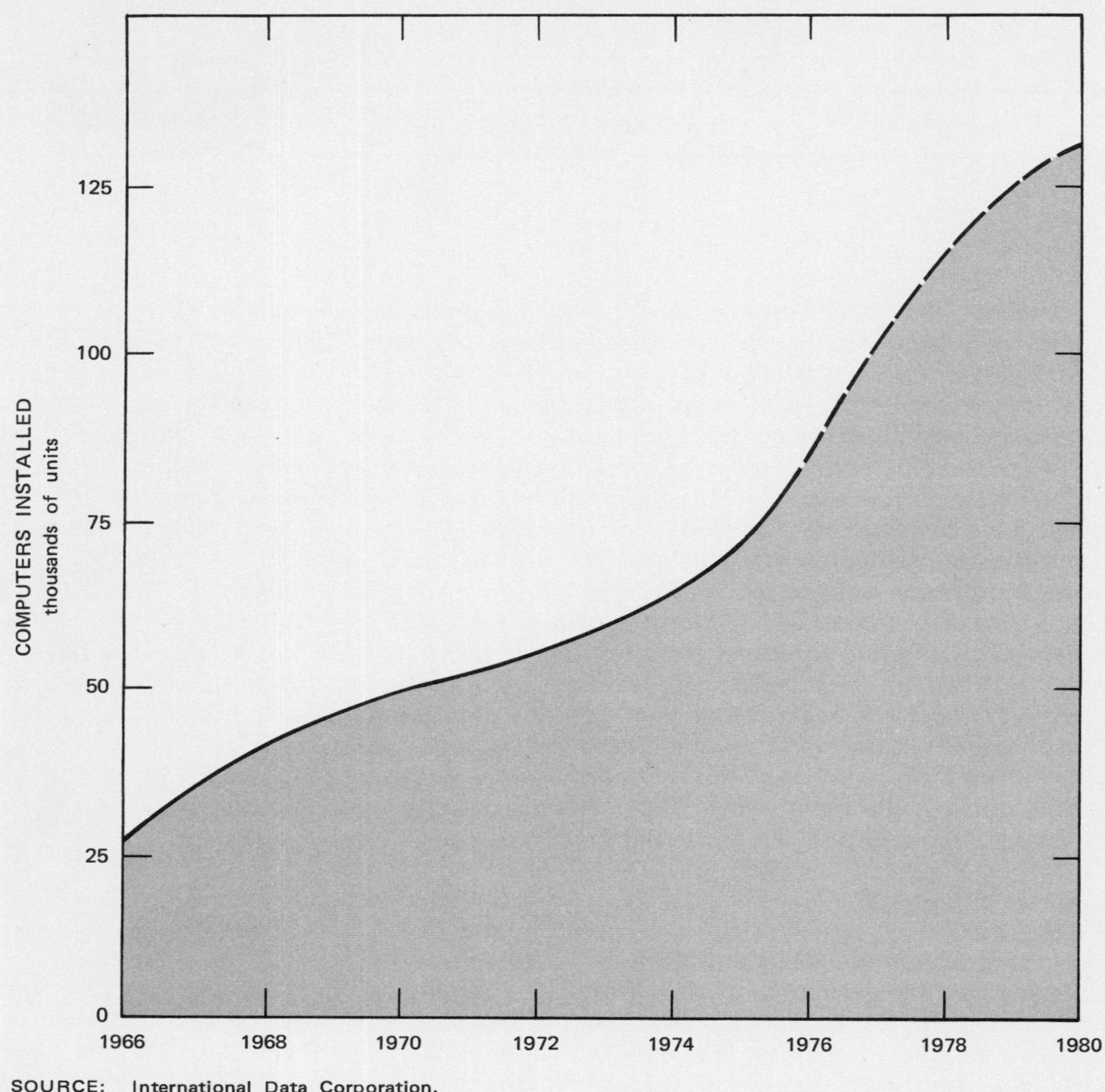

FIGURE 2-1 GENERAL-PURPOSE COMPUTER SYSTEMS INSTALLED, 1966-1980 (U.S.)

processing management, and internal audit management in SRI's Primary U.S. Mail Survey sample were asked, "What governmental, professional, or other trends do you see emerging that will have a definite impact on your data processing and internal auditing operations?" Government regulation and reporting were the most frequently reported trends. Privacy legislation was one form of regulation frequently mentioned. A second frequently cited governmental trend was the Securities and Exchange Commission's requirement for quarterly reviews. National health insurance, affirmative action programs, new rules for pension plan reporting, and consumer protection laws require modifications and extensions to the computer application systems maintained by many firms. Such reporting is quite often different from the usual reports prepared for management and necessitates modification and expansion of existing systems in many instances. Government regulation and regulatory reporting present substantial new requirements for computer application systems.

INCREASING DATA PROCESSING CAPABILITIES

The business trends described above (i.e., growth in transaction volumes, geographic distribution of operations, and increasingly complex product line reporting needs) have occurred during a period when important advances were being made in data processing technology and its application. These advances include:

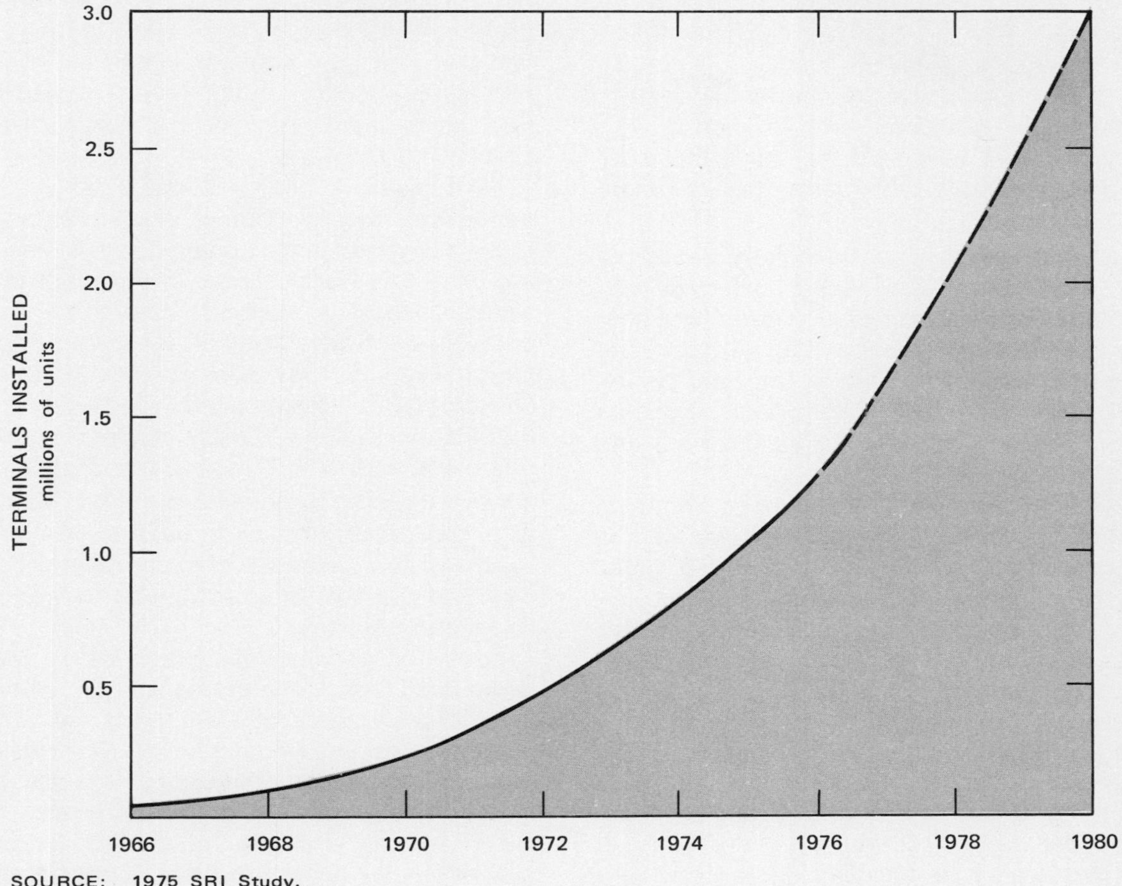

FIGURE 2-2 DATA COMMUNICATION TERMINALS INSTALLED, 1966-1980 (U.S.)

- Increased computer system usage
- Increased use of data communication facilities
- Net data processing application areas
- Distributed data processing
- Integrated computer application systems
- Centralized shared data files.

Figure 2-1 shows the increasing number of business-oriented computer systems installed during the past 10 years. In 1966, more than 25,000 general-purpose computer systems were installed in the United States. In 1975, over 70,000 were installed. This reflects the increasing use of data processing to provide the information that management needs to evaluate, control, and plan business operations.

Figure 2-2 shows the increasing number of installed data communications terminals. This characterizes the growing use of data communications in bringing computer capabilities closer to users and improving the flow of information between remote facilities. For example, a large automobile manufacturer has data communication links to its widespread suppliers, thus providing overall production control from the suppliers' facilities to the manufacturer's assembly plant. In another situation, a manufacturer has data communication links between its facilities and its distributors to provide nightly order entry for replenishment of the distributors' inventories. In the financial services industry, bank clearing systems are being linked using data communication facilities to speed interbank fund transfers and settlements.

The use of data communications has become substantial during the last five years. The use of data communications is expected to continue to grow in the years ahead, as shown by the projections in Figure 2-2.

Electronic funds transfer is an example of a new data processing application area that will require extensive use of data communications. Developments in electronic funds transfer affect financial institutions, retailers, and the consumer. This will be, perhaps, the area of greatest data processing growth during the next 10 years. Electronic funds transfer is in its early stages of development. The concept usually encompasses:

- Electronic interbank clearing.
- Automated teller machines and unattended remote terminals to dispense currency.
- Retail point of sale terminals that combine retail and banking transactions at supermarket checkout counters, for example.

Many regulatory and business problems remain to be resolved before electronic funds transfer application systems are available and widely used. Consumer acceptance is an important factor that will pace and perhaps constrain their wide use in the near future. Electronic funds transfer is an example of how data processing technology can affect both business and the consumer public.

The use of minicomputers in business began in 1969. By 1975, minicomputers installed for use in business applications reached nearly 40,000 units. The number of minicomputers used for business applications is expected to grow to 86,000 units in 1980.

The concept of distributed data processing based on the use of minicomputers is gaining importance with the increasing geographic distribution of business operations and the acceptance of minicomputers for business data processing. During the 1960s there was a trend toward consolidating data processing on large centralized computer systems. Such computer systems were several times faster than their smaller counterparts. They could perform the work of four or five smaller computers concurrently and in less elapsed time. Accordingly, there were economies of scale that resulted in consolidation and centralization of computing resources. Distributed processing is a currently growing countertrend resulting from the adaptation of low-cost, high-speed minicomputers to business needs.

For example, a midwestern manufacturer has 15 geographically distributed plants. Product transportation costs are a potentially large component of product cost, so plants are located in the areas they serve. The firm maintains a central accounting department and data processing facility with communication links to terminals at each plant location. It has recently installed minicomputers in each plant location to handle order entry, customer billing, and accounts receivable. This equipment replaced manual bookkeeping machines and is connected to the firm's central computer system. Order entry, production backlog reporting, billing, and accounts receivable are performed locally at each plant. Sales, production, and accounts receivable information is transmitted to the central data processing facility each night and used to prepare consolidated operating reports. In selecting this approach, the firm considered a larger central computer system with remote terminals at each location. They concluded it was more economical for them to process detailed information locally and transmit only summary statistics to the central facility. In specific situations, distributed processing may have advantages over totally centralized data processing facilities.

As a result of changing management information needs and the availability of new data processing technology, computer application systems are changing from traditional forms. In the past, for example, order processing, customer billing, and accounts receivable were developed as separate computer application systems. They were processed separately with files of related transactions passed between computer application systems. Order processing might occur one night, with billing the next, and accounts receivable processing only twice a month. Manual control logs and procedures were used to ensure the accuracy and completeness of successive processing cycles and the flow of transactions between computer application systems.

Computer application systems being designed and developed today involve the use of remote terminal entry, transaction processing, and central data base concepts. Remote terminal operations were described earlier. Transaction processing is a complementary concept. It involves integrating processing procedures so that a single transaction is entered and processed by all appropriate computer application systems in a single sequence. For instance, order entry, inventory control, billing, and accounts receivable application systems can be integrated into a single transaction that automatically flows through the entire sequence. Orders are entered and customer acknowledgments prepared, inventory records posted, warehouse packing documents prepared, and customer records posted. Terminal operators entering orders are automatically notified if discrepancies, such as items out of stock, are encountered during the processing sequence.

The concept of centralized shared data files (i.e., a "data base") has been a factor in the integration of computer application systems as described above. The data base concept is to capture and maintain data in a single central file, which can be accessed by those programs that have a need for specific data elements. In the past, each computer application system was designed around its own files. The same data elements would occur in different files, and would even have different values because of inconsistent processing procedures and/or schedules. Centralized files eliminate redundancy. When this concept is first explained, one might assume that all an organization's data reside in a single file. In fact, most data bases represent a federation of files serving logically related computer application systems. The elimination of redundant files and the logical association of data files with computer application systems are fundamental to the data base concept.

Several important changes in the data processing environment are summarized in Table 2-1.

In summary, management's needs and data processing capabilities have both become more complex and have merged. As more business functions have been computerized, business operations and management have become dependent upon data processing and the internal controls that ensure accuracy and completeness. Traditional control and audit methods, tools, and techniques have become outmoded as a result of changes in the structure and form of computer application systems. With greater reliance on data processing have come new potentials for loss. Loss exposures are described in the following section.

LOSS EXPOSURE

The potential for loss associated with the use of data processing is increasing and taking new forms, as procedures once performed manually are automated. Traditional systems and procedures relied on manual checks and verifications to ensure the accuracy and completeness of data and records. In such an environment, exceptions could be handled as they were encountered. Decisions could be made without much delay in processing. Manual control was maintained over most, if not all, phases of transaction processing and record keeping.

Computer Application Systems Error Potential

As business data processing expands, manual controls are replaced by computer application program control functions. Computer application program routines are needed that anticipate exceptions previously handled manually on an ad hoc basis. Without such control routines, incomplete or incorrect transactions can be processed unnoticed. When computer application systems are linked and integrated, an undetected error that is accepted by one application can result in errors in several others. Once accepted, an erroneous transaction can be processed against several files without any manual checking until the processing cycle is complete. The potential effects of a single error are much greater in this environment. When such errors are detected, their correction can require extensive manual analysis in order to determine what files and records have been affected, and to prepare proper correcting entries.

Internal audit and data processing management interviewed report that the primary area of emphasis for a further reduction in loss exposure will be computer application systems.

Computer Service Center Loss Potential

Increasing dependence upon data processing facilities and a continuing trend toward centralization and concentration of data processing resources are major concerns of a majority of top executives interviewed by SRI. Interruptions in the availability of either data or processing capability can have catastrophic consequences for organizations highly dependent upon data processing. Top management as well as data processing and internal audit management are concerned that effective programs be developed to protect data processing facilities and minimize this loss exposure. Controls in use generally include:

- Computer service center security (i.e., limited access, special fire protection, standby or uninterrupted power sources).
- Backup processing and data files, including alternative processing facilities and off-site storage of important data files.

Table 2-1
CHANGES IN THE DATA PROCESSING ENVIRONMENT

Areas of Change	1956-1965	1966-1975
Processing equipment	Separate, stand-alone installations	Computers and terminals linked with data communication facilities
Computer application system development	Limited coordination and discipline	Formalized coordination of development and use of standards within individual organizations
Computer application system design	Single-function batch processing applications	Interdependence among application systems
File usage	Overlapping and partial data files	Common masterfiles shared by several application systems
User relationship with data processing	Limited direct links to processing equipment	User has direct access to processing equipment and data files

■ Disaster planning, including documented recovery plans for various disaster situations such as fire, vandalism, flood, accidental or intentional destruction of vital data files.

Most of the firms interviewed have implemented improved computer service center security programs. Steps to enhance the security of computer facilities and to develop disaster plans require relatively short lead times and expenditures compared with the lead time to review computer application systems and eliminate vulnerabilities.

Loss Identification and Reporting

Despite a growing awareness of the potential for loss, top management interviewed by SRI seems confident that losses are minimal. Several of the managers said that they had no knowledge of loss relating to data processing within their organizations, but at the same time indicated that they had no formal procedures to identify and report incidences of data processing loss. In confirmation of this, in only 17% of the organizations in the Primary U.S. Mail Survey does top management receive periodic reports of time or dollars lost due to data processing errors and omissions.

A few of the organizations visited by SRI indicated that they had formalized procedures for reporting data processing losses and believe such reporting and subsequent investigation discourage loss due to fraud, embezzlement, or inadequate computer application system controls. These procedures are used to report individual instances of loss. No one interviewed had been able to establish a method of measuring or estimating the overall extent of loss, either detected or undetected loss, or loss potential associated with data processing. As part of the Primary U.S. Mail Survey, data processing and internal audit management were asked to identify the areas of potential loss exposure within data processing. Their responses, which are given in Table 2-2, show that, whereas internal auditors most often indicate a major concern is loss from improper controls, data processing management most often indicate a major concern is loss from errors and omissions. In response to the same question, about 85% of Japanese and 50% of European data processing management indicate their highest ranking concern is with potential loss resulting from inadequate system design. Of the Japanese internal auditors who responded, 60% indicate their highest ranking concern is with errors and omissions, while 50% of the European internal auditors indicate their highest ranking concern is with improper controls. Internal auditors interviewed reported that proper manual controls governing the origination, transmittal, and balancing of transactions in user

Table 2-2

DATA PROCESSING LOSS POTENTIAL

Which *two* of the following areas of potential loss exposure in the data processing department are you most concerned about? (Check two)

	Percentage of Organizations Selecting Each Category*	
	Data Processing	**Internal Audit**
Potential loss from errors and omissions	61.8%	46.8%
Potential loss from improper controls	47.4	67.1
Potential loss from inadequate system design	43.3	41.2
Potential loss from fraud and defalcation	17.1	15.6
Potential loss from failure to comply with standards or procedures	14.9	20.9
Potential loss from inadequate conversion methods	7.5	6.7
Other	8.0	1.7

Note: Number of respondents = 222 from data processing and 221 from internal audit.

*Percentages equal 200% because each respondent checked two categories. Percentages are based on actual responses weighted to reflect the probable response distribution of all organizations in the sampling frame. See the appendix for further description of weighting procedures.

areas can significantly reduce errors and omissions relating to source transactions. Improved computer application system controls can ensure the detection of errors and omissions and prevent their subsequent processing.

As part of the Primary U.S. Mail Survey, data processing managers were asked in which two areas improvements are needed most to reduce the potential loss exposure about which they were most concerned. The responses of those who checked the top three categories listed in Table 2-2 are shown in Table 2-3. The latter table indicates that among data processing management who are most concerned about losses from either errors and omissions or improper controls, controls on processing procedures are most often reported as being in need of improvement. Among those who are most concerned about losses from inadequate system design, however, controls on analysts and programmers are most often reported as being in need of improvement. Data processing managers interviewed by SRI also stressed the importance of procedures governing the handling and processing of data within the data processing organization. Many also reported that improvements are needed in the controls governing system analysts and programmers involved in computer application systems development and maintenance. Controls governing computer application systems development are required to ensure that adequate control procedures are built into computer application systems and programs being developed and maintained, and that adequate acceptance testing is performed.

In a related Primary U.S. Mail Survey question, top management was asked to identify its two major concerns about data processing. Table 2-4 summarizes the results of this question. The top management concerns most frequently reported are insufficient controls, the complexity of data processing, and insufficient user involvement. Despite the attention computer abuse and fraud have received in the media, potential loss due to fraud was only the fifth most frequently reported concern.

The top-ranking concern about data processing, as expressed by about 40% of the Japanese and 30% of the European top management, was with an inadequate return on investments. While insufficient controls were the second-ranking concern of European top management (about 25%), insufficient control was only the fourth-ranking concern of Japanese top management (about 20%). The top four concerns of Canadian top management are the same as those in the Primary U.S. Mail Survey. It is interesting to note that 65% of state government organizations responding to this question indicate insufficient controls as a major concern.

Table 2-3
CONTROLS NEEDED BY DATA PROCESSING TO REDUCE LOSS POTENTIAL

In which *two* of the following areas are improvements needed the most to reduce the potential loss exposure you checked above? (Check two)

	Percentage of Organizations That Are Concerned about Potential Loss from*		
Controls On	**Errors and Omissions**	**Improper Controls**	**Inadequate System Design**
1. Processing procedures	55.2%	67.8%	46.0%
2. Analysts/programmers	33.6	27.5	58.2
3. Operations personnel	31.0	31.2	22.3
4. Data access	24.0	32.7	14.0
5. Applications programmers	15.7	6.4	11.2
6. Data conversion (source data entry)	15.3	14.2	10.5
7. Systems programmers	11.3	3.8	18.0
8. Contingency planning	4.6	2.8	7.1
9. Physical access	4.0	10.2	2.8
10. Other	5.3	3.4	9.9

Note: Number of respondents = 214

*Percentages equal 200% because each respondent checked two categories. Percentages are based on actual responses weighted to reflect the probable response distribution of all organizations in the sampling frame. See the appendix for further description of weighting procedures.

Table 2-4
TOP MANAGEMENT'S DATA PROCESSING CONCERNS

What are your *two* major concerns about data processing in your organization? (Check two)

	Percent of Total*	Percentage of Organizations with Major Concerns Selecting Each Category*†
Organizations indicating no major concerns	5.3%	
Organizations indicating two of the following concerns	94.7	
Insufficient controls		39.4%
Complexity of data processing		29.5
Insufficient user involvement		25.1
Lack of data processing standards		23.9
Exposure to fraud		21.3
Lack of adequate independent review		19.8
Inadequate return on investment		17.1
Other		13.3

Note: Number of respondents = 214

*Percentages are based on actual responses weighted to reflect the probable response distribution of all organizations in the sampling frame. See the appendix for further description of weighting procedures.

†Percentages sum to 189.4% = 2 x 94.7% because respondents with major concerns checked two categories.

SUMMARY

Economic growth in the private sectors and growth in the scope of government activities have resulted in increasingly complex management information requirements. As data processing technology has been successfully applied to these management information needs, management at all levels has become increasingly reliant upon data processing for the information needed to effectively plan, evaluate, and control its organization's activities. The degree of reliance upon data processing is often not fully realized. However, a prolonged interruption of data processing can result in business disruption of catastrophic proportions.

Changes in data processing technology have occurred concurrent with the expansion of management's information needs. Data processing has become more complex as more business functions are automated and as advanced data processing technology is applied. As a result, traditional control techniques and procedures as well as audit techniques used in the past must be reevaluated in light of these developments. New audit and control techniques are needed to ensure the integrity of data processing. Changes in the role of the internal auditor are occurring and are presented in a subsequent chapter.

With the broader application of, and greater reliance upon, data processing, the potential for losses resulting from undetected errors and omissions has increased. Error potential exists in the areas of computer applications systems, computer service center operations and application systems development. Many organizations have taken steps to improve computer service center control procedures. The security of computer facilities has received much emphasis. Steps to improve controls in these areas are relatively easy to implement; relatively short lead times and only modest expenditures are usually involved. In contrast, action programs to improve computer application system controls involve more cost and are longer term. Because of the progress that has been made with computer service center control procedures, the primary emphasis in the future will be on application system controls.

Few of the organizations interviewed by SRI, or who responded to the SRI mail survey, have established formal programs to identify, report, and investigate losses associated with data processing. Those interviewed who have such programs, however, report them to be effective in preventing losses. No organization contacted during the study reported having a satisfactory method of measuring overall loss or loss potential. In general, existing programs handle loss reporting and investigation on an individual basis. The potential losses most frequently reported by data processing and internal audit are errors and omissions, inadequate systems design, and improper controls. In addition, internal auditors report that a better integration of manual and automated controls can reduce undetected errors and omissions originating during source documents preparation. Improved automated controls are important to ensure the detection of input errors and omissions and subsequent processing errors. Data processing management report controls governing processing procedures and systems development activities are the areas that need the most improvement.

EVALUATION AND OUTLOOK

The outlook is for a continuation of the trends that have characterized the growth of data processing in recent years: the automation of more business functions, an increasingly complex data processing environment, and greater management reliance upon computer-based information systems. However, because internal audit and control capabilities have not kept pace with the expansion of data processing and the introduction of new technology, new data processing control techniques and internal audit approaches are needed to ensure the accuracy, completeness, timeliness, and security of computer application systems. Greater emphasis is needed on systems auditability and control if they are to catch up and keep pace with rapidly advancing data processing technology.

Management programs are needed to improve the effectiveness of internal audit and control. These programs should focus attention on three areas: first, closer cooperation and coordination between data processing and internal audit to ensure that effective control procedures and audit facilities are established; second, more emphasis on the importance of controls, particularly computer application system controls in situations that involve the use of new technology or new system design concepts; third, formalized programs to develop needed data processing skills, knowledge, and capabilities within the internal audit organization.

Management attention and follow-up are needed to ensure that plans for greater cooperation and the upgrading of internal audit capabilities are prepared and executed. It is also important that the expanding role of internal audit is understood throughout the organization. Each of these areas is further discussed in the chapters that follow.

Chapter 3

INTERNAL CONTROL IN ORGANIZATIONS USING DATA PROCESSING

Internal controls are of increasing importance in the data processing environment to ensure the accuracy and completeness of transaction processing, record maintenance, and reporting, as well as the physical security of the computer environment and data files. Computer application system controls are taking new forms and becoming highly structured as a result of technological innovations such as data communications and integrated computer application systems sharing common data files. Increasingly complex control procedures are being developed as computer application systems are developed to handle more business functions and more exception conditions. Complementary manual phases of computer application systems are also becoming increasingly complex. Extensive testing is needed prior to production acceptance to verify the accuracy and completeness of computer application systems and to verify that associated controls are effective. In addition, periodic postimplementation examinations are being made by internal auditors to verify the accuracy and completeness of processing. This chapter describes internal controls as they relate to the data processing environment.

INTERNAL CONTROLS IN THE DATA PROCESSING ENVIRONMENT

Internal controls in the data processing environment pertain to the processing and recording of an organization's transactions and to resulting management reporting. They are the procedures that ensure the accuracy and completeness of manual and automated transactions, records, and reports, and the avoidance, detection, and correction of errors. They encompass source document origination, authorization, processing, data processing record keeping and reporting, and the use of data processing records and reports in controlling an organization's activities.

Internal controls governed manual transaction processing and record keeping for many years before the advent of electronic data processing. Data processing has, however, caused traditional controls to be revised. As a result, internal controls have taken new forms and become highly structured, particularly during the last decade.

This chapter provides an overview of, and conceptual framework for, internal control in the data processing environment. It presents a synthesis of information resulting primarily from SRI interviews conducted with leading U.S. and Canadian organizations. It describes the controls that govern computer application systems and data processing activities. The next chapter describes the role of the internal auditor.

Internal controls in the data processing environment govern transaction processing, and resulting record keeping and reporting; internal audit is the evaluation and verification of these controls and the results of data processing. Internal controls and the the object of internal audit. Based on SRI's field interviews it was concluded that most internal auditors and data processors do not clearly understand this perspective. To fully appreciate the role of the internal auditor in the changing data processing environment, one must understand the changes in internal control being brought about by the increasing dependence on data processing.

THE SCOPE OF INTERNAL CONTROL

The scope of internal control in a manufacturing firm is illustrated in Figure 3-1. Organizational elements, such as marketing, distribution, manufacturing, accounting and finance, and data processing, are established to achieve certain business plans and objectives. These organizational elements are bound together by various management and operational relationships. Internal control ensures that the interrelationship among the organizational elements is in accordance with management policies.

Internal control includes the following elements:

- Management policies.
- Organization and the assignment of tasks and responsibilities within the organizational structure.
- Business plans and projections used by management to guide the organization and evaluate achievement.
- Operating policy and procedures.
- Manual transaction processing procedures and record keeping.

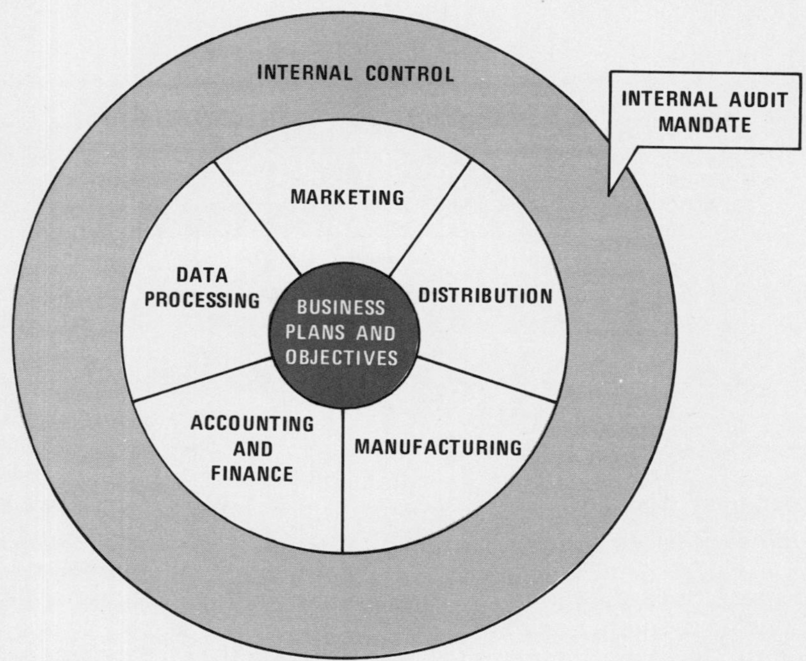

FIGURE 3-1 SCOPE OF INTERNAL CONTROL

The scope of internal control encompasses computer-based information and record keeping systems as well as those independent of data processing.

Management expects internal audit to review, evaluate, and verify controls in all areas, whether or not they involve computer application systems. Figure 3-1 illustrates this responsibility by showing that the whole of internal control may be included in the internal audit mandate. Chapter 4 of this volume presents specific SRI findings and conclusions relating to the role of the internal auditor and the internal audit mandate. See page 4-2 for a discussion of the latter.

Data processing is typically given the responsibility to develop and operate computer application systems that process transactions and maintain records on an accurate and timely basis. These systems are based on policy, organization, and procedures that are both explicit and implicit. Computer application systems developers work with personnel from user groups to develop new systems. They look to these users to provide definitions of the performance characteristics desired.

As more business functions have become automated, the roles of both the system designer and the internal auditor have expanded, as illustrated in Figure 3-2. The system designer has had to become more concerned with the manual procedures that precede (transaction origination and approval) and follow (the use of data processing outputs) the automated phases of computer application systems. Internal auditors have had to become more concerned with procedures and controls within the automated phases of computer application systems. This change and expansion of perspective is occurring in some organizations. It is not, however, a general trend and progress is slow.

ELEMENTS OF INTERNAL CONTROL

The typical data processing function includes three elements:

- Computer application systems, which encompass manual procedures to originate and transmit input transactions to the data processing department; computer application programs that control the processing of transaction data, record maintenance, and output report preparation; and procedures that guide computer service center personnel in the use of specific computer application programs and the handling of the associated input data and output reports.

- Computer service center operations, which encompass the facilities, equipment, personnel, and general procedures that govern computer center operations, as opposed to procedures specific to individual application systems.

- Application systems development, which encompasses the personnel and general procedures governing the design, development, testing, and implementation of the manual procedures and computer application programs that make up computer application systems. This element also includes the modification and improvement of existing computer application programs. Some of the organizations interviewed by SRI reported as much as two-thirds of

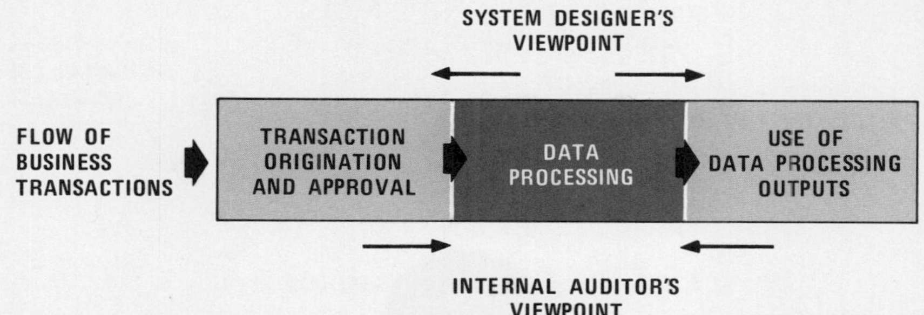

FIGURE 3-2 CHANGING DATA PROCESSING AND INTERNAL AUDIT VIEWPOINTS

their systems development work involved modifications and improvements to existing computer applications.

Figure 3-3 shows these three data processing elements in their relationship to internal control and the internal audit mandate. The components shown in Figure 3-3 are interrelated. The three data processing elements are planned, organized, and managed to achieve various management information system objectives. They are also interdependent. For example, systems development may be constrained by the availability of processing capacity or specialized resources. In contrast, processing capacity may be increased and special features added to accommodate new systems development requirements.

A similar interdependency exists between computer application systems and the computer service center. Poorly designed application programs can degrade overall center operations. Intervention required by center personnel tends to be error prone and to make inefficient use of expensive computer resources. Computer service center operations can have a significant impact upon computer application systems. Poorly or inadequately trained staff are frequent causes of processing problems that affect application systems and their users. Inadequate procedures within the computer service center can cause or allow errors to pass undetected in the preparation, scheduling, and handling of input transactions, data files, and output reports. Such undetected errors can defeat the intent of controls built into computer application programs, at considerable expense in terms of development time and money.

The internal controls that govern computer service center operations and the computer application systems development process are described as general controls, as opposed to application controls, because they are not related to specific computer application systems.

The terms "application controls" and "general controls" are taken from accounting literature used by internal auditors. The terms are used throughout the following chapters and are key to the classification of audit and control techniques made there. Figure 3-4 illustrates the relationship of these terms to the three data processing elements described earlier.

GENERAL CONTROLS GOVERNING APPLICATION SYSTEMS DEVELOPMENT

The adequacy of controls built into a computer application system can be constrained by the lack of knowledge, skill, or experience of the system designers and computer programmers performing the development work. Experience is critical to the successful development of computer application systems, particularly in regard to their internal control aspects. Unfortunately, no comprehensive reference work or standard for computer application controls has, to date, been compiled. The transfer of such knowledge has been slow despite a high level of interest and cooperation among people in the data processing field.

Formal procedures can be adopted to govern the systems development process and ensure that computer application systems are methodically designed, tested, and installed. With careful control of the systems development process, it is possible to achieve higher levels of accuracy and completeness. This is achieved by many data processing organizations through the use of standards and procedures governing computer program structure and coding, testing and user acceptance, documentation, and program change authorization and control. Formalized systems development planning and monitoring techniques, often called "systems development life cycle," are used to ensure that periodic technical and user reviews and approvals occur. These techniques are further discussed in Chapter 12 of the Control Practices Report. Their value is widely accepted in larger installations or where advanced computer application systems are being developed. They ensure a methodical systems development process, which in turn ensures more reliable and accurate computer application programs. Because the controls that gov-

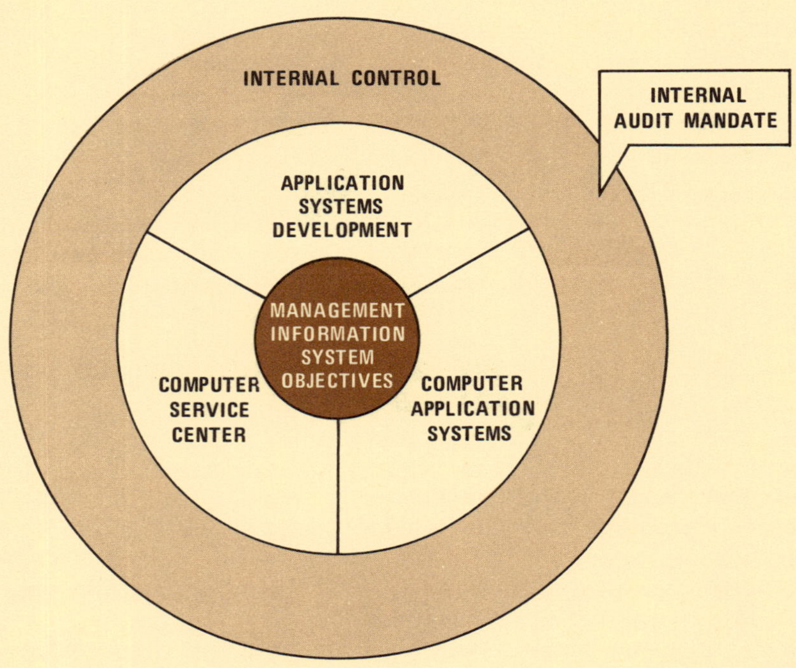

FIGURE 3-3 INTERNAL CONTROL IN THE DATA PROCESSING ENVIRONMENT

ern the systems development process can ultimately affect application controls and the accuracy and completeness of processing, internal auditors are concerned with the adequacy of these controls and may periodically audit for compliance.

COMPUTER SERVICE CENTER

Internal controls are required within the computer service center, independent of, and in addition to, those built into computer application systems. The accuracy and completeness of records and reports produced by data processing depend upon the general controls governing center operations. Inadequate procedures within the center, or failure to comply with established procedures can result in errors in data preparation and handling, production scheduling, file updating, and output report preparation. Controls within the center are functionally independent of the controls built into computer application systems. Important control functions maintained within the computer service center include:

- An input/output control section that schedules computer processing, receives and prepares user data for processing, checks balances and reconciles data processing output, and distributes data processing outputs to users.
- Media library facilities and procedures to provide for the physical storage of data files on such media as magnetic tapes, disk packs, and removable drums.

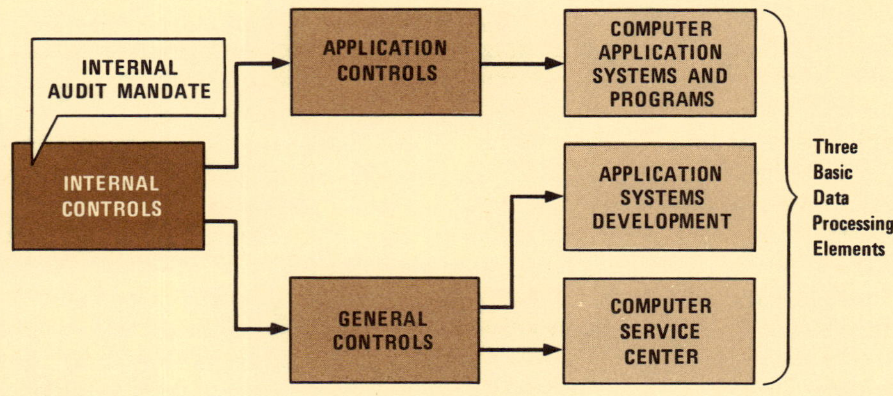

FIGURE 3-4 INTERNAL CONTROL RELATIONSHIP

- Malfunction reporting and preventive maintenance procedures to ensure that data processing equipment and operating system software are maintained in optimum condition so as to prevent undetected errors and omissions from occurring in records and reports produced by data processing. This includes environmental controls and physical security to ensure the continued availability of data files and processing resources and the protection of such resources against hazards such as fire and accidental or intentional destruction.
- Separation of duties to prevent the fraudulent use or misuse of computers, data files, or other critical items, such as negotiable instruments. Separation of duties applies within the data processing organization, as well as between data processing and its users.
- Supervision to ensure that appropriate procedures are followed, personnel are competent to perform their duties, and processing exceptions are properly documented and handled.
- Resource planning to ensure that adequate computing and human resources are available to provide continuity in the processing of existing applications and the development of new applications. Planning typically includes facilities, equipment, general-purpose software, and personnel.
- Disaster recovery procedures to ensure that an organization can respond rapidly to disaster situations that might otherwise cause interruption in the organization's business activities. Disaster recovery is particularly important as data processing resources are concentrated and management comes to rely on data processing for the day-to-day information necessary for evaluating operations and planning.

These computer service center controls are important from two points of view. First, improper scheduling or handling of input documents and/or outputs can directly contribute to inaccuracies in data processing results. Inadequate media library controls can result in the use of incorrect masterfiles during data processing. Separation of duties is necessary to reduce the risk of unauthorized transactions or processing controls being circumvented. If adequate procedures governing these areas are not established and maintained, the accuracy and completeness of data processing results can be compromised despite the controls that may be built into computer application systems and programs used during processing.

Second, controls such as those that govern malfunction reporting and preventive maintenance, the computer environment, and physical security are important to ensure the continuing availability of the equipment, data files, and application programs necessary to process an organization's information on a day-to-day basis. If these important resources are not protected and properly maintained, the flow of needed information to management can be disrupted.

Controls governing the systems development process and computer service center operations are typically the responsibility of data processing management because the control procedures themselves are not directly performed by other organizational elements. Various control techniques have evolved as new data processing technology and practices have been adopted.

While data processing users are involved with the general controls used within data processing, they are concerned that the general controls be appropriate and consistently applied to ensure that processing results are timely, accurate, and complete. Such controls have become of increasing interest to internal auditors because they can directly affect processing results.

APPLICATION SYSTEM CONTROLS

Computer application system controls, as previously described, involve both manual and automated procedures. Automated procedures may include terminal data entry performed in user areas outside data processing, as well as computer program procedures that control the flow of data within a computer system. Manual procedures in user areas are developed to ensure that the transactions processed by data processing are correctly prepared, authorized, and submitted to data processing. Manual application control procedures are also required within data processing. For example, balancing and reconciling input to output are frequently performed by the data processing input/output control section. File retention and security procedures may be required and specified for individual computer application systems. Such controls are unique to the requirements of a computer application system and complement general controls that govern input/output control and the media library.

Six steps in the flow of transactions through a computer application system are shown in Figure 3-5. Transaction flow has been used as a basis for classifying application controls because it seems, based on field interviews, to provide a common framework for internal auditors, data processing personnel, and others interested in computer application systems.

The two shaded blocks on the figure are activities primarily involving the data processing user organization. The following paragraphs briefly describe each element of the figure.

Transaction Origination — Application controls govern the origination, approval, and processing of source documents, and the preparation of data processing input transactions and associated error detection and correction procedures.

Data Processing Transaction Entry — Application controls govern the data entry, either remote terminal

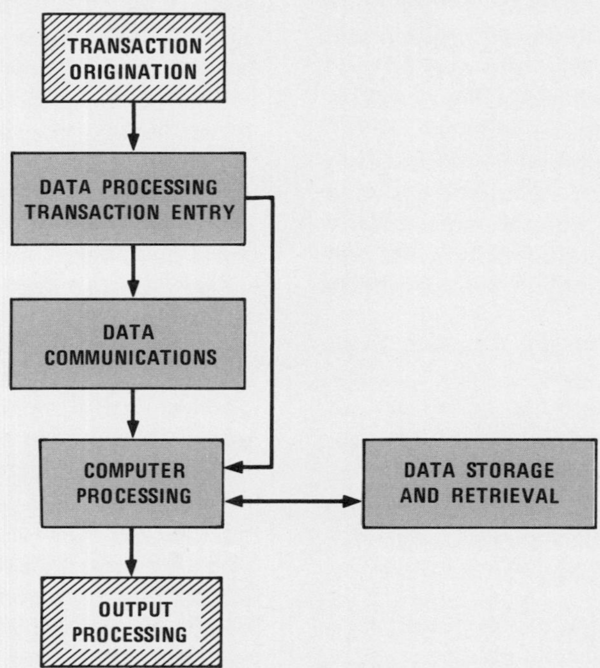

FIGURE 3-5 SCHEME FOR CLASSIFICATION OF APPLICATION SYSTEM CONTROLS

or batch, data validation, transaction or batch proofing and balancing, error identification and reporting, and error correction and reentry.

Data Communications — Application controls govern the accuracy and completeness of data communications, including message accountability, data protection hardware and software, security and privacy, error identification, and reporting.

Computer Processing — Application controls govern the accuracy and completeness of transaction processing, including the appropriateness of machine-generated transactions, transaction validation against masterfiles, error identification, and reporting.

Data Storage and Retrieval — Application controls govern masterfile data accuracy and completeness, correct transaction/masterfile cutoff, data security and privacy, and error handling, as well as backup, recovery, and retention. Note that file integrity controls reflect the growing use of general-purpose file handling, data base software, and an attendant trend to view processing procedures as independent of data files.

Output Processing — Application controls govern the manual balancing and reconciling of data processing input and output (both within the data processing input/output control section and at user locations), distribution of data processing output, control over negotiable documents (both within data processing and user areas), and output data retention.

This scheme, which illustrates the flow of transactions through a computer application system and the classification of application controls, is consistent with the way both data processing and internal audit personnel view computer application systems. Furthermore, it illustrates the complete scope of a computer application system, starting with controls governing the authorization and origination of source documents, and it provides a total system context in which to view internal controls, both manual and automated.

WHO IS RESPONSIBLE FOR INTERNAL CONTROLS?

When this question is asked, one can expect many different responses. The results of field interviews and other related SRI experience indicate that the responsibility for internal controls is not well-defined or understood.

There is agreement that the ultimate responsibility for internal controls resides with top management. At lower levels within an organization, however, the responsibility for internal control tends to be fragmented. Internal controls governing the manual phases of transaction processing and record keeping tend to be the responsibility of line management in charge of specific organizational units. Users can be viewed as being responsible for establishing the requirements for controls within the computer processing phase of an application system. Data processing management typically is responsible for designing and implementing the controls governing automated phases of computer application systems, and controls governing other phases of data processing activities. In many situations, controls in these two areas reflect accounting and financial reporting control objectives. Unfortunately, controls are often established to meet the needs of various stages of manual and computer processing without being evaluated within the context of the total computer application system and its associated control objectives.

System designers from data processing often have the broadest understanding of total system operations and requirements. However, they are often more technically oriented than controls-oriented, and the pressures of their implementation schedules frequently prevent a proper overall evaluation of internal control, particularly those controls not directly related to data processing, transaction processing, and record keeping. In contrast, users and accountants usually have a good understanding of overall financial control objectives, but lack the familiarity with computer application system procedures and related controls. As a result, internal controls associated with computer application systems are frequently fragmented and not evaluated within the context of total computer application systems requirements. Often, multiple controls, in various locations, may be designated to achieve a common objective.

Internal auditors are becoming increasingly involved in evaluating internal controls relating to computer application systems. This is a result of their relatively independent perspective in reviewing internal controls in user areas as well as within data processing. Changes in the internal auditor's role in this regard are discussed in the following chapter. It is important to note, however, that although the internal auditor may be used effectively in the review of internal controls and may even make control recommendations, the responsibility for internal controls properly resides with data processing and the user groups responsible for the preparation and processing of transactions, record keeping, and resulting management reports. The role of the auditor is to judge the adequacy of controls and to recommend control improvements. Responsibility to implement and maintain appropriate controls resides with data processing function and user organizations.

From a philosophical point of view, the primary responsibility for internal controls resides with those organizations requesting data processing services and establishing associated service requirements. Although they may look to data processing management to recommend and maintain certain controls, data processing is, in fact, a service organization. Therefore, the responsibility for the accuracy and completeness of records and associated management reports resides with those organizations to which management has assigned a functional information system responsibility (e.g., payroll, accounts payable, inventory control). In practice, data processing often assumes considerable responsibility for the accuracy of management information and associated controls. This occurs for two reasons. First, as information systems have been automated, management in groups using data processing has assumed that all aspects of those systems were the responsibility of data processing. This is often because top management has improperly placed the primary responsibility for the implementation of such systems with data processing, which has tended to relegate users to a secondary role in the implementation process. A complementary factor is the willingness of users to let data processing accept this responsibility. Second, user groups often lack the data processing experience and knowledge needed to evaluate control alternatives and to select proper control techniques. They have looked to data processing to provide the guidance in all things relating to computer application systems. These trends have blurred the lines of responsibility for the accuracy and completeness of computer-based information systems.

The primary responsibility for computer-based information systems can be restored to data processing users by requiring users to define the control requirements of their systems and then to work with data processing personnel to ensure that the systems are designed with control and audit features appropriate to meeting the control requirements. Adequate systems design will then include controls and audit features that allow users to verify all aspects of the data processing performed on their behalf. Many firms have established this criterion as a primary guideline for application systems development. It is necessary to restore the proper accountability for accurate and complete management information. In such a situation, the proper role of internal audit can be maintained as a function that reviews and evaluates the effectiveness and adequacy of controls, and verifies the accuracy and completeness of records and reports.

SELECTION OF APPLICATION SYSTEM CONTROLS

The selection of appropriate application system controls is typically not a formalized or structured process. Decisions as to what controls are appropriate to ensure the accuracy and completeness of data processed are usually not considered separately from other system design criteria. Data processing management interviewed by SRI frequently said that they view controls as secondary to the functional requirements of an application system. Such a view does not minimize the importance of application controls, but reflects typical systems development methodology. In developing computer application systems, data processing personnel first establish the functional requirements of the systems to be developed. They then establish appropriate procedures and application control techniques. In contrast, internal auditors interviewed by SRI place primary importance on the controls that ensure the accuracy and completeness of data. The adequacy and effectiveness of such controls gives them confidence in the reliability and accuracy of the data processed.

Some organizations have attempted to establish a control philosophy early in the development of application systems as a basis for evaluating and selecting application controls. They report that this is a desirable approach because control structures can be integrated with processing procedures from the outset of system design and development. In addition, all participants in the systems development effort have a common control philosophy or frame of reference. With this approach, selection and development of specific control techniques can be evaluated in terms of functional requirements of the application system and the preestablished control philosophy.

Even in situations where control philosophies or general guidelines to application controls have been adopted, the evaluation and selection of individual control techniques are generally unstructured. Application system designers rely on their own prior experience and ingenuity when new situations are presented. When new technology is applied requiring new control techniques, assistance is most often secured from the organization's computer vendor and other system designers who have been faced with similar application control problems.

A number of the larger organizations visited by SRI have developed control guidelines for application systems development. Such guidelines represent a substantial contribution in terms of knowledge transferred between system designers and other people concerned with the adequacy of application controls. Much of the material included in the Control Practices Report has been documented and presented to improve the exchange of knowledge relative to application controls.

One firm interviewed includes a controls evaluation as part of their design review of progressive application systems. In this situation, controls are evaluated independent of other design criteria. Functional requirements and technical approach are assumptions against which application controls are evaluated on a system flow-through basis. This review includes manual controls as well as automated controls.

A comprehensive philosophy for application system controls necessarily includes the following perspectives:

- Automated procedures and controls that are incorporated within computer application programs (e.g., data validation, error checking).
- Manual procedures and controls that have been designed to complement computer application controls (e.g., data entry procedures, batch or transaction control totals, batch balancing and reconciliation).
- Manual procedures and controls not directly interdependent with computer application system programs (e.g., policies and procedures governing the origination of business transactions that are eventually entered into data processing, or management's uses of information produced by data processing).
- Organizational controls that provide proper statements of procedures, assignment of responsibilities, and competent, trained personnel.

Establishing a comprehensive application control philosophy or approach often requires more than one point of view. For example, a financial officer may have to review and confirm basic financial control policy, on issues such as accruals, to recognize income earned but not billed. Such transactions may require unique controls to ensure correct preparation and approval. In addition, special application systems provisions may be required to enter and record such transactions. These typically entail functional processing procedures within computer application programs, as well as complementary manual procedures for data entry, balancing, and reconciliation. The development of such a comprehensive application control structure involves accounting policy, accounting procedures, and computer application systems procedures, both manual and automated. Although this is a simplified example, organizations interviewed that had successfully approached application control in a total systems context have found that several people may become involved before internal control requirements are fully understood and satisfied. This is because different organizations, organizational levels, and disciplines are entailed.

SRI's field findings indicate there is no widely used approach to the evaluation of control alternatives and the selection of appropriate application system controls. This is because the functional and procedural requirements of computer application systems vary significantly from organization to organization, and among applications within an organization, and because data processing systems development personnel think of application controls as being derived from the functional and procedural requirements of an application system. Accordingly, data processing personnel have done little to develop generalized approaches or criteria for application controls. Progress is being made within some organizations as a result of cooperation between internal auditors, accountants, and data processing system designers in establishing application control guidelines and in conducting evaluations of the adequacy and appropriateness of application controls during the systems development process.

EVALUATION AND VERIFICATION OF CONTROLS

Reviews to evaluate and verify controls are usually performed during final implementation and before acceptance of business systems as fully operational. A review of controls is also performed subsequent to initial implementation to ensure that controls have not become obsolete because of changes in the business environment since original installation or have fallen into disuse due to system change or employee apathy. These tests or reviews include preinstallation testing, postinstallation testing, and verification of manual procedures.

Preinstallation Review

The verification of computer application program controls requires careful planning and methodology. Application programs are becoming increasingly complex in terms of the number of controls and interrelationships between controls. Many control points are required within application programs to direct the flow of transactions during processing. Transactions may take different paths through an application system before processing is complete. The transaction type and associated controls built into the application programs are used to determine the routing and processing appropriate to each input transaction. As a result, transaction flow is often circuitous and a multitude of control points are involved. Comprehensive verification requires tests to provide evidence that all prescribed controls are operating properly.

The growing complexity of computer application controls and resulting verification tests reflect three automation trends:

- Procedures to detect errors and handle exceptions, which were once performed manually, are being automated.
- Computer application programs are being integrated with one another through the development of interrelated processing procedures and common or shared data files.
- Fewer opportunities for manual checks during the process are a result of automation of exception routines and the integration of computer application systems, for example, order entry transactions that flow to, and are processed by, inventory accounting and billing applications without intermediate manual review.

The elimination of manual intervention removes opportunities for errors and reduces overall processing time. However, it dramatically increases the size of application programs, the number of controls, and the testing required to verify controls.

As a result, computer application systems require extensive preinstallation testing to verify controls and ensure that processing results conform to specifications developed with users. Preinstallation testing is usually conducted with users and data processing personnel. Internal auditors are also becoming involved in preinstallation, as will be discussed in the following chapter. In some organizations, the scope of preinstallation testing has become so large and complex that separate task teams have been set up within development projects to prepare test data and perform verification tests. More often, such testing is performed by the same data processing and user personnel who participated in the development of application systems and programs, a practice that tends to reduce the rigorousness of testing and violates the principle of independence.

The time and cost of comprehensive preinstallation testing of computer applications are justified for two reasons: First, undetected errors and omissions can result in incorrect and misleading processing results (e.g., reports and records); second, once verified, processing procedures and associated controls will be executed consistently, barring program modifications, unauthorized computer operator intervention, equipment malfunction or failure, or incorrect manual input preparation. Proper preinstallation testing and verification gives assurance that processing results will be reliable and complete.

Postinstallation Review

Postinstallation testing is performed by internal audit periodically to verify controls governing computer application systems. Such testing is typically not comprehensive and is used to verify specific computer applications procedures, calculations, and control routines such as audit trail adequacy, user identification controls, and user documentation. Postinstallation testing performed by internal auditors is described in Chapter 4.

Verification of Manual Procedures

The accuracy and completeness of data processing results are dependent upon compliance with manual procedures designed to complement application program controls. Once application programs are properly tested and verified, they will execute consistently thereafter. In contrast, the manual phases of computer application system operation are subject to the inconsistency of human performance. Consequently, periodic verifications of compliance are necessary.

Compliance with manual application system requirements is important because of the interdependency between automated and manual controls. The manual interface with automated application systems is a weak point. As application systems have been designed to perform more functions and handle more exceptions, supporting manual procedures have become intricate and highly structured. Thorough user documentation and training are required to ensure a high level of compliance with manual requirements. A comprehensive review-and-verification of the manual phases of automated applications requires an understanding of application program controls.

SRI field interviews confirm that preinstallation testing and periodic postinstallation reviews are used to verify internal controls in the data processing environment. Preimplementation tests are usually performed by data processing and user personnel and place emphasis on computer application program verification. Periodic reviews subsequent to implementation are performed primarily by internal auditors and emphasize manual procedures.

SUMMARY

Internal control in the data processing environment is becoming increasingly important as more business functions are automated and as management becomes more dependent on data processing results. Management relies on internal controls to ensure the accuracy and completeness of such results. As a result of automation, internal controls governing computer-based information systems and data processing are taking new forms and are becoming highly structured.

Three areas requiring internal control in the data processing environment are computer application systems, computer service center operations, and the application systems development process. The areas are interdependent because they each affect the accuracy and completeness of data processing. Accordingly, control objectives must be considered within the context of the total management information and data processing process.

Audit cannot be separated from control. Internal controls in the data processing environment govern transaction processing, record keeping, and reporting; internal audit is the evaluation and verification of these controls and the results of data processing. Thus, internal controls and the records and reports produced by data processing are the objects of internal audit.

Internal auditors and system designers usually have different perspectives concerning controls. In developing computer application systems, system designers first design the functional requirements of the application system and secondly consider application controls. Such a perspective does not necessarily minimize the importance of application controls; rather, it reflects a logical sequence of thought during the systems development process. In contrast, however, internal auditors place primary emphasis on controls. This is because they evaluate the accuracy and completeness of data processing results. This difference in viewpoint has not helped bring data processing and internal audit professionals together.

Little progress has been made in developing comprehensive control guidelines or criteria for systems development. This lack of progress is particularly important to internal auditors who, therefore, have few standards against which to evaluate the adequacy of specific controls. The evaluation of alternatives and the selection of appropriate application controls represent, today, an unstructured and rather informal process.

The primary responsibility for internal control resides with top management. The responsibility for internal controls relating to specific computer application systems should reside with those organizational elements to whom management has assigned the functional responsibility (i.e., payroll, accounts payable, accounts receivable, inventory control). Current practice in many organizations sees this responsibility as shared between users and data processing. The first-line responsibility for accuracy and completeness should reside with data processing users, instead of with data processing itself. The relationship between data processing users, internal auditors, and the data processing department should be reviewed and clear statements of responsibility established relating to the development of appropriate controls and the continuing accuracy and completeness of data processing results.

The review of application controls occurs both before and after the installation of computer application systems. Preinstallation testing is performed by data processing personnel to verify computer application procedures and controls. Periodic postinstallation reviews are performed primarily by internal auditors. Such tests and verifications are performed to ensure that application procedures and controls have not become obsolete due to changes in the business environment, and that application procedures and controls are being followed. Emphasis in most organizations is currently on manual procedures and data processing outputs, but emphasis is shifting to include internal controls governing the automated phases of application systems. Management should ensure that effective periodic postinstallation verifications are performed.

Despite the need for greater emphasis on the automated phases of application system processing, system designers and internal auditors will continue to be concerned with the adequacy of manual procedures that must be designed to complement increasingly complex application system programs. The interface between manual and automated steps is one of the most vulnerable areas and requires careful design of both the manual and automated controls that prevent undetected errors and omissions.

EVALUATION AND OUTLOOK

Inadequate attention has, in the past, been given to the importance of internal controls, both by individual organizations and the data processing industry in general. The importance of controls for computer application systems and data processing applications has been more recently highlighted as a result of the errors, omissions, losses, and fraud that have been reported in the media. Improvements are being made, but several years may be required to incorporate needed controls into existing application systems by organizations with large data processing functions.

Improvements are needed in three areas. First, control objectives should be identified during the system development process and recognized as separate system development requirements. Several organizations have successfully developed and used control checklists and guidelines to aid system designers in evaluating and selecting appropriate control techniques to satisfy their control objectives. As new technology and application system design concepts are introduced, appropriate control techniques and alternatives need to be established and integrated into existing guidelines. Formalized control guidelines not only assist system designers but also provide a standard for internal auditors. It is particularly beneficial if data processing and internal audit personnel jointly establish the control guidelines.

Second, manual procedures designed to complement computer application programs are becoming increasingly complex as more business activities are automated. The design and development of application programs that perform more functions and handle more exception conditions cause supporting manual procedures to be intricate and highly structured. Increasingly complex manual procedures can contribute to higher levels of errors. Therefore, system designers must give careful consideration to the human factors affecting the manual phases of computer application systems and data processing operations. To this end, system designers must view all controls, both manual and automated, within the context of the total information handling process.

Third, internal control guidelines need to be developed jointly by The National Bureau of Standards, data processing user groups such as GUIDE, professional associations such as The Institute of Internal Auditors and the American Institute of Certified Public Accountants (AICPA) and equipment manufacturers. A framework of guidelines and objectives would be of great benefit to system designers and internal auditors. The control techniques documented and reported as a result of this study will be useful, as will the scheme used for their presentation. However, more comprehensive work that is directed specifically to the establishment of control guidelines and techniques is needed. Such work must integrate audit and control standards and guidelines promulgated by organizations such as the AICPA, and control techniques that have evolved through the successful experience of data processing professionals. Although it is proper, useful, and timely for data processing and internal audit personnel to work together within individual organizations to develop controlled guidelines, industry-wide effort is necessary to provide effective guidelines and suggested techniques that can be widely distributed and applied. Management should support such industry-wide efforts to establish effective control guidelines.

In proceeding with such a development program, it is important that representatives be included from all the segments of business and government that are concerned with systems auditability and control.

Chapter 4

THE ROLE OF INTERNAL AUDIT IN ORGANIZATIONS USING DATA PROCESSING

The role of the internal auditor is changing and taking on a new importance relative to data processing, as more functions within the organization are automated and as management places greater reliance on computer application systems. Internal audit's increasing involvement with data processing is an extension of traditional internal audit responsibilities, as management seeks assurance that computer application systems are accurate and reliable. The EDP audit function within internal audit is an important and relatively recent trend and is expanding to include computer application systems development, computer service center operations, and controls internal to computer application programs. Emphasis is shifting from the evaluation and verification of processing results (e.g., data files, records, and reports) to the evaluation and verification of the controls that ensure the continuing accuracy and reliability of processing results. This emphasis is resulting in new internal audit approaches and techniques.

NEED FOR INTERNAL AUDIT

Insufficient control is the most frequently reported concern of top management in the United States, Canada, and Europe, according to the SRI mail survey. Interviews with top management indicate that this concern is based on two related factors:

- Increasing dependence upon computer application systems.
- The belief that opportunities for errors and omissions increase as computer application systems become more comprehensive and complex.

The latter factor is supported by the Primary U.S. Mail Survey findings, wherein loss from errors and omissions is one of the two most frequently reported concerns of both data processing managers and internal auditors.

Related Primary U.S. Mail Survey findings indicate that, within organizations having internal auditors, about 78% of top management feel that internal auditors' reviews provide assurance of adequate internal controls. An almost equal percentage feel that external auditors provide such assurances. However, in organizations that have no internal auditors, about 62% of top management look to external auditors for assurance of adequate internal controls. Of Japanese top management responding to this question, 60% look to the users and data processing review groups to assure themselves that application systems contain adequate control, while only 10% rely on external auditors. Canadian and European top management indicate the same sources of assurances as expressed in the Primary U.S. Mail Survey. See Table 4-1 for further information relating to the Primary U.S. Mail Survey.

INTERNAL AUDIT MANDATE

During the field interviews, SRI talked with top management and internal audit management regarding their organizations' mandates for the internal audit function. These discussions reflected a wide range of variation. One reason for such variation is the corresponding variation in organizational structure and objectives. Another reason is differences in the internal audit department's relative involvement in the types of information systems for which computer application systems have been developed. Primary emphasis in most organizations was on the verification of financial and accounting application systems.

The following objectives and scope are included in the statement of responsibility issued by The Institute of Internal Auditors to its members:

"The objective of internal auditing is to assist all members of management in the effective discharge of their responsibilities, by furnishing them with analyses, appraisals, recommendations and pertinent comments concerning the activities reviewed. The internal auditor is concerned with any phase of business activity where he can be of service to management. This involves going beyond the accounting and financial records to obtain a full understanding of the operations under review. The attainment of this overall objective involves such activities as:

- Reviewing and appraising the soundness, adequacy, and application of accounting, financial, and other operating controls, and promoting effective control at reasonable cost.
- Ascertaining the extent of compliance with established policies, plans, and procedures.

Table 4-1
TOP MANAGEMENT'S ASSURANCE OF ADEQUATE APPLICATION CONTROLS

What assurances do you have that your organization's computer applications contain adequate internal controls? (Check all that apply)*

	Percentage Selecting Each Category†		
	Organizations with Internal Auditors	Organizations Without Internal Auditors	All Organizations
Reviews by external auditors	78.9%	62.2%	75.5%
Reviews by users	64.3	62.8	64.0
Reviews by internal auditors	77.7	0.0	59.4
Reviews by data processing review group	38.1	26.7	35.6
Executive management signoffs on approval	21.3	20.4	21.1
Other	9.2	7.8	8.9
Currently have no such assurances	4.6	8.2	5.4

Note: Number of respondents = 249

*Percentages sum to more than 100% because each respondent checked all applicable categories.

†Percentages are based on actual responses weighted to reflect the probable response distribution of all organizations in the sampling frame. See the appendix for further description of weighting procedures.

- Ascertaining the extent to which company assets are accounted for and safeguarded from losses of all kinds.
- Ascertaining the reliability of management data developed within the organization.
- Appraising the quality of performance in carrying out assigned responsibilities.
- Recommending operating improvements."

This statement provides a broad framework that may be useful to top management in formulating an appropriate mandate for their organizations.

INTERNAL AUDIT INDEPENDENCE

Top management and internal audit management interviewed by SRI reported that they believe internal audit should have a high degree of independence in selecting areas to be audited and in the performance of their work. They believe greater independence results from higher levels of reporting within the organization. An estimated 50% of the U.S. firms in the Primary U.S. Mail Survey have an audit committee of the board of directors. No Japanese firms reported the existence of an audit committee, while less than 10% of the European and about 33% of the Canadian firms reported having one. On the other hand, over 69% of the leading U.S. companies visited by SRI reported an audit committee. Survey results also indicate that, in 53% of the U.S. firms with an audit committee, internal auditors periodically prepare reports that are submitted directly to the audit committee, and in 22% the auditors report directly to that committee.

Audit committees are increasingly interested in their organizations' data processing activities. The Primary U.S. Mail Survey of top management of large corporations indicated that, in 70% of the organizations with an audit committee, that committee had communicated directly with the organization's internal auditors regarding data processing activities, and 77% indicated that the audit committee had communicated directly with external auditors regarding data processing.

SRI field interviews suggest that six factors relating to independence are important to a successful and effective internal audit function:

- A written policy statement specifying the internal audit mandate that includes the objectives and prerogatives of the internal audit functions; such a policy need not be either lengthy or detailed.
- Independence to plan and pursue audit work within the scope of the written mandate.
- Access to and support from top management for internal audit plans and programs.
- Support of the organization's external auditors.
- Access to consultants from outside the organization.
- Access to all phases of the organization including data processing.

Given these conditions, the internal audit function must make effective use of its prerogatives and independence without unnecessarily alienating operating management in the areas being audited.

These six factors seem to apply equally to large and small organizations that have an internal audit function. The primary differences between the larger and smaller organizations are, aside from the number of internal auditors, the degree of formality that exists. Larger internal audit functions have formalized the mandate, reporting relationships, and internal audit programs. Smaller internal audit functions tend to be more informal and to rely upon more personal relationships with top management and operating management.

EVOLVING ROLE OF THE INTERNAL AUDITOR IN DATA PROCESSING

An EDP audit specialty is evolving within internal audit. This is a result of the need for internal auditors to possess data processing knowledge and skills in order to do their work independent of the data processing department. As more business functions are automated, internal auditors are faced with the problem of being able to audit effectively and independently in a data processing environment.

The evolution of the EDP audit specialty is still in its early stages. Primary U.S. Mail Survey results from U.S. firms indicate that 78% have an internal audit function, while only 62% have EDP auditors. Table 4-2 shows the growth of EDP audit functions among U.S. firms that currently have EDP auditors.

Table 4-2
TREND IN ESTABLISHING AN EDP AUDIT FUNCTION

What year was your organization's EDP audit function established?

Year Established	Percentage Established*
Before 1950	0.7%
1950-1959	3.2
1960-1964	10.8
1965-1969	15.1
1970-1974	42.0
1975-1976	28.1

Note: Number of respondents = 172

*Percentages are based on actual responses weighted to reflect the probable response distribution of all organizations in the sampling frame. See the appendix for further description of weighting procedures.

Note that 70% of the organizations that now have EDP audit functions founded that function since 1970, indicating that EDP audit is a relatively recent innovation. Its development in larger organizations reflects greater reliance on data processing, increasingly complex management information systems, and increasing reliance upon internal audit to verify the accuracy and completeness of data processing results. Smaller organizations have tended to implement less complex computer application systems and to rely more on external auditors.

The Primary U.S. Mail Survey was structured to allow an analysis to identify differences in audit practices, if any, between organizations in regulated versus those in nonregulated industries. Key questions were selected that SRI believed could identify such differences. Analysis of these questions revealed no important differences in questionnaire responses between regulated and nonregulated industries, with the following two exceptions. First, nonregulated industries are less likely to have internal auditors than are regulated industries. An estimated 95% of the regulated companies have internal auditors, as compared with only 71% of the nonregulated companies. However, mail survey results indicate that regulated and nonregulated firms with internal audit are equally likely to have an EDP audit function. Second, regulated firms report involvement in the later stages of application systems with slightly greater frequency than do nonregulated firms. These findings are notable because it was assumed at the outset of the study that there would be important differences in the audit practices between regulated and nonregulated organizations. This assumption was not supported by the SRI analysis.

TRADITIONAL INTERNAL AUDIT APPROACH

Internal audit has traditionally placed emphasis on the verification of records, controls, and the adequacy of controls in the manual systems. This approach was developed to ensure the accuracy and completeness of records and reports. In a traditional manual systems environment, internal auditors could directly observe transaction processing, record keeping, and the preparation of reports. The verification of records was performed manually from ledgers and other written documents.

The early stages of business automation typically involved single-function application systems. Individual parts of the manual system were automated. These application systems were typically run on a batch basis. Input transactions were accumulated to create a batch for processing. Batch controls were usually computed by users and used by data processing personnel to verify subsequent processing steps. For example, tabulating card applications and early computer application systems automated individual steps in an accounts payable application. After each step there were manual checks to ensure the accuracy and completeness of processing in such data processing applications; typically, users and/or computer operations personnel verified control totals after each step in the processing procedure. If errors were encountered during processing, processing was suspended until errors were resolved. The users normally had complete control over the origination and cutoff of transactions affecting the records maintained for them by the data processing department. Verification of the accuracy and completeness of data processed was easily performed by reconciling beginning and ending balances with the total balance of transactions submitted for computer processing.

In a similar manner, internal auditors verified processing results without reviewing controls internal to data processing or tracing transactions through data processing. This internal audit approach is often described as "auditing around the computer" and is illustrated in Figure 4-1. Internal audit tests to verify the accuracy and completeness of processing results were performed using reports produced as normal processing outputs. Little specialized knowledge and few specialized tools or techniques were required by internal auditors.

CHANGING APPLICATION SYSTEMS STRUCTURE

Computer application systems have become more complex and present new problems for internal auditors. For example, computer application systems are being tied together so that a transaction entered into one application system may eventually be processed against a number of previously independent masterfiles. A customer order transaction may result in changes in the balances of several masterfiles without intermediate manual review. An inventory masterfile may be credited for the quantity to be shipped and retail value or cost of the items ordered. In so doing, the quantity on hand may drop below the order point, subsequently triggering the preparation of a procurement notice or purchase order. The order transaction may also automatically trigger the preparation of warehouse shipping instructions and a customer invoice, and may update the customer's accounts receivable record.

Not all organizations have implemented computer application systems using such advanced data processing design concepts. Various changes in the structure of application systems are taking place, however, in both large and small organizations:

- Input transactions are being entered for immediate, on-line processing from remote terminal locations, in contrast to the single-entry point batch input, typical of earlier years. Approximately 79% of the organizations in the Primary U.S. Mail Survey indicate expenditures of at least $1 million for data communications equipment from the data processing budget, exclusive of terminals. This is one measure of the increasing use of data communications. Data processing industry statistics also reflect the growing use of data communications.
- Applications are being tied together so that a single input transaction performs multiple functions as described in the previous example. Transactions are also being generated within application programs and automatically flow into others.
- Audit trails in hardcopy form are being eliminated. For example, detailed lists of input transactions and periodic master data file listings are being replaced by transaction logs on magnetic tape that can be printed if a need arises, and by on-line data bases for master data file interrogation.

Internal auditors working in this data processing environment report they can no longer audit around the computer and satisfy their managements' mandate. This is because so many of the controls that ensure the accuracy and completeness of data processing results are now automated and can no longer be reviewed and verified through direct observation.

AUDITING COMPUTER APPLICATION SYSTEMS

Auditing in this environment encompasses three primary areas, from the internal auditor's point of view. Each of these areas (listed below) should be reviewed based upon organization controls that provide for appropriate definition and segregation of responsibilities.

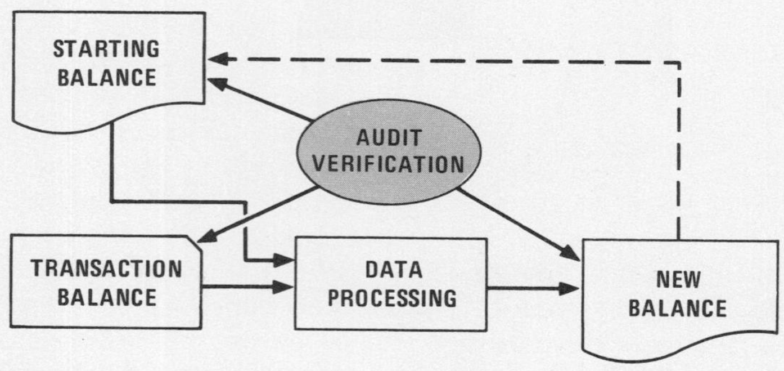

FIGURE 4-1 AUDITING AROUND THE COMPUTER

■ Manual procedures that have been developed to complement controls internal to computer application programs (e.g., input preparation, input control, error handling, and output balancing and reconciliation).

■ Application system controls internal to computer application programs (e.g., data validation, control total verification, batch or transaction balancing and proofing, and error identification and reporting).

■ Data files and reports produced as a result of computer application processing (e.g., data processing masterfiles, transaction logs, and output reports).

Figure 4-2 illustrates these three areas.

Auditing these areas includes a review of controls to determine their adequacy, tests to verify controls, and tests to verify data (i.e., masterfiles and reports). Each of these is discussed below.

Review Adequacy of Controls

The review of application system controls is performed to evaluate the adequacy of application controls, both manual and automated. The controls review phase of an audit is usually performed before the verification of controls; it is not so much a separate activity as it is a separate audit objective. Some internal audit organizations perform the controls review before installation of a new application, usually during systems development. Most internal auditors interviewed by SRI perform an evaluation of the adequacy of application controls as a part of periodic application audits. The objectives of such reviews are to determine if application controls are adequate to:

■ Ensure the accuracy and completeness of processing results (i.e., data files and reports).

■ Prevent undetected errors and omissions.

■ Ensure the continuing reliability of data processing results.

An additional objective is to determine if control techniques have become outmoded because of changes in the business environment that are not reflected in computer application systems. In conducting such evaluations, internal auditors observe and test manual input preparation, error handling, and output balancing and reconciliation procedures.

Verify Controls

Application system audits performed by internal auditors include a verification of controls. Such tests provide evidence of compliance with established control procedures, both manual and automated. Compliance testing is a public accounting term that some internal auditors who were interviewed used to describe the controls verification phase of their work. Compliance testing is not, however, a widely used term among internal auditors.

The internal auditor's objective in performing control verifications is to determine that manual controls are properly and consistently applied, and that automated controls are operating properly and have not been modified in some manner inconsistent with overall control objectives. Some internal auditors interviewed by SRI place emphasis on the manual phase of computer application operations because manual control procedures are more susceptible to inconsistent or incorrect application. During SRI field interviews, data processing and internal auditors reported that most incorrect data processing results can be attributed to the failure to follow manual control procedures or to the inadequacy of manual pro-

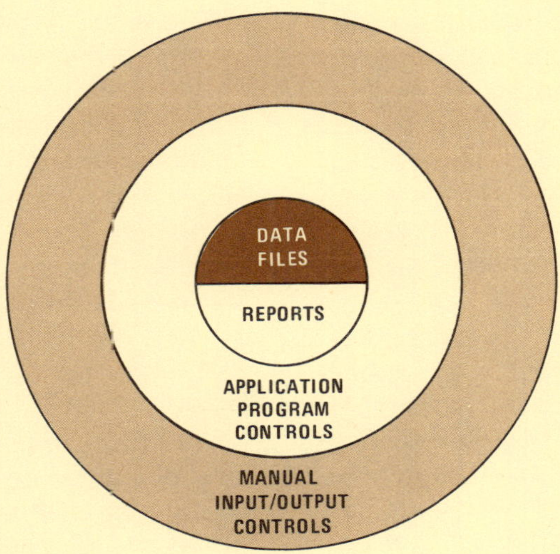

FIGURE 4-2 THREE AREAS OF AUDITING COMPUTER APPLICATION SYSTEMS

cedures. In contrast, when computer application programs are properly tested, they execute consistently, time after time, barring equipment malfunction or improper program modification.

The techniques internal auditors use in verifying manual application controls include observation, manual tracing of transaction handling and preparation, and examination of supporting source documents and logs. Primary U.S. Mail Survey findings indicate that one or more automated tools and techniques are used by an estimated 69% of the internal auditors of U.S. firms. These include techniques such as test data, parallel simulation, integrated test facilities (ITFs), and generalized audit software. Such automated techniques use the computer in auditing and, therefore, require internal auditors with data processing knowledge and experience.

Verify Data

Verifications of data processing files and reports are performed to secure evidence that processing results are accurate and complete. Public accounting literature refers to such tests and reviews as substantive tests. Few internal auditors interviewed by SRI used this term. Whereas controls verification focuses on the procedures governing data processing, the objective of data verification is to examine data files and output reports to determine their reliability.

Data verification and control verification are complementary. If a sufficient quantity of processing results are consistently accurate and complete, it seems to follow that application controls must be adequate and are being followed. Neither of these examinations is, however, entirely adequate. Data verification techniques confirm the accuracy and completeness of processing during a past period. Control verification is needed to give assurance of continued reliability. Data verification techniques used by internal auditors are both manual and automated. Manual sampling, verification of balances, and confirmation preparation are still used. An estimated 33% of the internal auditors of organizations in the Primary U.S. Mail Survey, however, use generalized audit software for data verification. A number of firms interviewed by SRI are using specialized audit software to interrogate and verify the controls of data files.

The process of auditing computer application systems is necessarily selective. Few computer applications are audited on a continuous basis. Most of the internal auditors interviewed audited computer applications only periodically. A typical approach may result in annual verification of certain data such as customer balances, retirement funds, or pension funds. Complete control reviews and verifications may be performed only every few years for a particular application system.

AUDITING COMPUTER SERVICE CENTERS

Procedures and controls governing computer center operations are of concern to internal auditors because they affect the accuracy and completeness of processing results. Several internal auditors interviewed by SRI reported that they have performed computer center audits that include procedures for physical security, program and data library control, fire protection, backup and disaster recovery, and input/output scheduling and control. This appears to be a common practice in EDP audit, although no statistical data were developed during this study. Larger organizations are developing a capability within internal audit to perform such reviews periodically. Smaller organizations use consultants or specialists from public accounting firms to review and evaluate center operations. As internal auditors become involved in computer service center audits, specialized knowledge of data processing capabilities and practices is being acquired, adding to their EDP audit capability.

AUDITING DURING SYSTEMS DEVELOPMENT

Internal auditor involvement during the development of application systems ensures that adequate controls are included for accuracy and completeness. Two points of view are reflected. Some internal auditors believe they should review systems only after their development is completed. They believe independence and objectivity are lost if they participate in the development of applications. This frequently encountered viewpoint seems to be giving way to the viewpoint of internal auditors who believe that their early participation is key to ensuring that adequate controls are considered. They believe that the evaluation of controls being designed into a system is no different from the evaluation of controls after the system is operational. They argue that it is too expensive to modify computer applications after they are completed.

Internal auditor participation took two forms in the organizations interviewed:

- Internal auditors were assigned to application development teams to present an internal audit point of view. In this situation the auditor participated but did not take direction from the project team leader. Written recommendations were prepared, but the emphasis was on cooperatively developing well-controlled computer applications.
- Internal auditors developed control guidelines for new computer applications systems. In one case reported, the EDP auditor worked with data processing personnel to develop guidelines for a remote terminal application. Other internal auditors have developed control guidelines for computer application systems development.

The primary constraint reported in achieving such internal audit involvement is the technical knowledge of the EDP auditor. Field interview results indicate that internal auditors can make an important contribution and will be accepted by data processing personnel if they are competent and current in data processing technology and practice. Interestingly, the Primary U.S. Mail Survey indicates that almost two-thirds of data processing managers believe that benefits have resulted from internal audit efforts. This belief was reinforced by other mail surveys in which 90% of the Japanese and 80% of the European and Canadian data processing managers indicate that benefits result from internal audit effort.

One of the objectives of the Primary U.S. Mail Survey was to determine the levels of internal audit involvement in various areas within data processing. Involvement in the systems development process and in reviewing computer application systems subsequent to implementation was an area of particular interest. To determine internal auditor involvement in this area, questionnaire recipients were asked, "How involved are the internal auditors in your organization in the following phases of computer application systems involvement?"

Respondents were asked to rate internal audit involvement in six areas using a five-point scale (1, 2, 3, 4, 5) ranging from heavy involvement, to moderate involvement, to no involvement. In addition, respondents could indicate that they did not know the level of involvement. Internal auditors and data processing management were asked to report what they believed to be the current level of involvement within their organizations. Top management, however, was asked to report what they believed internal audit involvement should be. An analysis was performed by SRI to identify differences among the responses from management, internal audit, and data processing.

Figure 4-3 shows the percentage from each questionnaire who indicated any involvement (i.e., scale position 1, 2, 3, or 4) by auditors in each of the various phases of application system development and use. In general, auditors believe that they are somewhat more involved than data processing representatives feel them to be, and less involved than management thinks they should be. This important finding indicates that management's expectations for internal audit are not being realized, which suggests that better understanding is needed between internal auditors and management regarding the scope and content of EDP audit activities.

Figure 4-3 also indicates that although some internal auditors are involved in computer application development before installation, the largest number is involved after installation. In other words, involvement is less widespread during the earlier stages of the systems development life cycle and increases during later stages.

Figure 4-4 shows the results from the five U.S. mail surveys and from the SRI site visits. The ordinate represents the percentage of respondent in organizations with internal auditors who indicated any involvement. The abscissa represents the six phases of computer application systems development included on the mail survey questionnaire. The number of firms reporting involvement in all phases is higher among those organizations selected to be visited by SRI than for those organizations responding in any other surveys. This is not surprising, since the organizations visited were selected because of their established EDP audit programs. Figure 4-5 shows the results of the Canadian, European, and Japanese mail surveys. The patterns and levels of involvement are similar to those shown for the U.S. surveys. Aside from the responses received from those organizations visited by SRI, no important differences exist between the various surveys. (For this evaluation, important differences are defined as being any difference greater than 25%).

The Primary U.S. Mail Survey results indicate that about 60% of internal audit programs include some involvement during application systems development. The results of field interviews conducted with U.S. and Canadian firms indicate that involvement in systems development is increasing. Several firms interviewed have active internal audit programs in this area. The experience of the firms interviewed does not, however, reflect trends in general. Smaller organizations have some involvement in the application systems development process; only about 16% indicated heavy involvement.

Figure 4-6 provides information obtained from the Primary U.S. Mail Survey regarding the degree of internal audit participation in the systems development process. The results indicate that fewer than 10% of the organizations surveyed had heavy internal audit participation during any phase of the system development process. With the exception of the Smaller U.S. Business and SRI Site surveys, in which the highest percentage of involvement was about 16% and 17% respectively, all other mail surveys indicated a smaller percentage of heavy involvement by internal auditors in any phase of the system development process than did the Primary U.S. Mail Survey organizations.

In a related Primary U.S. Mail Survey question, data processing managers were asked, "Who in your organization initiates internal auditor's participation in EDP application systems development?" Primary U.S. Mail Survey results indicate that, in 63% of the firms, data processing management itself is most likely to initiate the internal audit participation. This result is reinforced by non-U.S. surveys, which indicate that

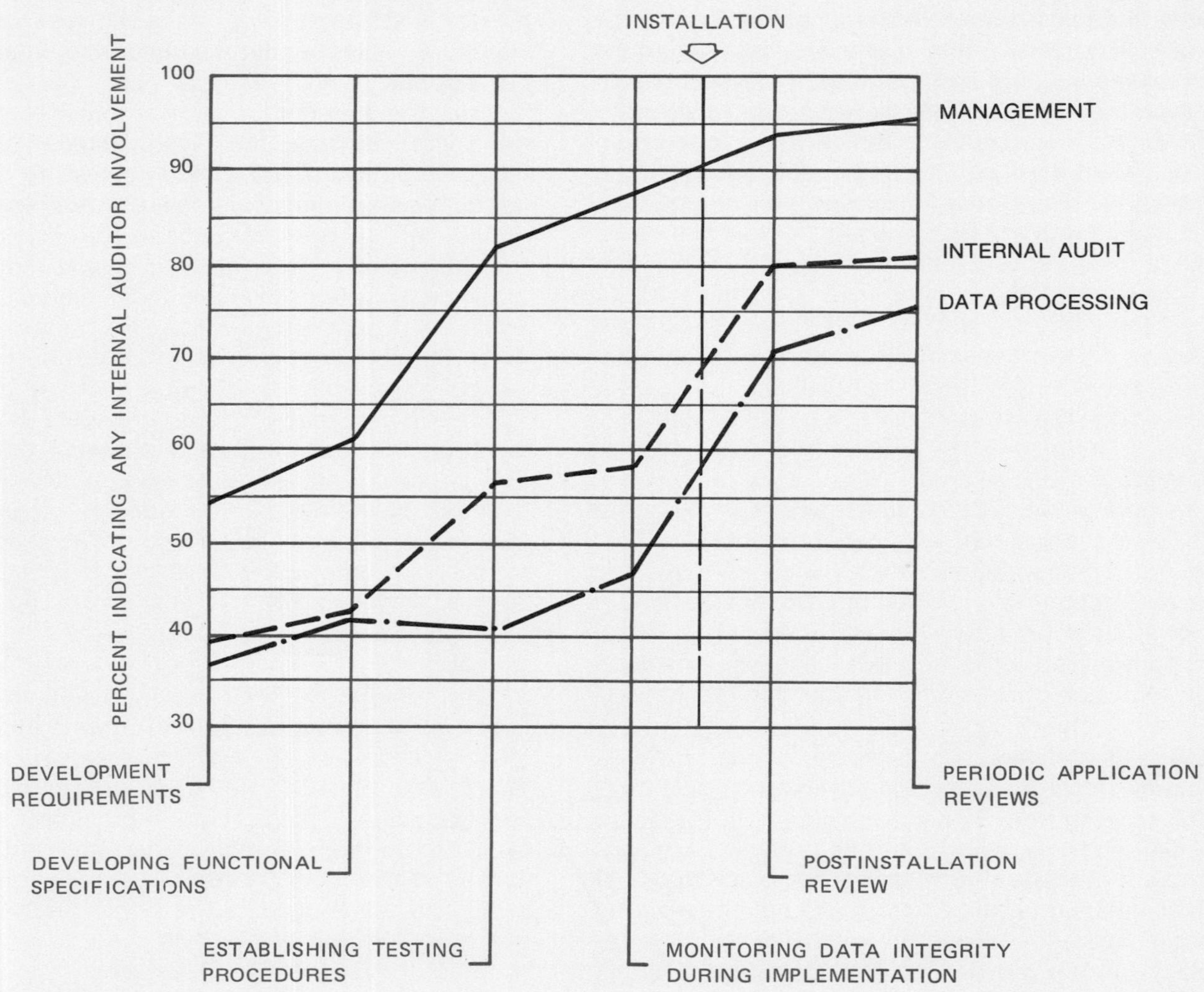

FIGURE 4-3 INTERNAL AUDIT INVOLVEMENT WITH COMPUTER APPLICATION SYSTEMS—PRIMARY U.S. MAIL SURVEY

Percentages are based on actual responses weighted to reflect the probable response distribution of all organizations with internal auditors in the sampling frame. See Appendix for further description of weighting procedures.

70% of the Canadian and 60% of the Japanese and European data processing management initiate internal audit participation. Data processing managers were also asked to report the areas in which internal auditors work with data processing in developing controls. They responded that over 50% of the internal auditors are involved in the development of application system controls, whereas 28% are not involved at all. The Canadian and European surveys suggest similar involvement; however, the Japanese survey indicated only one-third of the internal auditors worked in developing controls for application systems.

As part of the Primary U.S. Mail Survey, data processing managers were also asked to characterize internal audit involvement in terms of the following four criteria:

- Causes increased or decreased costs
- Harmful or helpful
- Worthless or valuable
- Unavailable or responsive.

The results indicate that internal audit involvement is viewed as both helpful and valuable. It is more often characterized as responsive than not. In terms of costs, slightly more than one-half the data processing representatives feel that auditing involvement neither increases nor decreases costs; the remainder are about evenly split between those who believe that internal auditors decrease costs and those who indicate that internal auditors increase costs.

Finally, data processing managers were asked to identify two ways that data processing has benefited most from the efforts of internal audit (see Table 4-3). The three most frequently checked areas of benefit were improved application system controls, reduced fraud/loss exposure, and increased user confidence and satisfaction. Interestingly, however, almost one-third of data processing managers believe that no significant benefits have resulted from internal auditors' efforts.

EDP AUDIT TOOLS AND TECHNIQUES

SRI has identified 28 EDP audit tools and techniques used by internal auditors in auditing applica-

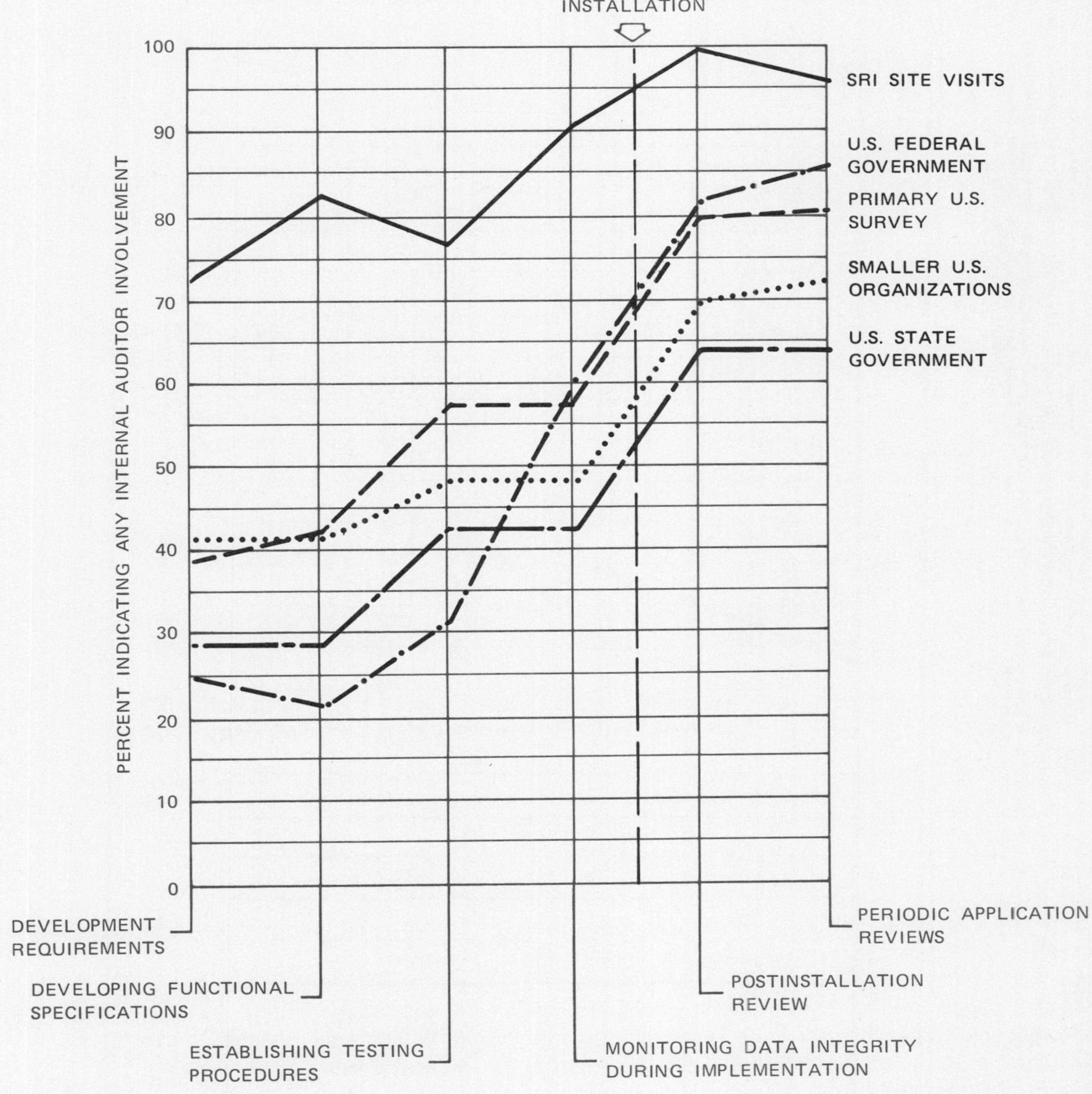

FIGURE 4-4 INTERNAL AUDIT INVOLVEMENT WITH COMPUTER APPLICATION SYSTEMS — UNITED STATES

Percentages for the primary U.S. survey are based on actual responses weighted to reflect the probable response distribution of all organizations with internal auditors in the sampling frame. See Appendix for further description of weighting procedures. All other percentages are based on unweighted responses.

tion systems, computer service center operations, and the controls governing the systems development process. Most of these tools and techniques have been developed to aid EDP auditors in evaluating and verifying the application system controls and processing results, such as data files and reports. The number and variety of tools and techniques reflect the desire of internal auditors to find effective and efficient tools and techniques appropriate to the new data processing environment. The tools and techniques most frequently reported as being used, based on the Primary U.S. Mail Survey results, are generalized audit software, manual tracing and mapping, and test decks. See Table 4-4 for a list of tools and techniques reported.

Although an increasing number of internal auditors are using the computer to assist them, many are still only auditing around data processing. These auditors

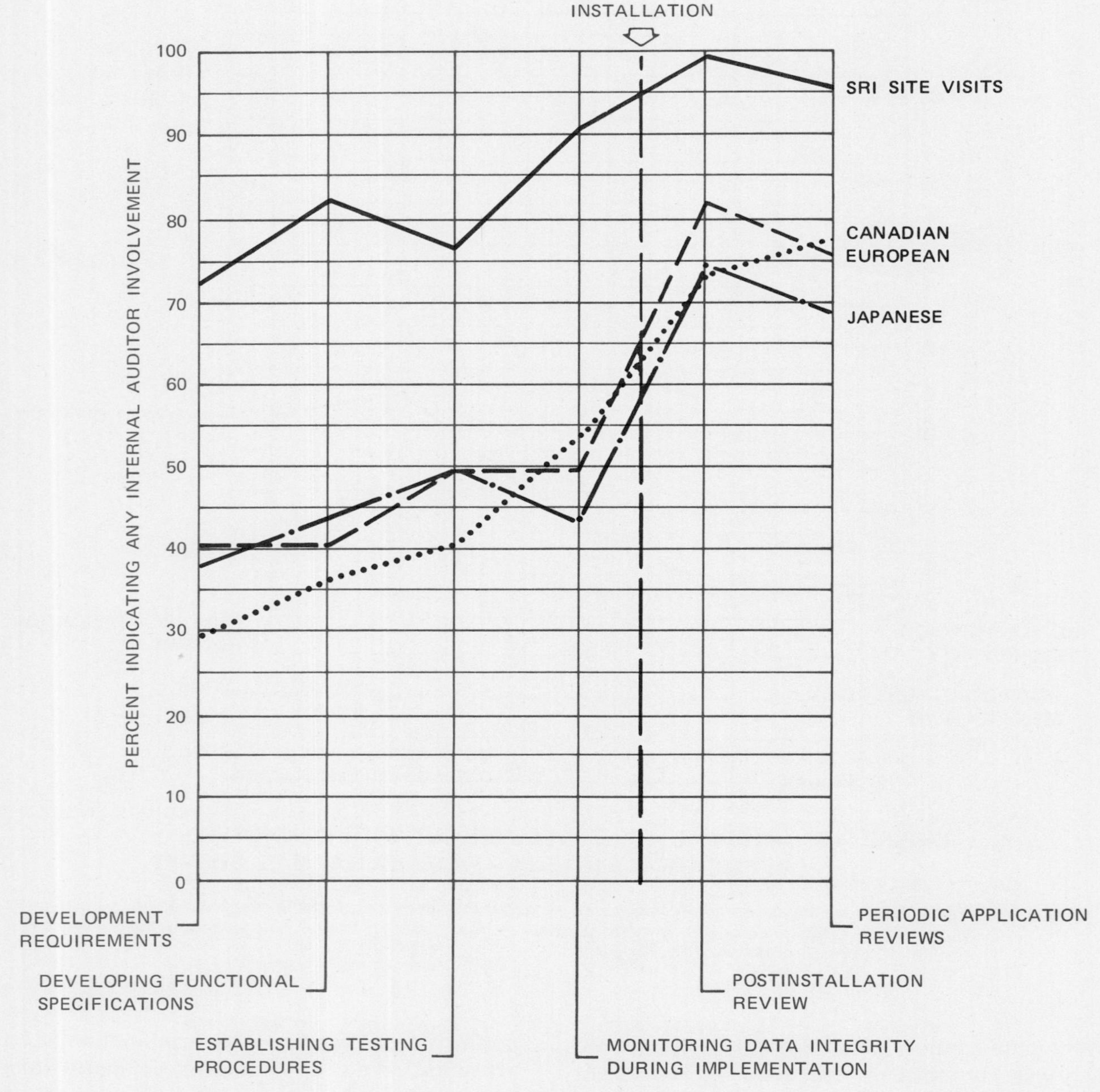

FIGURE 4-5 INTERNAL AUDIT INVOLVEMENT WITH COMPUTER APPLICATION SYSTEMS – SITE VISITS AND FOREIGN SURVEYS

All percentages are based on unweighted responses.

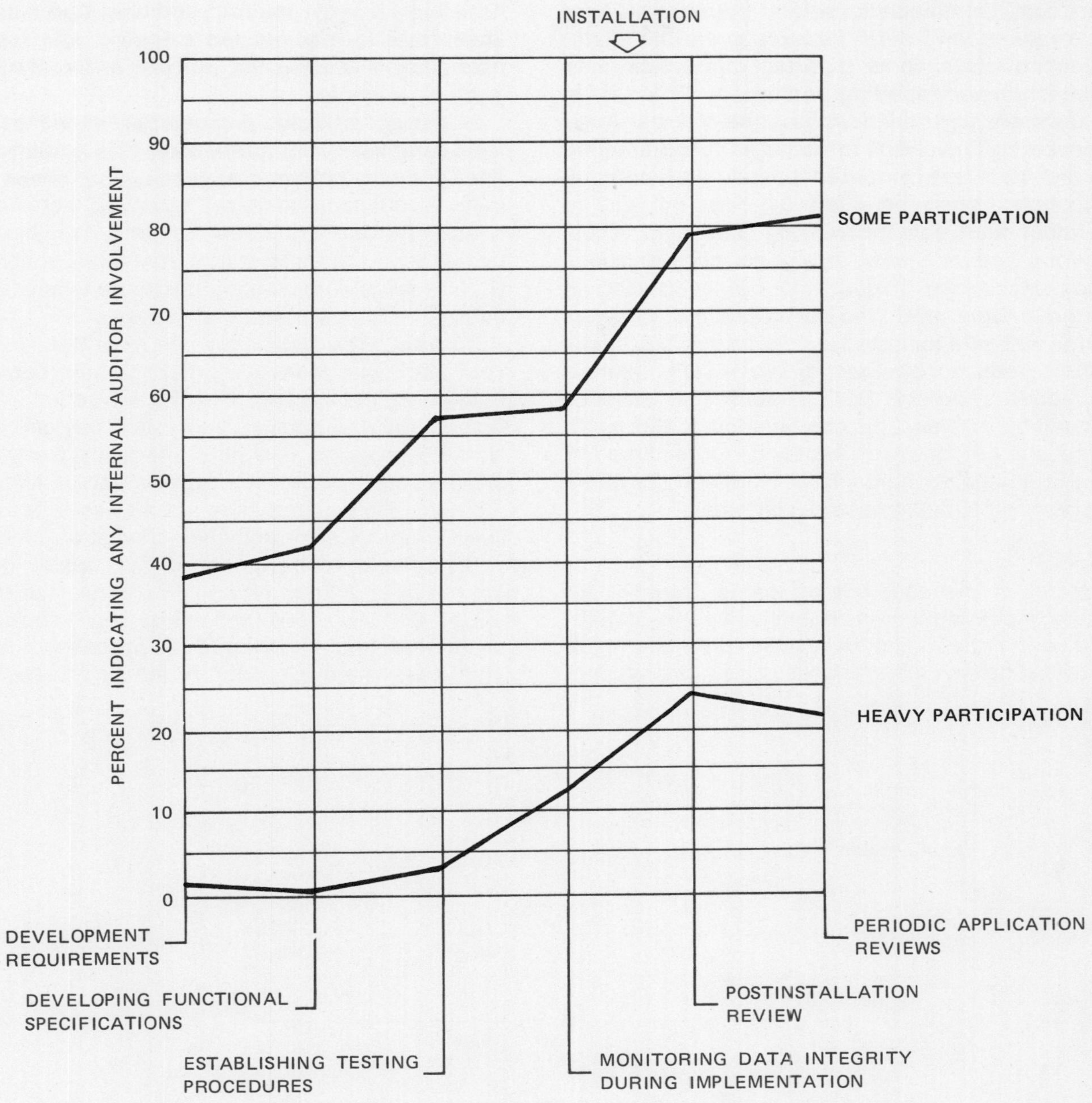

FIGURE 4-6 INTERNAL AUDIT INVOLVEMENT WITH COMPUTER APPLICATION SYSTEMS – PRIMARY U.S. MAIL SURVEY

Percentages are based on actual responses weighted to reflect the probable response distribution of all organizations with internal auditors in the sampling frame. See Appendix for further description of weighting procedures.

are ignoring the controls within application programs, believing that if processing results are verified, application controls must be effective.

Other internal auditors interviewed approached evaluation and verification of controls by performing a detailed examination of application program logic and coding. However, such examination is costly, is time-consuming, and requires extensive data processing knowledge and skill. As a result, such an approach is often not cost-effective, even though computer-aided tools are available to assist internal auditors in their examination.

An alternative approach is successfully used by many organizations. It includes a thorough data verification, complemented with selective functional testing to evaluate and verify application system and program controls, such as important computations or error detection and reporting procedures. These functional tests are performed without the internal auditors becoming involved in detailed programming logic; test data are prepared based on functional specifications, often provided by data processing users rather than data processing personnel. Thus, the internal auditor's work is less complex and less time-consuming than if audit work is conducted at the program logic level. The combination of generalized audit software for data verification and functional testing methods, such as test decks or ITFs, offers a cost-effective approach to EDP audit that satisfies basic audit objectives. This combination of EDP audit techniques is not, however, widely used because ITF capability is typically built into an application system during its original design and development.

SUMMARY

As a result of management concerns, internal auditors are becoming increasingly involved in evaluating and verifying application system controls and the controls that govern other phases of data processing, such as computer operations and application system development. Involvement in these areas is a new experience for most internal auditors, and specialized knowledge is required. As a result, EDP auditing is becoming a specialized activity within the internal audit organization.

A number of leading organizations visited by SRI have established comprehensive EDP audit programs. The scope of such programs includes reviews of computer application systems, computer service center operations, and application systems development activities. The expansion of internal audit activities into such areas is a logical and desirable extension of the internal auditor's traditional mandate.

Current EDP audit activities have not, in general, kept pace with increasing management dependence upon data processing and the introduction of new technology and application system design concepts. Notable progress has been made by many leading organizations in both the private sector and in government. Such progress is not, however, representative of internal audit activities in most organizations.

Three factors have tended to impede desirable growth of EDP audit capabilities. First, traditional internal auditors have minimized the importance of evaluating and verifying data processing controls. They have failed to recognize the significance of fun-

Table 4-3
INTERNAL AUDIT BENEFITS TO DATA PROCESSING

In which *two* of the following ways, if any, has data processing benefited *the most* from the efforts of internal auditing? (Check two)

	Percent of Total*	Percentage of Organizations That Indicated Benefits*†
Organizations indicating no significant benefit	31.6%	
Organizations indicating two of the following benefits	68.4	
Improved application system controls		45.3%
Reduced fraud/loss exposure		33.0
Increased user confidence and satisfaction		29.3
Reduced operations errors and omissions due to better controls		16.6
Reduced data processing operating costs		4.4
Improved equipment use and operating efficiency		4.4
Reduced application systems development time and cost		1.6
Other		2.2
No significant benefits		63.1

Note: Number of respondents = 169

*Percentages are based on actual responses weighted to reflect the probable response distribution of all organizations with internal auditors in the sampling frame. See the appendix for further description of weighting procedures.

†Percentages sum to 136.8% = 2 x 68.4 because respondents indicating significant benefit checked two categories.

damental changes in management information systems that have been brought about by data processing technology. Second, until recently, management has not fully appreciated the importance of the internal auditor's role in data processing. Third, audit of data processing is a relatively new activity for most internal auditors and requires new and specialized knowledge, programs, and approaches. Because the needed skills and capabilities are still in a formative stage, the internal audit manager who wants to upgrade his staff's data processing capability is faced with a wide range of experience, most so recent that its value is not clearly established.

Two viewpoints exist relative to the desirability of internal audit participation in the systems development process. Some internal auditors believe they should review systems only after a development process is completed. Others, who hold a viewpoint that seems to be gaining in importance, believe that their early participation is key to ensuring that controls are given proper consideration.

A better understanding is needed between internal auditors and both top management and data processing management regarding the scope and content of EDP audit activities. Moreover, the three groups must clearly define and understand internal audit goals and objectives.

Data processing managers surveyed characterized internal audit involvement with data processing in generally positive terms. Survey results indicate that such involvement is both helpful and valuable. The three most frequently identified benefits were improved applications system controls, reduced fraud/loss exposure, and increased user confidence and satisfaction.

Table 4-4
USE OF EDP AUDIT TOOLS AND TECHNIQUES

Which of the following tools and techniques are used in auditing EDP applications systems in your organization?

EDP Audit Tool/Technique	Percentage Used in Auditing Systems Developments and Modifications*	Percentage Used in Auditing Production Systems*
Generalized audit software	12.5%	32.6%
Manual tracing and mapping routines	22.9	31.2
Test data method (e.g., test-decking)	27.1	26.6
Parallel operation	32.2	23.1
Tagged transactions (flagging transactions in "live" operations for later review)	12.0	20.9
Snapshot (picture-taking of selected transactions through the flow of transactions)	10.0	18.4
Systems performance monitoring and analysis (e.g., SMF, SCERT)	8.2	15.8
Program source code comparison	9.6	14.5
Control flowcharting	8.3	9.0
Program object code comparison	4.7	8.9
Integrated test facility (mini- or dummy-company)	4.2	5.0
Modeling (simulation)	9.5	7.6
Automatic tracing and mapping routines (analysis of source language and logic to determine if any program segments are not being utilized)	3.6	3.9
Other	6.5	10.5

Note: Number of respondents = 221

*Percentages are based on actual responses weighted to reflect the probable response distribution of all organizations in the sampling frame. See the appendix for further description of weighted procedures.

New internal audit approaches, methods, tools, and techniques are needed. Conventional internal audit techniques are, in general, not adequate for the specialized requirements of auditing data processing. Internal auditors have recognized this need and adopted various data processing methods to audit computer application systems and other phases of data processing.

Finally, SRI selected key questions from the Primary U.S. Mail Survey to identify differences in audit techniques in regulated and nonregulated organizations. Subsequent analysis identified no important differences.

EVALUATION AND OUTLOOK

Internal audit programs must be updated in scope and content if internal auditors are to be responsive to their mandate from management. The scope must be expanded to encompass all phases of data processing. Traditional internal audit programs limited to the verification of records and reports are not adequate and do not reflect trends being set by leaders in EDP audit or trends in public accounting that emphasize the evaluation and verification of control procedures.

First, the internal audit mandate must reflect the expanded scope of internal audit, which encompasses computer applications systems, computer service center operations, and application systems development. Top management should make sure all affected elements of the organization understand this expanded scope and why it is desired by management. Affected elements of the organization must also understand that some time may be required to realize completely the objectives underlying this change in mandate.

Second, formalized programs with specific objectives are needed for guiding the development of desired EDP audit capabilities. Objectives may include recruiting, staff training, and initial audit in areas new to internal auditing, such as the computer service center. Objectives should reflect a reasonable balance between the present level of capabilities and the level of capabilities ultimately desired. Because several years may be required to develop the desired capabilities, specific intermediate objectives should be targeted.

Third, as skill and knowledge of data processing are acquired, internal auditors should become progressively more involved with data processing. Cooperation and coordination with data processing are important to the rapid development of desired EDP audit skills. Internal auditor participation in data processing training programs is highly desirable. One of the goals of such involvement is to achieve a better understanding between data processing and internal auditors regarding their respective perspectives. Particularly beneficial is the joint development of application system control guidelines and internal auditor participation in systems development.

Participation during systems development is important so that necessary audit and control features can be built into new application systems. Many of the current audit tools and techniques are "Band-Aids," necessary only because adequate audit features have not been built into application systems. Designs for such systems should include an explicit identification not only of the controls necessary to ensure accuracy, completeness, and security, but also of the features needed to facilitate verification of such controls.

Efforts to develop more effective EDP audit tools and techniques can be accelerated in two ways. First, development programs within organizations should be based on cooperation between internal audit and data processing personnel and, possibly, the organization's public accounting firm. Close cooperation between internal audit and data processing is critical to success in developing effective tools and techniques. In most organizations, relatively little cooperation occurred in the past because internal audit and data processing personnel lacked a mutual understanding of internal audit's responsibilities, goals, and approach to auditing. Close cooperation during system development is particularly important so that audit features can be built into new applications, such as ITFs and terminal audit software capabilities. Integrated audit techniques are far more effective than elaborate audit techniques developed after the fact and seem to hold the most promise for effective EDP audit in the future.

The development work within individual organizations must be complemented by the coordinated, industry-wide efforts of data processing user groups, professional groups such as The Institute of Internal Auditors and AICPA, and equipment and software suppliers. Although useful tools and techniques can be developed within individual organizations, improvements on a broad scale cannot be expected without bringing together interest groups that broadly represent the accounting and auditing professions, the data processing profession, and equipment and software designers. All representatives of interest groups contacted during this research expressed a high level of interest in better understanding systems auditability and control requirements in a data processing environment, particularly as new technology and application systems concepts are introduced.

Part II

COMPUTER APPLICATION SYSTEM CONTROLS

Part II of this report delineates the application system controls that are in use at the various organizations visited and about which detailed data were gathered. This part of the report is organized into six chapters (Chapters 5-10), each representing a phase of the flow of transactions through a computer application system. Transaction flow has been used as a basis for classifying application controls because it provides a common framework for reviewing internal controls. Figure II-1 depicts the six phases of this classification scheme.

These six phases are described as follows:

- *Transaction Origination* — Application controls governing the origination, approval, and processing of source documents, the preparation of data processing input transactions, and associated error prevention, detection, and correction procedures.
- *Data Processing Transaction Entry* — Application controls governing both remote terminal and batch data entry, data validation, transaction or batch proofing and balancing, error identification and reporting, and error correction and reentry.
- *Data Communications* — Controls governing the accuracy and completeness of data communications, including message accountability, data protection, hardware and software, security and privacy, error identification, and reporting.
- *Computer Processing* — Application controls governing the accuracy, correctness, and completeness of transaction processing, including transaction validation against masterfiles, error identification and reporting.

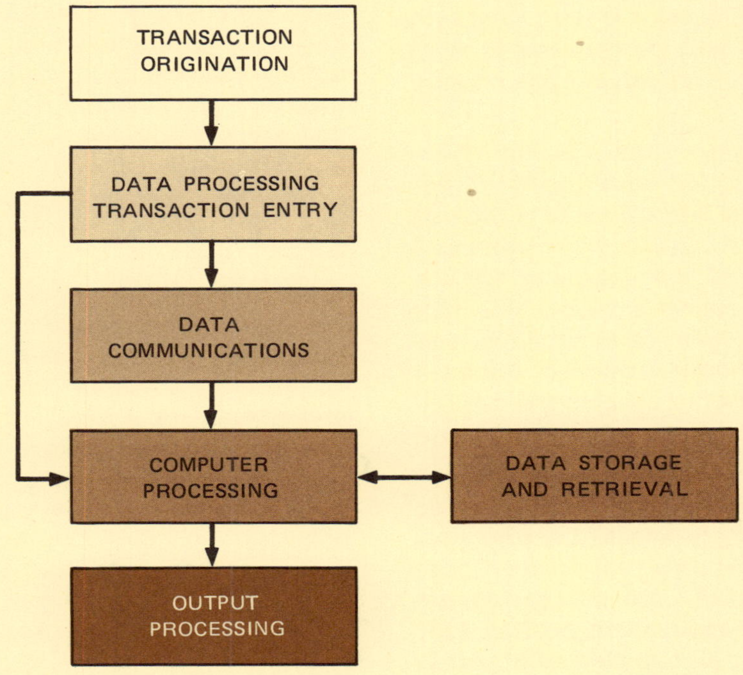

FIGURE II-1 SCHEME FOR CLASSIFICATION OF APPLICATION SYSTEM CONTROLS

- *Data Storage and Retrieval* — Application controls to ensure masterfile data accuracy and completeness, correct transaction/masterfile cutoff, data security and privacy, error handling, and backup, recovery, and retention. Note that file integrity controls reflect the growing use of general-purpose file handling and data base software, and an attendant trend to view processing procedures as independent of data files.
- *Output Processing* — Application controls governing manual balancing and reconciliation of data processing input and output (both within the data processing input/output control section and at user locations), distribution of data processing output, control over negotiable documents (both within data processing and user areas), and output data retention.

Within each of the six phases are various control areas, which are described in Chapters 5-10. Each area deals with a general function that requires control. Within the control areas are control types that address specific functions. Finally, for each control type are listed the specific controls that were collected during the field interviews.

The controls described in the following chapters are those that the organizations interviewed have found to be beneficial. The controls themselves are not dependent on a specific application; therefore, the reader can review them and consider incorporating them in computer application systems with which he is concerned. Generally, there are multiple controls within any one area. For this reason, the data processor or the auditor may treat these controls as a checklist, selecting the most appropriate controls for the system in question. Data processing personnel may review these controls with the objective of enhancing control within systems already developed or currently in development. The auditor, on the other hand, may review these controls with an eye toward recommending those controls be built into systems during development or retrofitted to current systems where control is judged inadequate.

Data processing personnel and internal auditors may use the material in these chapters to select or recommend the most appropriate controls. For example, a system analyst may be interested in designing controls into a specific application system and consequently may reference a specific control to satisfy a specific control objective, or reference the complete set of controls with a phase of the application system flow (e.g., data processing transaction entry). On the other hand, the internal auditor may review these controls in search of some specific manual control or automated control that may be used to obtain a specific control objective.

The list of controls in Chapters 5-10 includes the controls that were collected during the on-site interviews conducted by SRI. This list is not meant to be all-inclusive, but the controls that are listed are being used in practice. The majority of the controls listed are applicable to computer application systems designed for most data processing systems.

Chapter 5

TRANSACTION ORIGINATION

Transaction origination controls are used to ensure the accuracy and completeness of data before they enter the computer application system. The scope of the transaction origination control area includes controls up to the point of converting data to a machine-readable format. Management, systems personnel, and auditors are placing increasing emphasis on transaction origination controls to ensure that the information prepared for entry into the system is valid, reliable, cost-effective, and not subject to compromise.

Transaction origination controls are those controls that govern processes in five control areas: source document origination, authorization, data processing input preparation, source document retention, and source document error handling. Figure 5-1 shows the relationship of these five control areas. Three are in the direct flow of transaction processing. Source document retention is an offshoot of this flow, and source document error handling is part of a feedback loop to source document origination. The transaction entry phase follows this phase. Some of the controls in these two phases are manual because they are effected before the entry of data into the application system. Some are automated, being automatically applied during the entry or attempted entry of data into the application system.

The difference between a transaction origination control and a transaction entry control is that a transaction origination control occurs prior to the conversion of data into transaction entry format (e.g., keypunching, terminal entry). Both transaction origination and transaction entry controls may restrict the entry of data into the computer application system. Computer processing controls will not come into effect until the data have been entered into the application system and the application programs attempt to process them.

NEED FOR TRANSACTION ORIGINATION CONTROLS

Transaction origination controls are necessary to ensure that complete and accurate information is prepared for entry into the computer application system. The effectiveness of any computer application system is directly dependent on the source data on which it is based. The validity and accuracy of data in computer application systems relate directly to the functioning of controls from the inception of data origination. Consequently, it is important to establish control of data as close to the point of origination as possible.

In developing transaction origination controls, an organization may wish to ensure that:

- Transaction origination authorization is not performed by personnel having custody of assets or access to records thereof.
- Transaction origination is not performed by computer operations personnel.
- Instructions governing the preparation of source documents are specifically described in writing.

For examination of how to satisy control objectives through the use of application system controls, the process of transaction origination is separated into control areas. Within each control area are one or more types of controls. Each control type includes one or more specific application controls that organizations have used to control transaction origination. Table 5-1 shows the structure of transaction origination, broken down by control type within area, and by individual control within type.

CONTROL AREA — SOURCE DOCUMENT ORIGINATION

These controls include procedures and methods used to ensure the proper and timely recording of data. This recording of data may be in a machine-sensible form directly, or may occur after the initial recording of data on a human readable document. Control types discussed include written procedures, source document design, source document storage, and source document handling (see Figure 5-2).

Control Type — Written Procedures

Control Documentation — Control documentation is used to define system control points. System control points are points in the system where the integrity of the data is verified. For example, assume a merchandise billing system supplies data to an accounts receivable system. The dollar amount of accounts receivable updated as the result of a billing run may be printed on a report and verified manually, or it may be automatically "passed" to the accounts receivable

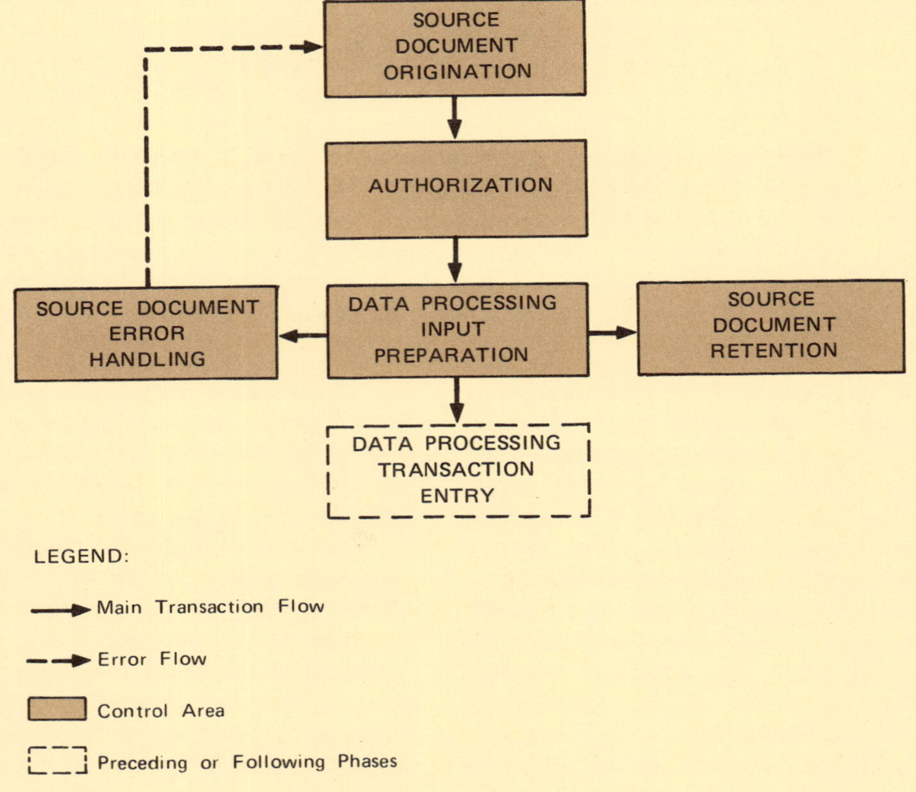

FIGURE 5-1 TRANSACTION ORIGINATION

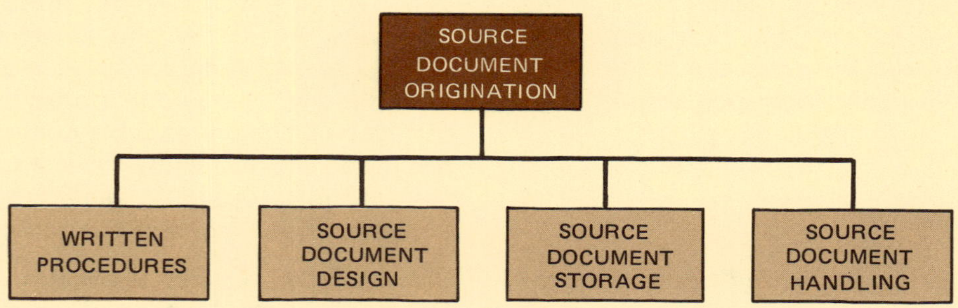

FIGURE 5-2 SOURCE DOCUMENT ORIGINATION

Table 5-1
TRANSACTION ORIGINATION CONTROL STRUCTURE

Control Area	Control Type	Control
Source document origination	Written procedures	Control documentation User procedures and manuals
	Source document design	Special purpose forms Source document numbers Transaction identification Cross reference Sequence log
	Source document storage	Restricted access Accountable source document storage Intermediate storage and transportation
	Source document handling	Dual custody
Authorization	Source document preparation	Separation of duties Signatures
	Written procedures	Written authorization
	Approval of source documents	Evidence of approval Transaction conflicts matrix
Data processing input preparation	Transaction identification	Transaction numbering User identification Schedule desk
	User review of input	Manual review
	Batching	Batch serial number Limit the number of transactions in a batch Batch and balance source data at point of origin
	Logging	Logs of source document transmittal between organizations
	Transmittal	Transmittal document Mail and message carrier Physically secure input
Source document retention	Source document retention characteristics	Source turnaround Retention dates on source documents Source document storage index
	Filing of source documents	File of source documents Batch storage Source documents maintained at origin
	Retention storage	Filing in user areas Limited access to retention facilities Removal from retention
Source document error handling	Error procedures	Written error handling procedures Source document correction procedures Responsibility for error correction
	Error detection	Error logging Visual review of source documents
	Error correction processing	Error notification Identification of error correction
	Corrected data resubmission	Verification of reentered data Monitoring of error corrections

system, where it is verified by accumulating the debit and credit billings, and mechanically comparing that total with the total supplied by the billing system. The important point is not the method of control used, but the fact that the system has been analyzed from a control viewpoint. The result of such analysis is specified in writing, in the form of control documentation.

User Procedures and Manuals — Written user procedures are used to guide the proper initiation, review, and authorization of input transactions. Such written instructions cover controls that must be used to:

- Prepare the document.
- Regulate document flow.
- Promote adherence to schedules (e.g., cutoff dates).
- Control the use of special codes (e.g., overrides).
- Describe input keying requirements.
- Promote the use of response interpretations (action on behalf of the user).

Written user procedures are the result of a procedural analysis of the business functions, which determines precisely what must be accomplished and the steps used to accomplish the functional objective. Written user procedures are part of a user's manual. In addition to the written user procedures, the user's manual may contain responsibilities for system control, administrative organization, and authorization responsibility.

Control Type — Source Document Design

Special-Purpose Forms — Special-purpose forms are used to guide the initial recording of transactions in a uniform format. Forms design is an important application control that provides assurance that the entry of data conforms to a predetermined, uniform format. Proper form design encourages the completeness and accuracy of data by preventing omissions, ensuring proper authorization, and providing accountability.

Characteristics of special-purpose forms most frequently used by respondent organizations to encourage the completeness and accuracy of data are:

- Preprinted information (forms numbering, repetitive data such as transaction code, product number).
- Authorization blocks.
- Control totals.
- Foot and crossfoot balancing.
- Retention dates.

Source Document Numbers — Source documents with preprinted sequential numbers are designed to establish control over source document accountability. Sequential numbers allow the serialization of document presentation. This serialization may be done in a manual operation by the filing process or may be part of an anticipatory control to see that all input documents are accounted for. Source document identification and serialization facilitate the tracing of transactions to and from their originating source documents.

Transaction Identification — Each transaction to be entered in a computer system must carry a transaction identification. Such transaction identification may be done in a variety of forms (i.e., serial number, sequence number, transaction code). It is essential that the transaction identification contain all the information necessary to uniquely identify a specific transaction.

Cross-Reference — Transactions as they are formatted in the computer often include a field in the record that identifies the source document. Where the source document number is part of the transaction identification, it will provide a cross-reference useful in tracing information to and from the source document to computer processing. For example, an accounts receivable transaction record contains a field for the billing document reference number. This cross-reference may then be used to retrieve source documents. Cross-reference identification used in connection with the number on hardcopy establishes control over the recording of transactions and facilitates the future reference. Such procedures enhance the system's ability to provide a system audit trail.

Sequence Log — The user identifies transactions with a sequence number and maintains an internal log of sequence numbers. The sequence log is an important control in assuring the completeness of data entry.

Control Type — Source Document Storage

Restricted Access — The authorized use of source documents and data processing input forms is aided by restricting the access to forms inventory. Access to source documents and blank input forms is limited to specifically authorized employees.

Accountable Source Document Storage — Accountable documents are those documents that have been specified by the organization as a form for which there must be a strict accounting (e.g., blank check stock). Accountable documents are stored in a secure location. Secure storage used in conjunction with other controls (e.g., sequential numbers) provides a mechanism to account for such documents.

Intermediate Storage and Transportation — Modifications to data on source documents are controlled by limiting access to forms during their intermediate storage and transportation. A number of controls, such as dual custody and mail and message carrier controls (see below), are useful in preventing access to forms during their intermediate storage and transportation.

Control Type — Source Document Handling
Dual Custody — A system of dual custody is used to maintain control over accountable forms. This method calls for a member of data processing and a member of the user department to jointly authorize the release of prenumbered forms from the storage area. This method is then followed through the processing cycle until the unused forms have been returned to the storage area.

Dual custody also entails the maintenance of other items (e.g., signature stamp) by individuals not associated with the previous processes.

CONTROL AREA — AUTHORIZATION

The process of source document authorization is broken down into the control types related to source document preparation, written procedures, and approval of source documents (see Figure 5-3).

Controls in this area include procedures and methods used to ensure that source data have been properly authorized. After the source document has been originated, control techniques are used to ensure that the source data have been properly authorized. Evidence of authorization may be reviewed by manual procedures (internal control group) or computer processing (transaction identification). Given today's advancements in computer hardware and software, the computer is being used more and more to verify the authorization of input. As this trend continues, it becomes critical that the auditor have the tools to test in this environment. Authorization procedures discussed here apply only to those concerned with source origination. Programmed processing controls and authorization procedures associated with terminal usage are discussed in later sections of the report.

Control Type — Source Document Preparation
Separation of Duties — Separation of duties as related to computer application systems normally involves three levels, at a minimum:

- Separation of the data processing department from its functional users.
- Segregation of duties within the data processing department (e.g., programming separate from operations).
- Separation in the user department between source data generation and other functions.

For example, segregation should exist between the functions of transaction origination, transaction entry, and the associated custody of assets. One method of doing this is to establish an independent person or group responsible for the entry of data.

Signatures — Signatures on source documents are used to provide an audit trail to the origination source. Approval signatures on source documents are used to provide evidence of proper transaction authorization.

An authorization hierarchy usually implies the empowering of individuals to approve specific transactions. Input processing procedures provide evidence of authorization. This evidence of authorization may be indicated by a signature on an input document, or by the use of specific security and password control in a terminal environment. The use of authorization controls in a terminal environment (programmed control) will be discussed in Chapter 6.

Control Type — Written Procedures
Written Authorization — Written authorization procedures are established for all transactions to ensure the entry of authorized transactions only. All transactions that may be entered in the application systems are listed and reviewed. The review of transactions is conducted by the person in authority to grant approval responsibility. Such a review of transaction authorization promotes an automatic separation of duties for transactions that are handled by different people. The completion of the review results in a document that provides authority to individuals to approve specific transactions.

Control Type — Approval of Source Documents
Evidence of Approval — The approval of specific transactions may occur by several mechanisms.

Input documents provide evidence of approval. This approval can then be related to the authorization

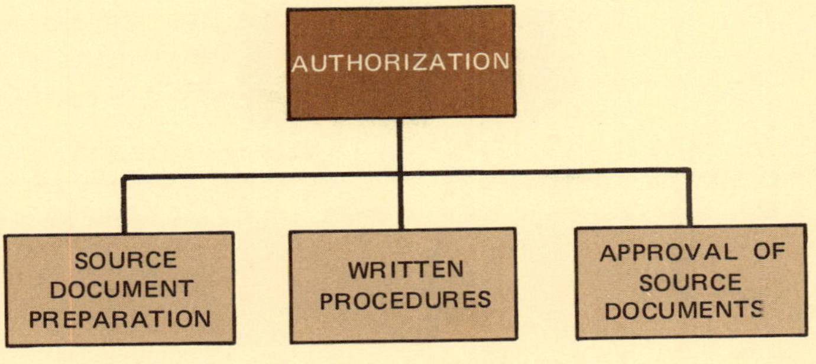

FIGURE 5-3 AUTHORIZATION

process. For example, assume the company organization provides that levels of management may authorize specific transactions. Credit supervisors are authorized to approve refunds up to $25. Credit managers are authorized to approve refunds up to $500. The assistant controller is required to approve refunds in excess of $500.

The important point is that whatever mechanism is chosen, the approval process is documented in writing.

Transaction Conflicts Matrix — A transaction conflicts matrix is prepared that covers all transactions within a computer application system, and between application systems. The transaction conflicts matrix has been used to detect such conflicting transactions as those that allow a user to pay refunds, and that allow the same user to make changes in the customer records during cash applications. It was felt such transactions did not allow the proper separation of duties. Therefore, the transaction conflicts matrix has been used to place restrictions on personnel having input transaction authority.

CONTROL AREA — DATA PROCESSING INPUT PREPARATION

After source documents have been originated and authorized, it is necessary to prepare the data further for data processing input. Controls included in the data processing input preparation are necessary to ensure the accuracy and completeness of data, from origination through the data conversion process in preparation for further computer processing. Control types to be discussed include transaction identification, user review of input, batching, logging, and transmittal (see Figure 5-4).

Control Type — Transaction Identification

Transaction Numbering — Each transaction to be entered in a computer system is identified by a consecutive number. Transaction numbering is used to provide a method of transaction accountability. Transaction numbering also facilitates the future referencing of source documents.

User Identification — A unique user identification (i.e., employee number and/or user department security code) is used to restrict the transaction that the user may process as well as the files the user may access.

Schedule Desk — The control desk function within the user department is used to monitor the timely receipt of transactions and/or batches, and to maintain proper source transaction schedules and compliance with requirements to that point.

Control Type — User Review of Input

Manual Review — A manual review of source documents is performed by user personnel in order to ensure the completeness and accuracy of data processing input.

Control Type — Batching

Batch Serial Number — Batches are identified by serial number or sequence number to provide accountability of data. Batch numbers are used in conjunction with logging techniques to account for the receipt of data.

Limit the Number of Transactions in a Batch — The number of transactions in a batch is limited to simplify the reconciliation process required when batches are out of balance. In addition, restrictions on the number of transactions included in a batch are established in order to facilitate transportation of batches of transactions between user department and data processing.

Batch and Balance Source Data at Point of Origin — Source data are batched and balanced as close to the point of origin as possible in order to establish control over source data origination. Transactions are grouped by output classifications such as corporate headquarters, regional office, or branch office. Data processing transactions are organized in batches to facilitate their further processing. Batching is one method used to avoid a loss of individual transactions during processing.

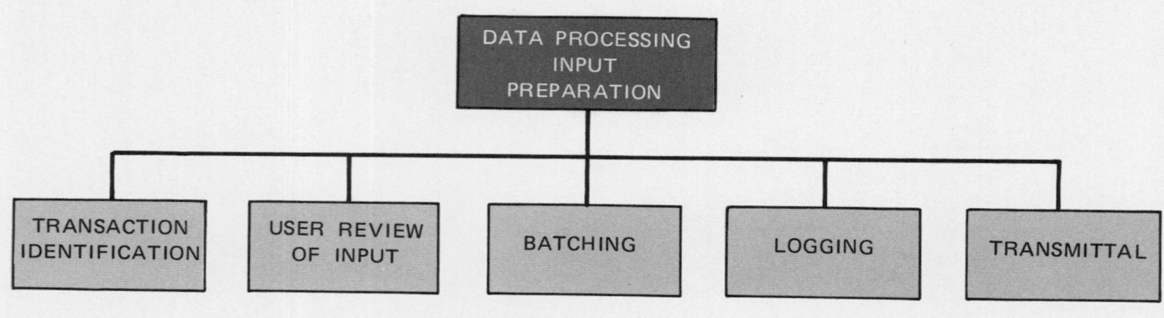

FIGURE 5-4 DATA PROCESSING INPUT PREPARATION

Control Type — Logging

Logs of Source Document Transmittals Between Organizations — Logging techniques (e.g., record counts, control totals) are used to record the flow of transactions and/or batches between organizations processing source documents to identify missing items and maintain accountability. Manual control logs in the primary user area are used to establish control close to the source of origination.

Control Type — Transmittal

Transmittal Document — A formal transmittal document is used to control the movement of paperwork between various users and the data entry function. Transmittal documents prepared at or near the source are used throughout the processing cycle. This means they follow the transaction flow during the movement of input from user department through the data processing input/output control function and back to the user area.

Mail and Message Carrier — Mail and message area controls such as packaging, labeling, registry, delivery receipts, and document receipts are used to establish audit trails within the system. Metal containers, plastic or canvas pouches, envelopes, or other suitable packaging techniques are used to ensure the integrity of batches during their transportation between user departments and the data processing function.

Physically Secure Input — The method of transportation of source data is dependent upon the classification of information. While locked boxes are appropriate for some types of information, paper envelopes tied together may be appropriate for other classifications. In any event, input when transferred from the user function to the data entry function is physically secured.

CONTROL AREA — SOURCE DOCUMENT RETENTION

These controls include procedures and methods used to ensure the proper retention of source documents, including the adequate backup of source data maintained to provide the capabilities to recreate data lost or data destroyed during processing. Types discussed (see Figure 5-5) include source document retention characteristics, filing of source documents, and retention storage. The identification and filing of source documents facilitate the historical referencing necessitated by statute, company policy, or purposes of recovery.

Control Type — Source Document Retention Characteristics

Source Turnaround Documents — Turnaround documents promote the accuracy of input preparation by eliminating all or part of the data to be recorded. The turnaround portion of the document contains prerecorded data that are used as the input medium for computer processing. For example, a bill received from a retail store usually contains a turnaround portion that includes precoded information, such as an account number. This requires the receiving organization to record only the amount of cash received while the rest of the data are reproduced automatically. Source turnaround documents provide one method for the retention of source information. Source data information entered on the document follows processing through the computer system and back to the user area to be retained.

Retention Dates on Source Documents — Retention dates are placed on source documents. They are placed on accompanying documents such as batch slips and/or source document containers. Each document contains the retention period as an identifying characteristic. The retention date placed on source documents is based on legal requirements and/or management policy.

Source Document Storage Index — A cross-index system is maintained by retention expiration date when source documents are stored in a sequence other than expiration date. A schedule is produced to control the purging of source documents from the files.

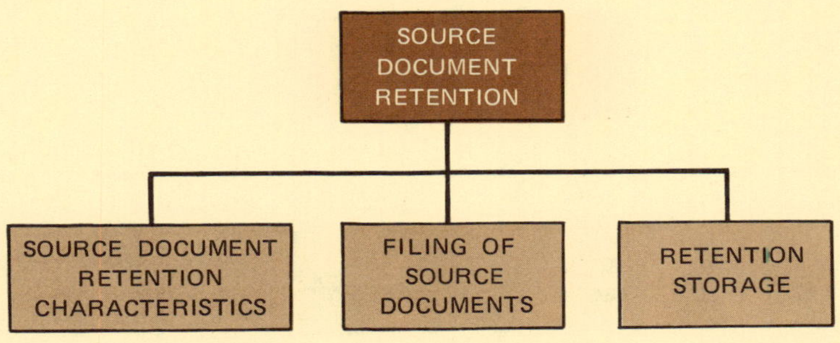

FIGURE 5-5 SOURCE DOCUMENT RETENTION

Control Type — Filing of Source Documents

File of Source Documents — The file of source documents should be in the sequence that best fits the situation. A file of source documents by identification numbers is used where it is necessary to have information readily retrievable. This procedure necessitates the development of the method of elimination of documents when retention dates are reached.

Batch Storage — Where information does not need to be readily retrievable, source documents are stored in batches by retention period expiration date.

Source Documents Maintained at Origin — Copies of source documents are maintained at the point of origin in order to provide backup in the event source documents are lost or damaged during subsequent transportation and processing. A copy of the source document is maintained in the user department whenever the source document leaves the department.

Control Type — Retention Storage

Filing in User Areas — Source documents are filed in user areas for convenient access during interim periods of storage. After a specified length of time, source documents are either destroyed or removed and stored as part of the long-term records retention program. In this manner, filing provides for both rapid access to information when needed as well as longer term security and legal considerations.

Limited Access to Retention Facilities — Access to record retention storage facilities is controlled and limited to authorized personnel.

Removal from Retention — Records, removed from retention facilities upon reaching their expiration dates, are destroyed according to their classifications. For example, some classifications of material call for dual custody removal from retention and observed shredding or burning. Other classifications of material may simply be removed from storage and discarded in the trash container.

CONTROL AREA — SOURCE DOCUMENT ERROR HANDLING

These controls include procedures and methods used to ensure that all transactions rejected at this point in the system are corrected and reentered in a timely manner. Controls in this area ensure that all errors are accounted for at the end of any processing cycle. Areas to be discussed include error procedures, error detection, error correction processing, and corrected data resubmission (see Figure 5-6).

Control Type — Error Procedures

Written Error Handling Procedures — Written error handling procedures are used to provide user personnel with comprehensive instructions for source document error detection, error correction, and corrected data resubmission.

The degree of formality and detail of written procedures governing the manual reviewing of data is usually dependent on two primary factors:

- The criticality of data.
- The degree and form of computer editing to follow.

For example, most firms tend to have more specifically developed procedures review (e.g., visual verification of approval signatures) for their financial applications systems. However, the trend is to have the computer perform as much of these compliance and verification procedures as possible.

Source Document Correction Procedures — Error correction procedures are defined in writing (e.g., in the user's manual). These correction procedures include the types of error conditions that will occur, the correction procedures to be followed, and the method to be used for the reentry of corrected data.

Responsibility for Error Correction — The assignment of error correction responsibility is specified in writing (e.g., in the user's manual). This includes the responsibility for the correction of transactions with multiple sources.

Control Type — Error Detection

Error Logging — Error logs are used to follow up on unresolved errors and to ensure their correction and timely reentry to the system. Such error logs are maintained in the user area to record and monitor the errors reported by the data processing input preparation function.

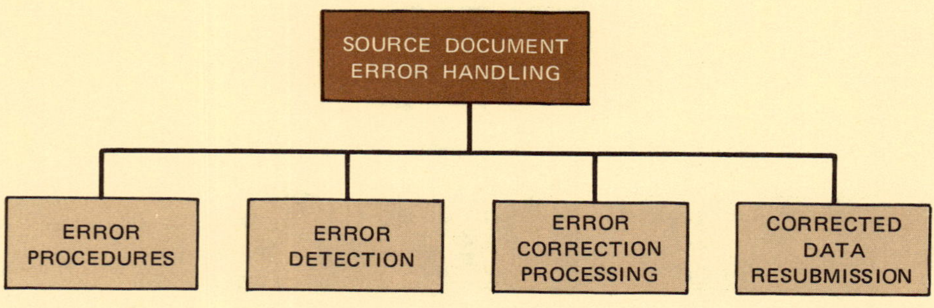

FIGURE 5-6 SOURCE DOCUMENT ERROR HANDLING

Visual Review of Source Documents — This procedure includes scanning the document for accuracy and completeness as well as evidence of document authorization.

Control Type — Error Correction Processing

Error Notification — The user is notified immediately of all source document error conditions.

Identification of Error Correction — Source documents in error are identified to facilitate the correction of the data in error. This involves the recording of a cross-reference between the transaction data in error and the originating source document.

Control Type — Corrected Data Resubmission

Verification of Reentered Data — The data fields on resubmitted source documents are subjected to the same verification procedures as the original source document. In some instances, when the original document has initially undergone a complete edit, only corrected data are reexamined.

Monitoring of Error Corrections — A log of all errors detected is used to monitor the timely resubmission of corrected data. As each corrected source document is resubmitted, it is crossed off the log and the date of resubmission is entered on the log. A report of source documents being held pending error correction resubmission is provided to the user area before the end of each processing cycle. This report is used to clear the system before the conclusion of the processing cycle so that proper system cutoffs will be observed.

SUMMARY

The accuracy, completeness, and validity of data contained in computer application systems are dependent on the proper functioning of a system of internal controls. So that an organization may be assured of a high degree of effectiveness of controls within computer application systems, it is necessary to start with a set of well-developed internal control objectives for that organization. These control objectives must then be carried forward in developing computer application systems. For example, if good internal control for the organization requires that the accountant should not be responsible for the cash receipts function, this same division of responsibilities must be maintained in the functioning of the computer application system (e.g., cashier cannot authorize a journal entry transaction to reduce the cash figure in the general ledger).

To provide maximum benefits in terms of accuracy, completeness, and validity, application controls are instituted at the point of source data origination. Procedural controls are then imposed to control the step-by-step processing of data. The need for good internal control in organizations has not changed. However, with today's capabilities in terms of hardware and software, the computer will be used more and more to provide verifying evidence that the process of transaction origination is providing complete and accurate data for further processing by computer application systems

Chapter 6

DATA PROCESSING TRANSACTION ENTRY

Transaction entry controls are used to ensure the accuracy and completeness of data during their entry into the computer application system. The scope of the transaction entry control area includes controls up to the point of data entering the communication link or, in a nondata communication environment, entry into computer application programs for further processing.

Transaction entry controls are a combination of manual and automated control routines. They are of particular importance because they control two important application areas: data conversion and edit and validation. Increasingly, the emphasis is on automating as many control routines as possible, to take advantage of computer hardware capabilities as well as to promote consistency in the application of controls.

Transaction entry controls are those controls that govern processes of transaction data entry in the following control areas: data entry (terminal or batch), transaction data validation, batch proof and balancing, and transaction entry error handling.

Figure 6-1 shows the relationship of these control areas. From the transaction origination phase, the mainline of flow passes through terminal or batch data entry, through transaction data validation, and on to either the data communications phase or the computer processing phase. Transaction error handling control is part of a feedback loop to either transaction data entry or transaction origination, depending on the nature of the errors.

Some of the controls within the transaction entry process may be instituted during the entry of data into the system. As such, they may be a combination of manual and automated control routines. Many of the newer on-line systems tend to have most of the controls within the transaction entry process automatically applied during the entry of data into the application system.

The difference between a transaction entry control and the subsequent data communication or computer processing controls is that a transaction entry control occurs during the conversion of data into a transaction entry format (e.g., keypunch, terminal entry). While a transaction entry control may restrict the entry of data into the computer application system, computer processing controls will not come into force until the data have been entered and the application programs attempt to process them.

NEED FOR TRANSACTION ENTRY CONTROLS

Transaction entry controls are necessary to ensure that complete and accurate data are entered into the computer application system. The validity and accuracy of data are dependent upon the functioning of controls from the inception of data origination.

The transaction entry process is of particular importance since it involves a data conversion phase. In this context, data conversion is the process of converting source data to a machine-readable format. Consequently, it is important to establish controls to ensure that this conversion is accurately performed.

In developing transaction entry controls, the following are the most important control objectives an organization may wish to satisfy:

- Transaction entry processing is performed accurately for all source data received.
- Transaction entry processing allows optimum validation of source data.
- Transaction entry error-handling procedures allow for the detection of errors, correction of data in error, and the timely resubmission of corrected data for further processing.

For examination of how to satisfy transaction entry control objectives through the use of specific application system controls, the process of transaction entry is separated into control areas. Within each control area are one or more types of controls. Each control type includes specific application controls that are currently being used in this phase of applications system processing. Table 6-1 shows the structure of transaction data entry, broken down by control type within area, and by individual control within type.

CONTROL AREA—TRANSACTION (BATCH) DATA ENTRY

These controls include procedures and methods used to ensure the proper collection of data for recording. The collection of data for computer processing is usually dependent on the application system processing cycle. The entry of data is controlled to allow the

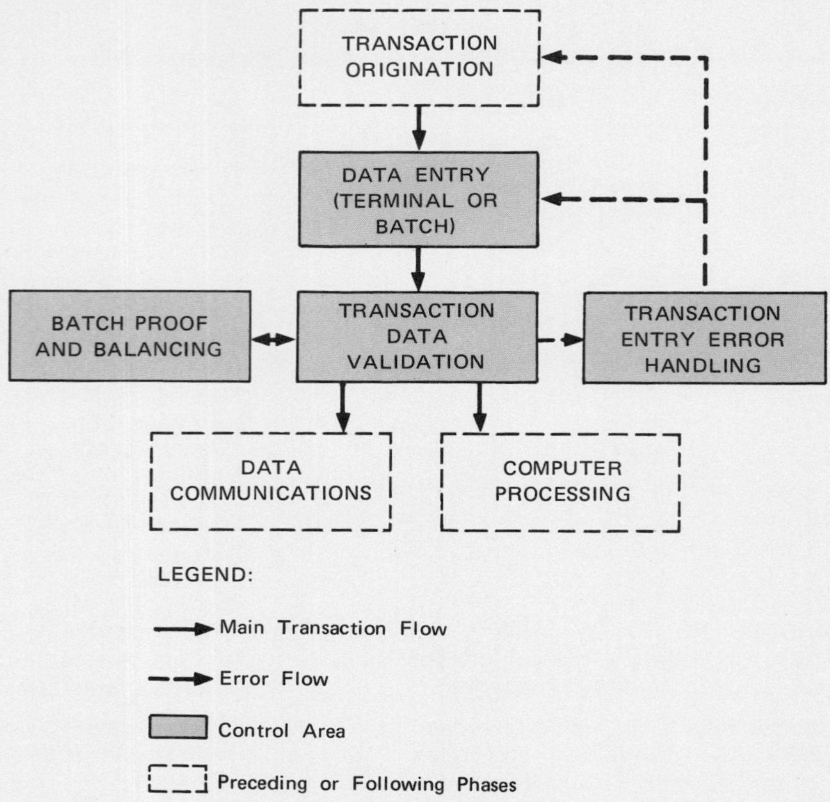

FIGURE 6-1 DATA PROCESSING TRANSACTION ENTRY

proper cutoff of input data. The objective to be accomplished is to place accurate and valid information within the appropriate processing cycle. For example, it is of little value to run a report on the aging of accounts receivable before the programs that do the cash application processing. The control of data entry allows the proper movement of data from the initiation to its entry into the computer application system (see Figure 6-2).

Control Type — Written Procedures

Control Documentation — Control documentation defines the system control point at which data entry procedures are verified. System control points are those points in the system where the integrity of the data is verified. The important point is not the method of control used, but the fact that the system has been analyzed from a control viewpoint. The result of such analysis is specified in writing and is used during the transaction entry process.

User Procedures — Written user procedures are used to guide the proper recording of input transactions. Such written instructions cover controls that must be used, data entry devices, schedules that must be observed (cutoff dates), and other procedures that are unique to the transaction entry process. Such user

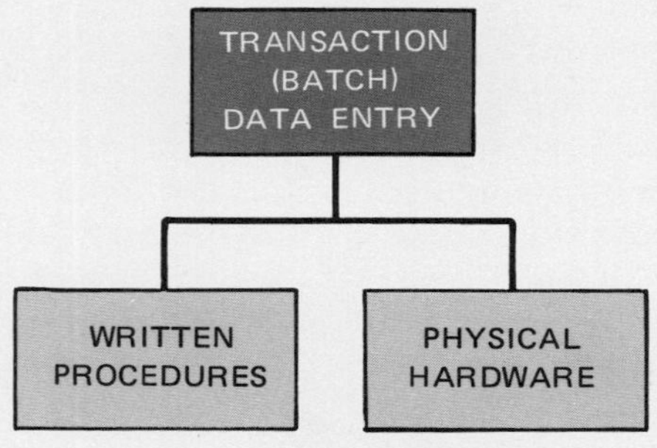

FIGURE 6-2 TRANSACTION (BATCH) DATA ENTRY

Table 6-1
TRANSACTION ENTRY CONTROL STRUCTURE

Control Area	Control Type	Control
Transaction (batch) data entry	Written procedures	Control documentation User procedures
	Physical hardware	Location of data conversion operation Simultaneous recording
Terminal data entry	Terminal software features	Security of data entry terminal Preformatting Interactive display Computer-aided instruction User application system access Terminal authority levels Data access matrix Master commands Terminal sign-on procedures Review of terminal assignments
	Hardware control features	Terminal features Intelligent terminals
Transaction data validation	Transcription verification techniques	Key verification Preprogrammed keying formats
	Data content validation techniques	Editing and validating routines Transaction data cutoff Passwords
Batch proof and balancing	Data input controls	Processing schedules Turnaround documents Cancellation of source documents Logging
	Proof and balancing methods	Manual check of control figures Batch control Batch header records
Transaction entry error handling	Error detection	Error display Unauthorized access attempts Error listings
	Error correction	Corrective action Warning messages Error message
	Corrected data resubmission	Corrected data editing Control totals and rejects

procedures may describe input keying requirements, response interpretations, and required actions on behalf of the user.

Written user procedures are the result of a procedural analysis of the business functions that determine precisely what must be accomplished and the steps used to accomplish the transaction entry process.

Control Type — Physical Hardware

Location of Data Conversion Operation — Data conversion operations are established as close to the source of information as possible to minimize the transmittal exposure of data and the time loss during transmittal.

Simultaneous Recording — Simultaneous recording on computer-readable media (e.g., cards, tape) is

... source of origination. ... Touchtone telephone sys- ... information coming in on tel- ... captured directly on computer ...rds) with no direct human interven- ...urce document (customer order) is then ... simultaneously with the recording of data on computer media.

Simultaneous recording is a method used to minimize the human errors that occur during a transaction entry process.

CONTROL AREA — TERMINAL DATA ENTRY

Current developments in data entry terminals represent another family of potential control mechanisms. These developments offer the opportunity to take advantage of the speed and accuracy of computer processing in the application of data entry controls. See Figure 6-3.

Control Type — Terminal Software Features

Security of Data Entry Terminal — Data entry terminals are physically secured. Security may be implemented by locking up the terminals in a secure room, putting a keylock on the terminal itself, or by placing a lockable cover over the terminal device when not in use.

Preformatting — A predesigned format is used to guide terminal operators in supplying input data necessary for the application system. Such procedures maximize the consistency of data entry.

Interactive Display — Interactive display allows the terminal operator to interact with the system during data entry, thus assisting correct inputs.

Computer-Aided Instruction — Computer-aided instruction is utilized in some systems using on-line dialogue in order to reduce the number of operator errors. Computer-aided instruction is a prompting method for educating on-line system users. Terminal operators receive specific instruction from the application system during transaction entry.

User Application System Access — Each individual user of an on-line system is limited to certain application transactions. This may be accomplished through limiting physical access to transaction entry devices or through a hierarchy of software protection (e.g., see discussion of passwords).

For a system that requires a high level of control, the user may be required to enter first his user number, second his personal security password, and third a special authorization code (secret number) before he is granted access to a specific file.

Terminal Authority Level — A list of authority levels may be maintained for each terminal in use. Authority levels for each terminal are defined by the system administrator. One system reviewed by SRI allows the use of 16 authority levels.

The work that may be entered on a terminal is restricted by the authority level assigned. For example, one terminal may be assigned for cash applications while another terminal is used for training new credit personnel. By designating the second terminal as "training," the system administrator allows the use of the terminal and the application system does not update the active files for transactions entered on this terminal.

Data Access Matrix — Software protection is used to restrict data access. This involves a matrix of data access authorities that is automatically checked against the user identification (password). This matrix is updated as passwords are changed periodically and different levels of access to files are granted. For a system that has been identified as critical, the "secret" password may be changed on a daily basis. In this way, an individual is restricted to the data within a specific system that is accessible to him.

Master Commands — A master command is a computer program to control the operation of a particular application system. Such commands control programs to be processed, initiating segments of the program controls on an input/output device, operator intervention, and corrective action to be taken on system malfunctions. The entry of master commands is restricted to a limited number of operations personnel using a master command terminal.

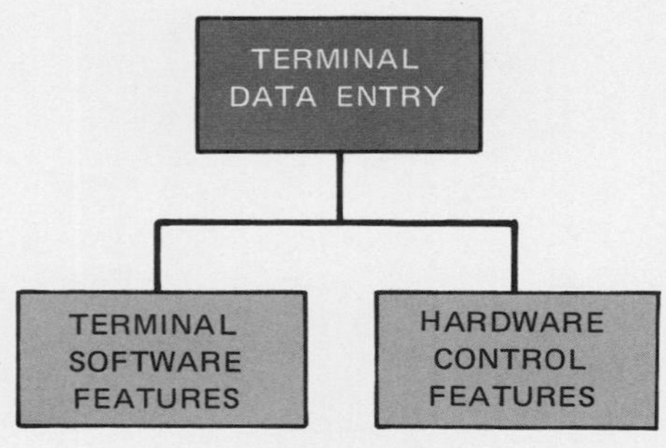

FIGURE 6-3 TERMINAL DATA ENTRY

Terminal Sign-On Procedures — Supervisory management sign-on procedures are used to initialize terminals before any operators can sign on. Supervisory management personnel are also required to sign off at the end of the day's use.

Review of Terminal Assignments — Management reviews the propriety of terminal authority level assignments periodically or in the event of some concern of security violation.

Control Type — Hardware Control Features

Terminal Features — Terminals are used that have features that enhance the ability to control data input and the correction of data entry errors. These features include:

- Erase and backspace keys and related text editing features.
- Terminal logs — These logs allow the terminal to record all transactions processed.
- Built-in terminal IDs — Terminals are provided with electronic identification that can be queried by the computer. This identification is used to validate proper terminal authorization.

Intelligent Terminals — Intelligent terminals are used as front-end input devices that have programming capabilities. These capabilities are used to detect errors and do editing before the transmission of the data entry to the central computer facility.

Intelligent terminals are most often used for front-end edit and validating terminals to minimize transmission traffic in operations that tend to be interactive. In this role, intelligent terminals are programmed to perform content-based, application-specific editing, accumulation of batch totals, and specialized operator prompting.

CONTROL AREA — TRANSACTION DATA VALIDATION

Transaction data entry information is subjected to a comprehensive edit and validating routine (Figure 6-4) to ensure the accuracy and completeness of data before its input to the computer applications systems. There are two types of controls: those that address the correct transcription of data from human-readable to computer-readable form, and those tha[illegible] data content to ensure its correctness.

Control Type — Transcription Verification Techniques

Key Verification — Key verification is a method used to remove human errors from the transaction entry process. To verify the accuracy of keying operations, a second operator, reading the same source documents, keys input data into a verifier. The machine compares the depressed key with the hole in the punched card (or its electronic equivalent). Differences between the original and verifying data are noted. A small perforation on the right margin of the card (or an electronic equivalent for tape or disk data) indicates the card has passed the verification process.

Preprogrammed Keying Formats — Formats for data entry, tailored to the application system, are prepared and used in conjunction with the format control features of the data entry device (keypunch, verifier, key-tape, or key-disk unit) to ensure that data are recorded in the proper fields, formats, and characters.

Control Type — Data Content Validation Techniques

Editing and Validating Routines — With today's hardware capabilities, edit and validating routines are becoming increasingly important processes performed by the computer application system. The editing and validating routines are normally performed for all input data fields even though an error may be detected in an early field.

Editing and validating routines may be performed in remote software such as the data entry input terminal or may be part of the computer application program. Today, there is a tendency to edit and validate data entry transactions as early as possible in the data flow to ensure that the system rejects any incorrect transaction before its entry into the system for updating.

Editing and validation routines are generally unique to the application system being used, although some general-purpose routines may be incorporated. An application program or intelligent terminal can

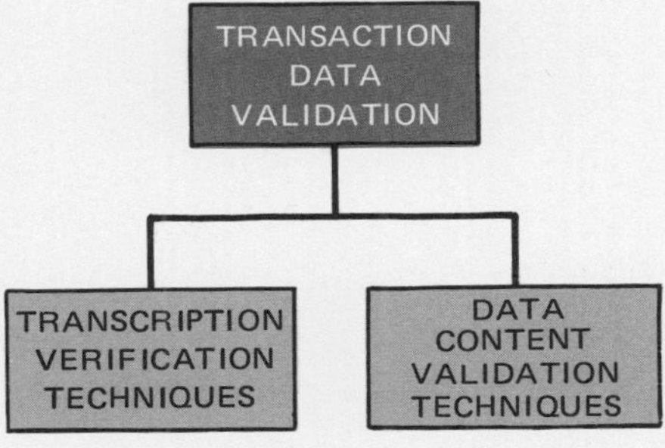

FIGURE 6-4 TRANSACTION DATA VALIDATION

...tines that may include ...es, record length, range, ...ids in a record, reasonability ...th.

...minals have the capability to perform ...ion and correction at the terminal site as ... to transmitting the data into the central computer site for error detection.

Edit and validating routines are placed in a system to aid in ensuring the completeness and accuracy of data. Therefore, the overriding of edit routines should not be taken lightly. In most systems the user is not provided this capability. Overriding of edit is allowed only from a master terminal and only by specialized user department personnel.

Transaction Data Cutoff — A special routine is often used that will automatically compare transaction dates to a table contained in the system. Transactions entering after a specific cutoff date are suspended until after closing. Suspended items are listed on a report for the user.

Passwords — Passwords are used to verify input as being received from an authorized source. Passwords provide the means for a terminal operator to access a file. A validity check of the passwords is performed before any transactions are accepted.

Procedures are established that govern periodic issuance of passwords. In addition, the procedures cover the process to be followed should a password need to be changed. The printing of passwords on hardcopy or on the terminal display may be suppressed to avoid the possibility of casual observance. Each person allowed to use the terminal receives an individual user number in conjunction with a password. A list of these user numbers and passwords is maintained by supervisory personnel.

CONTROL AREA — BATCH PROOF AND BALANCING

Transactions entering a computer for processing normally undergo a batch proof and balancing operation. These operations are performed to serve as an interface between the user and the data processing department. Batch proof and balancing operations may be performed by a control clerk or group, or the operations may be computerized. See Figure 6-5.

Control objectives normally accomplished by the batch proof and balancing operation are as follows:

- Input is submitted on schedule.
- Appropriate control fields are in balance.
- The transaction entry error handling process is controlled.

Typical functions performed by the control groups may be to receive data processing input, maintain control logs for verification of batch control totals, and coordinate the correction and reentry of errors identified and reported by the data processing department.

Control Type — Data Input Controls

Processing Schedules — A schedule of processing is used to determine that all transactions have been received and entered on time. Compliance monitoring with these schedules is performed to ensure that the user is submitting input data in accordance with processing requirements. This function is performed to avoid incomplete reports resulting from missing cutoff dates.

Turnaround Documents — Where data are entered from source documents, the documents are retained at the input terminal until the system accepts the entire transaction. The use of turnaround documents in conjunction with prerecorded information eliminates much of the need to re-record information being reentered into the application system.

For example, a department store sends out a monthly statement with a place to fill in the amount paid and return the check with a tear-off portion to the statement. The information, with the exception of the paid amount, is prerecorded on an input medium. This prerecorded information from the billing system is used during the cash application process.

The use of turnaround documents eliminates much redundant data entry operation and provides consistency between interfacing systems.

Cancellation of Source Documents — Source documents that have entered the data processing data

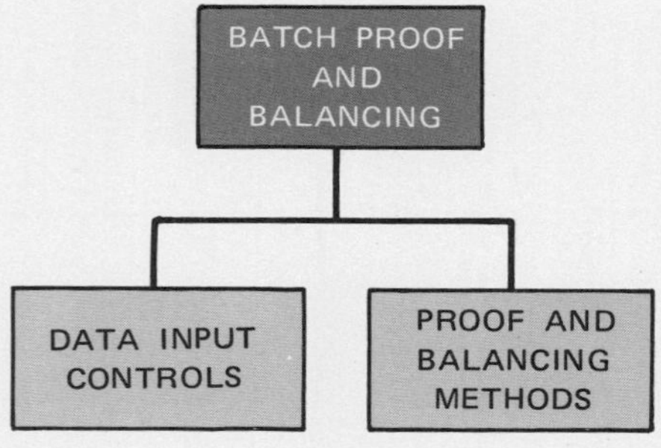

FIGURE 6-5 BATCH PROOF AND BALANCING

entry phase are cancelled or an indication is made on the source document that it has been processed. This is performed to prevent the accidental duplication or reuse of data. In one case the control group was required to sign source documents as evidence of its review. This signature indicated responsibility for the recording of a transaction and the verification of authorization signatures.

Logging — A record shows the receipt of data and actual disposition of data and provides for the accounting for all batches received. These document receipt logs are used to establish an audit trail within a system. This log generally contains batch number, time received, job name, received from, received by, and quantity.

Control Type — Proof and Balancing Methods

Manual Check of Control Figures — A manual check of source documents is made for control figures to determine that they are in balance before releasing the information to the computer operations area.

Batch Control — Terminal operators are required to enter their work in batches. In this manner, batch control totals are maintained close to the point of origination. The terminal operator creates the batches, and various processing controls and systems edit routines check totals within data fields. Control totals are recomputed and compared with manually calculated totals. This function prevents the loss of data during the conversion of source data to a machine-readable format.

Batch Header Records — Batch-control totals are used to establish controls on information to be processed by the system. Batch totals developed in the user department are submitted to data processing in the form of batch header records. These are subsequently used to prove the completeness of batches received. Where bad data are received within a batch, they are rejected. Batch header records are then adjusted to reflect control totals of the data to be carried forward to the processing cycle.

CONTROL AREA — TRANSACTION ENTRY ERROR HANDLING

These controls include the procedures and methods used to ensure that transactions rejected at this point in the system are corrected and reentered in a timely manner. Controls in this area ensure that all errors are accounted for at the end of any processing cycle. As shown in Figure 6-6, this area includes three types of controls: error detection, error correction, and corrected data resubmission.

Control Type — Error Detection

Error Display — A terminal system displays errors immediately upon detection. Corrections are made immediately by the terminal operator.

Unauthorized Access Attempts — An immediate report is displayed of unauthorized attempts to access the system. This report includes the location of the terminal, date, time, number of attempts, and the operator signed on at the time of the violation. The system takes preventive action at this point. It shuts down the terminal in question and allows access from that particular terminal only after special intervention by system administration personnel.

Error Listings — Preprocessing edit error listings are issued to help remove errors before on-line processing of data. In one case examined, this list included valid as well as invalid data. Therefore, the list contained *all input* transactions and identification of invalid data and out-of-balance controls.

Control Type — Error Correction

Corrective Action — When an error is detected in a transaction being processed, it is displayed at the time of detection. The entire transaction is displayed on the terminal. This display contains an error message along with the suggested corrective action to be taken for each data field in error.

Warning Messages — A warning message is displayed for each transaction that contains data that do not meet edit routine requirements. A warning message is issued to the user, but the data are accepted by the system for further processing.

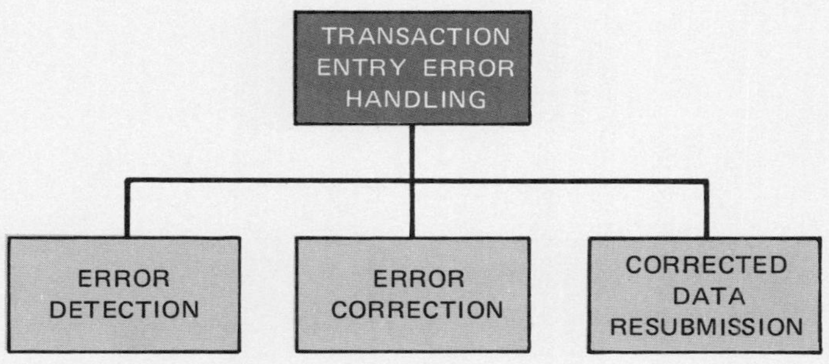

FIGURE 6-6 TRANSACTION ENTRY ERROR HANDLING

Error Message — An error message is given for each transaction that contains data that do not meet edit routine requirements. The transaction is rejected from further processing by the system.

Control Type — Corrected Data Resubmission

Corrected Data Editing — Corrected data editing is done by using the same rules as for processing the original transaction. When it is necessary to resubmit the entire transaction, the corrections are edited by the same module that was used for the original transaction. Even though an error is detected, processing continues to edit all fields of the transaction.

Control Totals and Rejects — Control totals are produced for all rejects. These totals reflect new rejects as well as the elimination of accepted data resubmission. Reconciliation of control totals may be accomplished through a manual monitoring of data resubmission or a computer control using suspense file principles.

SUMMARY

The accuracy, completeness, and validity of data contained in computer application systems are dependent on the proper functioning of a system of internal controls. Transaction entry controls ensure that complete and accurate data move forward from the transaction origination process into the data communications links or computer processing by the application program. The transaction entry process is of particular importance in the controlling of computer application systems because it entails two important phases: the data conversion process, which entails converting of data to a machine-readable format, and the edit and validation routines that occur before the transaction is entered into the computer application system.

The transaction entry process is subdivided into the following control areas: transaction data entry, transaction data validation, batch proof and balancing, and transaction entry error handling.

Many of the newer on-line systems have most of the controls within the transaction entry process automatically applied during the entry of data into the computer system. In the future, manual control routines will continue to be automated. This continuing trend takes advantage of computer capabilities to provide maximum benefits in terms of system control effectiveness and efficiency.

Chapter 7

DATA COMMUNICATION CONTROLS

Data communication controls are primarily concerned with ensuring the integrity of data as they pass through communication lines from the message input devices to the message reception devices. These controls are important because most data communication equipment is owned and controlled by organizations other than the sending or receiving organizations. These controls are also important because there is a fast-growing trend by many organizations to use data communication services as an integral part of their computer application systems. Consequently, to ensure the accuracy and completeness of data for the entire application system, internal auditors are expected to understand and review this area.

Data communication controls are those controls that govern the three control areas of message input, message transmission, and message reception and accounting. Figure 7-1 provides a pictorial description of the three basic elements of data communications. For this chapter, the term "message" is used rather than "transaction" because message is a more appropriate communications unit to discuss. A message may include one or a number of transactions or it may contain only a partial transaction. Of course, messages travel in both directions between remote terminals and computers. For the sake of simplicity, this chapter discusses controls only in the context of messages from a terminal to the computer. When messages travel in the reverse direction, the controls herein still apply.

The message input area refers to terminal-oriented input after the data are keyed into the communication system (i.e., data entry controls, as addressed in Chapter 6). The message transmission area refers to the hardware and software required to move the message from the terminal to its destination. The message reception and accounting area refers to the hardware, software, and procedures necessary to receive and account for all messages transmitted through the system before actual computer application processing of the message.

Traditionally, data communication controls have been more closely associated with application than with computer operating systems. Technological advances in the design of computer operating systems software have created a growing family of data communication controls that properly belong in the category of general, rather than application, controls. However, data communication controls falling into either category will be discussed in this chapter without making a distinction each time.

Controls in each area are divided into two types — hardware-related and software- and procedures-related, depending on the primary method or means of implementation.

NEED FOR DATA COMMUNICATION CONTROLS

Data communication controls are necessary to ensure that the integrity of the data is not lost or compromised from the time the data are entered at the terminal until the time they are received for computer processing. During the time of transmission, data usually are outside the control of the originating or processing organizations (i.e., most communication lines are either commercial dial service or are leased from a common carrier). Due to this lack of physical control, proper use of available communication controls is especially important to ensure the accuracy and completeness of data transmited over communication systems.

Organizations using communication systems attempt to satisfy the following objectives:

- Ensure that adequate data communication controls are operating in support of each application system affecting data transmitted within the organization and data transmitted over common carrier.
- Verify that data communication controls in use function as specified.
- Identify and satisfy changing data communication control requirements.

To provide organizations with information that will assist them in satisfying these control objectives, this chapter addresses controls currently in use by organizations that rely heavily on data communications. Table 7-1 shows the structure of data communications, by control area, control type, and specific controls identified in this chapter. Hardware-related control types are those controls that are heavily dependent on hardware for their application. Software- and procedure-related control types are those controls that are primarily based in software and procedures, but hardware may be involved in some instances.

CONTROL AREA – MESSAGE INPUT

Controls in this area include those relating to terminal identification and security as well as software mechanisms and procedures to monitor message activity.

Control Type – Hardware Related

Electronic Identification Code – A hardware identification code requiring no human intervention for its use is built into the terminal; the code is checked and validated periodically by the computer to ensure that no unauthorized terminals are being used.

Control Type – Software and Procedure Related

Secure Phone Equipment Rooms – Locks and alarms are used to control access to all phone equipment rooms throughout the organization to prohibit wiretapping or destruction of lines.

Network Configuration Polling Table – A table of all authorized terminal polling addresses within the communication network is maintained in the computer and used to ensure that the system does not leave open addresses for unauthorized terminals to gain access to the system.

Sending Message Identification – Each message from the sending terminal is identified by the sequence number of the message, date and time, transaction number, or video screen number to ensure that messages can be properly tracked through the system.

Security Table – A table relating what transaction types are authorized from specific terminal addresses is used to control user commands and, consequently, user access to sensitive data. This table can be part of the operating or application system.

Communication System Control Log – The communication system control log is reviewed periodically for network supervisor terminal commands issued. Commands reviewed include those for disabling or enabling a line or station to determine the status of the network at any point in time, those used for directing alternative routing or traffic from one station to another, and those used to change the order or frequency of line or terminal polling.

CONTROL AREA – MESSAGE TRANSMISSION

Controls or techniques in this area relate to message checking as the messages progress through the communication system, as well as to certain physical aspects of the communication lines themselves.

Control Type – Hardware Related

Communication Line Routing – Data communication lines are not put through the public switchboard (PBX), thus reducing the error rate and the chance for someone to "listen" into the data transmission

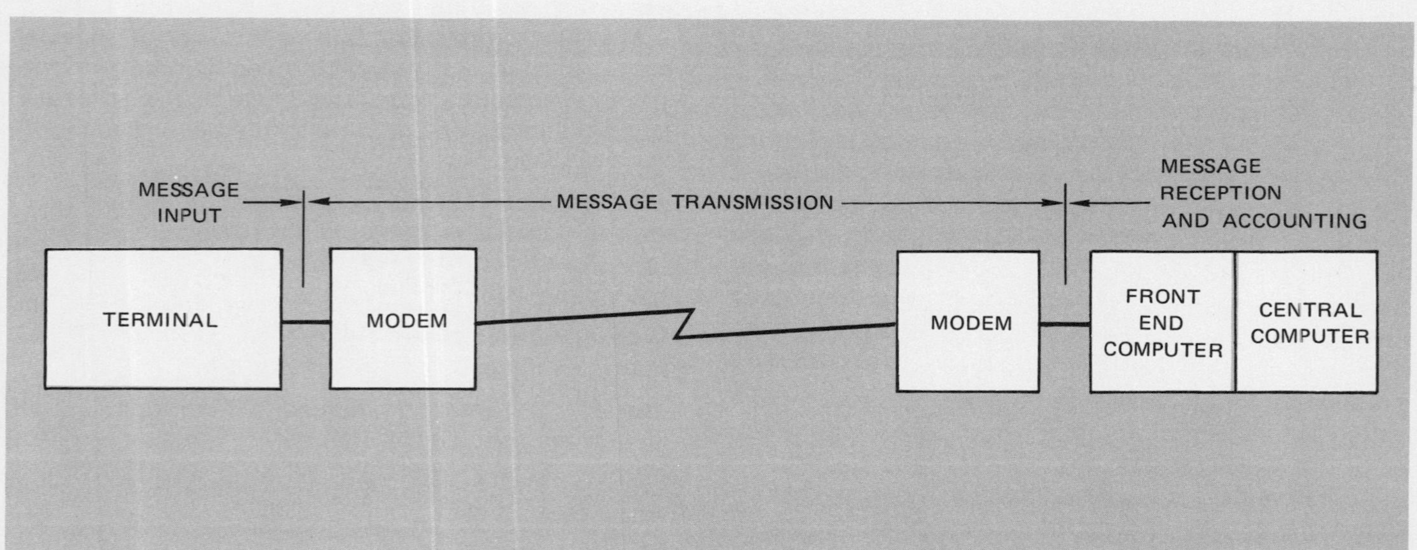

FIGURE 7-1 DATA COMMUNICATIONS SYSTEM CONTROL AREAS FOR MESSAGES FROM TERMINALS TO THE CENTRAL COMPUTER

Table 7-1
DATA COMMUNICATION CONTROL STRUCTURE

Control Area	Control Type	Control
Message input	Hardware related	Electronic identification code
	Software and procedure related	Secure phone equipment rooms Network configuration polling table Sending message identification Security table Communication system control log
Message transmission	Hardware related	Communication line routing Line conditioning Automatic store and forward Automatic dial backup Modem loop-back switch Forward error correction Validity check Echo checking Message intercept function Packet switching networks Local loop security Encryption techniques Multipurpose modems Backup modems Backup lines
	Software and procedure related	Transmission batch controls
Message reception and accounting	Hardware related	Detection with retransmission Backup electrical power
	Software and procedure related	Validation Line usage records Message sequence number Input/output message log Dial-up modems Message backup log Error recording Error correction procedures

Line Conditioning — Voice grade lines are specially conditioned to reduce transmission errors. This technique helps maintain the accuracy and integrity of data during transmission.

Automatic Store and Forward — An automatic store and forward capability is used to maintain control over messages queued for a busy device such as a terminal.

Automatic Dial Backup — An automatic dial backup capability is used with leased lines to ensure that, when leased lines fail, an automatic switchover to dial facilities is accomplished for the duration of the outage.

Modem Loop-Back Switches — Modems equipped with loop-back switches for fault isolation are used. These switches allow the organization to determine whether a failure or an increase in errors is being caused by the modem itself or the line to which the modem is connected.

Forward Error Correction — Forward error correction techniques are used for the detection and reporting of data communication errors associated with message units. Forward error correction uses sophisticated codes that contain sufficient redundancy to detect and correct errors without retransmission.

Validity Check — Parity and other validity checks are used to detect errors in transmission of data at the character level.

Echo Checking — Echo checking is used in the detection and reporting of data communication errors.

Echo checking is the technique in which each character is echoed back to the sending site. This type of error detection mechanism requires a 100% redundancy in transmission, decreasing effective line capacity because the data are transmitted twice.

Message Intercept Function — A message intercept function is used to receive messages directed to inoperable terminals. This equipment also performs periodic checking to detect errors, correct them, and initiate retransmission of messages found to be in error.

Packet Switching Networks — Packet switching networks are common carrier networks that offer many alternative routes between terminal points and that transmit information in standard-sized "packets." This procedure offers a high measure of security against unauthorized intercept and high reliability of transmission.

Local Loop Security — The local loop is the line that extends from the organization's premises to the phone company's nearest branch office. Because all the messages that come into the central computer must pass over the local loop, physically securing the local loop is important.

Encryption Techniques — Scrambling or encryption techniques are used by organizations in transmitting sensitive data to prevent unauthorized persons from using any information they may obtain accidentally or intentionally.

Multipurpose Modems — Modems that have the ability to handle both voice and data communications are used in the event that troubles either delay or stop the data communication process. In alternative voice communication, the operator at one terminal can talk to the operator at the other end over the same line on which the data are being transmitted.

Backup Modems — Backup modems are maintained at critical terminals for use when one of the operational modems fails.

Backup Lines — Key communication lines are duplicated to lower the probability that a communication link will be lost due to a communication line failure.

Control Type — Software and Procedure Related

Transmission Batch Controls — Transmission batch controls are used over high-speed transmission lines between regional concentrators and the central computer. Many terminals feed into regional concentrators in a real-time dialogue. The regional concentrator batches groups of transactions and creates internal batch control totals as it transmits them to the central host computer.

CONTROL AREA — MESSAGE RECEPTION AND ACCOUNTING

Controls in this area relate to the hardware and software usually associated with the central computer system to receive and account for all messages in the system.

Control Type — Hardware Related

Detection with Retransmission — Detection with retransmission is one of the most common forms of detection and reporting of data communication errors. Detection involves using redundancy checks to detect errors in transmission. The retransmission occurs when the receiving unit determines there is an error in the message. The receiving unit responds to the transmitting unit and tells it to resend the same message. In this way, only messages that are in error are transmitted. This is one of the most effective methods of error detection in the control of data communications.

Backup Electrical Power — Backup electrical power and air conditioning are provided for all equipment within the communication systems that require them.

Control Type — Software and Procedure Related

Validation — Both incoming and outgoing messages are checked for valid address and are edited for specific data-communication-oriented functions, such as routing, heading to the message, and reformatting.

Line Usage Records — A complete list of line usage records, individual messages, and processing statistics is maintained for audit trail purposes.

Message Sequence Number — A message sequence number is automatically assigned for all messages in and out of the computer system by the central computers. Regional terminals or regional concentrators can also assign message sequence numbers for all messages emanating from that equipment. This provides a traceable message log for each station or terminal that transmits a message within the communication system. It also allows for the balancing of all incoming and outgoing messages between the central computer and each of the terminals or concentrators to which it transmits.

Input/Output Message Log — A log of all input and output messages is maintained on a magnetic recording device to assist in system recovery or restart and in tracing messages.

Dial-Up Modems — For organizations that use the public switched network and dial-up modems at the computer, the following controls may be used:

- Phone numbers of modems are changed regularly.
- Phone numbers are kept confidential.
- Phone numbers are not placed on modems.
- Automatic call receipt is not allowed. An operator in the computer room intercepts all calls to obtain verbal identification as to who is placing the call.
- Terminals have an electronic identification circuit that the computer interrogates initially and periodically when active.

- Dial-out is used only where a dial-in call triggers an automatic dial-out.

Message Backup Log — All messages awaiting transmission are placed on a backup log before putting them into the transmission queue. As messages are transmitted and received, the receiving terminal sends a reply that the message has been received correctly; the backup log is then purged.

Error Recording — All errors in retransmission of messages in the system are logged. This log includes the type of error, the time and date, the terminal, the operator, and the number of times the message was retransmitted before it was correctly received.

Error Correction Procedures — A user's manual specifies a cross-reference of error messages to the appropriate error code generated by the system. These messages help the user interpret the error that has occurred and suggest corrective action to be taken.

SUMMARY

The accuracy, completeness, and validity of data received for processing by the computer application system over communication lines depend not only on the controls used during data handling and data entry, but also on the controls used within the data communication system itself. While many of the data communication controls are transparent to the user and internal auditor, the controls are still important to ensure the integrity of data and, as such, internal auditors, users, and data processing personnel must ensure that data communication controls are in place. Good data communication controls are also important because data passing through the communication system leave the control of the sending and receiving organizations. To understand the types of data communication controls in use and their adequacy for maintaining the integrity of the data, internal auditors are expanding their area of expertise to data communications.

The primary control areas of concern to internal auditors in data communications are in the message input and the message receiving areas. Controls used during data transmission are important, but, because almost all are implemented by hardware, most major data communication suppliers provide similar control capabilities. Internal auditors are primarily concerned with ensuring that their organizations use data communication control capabilities commensurate with the value of the data passing through the data communication system.

In the message input area, controls are basically concerned with ensuring that terminals in use are authorized for use and that all messages issued through terminals are identifiable. In the message reception area, controls are basically concerned with ensuring the data are complete and accurate as sent and that a log or journal of all messages is kept for traceability and recovery.

There is a rapidly growing trend to the use of data communications as an integral part of computer application systems. This trend, which can be expected to continue, is causing internal auditors to develop new areas of expertise in order to monitor the entire application system process from transaction origination to output processing. It is clear that internal auditors are increasingly being required to perform data communication audits in the same way they have conducted audits of data preparation, handling, and entry. Only after data communication controls are in place and audited can the accuracy, completeness, and validity of the data processed by the complete application system be ensured.

Chapter 8

COMPUTER PROCESSING

Computer processing controls, which are used to ensure accuracy and completeness of data during computer processing, are the controls that govern computer process integrity and computer process error handling. These controls are applied after the entry of data into the computer application system as application programs process the data. File interface and program interfaces are also included in this chapter.

The scope of computer processing controls discussed here includes application level controls that are built in and around the central processing unit. These controls are built into each individual application program and control application program data input, processing, and output. Application controls are unique and specific in one application and therefore may or may not be transferable between applications. During the continuing development of computer processing controls, it is important to ensure that the principles of internal control (e.g., separation of functions) are being carried forward to the functions performed by the computer application system.

NEED FOR PROCESSING CONTROLS

Computer processing controls are necessary to ensure that complete and accurate information is processed from data entry to output. As previously stated, the integrity of data in computer application systems is dependent on the functioning of controls from the inception of data origination through the processing of output. Consequently, it is important to establish adequate control during each process that occurs.

In developing computer processing controls, the following are among the important control objectives an organization may wish to satisfy:

- Verify all transactions that are entered as input for processing.
- Verify significant control totals.
- Verify processing using validity testing techniques.
- Verify that processing controls cannot be bypassed.
- Verify that the separation of functions principle necessary for the control of the application area is carried forward to the functions performed by the computer operation.

Computer processing has many characteristics that make the development and review of application controls a challenging task. It is not possible to physically observe the sequence of operations performed with the computer, as can be done with manual systems. Further, the results of operations are then stored on magnetically recorded files, which are also not subject to visual verification. Therefore, controls in this phase tend to be indirect, preventive, or ex post facto in nature.

For assistance in satisfying the control objectives through the use of application system controls, the computer processing control phase is separated into control areas. Within each control area are one or more types of controls. Each control type includes one or more specific controls that organizations are using to control computer processing. Table 8-1 lists all control areas of this phase, broken down by control type within area and by individual control within type.

CONTROL AREA — COMPUTER PROCESS INTEGRITY

These controls include procedures and methods used to ensure the completeness and accuracy of data during the computer processing of the application system. The computer processing control types to be discussed include transaction identification, computation and logic, file maintenance, and computer operations personnel (see Figure 8-1).

Control Type — Transaction Identification

Transaction Codes — A unique identifier, usually referred to as a transaction code and sometimes used in conjunction with transaction data (e.g., date), is used to direct the transaction to the proper portion of the application program for processing.

Monitoring of Computer-Generated Transactions — Computer-generated transactions are controlled by programs that print out all computer-generated transactions for direct feedback to users. This control provides for the use of computer-generated output figures that are checked manually.

Computer-generated transactions are also controlled by building in balance controls between program modules. These balance controls are automated internal cross-checks. Such controls may take the form of reasonableness checks or specific run-to-run control totals.

Control Type — Computation and Logic

Control Totals — Control totals are passed between jobs and job steps during production. A system of automated controls includes balancing the entire system, balancing between systems, and balancing and reconciling other files used. A common example of this type of control is the run-to-run total.

Default Option — A default option is developed where critical decisions must be made in a computer program. In this way, standardized action is taken whenever the user does not select a specific alternative action.

Anticipation Control — Anticipation controls are used as a method of ensuring accountability of input. Sequence checking is a common example of such a control in which the computer application system is programmed to anticipate each transaction and detect any missing transactions. In another example, the application program, before updating a masterfile, anticipates the result of the update and compares it to a reasonableness range for that field. All amounts outside the range are rejected, or a warning message is reported.

Dual Fields — Dual field input enters data twice on the input medium and subsequently checks the redundant data. For example, in an accounts receivable system the same amount may be added as a debit to the customer's account as well as to a file balance total. At the end of the day's processing, debit and credit amounts are added and compared with the file balance total.

Arithmetic Accuracy — Arithmetic accuracy is ensured through the use of techniques such as double arithmetic, arithmetic overflow checks, and reverse multiplication. These checks are placed at critical points in the application program calculations.

Exception Reporting — An exception report is prepared each time a program control is overridden or bypassed.

File Control Totals — Application file control totals containing the record count and critical dollar amounts are balanced automatically to file control totals from the previous program run. This type of control is used after each program run.

File Completion Check — A file completion check is used to determine that the application file has

Table 8-1
COMPUTER PROCESSING CONTROL STRUCTURE

Control Area	Control Type	Control
Computer process integrity	Transaction identification	Transaction codes Monitoring of computer-generated transactions
	Computation and logic	Control totals Default option Anticipation control Dual fields Arithmetic accuracy Exception reporting File control totals File completion check
	File maintenance	Balancing the computer file Dummy records
	Computer operations personnel	Operator instructions Computer program run books Computer console Display messages
Computer processing error handling	Error reporting	Error reporting Batch control header balancing Production report of rejected conditions
	Error correction	Automated error suspense file Discrepancy report Error serial numbers
	Corrected data resubmission	Destructive update Error suspense reentry

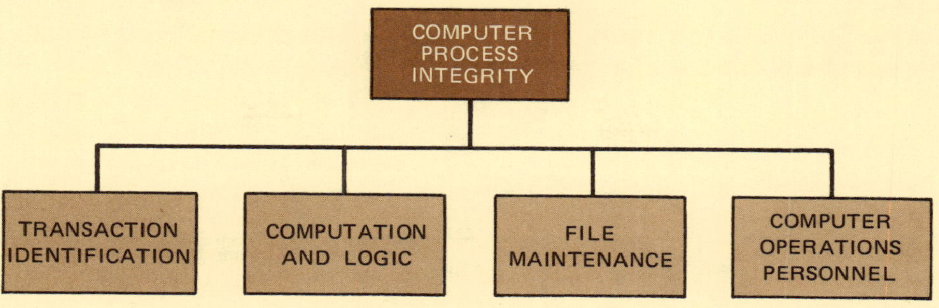

FIGURE 8-1 COMPUTER PROCESS INTEGRITY

been completely processed including both the transaction file and the masterfile.

Control Type — File Maintenance

Balancing the Computer File — The number of records on the opening of a data file is balanced against the changes made during the day and the closing balance. A control record contains the totals of field amounts and total record counts for each field maintained. On a regular basis the total of detail records is compared to the totals in the control records. All discrepancies are reported. For example, a master control record containing opening and closing day's master control record counts as well as daily transaction processing is maintained. This record is used to balance the difference between closing and opening day's record counts by adding total transactions processed for the day.

Dummy Records — No dummy records are allowed to be used to hold erroneous data.

Control Type — Computer Operations Personnel

Operator Instructions — A specific set of operator instructions is used for each application to limit computer operator intervention. These procedures include system start-up, terminal backup assignments, emergency message broadcasting, system shutdown, communication debugging, and systems and job status reporting. These computer instructions prohibit unauthorized access to the computer system by the operator.

Computer Program Run Books — Computer program run books are used by operators in running each application. The run books cover console message instructions, error message instructions, program halt instructions, rerun procedures, checkpoint and restart instructions, checkpoint control totals, job setup instructions, and narrative descriptions of the system, file layouts, and system flowcharts. A program-run manual for each job is developed that includes operator instructions, setup information, and notes on forms, carriage control, tapes, disks, and restart procedures and checkpoints.

Computer Console — The application programs do not accept data from the central computer console.

Display Messages — Application programs do not display messages on the central computer console only. Display messages are printed on the line printer as well as on the console. These messages are then available for review by personnel other than the machine operator.

CONTROL AREA — COMPUTER PROCESSING ERROR HANDLING

These controls include procedures and methods used to ensure that all transactions rejected during computer processing are corrected and reentered in a timely manner. Controls in this area provide for the detection of data loss or nonprocessing of transactions. Control types to be discussed include error reporting, error correction, and corrected data resubmission (see Figure 8-2).

Control Type — Error Reporting

Error Reporting — The information on error reports indicates all data fields in error. These reports also contain corresponding messages that describe the error condition incurred. The entire rejected transaction appears on the report. Processing of a transaction is discontinued when an error is detected. Processing resumes after the error has been corrected and corrected information is reentered into the system.

Batch Control Header Balancing — A report is produced from the application program that displays the contents of batch control header cards as well as the corresponding detail elements that make up the control figure. All out-of-balance conditions are flagged.

Production Report of Rejected Conditions — A production report is provided that will ensure all rejects have been corrected and resubmitted and the proper cutoff has been used.

Control Type — Error Correction

Automated Error Suspense File — An automated suspense file that includes all rejected transactions is maintained by data processing. Such error sus-

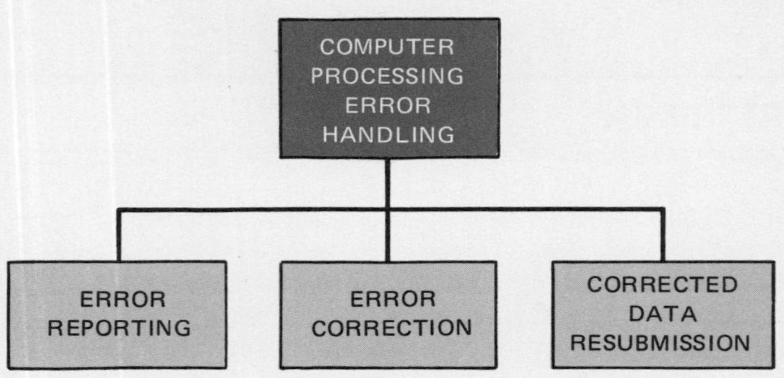

FIGURE 8-2 COMPUTER PROCESSING ERROR HANDLING

pense files are prepared in transaction sequence number within batch number by date.

Error suspense files are used to follow up, correct, and reenter corrected transactions rejected by data processing. Error suspense files are reviewed periodically by user management to monitor levels of transaction errors as well as status of uncorrected transactions.

Discrepancy Report — Discrepancy reports are used to ensure that the handling of errors results in their correction and reentry in a timely manner. All error items are printed on the discrepancy report and also recorded on the error suspense file. All errors stay on the file until they are corrected; this ensures that all errors are ultimately corrected. The error suspense file is periodically printed and distributed to all user departments. Information contained on the distributed reports includes aged errors, frequency of errors, types of errors, frequency by user area, and the date of original error.

Error Serial Numbers — Unique serial numbers are automatically assigned to transactions entered into automated error suspense files. Such serial numbers are used to control subsequent updating of correction data and reentry for normal processing.

Control Type — Corrected Data Resubmission

Destructive Update — Debit and credit type entries, not delete or erase commands, are used to correct error conditions. The system is constructed so that it cannot accept a delete command.

Error Suspense Reentry — Errors are corrected and reentered by making corrections on the error suspense listings. Corrected error suspense listings are subsequently resubmitted to data processing, where the corrections are posted to corresponding error transactions on the error suspense file.

SUMMARY

The accuracy, completeness, and validity of data contained in computer application systems are dependent on the proper functioning of the total system of controls. Computer processing controls begin with the entry of transaction data into the central computer and end with the maintenance of data (data storage and retrieval) or output processing. Application controls in this area are used to ensure the integrity of data during the computer processing phase of the application system.

Computer processing controls are an increasingly important part of the total system of control. With the rapid growth of technology, organizations are currently faced with several modes of computer usage (e.g., distributed systems, centralized processing, data base usage, terminal network, integrated systems). Currently, many organizations are faced with the decision to allocate large or small amounts of resources for the development of control policies and procedures for the control of computer processing. Little concrete feedback, other than reviews by internal and external auditors, for example, is available to measure the effectiveness or efficiency of this resource allocation.

In addition to the lack of "standards" or "measures" of control effectiveness and efficiency, computer processing controls have characteristics (e.g., media storage, media processing, data communications) that make them difficult to review using traditional methods.

As technology continues to advance, management, data processors, and auditors will need to work together to develop computer processing controls as well as methods to evaluate their efficiency and effectiveness.

Chapter 9

DATA STORAGE AND RETRIEVAL

Data storage and retrieval controls are important to ensure the accuracy and completeness of data during the process of data storage and retrieval.

The scope of computer data storage and retrieval controls includes those controls in effect during file handling and file error handling. These controls govern the file-handling processes that are not directly associated with the computer processing of the application system.

Data storage and retrieval controls are of particular importance because they involve a high degree of human intervention and data handling. For this reason it is important to provide for the facility and personnel procedures necessary to control the integrity of data files and programs during intermediate storage and retrieval.

Data storage and retrieval controls are those controls that govern the process of file handling and file error handling. A number of the controls within the data storage and retrieval process are dependent on human intervention in the computer process. As such, they may be a combination of manual and automated control routines. Many of the newer on-line systems tend to have most of the controls within the data storage and retrieval process automatically verified during the computer processing of the application system. Since 1970, computer manufacturers have developed more sophisticated data-base-oriented software that requires increased emphasis on auditability and control. Another reason for emphasis on file controls is the growing use of general-purpose file-handling, data base software and an attendant trend to view processing procedures as independent of data files.

The difference between data storage and retrieval controls and computer processing controls is that a data storage and retrieval control is applied during the preparation of files for storage or removal from storage for use by the application system. A computer processing control does not come into force until the data have been entered into the application system and the application programs attempt to process them.

NEED FOR DATA STORAGE AND RETRIEVAL CONTROLS

Data storage and retrieval controls are necessary to ensure that complete and accurate data are maintained during periods that the data are not being used in the computer application system. The validity and accuracy of such data are dependent upon the functioning of controls from the end of one computer processing cycle to the beginning of the next.

The data storage and retrieval process is of particular importance since it involves a high degree of human intervention, in particular by the media librarian and computer operations personnel. Consequently, it is important to establish controls to ensure that file-handling tasks are accurately performed.

In developing data storage and retrieval controls, an organization may wish to satisfy the following important control objectives:

- Data storage facilities and personnel procedures provide for the protection of data files and programs from loss, destruction, or unauthorized changes.
- Data storage and retrieval procedures allow for maximum ease in use of files and programs.
- Data storage and retrieval procedures allow for backup facilities and procedures for the reconstruction of files.
- Data storage and retrieval error-handling procedures ensure the detection of errors, correction of error condition, and timely reprocessing.

For examination of how to satisfy data storage and retrieval control objectives through the use of application system controls, the process of data storage and retrieval is separated into control areas. Within each control area are one or more control types. Each control type includes one or more specific application controls that are currently in use by organizations to control data storage and retrieval.

Table 9-1 lists all controls discussed in this chapter, grouped by control area and by control type within the control area.

CONTROL AREA – FILE HANDLING

Computerized records are a basic source of information in most of today's business organizations. Current data as well as historical data are recorded on computer files.

Table 9-1
DATA STORAGE AND RETRIEVAL CONTROL STRUCTURE

Control Area	Control Type	Control
File handling	Library	Operating procedures
		On-line library
		Source program statement library
	File access	Conflict prevention feature
		Group files
		File classification
		Data base control table
		Passwords
		Program linkage control table
		Header/trailer labels
		System inquiries
		System logging
		Manual authorization of security table
		Program modification
	File maintenance	Folio number
		Before and after looks
		Masterfile changes
		Dormant files
		Excessive activity
		Scanning of critical files
	Backup	Activity tape
		Separate computer
		Copy masterfiles
		Backup procedures
		Disaster plan
		Recovery procedures
File error handling	Error reporting	Operator intervention
		Comparison programs
	Error correction	Restart procedures
		Backup file usage
	Correction reentry	Job stream log

File-handling controls are important for two reasons. First, loss of the basic files (data base or other file structures) could be serious enough to cause bankruptcy or cost an organization thousands of dollars in recovering lost data. Monetary damage from the loss of various files could be excessive for an organization using on-line real-time systems that interact with data base files.

Second, file-handling controls are necessary to meet the requirements of government regulations. For example, the Privacy Act, which affects governmental installations, makes it mandatory for governmental organizations to impose stringent controls on who has access to data and how the data may be used. The Privacy Act increases the need for file integrity control in government organizations.

The federal government, as well as some state governments, are currently drafting and reviewing privacy acts that would affect the private business sector. Should this legislation be enacted, private business enterprises may be required to implement more stringent file integrity controls over areas such as access and use of data.

The file-handling control area includes procedures and methods used to ensure the proper storage and retrieval of data files. Control types that govern the tasks associated with this area are shown in Figure 9-1.

Control Type — Library

Operating Procedures — A formal library system is developed that indicates the disposition of all application system data files, disks, tapes, and documentation. See Chapter 11 for a discussion on general controls in the media library.

On-Line Library — Besides the media library, two separate libraries are maintained within the data processing operation. One library is the regular production load library for on-line application jobs. The other library stores programs or program modules during the testing phases of the application system development.

Source Program Statement Library — A source program statement library is used to save the old application source program when a new one is entered. The source program statement library procedure keeps track of the day, date, sequence, who made the change, and the update or revision number, as well as new and old application program listings.

Control Type — File Access

Conflict Prevention Feature — A feature in the file accessing routines prohibits two programs from simultaneously updating the same application record.

Group Files — Files in large systems are divided into groups for control purposes. Control is administered by subgrouping, division groupings, or overall groupings. When a file is maintained in groups, totals are provided for like groupings or for a selection of groupings. These can be verified against the totals maintained by the user area.

File Classification — Each application file is classified by security levels such as registered, confidential, company confidential, and critical. Access restrictions for fields, records, and files are based on such classifications. These access restrictions are used as a basis for the development of passwords and transaction authorizations.

Data Base Control Table — A data base control table is developed to control data base accesses from application program modules. In other words no data base access is allowed unless it comes from an authorized program module.

Passwords — Sensitive files are protected with the use of passwords. (See discussion of passwords in Chapter 6.)

Program Linkage Control Table — Program linkage control tables (i.e., tables that specify which programs access other programs) are used to ensure file and program integrity. These tables control the authorized module linkages between programs. All unauthorized linkages are identified, and programs are not allowed to make unauthorized linkages.

Header/Trailer Labels — Header and trailer labels are used in production jobs. These labels identify files by name, serial number, creation date, and the like. At each point the data enter the computer, internal file label checks are performed to ensure proper file usage.

System Inquiries — All application system inquiries are retained on an independent file. Depending on the level of security required, the information recorded on the independent file includes the originating terminal and terminal operator identification, date, and time.

System Logging — All transactions and messages entering the application system are retained on independent files. Such files include as part of each transaction a serial number, as well as the date and time the transaction entered the system. These history files include the originating terminal, user department security code, and individual password.

Manual Authorization of Security Table — All changes to security tables receive appropriate external (manual) authorization before the change is allowed to take effect in the computer system. All changes to security tables are authorized by more than one department. A member of the security department, data processing department, and user personnel are all required to authorize a change to security tables.

Program Modification — All application program modifications that were used to create the present version of the system are saved. Information in these records includes data and time sequence numbers of the change as well as the identification of the person making the change and the programmer responsible for the change. (See Chapter 12 for a description of a program change methodology.) The user (not the programmer) is the only one authorized to approve programmer fixes on corrections. The user is also the one responsible for updating the data base in the daily mode of operation.

Control Type — File Maintenance

Folio Number — Each record in a machine-sensible file has a unique identifier called a folio number. A folio number is attached to each record in a data

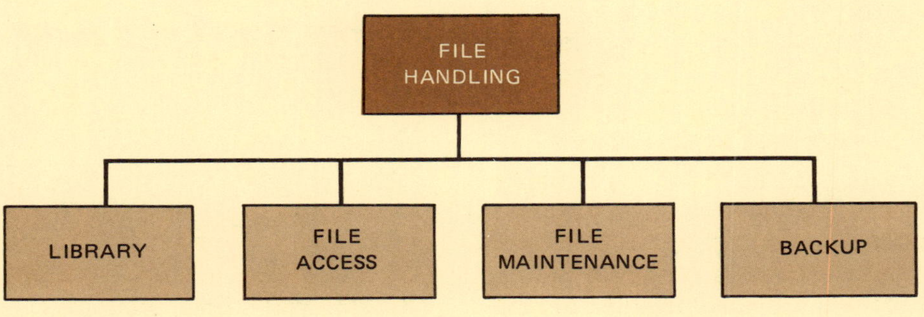

FIGURE 9-1 FILE HANDLING

base. The folio number is used to trace back to the previous good record should the data base need reconstruction. This folio number is changed daily and is constructed along with the day's date, so that each record contains a current folio number.

A separate logging tape contains both the old folio number and the new one that is added whenever the data base record is updated. This tape is used to reconstruct the data base should the program fail. In other words, whenever a data base record is updated, the new folio number is inserted in the updated data base record and a copy of the data base record is written onto the data base file journal (logging tape), along with the old folio number and the new folio number.

Before and After Looks — When a masterfile update program is used to update data base files, the program records the transaction in a corresponding masterfile record showing both "before" and "after" looks. In other words, a picture of before updating and after updating of the data base file is maintained. An independent file is maintained that reflects all updated master records since the last masterfile was dumped. It records all data base updates including the date, time, operator identification, and the content of the change, as well as before and after pictures of the data base files that were changed.

Masterfile Changes — Serially prenumbered forms, recorded and controlled at the source, are used to ensure that masterfile changes are authorized in writing by the initiating department. These forms are checked to ensure that the appropriate approval signatures are given to authorized changes to the files.

Dormant Files — The system reports master records and data fields that exhibit no activity (dormant records). Records are classified as dormant if they experience no activity for six months.

Excessive Activity — The system reports records and data fields that exhibit excessive activity. Excessive activity can be judged only with regard to the business function being used.

Scanning of Critical Files — Critical files are scanned periodically to review their content. Report writer programs and generalized audit software are used to perform such reviews. The purpose of such reviews is to uncover illogical or incorrect file content. For example, one firm used its generalized software program to check regularly for large debits or credits on customer accounts; another firm used its generalized software package to scan a file for payroll name and address duplication.

Control Type — Backup

Activity Tape — An activity tape is prepared during on-line hours of processing. Control records are kept to balance the total number of records in the activity tape and the dispersal of these records to individual files when processed. Whenever there is a general file update, all changes are printed on the activity tape. This tape is sent to the user for his approval of the general file update to the data base.

The activity tape is used to record all data base updates. This tape is a current activity tape for data update and is used for reconstructing the data base (using the folio numbers) whenever a program fails in midstream. This tape is used to downdate the data base to its original picture before the rerunning of the programs that failed.

The activity tape contains a security code of the user, the user authorization level, location of user, user number, terminal identification number, time of day, total number of displays used, and the number of lines of printed output. This tape is also used to trace the path of a specific user's transaction as it moves throughout the system during processing.

Separate Computer — A separate computer is used for backup, testing, and debugging new systems. This computer is separate from the computer used for a production job.

Copy Masterfiles — A copy is made of the application masterfiles. In addition to copying the masterfiles, a transaction log of all changes is made. This transaction log contains time and date sequence as well as the number of the change. A copy of the most current masterfile and the transaction log of all the changes made subsequent to that copy are saved off-line to be used to recover from a disaster or to provide an audit trail in the system.

Backup Procedures — Backup procedures are developed for all critical files. Critical files and critical programs are identified. These procedures provide for off-site data and program backup as well as hardware backup.

Disaster Plan — A disaster plan based on specified application requirements is prepared. The plan incorporates procedures to be invoked in case of application data loss or hardware loss (see Chapter 11 for a complete description of disaster recovery controls).

Recovery Procedures — Recovery procedures are developed for all critical application systems.

CONTROL AREA — FILE ERROR HANDLING

These controls include the procedures and methods used to ensure that file errors detected are corrected and reentered in a timely manner. Controls in this area ensure that all errors are accounted for at the end of any processing cycle. As Figure 9-2 shows, control types discussed include error reporting, error correction procedures, and correction reentry.

Control Type — Error Reporting

Operator Intervention — A log is prepared of all application system processing halts and operator interrup-

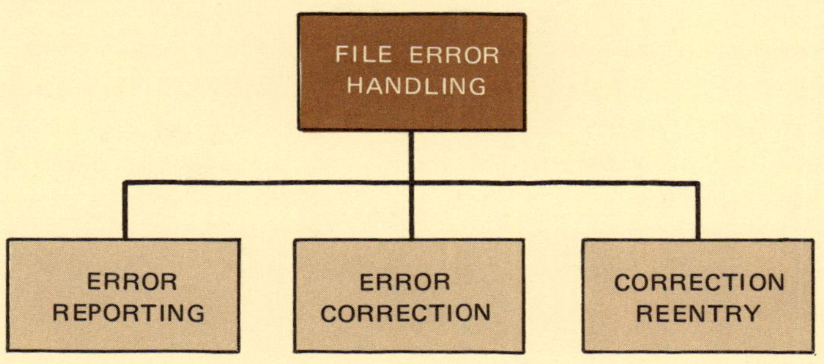

FIGURE 9-2 FILE ERROR HANDLING

tions. This log shows location, date, time, type of intervention, and corrective action taken.

Comparison Programs — A program compares a control duplicate application program to the application program that is currently being used to ensure file integrity. The frequency with which programs are compared varies depending on the criticality of the program. This type of comparison is also used between successive data file generations.

Control Type — Error Correction
Restart Procedures — A record is maintained of all restart procedures used by the computer operator.

Backup File Usage — Application backup files are never used without first copying them onto a second medium before correcting the fault that destroyed the original medium. Backup procedures allow for an application system to produce grandfather, father, and son files.

Control Type — Correction Reentry
Job Stream Log — The data processing department maintains a printout of application job steps to ensure that all errors are corrected. Responsibility is assigned to the computer operator for correcting errors and entering omitted data. The job stream log is an automated system that creates a record as errors are reported, corrected, and reentered.

SUMMARY

File-handling controls are necessary to preserve the accuracy, completeness, and integrity of data during the process of data storage and retrieval. Emphasis must be placed on data storage and retrieval controls because it is an area highly dependent on proper human intervention in the computer process. Data processing file characteristics necessitate a close monitoring of controls. For example, the physical bulk of computer media files is considerably smaller than manual records. This increases the exposure of larger amounts of data to destruction and/ or misuse by a single error or intentional act.

Because computerized records are a basic source of information in today's business, external forces (e.g., Internal Revenue Service, Privacy Study Commission) are beginning to influence organizational control practices.

Chapter 10

OUTPUT PROCESSING

Output processing controls are used to ensure the integrity of output data from the conclusion of computer processing until their delivery to the functional user.

The functional user is dependent upon the timely delivery of complete and accurate data to conduct his day-to-day business functions. If the organization has proper input and processing controls, computer output is usually correct. However, output controls play an important part in achieving the control objectives associated with the overall computerized record-keeping system. The function of output control is to ensure that processed information includes authorized, complete, and accurate data. The scope of output controls includes the control areas of data processing balancing and reconciliation, output distribution, user balancing and reconciliation, records retention, accountable documents control, and output error handling.

Output controls are important as a control interface between the functional user and data processing. The primary method by which data processing and users ensure that the integrity of data has been maintained during processing is by monitoring application system output.

Output controls are those controls that can be used to control the output and distribution of information from the computer application system.

Output controls take many forms, including:

- Control totals that are reconciled back to processing of inputs.
- Control of the distribution of reports after they are printed.
- Evidence to ensure that processed data include only authorized data.

The difference between an output control and its corresponding input and processing controls is that an output control is either a physical control that can be verified after the processing takes place, or it is a control that comes into play only when an exception has been processed. On the other hand, an input control restricts the entry of data into the system, and a processing control does not come into force until the data have been entered and accepted by the system and the various applications and system level programs attempt to process them.

NEED FOR OUTPUT CONTROLS

Output controls are required to ensure that the information coming from the computerized record-keeping system is complete and accurate. In addition, output controls ensure that the output is distributed only to authorized personnel, and that privacy and security of information are maintained.

Whereas the user is responsible for the accuracy of data to the point of having correct input into the system, the data processor is responsible for its accuracy during input preparation, throughout processing, and during preparation of output and distribution of final results.

This phase is divided into six control areas:

- Balancing and reconciliation in data processing
- Output distribution
- Balancing and reconciliation in the user department
- Accountable document control
- Records retention
- Error handling.

Figure 10-1 shows the relationship of the six control areas of this phase. Balancing and reconciliation in data processing and in the user department, output distribution, and records retention lie in the main flow of processing. Accountable document control has aspects that affect the first three of these areas. Error handling is part of a feedback loop to computer processing, the prior phase. Table 10-1 lists all the controls in this phase, grouped by control area, and within area by control type.

CONTROL AREA — DATA PROCESSING BALANCING AND RECONCILIATION

This function has responsibility for the monitoring of data processing-related controls. As part of the data processing department, this function determines that the integrity of data has not been lost during the data processing cycle. This group functions by reviewing

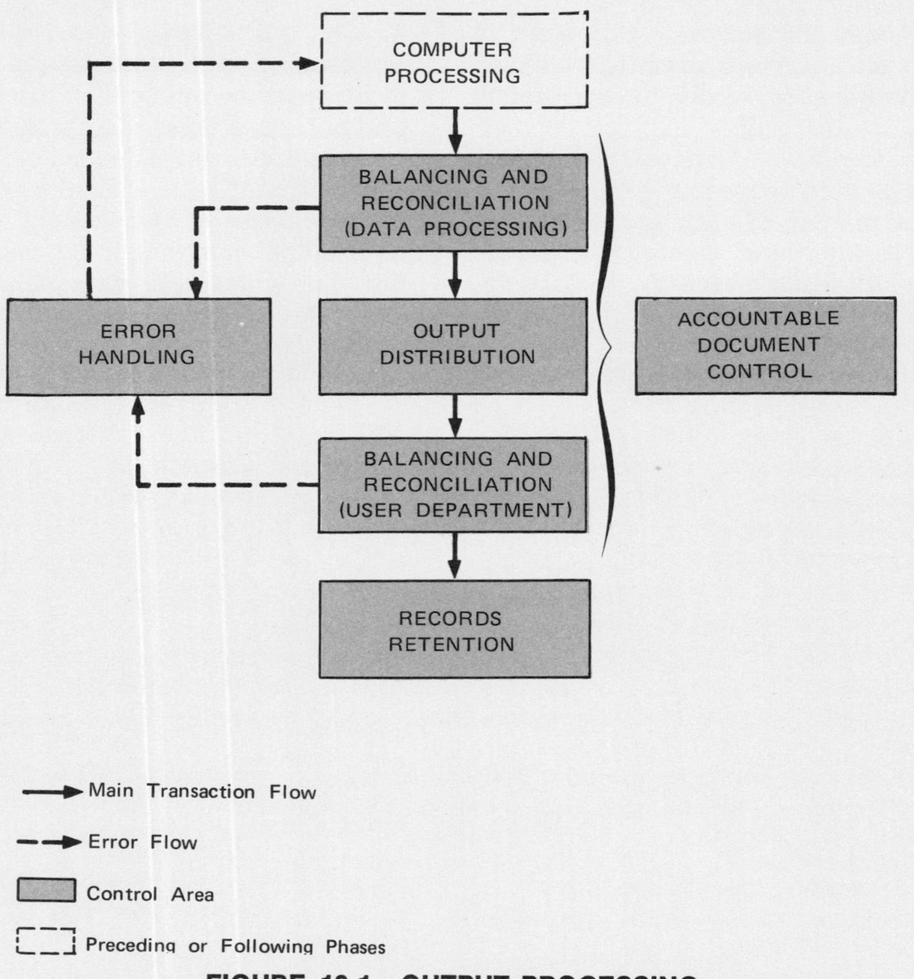

FIGURE 10-1 OUTPUT PROCESSING

the application systems output for completeness and accuracy of data before turning it over to the functional user. For example, the reconciliation of the number of output documents to the application system count of documents produced is a responsibility of this function.

In recent years, the trend toward integrated application systems has added responsibility to this area. The monitoring of critical system interfaces (e.g., billing system output becomes input to accounts receivable) has also added significant control responsibility to this area.

Control Type — Data Processing Control Group

Reconciliation — The output control totals for each application are reconciled with input totals before the release of the report from data processing. For example, the total value of cash entered to the application system is reviewed by the control group to ensure that all cash has been processed by the application system.

This activity includes the reconciliation of batch input logs to the computer report. Such reconciliation procedures are used to identify missing transactions and/or batches.

Transaction Log — The transaction log maintained by the computer system is compared with a transaction log maintained at each output device on a regular basis. These totals are verified against individual application control totals established at other steps in the processing stream to verify that everything has been properly processed to its final step.

Computer Console Log — A copy of the computer console log is reviewed to determine the number of computer operator interrupts during the running of the application.

Systems Output Logs — Systems output logs are maintained to provide an audit trail for the applications being run. These logs may be reviewed daily or placed on computer output microfilm devices for subsequent review and storage.

Record of Output Reports — A report is established summarizing the number of application reports generated, number of pages per report, cost per report, and number of lines per report. This report is used to verify the completeness and accuracy of outputs. In some cases, such statistics are used to "bill-out" computer service charges for running the application system.

Monitoring Process Flow — A record is kept that indicates the average time between the input of user data and the actual starting of each application run utilizing the specific data input. One of the sources that is used for this purpose is automatic job accounting routines in the system software.

Job Control Card Review — The control group receives a listing of all job control language cards used to produce the application system outputs. This department uses these job control cards to ensure that unauthorized programs have not been executed.

Graphical Charts — Charts are used to keep track of the number of transactions per terminal per period. Output control data are balanced against the input transactions whenever possible. These graphical charts are real-time system control guides because,

Table 10-1
OUTPUT PROCESSING CONTROL STRUCTURE

Control Area	Control Type	Control
Data processing balancing and reconciliation	Data processing control group	Reconciliation Transaction log Computer console log Systems output logs Record of output reports Monitoring process flow Job control card review Graphical charts
Output distribution	Output handling	Handling procedures for computer output Output report distribution Report copies
User balancing and reconciliation	Monitoring procedures	User department changes in masterfiles Report heading Transaction tracing list Internally generated transactions Control totals
	Testing procedures	Statistical sampling of final report List of all transactions
Records retention	User retention and disposal methods	Waste disposal procedures Deletion of unused reports
Accountable documents	Accountable document handling	Negotiable documents storage Printing of additional sequence number on preprinted forms
Output error handling	Error reporting	Independent history file of errors Aging open items Error logging by control groups Output activity review
	Error correction	Error correction processing Identification of error correction Correction procedures Responsibility for error correction
	Correction reentry	Error logging Verification of reentered data Monitoring of error conditions

as experience is gained, any variances between input versus output quantities may be an indication of problems.

CONTROL AREA — OUTPUT DISTRIBUTION

Output distribution controls are used to ensure the delivery of complete and accurate reports to the authorized recipients in a timely manner. This function is normally the responsibility of the computer service center. However, the instructions necessary for accomplishing this function must be jointly developed and understood by both data processing and the application system users.

Control Type — Output Handling

Handling Procedures for Computer Output — Output handling procedures for each application are established in the systems manual. These procedures include the following:

- The cover sheet of each report for every application is clearly labeled with the recipient's name and location.
- A log of all reports that are part of an overall application system leaving the data center shows the time, date, job name, dispatcher, and quantity.
- Control logs of each system output report record are maintained by the output control group. These logs keep track of who gets the report, when it was distributed, and any exceptions such as errors or reruns.
- Each output report is scheduled so the user knows when to anticipate it, and follow-up action is taken when reports are delayed.

Output Report Distribution — Application system output reports are delivered to authorized recipients only. A list of different report numbers and the recipients for each report is prepared. This list states whether it is a daily, weekly, or monthly report. An acknowledgment receipt is used to ascertain that the report output has been received by the proper personnel. In addition, a formalized output distribution checklist is provided to show the distribution of each copy of the report.

Report Copies — Report distribution is limited to the authorized number of report copies.

CONTROL AREA — USER BALANCING AND RECONCILIATION

User balancing and reconciliation controls are used to ensure that the integrity of data has not been lost during the processing by the application system. The user function is normally assigned specific tasks to perform that verify output integrity. In recent years, the trend has been to move many of the validation controls to the user area. The assignment of control responsibility to the user area promotes user acceptance of the application system and facilitates the correction of application system errors.

Control Type — Monitoring Procedures

User Department Changes in Masterfiles — The user department is furnished with a register showing changes to the application system masterfile data or programmed data.

Report Heading — The following elements are included in an application system output report heading to aid user balancing and reconciliation:

- Date prepared
- Processing period covered
- Descriptive title of the report contents
- User
- Processing program number.

Transaction Tracing List — A transaction tracing list is generated from the system. This is a list of transactions processed in accordance with the "accepted transaction listing" and is matched against the original source documents the following day to ensure the completeness of data processed by the system.

Internally Generated Transactions — A summary report listing of all internally generated transactions produced by the application system is sent to the functional user area.

Control Totals — The user department is furnished with a report to compare manually maintained batch totals to the equivalent accumulated totals produced by the computer application system.

Control Type — Testing Procedures

Statistical Sampling of Final Report — Final application reports are checked for accuracy and completeness using statistical sampling techniques for transactions selection. For example, in the billing system reviewed, 2% of the invoices were selected for a manual review and verification.

List of All Transactions — On a random basis, a listing of all transactions for one specific system is periodically given to the functional user area as a means of verification that the personnel are performing their duties correctly.

CONTROL AREA — RECORDS RETENTION

Records retention controls are used to guide the retention and disposal of computer application system output. Used in this context, the controls govern only those outputs received by the functional user area.

Control Type — User Retention and Disposal Methods

Waste Disposal Procedures — Appropriate waste disposal procedures are used to ensure that the confidential data for each application system are disposed of in the proper manner. These procedures specifically include the disposal of aborted computer runs. Aborted computer runs are destroyed by sending them through a paper shredder.

Deletion of Unused Reports — Periodic review is made of all computer application system reports received by the user. The express purpose of this review is to determine if the report still needs to be prepared.

CONTROL AREA — ACCOUNTABLE DOCUMENTS

The controls over the handling of accountable documents (e.g., blank check stock) may be an assigned responsibility of computer services, the user, or both (dual custody).

Accountable documents are discussed separately here because their handling usually entails the development of specific control responsibilities in addition to the other application system controls.

Control Type — Accountable Document Handling

Negotiable Documents Storage — Negotiable documents storage includes the movement of documents from the storage area to the computer line printer and back to the storage area under dual custody, where a member of data processing and a member of the functional user department are present during the movement and processing of documents.

Printing of Additional Sequence Number on Preprinted Forms — The processing program prints its own sequence number on preprinted forms. The differences between the beginning and ending preprinted numbers and the beginning and ending computer-generated numbers are then reconciled during the output reconciliation for control of accountable documents.

CONTROL AREA — OUTPUT ERROR HANDLING

These controls include procedures and methods used to ensure that all transactions rejected during the system processing are corrected and reentered in a timely manner. It is particularly important to ensure that controls in this area provide accountability of transactions at the end of a processing cycle. As shown in Figure 10-2, the areas to be discussed include procedures for error reporting, error correction, and correction reentry. Since this is the exception phase, most firms tend to have specific procedures for review, correction, and reentry.

Control Type — Error Reporting

Independent History File of Errors — An independent history file of errors, which is independent of all processing files, is regularly analyzed to report error trends and statistics by type, source, and frequency of errors in each application system.

Aging Open Items — Aging open items on error reports on each application are investigated regularly by the user to ensure their correction and timely reentry into the system.

Error Logging by Control Groups — All data rejected from a processing cycle of an application are entered in an error log by a control group. This log is then used to ensure the correction and reentry of data. The control group maintains the control log of rejected transactions and follows an established routine for the correction and resubmission of transactions.

Output Activity Review — Real-time statistics such as the number of terminals on-line, transaction quantities, and circuit traffic are reviewed by the appropriate management. Output reports affecting subjective judgments, such as credit authorization, are reviewed by user area management.

Control Type — Error Correction

Error Correction Processing — The user is notified immediately of all document error conditions.

Identification of Error Correction — A means of identification of the source document in error is established to facilitate the correction of the data in error. This involves the recording of a cross-reference between the transaction data in error and the originating source document.

Correction Procedures — Error correction procedures are defined in writing in the user's manual for the application. These correction procedures include the types of error conditions incurred and the correction procedures to be followed.

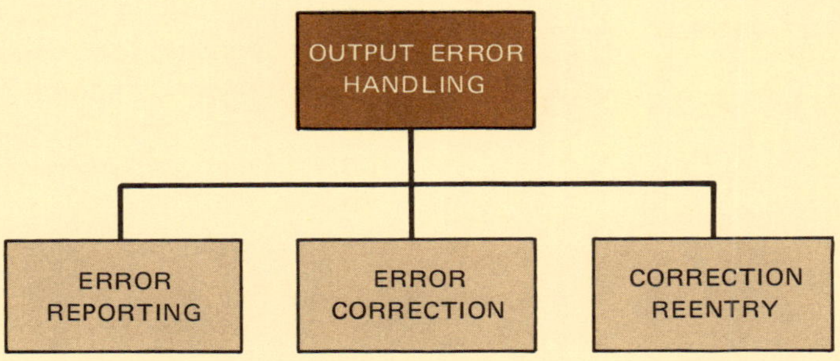

FIGURE 10-2 OUTPUT ERROR HANDLING

Responsibility for Error Correction — The assignment of error correction responsibility is specified in writing (e.g., user's manual). This includes the responsibility for the correction of transactions with multiple input sources.

Control Type — Correction Reentry

Error Logging — Error logs are used to follow up on unresolved errors and to ensure their correction and timely reentry to the system. Such error logs are maintained in the user area to record and monitor the errors reported to them by data processing.

Verification of Reentered Data — The data fields on resubmitted source documents are subjected to the same verification procedures as the original source document.

Monitoring of Error Conditions — The log of all errors detected is used to monitor the timely resubmission of corrected data. As each corrected source document is resubmitted, it is crossed off the log and the date of resubmission is entered on the log. A report of source documents being held pending error correction and resubmission is provided the user area before the end of each processing cycle. This report is used to "clear" pending items from the system.

SUMMARY

Output controls are necessary to ensure the integrity of data from the conclusion of computer processing until their return to the functional user. Normally, if application controls have been effective up to this point, the output will contain complete and accurate data. Output controls then emphasize balancing and reconciliation, output distribution, and records retention.

Whereas the functional user is responsible for the accuracy of data to the point of having correct input, the data processor is responsible for maintaining this integrity during input, processing, and output. Output controls are an important interface between the functional user and the data processor. Just as input controls are necessary to ensure the integrity of data for entry, output controls are necessary to ensure that data integrity has been maintained during processing and output handling and distribution.

Part III

GENERAL CONTROLS

Part III of this report delineates general controls that are independent of application systems. These controls were gathered during field site interviews and are representative of general controls in use at the various organizations visited by SRI. This part of the report is organized into two chapters — computer service center controls and application systems development controls.

These chapters explain both the control area and the flow of work through the control area. Each chapter has a summary table that lists control areas and a short description of the specific controls within each of these areas.

These controls can be used by data processing management to enhance control over computer service centers and application systems development. They can be used by the internal auditor to review and recommend better control practices within these same specific functional areas.

The two chapters and the control areas within each chapter are structured as follows:

Computer Service Center Controls (Chapter 11)

- Input/output scheduling and control
- Media library control
- Malfunction reporting and preventive maintenance
- Environmental controls and physical security
- Separation of duties
- Resources planning
- User billing/charge-out procedures
- Disaster recovery

Application System Development Controls (Chapter 12)

- System development life cycle
- Project management
- Structured programming
- Acceptance testing
- Program change control
- Documentation
- Data base administration

The controls listed in these two chapters are not meant to be all-inclusive, but they are controls that are being used in organizations visited by SRI.

Chapter 11

COMPUTER SERVICE CENTER CONTROLS

The accuracy and completeness of records and reports produced by the data processing function depend upon the general controls governing computer service center operations as well as on the application controls previously presented in Chapters 5-10. Inadequate controls within the computer service center or failure to comply with established controls can result in errors in data preparation and handling, production scheduling, file updating, and output report preparation. The controls are functionally independent of application controls but are of equal importance to the accuracy of the results of data processing. The failure of general controls within the computer service center can defeat the objectives of the most elaborate application controls, and controls are therefore of great concern to both data processors and internal auditors. The importance of this is borne out by the mail survey results, which state that the most important goals or objectives of internal auditing when reviewing the data processing department were: Development of more built-in audit controls, enhancement of security (data access, separation of duties, and so forth), monitoring methods and procedures to ensure accurate data processing performance.

Computer service center controls can contribute substantially to the fulfillment of all of these objectives.

This chapter presents the general controls applicable to the functions of computer service centers. Among these controls are those related to input/output, libraries, data security, disaster recovery, and the like. These controls are administered by the data processing department. For example, Primary U.S. Mail Survey findings indicate that about 90% of internal audit management felt that the data processing department is at least one of the groups in their organizations with explicit responsibility for maintaining data security. The majority of these controls are procedural and relate to the use and maintenance of the resources of the computer service center. Four categories of resources are covered: hardware, personnel, software, and data. However, other aspects of management responsibility in computer service centers must be controlled. In addition to resource use and maintenance, service center management must deal with acquisition or development of resources, and their modification (both temporary and permanent). Figure 11-1 presents aspects of resource management responsibility relative to resources and identifies control activities that fall in the corresponding categories.

In current field practice, these activities have not received equal emphasis. For example, little audit attention is directed toward hardware or personnel acquisition. However, software development and data file creation are an ever-increasing audit concern. Management is concerned with change, and emphasis is placed on planning for the sudden changes that are occasioned by fire, power failure, and the like. Here, the primary concentration has been on the plans and procedures for maintaining operational capability.

THE NEED FOR COMPUTER SERVICE CENTER CONTROLS

The data processing function is becoming more involved with the internal audit function. Currently, internal auditors are performing a constantly increasing number of in-depth reviews of the operational aspects of the data processing function. The data processing manager is also concerned with assuring his organization that its data processing function is carried out prudently and in accord with accepted practices. Data processing facilities represent a dual concern. Not only is the physical facility itself an asset, but, in use, it is a principal handler of asset-related records. Management must consider both the role of the internal auditor and the role of ensuring that the data processing function is carried out effectively when making a full assessment of the data processing function.

For data processing to operate effectively, it must be based on a background of general control standards, either explicitly described or implicitly derived from industry practice. In many functional areas of the service centers surveyed, such standards are lacking. In some cases, assessment of compliance to data processing control practices is not possible and only

RESOURCE / ASPECTS	HARDWARE	PERSONNEL	SOFTWARE	DATA
ACQUISITION OR DEVELOPMENT	Evaluation Benchmarking	Hiring Background checks Indoctrination	Package evaluation Development	Creation Definition
USE AND MAINTENANCE	Management information Utilization monitoring Performance analysis Security	Organization Separation of duties Performance analysis Security	Programmed controls Performance analysis Security	Data edits Batch totals Performance analysis Security
MODIFICATION -TEMPORARY -PERMANENT	Disaster plans Emergency repair Expansion planning	Disaster plans Promotion, training	Change control Conversion	Change control Conversion

FIGURE 11-1 ASPECTS OF RESOURCE MANAGEMENT RESPONSIBILITY IN COMPUTER SERVICE CENTERS

comparison to general control standards, such as are presented herein, can be performed.

The computer service center controls covered in this chapter are categorized into eight control areas: input/output control, media library controls, malfunction reporting and preventive maintenance, environmental controls and physical security, separation of duties, resources planning, user billing, and disaster recovery. The eight areas are discussed below and are summarized in Table 11-1, by control area, and within area by control type.

The controls listed in this chapter were collected and documented during the field site visits.

INPUT/OUTPUT SCHEDULING AND CONTROL

Input/output control entails maintaining a continuous control over the work submitted to and emanating from the computer service center, including scheduling of work and quality control checking of incoming source data and outbound reports. An input/output control function is maintained by computer service centers to ensure the accuracy and completeness of data received and distributed as well as to respond to customer complaints. Effective scheduling is an important part of this area because of the interdependence between manual and automated financial record-keeping processes. Application processing schedules must be established to accommodate input availability, data preparation time (such as time to accomplish keypunch and key verification), and the time required for processing and for output distribution. Timing of the flow of data between financial applications is also important to ensure the accuracy and completeness of financial data as well as to meet the various cutoffs required to produce logically consistent and timely reports.

The basic flow of work for a typical computer center is relatively straightforward. Local users submit their work through input/output control, who in turn submit the work to data entry. Then all of the necessary tape and disk files and other materials are assembled, and the scheduler submits this assembly to the computer room for processing.

Remote job entry (RJE) users, on the other hand, submit their work directly to the computer's task queue, and the computer operators must mount any necessary tapes or disks requested by the user. Outputs for local users must be moved out of the computer room and returned to input/output control for distribution to the user, whereas outputs for remote users are returned via their RJE station.

Table 11-1
COMPUTER SERVICE CENTER CONTROL STRUCTURE

Control Area	Control
Input/output scheduling and control	Input/output control group Job handling procedures Scheduling procedures Processing schedules Cutoff dates Job submission/authorization Input/output control group Daily work schedules
Media library controls	Access controls File release Separate library area Physical security Media restriction issuance Media inventory control procedures Media restriction quantity Media use records Handling equipment Security vaults Temperature and humidity control Off-site storage Duplicate file storage Redundancy and backup procedures
Malfunction reporting and preventive maintenance	Procedures reporting Problem documentation System utilization report System utilization reports review Vendor failures logging Resolutions problem logging Trouble reporting responsibility
Environmental controls and physical security	Physical security Access controls Backup for power, cooling, etc. Software backup Hardware backup
Separation of duties	Separation of duties within data processing Separation of data processing from other organizational units Computer programs to enforce separation between systems Automated controls to separate on-line users
Resources planning	Plan for facilities, equipment, software, and personnel Variance between actual and planned goals
User billing/charge-out procedures	Service contracts between the user and data processing Procedures to arbitrate disputes Chargeable versus free services Billing procedures tied to the computerized job accounting system Billing algorithm, periodic user billing statements, rerun cost allocation procedure
Disaster recovery	Disaster plan Disaster scenarios to update the disaster plan Top management's commitment to the disaster plan Maintenance and updating of the disaster plan User responsibility for the disaster plan Testing of the disaster plan User training in use of the disaster plan

In addition to being the place where users submit jobs for processing and pickup output, input/output control is also the place where users can receive information regarding the status of their jobs. Even though RJE users do not submit their jobs through input/output control, they also often must inquire about the status of their work. Usually the computer room production control staff gives input/output control a schedule listing all the regularly scheduled work that must be run on a given day. This schedule also shows periods set aside for maintenance and for special processing, such as payroll or erasing tapes. Input/output control must then receive the unscheduled work and fit it into the overall schedule. Input/output control is responsible for checking that all work submitted to it is properly prepared and that the person submitting the work is an authorized user. After these checks have been made, input/output control sorts out the work according to priority and takes it into the computer room for processing. The computer console operator must keep input/output control informed of the status of the equipment. For example, if certain classes of work are not being done, the console operator must ask input/output control how to adjust the work load to meet user demands. Input/output control, not the operator, is responsible for this decision.

In summary, in the area of input/output control, it is important to develop and apply procedures for:

- Receiving jobs from users
- Communicating status of jobs
- Returning output to users
- Scheduling computer usage.

MEDIA LIBRARY CONTROLS

Data processing management is directly responsible for the continued availability of data stored on data processing media, such as magnetic tapes and disks. Control over access to sensitive or confidential data is also a related internal audit concern. Therefore, access to the media library should be limited to the librarians and a small staff.

The media library is necessary in all but the smallest computer facilities to provide physical storage for all magnetic tapes and disk packs. The library must provide for the security of the media, including security from physical destruction and from loss of the file data stored on the media. The library function has the responsibility for ensuring the quality of the media, thus guaranteeing that stored files can be read and blank media written upon. The reason for maintaining a library is to provide a storage location, control the usage of the media, and provide speedy access to files and blank media. To perform and facilitate all the above functions, the library must maintain records that provide the necessary information and control.

The library must be located in a space separated by walls from any other area. The space should have very limited and controlled access to facilitate the policing of personnel access and physical security.

Various types of equipment are required. Racks are necessary for storing magnetic tape reels. Cabinets are necessary for the storage of disk packs. If confidential files are to be stored in the library, adequate locked racks and cabinets must be provided. If some media are to be stored for long periods, several alternatives may be provided: They may remain in the assigned place, an alternative (but protected) place within the main library may be assigned, or a physically separate location may be provided. Of the data processing respondents to the Primary U.S. Mail Survey, 89% had copies of both programs and masterfiles in an off-site storage area. If the latter approach is chosen, the environment in the separate space may not require as rigid control as the main area if the media are packed for long-term storage. Depending on the size of the computer machine facility and the library, various pieces of maintenance equipment may be desirable, such as tape cleaners, tape winders, tape erasers, and tape testers.

The temperature and humidity must be controlled because media can be damaged in many ways. The temperature and humidity control may be the same as in the machine room or slightly more relaxed. However, if it is more relaxed, media may need to be held up to two hours in the machine room environment before use. No smoking or food is allowed in the library area. The incoming air must be filtered, and the air filter elements must be changed at frequent intervals.

Physical security is required to protect the media from destruction. The security is partially provided by the construction and equipping of the library to protect the media from fire, water, bomb damage, and the like. Other methods include duplicate files or storing two generations of a file in separate library spaces. Since a person might purposely destroy media, access to the library must be limited to library personnel only. Authorized persons must be checked carefully, and, if possible, no one should ever be left alone in the library. Another method of physical security is to tightly control and limit the quantity of media checked out of the library at any given time. Media can be damaged by improper handling. Unfortunately, most handling takes place outside of library control in the machine room, but in the library area proper handling procedures can be enforced.

The release of data tapes or disks means providing them for other use (i.e., the original data contained thereon are destroyed). The release of tape reels or disks that contain operation data is one major area needing tight control. The control can generally be provided only by the librarian. The librarian may require that before a tape or disk is released it must have reached its release date and the appropriate replacing generation file must have been created. Only a librarian has the authority to release media.

After a file has been used or created, it is returned to the library. As the tape or disk is checked in, the media-use record (which tracks the use of specific media by serial number) is updated. Use may be determined by the record that shows the tape being checked out of the library and/or by operator's report (e.g., significant number of errors). When new files are created, the file records must also be updated; a check is then made to determine correctness of the external file label, and a check is also made to determine if the creation of a new generation of the file triggers the release of an earlier generation of the same file. A check is also made to determine if a returned file has an accompanying new file. Then all media are returned to storage.

Two kinds of records are maintained by the library. These records can be manual or automated. The first type of record is the media-use record. It is identified by serial number and records the number of passes of media (when known or applicable), number of read and/or write errors (when known or applicable), and maintenance of media by type and date. The second type of record is the file record. It is identified by a file identification. On this record will be multiple occurrences of the same data, because all generations of the file are recorded together. Also, a file may occupy more than one reel of tape. For a given generation of a file, the following is noted: the creation date, the release date, the generation of the replacing file (if any), the transaction file used to update to this generation, and the serial number(s) of media used.

In summary, in the area of the media library it is important to:

- Physically separate the media library from other data processing functions.
- Develop and apply procedures for the control of media inventory and their release and return.
- Develop and apply procedures for media redundancy and off-premises storage for critical files.
- Control access to the media library.
- Properly safeguard the contents of the media library against hazards by water, fire, or other environmental risks.
- Limit the issue of media to authorized personnel only.
- Develop and apply media inventory and control procedures.
- Develop and apply retention and release criteria for data stored on media.
- Establish erasure controls that adequately protect sensitive information.

MALFUNCTION REPORTING AND PREVENTIVE MAINTENANCE

Formal procedures for reporting the occurrence of hardware or operating system malfunctions and personnel or procedural failures are required for several reasons. Malfunction reporting provides a measure of the adequacy of preventive maintenance, the level of vendor maintenance service provided, and the rate of failure associated with the computer system. Because failures from the computer system can result in errors and omissions in financial and statistical records maintained by data processing, malfunction reporting is a concern of the data processing manager and the auditor.

One procedure that was uncovered during the field interviews was the use of regular weekly reports of system use, which are prepared from the operation logs. These reports include not only hardware use by component class, but also show the software use by application. By analyzing these reports, data processing management is able to identify areas where improvements can be effected and to spot the development of situations that may prove to be troublesome if unchecked. Analysis of the records is also used by both data processors and auditors to determine whether unusual patterns of work are present. Such abnormal situations may be the clue that unauthorized work is being done or that development is being treated as production to the detriment of control.

Regular analyses are made to better identify the causes for rerun. By analysis of the reasons, corrective steps can be taken to improve operations to decrease the incidence of reruns. Certainly, one important ingredient in making efficient use of the data processing facility is to minimize reruns. Not only do they reduce available computer system throughput, but rerun situations are often less well controlled than are normal operations, particularly if emergency repairs must be made to accomplish the rerun.

In addition to software maintenance function controls, which the system programming function must exercise when making changes to the operating system, a corresponding discipline must be exercised by systems programming in accumulating, noting, and following up on problems allegedly related to the operating system. This discipline must ensure that a particular symptom can be determined to be the fault of a user, an operator error, a hardware malfunction, or a problem with system software. This function must also maintain control of the relative priority for resolving different problems and must be capable of revising job priorities in accordance with the effect that particular problems have on day-to-day operations.

The maintenance or establishment of a log of problems and alleged problems provides a convenient opportunity to monitor and document the performance of vendors of hardware and software services. Therefore, the problem log must include specific resolutions for every item, even if that resolution is nothing more than a statement that the problem has been eliminated from further consideration.

Reporting facilities must be available to list all current problems, all problems whose resolution is pending, all problems associated with a given problem number, and all problems associated with or attributed to a given vendor. Problems associated with a given vendor are particularly important because they provide the basis for detecting, verifying, and proving adequate or inadequate vendor performance.

In summary, in the area of malfunction reporting it is important to:

- Develop a formal documentation procedure for recording and resolving alleged problems in:
  - Hardware
  - Software
  - Personnel
  - Procedure.
- Keep records of failures of vendors to supply satisfactory response.
- Have a single function responsible for:
  - Logging the trouble report.
  - Determining its priority.
  - Assigning it to someone for resolution by a certain date.
  - Exception reporting if it is not resolved by that date.
  - Determining if a given vendor is providing a satisfactory response.
  - Determining if this trouble report is similar to a past report.

ENVIRONMENTAL CONTROLS AND PHYSICAL SECURITY

Data processing facilities, as an asset, must be so managed as to minimize loss of data processing capability. This implies physical protection against natural hazards such as fire and power interruption. It also implies that only authorized individuals use the data processing facilities. Thus, in most computer service centers, access is controlled so that normally only properly authorized operators are permitted in the computer service center.

One field interview site, where an addition was being made to the facilities, took the opportunity to provide a computer service center that could be effectively protected against unauthorized access, loss of power, and fire. The new central facility is housed in two separate rooms. Each is separately powered and provided with individual backup power sources. The two rooms are capable of being isolated one from the other by a fire-resistant door. Thus, a fire in one installation can be contained. Each installation contains fire protection apparatus to further minimize the risk of loss due to fire.

Access to the installation is under badge control. Authorized employees are issued special badges containing their pictures. Each visitor, including employees who are not assigned to the computer service center, must trade his identification card for a vistor's badge and must sign in before entry. Visitors must also be accompanied by an authorized computer service center employee. One frequent test made by the internal auditors is to attempt to gain access without going through all these checks.

In addition to protecting the physical facilities, most large computer service centers make adequate provision for redundant equipment. This backup capability permits processing to continue despite the loss of some or all of the primary equipment. In many cases, the primary equipment is protected by such devices as automatic fire extinguishing apparatus and an uninterruptible power supply. The backup equipment may be a duplicate center that is separately powered and separately housed. In smaller centers, cooperating with nearby users of similar equipment provides mutual backup support.

Computers are extremely valuable pieces of equipment that are easily damaged, either accidentally or maliciously. Most computer centers today require extensive air conditioning and some form of augmentation of the existing power supply. Similarly, the extent to which backup power supplies and/or facilities for smoothing unusual voltage peaks are utilized must be reviewed. Sometimes centers experience unnecessary interruptions of service because of power-line voltage surges that can be smoothed by special devices. Centers processing especially critical work loads often need to have a backup power supply so they can continue to function even if the primary power has been lost.

In summary, in the area of environmental controls and physical security it is important to:

- Control physical access.
- Provide adequate fire protection, power backup, air-conditioning backup, and so forth.
- Maintain adequate redundant hardware.

SEPARATION OF DUTIES

Both data processors and internal auditors must determine that separation of duties is adequate to prevent fraudulent use of computers, data files, or supplies such as negotiable instruments. The scope of concern in this area includes a proper separation of duties within the data processing organization as well as between data processing and its users. The separation of system analysis and programming personnel from computer operations makes it more difficult for the programmers, who have the knowledge, to manipulate programs and data files.

More specifically, application programmers and system programmers must be separated from each other and from computer operations personnel as much as is practical in order to avoid any illegal program changes (Chapter 12 has a section on program change control).

The data processing department itself is structured to minimize the opportunities for mishandling asset-related records during normal operations. The data processing structure is chosen to separate program development from operations. Further, input/output control must be separated from data entry, from media library control, and from computer operations. This basic structure is used by nearly all organizations that have data processing. Smaller organizations will often combine some of the suggested functions but try to preserve this separation of duties and responsibilities. The Primary U.S. Mail Survey showed that "separation of responsibilities/duties" was the first choice by both internal auditors and data processors as a technique or procedure to deter personnel from circumventing control procedures.

One major concern of management, as stated during the site interviews, is the rapid growth of on-line systems. While such systems can vastly increase the efficiency of data entry operations in the user organizations, they also decrease the opportunity for physically separating source data initiation (the user function) from data entry. In batch systems, the data requests are typically initiated in the user department and then physically transferred to a data entry group for transcription to machine-sensible form. The physical separation of the two groups provided an opportunity for control of the entire process. With the advent of on-line data entry by the user department, this opportunity disappears. Its place can be taken only by the computer programs that are used to govern the on-line data entry terminals. Thus, the human-directed controls of the earlier system are replaced with programmed controls. The main consequence is that it is now necessary to specify controls fully before implementing the system, but such full specification has proved difficult to accomplish without unduly restricting the user. That combination of other forms of control and separation of duties that is possible with manual systems is effected with computerized systems by utilizing some of the controls listed previously in Chapter 5 and in Chapter 8.

In summary, in the area of separation of duties it is important to:

- Maintain adequate separation of duties both within the data processing department and between data processing and user areas.
- Develop automated program controls to control on-line systems.

RESOURCES PLANNING

Data processing management has a mandate to plan for the data processing function. Planning must occur to ensure that adequate computing and human resources are available to provide continuity in the processing of existing applications and to develop new applications as the organization's data processing needs grow. Adequate data processing planning includes facilities, equipment, software, and personnel.

The management function of a computer service center involves planning that takes into account future needs for services and translates them into resource requirements. Management, therefore, must be able to predict the change in work load of present applications, changes in the mode in which they will be provided, and the effect of such change on the resources. Management must also factor in the effect that new applications may have and the possible evolution of both hardware and software technology and its influence on performance and cost.

Proper planning for the computer service center thus must be based on a combination of thorough knowledge of the internal situation and potential internal changes. Management also must be able to determine the likelihood of external changes that may influence the computer service center operation, the areas in which they may take place, and their impact on services. Furthermore, planning must take into consideration any possible change of customer demands for type or volume of services. Finally, it must be able to translate the anticipated needs into resource configurations that are both available and efficient.

In summary, in the area of resources planning it is important to:

- Develop formal planning methods for:
  - Facilities
  - Equipment
  - Software
  - Personnel
- Assess variances between actual situations and planned goals.

USER BILLING/CHARGE-OUT PROCEDURES

An evaluation of the administrative controls governing the billing or charge-out of data processing costs to users is of concern to data processing management. Management wants to be assured that there is an equitable basis for such charges and that billing is made in accordance with the prevailing policy, procedures, and documented user agreements, if any.

The field site interviews uncovered concern over whether the user receives a fair value for data processing services in relation to the internal charges for that service. One field site used the internal auditors to evaluate and verify these charges.

In summary, in the area of user billing it is important to:

- Develop a formal procedure for the establishment of contracts between the computer service center and its users.
- Define the services chargeable to the user and job accounting system.
- Tie the billing procedures to the computerized job accounting system.
- Establish a billing algorithm.
- Prepare periodic user billing statements.
- Develop a rerun cost allocation procedure.
- Develop a procedure that handles the arbitration of disputes with a user.

DISASTER RECOVERY

Experience has demonstrated that the best-controlled data processing organizations often fail to maintain the appropriate level of control when faced with a change in operations resulting from an emergency situation. The Primary U.S. Mail Survey indicates that only 33% of data processing respondents have a published disaster plan covering the data processing operations, and that 29% of those plans had never been tested. There must be well-thought-out plans for meeting most emergency problems that are likely to arise. Thus, in addition to protecting and backing up computer data files, programs, and run documents, the data processor must keep them in duplicate and in separate locations. Moreover, it is not enough to maintain duplicate files, programs, and so on, there must also be well-controlled procedures for reestablishing the data processing function using the duplicated facilities. These procedures must not only be fully developed, they must also be tested. The disaster planning at one field interview site, a highly centralized computer user with significant on-line activity, can be described as follows:

- Their ongoing contingency plan has provision for facilities, communications, hardware, software, personnel, and other considerations including outside users. The plan takes into account several contingency scenarios ranging from short disruptions through longer disruptions to loss of the total data processing resources for an extended period of time.
- The plan goes beyond the usual data processing considerations and extends to the functional user areas. Each user is responsible for contingency planning to the extent that he is responsible for maintaining his portion of the backup function. By a continuing planning process, with semiannual reviews by data processing and monitored by the internal audit department, the contingency plan is kept up to date to provide continuous protection. The planning technique includes identification and selection of the threat scenarios and quantification of loss due to different scenarios on which policy and decision guidelines are based. These are used by senior management to perform a risk analysis. This analysis results in broad guidelines to direct data processing in implementing a full contingency plan. Initially, three person-years of senior staff effort were required to develop the plan. The result of this three-year effort is that the company is backed up to the extent that, if it were to lose the main data processing facility, the contingency plan provides sufficient capability to allow it to do all the critical jobs that must be done if the company is to remain operative. A major reason for the success of the plan is management directives to all major functional areas to ensure that they continue to maintain their part of the ongoing plan.

The major benefit of a thorough contingency plan comes from the ability of an organization to respond rapidly to disaster or exceptional situations that might otherwise cause considerable loss to, or total disruption of, the organization. With the increasing reliance on data processing resources, particularly in centralized operations with major on-line requirements, the need for contingency planning cannot be overemphasized.

Contingency planning is only as effective as the variety and plausibility of scenarios considered. A major limitation therefore is the skill and imagination required to develop encompassing scenarios. The scenarios addressed should include loss of the computer for a one- to four-day period, loss of the computer for a one- to two-week period, and loss of the computer for a month or more. For each of these alternatives, full fallback provisions should be defined for each application system. Further, contingency planning cannot be done once and forgotten. It must be an ongoing operation with modification on a continuing basis as new situations arise that might render the plan ineffective.

The major steps in implementing an effective contingency plan are:

1. Obtain top management concurrence with the need for contingency planning.
2. Have appropriate key individuals assigned to the analysis of threat scenarios for contingency planning.
3. Involve user departments in quantifying the impact of the operations loss.
4. Perform risk assessment and threat analysis functions that involve users, data processing management, and audit personnel.

5. Develop a plan outline with full consideration of implementation costs.
6. Obtain plan approval by senior management, even at the board level, to ensure that management backs the plan and its maintenance.
7. Assign implementation tasks to ensure that the plan is implemented as designed.
8. Create an independent group to maintain the plan and to perform regular testing to ensure that users are properly maintaining the plan.

The ongoing commitment of management to monitoring the plan is most important. All systems changes or new systems have an impact on contingency planning that must be considered during the planning phases of new systems. Reviews of the contingency plans must incorporate ways to test the plan as it changes to ensure that the modified plan is effective. Finally, users must be trained and their training audited periodically to ensure that the plan can be carried out and that it is appropriately modified as user requirements change.

In summary, in the area of disaster recovery it is important to:

- Develop a contingency plan for:
  - Hardware
  - Software
  - Facilities
  - Personnel
  - Power
- Continuously maintain and update the contingency plan.

SUMMARY

Input/Output Scheduling and Control

An input/output control function is important to ensure the accuracy and completeness of data moving between data processing and user areas. Scheduling and controlling input data cutoffs are necessary to ensure that data processing outputs are produced on a timely basis and without omissions of data.

Media Library Controls

The media library is necessary to provide secure physical storage for data files, such as magnetic tapes and disk packs, to be retained in the data processing organization. The off-site storage of both data and computer application programs is included in the media library procedures for most of the companies participating in the SRI study.

Malfunction Reporting and Preventive Maintenance

Formal procedures for reporting occurrences of hardware and operating system software malfunctions and failures are required to assure that computer systems and software are properly repaired and maintained so as to prevent errors and omissions in the processing of financial and statistical records and reports.

Environmental Controls and Physical Security

Data processing facilities must be designed and maintained so as to minimize the opportunity for interruptions in data processing capacity. Controls include proper cooling, fire detection and prevention devices, uninterruptible power sources, and restricted personnel access.

Separation of Duties

An adequate separation of duties is important to prevent fraudulent use or misuse of computers, data files, or supplies such as negotiable instruments. Separation of duties applies to functions within the data processing organization as well as between data processing and its users. Participants in the SRI study report that the separation of responsibilities and duties is an important technique to deter personnel from circumventing control procedures.

Resources Planning

Planning is necessary to ensure that adequate computing and human resources are available to provide continuity in processing existing applications and to develop new computer applications as an organization's data processing needs grow.

User Billing/Charge-Out Procedures

The billing or charge-out of data processing costs must be equitable to provide a basis for the distribution of data processing costs without alienating users.

Disaster Recovery

Contingency planning is important to assure that an organization can respond rapidly to a disaster that might otherwise cause considerable loss to or total disruption of the organization as a result of its loss of data processing capabilities.

RESULTS

The field visits clearly demonstrated that, over the past three to five years, physical security has been a major influence on data processing. This concern is still present, but it is decreasing as more data processing departments achieve adequate physical security.

The current major influence upon computer service centers is data security. Data processing departments are concerned with, for example, protection of tapes, disks, program libraries, files, and the like. Computer service center personnel are also conducting more data processing security reviews aimed at the overall security posture of the organization's data processing function.

The data processing department is primarily responsible for maintaining data security, whereas Primary U.S. Mail Survey results indicate that enhancement of security (e.g., data access, separation of duties) rates highly among internal auditors. Specifically, internal audit management was asked, "What are currently the *two* most important goals or objectives of internal auditing *Regarding the auditing of the data processing department?*" The two most frequently checked categories were "development of built-in audit controls" (45%) and "enhancement of security" (40%).

In the Primary U.S. Mail Survey, of those organizations that have internal auditors, about 70% indicate that the internal auditors perform audits of the data processing department.

The Primary U.S. Mail Survey results indicate that the most frequently used technique or procedure for deterring personnel from circumventing control procedures is "separation of responsibilities/duties," checked by 81% of the data processing respondents.

Some organizations use service bureaus instead of their own computer service centers. Another mail survey finding is that, in 75% of those survey organizations that use a service bureau, the auditing of the service bureau's work is done primarily by data processing personnel. According to the data processing respondents, in only 21% of these organizations are the internal auditors involved in this work.

In the future, computer service center controls will increase in importance as data base and data communications technologies centralize the organization's data. In this area internal auditors will increase their emphasis on both hardware acquisitions and the personnel aspects of the computer service center.

Chapter 12

APPLICATION SYSTEM DEVELOPMENT CONTROLS

The adequacy and effectiveness of controls included in computer application systems are affected by the methods and procedures used during the system development process. Controls over the system development process are important for three reasons. First, good development controls assist in managing costs and schedules. Second, they help ensure that appropriate application controls are built into application systems being developed. Third, they ensure that application controls are properly tested before application systems become operational. By carefully controlling the system development process, one can achieve higher levels of accuracy and reliability in the computer application systems developed and satisfy the goals of developing quality application systems within cost and on schedule.

Elements of the application system development process documented by SRI include project management, programming techniques, development and acceptance testing, program change control, documentation, and data base administration. Each of these elements is discussed in this chapter. Specific techniques and controls within each element identified during the study are presented within the relevant sections of the chapter.

This chapter presents a list of controls and techniques currently being used by organizations during the application system development process to develop more reliable and accurate systems within cost and on schedule. Table 12-1 presents a list of all controls and techniques, organized by control area and by control type within area.

The first technique presented is the systems development life cycle (SDLC). This is presented first because it provides a structure for the application system development environment that encompasses all the above-mentioned elements of the application system development process. All of the other elements mentioned above will be discussed separately in the logical order in which they occur within the SDLC.

A System Development Life Cycle Example – The SDLC is a technique used to divide the system development process into a small number of distinct phases with formal management control points placed between and during each phase. The objectives in using an SDLC technique are twofold: to provide a more structured management scheme for controlling costs and schedules, and to ensure proper and responsive communications channels among users, EDP auditors, hardware planning personnel, top management, and the data processing personnel responsible for developing the application systems.

The majority of companies interviewed which were using an SDLC technique did so to ensure that major application systems were developed on schedule, within cost, and to the user's satisfaction. In addition, interviews indicated that federal and state legislation relating to controls over personal privacy, electronic funds transfer, and other such activities was becoming a major concern of top management. As this legislation specifies certain legal liabilities that, if incurred, could seriously damage the entire organization permanently, top management is seeking more assurance that computer applications systems are designed, implemented, tested, and operated in the best possible ways. Many organizations felt that a properly specified and controlled SDLC was the best technique available today to accomplish this task.

The following representative example of how one large government organization has defined and uses the SDLC serves as a basis for discussion of the general controls and techniques identified in use during the study. However, other organizations define and use slightly different SDLC techniques, and such differences are discussed after the example. The government organization defines the SDLC as follows:

- Project definition – That phase whose primary purpose is to define the user requirements and uses for the system.
- System analysis and design – That phase in which an overall description of the system is prepared.
- Detailed design and programming – That phase that focuses on the internal components of the system and the development of computer programs needed to form the system.
- System test – That phase in which the system is exercised to determine the correctness and com-

Table 12-1
APPLICATION SYSTEM DEVELOPMENT CONTROL STRUCTURE

Control Area	Control
System development life cycle	Review user requirements
	Review project organization
	Review hardware requirements
	Review internal controls
	Require user or internal auditor sign-off
	Review detailed design documents
	Review file requirements
	Review costs and schedules
	Review test plan
	Review user and operational documentation
	Review test results
	Require user and internal audit sign-off
	Review conversion plan
	Review adequacy of documentation
	Identify user problem areas
	Identify system development problems
Project management	PERT control technique
Structured programming	Audit trail
Acceptance testing	Comparison of base case data to system produced data
	Manual review of output reports
Program change control	Require formal written request
	Review all changes
	Use of change control committee
	Restrict number and type of persons who make changes
	Require operator and programmer to make changes
	Modify SMF to obtain reports of all changes to load libraries
	Require report of quick fixes
	Limit number of times changes are made per time period
	Use program packages to control access to source libraries
Documentation	Provide flow of all application system data flow
	Specify how the programs implement controls
	Specify how programs are to be operated, backed up, and recovered
	Maintain up-to-date changes to accepted documents
	Specify allowable user commands and functions
Data base administration	Develop standards
	Establish and monitor standards
	Document and provide procedures to control operations
	Measure effectiveness of performance and integrity controls
	Develop security/control education programs

pleteness of implementation to the user requirements as manifest in the design documents.

■ Conversion — That phase in which the tested system and operational procedures are initiated to move the system into a full operational mode.

Other organizations include one or two additional phases broadly defined as:

■ Operational — That phase concerned with ongoing operation, program changes, and maintenance.

■ Postimplementation — That phase concerned with whether the system performs as intended by the user, with focus on methods to improve the development process.

Figure 12-1 shows details of the five phases of the development cycle and the 15 control points used by that government organization. During the development of application systems, all requirements specified at each control point must be satisfied before that phase or the next phase can be continued.

Basically two types of control points are used in this SDLC: those affecting the quality of systems being developed from a computer processing point of view and those used to interface to users and others outside the data processing department. System quality control takes place primarily at Points 1 and 4-13.

■ Control Point 1 — The EDP auditor, user, and the project leader review the project organization, the arrangements with the user for communications, and the plans and work program for the design. This central point helps the project leader to establish a good working relationship with the user to ensure that the system reflects user requirements.

■ Control Point 4 — The user, EDP auditor, and project leader review the project organization resulting from the first phase, the communication links established between team members, users, and EDP auditors, schedules and work plans, and other items germane to the specific project.

■ Control Point 5 — The EDP auditor, user, project leader, and design analysts review the detailed design output reports for completeness and clarity. The EDP auditor attempts to ensure that sufficient design documentation exists to allow for a clear understanding by the test team and the EDP audit staff.

■ Control Point 6 — The user, EDP auditor, project leader, and design analysts review the file requirement specifications and the input requirements associated with them. The user attempts to ensure that the file requirements do not implicitly or explicitly change the original system specifications.

■ Control Point 7 — The user, project leader, EDP auditor and other data processing personnel responsible for hardware planning review the equipment requirements to meet the requirements of the designed systems. Completeness of the equipment requirement is important to avoid unanticipated equipment costs at a later date.

■ Control Point 8 — The EDP auditor, user, and project leader review the design from cost, data processing standards, and general management points of view. The project leader is interested in ensuring that all loose ends from the past two phases are in place before moving into the detailed design phase.

■ Control Point 9 — The EDP auditor, project leader, user, and data processing personnel make a final review of plans, equipment, costs, project organization, and communications channels to ensure that all participants have agreed upon the status and direction of the project. The project leader is primarily concerned with assuring top management that sufficient systems analysis and design have taken place before the detailed design phase.

■ Control Point 10 — The EDP auditor, user, and project leader review the documentation scheme and documents available describing the file systems, interface data handler programs, and program run documents for compliance to standards, completeness, accuracy, and clarity. The project leader is primarily concerned with ensuring that the project team is providing adequate documentation to meet data processing and user documentation standards.

■ Control Point 11 — The EDP auditor, the project team members, testers, and user review the detailed system design to ensure that it follows from the general system design and still meets the user's requirements. In addition, the test plan is reviewed for completeness, timing, and cost. The conversion plan and associated paperwork are reviewed for reasonableness, completeness, and clarity. As this is the last checkpoint before the test phase, the project leader takes special care to ensure that the original design requirements are still intact or that a traceable trail exists that explains to top management and users why the system has changed.

■ Control Point 12 — The EDP auditor, testers, user, and project leader review the test team organization to ensure that the proper people are present and that the project test plan is complete and consistent. The project leader is primarily concerned with assuring himself that the test plan will completely test the system and in particular will test the internal controls designed in the system.

■ Control Point 13 — The EDP auditor, user, and testers develop test data, build masterfiles, review test results, and monitor the test plan progress to ensure that it is adhered to throughout the test phase.

General management and other organizational interface controls occur primarily at Control Points 1, 2, 3, 4, 14, and 15. As Control Points 1 and 4 have been described, only Points 2, 3, 14, and 15 are discussed below.

■ Control Point 2 — The user, EDP auditor, and project leader review the analysis and planned cost for completeness and accuracy. In addition, the project control and communications plan is discussed and changed if necessary. The user plays a major role at this control point in assuring himself that proper analysis has taken place.

■ Control Point 3 — The user, EDP auditor, and project leader review the conceptual design documentation for accuracy, completeness, and any changes that may have occurred. A revised cost-benefit plan is developed, and the EDP auditor presents the findings to top management.

■ Control Point 14 — The user, EDP auditor, computer operation personnel, and the project leader review the conversion plan for completeness of detail and personnel involved. Plans for communicating the production schedule to top management are discussed as well as other miscellaneous considerations germane to the specific project.

■ Control Point 15 — The user, EDP auditor, and project leader review all problems not yet resolved, adequacy of documentation, and any incomplete activities identified. Final reports on the project status can then be written by the EDP auditor.

Management at the government organization using the above SDLC told SRI that they would like to include a postimplementation phase in their current cycle. They feel that after the application system has been used for a few months, problems can be identified by the users that will point out methods to improve the application system in question, as well as improve the entire SDLC technique used.

Controls and techniques used in connection with the SDLC by other companies interviewed include:

■ Daily reports to the managers of the functional areas during the critical stages of application system development.

■ Required sign-off by the internal audit department on all new application systems developed. This control forced the internal auditors to become involved with the project team at an early stage of the SDLC.

■ Postimplementation performance reviews conducted by the internal auditors and users to determine whether the operational system functions as expected and has been adequately documented from a user's point of view.

In summary, using some type of SDLC does provide more management structure and an opportunity for users and EDP auditors to participate in all stages of application system development. It does not ensure that users and EDP auditors will do their respective jobs well or that project leaders will communicate as well as everyone would like. SDLC is a good application system development technique because it provides a means to develop more reliable and higher quality systems that can provide a high degree of data integrity. SRI believes that there is a definite trend to the use of some types of SDLC in organizations that are heavily involved in application system development.

PROJECT MANAGEMENT

Project management is a control technique that provides a formalized means of measuring progress of application system development through use of reports, such as periodic project status reports. The objective of project management is to provide a well-defined and structured management environment that offers a means of measuring progress during application development. The main elements of project management include:

■ A means for establishing intermediate work products that can be approved by users participating in the development process. The SDLC noted above is one technique for providing the required structure and work products.

■ A means of providing project status reports that indicate expenditures versus budget as work progresses and actual completion dates versus scheduled dates.

■ A means of providing periodic status reports to top management.

Basically, two project management techniques were used for controlling the development process reported during the study: the team approach and the program management group.

Team Approach — The team members included persons from data processing, the user group, the internal auditors group, and the hardware planning group. This team was usually coordinated by the project leader from data processing. Team members worked together throughout the development process, although not all team members were required at all phases. The SDLC example above is an example of this technique.

Program Management Group — This group is usually within the data processing department, whose charter is to monitor application system progress and to ensure that proper controls are included in the application system.

A large company interviewed formed a System Acceptance Group (SAG). The SAG plays a significant role in the early system design stage of the system development process, during the time just before actual operation of the system, and to a lesser degree during acceptance testing. It plays only a passive role in the detail design, conversion, and operations phases. One of the prime purposes of the SAG is to ensure that proper controls are included in the design of the application system. It also maintains up-to-date manuals describing control standards in a form that permits application of the standards in effective ways in an information system design.

The function of the SAG is split between overall control of the system development process and ensuring that controls are included in any system design. As such, the group is more or less continuously involved in the control aspects of systems in both the design and general production use of the system. While administering controls for system development, the group also develops and enforces standards in a form that permits their implementation in an information system.

Regardless of which project management technique was employed, a number of organizations interviewed were using Gantt charts and computer-based PERT control techniques to assist project management in keeping abreast of schedules and costs.

In summary, project management techniques assist the project leader in monitoring the system development process in a formalized manner. In addition, they provide the users and EDP auditors with opportunities to track the progress of the application system from their points of view. Project management techniques do not, in and of themselves, make a non-manager become a manager. Rather, they help a good manager do a better job. There is a rapidly accelerating trend to the use of project management techniques in large and small organizations for all application system development, be it a large or a small project.

STRUCTURED PROGRAMMING

Structured programming is a technique that provides specific guidelines to programmers on how they may use a programming language and how each program fits together to form an application or operating system. The objective in using structured programming techniques is to develop more usable and effective programs. "Usable" implies that the program can be read and understood by technical persons who did not write it, including users and EDP auditors. "Effective" implies that the program is designed to fit into an overall application system scheme so as to reduce redundancy and ensure processing efficiency.

Structured programming is a technique for system builders that renders systems easier to build, maintain, and alter. It is a discipline that is used primarily in the detail design and programming stages of the development process. As such, it uses a stepwise top-down approach, in which program modules are organized by functional specifications into a balanced hierarchical structure with minimum side effects on each module.

Structured programming involves a team approach to detailed design, with team members being used to "walk-through" the design and coding of components. The effect is that the design and code can be viewed by other than the originator to detect faulty logic, hard-to-follow code, and the extent to which the design meets prespecified objectives.

An example of using structured programming as a control over the production of code was reviewed at a major insurance company. This approach is relatively new for this organization, but the success attributed to it has been significant. The main advantage has been that the company finds programs easier to read, correct, test, and modify. It has also facilitated rapid training and made cross-training easier. This organization believes that, in spite of a high turnover rate in the programming staff of a large project, the project was completed on time because structured programming was used. This is perhaps the strongest testimony for this organization's experience with the use of structured programming.

The main areas of structured programming used by this organization include the use of:

- A semistrict program structure allowing GO TO statements in a downward direction within a section domain.
- Fixed column indentation for both procedure division and data division sections; in addition, a maximum of one verb per line and specific columns for operators.
- Structured walk-throughs whereby at least two peers completely trace or walk through the code generated by another programmer.

Another large insurance company has experimented with structured programming techniques on a pilot project. In most cases, the techniques were of significant value and could be used with little conflict with current methods and procedures. The overall results of the pilot project proved that the techniques were effective in increased quality of the system and reductions in time spent to produce the system. In system test, less than 60% of the planned time was spent. This is primarily attributed to the walk-throughs and specification techniques. In terms of programmer productivity, approximately 6% savings were realized over what was budgeted. By far the most useful result of the test was the high quality of the system produced, which, in turn, resulted in greater user acceptance and confidence in the system.

The insurance company attempted the use of many techniques involved with structured programming. In each case, a postproject analysis was performed summarizing the advantages, problems, and recommendations for continued use. The major techniques that were used are described in the following paragraphs.

Team Organization — This technique calls for the establishment of an integrated team consisting of one project leader/analyst, two programmer analysts, one to three programmers, and one programmer librarian. The experience of the team approach was generally good. The difficulties encountered were mainly ones of separation of duties among team members and not specifying the roles each member would take in the specification and programming phases. The approach was recommended for continuance of other projects.

Top-Down Design — This technique consists of designing program logic by specifying higher level functions first and then determining the subfunctions required to implement these higher level functions. The main advantage of this approach is that it forces a thorough analysis before program design begins. The recommendation was enthusiastic for continuing this approach on new projects.

Segmentation — During detail design and programming, it is advantageous to keep programs and modules in the form of routines called segments, with each segment having but one entry and exit. This approach follows naturally from the top-down design. It was also felt useful from the point of view of reducing code redundancy and defining clean interface points for other parts of the system.

Structured Coding — This approach or discipline is used to depict the process of coding whereby there are conventions used for syntax, program format, restricted and controlled branching, and disciplines on logic.

Walk-Throughs — The walk-through consists of a planned review of all system specifications and coding by peers of the developers. The walk-throughs were instrumental in uncovering a majority of errors during the preinstallation and test phases of the system. In adopting this approach, the organization found it more worthwhile to allow others to review the specifications and code before a joint meeting. The review meeting then became mainly a question answering and resolution session.

Top-Down Testing — This approach requires that the skeleton control modules be tested first, then progressing down the module structure until finally the entire system is tested.

Programmer Librarian — The programmer librarian actually serves the purpose of documenting all source codes. This function is responsible for getting codes keypunched, updating the source library, and other general program documentation. The difficulty with this approach is that the librarian function may be unable to be responsive to program changes coming from the coders and, in general, to interface or integrate into the actual coding process. Another more subtle disadvantage is that programmers prefer to do some of the librarian tasks themselves, as a break in the routine of coding. It was recommended that future projects not incur the expense of a librarian, allowing the programmers themselves to be responsible for all librarian functions.

In summary, use of structured programming techniques does provide for more usable and auditable programs. As it is a relatively new concept, there are some problems in changing to it from traditional programming techniques. However, it is a good control technique because it does provide an improvement in the quality of the application system as well as the individual programs that make it up. SRI found a slowly developing trend toward the usage of structure design and programming techniques, primarily in large organizations that develop major application systems.

ACCEPTANCE TESTING

Acceptance testing is a process in which persons, usually not responsible for program implementation, check the application system prior to its becoming operational in order to ensure that it functions as user requirements dictate and in conformance to data processing operational standards. Tests are designed to exercise the application system for errors of omission and errors of commission, i.e., the application system should perform all functions it is intended to do and no more.

The type of acceptance testing must be planned for in the early phases of the system development process. The details of acceptance testing can be based on a class of transactions that are defined, in general, during the system definition and design phase. These transactions are used to depict data that is input to the system and output from the system. The design process then takes into account the volumes for each of the transactions and the types of processing that need to be performed between input and output.

The definition of transactions heavily involves the various user departments either supplying or receiving data processed by the systems.

Base Case Testing — An approach to system testing using transactions that is used by one manufacturing organization is called base case testing. Base case testing is a technique to execute computer application systems and/or programs using test data sets developed as part of a comprehensive testing program, and to verify processing accuracy by comparing processing results with predetermined test data results. The base case test consists of test files containing data to test valid and invalid conditions, a predefined set of input and output transactions, and

PROJECT DEFINITION STUDY (PHASE I)

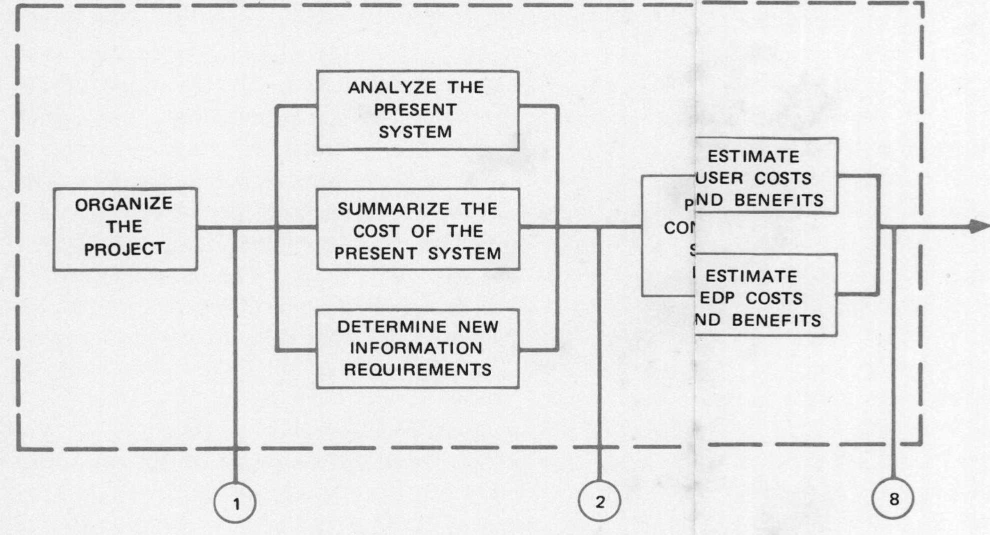

DETAIL DESIGN AND PROGRAMMING (PHASE III)

CONVERSION (PHASE V)

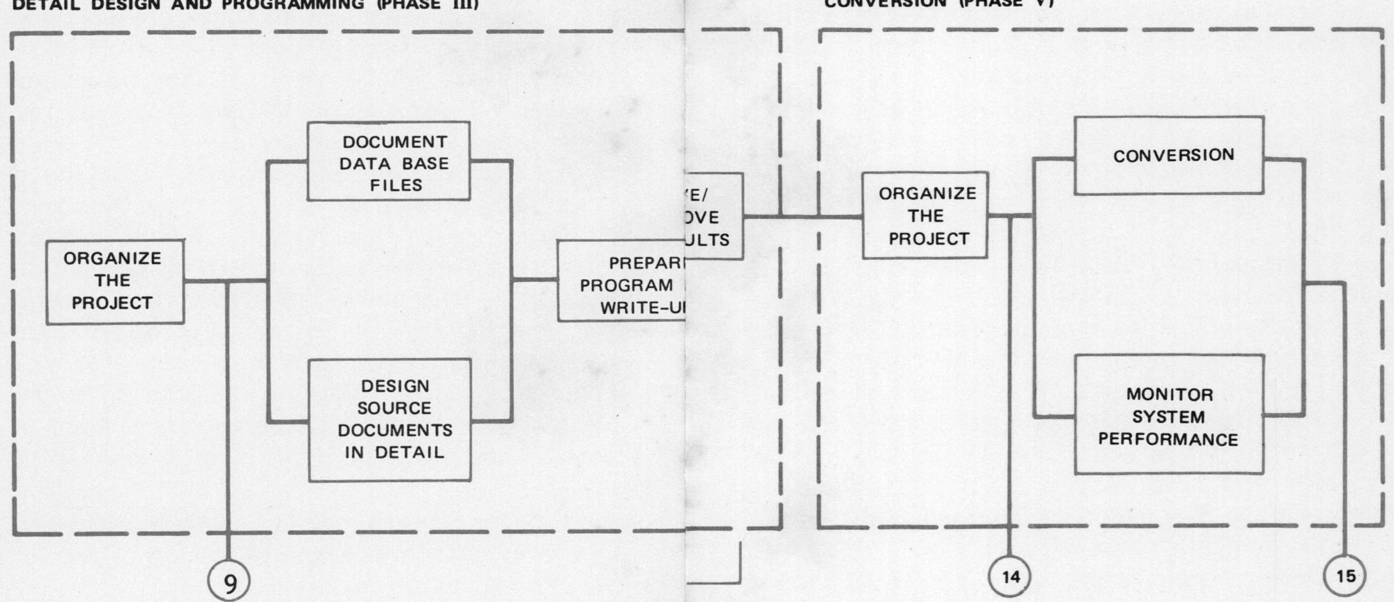

EDP Audit will work continuously with System Development and Operations thr

FIGURE 12-1 SYSTEM DEVELOPMENT LIFE CYCLE

an automatic or manual procedure to compare test results with predefined results.

The scope and composition of a base case are determined by consideration of input transaction types, computer programs, output reports, masterfiles, edits and validations, and system controls. The analysis and procedures for determining correct operation of the system using the base case consist of file comparison programs, program monitoring aids, file dump utilities, comparison of base case data to system produced data, and manual review of output reports.

This organization makes heavy use of representatives from users' departments in forming the base case. In addition, the organization believes that individuals responsible for the base case must be more than part-time participants. Sufficient time is planned for both the definition and use of the base case. The planning for the base case starts in the first phase of system development, the system definition phase. During the next phase of system development, the base case is defined in detail and also serves the purpose of assessing the design as it progresses toward detail design and programming.

The base case approach to testing is used for system test at the preinstallation stage, as well as during the production life of the system. As the system is used, modifications are bound to be made. As these modifications are made, the base case test is modified and used to test the new version of the system to ensure correct operation and avoid the bugs that inevitably result from minor changes.

Base case testing provides comprehensive system verification and compliance testing. However, it does require very substantial resources to maintain extensive data sets after initial installation. Consequently, it will probably be some time before extensive use of this technique is made in most organizations.

Transaction Driver Test — The transaction driver technique is a procedure that uses software to input transactions to an application system as part of the test procedure before the system becomes operational. The approach of testing systems through the use of transactions and an on-line transaction driver is being used by a major oil company. This company uses an on-line test system to exercise its new application systems. This system is used to generate and track transactions through the system being tested. The transactions do not impact the live data bases except for query purposes. In particular, they do not allow updates to the live data base during system test. All transactions from the on-line test system terminal are included on the log tape for comparison against predefined test tapes. The transactions that would normally go to posting on the data base are stripped away and stored on test tapes.

This approach is useful for the testing of on-line systems that are transaction driven. Through the use of this technique, any remote access to the system can be tested before actual production use. The approach is not directly applicable to nontransaction systems or to systems that are not on-line. In addition, the approach would be less effective in testing systems where there is a high incidence of file updating. However, for on-line transaction driven systems, the approach is extremely effective.

During the field interviews, the following general concepts of acceptance testing were identified:

- Acceptance test standards are required to ensure completeness.
- Acceptance testing planning must be started early in the application system development process.
- The user group must be heavily involved throughout all stages of acceptance testing and must approve the final test results.
- The test team members must maintain a posture independent from implementers.

Most organizations interviewed that used formal acceptance test teams noted that it is expensive to perform thorough testing of major application systems. However, the analysis does indicate that acceptance testing is cost-beneficial over the life of the application systems and there is a definite trend to use formal acceptance testing techniques.

In summary, adequate acceptance testing is very important and it does provide a mechanism for improving the quality of application systems and reducing the number of operation problems that are visible to users and top management. It does not guarantee a 100% error-free system or prevent bad design. It is an important control because it allows users, EDP auditors, designers, implementers, and other concerned parties an opportunity to view the application system in its final form before becoming an operational entity. It ensures processing accuracy, completeness, and reliability.

PROGRAM CHANGE CONTROL

Program change control, a formalized procedure for modifying application and operating systems, requires written approvals and supporting documentation. The objectives of program change controls are to prevent unauthorized and potentially fraudulent changes from being introduced into previously tested and accepted computer programs.

Change Authorization — This includes a formal change request and authorization form and procedure, approval procedures for programmers to gain access to source coding maintained in a source program library, and testing and certification of test results.

Program changes to existing systems are one area in which both internal auditors and data processing personnel have been increasing their efforts at control. Major changes are always preceded by planning of the kind that is associated with major development or acquisition efforts, and the internal auditors' roles are very much like those played in the system development process. Minor changes to existing programs and files pose a different problem because they usually occur with little notice and must be added to "keep the system running." Most organizations have their own special way of handling the problem.

One field interview site has set up a program change committee, through which all modifications to existing systems must pass. This program change committee must also pass on and approve new systems before they gain operational status. This program change committee consists of personnel from programming, operations management, technical service, and the systems and systems programming departments. This committee is meeting daily, but in the future it intends to appoint one full-time program change coordinator who will handle the day-to-day operations of approving program changes and will call committee meetings only when higher authority is required.

The committee evaluates the programmers' testing of the change, evaluates the validity of the change, examines operating instructions, and generally reviews all program changes before final implementation in the production system. This committee has absolute power and no system can be modified without committee approval.

The programmer submits his job control language (JCL), documentation, and changes to the committee for its approval. After being scrutinized and approved by the committee, the JCL, documentation, and changes are passed on to the operations department, which is responsible for modifying the load libraries.

This committee is an active control, but it does not preclude illegal program changes by programmers or systems personnel. To assist in the prevention and detection of illegal changes, the committee has inserted numerous other controls.

One control that is being used is a specialized usage of IBM's Systems Management Facilities (SMF) Reporting System. The SMF was modified to gather data automatically so a report on program changes in the production libraries is printed daily. Another report has been developed that lists all data base accesses that do not come from load libraries. In this way, the committee can have a report that shows potential unauthorized file accesses.

Another control used requires application programmers to submit suggested JCL specifications, and the operations personnel will actually insert all JCL cards in any update or program change. In this way, a programmer cannot embed JCL cards in the middle of a deck on a batch update to illegally modify some other program.

Another control exists for emergency cases in which a programmer must come in after hours to fix a system. The control requires that an emergency change report be sent to the program change committee the next morning. This report must include a comprehensive list of the program coding that was changed, a copy of the console log, and a copy of SYSOUT for the time the programmer was making the emergency changes. (SYSOUT is an IBM term for a class of operating system output that includes the devices that were used for an application run.) Internal auditing reviews the emergency call list to see who was in and when, and checks back to see if the program change committee was apprised of each emergency call.

Management estimates 500 man-hours were required to incorporate the above program change control system. This 500 hours involved up to 100 hours of programming effort to modify SMF and make other minor program changes, and about 400 hours writing the manual procedures and training the people in the use of the manual procedures to effect the program change control procedure.

Block Cut-In — Managing the number of changes can become a burdensome task unless steps are taken to minimize the frequency of change. One large organization used "block cut-in," in which program changes are collected and inserted into application programs as a group so that changes can be traced back to a block if errors occur.

Block cut-in of changes improves application control and control over operating systems. Unauthorized program changes can be detected more easily, whether they are operating-system or application-program changes. Finally, block cut-in improves the efficiency of general operations by batching changes and installing them into the system as a unit.

To implement block cut-in, data processing operations must do the following:

- Obtain agreement from the users that systems will be updated only a limited number of times a year.
- Develop a version numbering scheme to denote the releases (e.g., Payroll-Release 23).
- Develop a means of collecting and holding program changes as they are tested and approved, but before they are implemented into the system.
- Schedule cut-in dates and announce them, so a user has the option to change priorities of enhancements to be programmed and tested.
- Cut-in collected program changes at one time and announce the new release of the system.

This approach has two limitations. First, since only one to six releases per year are planned, some program changes might normally be held for several months. For program changes that are required quickly, such as a payroll withholding tax rate change, this may be impossible. The alternative is to have a variable cut-in schedule or a one-time emergency cut-in procedure. Second, when one change is made on a certain date, it may necessitate making changes in other related systems. This may mean departing from the planned schedule.

Program Packages — Some organizations interviewed used program packages to control changes to systems libraries. The packages allow for password protection of source libraries from which load libraries are created.

In summary, most organizations interviewed felt they could and would improve their program change controls and the procedures for using the controls. Program change controls allow data processing personnel to maintain the integrity of accepted systems and develop change lists that allow for traceability of the evolving application systems. Change controls frustrate programmers and sometimes cause delays in fixes to application systems. Program change controls are beneficial because they encourage data processing personnel to exercise more caution as they make changes to accepted production systems. SRI found a trend toward the use of some type of formal program change control procedures, but most organizations appear to be slow in moving to extensive use of this procedure.

DOCUMENTATION

Documentation is the process of describing on paper what functions an application system performs, how it performs them, and how the functions are to be used. The objectives of good documentation are to provide application system designers, implementers, testers, users, and EDP auditors with a clear means of understanding all aspects of the application system.

Documentation is important because it provides the primary communication channels between users, EDP auditors, and data processing personnel. It is important because it helps ensure correct and efficient processing within both data processing and user areas; it increases the ease and accuracy of computer program maintenance, and it provides internal auditors with an independent basis for evaluating application control.

System documentation occurs throughout system development. In the early stages, it is used to document system objectives and definitions. As such, it can be used within the system project staff and can serve as a vehicle for approval from units of the organization outside the data processing department. In the system development control approach, using control points discussed earlier in this chapter, we see this form of documentation used for approvals throughout the process.

Control elements provided by a comprehensive documentation program include the following:

- System documentation, including a clear statement of the system objectives, a flowchart showing the flow of information through the system and the interrelationship between manual and computer processing steps, system specifications that governed design and development, input forms and procedures, record formats and descriptions, descriptions of audit trails, and balancing and control procedures.
- Program documentation, including descriptions and flowcharts necessary to allow efficient and accurate maintenance subsequent to initial installation. Such documentation normally includes control cards and JCL, program listings, program test data, a testing log, input/output distribution instructions, data retention instructions, console operator instructions, and copies of program change request forms.
- Operations documentation, including instructions that provide the computer operations function with adequate instructions to accurately and efficiently run a computer application, balance inputs and outputs, and distribute reports. Restart and recovery procedures are also included. The requirements for operations instructions vary greatly from installation to installation depending upon the operating systems and the library procedures, and input/output controls that have been adopted.
- Library documentation, including procedures for backup, retention, restrictions on access to sensitive data, and inventory record keeping.
- User documentation, including a narrative description of the system's operation accompanied by a general flow diagram.

This basic user documentation is supplemented by specific instructions governing the proper completion of input forms and transactions. Control procedures provide users with instructions they need to balance, reconcile, and maintain overall control transactions, masterfiles, and the results of computer processing.

One approach to documentation control is used by a large food manufacturer. This organization makes use of a documentation test to be administered throughout the phases of system development. The primary purpose of the test is to ensure that appropriate documentation exists for the following major phases of system development: feasibility study, system proposal, system specifications, and installation, including turnovers to data processing and to program support.

In addition to verifying the existence of sufficient documentation, this technique also assesses various aspects of the documentation, including the following:

- Does the documentation give evidence that processing controls will be adequate?
- Have sufficient controls been built into the system to allow effective operation and maintenance?
- Can the documentation be used as a basis to prove that controls over operation and maintenance are adequate?

Within each of the major phases of system development, a detailed list of minimum documentation requirements is provided. For each phase, the required set of documentation must be present and assessed before the next phase can begin. The documentation test embodies a variety of levels of documentation to be used to control the actual overall processes and detailed control documents to be used within a phase. As such, it serves as an inventory for the documentation that should be present following actual system development and installation.

General documentation trends and concepts discovered during the study include:

- A desire by data processing personnel to develop application systems that are more self-documenting through use of techniques such as structured programming.
- A realization that documentation must be controlled. One company had gone so far as to require limited copies of sensitive documents and to require signatures each time a person is given a copy.

In summary, application system documentation is an important control technique because it provides a mechanism by which persons not directly associated with the development process can understand and evaluate the application system for usage and controls. Particularly important to internal auditors, it allows them to audit applications with general independence from data processing.

DATA BASE ADMINISTRATION

A data base is a collection of interrelated data stored together with controlled redundancy to serve one or many users or applications in an optimal fashion. In addition, the data are stored so that they are independent of programs that use them. The data base administrator (DBA) is the manager responsible for coordinating and controlling the design of the data base management system (DBMS) as well as the user interface and access to the data stored within the DBMS.

Data base administration and the role of the DBA are discussed in this chapter because the field interviews clearly indicated a trend toward the use of data base administration techniques to control data access and the early stages of the application system development process.

The objectives in creating a data base are to reduce the amount of data and the programs required to meet corporate needs, to control the user interfaces and access to the data, and to manipulate the data in the most efficient manner possible.

The objective of data base administration is to provide a focal point for defining and controlling all elements of data base systems. This requires that the DBA take an active part during the system development process, especially the early stages of it, to ensure that adequate controls exist.

The particular functions performed by a DBA have existed in one form or another for many years. Applications-oriented systems have been developed with the data base defined in direct support of the procedures. This is opposite from the data base design approach, in which the center of attention is the data. As systems become increasingly integrated, the importance of a data base design approach becomes critical to the successful design and development of integrated information systems. A data base environment supports a data base design approach. It is thus the management of the data base environment that will determine the success of a data base design approach and the resulting integrated corporate data base.

The Primary U.S. Mail Survey showed that, of the organizations using DBA techniques, over 70% used the DBA function at varying stages throughout the application system development process.

The five major areas of responsibility of the DBA as determined during interviews are data definition and data base design, administration, operations, system monitoring and improvement, and general support.

Data Definition and Data Base Design — The DBA is responsible for all standards related to the data base. These standards cover how data are defined and ultimately how data are stored, protected, and accessed by users of the data base.

Administration — The DBA enforces management's policies for disposition of the organization's data. The specific areas involved in this activity include the administration of data base standards used for data definition, use, protection, access, and documentation.

Operations — The DBA ensures that all resources within the data base environment operate in the most effective manner as the system becomes operational. The DBA is responsible for working with computer operations in developing both formal and documented procedures for operating the data base. These procedures include overall scheduling of computer time to ensure priority use of the data base, utilization of data base components, and general operational use of the data base. The DBA is also responsible for seeing that the system restart and recovery procedures are properly exercised and controlled.

System Monitoring and Improvement — The DBA continually monitors and measures the various aspects of performance to ensure an efficient level of service while maintaining data base integrity.

General Support — The DBA is the primary interface between the organization and computer vendors supplying hardware and software in support of DBMS. He must assess new products and their relative value to the data base environment.

The DBA conducts the necessary internal education. Education includes programs for new users and present users to ensure that all components and standards of the data base environment are being effectively and properly used.

In summary, both data base and data base administration are receiving increased attention in many large institutions. Data base use is growing because organizations are placing more types of related data into computer systems and the use of data base management systems provides the best means of control. Data base administration is growing to meet the requirement for controlling data bases and data base management systems. Data base systems place heavy emphasis on the data to be processed. Data base administration provides a centralized mechanism for controlling the definition of data and the access to and protection of the data, as well as a means for controlling the development of the application system. The concept of data base administration is relatively new, and consequently there is not a universally accepted method for its use. However, data base administration is a good control because it does encourage organizations to view application system development from the point of view of how the data are to be used.

SUMMARY

The controls and techniques governing the system development process are important because the adequacy and effectiveness of controls included in computer application systems are heavily affected by the methods and procedures used during the system development process. To ensure the accuracy, completeness, and validity of data being processed by complex computer application systems, internal auditors must consider an entire system of controls that encompass data preparation, data entry, data communications, data processing, and data distribution. To accomplish this goal, internal auditors are being required to participate actively in the system development process because retrofitting controls, or trying to understand internal controls after the application system has been implemented, is costly and difficult. In addition, internal auditors are responsible for evaluating and verifying operational and user controls associated with the computer application systems. Participating in the system development process broadens the internal auditor's perspective and understanding of the computer application systems and allows him to perform all his functions more completely.

The primary controls and techniques of concern during the system development process are documentation, project management, and application system change controls. Documentation is one of the most important controls from the internal auditor's point of view because it provides him with a means for conducting independent reviews of system specifications and design, system testing and operation requirements, and user interface and usage specifications. Matching all areas in an independent but coordinated manner allows for completeness. The project management technique provides for a management structure that forces periodic status reporting to keep all parties informed. These status reports allow the user and internal auditors to monitor progress and costs against plans and budget. Change controls are important because most computer application systems are large and complex and require periodic changes. After an application system has undergone formal acceptance testing, the integrity of the system must be maintained as it is changed.

The systems development life cycle technique is a rapidly growing trend in data processing because it encompasses the primary concerns of data processing and encourages the development of better application systems. System development controls and techniques tend to be more expensive than many other controls because of the requirements for skilled persons and new concepts. For example, SDLC is a technique that requires EDP auditors, users, and project management to meet on a regular basis, communicate technical ideas, and receive formal approvals from each other. The cost of system development controls must be weighed against the cost of the computer application system over its expected life. While the controls or techniques may be expensive over a short time, the cost over the expected life of the system is much more reasonable. Application systems developed with good management controls and techniques will require less maintenance and be less susceptible to fraud or other abuses.

Part IV
CONTROL ILLUSTRATIONS

Part IV of the Control Practices report delineates four on-line application systems currently installed in organizations interviewed by SRI. These application systems were documented for the purposes of providing a perspective on control practices as they relate to the total application system, illustrating how some of the control practices outlined in Chapters 5 through 10 have been implemented in data processing installations, and further describing areas of auditor interest in the data processing function.

The controls outlined in each application system do not necessarily represent all the controls that an organization might consider necessary. However, in the organizations interviewed, it has been determined that the level of control implemented satisfies their audit and control requirements.

The Internal Auditing and Data Processing Departments of the organizations interviewed have reviewed the control illustrations for completeness and accuracy. All areas of applications wherein it appears to the reader that a control point may be missing have been previously reviewed by the respective managements of the organizations interviewed. In their judgment, cost-benefit analyses indicated that the benefits did not justify the cost of implementing controls at those points.

The application systems were selected for their broad applicability and representation of key interest areas to data processing, audit, and user management. They are:

- Accounts Receivable
- Order Entry
- Inventory Management
- Point of Sale Credit Approval

Each of the application systems discussed contains a summary table of the application control points. The summary table is intended to assist the reader in obtaining additional information regarding control practices by referencing the control areas in Chapters 5 to 10.

Part IV is organized to meet the needs of data processing personnel as well as auditors. For example, data processing personnel who are concerned with how the controls listed in Parts II and III of this report are utilized will find these examples useful.

Chapter 13

ACCOUNTS RECEIVABLE CONTROL ILLUSTRATION

APPLICATION OVERVIEW

There are two basic approaches to performing an accounts receivable application: open-item and balance-forward processing. In open-item processing, a separate record is maintained in the accounts receivable system for each of the customer's unpaid invoices. As customer remittances are received, they are matched to the unpaid invoices. In balance-forward processing, the customer's remittances are applied against a customer's total outstanding invoice balance rather than against individual invoices. The following control illustration describes the cash application segment of an on-line open-item accounts receivable application system.

BACKGROUND

This accounts receivable application system is one of 16 on-line application systems installed at a large manufacturing organization located in a major eastern city. For control purposes and to ensure the continuity of daily business operations, the data processing hardware systems installed at this facility are completely backed up by a similar system configuration located in another eastern city.

The hardware systems supporting these application systems consist of one large-scale computer system, with four medium-sized front-end computers functioning as line concentrators for approximately 1,600 display terminals and approximately 800 hard-copy terminals in over 300 locations throughout the United States. Of the 38,000 business transactions processed daily through the total system, more than 1,000 are accounts receivable cash application transactions.

There are 11 major control points in the cash application segment of the accounts receivable system. A flowchart of the cash application segment and the control points associated with the system are illustrated in Figure 13-1.

APPLICATION DESCRIPTION AND CONTROL PRACTICES

At the completion of each billing cycle, the billing data are loaded, via batch processing, onto an Open Item Accounts Receivable File.

Control Point 1 — Data Processing File Control

At that time, a Divisional Control File, which is a summary of the open-item accounts receivable file by type of accounts receivable (e.g., installment, net 30, etc.) is updated to reflect the new billing data. A File Control Summary report is then generated to reflect the new updated file totals. Prior to the processing of daily cash remittances, this control report is reviewed and approved by Accounts Receivable management at the headquarters location to ensure that the Accounts Receivable File and Divisional Control File are in balance.

Customer payments are remitted to a special post-office box number, which corresponds to the bank into which the payments will be deposited. This approach separates the checks from other mail received by the organization's branch location, thereby eliminating manual sorting of the checks and reducing the number of individuals handling the checks when received at the organization's branch office.

Control Point 2 — Check Endorsement

When the checks are received from the post office by the organization's branch office, they are given to a control desk, where a control clerk restrictively endorses them. This stamped endorsement "For Deposit, Company Account, Account Number, Date" prevents the deposit of the remittance to any unauthorized bank account.

Control Point 3 — Cash Receipt Total

The control clerk then totals all checks by adding machine, and prepares deposit slips for each depository bank. This control is to ensure the accountability of checks received and their subsequent disposition. When the checks are deposited at the banks, the receipted deposit slips and adding machine tapes are filed in the branch office, at the control desk, to be later reconciled to the Daily Cash Summary Report (see Control Point 9).

For ease of handling, controlling, and reconciling, the payments are batched into control groups of 50 or fewer checks. When the checks are ready to be processed, a terminal operator requests access to the accounts receivable system through a display-type terminal. The operator keys into the terminal his unique security code and employee number and identifies

FIGURE 13-1 ACCOUNTS RECEIVABLE FLOWCHART

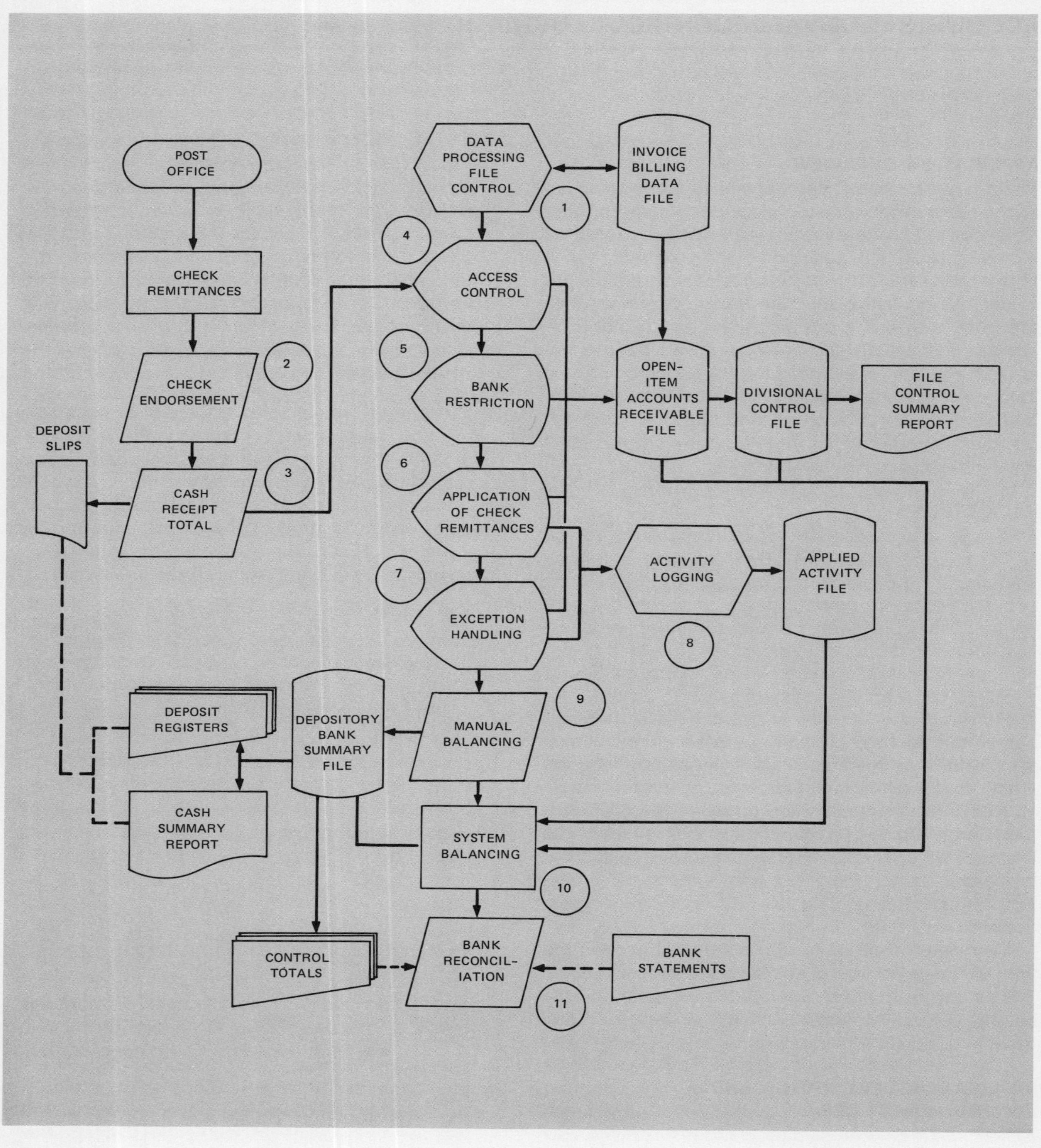

the transaction he wants to process (e.g., cash application — single invoice checks, cash application — multiple invoice checks).

Control Point 4 — Access Control

A security application, which controls access to all applications within the total system, verifies that the operator is an authorized user of the system and that his personal profile of clearances includes the transaction he has requested. Accounts receivable management may delegate or remove authority to process transactions, but the security application limits management to the delegation of transactions within the scope of its authority (as defined by a similar type manager's security profile) and to transactions that will not compromise good separation of duties when processed in combination with existing transaction authorities.

The terminal operator, upon being given access to the accounts receivable system, is given a choice of depository banks against which to apply payments.

Control Point 5 — Bank Restriction

The choice of depository banks is limited to the specific banks identified in a branch office profile maintained within the accounts receivable system. This control ensures that the cash is being applied within the accounts receivable system to one of the depository accounts that may be used by the branch office.

There are two basic processing procedures for applying remittance checks in the accounts receivable system. The first is for all checks within a batch that have a single invoice payment referenced on them. The second procedure is for checks with multiple or no invoice payments referenced on the customer's remittance advice. For single invoice payments, the terminal operator enters into a display terminal from the remittance advice the invoice number and check amount as an individual line item for as many lines as the terminal is capable of displaying. The accounts receivable system then compares the individual line items against the Open Item Accounts Receivable File. For those line items where an invoice number and check amount match a corresponding record in the Open Item Accounts Receivable File, the check amount is applied. If there are line items that do not have a complete match on invoice number and check amount, or the accounts receivable system notes that an entered invoice number was previously cleared, an error message is immediately transmitted back to the input terminal indicating the line item in error and the reason for rejection (e.g., no unpaid invoice number on file; check amount entered is under/over invoice amount on file).

Control Point 6 — Application of Check Remittances

All check remittances within a batch must be applied to a customer's account unless the check remittance was erroneously sent to the company. If a check remittance for some reason is not entered into the system and not subtracted from the batch control totals the discrepancy will be highlighted in Control Point 9. A line item that has been identified by the accounts receivable system as being incorrect must be reentered on the next display by the terminal operator or it must be processed within one of the options outlined in the following procedure.

For processing customer remittances with multiple or no invoice payments referenced on them, the terminal operator has the following options available for entering data. He can enter:

- One of the invoice numbers and the remittance check amount.
- The customer's number, if on the remittance advice, and the check amount.
- The customer's name and the check amount.

Depending on the option selected by the operator, the accounts receivable system will process the input as follows:

If the entered invoice number and check amount do not match a record on the Open Item Accounts Receivable File and there are multiple unpaid customer invoice numbers on the file, the accounts receivable system will display to the terminal operator all the unpaid invoice numbers and invoice amounts. The terminal operator then keys into the terminal the invoice number(s) to be applied against the check remittance, and the accounts receivable system applies the cash remittance to these invoices. If, after applying the cash amounts, the accounts receivable system determines that cash still remains to be applied, the accounts receivable system displays the remaining amount on the terminal. The terminal operator then selects one of the three alternatives outlined below. When the accounts receivable system makes a match on the invoice number, but the check amount does not match, and there are no other unpaid invoices for the customer, the accounts receivable system applies the check amount to the open invoice item and displays the calculated differences between the invoice amount and the check amount to the terminal operator. The terminal operator then selects one of the following alternatives which:

- Requests a display of associated customer accounts (affiliates, subsidiaries, etc.) to determine if the following check amount should be applied to an unpaid invoice number.

- Indicates to the system that the remaining check amount should be applied as balance on account to the customer. (The system will assign a sequential invoice number for the remaining check amount.)
- Establishes an invoice number based on the customer's remittance advice and enters it and the remaining check amount into the system as a balance on account for the customer.

When invoice numbers are not identified on the customer's remittance, the terminal operator may enter the customer number and the check amount. The accounts receivable system then displays a list of all the unpaid invoices for the customer, and the terminal operator, using the previously described procedure, selects the invoices to which the check amount should be applied. If the customer's name and check amount are entered by the terminal operator, the accounts receivable system will search the customer masterfile and display the customer name and address, the customer number, and a list of unpaid invoices. The terminal operator, after verifying the customer name and address, will apply the check remittance as previously described.

Control Point 7 — Exception Handling

The terminal operator is restricted by the accounts receivable system to applying cash remittances to a single customer account (or subsidiary accounts). The terminal can access only one customer account for each check remittance. The entire check remittance amount must be applied to that customer account. The terminal operator cannot apply the remaining check amount of one customer's payment to another customer's account. If a terminal operator is unable to apply a customer remittance because the customer's account is not on the Open Item Accounts Receivable File, then accounts receivable management follows up with the customer (usually the result of a misrouted check by the customer). If appropriate, the check amount is subtracted by the control clerk from the batch total and the check is returned to the customer.

As payments are applied against the unpaid invoice records on the Open Item Accounts Receivable File, the invoice records are updated to reflect the payment date, activity code (e.g., check payment, invoice adjustment), bank depository number, and a sequential check number generated by the system for each of the bank depository locations. The paid customer invoice records are retained on-line for one year and are available for inquiries.

Control Point 8 — Activity Logging

All cash remittance activity is logged on an Applied Activity File to provide an audit trail of all cash transactions processed against the Open Item Accounts Receivable File. The Applied Activity File is used in the daily balancing of the total accounts receivable system (see Control Point 10) and for preparing, upon request, listings that assist data processing system personnel in tracing any lost activity that may have resulted from a system error.

After a batch of checks has been applied by the accounts receivable system, the system updates a Depository Bank Summary File for the dollar amount of the batch of checks. Also, a deposit register detailing and totaling the invoice numbers and invoice amounts in the batch is printed on a hard-copy terminal at the branch location.

Control Point 9 — Manual Balancing

Daily, upon completion of the application of cash remittance, the accounts receivable system prepares on hard-copy terminals at the branch location a Cash Summary Report from the Depository Bank Summary File. This report lists the total number of checks and total dollars applied to each depository bank for the branch location during that day. The deposit registers are compared to the Cash Summary Report by the control desk clerk to ensure that the cash applied to the system is in balance. In addition, the bank-receipted deposit slips, referred to in Control Point 3, are reconciled by the control clerk to the Cash Summary Report. This reconciliation ensures that the cash deposited in the branch's specified banks was applied by the accounts receivable system to the appropriate bank account. After the control clerk has balanced the deposit registers and the cash summary report, the Cash Summary Report is given to the branch's accounts receivable management for review and signature and is filed for future reference. The deposit registers are filed with the day's customer remittance advices for future reference or reconciliation.

Daily, the Applied Activity File is summarized by bank depository number and compared to the bank depository totals in the Depository Bank Summary File. Also, the Applied Activity File totals by type of accounts receivable are subtracted from the Divisional Control File totals, which reflect the previous day's Open Item Accounts Receivable File data by type of accounts receivable. Finally, the current Open

Item Accounts Receivable File is accumulated by type of accounts receivable. These accounts receivable system processing steps are made daily before the Open Item Accounts Receivable File is updated with new billing data or invoice adjustment data. Monthly, the total amount of cash activity on the Applied Activity File is summarized and entered into the General Ledger application system.

Control Point 10 — System Balancing

The comparison of the Applied Activity File and the Depository Bank Summary File ensures that all cash that has been deposited has been applied and recorded on the Applied Activity File. The computed total derived from subtracting the Applied Activity File from the Divisional Control File should equal the summary totals by type of accounts receivable of the current Open Item Accounts Receivable File. This system balancing imposes a three-way check to ensure that each file within the accounts receivable system is in balance. As a result, any out-of-balance condition is readily identified and appropriate corrective action initiated prior to proceeding with the next day's accounts receivable processing procedures.

Control Point 11 — Bank Reconciliation

Monthly, Corporate Accounting Management receives statements from the banks. These statements are compared to the totals that are transmitted daily via hard-copy terminal to Corporate Accounting from the Depository Bank Summary File to ensure that the Depository Bank Summary File and the bank accounts are in balance. Any discrepancies in the totals are forwarded to the appropriate branch office location for follow-up and resolution.

Table 13-1 cross-references the 11 control points in this control illustration to the application system controls (Chapters 5-10) and the control areas within those chapters.

Table 13-1
SUMMARY OF ACCOUNTS RECEIVABLE CONTROL PRACTICES

Control Point	Description	Application System Control Phase	Control	Chapter Reference
1	Data Processing File Control	Data Storage and Retrieval	Before and after looks	9
2	Check Endorsement	Transaction Origination	Signatures	5
3	Cash Receipt Control	Transaction Origination	Batch and balance source Data at point of origination	5
4	Access Control	Transaction Entry	Data access matrix	6
5	Bank Restriction	Computer Processing	Transaction codes	8
6	Application of Check Remittances	Computer Processing	Error reporting or anticipation controls	8
7	Exception Handling	Transaction Origination	Responsibility for error correction	5
8	Activity Logging	Computer Processing		8
9	Manual Balancing	Output Processing	Manual output balancing	10
10	System Balancing	Output Processing	Reconciliation	10
11	Bank Reconciliation	Output Processing	Manual output balancing	10

Chapter 14

ORDER ENTRY CONTROL ILLUSTRATION

APPLICATION OVERVIEW

Order entry systems vary considerably; however, their basic objective is similar; namely, the accurate and timely completion of customer orders. The order-entry system reviewed in this chapter is described as follows:

> The customer calls a customer order representative and places his order. A terminal operator enters the customer order into a central computer, where information files are checked on the customer's credit rating and on the availability of the product, bills of lading are calculated, and shipping points are assigned. Information is then sent to a warehouse in the form of "packing" and "shipping" papers, and the materials are forwarded to the customer. The following control illustration describes the order entry segment of an order entry/inventory control system.

BACKGROUND

This control illustration describes an on-line order entry system that is being used by a large continuous process manufacturer. The order entry system is operated on a large-scale computer that is used for the actual processing of customer orders, a medium-scale computer that is used for controlling the communication lines and terminals, and a small special-purpose computer that is used as a connecting device or coupler between the two larger computers. The order entry system, which is part of a system that includes inventory control, utilizes 15 high-speed hard-wired leased lines that connect over 200 hard-copy and display-type terminals to the system. More than 4,000 customer orders, which represent approximately 16,000 order entry transactions, are processed weekly.

There are 15 control points in this system. These control points and the order entry system itself are illustrated in Figure 14-1.

APPLICATION DESCRIPTION AND CONTROL PRACTICES

To place an order, a customer calls toll free to a centralized order processing location. The call is routed to a customer order representative assigned to that customer's geographic region, who then completes a customer work order that includes the quantities and items ordered by the customer. The work order is then forwarded to a data entry operator within the order processing location for entry of the customer order data into the order entry system. The data entry operator, using a display type of terminal, requests the system to display the proper format for processing the specific type of order reflected on the customer work order (e.g., normal or consignment). The format request is made through the use of format codes.

Control Point 1 — Transaction Control

A table of transaction codes that indicates which terminals are authorized to transmit certain data is maintained in the order entry system. The codes and terminals were preidentified by data processing and order entry management during the system's design. All terminal requests are checked against this table and those transactions that do not match are rejected and the terminal does not have access to the data. As a further control, after five attempts by a terminal operator to access data that a terminal does not have clearance to access, the system will discontinue polling the terminal. The terminal can only be reinstated into the polling sequence by data processing operation personnel after having received a call from an authorized manager at the order processing location.

When the requested format is displayed, a computer-generated order control number is also displayed. This order control number consists of the terminal number, Julian date, the warehouse geographic location code, and a serial number assigned by the computer.

Control Point 2 — Customer Order Control

The order control number is assigned by the computer to eliminate the possibility of duplicate order numbers being assigned to customer orders. All order entry transactions must reference an order control number or they are rejected. Order control numbers cannot be established or altered by a terminal operator. This control establishes that the order entry system has a record of every customer work order entered into the system. The order control number also serves as a means of follow-up if something goes wrong during order entry processing.

The data entry operator then enters the data from the customer work order into the terminal. After entering all the items on the order, the operator enters a summary total of the quantity ordered, which was originally totaled by the customer order representative.

Control Point 3 — Data Entry Control
The order entry system validates against customer and inventory master records the customer number and the items being ordered to ensure that the data entry operator is entering valid customer and product data into the system. The system also totals the quantities ordered and compares this total with the hash total entered by the data entry operator. If there are any discrepancies in this validation process, the system records all the data on an Error Cycle File and redisplays all the order entry data to the terminal operator (see Control Point 6).

All data transmitted to and from the order entry system are first recorded on a computer log tape on the message switching computer. All transactions that update an order entry system data base are also recorded on a computer log tape on the order entry processing computer.

Control Point 4 — Activity Logging
The data recorded on the computer log tape of the message switching computer are used primarily for monitoring terminal and system transaction activity. Listings reflecting, by terminal, the date and number of transactions processed are prepared upon request. As an example, the Internal Auditing Department at times requests terminal activity reports when they are reviewing unusual inventory activity at warehouses.

The computer log tape for the order entry processing computer is maintained primarily for file and system recovery purposes. The computer log tape is only printed out when difficulties are experienced in file recovery.

After the data entry operator has correctly entered all of the customer's order into the system, the operator posts the order control number on the customer's work order and the work order is filed.

Control Point 5 — Source Document Control
The customer's work order, which now has the order control number posted to it, is filed in the customer's order file. The order control number serves as a cross-reference between the customer's work order and the processing of the customer's order through the order processing system. The filed work order is used for answering customer inquiries relative to items ordered.

If, in the order entry processing cycle, an error is detected (e.g., an invalid item number, an invalid terminal transaction, reference to a nonexistent customer), the entire order is displayed to the order entry operator with an asterisk and an error code beside the line item as an indicator of the type of error detected (e.g., not on the masterfile, data entry procedural error). These codes assist the data entry operator to isolate and correct the error.

Control Point 6 — Error Control
When an error is detected by the order entry system, the entire customer order is recorded on an Error Cycle File and an error control number is assigned by the computer and associated with the order control number. An order cannot be processed if any part of it is in error. Daily, a report is prepared on the terminals at the order processing locations reflecting all pending error control numbers and associated order control numbers on the Error Cycle File. This report is reviewed by the sales services supervisor at the order processing location to ensure that action is being taken on all pending error items.

When an error has been corrected at the order processing location, the data entry operator requests the pending customer order from the Error Cycle File by referencing the error control number.

Control Point 7 — Error Correction Routine
Access to the Error Cycle File can be made only by referencing the error control number. Upon identification of an error control number, the customer's order data will be released from the Error Cycle File for display to the data entry operator. When the data in error are corrected, the pending order data are deleted from the Error Cycle File and the entire customer order is again processed through the validation procedure of the order entry system.

Once the order entry system has determined that all the data entered for a customer's order are valid, then the actual processing of the customer's order data takes place. First, the customer masterfile is accessed to determine the terms and conditions for this customer (e.g., type of account, warehouse location, shipping instructions). Next, the value of the customer's order is calculated and a customer credit limitation check is performed.

Control Point 8 — Credit Check
This control point is to ensure that the customer's order does not exceed the credit limitations established for this customer by the credit de-

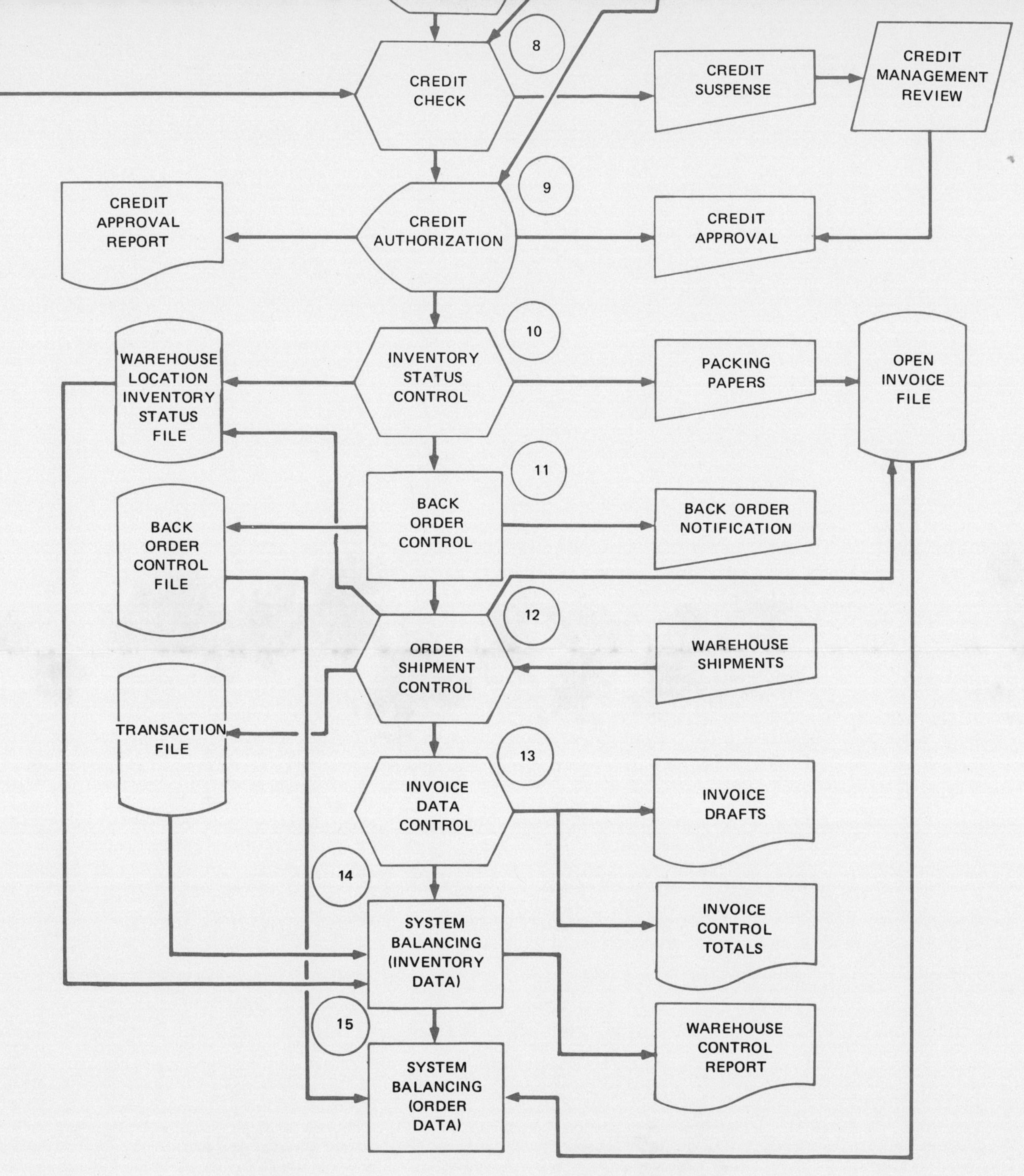

FIGURE 14-1 ORDER ENTRY FLOWCHART

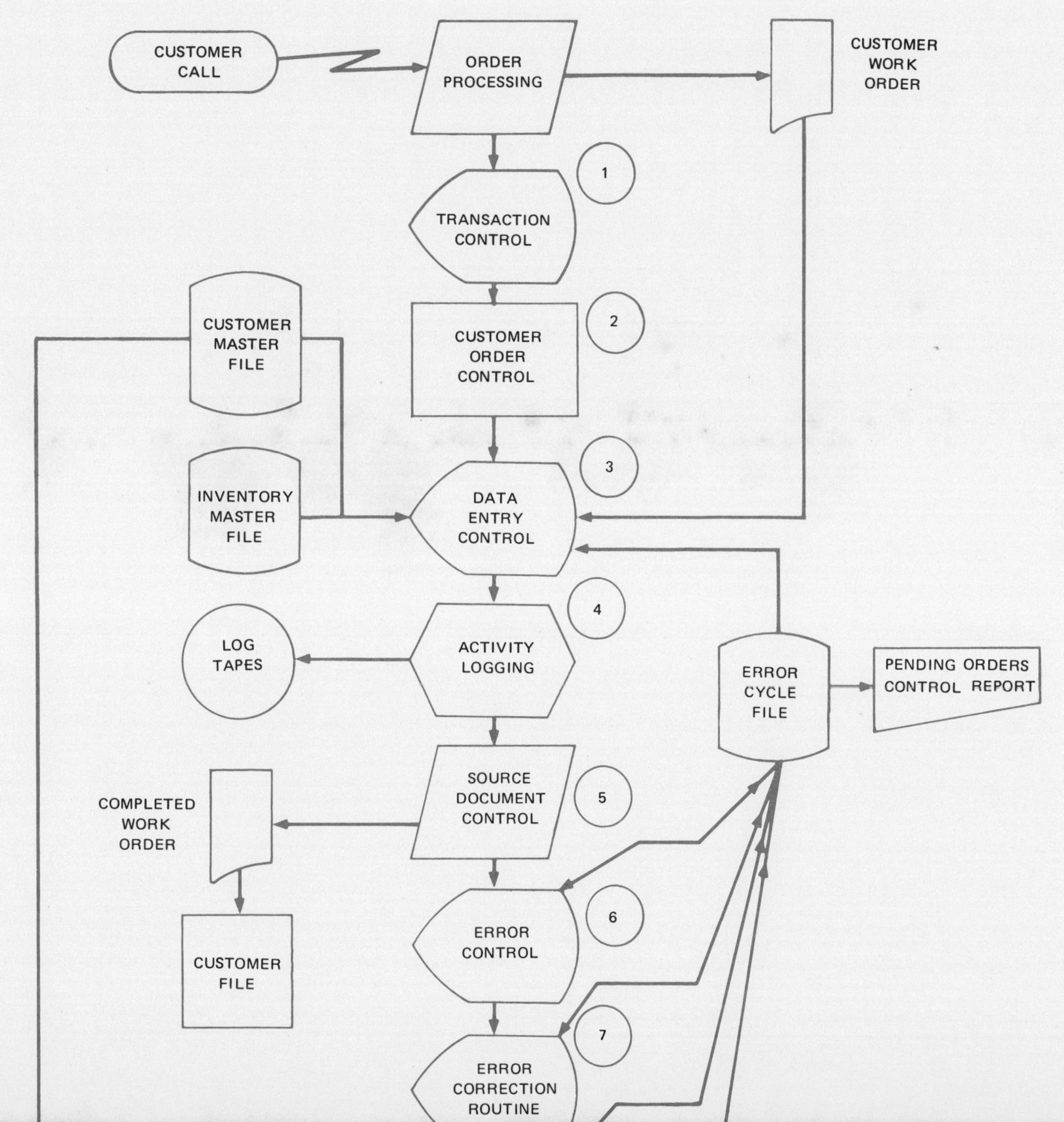
CUSTOMER CALL
ORDER PROCESSING
CUSTOMER WORK ORDER
1
TRANSACTION CONTROL
2
CUSTOMER ORDER CONTROL
CUSTOMER MASTER FILE
INVENTORY MASTER FILE
3
DATA ENTRY CONTROL
4
ACTIVITY LOGGING
LOG TAPES
ERROR CYCLE FILE
PENDING ORDERS CONTROL REPORT
5
SOURCE DOCUMENT CONTROL
COMPLETED WORK ORDER
CUSTOMER FILE
6
ERROR CONTROL
7
ERROR CORRECTION ROUTINE

justment) processed through the order entry system during the daily processing. Each inventory item record reflects the on-hand balance of the item prior to the transaction, the quantity of the transaction, the new on-hand inventory balance, and the invoice number of the transaction. The Transaction File data are maintained for at least seven years and are retrieved by the Internal Auditing Department when reviewing inventory activity related to a customer's shipment.

At the close of each business day, the order entry system prepares a draft of the customer invoices. The invoices are then forwarded to the Billing Department. The billing data include all customer shipping information, customer number, order number, items shipped, quantity shipped, and so on.

Control Point 13 — Invoice Data Control

For control purposes, the order entry system also prepares two summary control totals for the Billing Department. One total indicates the total number of invoices forwarded, and the other is a total of all the items shipped. Upon receipt of the invoices, the Billing Department counts the invoices and prepares an adding machine tape to verify the quantity shipped and to ensure that invoice data have been forwarded. If there is a discrepancy, the Billing Department contacts the Data Processing Department and the differences are reconciled. As required, new draft invoices are prepared. The preparation of the actual customer invoices is accomplished by the organization's billing application system.

At the close of each business day, the order entry system prepares a daily Warehouse Control Report for Warehouse Administration management. Each warehouse location is separately listed on this report, showing total warehouse inventory, inventory in-transit, inventory adjustments, orders shipped, and orders backlogged.

Control Point 14 — System Balancing (Inventory Data)

Daily, the Transaction File is balanced by item, by adding and/or subtracting the days inventory transactions to the previous day's ending balance to determine if the total equals the item's new on-hand balance. If the totals do not balance, then the Transaction File is printed out for the out-of-balance items and the individual transactions are reviewed by the data processing systems personnel to determine the error in systems processing and to initiate the appropriate adjustment. In addition, the Transaction File is sorted into items within location sequence and is processed against the Warehouse Location Inventory Status File. The ending on-hand balance for an item on the Transaction File should balance to the on-hand balance on the Warehouse Location Inventory Status File. If these balances agree, then it has been verified that all items identified as having been shipped from a warehouse have, in fact, been deducted from the on-hand inventory for that warehouse on the Warehouse Location Inventory Status File. If the two files do not balance, then the Transaction File is printed out and reviewed as above. A Warehouse Control Report is prepared as a by-product of the system balancing procedure. This report is forwarded to the Warehouse Administration group at the headquarters location, where it is reviewed as a control report to monitor overall daily warehouse activity and to reflect overall inventory status.

Control Point 15 — System Balancing (Order Data)

Also, daily the Open Invoice File and the Back-Order File are balanced by warehouse location for total units added to those files during the day's order entry processing, with the total units, by warehouse, that were entered into the order entry system that day. This balancing ensures that all valid order entry items that entered the order entry system have been accounted for, either as shipment items or as a back-ordered item. Again, if the files do not balance, the data processing system personnel review a listing of the items within the warehouse that are out of balance to determine the processing error and initiate the appropriate adjustment.

Table 14-1 cross-references the 15 control points in this control illustration to the Application System Controls (Chapters 5-10) and the respective Control Areas within those chapters.

partment. The credit limitation check is performed by calculating the value of this order and adding it to the sum of the customer's unpaid invoices. The new sum is then compared to the established credit limit. Should the customer's credit limitation check fail, then the entire customer order is recorded on the Error Cycle File (in a credit suspense category) and the regional credit location management is notified by terminal output that this customer order is being held in suspense. The terminal output includes customer name, credit terms, unpaid invoices dollar value, and current order dollar value.

To release a customer order that has been held in the Error Cycle File for credit limitation approval, the data entry operator at the order processing location must first receive authorization from the regional credit manager. The data entry operator then requests a display of the suspended order by referencing the order control number. The operator then enters on the terminal a credit authorization override code that deletes the order from the Error Cycle File and releases the customer order data for normal processing by the order entry systems.

Control Point 9 — Credit Authorization

The credit manager at the regional credit location must phone or wire the order processing location with approval to proceed with the processing of a customer order that has exceeded the customer's credit limitation. As a further control of this authorization procedure, a terminal printout is prepared daily for the regional credit managers and corporate headquarters, indicating all the previous day's credit approvals, as well as a list of all customer orders and order dates still being held pending credit authorization. These reports are reviewed by regional and corporate credit management to ensure that timely credit reviews are being initiated by the regional credit managers.

The next step in the order entry processing cycle is for the system to check the inventory status of the items on the customer's order to determine if sufficient quantity is on hand to fill the order. For those customer order items that have inventory on hand, the shipping weight for the items is calculated by the system, and a customer invoice number is automatically assigned by the computer. At this time, a set of packing and shipping papers is transmitted to a hard-copy terminal at the warehouse location. All the customer and shipment data included on the shipping papers are also updated on an Open Invoice File by invoice number.

Control Point 10 — Inventory Status Control

The order entry system checks the Warehouse Location Inventory Status File to determine if the items are available, and if so, to reserve the items and reduce the available inventory for subsequent orders. If there is insufficient quantity of an item, the customer's coded instructions are checked to determine whether this customer desires unfilled quantities to be back ordered or whether the unfilled quantity is to be cancelled.

If the out-of-stock items are to be back ordered, a Back-Order File is updated with the customer's order reference data, the back-ordered item(s), and the quantities.

Control Point 11 — Back-Order Control

A back-control number is assigned by the system to the items back ordered on the customer's order. The back-order control number, customer number, order control number, items, and quantities are also printed on the terminal at the order processing location. This is the customer's order representative's notification that all items ordered were not shipped, but were back ordered. The order representatives are responsible for releasing items from the Back-Order File. They do this by assigning inventory from another warehouse location that is under their control or by ultimately applying inventory from the original warehouse once that warehouse's inventory has been replenished.

After the warehouse personnel have shipped the items identified on the packing papers, a warehouse terminal operator transmits to the order entry system the invoice number, date shipped, and total quantity of all items shipped on this invoice number.

If there are any discrepancies in the quantity shipped and the quantities originally listed on the packing papers, the warehouse terminal operator also transmits the item number and quantity shipped for the item that was under- or overshipped.

Control Point 12 — Order Shipment Control

The Warehouse Location Inventory Status File is updated for the items shipped. For each item, the quantity shipped, which is the ordered quantity unless otherwise indicated by the terminal operator, is subtracted from the inventory on-hand balance; then the open order balance and the shipped-to-date balance are updated by the quantity shipped. The items and quantities shipped are also recorded on a Transaction File. The Transaction File consists of a record for every item that has had an inventory transaction (i.e., shipment, inventory receipt, or inventory ad-

Table 14-1
SUMMARY OF ORDER ENTRY CONTROL PRACTICES

Control Point	Description	Application System Control Phase	Control	Chapter Reference
1	Transaction Control	Transaction Entry	Data access matrix	6
2	Customer Order Control	Computer Processing	Transaction codes	8
3	Data Entry Control	Transaction Entry	Editing and validation routines	6
4	Activity Logging	Data Communications	Log input/output messages	7
5	Source Document Control	Transaction Origination	File of source documents	5
6	Error Control	Computer Processing	Error reporting	8
7	Error Correction Routine	Computer Processing	Error serial number or error suspense reentry	8
8	Credit Check	Computer Processing	Anticipation control	8
9	Credit Authorization	Transaction Origination or Output Processing	Evidence of approval output activity review	5/10
10	Inventory Status Control	Computer Processing or Transaction Entry	Anticipation control edit and validating	8/6
11	Back-Order Control	Computer Processing	Transaction codes	8
12	Order Shipment Control	Computer Processing	Masterfile access	8
13	Invoice Data Control	Output Processing	Manual output balance	10
14	System Balancing (Inventory Data)	Output Processing	Reconciliation	10
15	System Balancing (Order Data)	Data Storage and Retrieval or Output Processing	Before and after look or reconciliation	9/10

Chapter 15

INVENTORY MANAGEMENT CONTROL ILLUSTRATION

APPLICATION OVERVIEW

The basic objective of an inventory management system is to assist corporate management to maintain a level of inventory that achieves the optimum balance between on-order, on-hand, and out-of-stock. The inventory management system reviewed in this chapter is described as follows:

> The engineering department inputs its requirement into an inventory management system. This information, together with other inventory data, is used to calculate reorder points and quantities. Information files are checked regarding inventory part specification, suppliers, open purchase orders; and purchase orders are prepared for material planner review. Material buyers notify suppliers and the material is ordered. Upon receipt of the ordered material, receiving memos are prepared, the purchase order closed, and the material warehoused. The following control illustration describes in more detail the inventory management system.

BACKGROUND

This control illustration describes an on-line inventory management system that is currently being used by a large manufacturing company. This system, which operates in both an on-line and batch processing mode, has more than 400 terminals in daily operation, and operates on a large-scale computer with a second computer available for backup if necessary. The terminals that are being used are basically typewriter models, although audio response terminals are being used in the material-receiving operation. This inventory management system, in addition to controlling supplier files, purchase order files, and work order files, also controls five inventory data files that consist of four facility inventory files and one surplus inventory file. These inventory files consist of more than 80,000 separate inventory items, and approximately one-fourth of the inventory items are disbursed and received monthly.

The inventory management system and the 25 control points of the system are illustrated in Figure 15-1.

APPLICATION DESCRIPTION AND CONTROL PRACTICES

All the terminals are activated at the beginning of each business day. Those terminals that connect to the inventory management system through a dial-up system use a password sign-on feature, while those terminals that connect to the system through leased lines have no special password sign-on procedures. There is, however, a terminal/transaction matrix resident in the computer that governs the use of these controls.

> *Control Point 1 — Terminal Transaction Control*
>
> *A matrix of approved transaction codes is maintained by the inventory management system. This matrix, prepared by data processing and approved by the Materials Management Department, is checked as each terminal request is made. Those transactions not approved are rejected, and the terminal operator is not allowed access to the inventory management data base files. As a further control, special passwords stored in the matrix are used by those terminals that have approved transactions when changes such as payments and credit codes are being made to certain data elements of the Supplier File. All rejected transactions are recorded on the computer log tape (see Control Point 2).*

All information that is transmitted to and from the inventory management system is recorded on a computer log tape.

> *Control Point 2 — Transmission Log Control*
>
> *The data recorded on the computer log tape are used primarily for terminal statistical reporting. A monthly report is produced by terminal identification number that reflects all transmissions to and from the inventory management system. This report is used by data processing, EDP auditors, and material management personnel to monitor terminal activity and to review unauthorized attempts at terminal usage. Special reports may be requested from the computer log tape.*

All information that is to be processed by the inventory management system is first edited or validated by a generalized validation system that is used for all on-line application processing.

> *Control Point 3 — Data Validation Control*
>
> *Edit routines have been developed in a validation application system that is generalized for all*

the organization's on-line application systems. This validation system performs checks on all input transactions. Some of the data validation routines include verification that the number of input characters does not exceed the number allowed, check digit calculation, mandatory presence of a data element, and calendar data edit. Once an error is detected in a data element, no further checking on that data element is performed. However, editing on other data elements of the input transaction continue until all data elements have been checked or until a third data element in error is detected, at which time the input transaction is immediately rejected. After the data being entered by the terminal operator have been validated, the transaction is recorded on the generalized validation system log tape (see Control Point 5) and the transaction is then passed to the appropriate application system for processing, in this instance the inventory management system. Input transactions that are rejected are reentered by the terminal operator after corrections have been made by the department preparing the input. Rejected transactions are not recorded on the generalized validation system log tape as this log tape may be used for system recovery purposes.

Control Point 4 — Validation Parameter Control
The parameters within the generalized validation system can be changed as necessary to accommodate the validation requirements of an application. Changes to the parameters are made via a memo signed by the departmental manager responsible for the application system. A copy of this change memo is filed in the data processing department and is periodically reviewed by the EDP auditors.

Control Point 5 — Validation Log Control
The data recorded on the computer tape of the generalized validation system are used primarily for file recovery. Special reports are printed from this log tape when, as an example, the EDP auditors are reviewing validation parameter changes. The tape as a rule, however, is printed only when difficulties are being experienced in file recovery. All transactions that enter the inventory management system via batch processing are kept on magnetic tape. These tapes, which contain only valid transactions, are retained for three inventory management system update cycles. When it is necessary to restore the data files, these tapes are merged with the computer log tape of the generalized validation system. The tapes are not printed routinely but only when difficulties are encountered in file restoration.

When an engineering change has to be made to a product, an engineering blueprint is reviewed by a parts requirement analyst who prepares a parts requirements form for those sections of the engineering blueprint where parts will be required. The parts requirement form is given to a terminal operator for entry into the system. After the terminal operator enters the data, the part requirement form is filed by engineering drawing number.

Control Point 6 — Source Document Control
The parts requirement form that contains the engineering drawing number is filed by that number in a temporary file at the terminal operator's station, where it is used for correcting any data errors or answering part requirement questions as they relate to the drawing.

The part requirement transaction, after having been edited by the generalized validation program, is then processed by the inventory management system. The Work Order File, which is maintained and controlled by the Finance Department, is interrogated. The Schedule Assignment File, which is maintained and controlled by the Manufacturing Department, is also interrogated.

Control Point 7 — File Check
The Work Order File is checked to obtain the contract number and to validate the account number against which the items required will be charged. If neither the correct record on the file nor the account number can be verified, the input transaction is rejected (see Control Point 8). The Schedule Assignment File is checked to obtain the "need" date for the part. This data element is required as it is basic data input to ordering and stocking calculations of the inventory master update program. If the appropriate master record cannot be located on the Schedule Assignment File, the part requirement transaction will be rejected (see Control Point 8).

Control Point 8 — Input Error Control
All on-line input transactions that are rejected by the inventory management system are transmitted immediately to the inputting terminal, where the hard-copy printout of the transaction and the reason for rejection are attached to the source document (part requirement form) and returned to the originating department for correction and resubmission. The managers of the departments inputting data to the inventory

management system have the responsibility to ensure that all transactions that are rejected are corrected and resubmitted.

The next step in the inventory management system is the exploding of the part requirements into component or item inventory requirements. These requirements are held on magnetic tape for the next processing of the inventory control segment of the inventory management system. The item inventory requirements that will be processed weekly and in a batch mode will be checked against a Part Name and Specifications File.

Control Point 9 — Part Name/Specification Control
Each component or inventory item that resulted from the parts requirement explosion is checked against a Part Name and Specification File. If the item is not a new inventory item, it is only validated against the file. Any item that cannot be found on this file is printed on an error report and recorded on an error cycle file (see Control Point 10). The weekly error report that reflects the input transaction (after the parts explosion) and the reason for rejection is sent to the originating department for correction and resubmission.

Control Point 10 — Specification Error Correction Control
Most of the input transactions that are rejected are new inventory items that are input to the system as transactions prior to the updating of the Part Name and Specification File. The Error Cycle File is merged with weekly input transactions for reprocessing. If the transaction is rejected again, it is reported on a weekly error report, which is sent to a material planner and again recorded on the error file a maximum of six times, when it will be dropped. All transactions to be dropped are so noted on the weekly error report. A transaction on the Error Cycle File may be erased prior to the sixth cycle by the material planner entering a void transaction as part of the regular weekly update.

The data from the parts requirements explosion, as well as inventory adjustment and disbursement transactions, are processed by the Inventory Control Master Update Program. The Master Update Program contains all the formulae that have been developed to control the timing and quantity of stocking levels, replenishments, and stock locations of inventory items. The input transactions to the Inventory Control Master Update Program are checked against the Purchase Order File and the Facility Inventory Part Files. When the Inventory Control Master Update Program determines that inventory items are required, purchase records are created on the Purchase Order File and "to-be-ordered" quantities of the Inventory Parts Records are updated.

Control Point 11 — Inventory Update Master Check
The input transactions are checked against the Purchase Order File, to obtain status information regarding any open purchase orders for each inventory item that is required. This status information will later be printed on the Purchase Request to assist the material planner in controlling stocking levels and the buyer in placing the purchase order.

The input transactions are also checked against the Facility Inventory Files to validate the inventory part number and also to ensure that the amount of inventory to be disbursed does not exceed the allowed quantity to disburse. All transactions that are rejected because of invalid part numbers or disbursement quantity problems are printed on an error report, which is sent to the originating department for correction and resubmission. The error is also recorded on an Inventory Parts Error File.

Control Point 12 — Inventory Parts Error Control
The Inventory Parts Error File operates in the same manner as the Error Cycle File discussed earlier (see Control Point 10). The exception is that the transactions in error will not be eliminated after six processing cycles. Positive action, namely the inputting by the material planner of a transaction to erase the erroneous transaction, is the only way to eliminate an error transaction from the Error Cycle File.

A material position report together with purchase request forms are prepared by the inventory management system for the material planner's review.

Control Point 13 — Material Status Control
The material position report reflects the quantity on hand, quantity on order, and quantity to be disbursed for each item of inventory to be ordered. The material planner, in reviewing the report, may increase or decrease the quantity to be ordered. The material planner may even cancel the purchase request completely. When a purchase request is cancelled, the material planner stamps the request cancelled, initials it, and submits it to a terminal operator for entry to the inventory management system. The purchase request record on the Purchase Order File is erased and the "to-be-ordered" quantity of the Inventory Parts Record is reduced by the

quantity on the erased purchase request record. When the decision is made to increase or decrease the quantity to be ordered, the Inventory Parts Record is changed accordingly and the purchase request record on the Purchase Order File is also changed.

Control Point 14 — Purchase Request Number Control

When a purchase request is printed, the computer generates a purchase request number to eliminate the possibility of duplicate purchase request numbers being assigned to potential purchase orders. This request number, which is an eight-digit number, includes coding that identifies the department requesting the materials. This tie-back to the requesting department serves as a means of tracing a purchase request if something delays it in the purchasing order cycle. Manually prepared purchase requests are prenumbered forms, with the area for the requesting department number left blank. The department number is entered by the requesting department when the purchase request is completed. Purchase requests are prepared manually only when the requirement for an inventory item is such that the material planner cannot wait for the weekly processing of the Inventory Control Update program that prints the purchase requests. Manually prepared requests are entered via the terminal operator and the data are validated as discussed in Control Points 7, 8, 9, and 11. All errors detected are transmitted to the input terminal where they are corrected by the material planner and resubmitted.

When the material planner approves a purchase request, the request is stamped "approved" and initialed by the material planner. It is then submitted to a material buyer.

Control Point 15 — Purchase Request Authorization Control

The purchase request must be stamped "approved" and initialed before any material buyer action can take place. If the purchase request is not stamped, it is rejected by the buyer. Computer prepared purchase requests are sent to the material planning supervisor, where they are investigated and resubmitted for buyer action if appropriate. Manually prepared purchase requests that are not stamped "approved" are returned to the manager of the requesting department for investigation and resubmitted for buyer action if later approved by a material planner.

The material buyer, when processing a purchase request, prefixes the purchase request number with his two-digit buyer code.

Control Point 16 — Material Buyer Control

Each material buyer has a two-digit buyer code that is prefixed to the purchase request number. This code is entered into the computer by the terminal operator and becomes an integral part of the purchase request number. The buyer code serves as a means of tracing purchase orders and also as a means of monitoring and evaluating the performance of a buyer.

Before the buyer contacts the material supplier and obtains the purchase terms and conditions, the supplier information on record is checked in the inventory management system.

Control Point 17 — Material Supplier Control

The Material Supplier File is checked via a terminal located in the purchasing department to verify that the supplier is approved. If the supplier is not considered an approved supplier, because of such things as poor material quality or late deliveries, then another supplier's record is reviewed. If no other supplier is on the Supplier File, then the buyer notifies his supervisor and the purchase request is held until an approved supplier can be located.

When an approved material supplier is contacted and the purchasing terms and conditions are obtained, they are entered by the terminal operator into the inventory management system and recorded on the Purchase Order File.

Control Point 18 — Supplier Terms and Conditions Control

The final value of the purchase order, if it is more than a predetermined amount (this amount may vary by project), is reviewed by the buyer supervisor, who has the authority to cancel the order if he deems it appropriate. If the order is cancelled, then the terms and conditions recorded on the Purchase Order File are erased through the terminal by the terminal operator and another supplier is located. The purchase request, which is now considered an order, is further checked by representatives from product assurance and packaging. Any disagreements are resolved by the manager of the department requesting the materials.

When the ordered material arrives at the plant receiving dock, it is counted by a representative of the material inspection department.

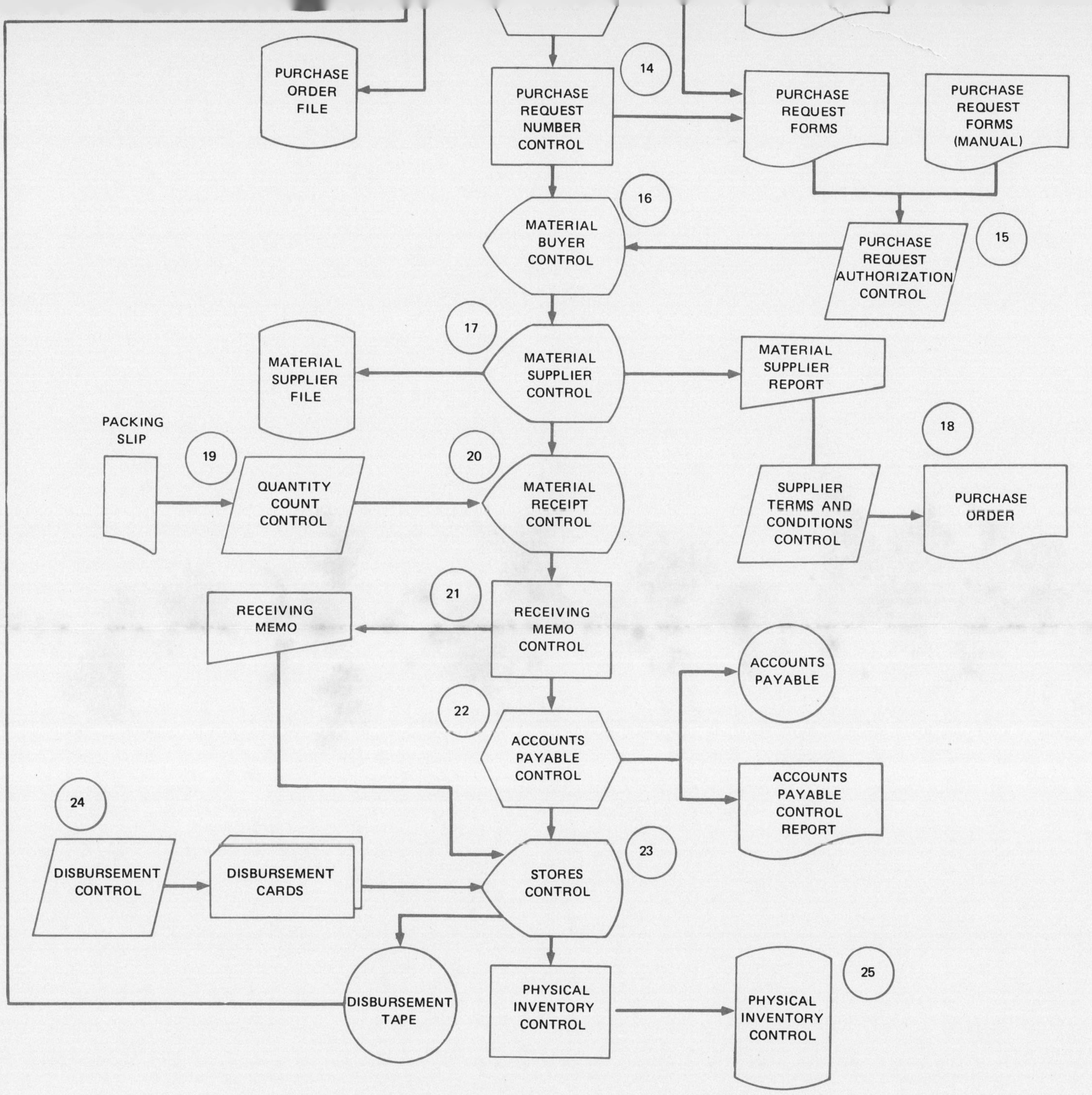

FIGURE 15-1 INVENTORY MANAGEMENT FLOWCHART

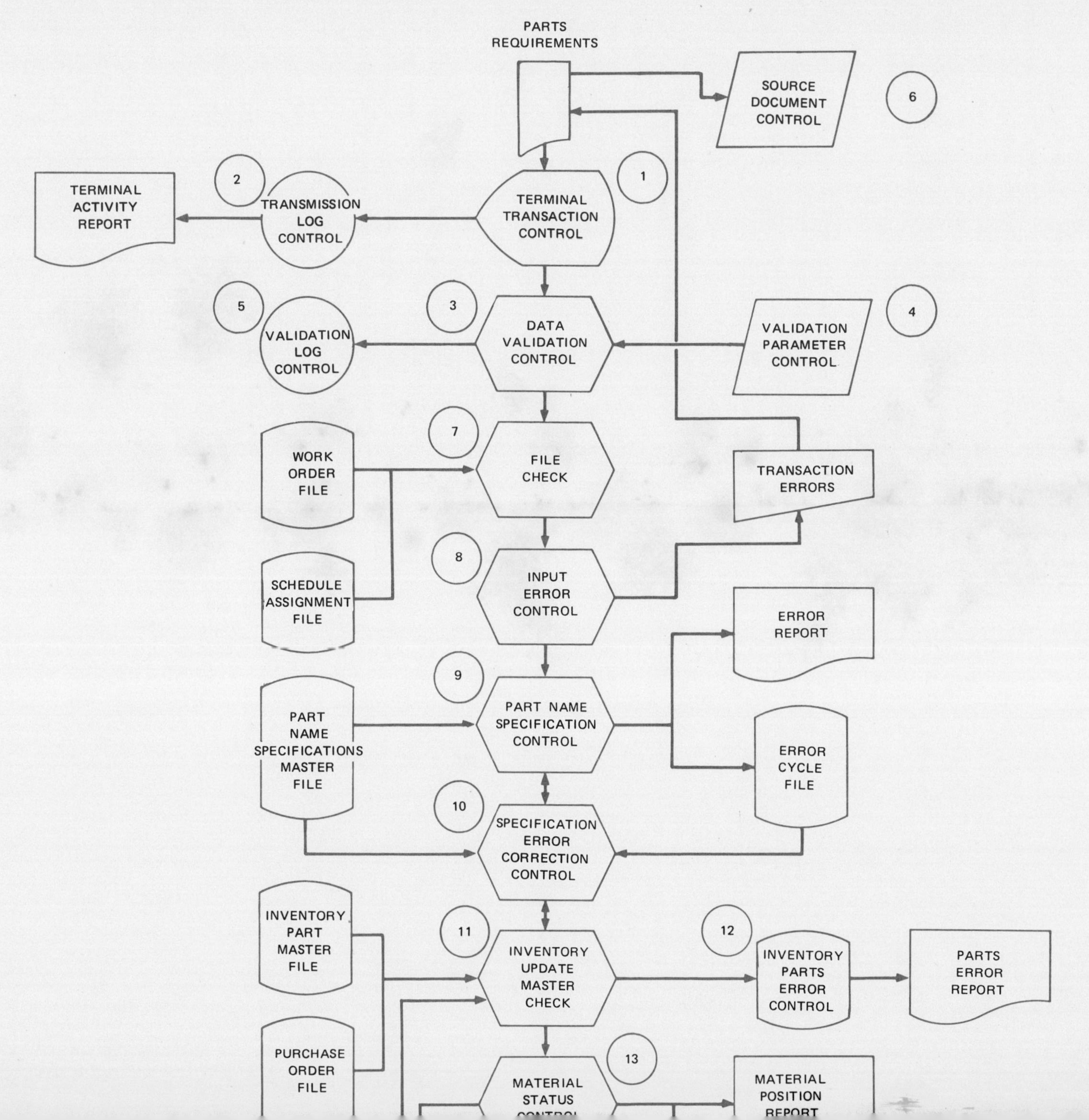
PARTS REQUIREMENTS
SOURCE DOCUMENT CONTROL
6
1
TERMINAL TRANSACTION CONTROL
2
TRANSMISSION LOG CONTROL
TERMINAL ACTIVITY REPORT
3
DATA VALIDATION CONTROL
4
VALIDATION PARAMETER CONTROL
5
VALIDATION LOG CONTROL
7
WORK ORDER FILE
FILE CHECK
TRANSACTION ERRORS
8
SCHEDULE ASSIGNMENT FILE
INPUT ERROR CONTROL
ERROR REPORT
9
PART NAME SPECIFICATIONS MASTER FILE
PART NAME SPECIFICATION CONTROL
ERROR CYCLE FILE
10
SPECIFICATION ERROR CORRECTION CONTROL
INVENTORY PART MASTER FILE
11
INVENTORY UPDATE MASTER CHECK
12
INVENTORY PARTS ERROR CONTROL
PARTS ERROR REPORT
PURCHASE ORDER FILE
13
MATERIAL STATUS
MATERIAL POSITION

Control Point 19 — Quantity Count Control

The material is counted and compared to quantity count on the attached vendor-supplied packing slip. If the count does not agree with the packing slip, the material inspection department manager is notified and the material is impounded until the quantity difference is resolved. Resolution usually results in the supplier authorizing the material inspection department manager to change the packing slip count to agree with the actual count.

When the actual quantity and packing slip quantity agree, the packing slip is submitted to a terminal operator in the material inspection department for entry into the inventory management system.

Control Point 20 — Material Receipt Control

The terminal operator enters the packing slip number, the purchase order number (from the packing slip), and the quantity received. If there is no match against the Purchase Order File, the packing slip and the material are held for a maximum of two days. The terminal operator reenters the information several more times in the two-day period. This mismatch is often caused by material being expedited before computer records can be updated. Failure to match the material data to the Purchase Order File within two days results in the buyer supervisor being notified by the material inspection department manager, and the matter is investigated. If the difference is a mismatch in terms of over or under shipment as compared to the quantity ordered on the purchase order, or if the arrival date is significantly different from that reflected on the purchase order, the following occurs:

If the material received arrives more than 30 days ahead of schedule, the material investigation group must be advised and a decision made as to whether to return the material or to impound it until such time as it is needed. If the material received is overshipped by 5% or $50, the material investigation group must be advised. If the overshipped material is accepted, then the requesting department must increase the purchase order request quantity to agree with the shipped quantity and these data must be recorded on the Purchase Order File. If the material is undershipped, usually by 5% or $50, and the purchase order is not being closed out (finalized), the shipment is accepted. If, however, there is an undershipment and the purchase order is being closed out, a special change order must be prepared by the material planner and recorded on the Purchase Order File. The purpose of this control point is to record the fact that the ordered material has arrived, but because of discrepancies is being held.

When the material is considered acceptable (shipped quantity equals ordered quantity and receiving date is within 30 days of requested date), a computer-generated receiving memo is prepared on the hard-copy terminal at the receiving location.

Control Point 21 — Receiving Memo Control

A receiving memo with a computer-generated control number is printed and attached to the material. The control number, which consists of eight digits including a check digit calculated using the modulus 10 weighted formula, is recorded on the purchase order record indicating that the material has been received and is currently located in the material inspection department.

When the receiving memo is printed by the inventory management system, an accounts payable transaction tape is generated for accounts payable application system processing.

Control Point 22 — Accounts Payable Control

In addition to supplying a tape for processing, an audit trail report of all transactions is prepared. This audit trail report, which reflects vendor name, purchase order number, and amount due, is reviewed by the personnel of the accounts payable department, as the policy at the organization interviewed is that all procurements under $5,000 are paid automatically. This represents 90% of all procurements. If, however, the value of the purchase order is over $5,000, then an accounts payable check is not issued, and the supplier will not receive payment until such time as an invoice is submitted.

When the material arrives at the stores location, the stores attendant, via an audio response terminal, enters the receiving memo control number from the receiving memo that is attached to the material.

Control Point 23 — Stores Control

When the receiving memo control number is entered into the inventory management system, the check digit is calculated and if there is an error, the audio response terminal responds, indicating an incorrect receiving memo control number. After several unsuccessful attempts have been made, stores management advises the data processing department, since a control number reject at this point is indicative of a software problem. When the control number is successfully entered, the quantity data from the

Table 15-1
SUMMARY OF INVENTORY MANAGEMENT CONTROL PRACTICES

Control Point	Description	Application System Control Phase	Control	Chapter Reference
1	Terminal Transaction Control	Data Communications	Security table	7
2	Transmission Log Control	Data Communications	Log input/output messages	7
3	Data Validation Control	Transaction Entry	Editing and validating routines	6
4	Validation Parameter Control	Transaction Entry	Editing and validating routines	6
5	Validation Log Control	Data Communications	Log input/output messages	7
6	Source Document Control	Transaction Origination	File of source documents	5
7	File Check	Transaction Entry	Editing and validating routines	6
8	Input Error Control	Transaction Entry	Error message	6
9	Part Name/Specification Control	Transaction Entry	Editing and validating routine and error message	6
10	Specification Error Control	Transaction Entry	Error message	6
11	Inventory Update Master Check	Transaction Entry	Editing and validating routines and error message	6
12	Inventory Parts Error Control	Transaction Entry	Error message	6
13	Material Status Control	Output Processing		10
14	Purchase Request Number Control	Transaction Origination	Sequential numbers	5
15	Purchase Request Authorization Control	Transaction Origination	Signatures	5
16	Material Buyer Control	Transaction Origination	Input preparation	5
17	Material Supplier Control	Transaction Entry	Editing and validating routines	6
18	Supplier Terms and Conditions Control	Output Processing		10
19	Quantity Count Control	Transaction Entry	Proof and balancing methods	6
20	Material Receipt Control	Transaction Entry	Editing and validating routine	6
21	Receiving Memo Control	Transaction Origination	Sequential numbers	5
22	Accounts Payable Control	Output Processing		10
23	Stores Control	Transaction Entry	Editing and validating routines	6
24	Disbursement Control	Transaction Origination	Signatures	5
25	Physical Inventory Control	Output Processing	User balancing and reconciling	10

Purchase Order File are entered on the Inventory Parts Record. The purchase order record on the Purchase Order File is retained for historical purposes and after approximately 12 months will be recorded on microfilm.

When inventory items are going to be disbursed from stores, disbursement cards that reflect part number, "need" date, unit of issue, issue quantity, and work order number are reviewed by the material planner.

Control Point 24 — Disbursement Control

The material planner must authorize inventory disbursement. The stores keeper is not allowed to disburse any inventory item without a disbursement card signed by the material planner.

When parts are disbursed from stores, the approved disbursement cards are transmitted via the card-reading terminal located in the stores area to the inventory management system. The disbursement information is stored on tape for weekly processing of the Inventory Control Master Update Program (see Control Point 11).

A physical inventory is taken on a cycle basis over at least a year. High-value parts, such as microelectronic parts, are counted more frequently. The inventory management system generates a card containing the part number, part description, and unit of issue when a physical inventory is to be taken.

Control Point 25 — Physical Inventory Control

The actual item count is entered on the card and is processed by the inventory management system. The actual count is compared to the "quantity-on-hand" count in the Inventory Parts Master and a report of exceptions is produced for the Material Management and Finance Departments. If the exception value is $200 or less, the "quantity-on-hand" count of the Inventory Parts Master is adjusted and the part dollar value is written off by the Finance Department. If the exception value is more than $200, then a part recount is ordered. If the exception still exists after the recount, the Material Management Department will review every transaction pertaining to that particular part since the last physical count. When the discrepancy has been resolved, the Inventory Parts Master is adjusted.

Table 15-1 cross-references the 25 control points in this control illustration to the application system controls (Chapters 5-10) and the control areas within those chapters.

Chapter 16

POINT OF SALE CONTROL ILLUSTRATION

APPLICATION OVERVIEW

There are many facets to a point of sale system and the system itself varies considerably according to the type of business in which it is being used. The system reviewed in this chapter is described as follows:

> A customer, with the merchandise to be purchased, approaches a salesperson who is operating a point of sale terminal. Sales tickets attached to the merchandise contain coded information that identifies the merchandise, the sales department, and the merchandise price. This information is entered into the point of sale terminal by the salesperson manually or, in some cases, through the use of a wand that reads the bar-encoded information. The information is transmitted to a central computer where credit approvals are obtained, inventory data are collected for later processing, and sales reports and customer billings are prepared.

BACKGROUND

The following control illustration describes an on-line credit approval application that is being used by a large retailing corporation. The Point of Sale (POS) system uses in its credit approval operation more than 900 cash register/POS terminals. These POS terminals, of which approximately 675 are equipped with wand readers for reading bar-encoded merchandise data, are connected to concentrators located in each of the 26 stores. Thirteen high-speed leased lines connect the concentrators to two minicomputers located at the computer center at corporate headquarters. The minicomputers perform primarily in a data collection mode that captures POS terminal activity for nighttime processing of customer accounts on a large-scale computer. The minicomputers also perform as message switching computers, by routing all credit approval transactions to the large-scale computer for immediate processing. The POS system on an average day processes more than 65,000 transactions, of which approximately three-fourths are credit approval transactions. There are 13 control points in this POS/credit approval system. The control points and the POS/credit approval system itself are illustrated in Figure 16-1.

APPLICATION DESCRIPTION AND CONTROL PRACTICES

All the POS terminals are activated at the beginning of each business day. To activate the system at each store, the local store manager or one of his assistants turns on the power system to the terminals.

> *Control Point 1 — Terminal Power Control*
>
> *The power switch for activating the terminals of a store is in a locked box in a locked room. The local store manager, or one of his assistants, must activate the system at the beginning of each business day. Any attempt to operate a POS terminal prior to its being activated results in the sounding of an alarm at the terminal. The local store security personnel immediately respond and investigate the cause of the alarm. After the system is activated, the power room and box are relocked and the room is not entered again until it is time to deactivate the system.*

To activate a point of sale terminal, the salesperson must insert a special key.

> *Control Point 2 — Terminal Access Control*
>
> *Each salesperson has two keys for accessing and operating the POS terminal. Failure to insert the first key, which activates the terminal, results in the POS terminal being totally inoperable. The second key, which locks and unlocks the cash drawer, cannot be used unless the terminal has been activated. Distribution and control of the terminal keys are the responsibility of the department manager.*

All merchandise tickets are printed with bar-encoded information at a central location. This information, which consists of codes to identify the merchandise, merchandise price, sales department, and stock-keeping unit, is also printed on the merchandise tickets in a non-bar-encoded form. This is to allow data entry by salespersons operating POS terminals not equipped with wand readers. When a person making a purchase elects to charge his account, the salesperson enters the sales function code, salesperson operator number, and the customer's account number, which is obtained from the customer's charge card or after contacting the local store's credit office.

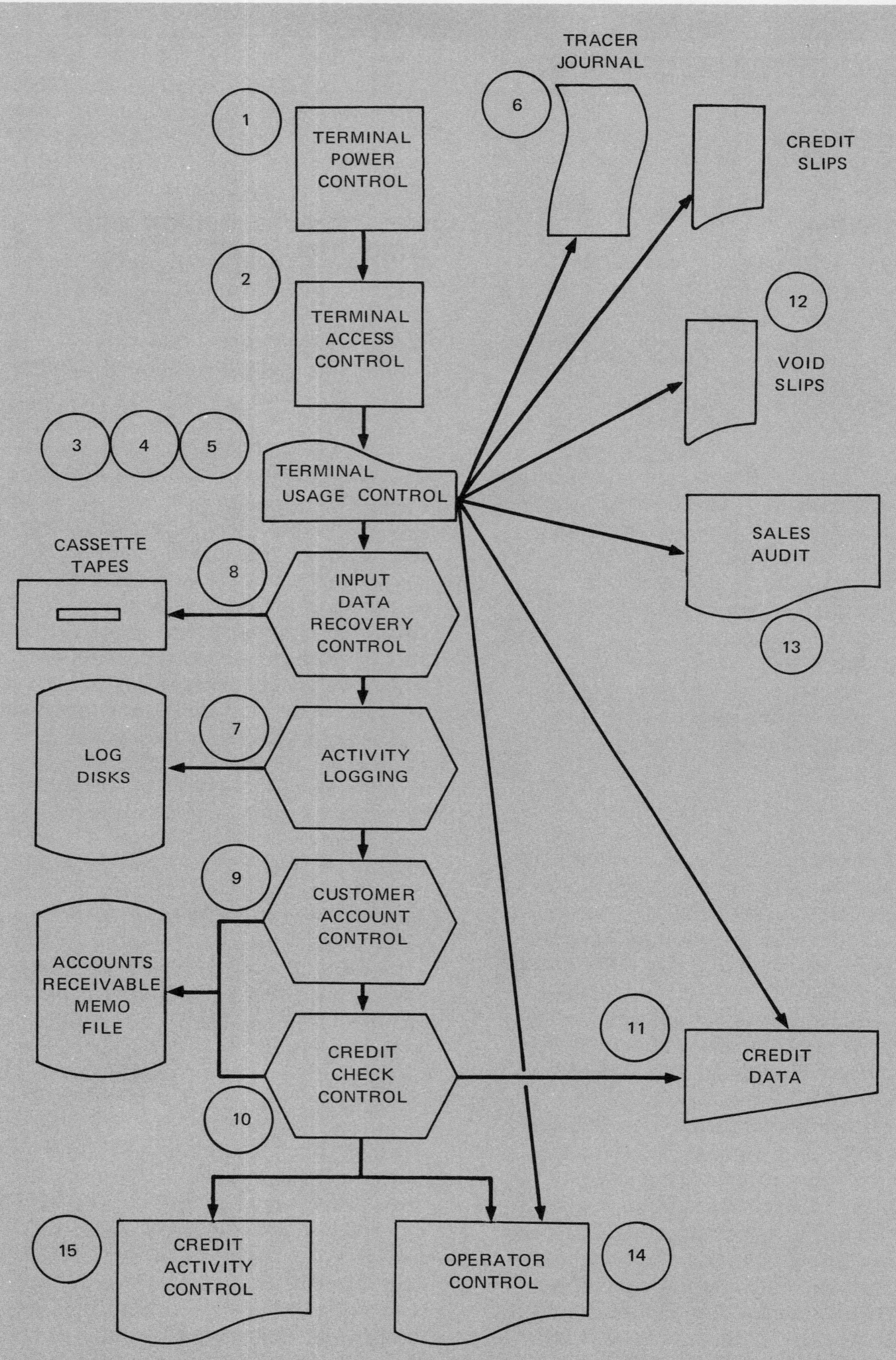

FIGURE 16-1 POINT OF SALE FLOWCHART

Control Point 3 — Function Control

A one-digit code, representing the type of terminal operation that is going to be performed, such as cash sale, refund, or no sale, must be entered as the first item of terminal information. Failure to enter this code results in the POS terminal flashing the word "Function." If the function code is not entered within approximately 10 seconds, an alarm at the terminal sounds and the department manager investigates the cause of the alarm.

Control Point 4 — Salesperson Number Control

Each operation of the POS terminal requires the entry of the salesperson number. Failure to enter the salesperson number results in the POS terminal flashing the word "Number." If the salesperson number is not entered within approximately 10 seconds, an alarm at the terminal sounds and the department manager investigates.

Control Point 5 — Customer Account Number Control

The customer account number is a nine-digit number that includes a check digit calculated using the modulus 10 weighted formula. Each time the account number is entered, the check digit is calculated. If the system will not accept the account number, the words "account number" are flashed on the POS terminal, and the terminal operator enters the account number again. Failure to enter the account number within approximately 10 seconds results in the sounding of an alarm at the terminal, and the department manager investigates. After several unsuccessful attempts to enter the customer account number, the salesperson cancels the transaction by depressing the Error Correct and Total keys and calls the central credit office. The central credit office advises the salesperson to keep the charge card, in the case of a stolen card, while at the same time advising local store security personnel. The central credit office may, however, advise the salesperson to keep the charge card and issue a temporary one-day pass in those cases where the old account number is going to be deactivated and a new account number issued. The one-day pass contains the new account number as advised by the central credit office.

At the time the salesperson operates the POS terminal, a tracer tape or journal tape is created in addition to the terminal transaction being recorded on the computer log (see Control Point 7).

Control Point 6 — Tracer Journal/Transaction Control

The POS terminal produces a tracer journal, often referred to as a journal tape, that contains a sequence number, a code that represents the function being performed on the terminal, and the dollar value of the transaction. The sequence number is a series number that is incremented each time the terminal is operated, and the function code is the same code the POS terminal operator enters (see Control Point 3). This tracer tape is collected from each POS terminal at the end of the business day and sent to the Sales Audit Department, in addition to a computer-generated terminal activity report, in balancing cash receipts with sales (see Control Point 13). If an error of less than $10 is uncovered, a record is kept of it and local store security personnel are notified; if there are continued occurrences, an investigation begins. If the error is more than $10, local store security personnel are notified, and there is an immediate investigation.

After the salesperson has entered the customer information and the merchandise information from the merchandise ticket, either by keying the data or by a wand reader, it is transmitted directly to the central computer. All transmissions to and from the central computer and the store POS terminals are recorded on the computer log disk of the large-scale computer. Also recorded on the log disk are POS system status changes, which are primarily the switching of local store processing from one minicomputer to the other.

Control Point 7 — Activity Logging

The computer log is used by the Data Processing Department primarily for researching software and hardware problems. The log disk is not printed routinely but only as required for diagnostic purposes.

Control Point 8 — Input Data Recovery Control

All the POS terminals are linked to the store's concentrator, where two tape cassettes are attached. These cassettes, which are used primarily as data recovery devices, are automatically activated and used only when the data circuits between the store and the central computer fail, or if the central computer itself fails. If there is a communication failure, the salesperson, when attempting to register a credit purchase, is so advised by the display of a communication failure code on the POS terminal. However, the salesperson continues to operate the POS terminals as though no failure has occurred. The credit sale transaction data are recorded on the tape cassette, and no computer credit approvals take place. In this event, all credit purchases above a certain amount (this amount varies by store) require the approval of the central credit office. When communication has been reestablished with the central computer, all the information recorded on the tape cassettes during the communication failure will be processed by the computer at the end of the business day.

When the customer and merchandise data are received at the central computer center, an abbreviated version of the Accounts Receivable Masterfile is interrogated by the credit approval system.

Control Point 9 — Customer Account Control

The abbreviated version of the masterfile, often referred to as a "Memo" file, is copied from the masterfile after each accounts receivable update, which is three times weekly. The memo file, which cannot be updated by transactions, is used rather than the masterfile because of cost considerations in keeping the entire masterfile on-line and the need for rapid inquiry. This file is interrogated first to verify the existence of the customer's account and then to determine credit authorization. The memo file contains customer's name, address, credit limits, outstanding balances, and payment history data. Failure to verify the existence of a customer's account results in the POS terminal flashing the words "Account Number" (see Control Point 5).

After the credit approval application system has verified the existence of the customer's account, the value of the customer's purchase is added to the customer's unpaid balance, and this sum is then compared to the customer's credit limit. If the credit is authorized, a proceed code is transmitted to the POS terminal and the sale is completed. A customer-signed credit sales slip is filed for later POS terminal balancing (see Control Point 13). If credit is not authorized, a code indicating that further credit checking is necessary is transmitted to the POS terminal. A telephone number at the central credit office is also displayed on the POS terminal.

Control Point 10 — Credit Check Control

When the credit restriction code is displayed on the terminal, the salesperson enters this code on the POS terminal and proceeds as if credit were authorized but retains the merchandise. This procedure is only to "free-up" the POS terminal for other use while the salesperson calls the telephone extension at the central credit office that was displayed on the POS terminal. Failure to call the central credit office within approximately 5 minutes after the telephone extension number is displayed on the POS terminal results in local store security personnel being notified by the central credit office, as well as a call being made to the store department where the terminal is located. Security personnel are notified to alert them to a possible physical problem, such as a robbery attempt or an irate customer.

At the same time that the credit restriction code is displayed on the POS terminal at the store, a two-line printout of the customer's account is printed out on a hard-copy terminal located at the central credit office. This printout is used by credit personnel to determine whether or not credit should be authorized and to so advise the salesperson when he calls. If more data than are available on the two-line printout are required, the personnel at the central credit office have available microfiche copies of the Accounts Receivable Masterfile.

Control Point 11 — Credit Data Control

The hard-copy printout of the customer's account has to be signed by the person at the central credit office who decides whether or not credit will be authorized. The credit decision will be based on such factors as the customer's payment history and the amount by which the credit limit is exceeded. These hard-copy printouts are reviewed daily by credit supervisors and the credit department manager to ensure that credit policies are adhered to. The hard-copy report is also used by credit checking personnel to ensure that the salesperson calls the central credit office (see Control Point 10).

If the credit is approved, the person at the central credit office authorizing it gives his name to the salesperson who enters it on the credit sales slip. A copy of the credit sales slip is retained by the salesperson and is forwarded to the Sales Audit Department (see Control Point 13) at the end of the business day. Since the credit sales data were already entered into the POS terminal, the sales transaction is concluded. If, however, credit is not approved, the salesperson notifies the customer and advises him to go to the local store credit office. The salesperson then voids the previously entered credit sale data by using a void sale function code.

Control Point 12 — Void Sale Control

The salesperson enters the sequence number of the credit sale that is printed on the tracer journal at the time the credit sale is entered and before credit is refused. This sequence number is obtained from the tracer journal (see Control Point 6). The salesperson then completes a void sales slip with the same information and forwards it to the Sales Audit Department at the end of the business day. The void sales slips are manually matched by the Sales Audit Department to the tracer journal of the appropriate POS terminal as well as to a computer-generated report of the previous day's void sales. Failure to have this three-way match results in the local store security personnel being notified. Repeat occurrences of this type by a salesperson result in an investigation by the store's security personnel.

At the conclusion of each business day, each store sends to the Sales Audit Department, located at corporate headquarters, the daily sales activity. This information, which is categorized by POS terminal, includes a report of cash receipts, the terminal tracer journal, and all slips relating to void sales, credit sales, and so on.

Control Point 13 — Sales Audit/Terminal Activity Control

The sales activity material, together with a computer-generated report of daily terminal activity, is physically matched and compared by sales audit personnel. Each POS terminal is audited to ensure that the tracer journal agrees with the computer-generated report of terminal activity, and that all void sale slips, credit sale slips, and so on agree with the tracer journal. Any discrepancies are immediately researched and if they cannot be resolved, security personnel are notified (see Control Point 6). The other types of discrepancies are usually failure of the local store to send to the Sales Audit Department all the noncash slips. If a noncash slip is missing and the amount is considerable, store security personnel are notified immediately. If the noncash slips do not arrive at the Sales Audit Department in the following two to three days, store security personnel are notified and the matter is investigated. Sales Audit Department supervisors, the department manager, and the corporate controller routinely review the activities of the Sales Audit Department personnel.

A monthly report of store POS terminal operator activity is sent to the Internal Auditing Department. This report reflects the number of times per day each function code (such as credit sale, no sale) is used and the dollar value by sales function.

Control Point 14 — POS Terminal Operator Control

This report, which reflects summary data of sales activity by each salesperson, is used to monitor salesperson activity. Higher counts than normal on certain function or sales codes, such as "No Sale" and "Refund," result in a review of Sales Audit Department data of that salesperson. Questionable activities result in the notification of store security personnel and the establishment of a salesperson monitoring program.

A daily report of all credit referrals is prepared for the Credit Department manager. This report is a summary report of all credit activity, not a detailed listing of all credit sales that required further credit checking by the central credit office.

Control Point 15 — Credit Activity Control

This report is used by the Credit Department manager to continually monitor the credit limits that have been established by the corporation. The report reflects the number of automatic credit approvals and the dollar amount, as well as those credit sales requiring further credit checking. For the latter category, the report reflects the number of credit sales authorized that are 10% above the credit limit, 20% above the credit limit, and 30% or more above the credit limit. If it is determined that the number of calls for further credit checking is excessive and that most calls result in credit being approved, then credit limits may be increased.

Table 16-1 cross-references the 15 control points in this control illustration to the Application System Controls (Chapters 5-10) and the Control Areas within those chapters.

Table 16-1 is found on the next page.

Table 16-1
SUMMARY OF POINT OF SALE CONTROL PRACTICES

Control Point	Description	Application System Control Phase	Control	Chapter Reference
1	Terminal Power Control	Transaction Entry	Terminal sign-on	6
2	Terminal Access Control	Transaction Entry	Security of data entry terminals	6
3	Function Control	Transaction Entry	Editing and validating routines	6
4	Salesperson Number Control	Transaction Entry	Passwords	6
5	Customer Account Number Control	Transaction Entry	Editing and validating routines	6
6	Tracer Journal/ Transaction Control	Transaction Entry	Logging	6
7	Activity Logging	Computer Processing or Data Communications	Data base activity log or message sequence number	8/7
8	Input Data Recovery Control	Data Communication	Log input/output messages	7
9	Customer Account Control	Transaction Entry	Editing and validating routines	6
10	Credit Check Control	Computer Processing or Transaction Entry	Anticipation control Edit evaluating	8/6
11	Credit Data Control	Output Processing		10
12	Void Sale Control	Transaction Origination or Transaction Entry	Verification of reentered data Concentration of source document	5/6
13	Sales Audit/Terminal	Output Processing	Reconciliation	10
14	POS Terminal Operator Control	Output Processing	Manual output balancing	10
15	Credit Activity Control	Output Processing	Output activity review	10

APPENDIX

RESEARCH METHODOLOGY

RESEARCH METHODOLOGY APPENDIX

INTRODUCTION

Research methodology was established by SRI in consultation with the Steering Committee and the Advisory Committee of The Institute of Internal Auditors (IIA). Two complementary objectives guided the formulation of the research methodology. First, specific audit and control techniques were to be identified, documented, and included in the final SRI reports based on visits to leading businesses and government organizations. The results of this phase of the research were intended to be the documentation of specific audit and control techniques of proven value. In addition, SRI field interviews were intended to obtain management perspectives relating to trends and expertise in EDP audit and data processing control.

Second, a mail survey was designed to identify practices and trends in internal audit and in data processing for broad segments of business and government, both domestic and international. The mail survey also was utilized to further identify management perspectives relating to trends and expertise in EDP audit and data processing control. The procedures used in both phases of this SRI research were coordinated with and approved by The Institute of Internal Auditors.

FIELD INTERVIEW METHODOLOGY

Field interviews were conducted at over 40 selected businesses and government organizations in the United States, Canada, Europe, and Japan. These companies were believed to be leaders in their approaches to data processing and/or internal auditing in the data processing environment. The two objectives of these field interviews were first, to document audit and control techniques proved to be of value in the experience of the company interviewed. The documentation of these findings was intended to be the basis for the knowledge transfer among practitioners in data processing and EDP audit. The second objective was to obtain a knowledge of management's perspective on data processing and internal audit through interviews with top management, data processing management, and internal audit management. Such information was intended to supplement that collected through the SRI mail surveys, and to provide insight to aid in analyzing and evaluating the results of the mail survey.

FIELD INTERVIEW DEVELOPMENT

Before designing the structured interview guidelines for the field interviews, SRI developed a general outline of the final reports. These final report outlines were reviewed and tentatively approved by members of the Steering Committee of The Institute of Internal Auditors. Utilizing these draft report outlines, SRI then identified all the data elements that would need to be collected to answer the appropriate questions and write the final reports. The data elements were also reviewed and tentatively approved by members of the IIA Steering Committee. The next step was to design a structured interview guide that would be used by all the interviewers during the on-site visits. This interview guide went through two iterations, after which members of both the IIA Steering Committee and SRI approved its final format. A pretest was conducted using the structured interview guide. The results of this pretest were reviewed with the IIA Advisory Committee. Comments and recommended improvements agreed upon between the IIA Steering Committee and SRI were then incorporated. This second draft of the structured interview guide was then fully field-tested at two independent and unrelated sites. After this test, the interview guide was slightly modified and put into its final format.

Company Selection and Interviews

A list of more than 175 organizations was selected jointly with The Institute of Internal Auditors from over 300 candidate organizations proposed by the Advisory Committee of The Institute of Internal Auditors. A subsequent telephone survey performed by SRI was used to qualify the audit techniques and controls in use at these candidate organizations. As a result of the telephone survey, the list was reduced to 75 organizations. Of these, 45 were ultimately visited by SRI (see Table A-1). In selecting the organizations to be visited, an effort was made to maintain a degree of representation in terms of industry groups and company size as well as not to duplicate the documentation of the same audit techniques and controls. Because only leaders in internal audit and data processing were sought, however, the companies visited tended to be large commercial, industrial, and governmental organizations. Company selection included organizations in Canada, Europe, and Japan as well as in the United States. Contact was also made with several small data processing users in an attempt to identify audit and control techniques that would achieve a degree of consistency in the information gathered and documented.

Early experience at conducting the field interviews indicated that the management-oriented questions in the interview guide were being answered repetitively e.g., management personnel from widely diversified industries and geographical areas were giving the same answers to the same questions. As a result of this, after the first 10 to 15 field interviews, the interview guide was simplified to the extent that less than one-half of the management-oriented questions were still used. This decision was made because it was felt that SRI had collected all the data that were necessary in this area. With regard to the portion of the interview guide that was used to document audit and control techniques, the interviewers found that it was difficult to secure information on cost factors, training requirements, and the effectiveness of audit techniques and controls.

Field interviews were scheduled not to exceed one week at each organization. When possible, a member of the organization's public accounting firm accompanied SRI during the interviews. This occurred in only about half of the interviews because of difficulties involved in scheduling or because some organizations requested that their public accountants not be present during the SRI interviews. In other cases, IIA personnel or Steering Committee personnel accompanied the SRI interviewer. Most of the interviews were conducted in two or three days, with an additional four to five days to document interview findings. Follow-up telephone calls were used to secure information to supplement that obtained during the on-site visits. In a few instances, a follow-up visit was made to secure supplementary information and to review documentation prepared as a result of the first visit. In many instances, documentation prepared by SRI as a result of the field visit was sent to the organization visited for its approval and/or revision.

Field Interview Data Analysis

The results of interviews with management were manually tabulated on cards for subsequent analysis and evaluation during the preparation of the final reports. This information was sorted into various topical areas for analysis in an attempt to identify management attitudes and concerns relative to internal audit and control in a data processing environment. Much of the information included in the final reports was based on a synthesis of these field interview data. Although one small data processing user, a midwestern municipality, was visited, most of the audit and control techniques that were documented and included in the final reports were secured from larger organizations with well-established internal audit and data processing programs.

Table A-1
ORGANIZATIONS VISITED DURING SRI FIELD INTERVIEWS

Aetna Life & Casualty
Arthur Andersen, Japan
Atlantic Richfield Company
Bell Canada
British Columbia Hydropower
Burlington Northern
Burroughs Corporation
City of Wyandotte, Michigan
Coopers & Lybrand, Tokyo
Del Monte Corporation
Eastman Kodak Company
Federal Home Loan Bank, Des Moines
Federal Reserve Bank, Kansas City
Fuji Bank, Japan
The B. F. Goodrich Company
Harris Trust and Savings Bank
The Hartford Insurance Group
IBM Corporation
Investors Diversified Services, Inc.
Lever Brothers, London
Lockheed Missiles and Space Division
Los Angeles County
3M Company
Manufacturers Hanover Corporation
Massachusetts Mutual Life Insurance Company
Mervyn's Department Stores
Michigan Bell
The Northern Trust Company
Pacific Gas and Electric Company
J. C. Penney Company, Inc.
N. V. Philips, Holland
Price Waterhouse, Japan
Shell Oil Company
Skandia Group, Sweden
Standard Oil Company (Indiana)
State Farm Insurance Companies
Tenneco, Inc.
Touche Ross & Co.
Twentieth Century-Fox
U.S. Department of Agriculture
United California Bank Association
United States Steel Corporation
Western States Bankcard
Xerox
Yale University

Interview Procedure

The interview procedure used included a preinterview questionnaire, a structured interview guide, and a specific format for the documentation of EDP audit tools and techniques. Before each field visit, the scheduled interviewer contacted the director of internal audit or the manager of data processing and explained the objectives of the research and the procedures to be used. A brief preinterview questionnaire was then sent to collect basic information about the organization and scope of the candidate's data processing and internal audit activities. Data processing and internal audit managers were asked to identify audit and control techniques they felt would be of interest for purposes of the research. When this questionnaire was returned to SRI, it was evaluated in terms of the tools and techniques in use at the specific organization and their applicability to the research. This usually led to another telephone conversation before the interview.

After receiving and analyzing the preinterview questionnaire, the SRI interviewer contacted the director of internal auditing or manager of EDP to establish a mutually convenient agenda and interview schedule. Interview agendas were subject to modification to avoid visits that would duplicate EDP audit or data processing controls documented during previous interviews.

Interview guides were established for visits with top management, data processing management, and internal audit management, respectively. Because a number of SRI staff members were involved in conducting field interviews, these guides were established to obtain a consistent and structured interview approach.

MAIL SURVEY METHODOLOGY

Questionnaire Development

Before designing the questionnaire, SRI developed general outlines of the final reports which were reviewed and tentatively approved by members of the IIA Steering Committee. These outlines were then used to develop both the structured interview guide and the mail questionnaires. SRI developed three separate questionnaires, one each for executive management, internal audit, and data processing respondents.

Using the tentative final report outlines, SRI identified all the data elements that would need to be collected to develop the appropriate questions and write the final reports. These data elements were also reviewed and tentatively approved by members of the IIA Steering Committee.

Next, SRI wrote the questions to be included in each of the three questionnaires. After these questions were assembled into their respective questionnaires, they were reviewed by the IIA Steering Committee and were substantially modified. Many of these modifications were suggested by the Advisory Committee to which the Steering Committee looked for guidance. After incorporating these modifications into the three questionnaires, SRI field-tested the questionnaire at four sites. SRI personnel hand-carried the questionnaires to selected sites and asked the appropriate management, auditing, and data processing personnel to complete the questionnaires. After this field test, the questionnaires were slightly modified again to improve clarity, brevity, and completeness.

These drafts were then reviewed by SRI and The Institute of Internal Auditors during a week of meetings held at Menlo Park, California. Substantial changes were made during these meetings. The drafts resulting from these meetings were submitted to The Institute of Internal Auditors and were reviewed one more time. This review resulted in final approval of the mail questionnaires. The final versions of the questionnaires were printed in three booklets (management, internal audit, and data processing), each of a different color.

Samples

The Institute of Internal Auditors and SRI chose seven different sampling frames from which to select organizations in the United States, Canada, Western Europe, and Japan. Four of these frames (lists) were used to select U.S. organizations, as follows:

1. A sample of 261 organizations in regulated industries (finance, insurance, utilities, and transportation) and 239 organizations in nonregulated industries (e.g., manufacturing, retail, education) was selected at random from Computer Intelligence, Inc.'s file of commercial, industrial, and institutional organizations that have computer installations with a monthly rental greater than $20,000. The organizations in this sample represent the approximately 3,000 largest (nongovernment) U.S. organizations with computer systems. This sample is referred to as the Primary U.S. Mail Survey.

2. A sample of 500 organizations was randomly selected from Dun and Bradstreet's Million Dollar Directory, which includes all (nongovernment) U.S. organizations with a net worth of $1 million or more. Organizations in this sample did not necessarily have computer installations. This sample is referred to as "smaller U.S. organizations."

3. The state auditor in each state was included in the survey. At a later date, questionnaires were readdressed to specific agencies (known to have computers) in 15 states from which a response had not been received.

4. A sample of 48 federal agencies was selected purposively (nonrandomly) on the basis of the likelihood that each would have information relevant to the study.

The Canadian sampling frame was defined as all organizations that were listed on International Data Corporation's file of Canadian computer installations and that had computer systems with a monthly rental value of at least $24,000. A random sample of 250 organizations was selected from this sampling frame.

The 150 Western European organizations selected comprise a systematic random sample of Europe's approximately 600 largest industrial firms. The following nations (and the number of organizations in each) were included in the survey: Austria (3), Belgium (6), Denmark (2), Finland (2), France (19), Germany (47), Great Britain (37), Italy (7), the Netherlands (8), Norway (1), Sweden (13), and Switzerland (5).

The Japanese sample consisted of the 73 largest industrial and commercial organizations in Japan, as listed in *Fortune* magazine, August 1975.

Of these samples, only the Primary U.S. Mail Survey was intended to provide statistically supportable generalizations. The other surveys were included to supplement this survey and to provide an international and governmental flavor to the study.

Survey Procedures

For all surveys of U.S. organizations, the following procedures took place: One week before the questionnaires were mailed, an "advance" letter was sent to the chief executive officer (CEO) of each organization in the samples. This letter informed the recipients that they were about to receive the questionnaires and told them of the nature of the study, its sponsors, and so on.

All three questionnaires (for management, data processing, and internal audit) were sent to the CEO in each organization. Included with each questionnaire was a cover letter from SRI, a brief study description, and a postage-paid preaddressed return envelope. The CEO was asked to complete and return the management questionnaire himself and to forward the other two questionnaires to the appropriate individuals in his organization. He was also requested to complete and return the enclosed postage-paid postcard asking for the names and titles of the individuals to whom he was forwarding the audit and data processing questionnaires.

Ten days after the questionnaires were mailed, reminder letters were sent to all CEOs, thanking them for their participation if they had already responded and urging them to respond if they had not yet done so. Ten days after this letter was sent, a second reminder was mailed to those who had not responded by that time. Reminders were also sent to persons whose names had been received on the returned postcards. In addition, thank-you letters were sent to each respondent.

Procedures for the Canadian, Japanese, and European surveys were similar to those described above, with the following exceptions: "Advance" letters were not sent to potential respondents in any of these surveys; Canadian CEOs received only one follow-up letter; some telephone reminders were made to CEOs in Japan. For the European survey, the cover letters were translated to each respondent's native language, but all questionnaires were in English. This fact almost certainly lowered the response rate from non-English-speaking countries.

Survey Response Rates

Table A-2 shows, for each survey, the number of organizations in the sample frame, the sample size, and the number of organizations from which at least one completed questionnaire was received.

Telephone Surveys of Nonrespondents

Two separate telephone surveys of nonrespondents were made. The first, a survey of nonrespondents in the smaller U.S. organizations sample, was prompted by a very low return rate and a high number of firms reporting having no EDP facilities. In this survey, 50 firms which had not responded to the mail survey were contacted to find out why the questionnaires had not been completed and returned to SRI. On the basis of the results of this survey, it was estimated that approximately 50% of the sampled organizations did not have EDP facilities.

The second telephone survey was of a sample of nonrespondents in the Primary U.S. Mail Survey sample. In this survey, 100 organizations were contacted to estimate the possible differences in response between mail survey respondents and nonrespondents. To this end, selected questionnaire items were asked of management, audit, and data processing representatives at each firm contacted. The telephone responses were then compared with the mail responses, and the results were reviewed by SRI in an effort to identify systematic differences between the two groups. Although some differences were found, it was concluded that they did not affect the conclusions presented in these reports.

Processing Survey Returns

All returned questionnaires were hand-edited for legibility and procedural mistakes and then were keypunched with 100% verification. Once entered onto the computer, the data were submitted to internal consistency and range checks.

Weighting Procedures

To make the returns from the Primary U.S. Mail Survey organizations as representative as possible of

Table A-2
SURVEY SAMPLE SIZES AND RESPONSE RATES

Survey	Size of Sample Frame	Size of Sample	Number of Organizations Responding	Percent of Organizations Responding
Primary U. S.	3,337	500	283	57%
Smaller U.S. Organizations	30,000	500	101	20
U.S. State Agencies	50	50	23	46
U.S. Federal Agencies	48	48	33	69
Canada	1,008	250	113	45
Europe	600	150	52	35
Japan	73	73	19	26

that sampling frame, two weighting procedures were performed:

1. As noted above, the sample for this survey consisted of 261 organizations in regulated industries and 239 organizations in nonregulated industries. These sample sizes represent an oversampling of regulated industries and a concurrent undersampling of nonregulated industries. (Approximately 25% of the regulated firms on the sampling frame were selected for the survey, while only about 10% of the listed nonregulated firms were selected.) Consequently, in order to combine the group's results in a meaningful way, it was necessary to weight the responses according to their original proportions in the sampling frame.
2. Early analysis of the returns of the Primary U.S. Mail Survey organizations indicated that larger companies were more likely to respond than were smaller companies, and that regulated companies were more likely to respond than nonregulated companies. To eliminate the unduly heavy effect of the larger companies and of those in regulated industries, the companies were grouped into categories on the basis of their size (gross sales and number of employees) and their regulatory status. Each category's responses were then weighted according to their proportions in the sample.

The computed weights are shown in Table A-3.

TABULATION OF SURVEY RESULTS

The results of each survey were tabulated by computer using the Statistical Package for the Social Sciences (SPSS). Response-frequency distributions were obtained for each question on each of the three questionnaires, and cross-tabulations of responses to each question by the seven surveys and the site visits were produced. For the Primary U.S. Mail Survey, cross-tabulations were also performed on selected questions within each questionnaire and between questionnaires. In addition, for selected questions, responses were tabulated separately for organizations in regulated industries and for those in nonregulated industries.

Table A-3
WEIGHTS ASSIGNED TO THE RESPONSES FROM THE SURVEY — PRIMARY U.S. MAIL SURVEY

Regulated Industries

Gross Sales (in millions)	Number of Employees 0-699	700-3999	4000+
Missing data	7 (n=11)*	5 (n=12)	6 (n=4)
$0-$49	7 (n=21)	6 (n=4)	———†
$50-$199	7 (n=15)	6 (n=46)	6 (n=3)
$200+	10 (n=2)	5 (n=27)	6 (n=32)

Nonregulated Industries

Gross Sales (in millions)	Number of Employees 0-699	700-3999	4000+
Missing data	28 (n=6)	33 (n=4)	13 (n=4)
$0-$49	37 (n=16)	24 (n=8)	9 (n=1)
$50-$199	———	20 (n=9)	18 (n=11)
$200+	———	17 (n=9)	14 (n=42)

*n = number of companies responding.

†A line indicates that no companies in that category appeared in the sample.

GLOSSARY

GLOSSARY

Every attempt has been made to avoid the use of technical terminology and jargon, either accounting, internal audit, or data processing. Some terms are, however, used that have a meaning that may not be clear to some readers. Accordingly, a brief glossary of selected terms is provided.

Auditability — Features and characteristics of an information system, either computer-based or manual, that allow verification of the adequacy and effectiveness of controls and verification of the accuracy and completeness of data processing results.

Audit Trail — Accounting control procedures that provide documentary evidence of processing so that original transactions can be traced forward to related records and reports, and records and reports can be traced back to their component source transactions.

Computer Application System — A computer-based information system that includes both manual and computerized procedures for source transaction origination, data processing and record keeping, and report preparation.

Data Base Management — A systematic approach to storing, updating, and retrieving information from central files, where many users or even remote locations have common access.

Data Communications — The movement of computer and coded information by means of electrical transmission systems.

Distributive Processing — An arrangement of computers within an organization that has several separate computer facility locations. The computers are interconnected to work in a cooperative manner rather than as conventional single-location facilities.

EDP Audit — A specialized phase of internal audit that pertains to the review, evaluation, and verification of the controls governing data processing, and the results of data processing, such as data files and reports.

Internal Controls — Procedures that ensure the accuracy and completeness of manual and automated transactions, origination and processing, record keeping and reporting, and the avoidance, detection, and correction of errors and omissions.

Systems Auditability & Control Study

DATA PROCESSING AUDIT PRACTICES REPORT

Prepared for:
THE INSTITUTE OF INTERNAL AUDITORS, INC.
Altamonte Springs, Florida

Researched by:
STANFORD RESEARCH INSTITUTE
BRIAN RUDER
TOM S. EASON MALIN E. SEE
SUSAN HIGLEY RUSSELL

Under a grant from:
INTERNATIONAL BUSINESS MACHINES CORPORATION

ABOUT SAC PROJECT ADMINISTRATION . . .

This project was administered by The Institute of Internal Auditors (IIA), an international, nonprofit organization devoted to the advancement of the auditing profession. IIA utilized its resources, over 14,000 members in 64 lands and a 51-member staff, to administer the project and publish the three reports which resulted from the study. For many years, The Institute of Internal Auditors has been concerned with the problem of system auditability and control. For this reason, a grant was sought and obtained from International Business Machines Corporation for the purpose of compiling the best known systems control and audit practices in use today. The grant of $500,000 from IBM permitted IIA to contract the services of the Stanford Research Institute (SRI). SRI's independent study produced three reports: Executive, Data Processing Control Practices, and Data Processing Audit Practices. To assure wide dissemination of the reports, The Institute distributed over 4,000 sets of the reports at no cost to the chief executive officer of organizations represented by its members. In addition, each IIA member received a complimentary copy of the Data Processing Audit Practices report. The Institute of Internal Auditors is pleased to have been of service to the auditing profession, to the business community and to government organizations by administering this unique project.

ISBN 0-89413-052-8

CONTENTS

CONTENTS

EXHIBITS

FIGURES

TABLES

FOREWORD

It is commonly accepted that the function of auditing and controlling data processing systems in many organizations is lagging behind the data processing capabilities. Expanding the use of the computer, discovering new applications, and putting these applications to use in processing and decision-making operations have appeared to be more important than simultaneously considering the development and implementation of adequate controls over these new applications.

This Systems Auditability and Control (SAC) research project was founded on the belief that audit and control techniques have been developed by many of the larger organizations. In concert with The Institute of Internal Auditors motto "Progress Through Sharing," it was felt that there would be considerable value in providing a compendium of these proven controls and techniques to the auditing and data processing communities. These project reports are designed to provide practitioners with practical solutions to the known current problems associated with computer audit and control.

The Institute believes this is the first definitive step in providing a current comprehensive framework for the auditability of computer system applications. The Institute is indebted to the organizations who participated in the fieldwork. Their experience should provide internal auditors and computer system analysts with an insight into the various methods with which practitioners approach their responsibilities in designing, controlling, and auditing the total information processing system.

The Institute of Internal Auditors expresses its appreciation to the IBM Corporation, which provided the funding for this project. The Institute expresses its appreciation to all those who contributed to the completion of this project, including the Stanford Research Institute who undertook the fieldwork, and the Advisory Committee whose interest, advice, and direction contributed a great deal to the successful completion of this project.

The Institute extends a special recognition to the project team headed by Mr. William E. Perry, director of EDP and research for The IIA and to the SAC Steering Committee who were so helpful to him, including: Mr. Edward T. Johnson of the IBM Corporation, Mr. Frederick B. Palmer of Colgate-Palmolive Company, and Mr. Frank F. George of Norton Company.

Stanley C. Gross, CIA
International President

PREFACE

PROJECT BACKGROUND

The internal audit community has for some time recognized that advances in data processing are causing important changes in both the internal controls governing data processing and associated internal audit requirements. It is believed that the adequacy of internal control practices in the data processing environment has not kept pace with the expansion of data processing and the introduction of new technology and new information system design concepts. It is also believed that progress has been made in developing new techniques for audit and control in the data processing environment, but that these development efforts have occurred within a variety of organizations and on an isolated basis. As a result, although many useful solutions to specific data processing audit and control problems have been developed, they have not been widely communicated or adopted. This study was conceived in an attempt to determine current internal audit and control problems, and to document solutions that have been successfully applied. The Institute of Internal Auditors conceived and organized this study to survey the state of the art in the audit and control of computer-based information systems and data processing.

STUDY OBJECTIVES

SRI was commissioned in 1975 by The Institute of Internal Auditors to research data processing audit and control practices on an international basis. This research was funded by the IBM Corporation. Study objectives that have guided the conduct of the research and the preparation of resulting reports are threefold:

- To survey the state of the art in the audit and control of computer-based information systems and data processing to identify current trends in audit and control and to document specific audit and control techniques now in use that have been demonstrated to be of practical value.
- To increase management's awareness of the changing data processing environment as it affects internal audit and the controls governing data processing, and the need to build appropriate controls and audit procedures into computer-based information systems.
- To place internal audit and control of computer-based information systems and data processing in a proper perspective within the total information system environment.

TERMINOLOGY AND REPORTS

The name of the study, Systems Auditability and Control Study, reflects the interrelationship between internal audit and control, and the scope of the research. Systems auditability pertains to the features and characteristics of information systems needed to verify the accuracy and completeness of data processing results. Systems control pertains to the internal controls governing information systems in the data processing environment that assure the accuracy and completeness of processing results, the security of the environment in which data processing is effected, and the effectiveness of computer system design and operations. Thus, the scope of this study includes both internal audit and internal control, two separate but closely related subjects. Because considerable research has been conducted on data security and computer fraud, these areas were excluded from the study.

Audit and control in the data processing environment need to be considered together because they are two sides of the same coin. Internal control in the data processing environment covers transaction processing, record keeping, and reporting. Internal audit is the evaluation and verification of these controls and the results of data processing. Thus, internal controls, records, and reports produced by data processing are the object of internal audit. Because of this interrelationship, to consider internal audit it is necessary to consider internal control. Similarly, a comprehensive examination of the subject of inter-

PREFACE

nal control requires consideration of internal audit as it relates to the evaluation and verification of controls. To deal with this interrelationship, two volumes, the Data Processing Audit Practices Report and the Data Processing Control Practices Report have been prepared. They are intended as reference works to aid in evaluating and establishing audit and control procedures.

The Data Processing Audit Practices Report presents information relating to auditing in the data processing environment. Current data processing audit methodology, tools, and techniques are presented. The report is written primarily for internal auditors and presumes that the reader has some auditing background. It will, however, be of interest to system designers and data processing managers who work with internal auditors or are concerned with improving auditability of computer application systems. Chapters 5-9 of the report provide a general description of auditing in the data processing environment. Chapters 6 and 10-33 present information on audit tools and techniques applicable to auditing in the data processing environment.

The Data Processing Control Practices Report presents information relating to control techniques applicable to computer-based information systems, computer service center operations, and the information system development process. It provides an overview of data processing control practices and describes, in Chapters 5-16, specific controls and techniques of practical value. The Data Processing Control Practices Report complements the audit information presented in the Data Processing Audit Practices Report and is written for system analysts, computer programmers, data processing users and auditors, and others concerned with effective auditability and control. The first four chapters in each of these reports are identical, with the exception of a few pages at the end of Chapter 4.

A third document, the Executive Report, provides a high-level overview of the study and presents the principal findings and conclusions.

SCOPE OF STUDY

The scope of SRI's research included visits to 45 organizations in Canada, the United States, Europe, and Japan. These organizations represent a variety of industry groups and government. In addition, over 1,500 organizations were contacted as part of SRI's mail survey program. The scope of the mail survey activities included Canadian, European, Japanese, and U.S. organizations in representative industry and government groupings. As a result of this fact-finding and of subsequent analysis, these reports have been prepared. Audit and control tools and techniques included in these reports are representative of the thought and experience of larger business and governmental organizations with internal audit programs that are more advanced than most. SRI findings are, however, not based exclusively on larger organizations. For more detailed information on the research methodology, see the appendix.

THESE REPORTS ARE NOT INTENDED TO BE USED AS AUDITING GUIDELINES OR STANDARDS, NOR DO THEY REPRESENT AN OFFICIAL POSITION OF THE INSTITUTE OF INTERNAL AUDITORS, ITS COMMITTEES, THE ADVISORS WHO CONSULTED WITH SRI DURING THEIR PREPARATION, OR THE IBM CORPORATION WHO FUNDED THE PROJECT.

ACKNOWLEDGMENTS

SRI appreciates and acknowledges the participation, assistance, and general cooperation of the people contacted during this study. The willing participation of firms visited by SRI has been essential in compiling much of the information upon which these reports are based. Similarly, the interest and response of firms included in the mail survey phase of the research have been essential in identifying broad trends in both internal audit and controls in the data processing environment.

SRI is particularly grateful to the advisory and steering committees formed by The Institute of Internal Auditors to review project progress and direction. Consultation with the research staff of The Institute of Internal Auditors has been important to the successful completion of this work. Their contribution is also gratefully acknowledged.

Systems Auditability and Control Steering Committee

Frank F. George, CIA
Chief Auditor
Norton Company

Edward T. Johnson
Program Manager
Information Systems Control & Auditability
IBM Corporation

Frederick B. Palmer, CIA
Project Manager — MIS Quality Assurance
Colgate-Palmolive Company

William E. Perry, CIA, CPA
Director of EDP and Research
The Institute of Internal Auditors

Project Coordinator

H. C. Warner, CIA
Assistant Director EDP and Research
The Institute of Internal Auditors

SYSTEMS AUDITABILITY AND CONTROL ADVISORY COMMITTEE

Donald L. Adams
Managing Director,
Administrative Services
AICPA

F. Andrew Best
Computer Audit Specialist
Advanced Techniques Consultants, Inc.
Affiliation: Former Director of
Advanced Techniques
Department of Agriculture

L. C. Bethards
Manager, Systems Auditing
Federal Reserve Bank of Kansas City
Affiliation: SHARE, Inc.

Richard C. Bluestine
Hurdman & Cranstoun

Wayne S. Boutell
Professor of Business Administration
University of California

J. D. Bradt
General Auditor
Imperial Oil Ltd.
Affiliation: Past President,
The Institute of Internal Auditors

Charles L. Brown
Divisional V. P. &
Director of Auditing
J. C. Penney Co., Inc.

John C. Burton
Deputy Mayor for Finance
The City of New York
Affiliation: Former Chief Accountant,
Securities and Exchange Commission

Benjamin Conway
Manager, Information System Audits
International Business
Machines Corporation

Garland Cupp
Director of Business Systems Services
McDonnell Douglas Corporation
Past President, GUIDE International

Gordon B. Davis
Professor
University of Minnesota

Ruth M. Davis
Director, Institute for Computer
Sciences and Technology
National Bureau of Standards

William J. Duane, Jr.
General Auditor
Manufacturers Hanover Trust Co.

David V. Dunbar
Director of Personnel & Administration
Comptrollers & Finance Departments
Bell Canada

J. R. Ellison
Manager Computer Security & Privacy
The National Computing Centre
Manchester, UK

Arthur Fields
Second Vice-President
The Chase Manhattan Bank N.A.

John C. Gambles
Partner
Deloitte, Haskins & Sells
Affiliation: Canadian Institute of
Chartered Accountants

George Glaser
Consultant
Affiliation: Past President, American
Federation of Information Processing
Societies

Richard J. Guiltinan
Partner
Arthur Andersen & Co.

Vico E. Henriques
Vice President
Computer and Business Equipment
Manufacturers Association

William W. Higgins
V. P. for Automated Systems
Advanced Technological Services, Inc.
Affiliation: Former Director for Data
Automation Department of Defense

Stephen Landekich
Research Director
National Association of Accountants

H. Clifford Lazarine
Manager Information Systems
Texas Instruments, Inc.

David H. Li
Associate Director
Cost Accounting Standards Board

William C. Mair
Partner
Touche Ross & Co.

Benjamin R. Makela
Research Director
Financial Executives
Research Foundation

Lynn J. McKell
Associate Professor
Institute of Professional Accountancy
Brigham Young University
Affiliation: American Accounting
Association

Mort Nelson
Director of Education
Society of Industrial Accountants
of Canada

Frederick L. Neumann
Professor of Accountancy
University of Illinois at
Urbana-Champaign

John Nuxall
Partner
Peat, Marwick, Mitchell & Co.

Robert W. Olsen
President
Computer Services Corporation
Affiliation: Past President ADAPSO

Robert W. Parker
V. P., Director of Corporate Systems
Merrill Lynch, Pierce, Fenner & Smith

E. Read Peirce
General Auditor
Burroughs Corporation

Charles R. Perkett
Assistant to the Financial Vice President
Norton Company

Ken Pollock, CPA
Assistant Director for ADP Policy
U.S. General Accounting Office

Shirley F. Prutch
Director, Advanced Systems
Martin Marietta Corporation
Affiliation: Past President SHARE, Inc.

James H. Reber
Manufacturing Control
Systems Administrator
Sperry-New Holland, European Division
Former member SAC Steering Committee

Richard A. Ress
Manager, Audit & Internal Control
Shell Oil Co.

Arnold Schneidman
Partner
Seymour Schneidman & Associates
Affiliation: ACUTE

Ilario Simonette
Principal
Peat, Marwick, Mitchell & Co.
Affiliation: GUIDE International

Harry Steele
Director of Services
Society for Worldwide Interbank
Financial Telecommunication S. C.
Brussels, Belgium

Berny L. Thurman, Jr.
Assistant Comptroller
U.S. Steel Corporation

George R. Troost
General Auditor
General Motors Corporation

Norman L. Vincent
Vice President — Data Processing
State Farm Mutual Automobile
Insurance Company

Joseph J. Wasserman
Consultant
Past President, Computer Audit
Systems, Inc.

Frederick Weingarten
Program Director — Special Projects
National Science Foundation

Harold Weiss
President
Automation Training Center

HOW TO USE THE AUDIT PRACTICES REPORT

The Data Processing Audit Practices Report presents information on auditing in the data processing environment. This report, developed through visits to large organizations throughout the world, presents those audit practices accumulated by SRI as a result of its fieldwork. No one organization uses all of the practices, nor can it be expected that any one organization should adopt all of these practices.

Material in this report will assist organizations to:

- Identify the role of internal audit as it relates to the data processing function.
- Establish EDP audit procedures and approaches.
- Close the gap between EDP audit capability and the rapidly advancing data processing technology.

Part I of the report discusses the state of the art of EDP auditing. This section discusses the importance of the EDP audit function and outlines a comprehensive role for internal audit as it relates to the data processing function. Information is also presented on establishing an EDP audit staff, selecting individuals for that staff, and training of EDP auditors.

Part II discusses the three areas of audit activity in the data processing environment. These areas are auditing computer-based information systems, auditing computer service centers, and auditing computer-based systems development. Discussions relate to what various organizations are doing in each of these areas.

Parts III through VI discuss the various audit tools and techniques being used by large organizations. The descriptions of these tools and techniques are designed to provide internal auditors with enough background information to evaluate the applicability of implementing these techniques in their organizations. Each technique contains a table showing the data processing knowledge level required by internal auditors to use the tool or technique effectively. A brief evaluation of the effectiveness of the technique is included as part of each description.

To make effective use of this report, internal audit management should perform the following steps:

- Read Parts I and II to gain an appreciation of what EDP auditing is doing in large organizations.
- Meet with top management and data processing management to define the role and scope of the EDP audit function in fulfilling needs and requirements of the organization.
- Determine jointly with top management the size and caliber of the EDP audit staff required for accomplishing the EDP audit function.

The techniques presented are designed to supplement and/or automate traditional audit methods. The EDP audit function should review each of the techniques in this report to become familiar with its characteristics. The evaluation, selection, and implementation of a particular technique will normally be dependent on the effectiveness and efficiency of the technique in accomplishing a specific audit requirement.

Part I

STATE OF THE ART

Chapter 1

MANAGEMENT SUMMARY

*Important changes in recent years have affected management's need for information to plan, evaluate, and control the operations of business and government. Increasingly, management requires more comprehensive information in order to make timely decisions. This growth in the need for management information has been paralleled by the growth of data processing. Management at all levels has become increasingly dependent on data processing and, consequently, more concerned about the continuing accuracy and completeness of data processing results. With the introduction of new technology and with this greater dependence on data processing, new audit and control techniques and procedures are required and are being developed. However, developments in audit and control have not kept pace with the growth of data processing. This chapter summarizes important SRI findings and conclusions relative to the improvements needed in audit and control in the data processing environment. Findings and conclusions are based on extensive field interviews and a large international mail survey.**

BACKGROUND

Economic growth in the private sector, widespread operational diversification, and growth in government activities have resulted in increasingly complex requirements for management information systems. As data processing technology has been successfully applied to meet these information needs, management at all levels has become increasingly reliant on data processing to effectively plan, evaluate, and control organizational activities. The growth in the number of computer systems installed is one measure of management's increasing reliance on data processing. In 1966, more than 25,000 general-purpose computer systems were installed in the United States. In 1975, over 70,000 general-purpose computer systems were installed.

Changes in data processing technology have occurred concurrent with the expansion of management's information needs. Data communications is one example of this growth in new technology. Only 25% of the general-purpose computers installed in 1970 were equipped with data communications terminals. By 1975, 54% had terminals. As a result of the introduction and use of this and other new technology and new computer-based system design concepts, traditional control techniques and procedures are becoming obsolete. Thus, new audit and control techniques are needed to meet the changing requirements and to ensure the integrity of data processing.

*Details of the research methodology and characteristics of the mail survey can be found in the appendix to this report.

The changes in data processing have caused changes in the traditional role of the internal auditor. To understand this changing role, one must understand the changes occurring in internal control that are being brought about by increasing automation and new data processing technology. In addition, audit and control must be considered together rather than separately, because they are completely interrelated. Internal controls in the data processing environment govern transaction processing, record keeping, reporting, and environmental security; internal auditing is the evaluation and verification of these controls and the results of data processing. Thus, internal controls and the records and reports produced by data processing are the objects of internal audit. Because of this interrelationship, one cannot consider internal audit without considering internal control.

The reports produced as a result of this study reflect both control and audit practices. Chapters 5-16 of the Data Processing Control Practices Report present information on control techniques applicable to computer-based information systems, computer service center operations, and system development. Chapters 6 and 10-33 of the Data Processing Audit Practices Report present information on audit tools and techniques applicable to auditing in the data processing environment. The first four chapters in each of these reports are identical, with the exception of a few pages at the end of Chapter 4. Chapters 5-9 of the Data Processing Audit Practices Report provide a general description of auditing in the data processing environment. A third document, the Executive Report, provides a high-level overview and the findings and conclusions of the study.

PRINCIPAL SRI CONCLUSIONS

Following are SRI's principal study conclusions, based on the results of field interviews and the mail survey. Each of these conclusions is briefly discussed in this chapter; later chapters provide more detail.

1. The primary responsibility for overall internal control resides with top management, while the operational responsibility for the accuracy and completeness of computer-based information systems should reside with users.
2. There is a need for improved controls because inadequate attention has been given to the importance of internal controls in the data processing environment.
3. Internal auditors must participate in the system development process to ensure that appropriate audit and control features are designed into new computer-based information systems.
4. Verification of controls must occur both before and after installation of computer-based information systems.
5. As a result of the growth in complexity and use of computer-based information systems, needs exist for greater internal audit involvement relative to auditing in the data processing environment.
6. An important need exists for EDP audit staff development because few internal audit staffs have enough data processing knowledge and experience to audit effectively in the data processing environment.
7. Few current EDP audit tools and techniques are adequate to the needs of the EDP auditors as they approach the task of verifying the accuracy and completeness of data processing activities and results. New tools and techniques are needed.
8. Many organizations are not adequately evaluating their audit and control functions in the data processing environment. Top management should initiate a periodic assessment of its audit and control programs.

The above conclusions indicate needs for the attention of top management and needs for investments of money, staff, and management time to ensure the adequacy of the audit and control functions for each data processing system.

Following is a brief discussion of each principal conclusion:

Top Management Responsibility for Internal Controls (Conclusion 1)

The primary responsibility for overall internal control resides with top management. The responsibility for internal controls relative to specific computer-based information systems resides with those organizational elements to whom management assigns the functional responsibility (i.e., users such as payroll or accounts payable). However, the current practice in many organizations is to distribute this responsibility between users and data processing. Because computer-based information systems and associated controls are developed to meet user needs, the operational responsibility for accuracy and completeness should reside with users. When data processing builds in adequate controls, users are in the best position to evaluate and verify the accuracy and completeness of data processing records and reports. It is improper to hold the internal auditor responsible for internal control and processing accuracy except within the context of periodic reviews and verifications. The relationships among users, internal auditors, and the data processing department should be clearly established by top management.

Need for Improved Controls (Conclusion 2)

The adequacy of internal controls in the data processing environment has not kept pace with the expansion of data processing and the introduction of new technology. In the past, inadequate attention has been given to the importance of internal controls in developing computer-based information systems and in establishing data processing operations. More emphasis is needed on internal controls governing computer-based information systems and data processing if such controls are to catch up and keep pace with the anticipated growth of data processing. Control guidelines must be developed, based on cooperation among data processing, users, internal auditors, and external auditors; these efforts should emphasize the development of more effective controls within the context of total information processing systems.

SRI believes that the following are among the elements that characterize effective internal control programs:

- Control objectives are identified during the system development process and are recognized as separate development requirements.
- Control objectives for computer-based information systems, computer service center operations, and system development are considered within the context of the total management information processing system.
- Before new data processing technology or system design concepts are introduced within an organization, they are evaluated in terms of associated control requirements, capabilities, and procedures.
- Design review programs that include an evaluation of the adequacy of planned controls are established

as part of the information system development process.

■ Control features are built into information systems to allow the organization using data processing to evaluate and verify the accuracy and completeness of data processing records and reports.

■ The operational responsibility for internal control resides with data processing users.

■ Clear statements of responsibility for controls are established to define the relationship among data processing users, the data processing department, and the internal audit function.

■ Data processing users, internal auditors, and data processing personnel work together to develop appropriate guidelines and standards for controls governing data processing.

■ System designers consider human factors affecting the reliability of computer-based information systems and data processing operations.

■ Preinstallation testing is not compromised in order to achieve system development and installation schedules.

■ Effective preinstallation evaluations are performed by internal auditors who also perform periodic postinstallation verification of controls and of processing results such as records and reports.

More detailed information on internal control in the data processing environment is included in Chapter 3.

Participation by Internal Audit in the System Development Process (Conclusion 3)

Internal auditors must participate in the systems development process to ensure that necessary audit and control features are built into new computer-based information systems. An evaluation of the adequacy of controls after a system is installed determines weakness too late in the development process. The cost and time for modifying the system after installation can cause operational delays and may be used to argue against the inclusion of desired controls.

Some internal auditors argue that objectivity is lost as a result of such participation. This objection is overcome by placing the responsibility for internal controls with data processing users and by limiting internal audit participation to reviews of controls that result in recommendations to data processing and its users regarding audit and control techniques appropriate for inclusion.

SRI concludes that effective involvement in computer-based information system development is possible when:

■ Internal auditors participate in the development process to ensure that appropriate audit and control features are included in the computer-based information systems being developed.

■ Audit tools and techniques are developed as an integral part of the design of computer-based information systems.

■ Data processing accepts the expanded mandate and role of internal audit regarding data processing activities.

■ Internal auditors are able to articulate their audit objectives in terms understandable to data processing personnel.

More detailed information regarding internal audit involvement in systems development is presented in Chapter 4, and in Chapter 12 of the Data Processing Control Practices Report.

Verification of Controls Before and After Installation (Conclusion 4)

Verification of controls must occur both before and after installation of computer-based information systems. It is important that adequate preinstallation testing be performed and not compromised in order to achieve system development or to satisfy installation schedules. In addition, effective, periodic, postinstallation reviews should be performed by internal auditors. Such reviews include the verification of controls and of processing results. The verification of controls, although a new task to many internal auditors, is important as a complement to more traditional data verification techniques. It is therefore important that management recognize the value of, and ensure the performance of, both pre- and post-installation reviews.

Need to Improve Internal Audit Involvement (Conclusion 5)

Based on the successful experience of leading organizations visited during the study, SRI concludes that greater involvement by the internal audit functions in all phases of data processing is necessary and proper in today's increasingly complex data processing environment.

As management has become more dependent on data processing, data processing responsibilities have become more diffused throughout each organization. Previously, a department such as payroll or purchasing was responsible for its files and processing. That responsibility is now shared with a separate service facility, data processing, and frequently with other departments that use integrated systems as sources of information or as users. This brings about an upward shift in the lowest level of common responsibility or line management control. As a result management increasingly looks to internal audit as the logical group to evaluate and verify the effectiveness of internal controls across the entire organization.

Formalized programs for progressively increasing internal audit involvement in the various phases of data processing and a parallel effort to develop the EDP audit skills and capabilities are needed. The evaluation/verification of controls is an important function that complements more traditional data verification techniques. The expansion of internal audit activities into computer-based information systems, computer service center operations, and systems development is a logical and desirable extension of internal audit's traditional mandate. Expanded EDP audit programs are based on two premises. First, an evaluation and verification of data processing controls are as important as the more traditional verification of data processing results; second, internal controls must be evaluated in the context of the total information handling process, rather than as individual control procedures.

As internal audit programs expand into data processing, a new type of internal auditor, called the EDP auditor, is coming into existence. EDP auditing is a specialized activity within the internal audit organization. Results of SRI's Primary U.S. Mail Survey indicate that currently about 60% of the large U.S. corporations have EDP audit functions. However, of those that have an EDP audit function, more than two-thirds were established since 1970, which indicates that the EDP audit specialty is a relatively recent phenomenon.

SRI believes that effective EDP audit programs are characterized by elements such as the following:

- Management's mandate to internal audit reflects an expanded scope of audit activities to include computer-based information systems, computer service center operations, and information system development.
- Formalized programs are maintained within the internal audit function to develop needed skills and knowledge through appropriate recruiting and/or training.
- Close cooperation is maintained between data processing and internal audit to coordinate programs that improve internal controls in the data processing environment.
- Internal audit plans and objectives are periodically updated to reflect the expanded scope of audit in the data processing environment as needed skills and knowledge are acquired.

More detailed information on internal audit involvement with data processing is presented in Chapter 4.

Need for EDP Audit Staff Development (Conclusion 6)

Few internal audit staffs have sufficient data processing knowledge and experience to effectively audit data processing. Thus, plans must be established to upgrade existing staff capabilities. Organizations have tried different approaches to acquire needed EDP audit expertise. The range of alternatives includes:

- Establishing a separate staff of data processing professionals trained in audit.
- Training existing internal auditors in data processing concepts and practices, and in the use of computer audit tools and techniques.
- Training existing internal auditors and supplementing this staff with a few data processing specialists.

It is preferable to develop required EDP audit capabilities by training existing internal auditors who have an interest in and desire to work in data processing, or to recruit experienced EDP auditors. Hiring or transferring data processing professionals to supplement the internal audit staff has met with only mixed success. Attracting and retaining qualified data processing professionals on the internal audit staff can prove to be difficult because they are not auditors by background and will be removed from the mainstream of their professional interest. In addition, data processing professionals generally lack the audit perspective necessary to work effectively with other internal auditors. However, it may be appropriate, as involvement with data processing increases, to add data processing personnel to the EDP audit staff to provide specialized assistance in areas such as data communications or data base software.

Elements that SRI believes characterize effective programs to train internal auditors in data processing include the following:

- Courses in the fundamentals of data processing are required for internal auditors with no prior data processing experience. It is appropriate that such courses emphasize system design concepts and data processing capabilities rather than computer program coding.
- Internal auditors involved in EDP audit work are required to acquire additional professional training in auditing in the data processing environment. Such training is offered through private organizations, public accounting firms, and professional associations.
- Internal auditors involved in advanced aspects of data processing, such as data communications or data base, are encouraged to attend data processing technical courses in relevant subject areas. Such courses are offered by private institutions, professional associations, and computer hardware and software suppliers.
- Internal auditors involved in EDP audit work are encouraged to attend seminars and conferences wherein recent experience with advanced EDP audit tools and techniques is discussed.

More detailed information on internal audit staff development and training is presented in Chapter 5 of the Data Processing Audit Practices Report.

Need for New EDP Audit Tools and Techniques (Conclusion 7)

New EDP audit tools and techniques are needed as computer-based information systems become logically and technologically more complex. Despite the number and variety of tools and techniques available, SRI concludes that few are adequate to the needs of the EDP auditor. Efforts to develop tools and techniques within individual organizations need to be complemented by more broadly based cooperative efforts among such groups as data processing user organizations, professional associations, and hardware and software suppliers. Emphasis in these efforts should be placed on audit techniques designed to be an integral part of computer-based information systems such as integrated test facilities (ITFs), rather than on after-the-fact techniques independently developed by internal auditors. SRI has identified and documented 28 EDP audit tools and techniques used by internal auditors in auditing computer-based information systems, computer service center operations, and the system development process.

Although an increasing number of internal auditors are using the computer, many are still only auditing around data processing. Auditing around data processing may efficiently verify historical results, but, if used exclusively, it overlooks the possibility that the programs and the programming process itself may not be properly controlled.

Even though the internal auditor may use the computer to perform data verification, two important audit objectives are not realized, namely, the evaluation of and verification of application program controls. A thorough data verification, complemented by selective functional testing, is an effective EDP audit approach to evaluating and verifying computer-based information system and program controls. The combination of generalized audit software for data verification and functional test methods, such as the use of test decks or ITFs, offers an approach to EDP audit that satisfies all basic audit objectives.

SRI believes that efforts to develop more effective EDP audit tools and techniques can be accelerated if:

- Development programs within organizations are based on cooperation between internal auditors and data processing personnel.
- The role of the internal audit function in the computer-based information system development process is defined as described elsewhere in this chapter.
- Audit objectives relating to the data processing environment are well-defined.
- Particular EDP audit techniques are based on the appropriateness of the technique to accomplish the audit objective.
- Representatives from the organization's public accounting firm are used to relate their experience in use and development of similar EDP audit approaches, tools, and techniques.

For more information regarding EDP audit tools and techniques, refer to Chapters 6 and 10-33 of the Data Processing Audit Practices Report.

Need for Audit and Control Assessment (Conclusion 8)

Top management should initiate a periodic assessment of the audit and control programs pertaining to the data processing environment. This review should ensure that the responsibility for control is clearly established and that the internal audit mandate includes appropriate data processing involvement. This review and evaluation should be performed jointly by internal audit and data processing management. Both perspectives are required in evaluating audit and control needs and capabilities. Such a review and evaluation should consider audit and control objectives, the adequacy of control guidelines, the scope of internal audit, internal audit involvement within data processing, the inclusion of control guidelines in design reviews performed for new information systems, internal auditor training, and the need for loss investigation reporting programs.

SRI concludes that an assessment of the audit and control function should include the following three objectives:

- An evaluation of current audit and control practices and an assessment of data processing capabilities within the internal audit staff.
- An identification of likely future trends in the development of computer-based information systems and data processing technology.
- Formulation of programs to improve both the audit and the control capabilities in the data processing environment.

Appropriate action plans should be prepared with related economic justification when possible. In reviewing the results of such a review, top management should realize that it may take some time to achieve audit and control program objectives after recommendations are accepted. Additional expenditures, or at least a reallocation of resources, may be necessary. Such expenditures are an investment in the continuing accuracy and reliability of data processing.

INDICATED MANAGEMENT ACTIONS

SRI has identified a number of areas of management responsibility for ensuring that computer-based information systems are developed with adequate controls, are auditable, and operate in a reliable manner. Top management, internal audit management, and data processing system management must work together to make sure that their actions are coordinated and complementary.

While it is not within the scope of the study to fix responsibility for the various management activities related to data processing control and audit, the following list is offered as indicative of the management concerns and the probable location of primary (P) and supporting (S) responsibility for each:

OUTLOOK FOR THE FUTURE

Although data processing and internal auditing have each been changing in recent years, there has been little coordination in the areas where the two disciplines interface. Due to the rapidly changing data processing environment, the internal auditors' mandate and the scope of internal audit activities are not clear to most internal audit and data processing managers. Internal audit management is being faced

Action	Responsibility: Executive Management	Responsibility: Audit Management	Responsibility: Data Processing Management
Ensure that all management realize the importance of internal audit in data processing.	P	S	S
Issue a clearly defined internal audit mandate that specifies the responsibility of internal audit as it relates to all phases of data processing.	P	S	S
Clearly define the working relationship among users, internal auditors, and the data processing department for the development and maintenance of computer-based information systems.	P	S	S
Encourage the development of new data processing control techniques and internal audit approaches to ensure the reliability of computer-based information systems.	P	S	S
Require the development of control guidelines.	P	S	S
Ensure that internal audit participates in the system development process.	P	S	S
Ensure adequate preinstallation testing of computer-based information systems.	S	S	P
Ensure that periodic postinstallation verification takes place.	S	P	S
When auditing computer-based information systems, computer service center operations, and system development, ensure that there are reviews of controls, tests to verify the controls, and tests to verify the data.	S	P	S
Encourage data processing and internal audit to work together to achieve improved system audit and control capabilities.	P	S	S
Ensure that training programs are developed to provide the needed skills to audit data processing, and also to reflect the internal audit discipline.	S	P	S
Upgrade the quality and quantity of EDP auditors. As a starting point, use individuals from the internal audit staff with a specific interest in data processing.	S	P	S
Add data processing personnel to the EDP audit staff for specialized data processing assistance.	S	P	S
Ensure that data processing, internal audit, and external audit work together to develop required EDP audit tools and techniques.	P	S	S
Ensure that assessments of the internal audit function are performed jointly by internal audit and data processing.	P	S	S

with increasing emphasis from top management to audit in the data processing environment, an environment in which it has only limited experience, knowledge, skills, or tools and techniques. The need for internal auditors to completely audit data processing functions is becoming recognized. However, most organizations still have to establish effective, comprehensive EDP audit programs.

Top management interest and direction are the keys to overcoming the inertia that has prevented the development and acceptance of effective EDP audit programs. The direction of top management is needed to ensure that an appropriate internal audit mandate is established for data processing and that specific programs are established in which data processing and internal audit work together effectively.

Chapter 2

THE CHANGING MANAGEMENT INFORMATION SYSTEMS ENVIRONMENT

Management's information needs have changed dramatically during the last 20 years as a result of the growth and diversification of business activities. Government regulation and regulatory reporting requirements have increased concurrently. These trends have resulted in the need for more comprehensive and sophisticated computer-based information systems. During this same period and particularly since the early 1960s, new data processing technology and concepts have been applied to satisfy management's information needs. As new technology is successively introduced and applied, computer application systems and controls have become more complex. For example, data communication capabilities bring data processing users closer to the computer, and thus allow faster access to needed data. The implementation of such technology has, however, resulted in fundamental changes in the structure of computer application systems and controls. As a result, audit and control techniques appropriate to earlier business operations have, to some extent, become outmoded. In addition, with increasing reliance upon data processing, management is increasingly concerned about insufficient controls and the complexity of data processing. These concerns are translated to data processing management's increasing concerns about losses arising from errors and improper controls that may occur and remain undetected. In this environment, the audit and control of computer application systems and supporting data processing activities are becoming more important to management.*

CHANGES IN MANAGEMENT'S INFORMATION NEEDS

The information needs of both business and government have increased dramatically in recent years. The private sectors of the economies in Canada, Western Europe, Japan, and the United States grew rapidly during the 1960s and early 1970s, until the slowdown was experienced. With economic recovery now under way in most areas, there is no reason to believe management's information needs will not continue to grow in the years ahead.

Economic growth has occurred as a result of an expansion of existing markets and products. Business activity has also expanded geographically within countries and across national borders. The latter is exemplified by the multinational corporation phenomenon, which became prominent during the mid and late 1960s. The geographic spread of business increases the need for communication facilities to allow the exchange of information between business locations. In response to this need, communication and digital computer technologies have been joined to provide the high-speed data communication capabilities now used by many businesses. Multinational business operations share the need for data communications capabilities, but also have other requirements that increase the complexity of management information needs. For example, multinational corporations must accommodate currency conversion, additional regulatory reporting, and variations in practices in developing computer-based information systems.

Expanding markets and product lines have involved acquisitions for many businesses. This has led to consolidation of operations in some situations and diversification in others. Consolidation is often accompanied by increased transaction volumes and an expansion of existing information systems. Diversification through acquisition has, in contrast, often required an information exchange between previously unrelated management information systems. In some situations, diversification has resulted in a significant expansion of data processing capabilities in order to provide necessary management information on a consolidated basis.

The rapid growth of the private sector of the economy has been paralleled by increasing government activities. Legislation and governmental regulation to control business increased significantly during the 1960s and early 1970s. Such regulation and associated regulatory reporting have caused an

*Definitions of selected data processing and internal audit terms are included in the Glossary.

increase in the amount and complexity of information that must be captured and processed. Top management, data processing management, and internal audit management in SRI's Primary U.S. Mail Survey sample were asked, "What governmental, professional, or other trends do you see emerging that will have a definite impact on your data processing and internal auditing operations?" Government regulation and reporting were the most frequently reported trends. Privacy legislation was one form of regulation frequently mentioned. A second frequently cited governmental trend was the Securities and Exchange Commission's requirement for quarterly reviews. National health insurance, affirmative action programs, new rules for pension plan reporting, and consumer protection laws require modifications and extensions to the computer application systems maintained by many firms. Such reporting is quite often different from the usual reports prepared for management and necessitates modification and expansion of existing systems in many instances. Government regulation and regulatory reporting present substantial new requirements for computer application systems.

INCREASING DATA PROCESSING CAPABILITIES

The business trends described above (i.e., growth in transaction volumes, geographic distribution of operations, and increasingly complex product line reporting needs) have occurred during a period when important advances were being made in data processing technology and its application. These advances include:

- Increased computer system usage
- Increased use of data communication facilities
- New data processing application areas
- Distributed data processing
- Integrated computer application systems
- Centralized shared data files.

Figure 2-1 shows the increasing number of business-oriented computer systems installed during the past 10 years. In 1966, more than 25,000 general-purpose computer systems were installed in the United States. In 1975, over 70,000 were installed. This reflects the increasing use of data processing to provide the information that management needs to evaluate, control, and plan business operations.

Figure 2-2 shows the increasing number of installed data communications terminals. This characterizes the growing use of data communications in bringing computer capabilities closer to users and improving the flow of information between remote facilities. For example, a large automobile manufacturer has data communication links to its widespread suppliers, thus providing overall production control from the suppliers' facilities to the manufacturer's assembly plant. In another situation, a manufacturer has data communication links between its facilities and its distributors to provide nightly order entry for replenishment of the distributors' inventories. In the financial services industry, bank clearing systems are being linked using data communication facilities to speed interbank fund transfers and settlements.

The use of data communications has become substantial during the last five years. The use of data communications is expected to continue to grow in the years ahead, as shown by the projections in Figure 2-2.

Electronic funds transfer is an example of a new data processing application area that will require extensive use of data communications. Developments in electronic funds transfer affect financial institutions, retailers, and the consumer. This will be, perhaps, the area of greatest data processing growth during the next 10 years. Electronic funds transfer is in its early stages of development. The concept usually encompasses:

- Electronic interbank clearing.
- Automated teller machines and unattended remote terminals to dispense currency.
- Retail point of sale terminals that combine retail and banking transactions at supermarket checkout counters, for example.

Many regulatory and business problems remain to be resolved before electronic funds transfer application systems are available and widely used. Consumer acceptance is an important factor that will pace and perhaps constrain their wide use in the near future. Electronic funds transfer is an example of how data processing technology can affect both business and the consumer public.

The use of minicomputers in business began in 1969. By 1975, minicomputers installed for use in business applications reached nearly 40,000 units. The number of minicomputers used for business applications is expected to grow to 86,000 units in 1980.

The concept of distributed data processing based on the use of minicomputers is gaining importance with the increasing geographic distribution of business operations and the acceptance of minicomputers for business data processing. During the 1960s there was a trend toward consolidating data processing on large centralized computer systems. Such computer systems were several times faster than their smaller counterparts. They could perform the work of four or five smaller computers concurrently and in less elapsed time. Accordingly, there were economies of scale that resulted in consolidation and centralization of computing resources. Distributed processing is a currently growing countertrend resulting from the adaptation of low-cost, high-speed minicomputers to business needs.

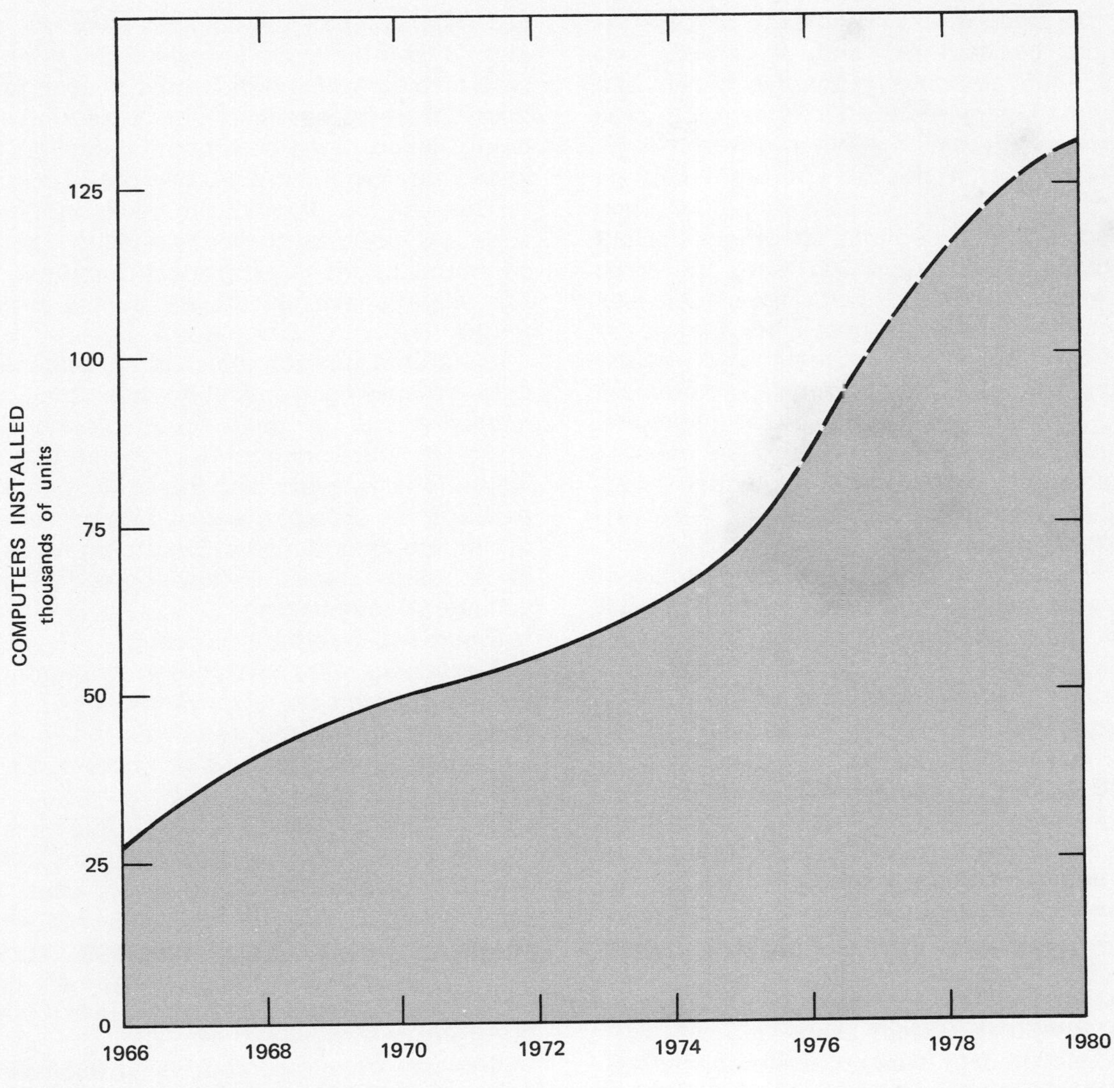

SOURCE: International Data Corporation.

FIGURE 2-1 GENERAL-PURPOSE COMPUTER SYSTEMS INSTALLED, 1966-1980 (U.S.)

For example, a midwestern manufacturer has 15 geographically distributed plants. Product transportation costs are a potentially large component of product cost, so plants are located in the areas they serve. The firm maintains a central accounting department and data processing facility with communication links to terminals at each plant location. It has recently installed minicomputers in each plant location to handle order entry, customer billing, and accounts receivable. This equipment replaced manual bookkeeping machines and is connected to the firm's central computer system. Order entry, production backlog reporting, billing, and accounts receivable are performed locally at each plant. Sales, production, and accounts receivable information is transmitted to the central data processing facility each night and used to prepare consolidated operating reports. In selecting this approach, the firm considered a larger central computer system with remote terminals at each location. They concluded it was more economical for them to process detailed information locally and transmit only summary statistics to the central facility. In specific situations, distributed processing may have advantages over totally centralized data processing facilities.

As a result of changing management information needs and the availability of new data processing technology, computer application systems are changing from traditional forms. In the past, for example, order processing, customer billing, and accounts receivable were developed as separate computer application systems. They were processed separately with files of related transactions passed

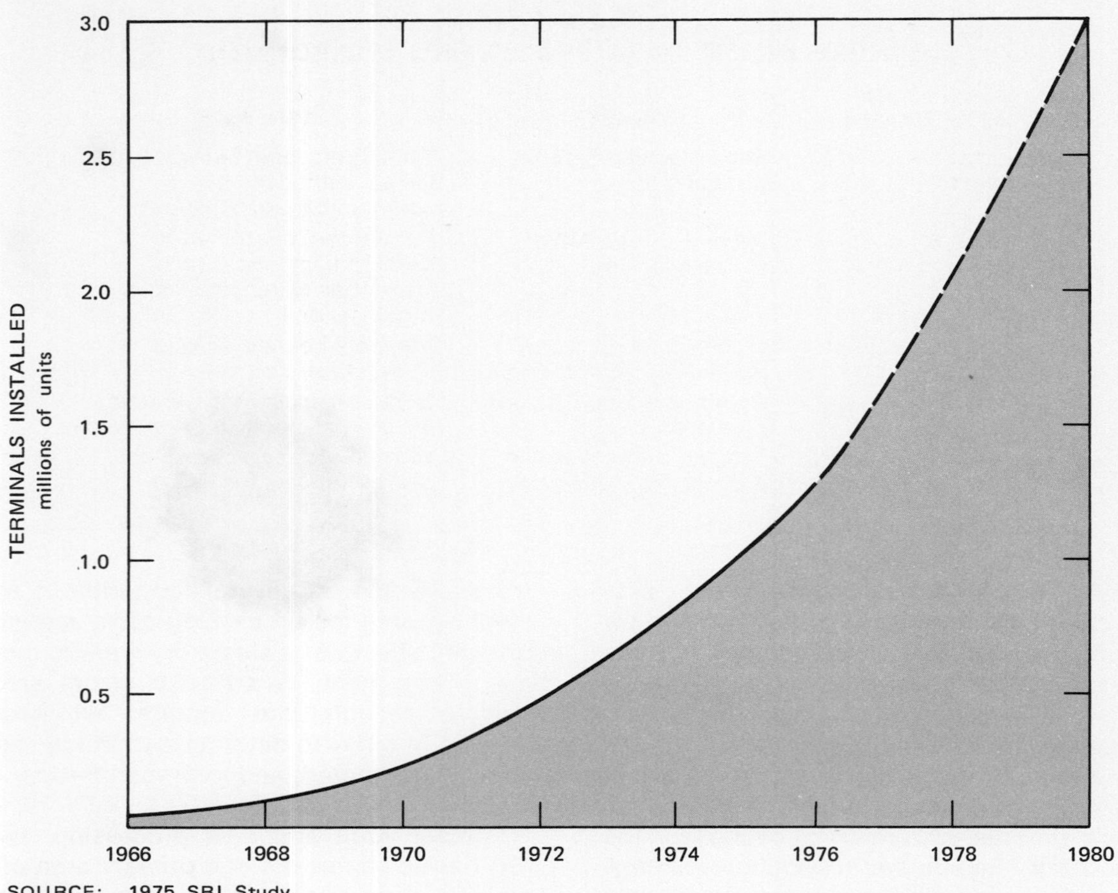

SOURCE: 1975 SRI Study.

FIGURE 2-2 DATA COMMUNICATION TERMINALS INSTALLED, 1966-1980 (U.S.)

between computer application systems. Order processing might occur one night, with billing the next, and accounts receivable processing only twice a month. Manual control logs and procedures were used to ensure the accuracy and completeness of successive processing cycles and the flow of transactions between computer application systems.

Computer application systems being designed and developed today involve the use of remote terminal entry, transaction processing, and central data base concepts. Remote terminal operations were described earlier. Transaction processing is a complementary concept. It involves integrating processing procedures so that a single transaction is entered and processed by all appropriate computer application systems in a single sequence. For instance, order entry, inventory control, billing, and accounts receivable application systems can be integrated into a single transaction that automatically flows through the entire sequence. Orders are entered and customer acknowledgments prepared, inventory records posted, warehouse packing documents prepared, and customer records posted. Terminal operators entering orders are automatically notified if discrepancies, such as items out of stock, are encountered during the processing sequence.

The concept of centralized shared data files (i.e., a "data base") has been a factor in the integration of computer application systems as described above. The data base concept is to capture and maintain data in a single central file, which can be accessed by those programs that have a need for specific data elements. In the past, each computer application system was designed around its own files. The same data elements would occur in different files, and would even have different values because of inconsistent processing procedures and/or schedules. Centralized files eliminate redundancy. When this concept is first explained, one might assume that all an organization's data reside in a single file. In fact, most data bases represent a federation of files serving logically related computer application systems. The elimination of redundant files and the logical association of data files with computer application systems are fundamental to the data base concept.

Several important changes in the data processing environment are summarized in Table 2-1.

Table 2-1
CHANGES IN THE DATA PROCESSING ENVIRONMENT

Areas of Change	1956-1965	1966-1975
Processing equipment	Separate, stand-alone installations	Computers and terminals linked with data communication facilities
Computer application system development	Limited coordination and discipline	Formalized coordination of development and use of standards within individual organizations
Computer application system design	Single-function batch processing applications	Interdependence among application systems
File usage	Overlapping and partial data files	Common masterfiles shared by several application systems
User relationship with data processing	Limited direct links to processing equipment	User has direct access to processing equipment and data files

In summary, management's needs and data processing capabilities have both become more complex and have merged. As more business functions have been computerized, business operations and management have become dependent upon data processing and the internal controls that ensure accuracy and completeness. Traditional control and audit methods, tools, and techniques have become outmoded as a result of changes in the structure and form of computer application systems. With greater reliance on data processing have come new potentials for loss. Loss exposures are described in the following section.

LOSS EXPOSURE

The potential for loss associated with the use of data processing is increasing and taking new forms, as procedures once performed manually are automated. Traditional systems and procedures relied on manual checks and verifications to ensure the accuracy and completeness of data and records. In such an environment, exceptions could be handled as they were encountered. Decisions could be made without much delay in processing. Manual control was maintained over most, if not all, phases of transaction processing and record keeping.

Computer Application Systems Error Potential

As business data processing expands, manual controls are replaced by computer application program control functions. Computer application program routines are needed that anticipate exceptions previously handled manually on an ad hoc basis. Without such control routines, incomplete or incorrect transactions can be processed unnoticed. When computer application systems are linked and integrated, an undetected error that is accepted by one application can result in errors in several others. Once accepted, an erroneous transaction can be processed against several files without any manual checking until the processing cycle is complete. The potential effects of a single error are much greater in this environment. When such errors are detected, their correction can require extensive manual analysis in order to determine what files and records have been affected, and to prepare proper correcting entries.

Internal audit and data processing management interviewed report that the primary area of emphasis for a further reduction in loss exposure will be computer application systems.

Computer Service Center Loss Potential

Increasing dependence upon data processing facilities and a continuing trend toward centralization and concentration of data processing resources are major concerns of a majority of top executives interviewed by SRI. Interruptions in the availability of either data or processing capability can have catastrophic consequences for organizations highly dependent upon data processing. Top management as well as data processing and internal audit management are concerned that effective programs be developed to protect data processing facilities and minimize this loss exposure. Controls in use generally include:

- Computer service center security (i.e., limited access, special fire protection, standby or uninterrupted power sources).
- Backup processing and data files, including alternative processing facilities and off-site storage of important data files.
- Disaster planning, including documented recovery plans for various disaster situations such as fire, vandalism, flood, accidental or intentional destruction of vital data files.

Most of the firms interviewed have implemented improved computer service center security programs. Steps to enhance the security of computer facilities and to develop disaster plans require relatively short lead times and expenditures compared with the lead time to review computer application systems and eliminate vulnerabilities.

Loss Identification and Reporting

Despite a growing awareness of the potential for loss, top management interviewed by SRI seems confident that losses are minimal. Several of the managers said that they had no knowledge of loss relating to data processing within their organizations but at the same time indicated that they had no formal procedures to identify and report incidences of data processing loss. In confirmation of this, in only 17% of the organizations in the Primary U.S. Mail Survey does top management receive periodic reports of time or dollars lost due to data processing errors and omissions.

A few of the organizations visited by SRI indicated that they had formalized procedures for reporting data processing losses and believe such reporting and subsequent investigation discourage loss due to fraud, embezzlement, or inadequate computer application system controls. These procedures are used to report individual instances of loss. No one interviewed had been able to establish a method of measuring or estimating the overall extent of loss, either detected or undetected loss, or loss potential associated with data processing. As part of the Primary U.S. Mail Survey, data processing and internal audit management were asked to identify the areas of potential loss exposure within data processing. Their responses, which are given in Table 2-2, show that, whereas internal auditors most often indicate a major concern is loss from improper controls, data processing management most often indicate a major concern is loss from errors and omissions. In response to the same question, about 85% of Japanese and 50% of European data processing management indicate their highest ranking concern is with potential loss resulting from inadequate system design. Of the Japanese internal auditors who responded, 60% indicate their highest ranking concern is with errors and omissions, while 50% of the European internal auditors indicate their highest ranking concern is with improper controls. Internal auditors interviewed reported that proper manual controls governing the origination, transmittal, and balancing of transactions in user areas can significantly reduce errors and omissions relating to source transactions. Improved computer application system controls can ensure the detection of errors and omissions and prevent their subsequent processing.

Table 2-2

DATA PROCESSING LOSS POTENTIAL

Which *two* of the following areas of potential loss exposure in the data processing department are you most concerned about? (Check two)

	Percentage of Organizations Selecting Each Category*	
	Data Processing	**Internal Audit**
Potential loss from errors and omissions	61.8%	46.8%
Potential loss from improper controls	47.4	67.1
Potential loss from inadequate system design	43.3	41.2
Potential loss from fraud and defalcation	17.1	15.6
Potential loss from failure to comply with standards or procedures	14.9	20.9
Potential loss from inadequate conversion methods	7.5	6.7
Other	8.0	1.7

Note: Number of respondents = 222 from data processing and 221 from internal audit.

* Percentages equal 200% because each respondent checked two categories. Percentages are based on actual responses weighted to reflect the probable response distribution of all organizations in the sampling frame. See the appendix for further description of weighting procedures.

As part of the Primary U.S. Mail Survey, data processing managers were asked in which two areas improvements are needed most to reduce the potential loss exposure about which they were most concerned. The responses of those who checked the top three categories listed in Table 2-2 are shown in Table 2-3. The latter table indicates that among data processing management who are most concerned about losses from either errors and omissions or improper controls, controls on processing procedures are most often reported as being in need of improvement. Among those who are most concerned about losses from inadequate system design, however, controls on analysts and programmers are most often reported as being in need of improvement. Data processing managers interviewed by SRI also stressed the importance of procedures governing the handling and processing of data within the data processing organization. Many also reported that improvements are needed in the controls governing system analysts and programmers involved in computer application systems development and maintenance. Controls governing computer application systems development are required to ensure that adequate control procedures are built into computer application systems and programs being developed and maintained, and that adequate acceptance testing is performed.

In a related Primary U.S. Mail Survey question, top management was asked to identify its two major concerns about data processing. Table 2-4 summarizes the results of this question. The top management concerns most frequently reported are insufficient controls, the complexity of data processing, and insufficient user involvement. Despite the attention computer abuse and fraud have received in the media, potential loss due to fraud was only the fifth most frequently reported concern.

The top-ranking concern about data processing, as expressed by about 40% of the Japanese and 30% of the European top management, was with an inadequate return on investments. While insufficient controls were the second-ranking concern of European top management (about 25%), insufficient control was only the fourth-ranking concern of Japanese top management (about 20%). The top four concerns of Canadian top management are the same as those in the Primary U.S. Mail Survey. It is interesting to note that 65% of state government organizations responding to this question indicate insufficient controls as a major concern.

SUMMARY

Economic growth in the private sectors and growth in the scope of government activities have resulted in increasingly complex management information requirements. As data processing technology has been successfully applied to these management information needs, management at all levels has become increasingly reliant upon data processing for the information needed to effectively plan, evaluate, and control its organization's activities. The degree of reliance upon data processing is often not fully realized. However, a prolonged interruption of data processing can result in business disruption of catastrophic proportions.

Changes in data processing technology have

Table 2-3
CONTROLS NEEDED BY DATA PROCESSING TO REDUCE LOSS POTENTIAL

In which *two* of the following areas are improvements needed the most to reduce the potential loss exposure you checked above? (Check two)

	Percentage of Organizations That Are Concerned about Potential Loss from*		
Controls On	**Errors and Omissions**	**Improper Controls**	**Inadequate System Design**
1. Processing procedures	55.2%	67.8%	46.0%
2. Analysts/programmers	33.6	27.5	58.2
3. Operations personnel	31.0	31.2	22.3
4. Data access	24.0	32.7	14.0
5. Applications programmers	15.7	6.4	11.2
6. Data conversion (source data entry)	15.3	14.2	10.5
7. Systems programmers	11.3	3.8	18.0
8. Contingency planning	4.6	2.8	7.1
9. Physical access	4.0	10.2	2.8
10. Other	5.3	3.4	9.9

Note: Number of respondents = 214

*Percentages equal 200% because each respondent checked two categories. Percentages are based on actual responses weighted to reflect the probable response distribution of all organizations in the sampling frame. See the appendix for further description of weighting procedures.

Table 2-4
TOP MANAGEMENT'S DATA PROCESSING CONCERNS

What are your *two* major concerns about data processing in your organization? (Check two)

	Percent of Total*	Percentage of Organizations with Major Concerns Selecting Each Category*†
Organizations indicating no major concerns	5.3%	
Organizations indicating two of the following concerns	94.7	
Insufficient controls		39.4%
Complexity of data processing		29.5
Insufficient user involvement		25.1
Lack of data processing standards		23.9
Exposure to fraud		21.3
Lack of adequate independent review		19.8
Inadequate return on investment		17.1
Other		13.3

Note: Number of respondents = 221

*Percentages are based on actual responses weighted to reflect the probable response distribution of all organizations in the sampling frame. See the appendix for further description of weighting procedures.

†Percentages sum to 189.4% = 2 × 94.7% because respondents with major concerns checked two categories.

occurred concurrent with the expansion of management's information needs. Data processing has become more complex as more business functions are automated and as advanced data processing technology is applied. As a result, traditional control techniques and procedures as well as audit techniques used in the past must be reevaluated in light of these developments. New audit and control techniques are needed to ensure the integrity of data processing. Changes in the role of the internal auditor are occurring and are presented in a subsequent chapter.

With the broader application of, and greater reliance upon, data processing, the potential for losses resulting from undetected errors and omissions has increased. Error potential exists in the areas of computer applications systems, computer service center operations and application systems development. Many organizations have taken steps to improve computer service center control procedures. The security of computer facilities has received much emphasis. Steps to improve controls in these areas are relatively easy to implement; relatively short lead times and only modest expenditures are usually involved. In contrast, action programs to improve computer application system controls involve more cost and are longer term. Because of the progress that has been made with computer service center control procedures, the primary emphasis in the future will be on application system controls.

Few of the organizations interviewed by SRI, or which responded to the SRI mail survey, have established formal programs to identify, report, and investigate losses associated with data processing. Those interviewed who have such programs, however, report them to be effective in preventing losses. No organization contacted during the study reported having a satisfactory method of measuring overall loss or loss potential. In general, existing programs handle loss reporting and investigation on an individual basis. The potential losses most frequently reported by data processing and internal audit are errors and omissions, inadequate systems design, and improper controls. In addition, internal auditors report that a better integration of manual and automated controls can reduce undetected errors and omissions originating during source documents preparation. Improved automated controls are important to ensure the detection of input errors and omissions and subsequent processing errors. Data processing management report controls governing processing procedures and systems development activities are the areas that need the most improvement.

EVALUATION AND OUTLOOK

The outlook is for a continuation of the trends that have characterized the growth of data processing in recent years: the automation of more business functions, an increasingly complex data processing environment, and greater management reliance upon computer-based information systems. However, because internal audit and control capabilities have not kept pace with the expansion of data processing and the introduction of new technology, new data processing control techniques and internal audit approaches are needed to ensure the accuracy, completeness, timeliness, and security of computer application systems. Greater emphasis is needed on systems auditability and control if they are to catch up and keep pace with rapidly advancing data processing technology.

Management programs are needed to improve the effectiveness of internal audit and control. These programs should focus attention on three areas: first, closer cooperation and coordination between data processing and internal audit to ensure that effective control procedures and audit facilities are established; second, more emphasis on the importance of controls, particularly computer application system controls in situations that involve the use of new technology or new system design concepts; third, formalized programs to develop needed data processing skills, knowledge, and capabilities within the internal audit organization.

Management attention and follow-up are needed to ensure that plans for greater cooperation and the upgrading of internal audit capabilities are prepared and executed. It is also important that the expanding role of internal audit is understood throughout the organization. Each of these areas is further discussed in the chapters that follow.

Chapter 3

INTERNAL CONTROL IN ORGANIZATIONS USING DATA PROCESSING

Internal controls are of increasing importance in the data processing environment to ensure the accuracy and completeness of transaction processing, record maintenance, and reporting, as well as the physical security of the computer environment and data files. Computer application system controls are taking new forms and becoming highly structured as a result of technological innovations such as data communications and integrated computer application systems sharing common data files. Increasingly complex control procedures are being developed as computer application systems are developed to handle more business functions and more exception conditions. Complementary manual phases of computer application systems are also becoming increasingly complex. Extensive testing is needed prior to production acceptance to verify the accuracy and completeness of computer application systems and to verify that associated controls are effective. In addition, periodic postimplementation examinations are being made by internal auditors to verify the accuracy and completeness of processing. This chapter describes internal controls as they relate to the data processing environment.

INTERNAL CONTROLS IN THE DATA PROCESSING ENVIRONMENT

Internal controls in the data processing environment pertain to the processing and recording of an organization's transactions and to resulting management reporting. They are the procedures that ensure the accuracy and completeness of manual and automated transactions, records, and reports, and the avoidance, detection, and correction of errors. They encompass source document origination, authorization, processing, data processing record keeping and reporting, and the use of data processing records and reports in controlling an organization's activities.

Internal controls governed manual transaction processing and record keeping for many years before the advent of electronic data processing. Data processing has, however, caused traditional controls to be revised. As a result, internal controls have taken new forms and become highly structured, particularly during the last decade.

This chapter provides an overview of, and conceptual framework for, internal control in the data processing environment. It presents a synthesis of information resulting primarily from SRI interviews conducted with leading U.S. and Canadian organizations. It describes the controls that govern computer application systems and data processing activities. The next chapter describes the role of the internal auditor.

Internal controls in the data processing environment govern transaction processing, and resulting record keeping and reporting; internal audit is the evaluation and verification of these controls and the results of data processing. Internal controls and the records and reports produced by data processing are the object of internal audit. Based on SRI's field interviews it was concluded that most internal auditors and data processors do not clearly understand this perspective. To fully appreciate the role of the internal auditor in the changing data processing environment, one must understand the changes in internal control being brought about by the increasing dependence on data processing.

THE SCOPE OF INTERNAL CONTROL

The scope of internal control in a manufacturing firm is illustrated in Figure 3-1. Organizational elements, such as marketing, distribution, manufacturing, accounting and finance, and data processing, are established to achieve certain business plans and objectives. These organizational elements are bound together by various management and operational relationships. Internal control ensures that the interrelationship among the organizational elements is in accordance with management policies.

Internal control includes the following elements:

- Management policies.
- Organization and the assignment of tasks and responsibilities within the organizational structure.
- Business plans and projections used by management to guide the organization and evaluate achievement.
- Operating policy and procedures.

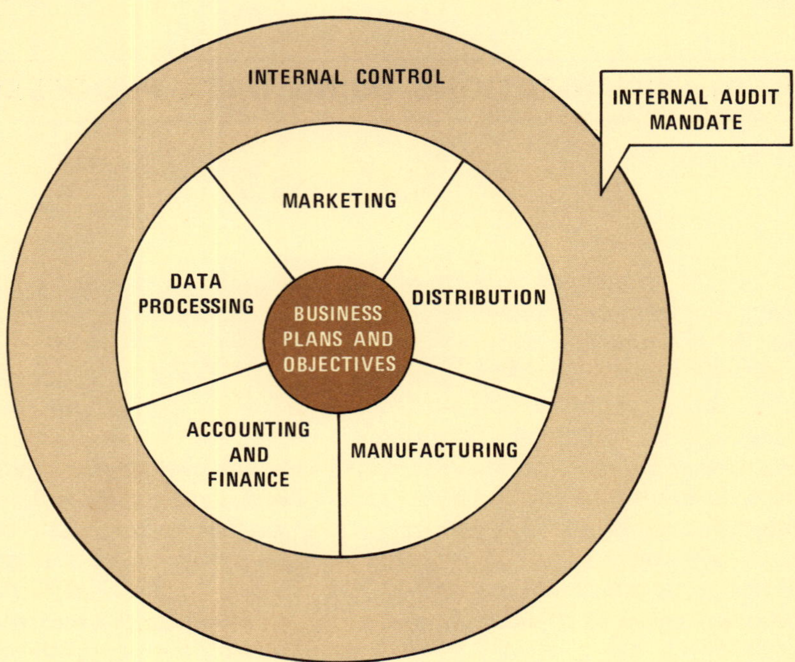

FIGURE 3-1 SCOPE OF INTERNAL CONTROL

■ Manual transaction processing procedures and record keeping.

The scope of internal control encompasses computer-based information and record keeping systems as well as those independent of data processing.

Management expects internal audit to review, evaluate, and verify controls in all areas, whether or not they involve computer application systems. Figure 3-1 illustrates this responsibility by showing that the whole of internal control may be included in the internal audit mandate. Chapter 4 of this volume presents specific SRI findings and conclusions relating to the role of the internal auditor and the internal audit mandate. See page 33 for a discussion of the latter.

Data processing is typically given the responsibility to develop and operate computer application systems that process transactions and maintain records on an accurate and timely basis. These systems are based on policy, organization, and procedures that are both explicit and implicit. Computer application systems developers work with personnel from user groups to develop new systems. They look to these users to provide definitions of the performance characteristics desired.

As more business functions have become automated, the roles of both the system designer and the internal auditor have expanded, as illustrated in Figure 3-2. The system designer has had to become more concerned with the manual procedures that precede (transaction origination and approval) and follow (the use of data processing outputs) the automated phases of computer application systems. Internal auditors have had to become more concerned with procedures and controls within the automated phases of computer application systems. This change and expansion of perspective is occurring in some organizations. It is not, however, a general trend and progress is slow.

ELEMENTS OF INTERNAL CONTROL

The typical data processing function includes three elements:

■ Computer application systems, which encompass manual procedures to originate and transmit input transactions to the data processing department; computer application programs that control the processing of transaction data, record maintenance, and output report preparation; and procedures that guide computer service center personnel in the use of specific computer application programs and the handling of the associated input data and output reports.

■ Computer service center operations, which encompass the facilities, equipment, personnel, and general procedures that govern computer center operations, as opposed to procedures specific to individual application systems.

■ Application systems development, which encompasses the personnel and general procedures governing the design, development, testing, and implementation of the manual procedures and computer application programs that make up

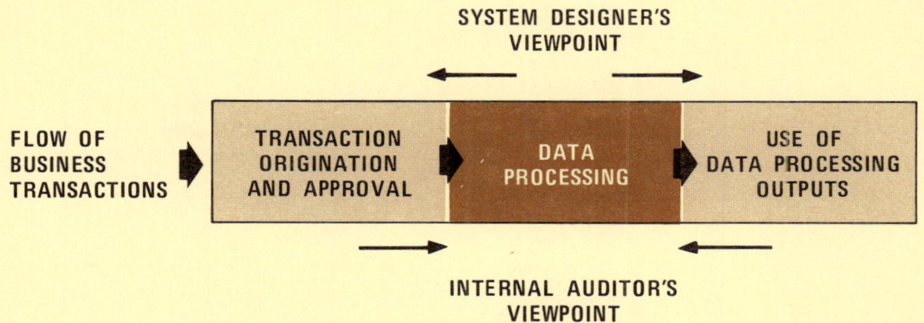

FIGURE 3-2 CHANGING DATA PROCESSING AND INTERNAL AUDIT VIEWPOINTS

computer application systems. This element also includes the modification and improvement of existing computer application programs. Some of the organizations interviewed by SRI reported as much as two-thirds of their systems development work involved modifications and improvements to existing computer applications.

Figure 3-3 shows these three data processing elements in their relationship to internal control and the internal audit mandate. The components shown in Figure 3-3 are interrelated. The three data processing elements are planned, organized, and managed to achieve various management information system objectives. They are also interdependent. For example, systems development may be constrained by the availability of processing capacity or specialized resources. In contrast, processing capacity may be increased and special features added to accommodate new systems development requirements.

A similar interdependency exists between computer application systems and the computer service center. Poorly designed application programs can degrade overall center operations. Intervention required by center personnel tends to be error prone and to make inefficient use of expensive computer resources. Computer service center operations can have a significant impact upon computer application systems. Poorly or inadequately trained staff are frequent causes of processing problems that affect application systems and their users. Inadequate procedures within the computer service center can cause or allow errors to pass undetected in the preparation, scheduling, and handling of input transactions, data files, and output reports. Such undetected errors can defeat the intent of controls built into computer application programs, at considerable expense in terms of development time and money.

The internal controls that govern computer service center operations and the computer application systems development process are described as general controls, as opposed to application controls, because they are not related to specific computer application systems.

The terms "application controls" and "general controls" are taken from accounting literature used by internal auditors. The terms are used throughout the following chapters and are key to the classification of audit and control techniques made there. Figure 3-4 illustrates the relationship of these terms to the three data processing elements described earlier.

GENERAL CONTROLS GOVERNING APPLICATION SYSTEMS DEVELOPMENT

The adequacy of controls built into a computer application system can be constrained by the lack of knowledge, skill, or experience of the system designers and computer programmers performing the development work. Experience is critical to the successful development of computer application systems, particularly in regard to their internal control aspects. Unfortunately, no comprehensive reference work or standard for computer application controls has, to date, been compiled. The transfer of such knowledge has been slow despite a high level of interest and cooperation among people in the data processing field.

Formal procedures can be adopted to govern the systems development process and ensure that computer application systems are methodically designed, tested, and installed. With careful control of the systems development process, it is possible to achieve higher levels of accuracy and completeness. This is achieved by many data processing organizations through the use of standards and procedures governing computer program structure and coding, testing and user acceptance, documentation, and program change authorization and control. Formalized systems development planning and monitoring techniques, often called "systems development life cycle," are used to ensure that periodic technical and user reviews and approvals occur. These techniques are further discussed in Chapter 12 of the Control Practices Report. Their value is

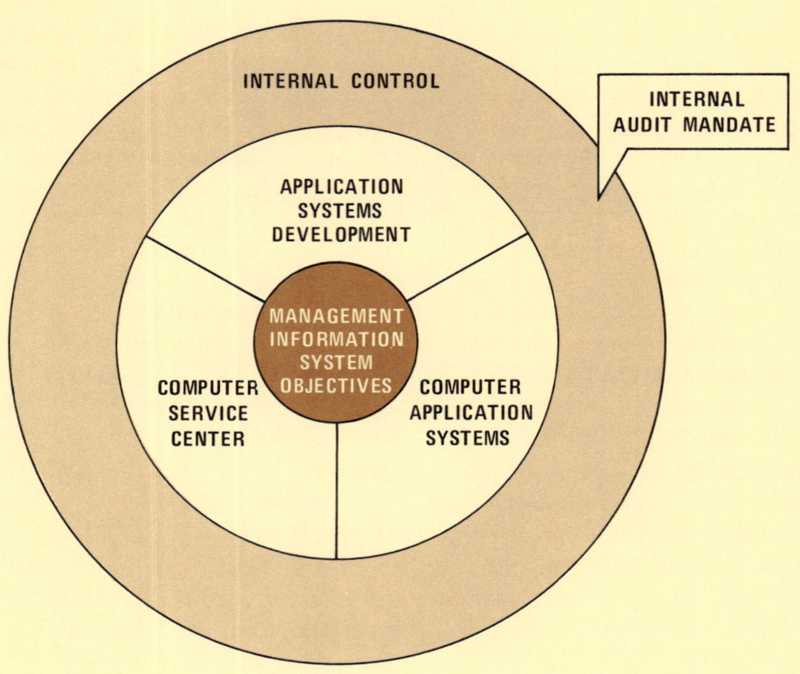

FIGURE 3-3 INTERNAL CONTROL IN THE DATA PROCESSING ENVIRONMENT

widely accepted in larger installations or where advanced computer application systems are being developed. They ensure a methodical systems development process, which in turn ensures more reliable and accurate computer application programs. Because the controls that govern the systems development process can ultimately affect application controls and the accuracy and completeness of processing, internal auditors are concerned with the adequacy of these controls and may periodically audit for compliance.

COMPUTER SERVICE CENTER

Internal controls are required within the computer service center, independent of, and in addition to, those built into computer application systems. The accuracy and completeness of records and reports produced by data processing depend upon the general controls governing center operations. Inadequate procedures within the center, or failure to comply with established procedures can result in errors in data preparation and handling, production scheduling, file updating, and output report preparation. Controls within the center are functionally independent of the controls built into computer application systems. Important control functions maintained within the computer service center include:

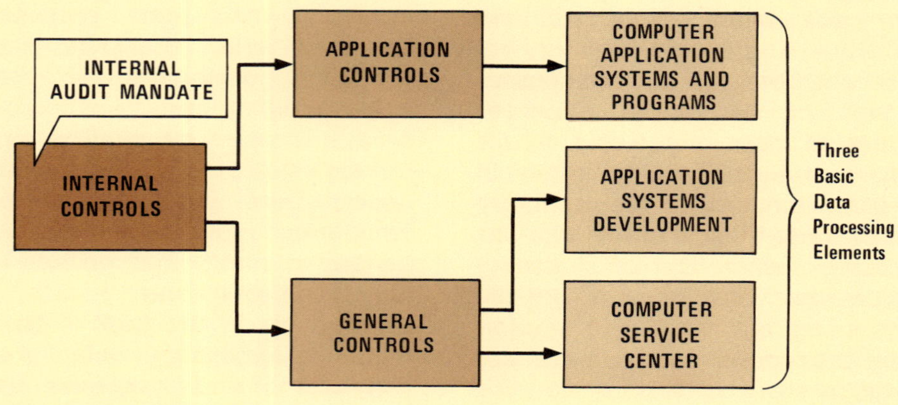

FIGURE 3-4 INTERNAL CONTROL RELATIONSHIP

- An input/output control section that schedules computer processing, receives and prepares user data for processing, checks balances and reconciles data processing output, and distributes data processing outputs to users.
- Media library facilities and procedures to provide for the physical storage of data files on such media as magnetic tapes, disk packs, and removable drums.
- Malfunction reporting and preventive maintenance procedures to ensure that data processing equipment and operating system software are maintained in optimum condition so as to prevent undetected errors and omissions from occurring in records and reports produced by data processing. This includes environmental controls and physical security to ensure the continued availability of data files and processing resources and the protection of such resources against hazards such as fire and accidental or intentional destruction.
- Separation of duties to prevent the fraudulent use or misuse of computers, data files, or other critical items, such as negotiable instruments. Separation of duties applies within the data processing organization, as well as between data processing and its users.
- Supervision to ensure that appropriate procedures are followed, personnel are competent to perform their duties, and processing exceptions are properly documented and handled.
- Resource planning to ensure that adequate computing and human resources are available to provide continuity in the processing of existing applications and the development of new applications. Planning typically includes facilities, equipment, general-purpose software, and personnel.
- Disaster recovery procedures to ensure that an organization can respond rapidly to disaster situations that might otherwise cause interruption in the organization's business activities. Disaster recovery is particularly important as data processing resources are concentrated and management comes to rely on data processing for the day-to-day information necessary for evaluating operations and planning.

These computer service center controls are important from two points of view. First, improper scheduling or handling of input documents and/or outputs can directly contribute to inaccuracies in data processing results. Inadequate media library controls can result in the use of incorrect masterfiles during data processing. Separation of duties is necessary to reduce the risk of unauthorized transactions or processing controls being circumvented. If adequate procedures governing these areas are not established and maintained, the accuracy and completeness of data processing results can be compromised despite the controls that may be built into computer application systems and programs used during processing.

Second, controls such as those that govern malfunction reporting and preventive maintenance, the computer environment, and physical security are important to ensure the continuing availability of the equipment, data files, and application programs necessary to process an organization's information on a day-to-day basis. If these important resources are not protected and properly maintained, the flow of needed information to management can be disrupted.

Controls governing the systems development process and computer service center operations are typically the responsibility of data processing management because the control procedures themselves are not directly performed by other organizational elements. Various control techniques have evolved as new data processing technology and practices have been adopted.

While data processing users are involved with the general controls used within data processing, they are concerned that the general controls be appropriate and consistently applied to ensure that processing results are timely, accurate, and complete. Such controls have become of increasing interest to internal auditors because they can directly affect processing results.

APPLICATION SYSTEM CONTROLS

Computer application system controls, as previously described, involve both manual and automated procedures. Automated procedures may include terminal data entry performed in user areas outside data processing, as well as computer program procedures that control the flow of data within a computer system. Manual procedures in user areas are developed to ensure that the transactions processed by data processing are correctly prepared, authorized, and submitted to data processing. Manual application control procedures are also required within data processing. For example, balancing and reconciling input to output are frequently performed by the data processing input/output control section. File retention and security procedures may be required and specified for individual computer application systems. Such controls are unique to the requirements of a computer application system and complement general controls that govern input/output control and the media library.

Six steps in the flow of transactions through a computer application system are shown in Figure 3-5 Transaction flow has been used as a basis for classifying application controls because it seems, based on field interviews, to provide a common

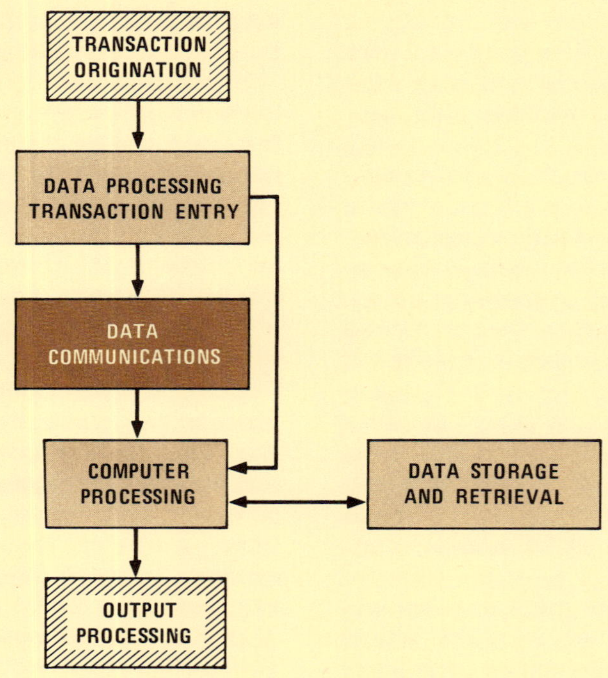

FIGURE 3-5 SCHEME FOR CLASSIFICATION OF APPLICATION SYSTEM CONTROLS

framework for internal auditors, data processing personnel, and others interested in computer application systems.

The two shaded blocks on the figure are activities primarily involving the data processing user organization. The following paragraphs briefly describe each element of the figure.

Transaction Origination — Application controls govern the origination, approval, and processing of source documents, and the preparation of data processing input transactions and associated error detection and correction procedures.

Data Processing Transaction Entry — Application controls govern the data entry, either remote terminal or batch, data validation, transaction or batch proofing and balancing, error identification and reporting, and error correction and reentry.

Data Communications — Application controls govern the accuracy and completeness of data communications, including message accountability, data protection hardware and software, security and privacy, error identification, and reporting.

Computer Processing — Application controls govern the accuracy and completeness of transaction processing, including the appropriateness of machine-generated transactions, transaction validation against masterfiles, error identification, and reporting.

Data Storage and Retrieval — Application controls govern masterfile data accuracy and completeness, correct transaction/masterfile cutoff, data security and privacy, and error handling, as well as backup, recovery, and retention. Note that file integrity controls reflect the growing use of general-purpose file handling, data base software, and an attendant trend to view processing procedures as independent of data files.

Output Processing — Application controls govern the manual balancing and reconciling of data processing input and output (both within the data processing input/output control section and at user locations), distribution of data processing output, control over negotiable documents (both within data processing and user areas), and output data retention.

This scheme, which illustrates the flow of auditor transactions through a computer application system and the classification of application controls, is consistent with the way both data processing and internal audit personnel view computer application systems. Furthermore, it illustrates the complete scope of a computer application system, starting with controls governing the authorization and origination of source documents, and it provides a total system context in which to view internal controls, both manual and automated.

WHO IS RESPONSIBLE FOR INTERNAL CONTROLS?

When this question is asked, one can expect many different responses. The results of field interviews and other related SRI experience indicate that the responsibility for internal controls is not well-defined or understood.

There is agreement that the ultimate responsibility for internal controls resides with top management. At lower levels within an organization, however, the responsibility for internal control tends to be fragmented. Internal controls governing the manual phases of transaction processing and record keeping tend to be the responsibility of line management in charge of specific organizational units. Users can be viewed as being responsible for establishing the requirements for controls within the computer processing phase of an application system. Data processing management typically is responsible for designing and implementing the controls governing automated phases of computer application systems, and controls governing other phases of data processing activities. In many situations, controls in these two areas reflect accounting and financial reporting control objectives. Unfortunately, controls are often established to meet the needs of various stages of manual and computer processing without being evaluated within the context of the total computer application system and its associated control objectives.

System designers from data processing often have the broadest understanding of total system operations and requirements. However, they are often more technically oriented than controls-oriented, and the pressures of their implementation schedules frequently prevent a proper overall evaluation of internal control, particularly those controls not directly related to data processing, transaction processing, and record keeping. In contrast, users and accountants usually have a good understanding of overall financial control objectives, but lack the familiarity with computer application system procedures and related controls. As a result, internal controls associated with computer application systems are frequently fragmented and not evaluated within the context of total computer application systems requirements. Often, multiple controls, in various locations, may be designated to achieve a common objective.

Internal auditors are becoming increasingly involved in evaluating internal controls relating to computer application systems. This is a result of their relatively independent perspective in reviewing internal controls in user areas as well as within data processing. Changes in the internal auditor's role in this regard are discussed in the following chapter. It is important to note, however, that although the internal auditor may be used effectively in the review of internal controls and may even make control recommendations, the responsibility for internal controls properly resides with data processing and the user groups responsible for the preparation and processing of transactions, record keeping, and resulting management reports. The role of the auditor is to judge the adequacy of controls and to recommend control improvements. Responsibility to implement and maintain appropriate controls resides with data processing function and user organizations.

From a philosophical point of view, the primary responsibility for internal controls resides with those organizations requesting data processing services and establishing associated service requirements. Although they may look to data processing management to recommend and maintain certain controls, data processing is, in fact, a service organization. Therefore, the responsibility for the accuracy and completeness of records and associated management reports resides with those organizations to which management has assigned a functional information system responsibility (e.g., payroll, accounts payable, inventory control). In practice, data processing often assumes considerable responsibility for the accuracy of management information and associated controls. This occurs for two reasons. First, as information systems have been automated, management in groups using data processing has assumed that all aspects of those systems were the responsibility of data processing. This is often because top management has improperly placed the primary responsibility for the implementation of such systems with data processing, which has tended to relegate users to a secondary role in the implementation process. A complementary factor is the willingness of users to let data processing accept this responsibility. Second, user groups often lack the data processing experience and knowledge needed to evaluate control alternatives and to select proper control techniques. They have looked to data processing to provide the guidance in all things relating to computer application systems. These trends have blurred the lines of responsibility for the accuracy and completeness of computer-based information systems.

The primary responsibility for computer-based information systems can be restored to data processing users by requiring users to define the control requirements of their systems and then to work with data processing personnel to ensure that the systems are designed with control and audit features appropriate to meeting the control requirements. Adequate systems design will then include controls and audit features that allow users to verify all aspects of the data processing performed on their behalf. Many firms have established this criterion as a primary guideline for application systems development. It is necessary to restore the proper accountability for accurate and complete management information. In such a situation, the proper role of internal audit can be maintained as a function that reviews and evaluates the effectiveness and adequacy of controls, and verifies the accuracy and completeness of records and reports.

SELECTION OF APPLICATION SYSTEM CONTROLS

The selection of appropriate application system controls is typically not a formalized or structured process. Decisions as to what controls are appropriate to ensure the accuracy and completeness of data processed are usually not considered separately from other system design criteria. Data processing management interviewed by SRI frequently said that they view controls as secondary to the functional requirements of an application system. Such a view does not minimize the importance of application controls, but reflects typical systems development methodology. In developing computer application systems, data processing personnel first establish the functional requirements of the systems to be developed. They then establish appropriate procedures and application control techniques. In contrast, internal auditors interviewed by SRI place primary importance on the controls that ensure the accuracy and completeness of data. The adequacy and effectiveness of such controls gives them confidence in the reliability and accuracy of the data processed.

Some organizations have attempted to establish a control philosophy early in the development of application systems as a basis for evaluating and selecting application controls. They report that this is a desirable approach because control structures can be integrated with processing procedures from the outset of system design and development. In addition, all participants in the systems development effort have a common control philosophy or frame of reference. With this approach, selection and development of specific control techniques can be evaluated in terms of functional requirements of the application system and the preestablished control philosophy.

Even in situations where control philosophies or general guidelines to application controls have been adopted, the evaluation and selection of individual control techniques are generally unstructured. Application system designers rely on their own prior experience and ingenuity when new situations are presented. When new technology is applied requiring new control techniques, assistance is most often secured from the organization's computer vendor and other system designers who have been faced with similar application control problems.

A number of the larger organizations visited by SRI have developed control guidelines for application systems development. Such guidelines represent a substantial contribution in terms of knowledge transferred between system designers and other people concerned with the adequacy of application controls. Much of the material included in the Control Practices Report has been documented and presented to improve the exchange of knowledge relative to application controls.

One firm interviewed includes a controls evaluation as part of their design review of progressive application systems. In this situation, controls are evaluated independent of other design criteria. Functional requirements and technical approach are assumptions against which application controls are evaluated on a system flow-through basis. This review includes manual controls as well as automated controls.

A comprehensive philosophy for application system controls necessarily includes the following perspectives:

- Automated procedures and controls that are incorporated within computer application programs (e.g., data validation, error checking).
- Manual procedures and controls that have been designed to complement computer application controls (e.g., data entry procedures, batch or transaction control totals, batch balancing and reconciliation).
- Manual procedures and controls not directly interdependent with computer application system programs (e.g., policies and procedures governing the origination of business transactions that are eventually entered into data processing, or management's uses of information produced by data processing).
- Organizational controls that provide proper statements of procedures, assignment of responsibilities, and competent, trained personnel.

Establishing a comprehensive application control philosophy or approach often requires more than one point of view. For example, a financial officer may have to review and confirm basic financial control policy, on issues such as accruals, to recognize income earned but not billed. Such transactions may require unique controls to ensure correct preparation and approval. In addition, special application systems provisions may be required to enter and record such transactions. These typically entail functional processing procedures within computer application programs, as well as complementary manual procedures for data entry, balancing, and reconciliation. The development of such a comprehensive application control structure involves accounting policy, accounting procedures, and computer application systems procedures, both manual and automated. Although this is a simplified example, organizations interviewed that had successfully approached application control in a total systems context have found that several people may become involved before internal control requirements are fully understood and satisfied. This is because different organizations, organizational levels, and disciplines are entailed.

SRI's field findings indicate there is no widely used approach to the evaluation of control alternatives and the selection of appropriate application system controls. This is because the functional and procedural requirements of computer application systems vary significantly from organization to organization, and among applications within an organization, and because data processing systems development personnel think of application controls as being derived from the functional and procedural requirements of an application system. Accordingly, data processing personnel have done little to develop generalized approaches or criteria for application controls. Progress is being made within some organizations as a result of cooperation between internal auditors, accountants, and data processing system designers in establishing application control guidelines and in conducting evaluations of the adequacy and appropriateness of application controls during the systems development process.

EVALUATION AND VERIFICATION OF CONTROLS

Reviews to evaluate and verify controls are usually performed during final implementation and before acceptance of business systems as fully operational. A review of controls is also performed subsequent to initial implementation to ensure that controls have not become obsolete because of changes in the business environment since original installation or have fallen into disuse due to system change or employee apathy. These tests or reviews include preinstallation testing, postinstallation testing, and verification of manual procedures.

Preinstallation Review

The verification of computer application program controls requires careful planning and methodology. Application programs are becoming increasingly complex in terms of the number of controls and interrelationships between controls. Many control points are required within application programs to direct the flow of transactions during processing. Transactions may take different paths through an application system before processing is complete. The transaction type and associated controls built into the application programs are used to determine the routing and processing appropriate to each input transaction. As a result, transaction flow is often circuitous and a multitude of control points are involved. Comprehensive verification requires tests to provide evidence that all prescribed controls are operating properly.

The growing complexity of computer application controls and resulting verification tests reflect three automation trends:

- Procedures to detect errors and handle exceptions, which were once performed manually, are being automated.
- Computer application programs are being integrated with one another through the development of interrelated processing procedures and common or shared data files.
- Fewer opportunities for manual checks during the process are a result of automation of exception routines and the integration of computer application systems, for example, order entry transactions that flow to, and are processed by, inventory accounting and billing applications without intermediate manual review.

The elimination of manual intervention removes opportunities for errors and reduces overall processing time. However, it dramatically increases the size of application programs, the number of controls, and the testing required to verify controls.

As a result, computer application systems require extensive preinstallation testing to verify controls and ensure that processing results conform to specifications developed with users. Preinstallation testing is usually conducted with users and data processing personnel. Internal auditors are also becoming involved in preinstallation, as will be discussed in the following chapter. In some organizations, the scope of preinstallation testing has become so large and complex that separate task teams have been set up within development projects to prepare test data and perform verification tests. More often, such testing is performed by the same data processing and user personnel who participated in the development of application systems and programs, a practice that tends to reduce the rigorousness of testing and violates the principle of independence.

The time and cost of comprehensive preinstallation testing of computer applications are justified for two reasons: First, undetected errors and omissions can result in incorrect and misleading processing results (e.g., reports and records); second, once verified, processing procedures and associated controls will be executed consistently, barring program modifications, unauthorized computer operator intervention, equipment malfunction or failure, or incorrect manual input preparation. Proper preinstallation testing and verification gives assurance that processing results will be reliable and complete.

Postinstallation Review

Postinstallation testing is performed by internal audit periodically to verify controls governing computer application systems. Such testing is typically not comprehensive and is used to verify specific computer applications procedures, calculations, and control routines such as audit trail adequacy, user identification controls, and user documentation. Postinstallation testing performed by internal auditors is described in Chapter 4.

Verification of Manual Procedures

The accuracy and completeness of data processing results are dependent upon compliance with manual procedures designed to complement application program controls. Once application programs are properly tested and verified, they will execute consistently thereafter. In contrast, the manual phases of computer application system operation are subject to the inconsistency of human performance. Consequently, periodic verifications of compliance are necessary.

Compliance with manual application system requirements is important because of the interdependency between automated and manual controls. The manual interface with automated application systems is a weak point. As application systems have been designed to perform more functions and handle more exceptions, supporting manual procedures have become intricate and highly structured. Thorough user documentation and training are required to ensure a high level of compliance with manual requirements. A comprehensive review-and-verification of the manual phases of automated applications requires an understanding of application program controls.

SRI field interviews confirm that preinstallation testing and periodic postinstallation reviews are used to verify internal controls in the data processing environment. Preimplementation tests are usually performed by data processing and user personnel and place emphasis on computer application program verification. Periodic reviews subsequent to implementation are performed primarily by internal auditors and emphasize manual procedures.

SUMMARY

Internal control in the data processing environment is becoming increasingly important as more business functions are automated and as management becomes more dependent on data processing results. Management relies on internal controls to ensure the accuracy and completeness of such results. As a result of automation, internal controls governing computer-based information systems and data processing are taking new forms and are becoming highly structured.

Three areas requiring internal control in the data processing environment are computer application systems, computer service center operations, and the application systems development process. The areas are interdependent because they each affect the accuracy and completeness of data processing. Accordingly, control objectives must be considered within the context of the total management information and data processing process.

Audit cannot be separated from control. Internal controls in the data processing environment govern transaction processing, record keeping, and reporting; internal audit is the evaluation and verification of these controls and the results of data processing. Thus, internal controls and the records and reports produced by data processing are the objects of internal audit.

Internal auditors and system designers usually have different perspectives concerning controls. In developing computer application systems, system designers first design the functional requirements of the application system and secondly consider application controls. Such a perspective does not necessarily minimize the importance of application controls; rather, it reflects a logical sequence of thought during the systems development process. In contrast, however, internal auditors place primary emphasis on controls. This is because they evaluate the accuracy and completeness of data processing results. This difference in viewpoint has not helped bring data processing and internal audit professionals together.

Little progress has been made in developing comprehensive control guidelines or criteria for systems development. This lack of progress is particularly important to internal auditors who, therefore, have few standards against which to evaluate the adequacy of specific controls. The evaluation of alternatives and the selection of appropriate application controls represent, today, an unstructured and rather informal process.

The primary responsibility for internal control resides with top management. The responsibility for internal controls relating to specific computer application systems should reside with those organizational elements to whom management has assigned the functional responsibility (i.e., payroll, accounts payable, accounts receivable, inventory control). Current practice in many organizations sees this responsibility as shared between users and data processing. The first-line responsibility for accuracy and completeness should reside with data processing users, instead of with data processing itself. The relationship between data processing users, internal auditors, and the data processing department should be reviewed and clear statements of responsibility established relating to the development of appropriate controls and the continuing accuracy and completeness of data processing results.

The review of application controls occurs both before and after the installation of computer application systems. Preinstallation testing is performed by data processing personnel to verify computer application procedures and controls. Periodic postinstallation reviews are performed primarily by internal auditors. Such tests and verifications are performed to ensure that application procedures and controls have not become obsolete due to changes in the business environment, and that application procedures and controls are being followed. Emphasis in most organizations is currently on manual procedures and data processing outputs, but emphasis is shifting to include internal controls governing the automated phases of application systems. Management should ensure that effective periodic installation verifications are performed.

Despite the need for greater emphasis on the automated phases of application system processing, system designers and internal auditors will continue to be concerned with the adequacy of manual procedures that must be designed to complement increasingly complex application system programs. The interface between manual and automated steps is one of the most vulnerable areas and requires careful design of both the manual and automated controls that prevent undetected errors and omissions.

EVALUATION AND OUTLOOK

Inadequate attention has, in the past, been given to the importance of internal controls, both by individual organizations and the data processing industry in general. The importance of controls for computer application systems and data processing applications has been more recently highlighted as a result of the errors, omissions, losses, and fraud that have been reported in the media. Improvements are being made, but several years may be required to incorporate needed controls into existing application systems by organizations with large data processing functions.

Improvements are needed in three areas. First, control objectives should be identified during the system development process and recognized as separate system development requirements. Several organizations have successfully developed and used control checklists and guidelines to aid system designers in evaluating and selecting appropriate control techniques to satisfy their control objectives. As new technology and application system design concepts are introduced, appropriate control techniques and alternatives need to be established and integrated into existing guidelines. Formalized control guidelines not only assist system designers but also provide a standard for internal auditors. It is particularly beneficial if data processing and internal audit personnel jointly establish the control guidelines.

Second, manual procedures designed to complement computer application programs are becoming increasingly complex as more business activities are automated. The design and development of application programs that perform more functions and handle more exception conditions cause supporting manual procedures to be intricate and highly structured. Increasingly complex manual procedures can contribute to high levels of errors. Therefore, system designers must give careful consideration to the human factors affecting the manual phases of computer application systems and data processing operations. To this end, system designers must view all controls, both manual and automated, within the context of the total information handling process.

Third, internal control guidelines need to be developed jointly by The National Bureau of Standards, data processing user groups such as GUIDE, professional associations such as The Institute of Internal Auditors and the American Institute of Certified Public Accountants (AICPA) and equipment manufacturers. A framework of guidelines and objectives would be of great benefit to system designers and internal auditors. The control techniques documented and reported as a result of this study will be useful, as will the scheme used for their presentation. However, more comprehensive work that is directed specifically to the establishment of control guidelines and techniques is needed. Such work must integrate audit and control standards and guidelines promulgated by organizations such as the AICPA, and control techniques that have evolved through the successful experience of data processing professionals. Although it is proper, useful, and timely for data processing and internal audit personnel to work together within individual organizations to develop controlled guidelines, industry-wide effort is necessary to provide effective guidelines and suggested techniques that can be widely distributed and applied. Management should support such industry-wide efforts to establish effective control guidelines.

In proceeding with such a development program, it is important that representatives be included from all the segments of business and government that are concerned with systems auditability and control.

Chapter 4

THE ROLE OF INTERNAL AUDIT IN ORGANIZATIONS USING DATA PROCESSING

The role of the internal auditor is changing and taking on a new importance relative to data processing, as more functions within the organization are automated and as management places greater reliance on computer application systems. Internal audit's increasing involvement with data processing is an extension of traditional internal audit responsibilities, as management seeks assurance that computer application systems are accurate and reliable. The EDP audit function within internal audit is an important and relatively recent trend and is expanding to include computer application systems development, computer service center operations, and controls internal to computer application programs. Emphasis is shifting from the evaluation and verification of processing results (e.g., data files, records, and reports) to the evaluation and verification of the controls that ensure the continuing accuracy and reliability of processing results. This emphasis is resulting in new internal audit approaches and techniques.

NEED FOR INTERNAL AUDIT

Insufficient control is the most frequently reported concern of top management in the United States, Canada, and Europe, according to the SRI mail survey. Interviews with top management indicate that this concern is based on two related factors:

- Increasing dependence upon computer application systems.
- The belief that opportunities for errors and omissions increase as computer application systems become more comprehensive and complex.

The latter factor is supported by the Primary U.S. Mail Survey findings, wherein loss from errors and omissions is one of the two most frequently reported concerns of both data processing managers and internal auditors.

Related Primary U.S. Mail Survey findings indicate that, within organizations having internal auditors, about 78% of top management feel that internal auditors' reviews provide assurance of adequate internal controls. An almost equal percentage feel that external auditors provide such assurances. However, in organizations that have no internal auditors, about 62% of top management look to external auditors for assurance of adequate internal controls. Of Japanese top management responding to this question, 60% look to the users and data processing review groups to assure themselves that application systems contain adequate control, while only 10% rely on external auditors. Canadian and European top management indicate the same sources of assurances as expressed in the Primary U.S. Mail Survey. See Table 4-1 for further information relating to the Primary U.S. Mail Survey.

INTERNAL AUDIT MANDATE

During the field interviews, SRI talked with top management and internal audit management regarding their organizations' mandates for the internal audit function. These discussions reflected a wide range of variation. One reason for such variation is the corresponding variation in organizational structure and objectives. Another reason is differences in the internal audit department's relative involvement in the types of information systems for which computer application systems have been developed. Primary emphasis in most organizations was on the verification of financial and accounting application systems.

The following objectives and scope are included in the statement of responsibility issued by The Institute of Internal Auditors to its members:

"The objective of internal auditing is to assist all members of management in the effective discharge of their responsibilities, by furnishing them with analyses, appraisals, recommendations and pertinent comments concerning the activities reviewed. The internal auditor is concerned with any phase of business activity where he can be of service to management. This involves going beyond the accounting and financial records to obtain a full understanding of the operations under review. The attainment of this overall objective involves such activities as:

- Reviewing and appraising the soundness, adequacy, and application of accounting, financial, and other operating controls, and promoting effective control at reasonable cost.

Table 4-1
TOP MANAGEMENT'S ASSURANCE OF ADEQUATE APPLICATION CONTROLS

What assurances do you have that your organization's computer applications contain adequate internal controls? (Check all that apply)*

	Percentage Selecting Each Category†		
	Organizations with Internal Auditors	Organizations Without Internal Auditors	All Organizations
Reviews by external auditors	78.9%	62.2%	75.5%
Reviews by users	64.3	62.8	64.0
Reviews by internal auditors	77.7	0.0	59.4
Reviews by data processing review group	38.1	26.7	35.6
Executive management signoffs on approval	21.3	20.4	21.1
Other	9.2	7.8	8.9
Currently have no such assurances	4.6	8.2	5.4

Note: Number of respondents = 249

*Percentages sum to more than 100% because each respondent checked all applicable categories.

†Percentages are based on actual responses weighted to reflect the probable response distribution of all organizations in the sampling frame. See appendix for further description of weighting procedures.

- Ascertaining the extent of compliance with established policies, plans, and procedures.
- Ascertaining the extent to which company assets are accounted for and safeguarded from losses of all kinds.
- Ascertaining the reliability of management data developed within the organization.
- Appraising the quality of performance in carrying out assigned responsibilities.
- Recommending operating improvements."

This statement provides a broad framework that may be useful to top management in formulating an appropriate mandate for their organizations.

INTERNAL AUDIT INDEPENDENCE

Top management and internal audit management interviewed by SRI reported that they believe internal audit should have a high degree of independence in selecting areas to be audited and in the performance of their work. They believe greater independence results from higher levels of reporting within the organization. An estimated 50% of the U.S. firms in the Primary U.S. Mail Survey have an audit committee of the board of directors. No Japanese firms reported the existence of an audit committee, while less than 10% of the European and about 33% of the Canadian firms reported having one. On the other hand, over 69% of the leading U.S. companies visited by SRI reported an audit committee. Survey results also indicate that, in 53% of the U.S. firms with an audit committee, internal auditors periodically prepare reports that are submitted directly to the audit committee, and in 22% the auditors report directly to that committee.

Audit committees are increasingly interested in their ogranizations' data processing activities. The Primary U.S. Mail Survey of top management of large corporations indicated that, in 70% of the organizations with an audit committee, that committee had communicated directly with the organization's internal auditors regarding data processing activities, and 77% indicated that the audit committee had communicated directly with external auditors regarding data processing.

SRI field interviews suggest that six factors relating to independence are important to a successful and effective internal audit function:

- A written policy statement specifying the internal audit mandate that includes the objectives and prerogatives of the internal audit function; such a policy need not be either lengthy or detailed.
- Independence to plan and pursue audit work within the scope of the written mandate.
- Access to and support from top management for internal audit plans and programs.
- Support of the organization's external auditors.
- Access to consultants from outside the organization.
- Access to all phases of the organization including data processing.

Given these conditions, the internal audit function must make effective use of its prerogatives and independence without unnecessarily alienating operating management in the areas being audited.

These six factors seem to apply equally to large and small organizations that have an internal audit function. The primary differences between the larger and smaller organizations are, aside from the number of internal auditors, the degree of formality that exists. Larger internal audit functions have formalized the mandate, reporting relationships, and internal audit programs. Smaller internal audit functions tend to be more informal and to rely upon more personal relationships with top management and operating management.

EVOLVING ROLE OF THE INTERNAL AUDITOR IN DATA PROCESSING

An EDP audit specialty is evolving within internal audit. This is a result of the need for internal auditors to possess data processing knowledge and skills in order to do their work independent of the data processing department. As more business functions are automated, internal auditors are faced with the problem of being able to audit effectively and independently in a data processing environment.

The evolution of the EDP audit specialty is still in its early stages. Primary U.S. Mail Survey results from U.S. firms indicate that 78% have an internal audit function, while only 62% have EDP auditors. Table 4-2 shows the growth of EDP audit functions among U.S. firms that currently have EDP auditors.

Table 4-2
TREND IN ESTABLISHING AN EDP AUDIT FUNCTION

What year was your organization's EDP audit function established?

Year Established	Percentage Established*
Before 1950	0.7%
1950-1959	3.2
1960-1964	10.8
1965-1969	15.1
1970-1974	42.0
1975-1976	28.1

Note: Number of respondents = 172

*Percentages are based on actual responses weighted to reflect the probable response distribution of all organizations in the sampling frame. See the appendix for further description of weighting procedures.

Note that 70% of the organizations that now have EDP audit functions founded that function since 1970, indicating that EDP audit is a relatively recent innovation. Its development in larger organizations reflects greater reliance on data processing, increasingly complex management information systems, and increasing reliance upon internal audit to verify the accuracy and completeness of data processing results. Smaller organizations have tended to implement less complex computer application systems and to rely more on external auditors.

The Primary U.S. Mail Survey was structured to allow an analysis to identify differences in audit practices, if any, between organizations in regulated versus those in nonregulated industries. Key questions were selected that SRI believed could identify such differences. Analysis of these questions revealed no important differences in questionnaire responses between regulated and nonregulated industries, with the following two exceptions. First, nonregulated industries are less likely to have internal auditors than are regulated industries. An estimated 95% of the regulated companies have internal auditors, as compared with only 71% of the nonregulated companies. However, mail survey results indicate that regulated and nonregulated firms with internal audit are equally likely to have an EDP audit function. Second, regulated firms report involvement in the later stages of application systems with slightly greater frequency than do nonregulated firms. These findings are notable because it was assumed at the outset of the study that there would be important differences in the audit practices between regulated and nonregulated organizations. This assumption was not supported by the SRI analysis.

TRADITIONAL INTERNAL AUDIT APPROACH

Internal audit has traditionally placed emphasis on the verification of records, controls, and the adequacy of controls in the manual systems. This approach was developed to ensure the accuracy and completeness of records and reports. In a traditional manual systems environment, internal auditors could directly observe transaction processing, record keeping, and the preparation of reports. The verification of records was performed manually from ledgers and other written documents.

The early stages of business automation typically involved single-function application systems. Individual parts of the manual system were automated. These application systems were typically run on a batch basis. Input transactions were accumulated to create a batch for processing. Batch controls were usually computed by users and used by data processing personnel to verify subsequent processing steps. For example, tabulating card applications and early computer application systems automated individual steps in an accounts payable application. After each step there were manual checks to ensure the accuracy and completeness of processing in such data processing applications; typically, users and/or computer operations personnel verified control totals after each step in the processing procedure. If errors were encountered during processing, processing was suspended until errors were resolved. The users normally had complete control over the origination and cutoff of transactions affecting the records maintained for them by the data processing department. Verification of the accuracy and completeness of data processed was easily performed by reconciling beginning and ending balances with the total balance of transactions submitted for computer processing.

In a similar manner, internal auditors verified processing results without reviewing controls internal to data processing or tracing transactions through data processing. This internal audit approach is often described as "auditing around the computer" and is illustrated in Figure 4-1. Internal audit tests to verify the accuracy and completeness of processing results were performed using reports produced as normal processing outputs. Little specialized knowledge and few specialized tools or techniques were required by internal auditors.

CHANGING APPLICATION SYSTEMS STRUCTURE

Computer application systems have become more complex and present new problems for internal auditors. For example, computer application systems are being tied together so that a transaction entered into one application system may eventually be processed against a number of previously independent masterfiles. A customer order transaction may result in changes in the balances of several masterfiles without intermediate manual review. An inventory masterfile may be credited for the quantity to be shipped and retail value or cost of the items ordered. In so doing, the quantity on hand may drop below the order point, subsequently triggering the preparation of a procurement notice or purchase order. The order transaction may also automatically trigger the preparation of warehouse shipping instructions and a customer invoice, and may update the customer's accounts receivable record.

Not all organizations have implemented computer application systems using such advanced data processing design concepts. Various changes in the structure of application systems are taking place, however, in both large and small organizations:

- Input transactions are being entered for immediate, on-line processing from remote terminal locations, in contrast to the single-entry point batch input, typical of earlier years. Approximately 79% of the organizations in the Primary U.S. Mail Survey indicate expenditures of at least $1 million for data communications equipment from the data processing budget, exclusive of terminals. This is one measure of the increasing use of data communications. Data processing industry statistics also reflect the growing use of data communications.

- Applications are being tied together so that single input transaction performs multiple functions as described in the previous example. Transactions are also being generated within application programs and automatically flow into others.
- Audit trails in hardcopy form are being eliminated. For example, detailed lists of input transactions and periodic master data file listings are being replaced by transaction logs on magnetic tape that can be printed if a need arises, and by on-line data bases for master data file interrogation.

Internal auditors working in this data processing environment report they can no longer audit around the computer and satisfy their managements' mandate. This is because so many of the controls that ensure the accuracy and completeness of data processing results are now automated and can no longer be reviewed and verified through direct observation.

AUDITING COMPUTER APPLICATION SYSTEMS

Auditing in this environment encompasses three primary areas, from the internal auditor's point of view. Each of these areas (listed below) should be

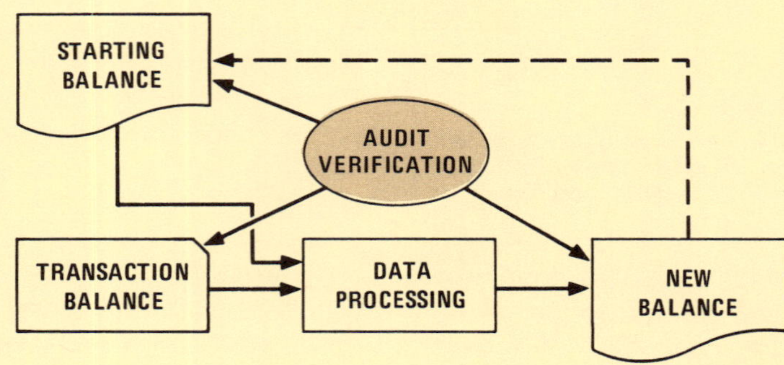

FIGURE 4-1 AUDITING AROUND THE COMPUTER

reviewed based upon organization controls that provide for appropriate definition and segregation of responsibilities.

- Manual procedures that have been developed to complement controls internal to computer application programs (e.g., input preparation, input control, error handling, and output balancing and reconciliation).
- Application system controls internal to computer application programs (e.g., data validation, control total verification, batch or transaction balancing and proofing, and error identification and reporting).
- Data files and reports produced as a result of computer application processing (e.g., data processing masterfiles, transaction logs, and output reports).

Figure 4-2 illustrates these three areas.

Auditing these areas includes a review of controls to determine their adequacy, tests to verify controls, and tests to verify data (i.e., masterfiles and reports). Each of these is discussed below.

Review Adequacy of Controls

The review of application system controls is performed to evaluate the adequacy of application controls, both manual and automated. The controls review phase of an audit is usually performed before the verification of controls; it is not so much a separate activity as it is a separate audit objective. Some internal audit organizations perform the controls review before installation of a new application, usually during systems development. Most internal auditors interviewed by SRI perform an evaluation of the adequacy of application controls as a part of periodic application audits. The objectives of such reviews are to determine if application controls are adequate to:

- Ensure the accuracy and completeness of processing results (i.e., data files and reports).
- Prevent undetected errors and omissions.
- Ensure the continuing reliability of data processing results.

An additional objective is to determine if control techniques have become outmoded because of changes in the business environment that are not reflected in computer application systems. In conducting such evaluations, internal auditors observe and test manual input preparation, error handling, and output balancing and reconciliation procedures.

Verify Controls

Application system audits include a verification of controls. They provide evidence of compliance with manual and automated control procedures. Compliance testing is a term used by public accountants and some internal auditors to describe the controls verification phase of their work. Compliance testing is not, however, a widely used term among internal auditors.

The internal auditor's objective in performing control verifications is to determine that manual controls are properly and consistently applied, and that automated controls are operating properly and have not been modified in some manner inconsistent with overall control objectives. Some internal auditors interviewed by SRI place emphasis on the manual phase of computer application operations because manual control procedures are more susceptible to inconsistent or incorrect application. During SRI field interviews, data processing and internal auditors reported that most incorrect data

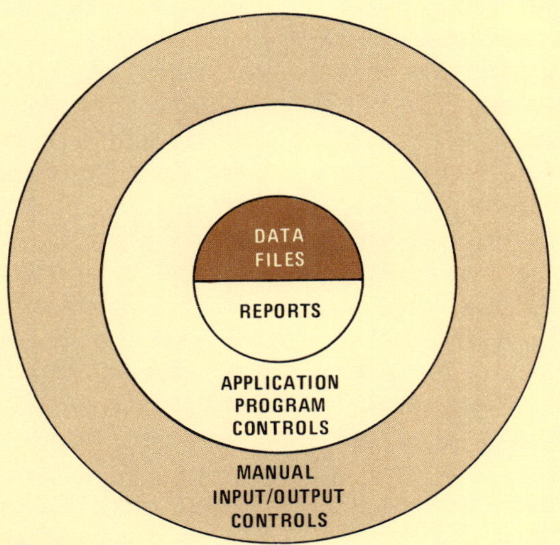

FIGURE 4-2 THREE AREAS OF AUDITING COMPUTER APPLICATION SYSTEMS

processing results can be attributed to the failure to follow manual control procedures or to the inadequacy of manual procedures. In contrast, when computer application programs are properly tested, they execute consistently, time after time, barring equipment malfunction or improper program modification.

The techniques internal auditors use in verifying manual application controls include observation, manual tracing of transaction handling and preparation, and examination of supporting source documents and logs. Primary U.S. Mail Survey findings indicate that one or more automated tools and techniques are used by an estimated 69% of the internal auditors of U.S. firms. These include techniques such as test data, parallel simulation, integrated test facilities (ITFs), and generalized audit software. Such automated techniques use the computer in auditing and, therefore, require internal auditors with data processing knowledge and experience.

Verify Data

Verifications of data processing files and reports are performed to secure evidence that processing results are accurate and complete. Public accounting literature refers to such tests and reviews as substantive tests. Few internal auditors interviewed by SRI used this term. Whereas controls verification focuses on the procedures governing data processing, the objective of data verification is to examine data files and output reports to determine their reliability.

Data verification and control verification are complementary. If a sufficient quantity of processing results are consistently accurate and complete, it seems to follow that application controls must be adequate and are being followed. Neither of these examinations is, however, entirely adequate. Data verification techniques confirm the accuracy and completeness of processing during a past period. Control verification is needed to give assurance of continued reliability. Data verification techniques used by internal auditors are both manual and automated. Manual sampling, verification of balances, and confirmation preparation are still used. An estimated 33% of the internal auditors of organizations in the Primary U.S. Mail Survey, however, use generalized audit software for data verification. A number of firms interviewed by SRI are using specialized audit software to interrogate and verify the controls of data files.

The process of auditing computer application systems is necessarily selective. Few computer applications are audited on a continuous basis. Most of the internal auditors interviewed audited computer applications only periodically. A typical approach may result in annual verification of certain data such as customer balances, retirement funds, or pension funds. Complete control reviews and verifications may be performed only every few years for a particular application system.

AUDITING COMPUTER SERVICE CENTERS

Procedures and controls governing computer center operations are of concern to internal auditors because they affect the accuracy and completeness of processing results. Several internal auditors interviewed by SRI reported that they have performed computer center audits that include procedures for physical security, program and data library control, fire protection, backup and disaster recovery, and input/output scheduling and control. This appears to be a common practice in EDP audit, although no statistical data were developed during this study. Larger organizations are developing a capability within internal audit to perform such reviews periodically. Smaller organizations use consultants or specialists from public accounting firms to review and evaluate center operations. As internal auditors become involved in computer service center audits, specialized knowledge of data processing capabilities and practices is being acquired, adding to their EDP audit capability.

AUDITING DURING SYSTEMS DEVELOPMENT

Internal auditor involvement during the development of application systems ensures that adequate controls are included for accuracy and completeness. Two points of view are reflected. Some internal auditors believe they should review systems only after their development is completed. They believe independence and objectivity are lost if they participate in the development of applications. This frequently encountered viewpoint seems to be giving way to the viewpoint of internal auditors who believe that their early participation is key to ensuring that adequate controls are considered. They believe that the evaluation of controls being designed into a system is no different from the evaluation of controls after the system is operational. They argue that it is too expensive to modify computer applications after they are completed.

Internal auditor participation took two forms in the organizations interviewed:

- Internal auditors were assigned to application development teams to present an internal audit point of view. In this situation the auditor participated but did not take direction from the project team leader. Written recommendations were prepared, but the emphasis was on cooperatively developing well-controlled computer applications.
- Internal auditors developed control guidelines for new computer applications systems. In one case

reported, the EDP auditor worked with data processing personnel to develop guidelines for a remote terminal application. Other internal auditors have developed control guidelines for computer application systems development.

The primary constraint reported in achieving such internal audit involvement is the technical knowledge of the EDP auditor. Field interview results indicate that internal auditors can make an important contribution and will be accepted by data processing personnel if they are competent and current in data processing technology and practice. Interestingly, the Primary U.S. Mail Survey indicates that almost two-thirds of data processing managers believe that benefits have resulted from internal audit efforts. This belief was reinforced by other mail surveys in which 90% of the Japanese and 80% of the European and Canadian data processing managers indicate that benefits result from internal audit effort.

One of the objectives of the Primary U.S. Mail Survey was to determine the levels of internal audit involvement in various areas within data processing. Involvement in the systems development process and in reviewing computer application systems subsequent to implementation was an area of particular interest. To determine internal auditor involvement in this area, questionnaire recipients were asked, "How involved are the internal auditors in your organization in the following phases of computer application systems involvement?"

Respondents were asked to rate internal audit involvement in six areas using a five-point scale (1,2,3,4,5) ranging from heavy involvement, to moderate involvement, to no involvement. In addition, respondents could indicate that they did not know the level of involvement. Internal auditors and data processing management were asked to report what they believed to be the current level of involvement within their organizations. Top management, however, was asked to report what they believed internal audit involvement should be. An analysis was performed by SRI to identify differences among the responses from management, internal audit, and data processing.

Figure 4-3 shows the percentage from each questionnaire that indicated any involvement (i.e., scale position 1,2,3, or 4) by auditors in each of the various phases of application system development and use. In general, auditors believe that they are somewhat more involved than data processing representatives feel them to be, and less involved than management thinks they should be. This important finding indicates that management's expectations for internal audit are not being realized, which suggests that better understanding is needed between internal auditors and management regarding the scope and content of EDP audit activities.

Figure 4-3 also indicates that although some internal auditors are involved in computer application development before installation, the largest number is involved after installation. In other words, involvement is less widespread during the earlier stages of the systems development life cycle and increases during later stages.

Figure 4-4 shows the results from the five U.S. mail surveys and from the SRI site visits. The ordinate represents the percentage of respondents in organizations with internal auditors who indicated any involvement. The abscissa represents the six phases of computer application systems development included on the mail survey questionnaire. The number of firms reporting involvement in all phases is higher among those organizations selected to be visited by SRI than for those organizations responding in any other surveys. This is not surprising, since the organizations visited were selected because of their established EDP audit programs. Figure 4-5 shows the results of the Canadian, European, and Japanese mail surveys. The patterns and levels of involvement are similar to those shown for the U.S. surveys. Aside from the responses received from those organizations visited by SRI, no important differences exist between the various surveys. (For this evaluation, important differences are defined as being any difference greater than 25%.)

The Primary U.S. Mail Survey results indicate that about 60% of internal audit programs include some involvement during application systems development. The results of field interviews conducted with U.S. and Canadian firms indicate that involvement in systems development is increasing. Several firms interviewed have active internal audit programs in this area. The experience of the firms interviewed does not, however, reflect trends in general. Smaller organizations have some involvement in the application systems development process; only about 16% indicated heavy involvement.

Figure 4-6 provides information obtained from the Primary U.S. Mail Survey regarding the degree of internal audit participation in the systems development process. The results indicate that fewer than 10% of the organizations surveyed had heavy internal audit participation during any phase of the system development process. With the exception of the Smaller U.S. Business and SRI Site surveys, in which the highest percentage of involvement was about 16% and 17% respectively, all other mail surveys indicated a smaller percentage of heavy involvement by internal auditors in any phase of the system development process than did the Primary U.S. Mail Survey organizations.

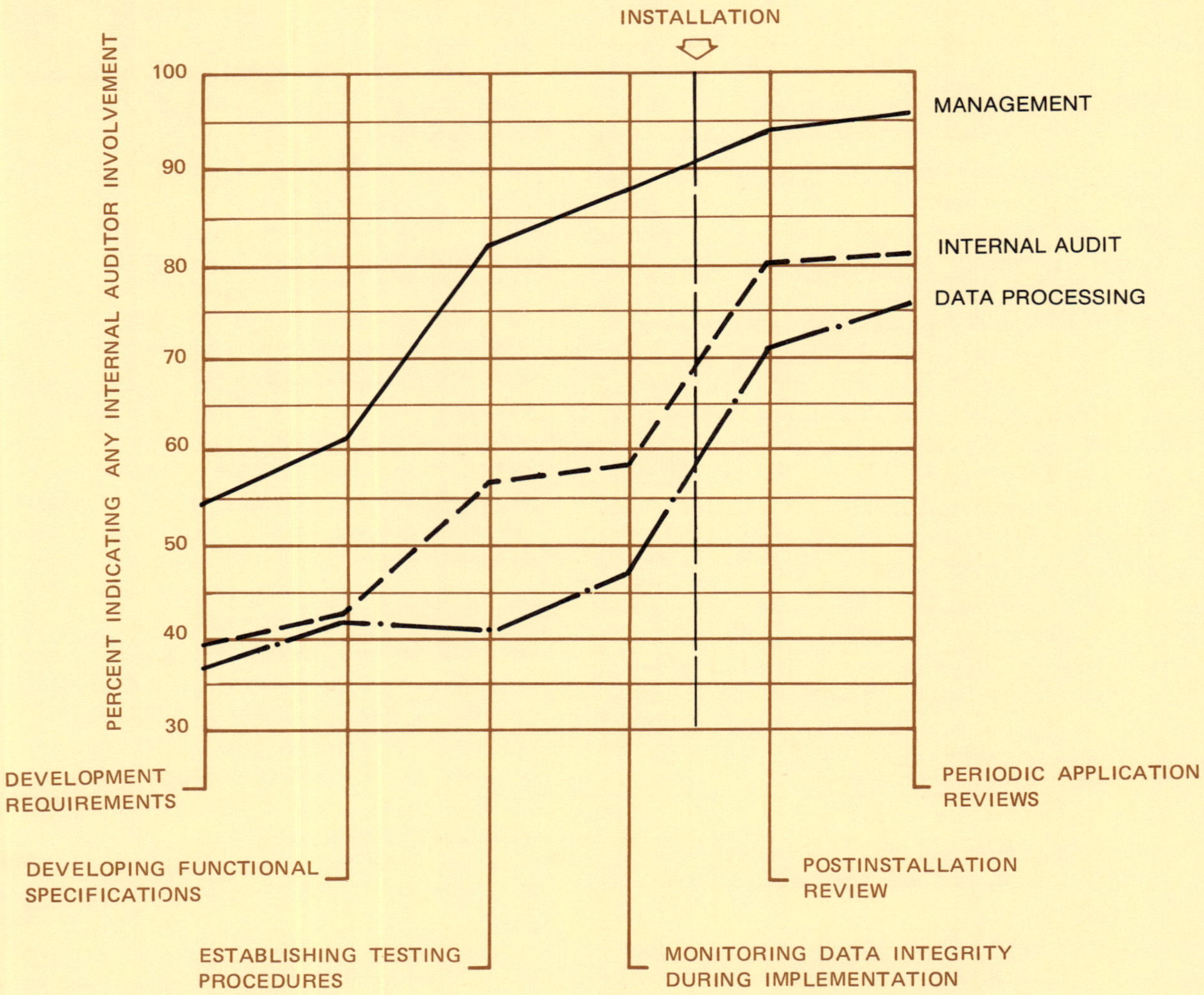

FIGURE 4-3 INTERNAL AUDIT INVOLVEMENT WITH COMPUTER APPLICATION SYSTEMS — PRIMARY U.S. MAIL SURVEY

Percentages are based on actual responses weighted to reflect the probable response distribution of all organizations with internal auditors in the sampling frame. See Appendix for further description of weighting procedures.

In a related Primary U.S. Mail Survey question, data processing managers were asked, "Who in your organization initiates internal auditor's participation in EDP application systems development?" Primary U.S. Mail Survey results indicate that, in 63% of the firms, data processing management itself is most likely to initiate the internal audit participation. This result is reinforced by non-U.S. surveys, which indicate that 70% of the Canadian and 60% of the Japanese and European data processing management initiate internal audit participation. Data processing managers were also asked to report the areas in which internal auditors work with data processing in developing controls. They responded that over 50% of the internal auditors are involved in the development of application system controls, whereas 28% are not involved at all. The Canadian and European surveys suggest similar involvement; however, the Japanese survey indicated only one-third of the internal auditors worked in developing controls for application systems.

As part of the Primary U.S. Mail Survey, data processing managers were also asked to characterize internal audit involvement in terms of the following four criteria:

- Causes increased or decreased costs
- Harmful or helpful

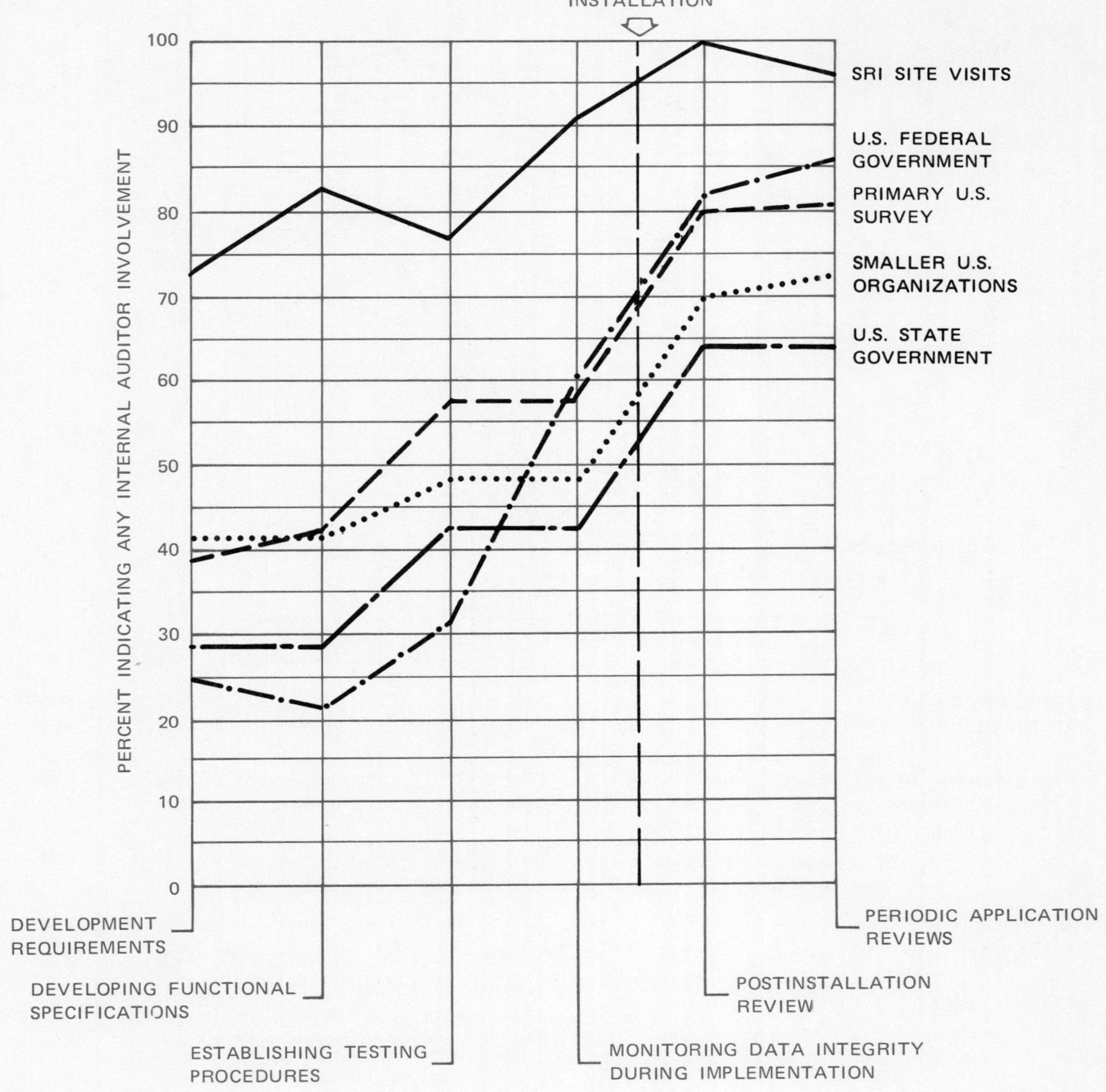

FIGURE 4-4 INTERNAL AUDIT INVOLVEMENT WITH COMPUTER APPLICATION SYSTEMS — UNITED STATES

Percentages for the primary U.S. survey are based on actual responses weighted to reflect the probable response distribution of all organizations with internal auditors in the sampling frame. See Appendix for further description of weighting procedures. All other percentages are based on unweighted responses.

- Worthless or valuable
- Unavailable or responsive

The results indicate that internal audit involvement is viewed as both helpful and valuable. It is more often characterized as responsive than not. In terms of costs, slightly more than one-half the data processing representatives feel that auditing involvement neither increases nor decreases costs; the remainder are about evenly split between those who believe that internal auditors decrease costs and those who indicate that internal auditors increase costs.

Finally, data processing managers were asked to identify two ways that data processing has benefited

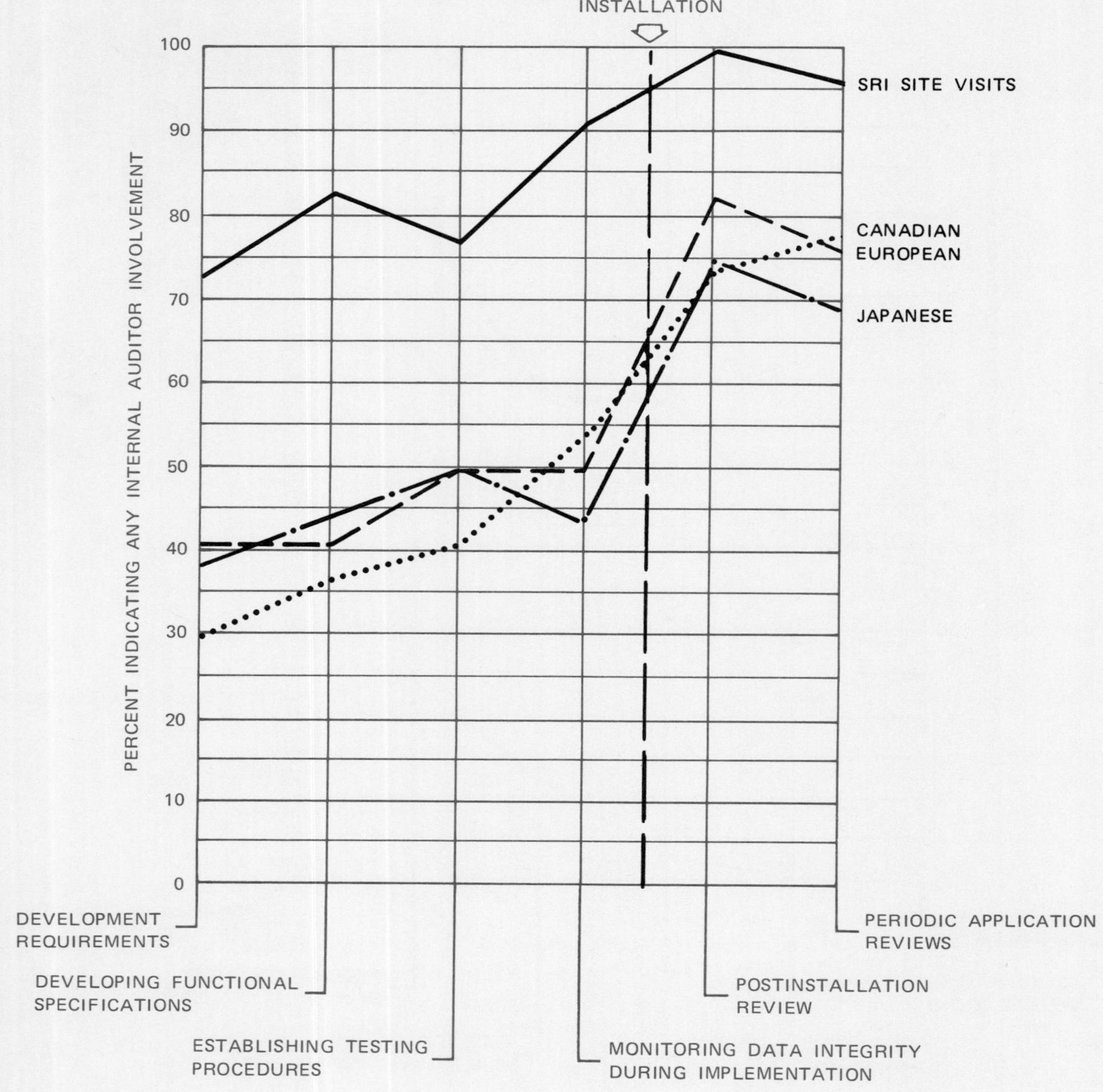

FIGURE 4-5 INTERNAL AUDIT INVOLVEMENT WITH COMPUTER APPLICATION SYSTEMS — SITE VISITS AND FOREIGN SURVEYS
All percentages are based on unweighted responses.

most from the efforts of internal audit (see Table 4-3). The three most frequently checked areas of benefit were improved application system controls, reduced fraud/loss exposure, and increased user confidence and satisfaction. Interestingly, however, almost one-third of data processing managers believe that no significant benefits have resulted from internal auditors' efforts.

SUMMARY

As management has become more dependent on data processing for the information needed to plan, evaluate, and control the activities of its organization, it has also become concerned about the increasing opportunities for efforts and omissions. Management looks to internal audit to verify the effectiveness of internal controls and the accuracy

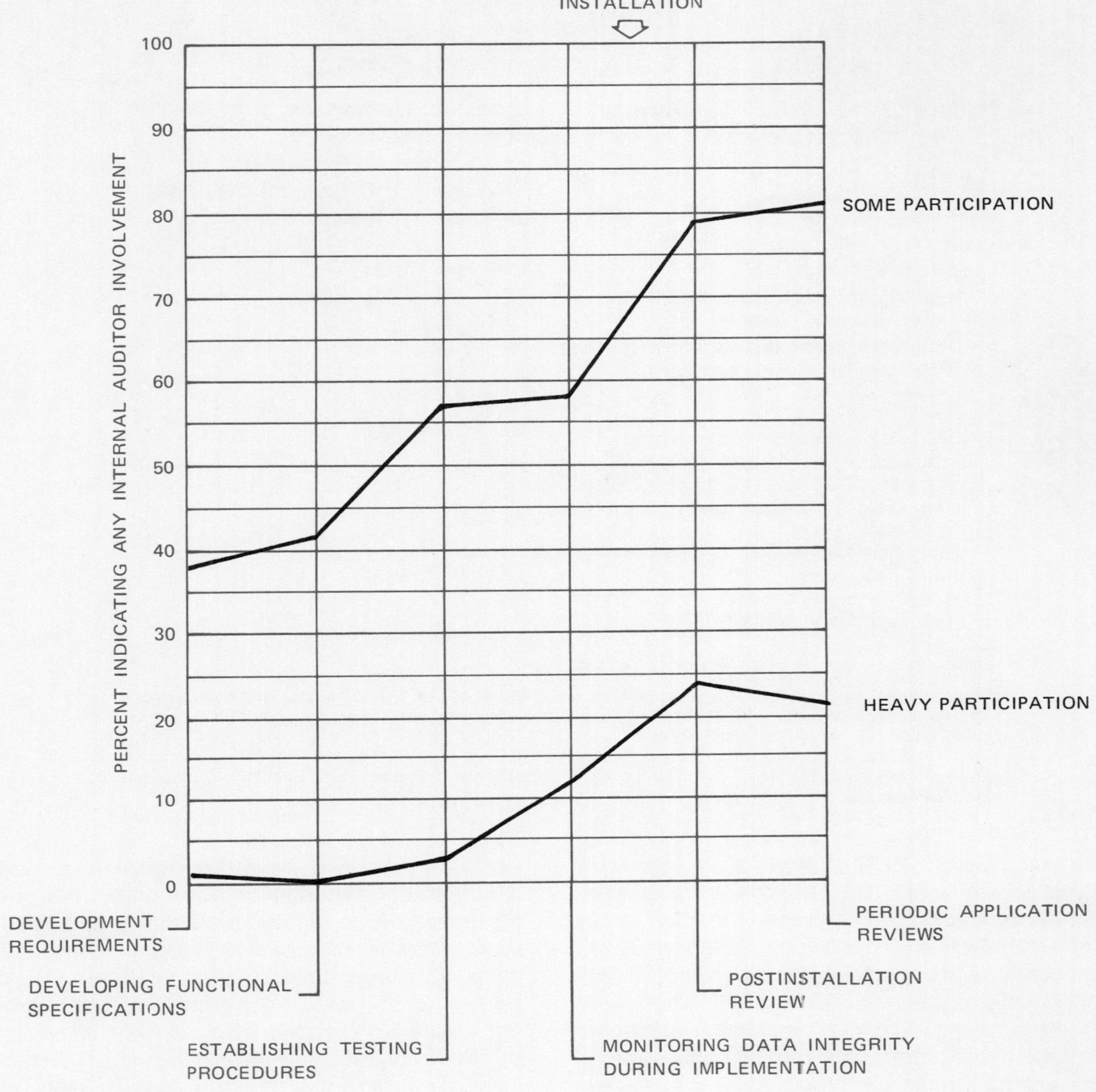

FIGURE 4-6 INTERNAL AUDIT INVOLVEMENT WITH COMPUTER APPLICATION SYSTEMS — PRIMARY U.S. MAIL SURVEY

Percentages are based on actual responses weighted to reflect the probable response distribution of all organizations with internal auditors in the sampling frame. See Appendix for further description of weighting procedures.

and completeness of data processing results. Thus, internal auditors are becoming increasingly involved in evaluating and verifying application system controls and the controls that govern other phases of data processing, such as computer operations and application system development.

Involvement in these areas is a new experience for most internal auditors, and specialized knowledge is

Table 4-3

INTERNAL AUDIT BENEFITS TO DATA PROCESSING

In which *two* of the following ways, if any, has data processing benefited *the most* from the efforts of internal auditing? (Check two)

	Percent of Total*	Percentage of Organizations That Indicated Benefits*†
Organizations indicating no significant benefit	31.6%	
Organizations indicating two of the following benefits	68.4	
Improved application system controls		45.3%
Reduced fraud/loss exposure		33.0
Increased user confidence and satisfaction		29.3
Reduced operations errors and omissions due to better controls		16.6
Reduced data processing operating costs		4.4
Improved equipment use and operating efficiency		4.4
Reduced application systems development time and cost		1.6
Other		2.2
No significant benefits		63.1

Note: Number of respondents = 169

*Percentages are based on actual responses weighted to reflect the probable response distribution of all organizations with internal auditors in the sampling frame. See the appendix for further description of weighting procedures.

†Percentages sum to 136.8% = 2 × 68.4 because respondents indicating significant benefit checked two categories.

required. As a result, EDP auditing is becoming a specialized activity within the internal audit organization. Statistics clearly indicate that the EDP audit specialty is a relatively recent phenomenon.

A number of leading organizations visited by SRI have established comprehensive EDP audit programs, the scope of which includes computer application systems, computer service center operations, and application system development activities. The expansion of internal audit activities into such areas is a logical and desirable extension of the internal auditor's traditional mandate. Comprehensive internal audit programs such as these are based on two premises:

- An evaluation and verification of data processing controls is as important as the more traditional verification of data processing results.
- Internal controls must be evaluated within the context of the total information handling process, rather than as individual control procedures.

Thus, internal auditors will continue to become increasingly involved in all phases of data processing.

The scope of current EDP audit activities and the capabilities of internal auditors to effectively evaluate and verify data processing controls are expanding, but have not, in general, kept pace with increasing management dependence upon data processing and the introduction of new technology and application system design concepts. Notable progress has been made by many leading organizations in both the private sector and in government. Such progress is not, however, representative of internal audit activities in a majority of organizations. Relatively few internal audit organizations have been able to develop needed data processing skills and experience at a fast enough pace. Three factors have tended to impede desirable growth of EDP audit capabilities.

First, traditional internal auditors have minimized the importance of evaluating and verifying data processing controls. They have failed to recognize the significance of fundamental changes in management information systems that have been brought about by data processing technology. Many internal auditors have kept to traditional methods despite the rapidly changing data processing environment.

Second, until recently, management has not fully appreciated the importance of the internal auditor in data processing. However, with the increasing incidence of computer errors and omissions, fraud, and computer abuse that has been reported in the media, management has recognized the need for greater internal audit emphasis relative to data processing.

Third, because the audit of data processing is a relatively new activity for most internal auditors and requires new and specialized knowledge, programs, and approaches to develop, the needed skills and capabilities are still in a formative stage. Thus, the internal audit manager who wants to upgrade the internal audit staff's data processing capability is faced with a wide range of experience, most so recent that its value is not clearly established. As more successful experience is gained and documented, the development of effective data processing audit programs can be accelerated.

Two divergent viewpoints exist relative to the desirability of internal audit participation in the system development process. Some internal auditors believe they should review systems only after a development process is completed. This viewpoint, however, seems to be giving way to that of internal auditors who believe that their early participation is key to ensuring that the controls are given proper consideration. This view was expressed by several leading organizations with internal audit programs that include involvement during system development. The experience of these organizations is not, however, representative of the majority of organizations contacted, particularly smaller organizations that have little if any involvement in the application system development process.

A better understanding is needed between internal auditors and both top management and data processing management regarding the scope and content of EDP audit activities. Internal audit goals and objectives need to be defined and understood by internal audit, data processing, and top management.

Data processing managers responding to the Primary U.S. Mail Survey characterized internal audit involvement with data processing in generally positive terms. The survey results indicate that internal audit involvement is both helpful and valuable. The three most frequently identified benefits reported by data processing managers were improved application system controls, reduced fraud/loss exposure, and increased user confidence and satisfaction.

Key questions were selected from the Primary U.S. Mail Survey that SRI believed would identify differences in audit techniques in regulated and nonregulated organizations. This SRI analysis identified no important differences.

EVALUATION AND OUTLOOK

Internal audit programs must be updated, both in terms of scope and content, if internal auditors are to be responsive to their mandate from management. The scope must be expanded to encompass all phases of data processing. Traditional internal audit programs limited to the verification of records and reports are not adequate and do not reflect trends being set by leaders in EDP audit or trends in public accounting that emphasize the evaluation and verification of control procedures.

First, the internal audit mandate must reflect the scope of internal audit, which encompasses appropriate areas of data processing, such as application systems, computer service center operations, and application system development. In many organizations, this will represent a whole new area of emphasis for internal auditors. Top management should make sure all affected elements of the organization understand this change and why it is desired by management. It is also important that affected elements of the organization understand that it may require some time to realize completely the objectives underlying this change in mandate.

Second, formalized programs with specific objectives are needed to guide the development of desired EDP audit capabilities. Objectives may include recruiting, staff training, and initial audit in areas new to internal auditing, such as the computer service center. Objectives should be set that reflect a reasonable balance between the present level of capabilities and the level of capabilities ultimately desired. Since it may take several years to develop the desired capabilities, specific intermediate objectives should be targeted.

Third, as skill and knowledge of data processing are acquired, internal auditors should become progressively more involved with data processing. Cooperation and coordination with data processing are important factors contributing to the rapid development of desired EDP audit skills. Internal auditor participation in data processing training programs is highly desirable. One of the goals of such involvement is to achieve a better understanding between data processing and internal auditors regarding their respective perspectives. One area of cooperation that is particularly beneficial includes the joint development of application system control guidelines and internal auditor participation in system development.

Participation during system development is important so that necessary audit and control features can be built into new application systems. Many of the audit tools and techniques are "Band-Aids," necessary only because adequate audit features have not been built into application systems. The strongest argument against participation given by internal auditors is that they lose their objectivity. This objective is overcome by ensuring that the user establishes application system requirements and that the internal auditor maintains a supporting role. Application system designs should include an explicit identification not only of the controls necessary to ensure accuracy, completeness, and security, but also of the features needed to facilitate verification of such controls.

Thus, audit tools and techniques can be developed as an integral part of the design of application systems. For such participation to work successfully, data processing must accept the expanded mandate and role of the internal audit regarding data processing activities, and internal auditors must be able to articulate their audit objectives in terms understandable to data processing personnel.

Chapter 5

EDP AUDIT STAFF DEVELOPMENT

With the growing organizational dependence upon internal auditors, the quality and quantity of EDP audit staff are a concern of top management and audit management. There are a number of alternatives in EDP audit staff development, ranging from hiring trained EDP audit personnel from outside the organization to developing comprehensive internal EDP audit training courses. Each has its advantages and disadvantages which must be evaluated relative to the organization's current EDP audit staff and requirements.

EDP audit training is important because internal auditors are being asked by management to audit through the computer rather than around it. This requirement means that internal auditors must understand the concepts of data processing and the tools and techniques available to them to perform a through-the-computer audit. In order to perform this task well, internal auditors must not only become more aware of data processing concepts, they must also keep up with computer technology and audit tools as they change.

EDP AUDIT STAFF DEVELOPMENT ALTERNATIVES

Internal audit and data processing are professions that have developed independently of one another until recent years. The increasing importance of and reliance upon data processing have caused internal audit management to recognize the need to acquire data processing competence independent of the data processing organization. Organizations have tried different approaches to acquire needed EDP audit capabilities. The range of alternatives includes:

- A separate staff of data processing professionals trained in audit.
- Training existing internal auditors in data processing concepts and practices, and in the use of computer audit tools and techniques.
- Training existing internal auditors and supplementing this staff with a few data processing specialists.
- Recruiting and training auditors specifically for EDP audit.

Each of these alternatives has been tried, frequently with variable results. Training existing internal auditors in data processing can prove to be long and costly. Many internal auditors lack the interest and motivation to work extensively with data processing. In contrast, adding data processing professionals to the internal audit staff can cause a career development problem.

The following analysis further contrasts the advantages and disadvantages of creating a staff of separate EDP specialists and of training the internal audit staff.

Separate Specialists

The formation of a separate EDP audit staff of data processing specialists is an attractive alternative because it provides a relatively quick infusion of EDP expertise. Among other advantages are the following:

- Specialized and current technical expertise becomes available to the internal audit staff without reliance upon the data processing staff.
- EDP auditors' credibility and acceptance by their data processing counterparts are improved, which facilitates acceptance of important internal audit findings and recommendations by data processing.

This approach is not, however, without important disadvantages, particularly in the long run. These include:

- Data processing personnel lack acceptance by traditional internal audit staff members. Experience of firms visited indicates this may result because data processing personnel do not typically have an appreciation of the audit perspective and because auditors tend not to embrace the data processing technicians' perspective.
- Technical knowledge can become obsolete unless the EDP auditor can continue to work closely with systems development personnel.

In addition, it may be difficult to acquire well-qualified data processing personnel because a shift to internal audit can represent a redirection of their career. Data processing personnel may see little attraction in shifting from a technology-oriented to an auditing-oriented career path where, in the long term, their specialized knowledge can become obsolete and is not a primary criterion for advancement. On the other hand, experience in more general aspects of business and accounting can be of great benefit to career data processing personnel and internal audit can be an ideal position from which to gain such a perspective.

Training the Auditing Staff

The issue underlying the feasibility of this approach to organizational development is whether or not the existing staff can acquire the necessary skills and knowledge to adequately perform the EDP audit function. Experience indicates that this can be done, subject to two important qualifications; first, formal courses in EDP auditing and data processing concepts and hands-on training are required over an extended period of time, and second, all internal auditors may not have the desire to acquire the necessary proficiency. The advantages of this approach are:

- Proper audit perspective and methods guide EDP audit programs and the use of computer audit tools and techniques.
- A total systems perspective is maintained.

Important disadvantages are also associated with this approach. These include:

- Training and hands-on experience can require many months. The effectiveness of the EDP audit program can be very limited during the interim.
- Internal audit personnel may lack credibility with data processing management and staff because they lack understanding of data processing concepts, problems associated with system development, computer service center operations, and new technology. The lack of credibility may not be material to the realization of internal audit goals and objectives, but it can be a significant deterrent.

The following examples of alternatives currently being used by companies help illustrate alternative approaches to staff development.

An Example of Training an Existing Staff

A midwestern financial corporation began to acquire EDP audit expertise several years ago when an internal auditor and his management recognized the growing importance of data processing knowledge required to properly perform internal audit duties. The firm encouraged the auditor to acquire basic training in data processing by attending technical seminars and evening college courses in data processing. He worked with data processing staff and their public accounting firm's management services staff to expand his knowledge of system auditability and control. As this first EDP auditor's knowledge increased, he was able to begin working with other internal auditors.

He was instrumental in introducing automated audit tools and techniques to other internal auditors. The advantages of EDP audit techniques became obvious to audit management and other internal auditors on the staff of over 40.

With greater acceptance came the question of how best to expand the EDP audit function. The second person added to the EDP audit staff was also an internal auditor. The EDP audit staff was then given a charter with three primary responsibilities:

- Use data processing tools and techniques to support the audit objectives assigned other internal audit staff personnel.
- Further develop and implement appropriate system auditability and control techniques, working with internal audit and data processing personnel.
- Train other internal audit personnel in the use of data processing tools and techniques so they may become generally self-sufficient.

As these tasks grew it was decided that further data processing competence was needed. At that time, two people with data processing backgrounds were added to the EDP audit staff. These individuals were chosen to provide more technical data processing knowledge and experience. Their work is directed by the EDP audit supervisor who was the first EDP auditor on the staff.

This organization reports that it is generally pleased with the evolution of its EDP audit function. It is currently working well and making an important contribution. One problem persists, relating to the newer data processing personnel who seem to be having trouble gaining rapport with other internal auditors. They use different jargon and do not have a common perspective. In addition, many audit personnel still have not developed an appreciation of the data processing perspective. This is being overcome slowly through improving working relationships with the data processing personnel.

An Example of Specialized Outside Recruiting

A large eastern financial institution interviewed hires experienced internal auditors from outside the organization. These auditors are hired with an understanding that they will specialize in EDP audit. They need not have prior data processing knowledge. When the new EDP auditors report for work, they first attend a 13-week data processing course. Upon completion of the course, they are then assigned to maintenance programming work within the data processing organization for five months. This provides practical experience in data processing and a familiarity with the procedures and standards used within the data processing organization. Upon completion of this eight-month technical training period, the EDP auditor is assigned to the internal audit staff and begins supervised work on EDP audits.

This approach was used in order to achieve a buildup of EDP audit capability within the organization. It represents substantial expenditures in terms of both recruiting and training. Extensive provisions for training new EDP auditors are required for the success of such a program.

This approach has the advantage of selecting experienced auditors who have made the commitment to the EDP audit specialty. It has the added advantage of providing eight months of controlled training and experience in the data processing environment within which the auditor will subsequently work. During this training period, EDP auditors become acquainted with their data processing counterparts and have an opportunity to gain specific application knowledge and rapport with data processing personnel. The approach has at least one major disadvantage, the level of expertise acquired by new EDP auditors is somewhat limited by their eight-month training program. They have little opportunity to gain true expertise in other than the most rudimentary concepts, principles, and practices of data processing.

An Example of a Hybrid Approach

An eastern manufacturing firm with a staff of 100 internal auditors located throughout the United States started a formal program to develop an EDP audit capability six years ago. Its original objective was to upgrade existing internal auditors and achieve an integration of data processing and traditional audit techniques. A single EDP audit coordinator was designated who had a good data processing background, and a training program was developed. However, the results of this effort were disappointing and three problems were identified:

- Training everyone on the internal audit staff was a slow and expensive process.
- Internal auditors felt training emphasized too much technical information that was beyond the context of internal audit.
- While some internal auditors had an interest and intellectual orientation to data processing, others had little interest and felt course content was not relevant to their work.

A high level of EDP auditing competence and involvement was not achieved. However, two important results were realized. First, the audit staff was exposed to the importance and complexities data processing could impose upon the future audit environment and the general EDP audit techniques available to deal with these growing complexities. Second, the program served to identify those individuals who had an aptitude for and/or interest in EDP audit. Thus a nucleus of interested people was identified.

This company took a different approach to training, starting approximately four years ago. Data processing technical specialists were added to the corporate audit staff to form a small EDP audit function. Their responsibilities were training and technical assistance for other internal auditors in performing data processing audits including participation in application system development. It is now concluded that it is not practical or necessary to train the entire internal audit staff in EDP audit techniques. In fact, it is preferable to identify individuals from internal audit with an interest and desire to work with data processing and train them in order to form a cadre of internal auditors with a strong data processing orientation. This group can support other internal auditors.

The technical support function has remained small so that little organizational distinction is made between EDP auditors and other internal auditors. It is expected that this staff will continue to be made up of internal audit personnel with some data processing personnel having fairly specialized knowledge in data base and data communications. This group will provide staff support to all audits performed within the data processing function and involving computer application systems.

Internal audit management believes that the success of this concept is dependent upon the personnel selected for the technical staff. Individuals have been chosen based upon their knowledge of the business in general and their accounting background, data processing technical knowledge, and potential for subsequent promotability.

By rotating these data processing personnel through EDP audit, other important disadvantages are overcome. For example, technical knowledge can be kept current within the EDP audit function, technically qualified and aggressive individuals are attracted and the position does not become a dead end; and the ultimate responsibility for traditional audit work remains with other internal auditors.

This experience reflects a change in original philosophy of training everyone, to a philosophy of selective internal auditor training, with a small technical group to provide training and support programs for all the corporation's internal auditors. As a result, appropriate use of EDP audit technicians is gaining acceptance by other internal auditors.

EDP AUDITOR TRAINING

For organizations that utilize data processing as a major component, training internal auditors in data processing concepts and in the use of EDP audit tools and techniques is an essential element in successful organization development. However, Primary U.S. Mail Survey results indicate that about half the large U.S. corporations with internal auditors have no budget for EDP audit training. Almost 90% of those organizations that have such a budget allocate less than 5% of the total internal audit budget for training.

The structure of an EDP audit training program depends upon the size and background of the staff to be trained, whether or not the staff is centralized or geographically dispersed, and the data processing activities of the organization. Small firms operating out of a single location can usually get by with more informally planned programs, while geographically dispersed organizations require more structured approaches. The content of EDP audit training programs depends upon the sophistication of data processing application systems, the data processing background of the internal auditors, and the EDP audit tools and techniques required to audit the organization's data processing activities. These subjects will be addressed in more detail later in this chapter.

EDP Audit Training Objectives and Elements

The primary objectives of EDP audit training determined during the study are to:

- Provide the internal audit function with sufficient EDP audit knowledge to effectively audit computer application systems and related data processing activities.
- Develop and maintain an awareness of the best EDP audit tools and techniques available to the internal auditor.
- Develop and maintain an awareness of computer technology as it relates to EDP auditing in order to anticipate new requirements.

To meet these EDP audit training objectives, organizations are using a number of available sources that include:

- Professional associations such as The Institute of Internal Auditors or the American Institute of Certified Public Accountants.
- Public accounting and consulting firms.
- Colleges and universities.
- Professional conferences.
- Audit software vendors.
- Computer hardware suppliers.
- Data processing training staff.

As an example, within an estimated 80% of the organizations included in the Primary U.S. Mail Survey with internal audit functions, the internal audit staff keeps pace with technical development in data processing in part by attending professional conferences and external courses.

Four basic areas for EDP auditor training are:

- Introduction to data processing
- General EDP audit training
- Advanced data processing
- Specialized EDP audit techniques.

EDP auditors may require an introductory course in data processing to familiarize them with terminology, concepts, software, hardware, and the data processing environment. This type of course can usually be provided by the data processing department, or the department can provide information on where to obtain such a course.

The Institute of Internal Auditors, the American Institute of Certified Public Accountants, and other professional organizations provide some of the best programs for general EDP audit training. This type of course introduces the EDP auditor to the state of the art, EDP audit tools available, software packages available, and, perhaps most important, introduces the EDP auditor to the emerging role of EDP auditors.

Advanced data processing training is required for organizations that are major data processing users—those that are heavily involved in large data base management systems, that develop more than one major application system per year, and so on. The advanced data processing course expands on the basic course by providing more depth of knowlede in each area of data processing covered in the basic course. In addition, it usually addresses the computer system architecture in some detail, covering such items as operating system characteristics, memory management systems, and communication systems. This course is usually available from the data processing department or their training department. In some instances, the computer supplier also provides this type of course, but the data processing department is the best point of contact.

Specialized EDP audit techniques are available from the audit software vendors and, to a degree, through professional audit associations and public accounting firms. In general, these courses address special tools, techniques, and audit software that are tailored to specific environments, such as financial systems.

In the following example, the company interviewed combined the basic data processing course with a basic EDP audit course. While combining the two courses provides some degree of continuity, in some cases it may require the internal auditor to comprehend too much information in too short a period of time. Each organization must evaluate the background, capabilities, and interest of the persons in the course to see which alternative works the best.

Training for Internal Auditors with Little or No Data Processing Experience

The following five-day course outline, used by one firm interviewed, serves as a good example of the type and content of short courses available to internal auditors as an introduction to data processing. This type of course is usually quite general and is applicable to internal auditors from different types of organizations. The primary objective of this type of course is to provide the internal auditor with an appreciation of data processing and the role of the EDP auditor within that environment.

- Introduction to the elements of data processing and computer application systems as viewed by an internal auditor.
- Computer hardware overview—includes a discussion of terminals, storage devices, processors, and the general terminology associated with them.
- Computer programming overview—Includes discussions of flowcharting, decision tables, and the COBOL programming language.
- Computer documentation overview—Includes discussions of documentation types, styles, and standards required by internal auditors.
- Introduction to internal controls—Discusses the objective of internal controls, methods for implementing controls, and methods available to audit the controls.
- Introduction to general controls—Discusses controls over data processing activities, data communications, and other areas requiring general controls.
- Case study that allows the participants to take part in an active audit case.

The time spent on this type of course varies among organizations interviewed. Although the above outline was for a five-day course, some organizations send their personnel to a one-semester college or university night course that provides the same material. Other organizations use cassettes and break the course into as many as 30 to 40 hours of one-hour courses that can be used by the person at his or her convenience. Under no circumstances is it possible to learn the amount of information required by EDP auditors in one or two such courses. It not only takes time, but experience in applying the knowledge. For this reason, it is especially beneficial for organizations to encourage cooperation between data processing and internal audit to develop and provide the training courses.

Training for Internal Auditors with Data Processing Experience

This type of course is more specific in its objectives, and it is usually not applicable to a wide spectrum of organizations. For example, it may be tailored to financial application systems or to manufacturing application systems, but usually not to both. Although there are advanced courses that apply across the board, most organizations indicate that internal auditors find tailored courses to be much more cost beneficial.

The following example of an advanced course used by a large insurance company serves to highlight the scope of this type of course. The company combines advanced data processing and specialized audit techniques training activities. A prerequisite for attending is knowledge of on-line systems and a basic systems control course.

- Introduction—Includes a review of the accepted control objectives and checklist.
- On-line systems control—Addresses identification, verification, and authorization of persons and terminals. This includes a review of techniques available through the computers to assist in controlling access to data and programs in a specific environment.
- Data communication control—Addresses message sequencing, control totals, message accounting, journaling, and error detection and correction. In addition, discussions of physical controls available in this area are included.
- Continuous operation controls—Includes discussions of data, terminal, communications, and processing equipment.
- Storage media/device control—Includes tape and disk, internal and external labeling, and access journals.
- Audit trace considerations—Includes discussions of how audit trails should be used to assist the internal audit function.
- Special audit software—Includes tools, techniques, and software available to meet the organization's requirements.
- Case study.

Additional elements in some courses reviewed by SRI include:

- Computer room security audit techniques
- Demonstrations of new software packages on the market.

The more advanced courses address the problems of on-line systems rather than batch systems. This does not imply that batch control training is not important, but rather that on-line systems present more of a problem and a challenge to internal auditors.

The Primary U.S. Mail Survey results indicate that almost half (43%) of the EDP auditors most recently added to the staffs of large U.S. organizations come from outside the company. Other mail survey results with the exception of the Japanese survey reinforced this finding. Japanese firms responding report no auditors are recruited from outside the company, as might be expected due to traditional Japanese employment patterns. Well-trained EDP auditors are being recognized as valuable professionals. As a consequence, it is anticipated that organizations with good EDP training programs may be forced to deal with higher salary requirements or higher turnover rates until the supply of EDP auditors meets industry needs.

SUMMARY

The training of internal auditors in concepts of data processing and EDP audit tools and techniques is important to successful organizational development because top management is placing more reliance on internal auditors to verify the accuracy and completeness of computer application systems. This reliance on internal auditors is forcing them to develop more technical data processing expertise. Several alternatives to upgrade the technical skills of internal audit are discussed in this chapter, of which the best, based on SRI field interviews, involves training a portion of the existing internal audit staff in data processing and supplementing the staff with a few data processing specialists on a rotational or well-defined basis. This alternative avoids some of the career path development problems associated with the other alternatives. In fact, it allows both data processing professionals and internal auditors an opportunity to expand their career potentials.

Any type of EDP audit training program developed should include two phases, a general introductory course for those internal auditors with no data processing experience, and a more advanced course tailored to the specific data processing and operations requirements of an organization. The amount of time and money required to develop an adequately trained staff varies among organizations, but top management should be made aware that for the next few years the training program will not be quick and easy. As the number of well-trained EDP auditors increases, organizations will require less resources for training, but some level will always be required to keep pace with rapidly changing computer technology.

EVALUATION AND OUTLOOK

Currently, there is a growing requirement in most organizations that are large users of data processing to upgrade the quality and quantity of EDP auditors within their organizations. There are not enough trained EDP auditors to meet the demand. Consequently, well-trained EDP auditors will continue to be sought after by large organizations. Although some organizations are attempting to train existing internal auditors in data processing and some are attempting to train data processing personnel in internal audit, a successful approach includes some mix of internal auditors and data processing personnel.

It is preferable to identify individuals from internal audit with a specific interest and desire to work with data processing and train them to form a cadre of internal auditors with a strong data processing orientation. Once a nucleus is formed, this group can support other internal auditors and encourage them in their greater involvement with data processing. The activities of this EDP audit staff include supporting the entire internal audit staff as well as performing specialized audits of computer application systems within the data processing department. It may be appropriate, as involvement with data processing increases, to add data processing personnel to the EDP audit staff to provide specialized assistance in areas such as data communications or the use of generalized data software.

SRI believes that effective programs to train internal auditors should include the following characteristics.

- Courses in the fundamentals of data processing for internal auditors with no prior data processing experience. It is appropriate that such courses emphasize system design concepts and data processing capabilities rather than computer program coding.
- Courses for internal auditors involved in EDP audit work that enable them to acquire additional formalized training in auditing in the data processing environment. Among organizations offering such training are colleges, universities, public accounting firms, and professional associations.
- Technical courses for EDP auditors involved in advanced aspects of data processing, such as data communications or data base. Such courses are offered by private institutions, professional associations, and computer hardware and software vendors.
- Attendance at seminars and conferences wherein recent experience with advanced EDP audit tools and techniques are discussed.

Finally, training of internal auditors will be a continuing process. Data processing technology will continue to change and grow. Internal auditors will be required to keep up with the changes and anticipated new requirements. This will require extensive training on a regular basis.

Part II

AUDITING IN THE DATA PROCESSING ENVIRONMENT

This part of the Audit Practices Report includes four chapters that present SRI findings and conclusions relating to the tools and techniques currently being used by internal auditors to evaluate and verify controls governing computer-based information system processing, computer service center operations, and the application system development process.

Chapter 6 provides an overview of EDP audit approaches, tools, and techniques identified and documented by SRI during field interviews. Discussions of 28 EDP tools and techniques are included, with usage information secured from respondents to the Primary U.S. Mail Survey. The complementary relationship between auditing the controls governing computer-based information system processing and auditing the results of such processing, e.g., data files and reports, is presented.

Chapter 7 describes audit and control practices relating to computer-based information systems. Controls and audit techniques are described, categorized in six areas: transaction origination, data processing transaction entry, data communications, computer processing, data storage and retrieval, and output processing. Important SRI findings and conclusions are presented relating to increasing internal auditor involvement in auditing computer-based information system controls and associated tools and techniques.

Chapter 8 describes audit and control practices relating to computer service center operations. Findings are presented, categorized in eight areas: input/output, media library, separation of duties, environmental physical security, disaster recovery malfunction reporting and preventive maintenance, resource planning, and user billing/chargeout procedures. Important SRI findings and conclusions are included relating to the increasing emphasis that internal auditors are placing on controls governing computer service center operations and the increasing knowledge required to effectively audit this area.

Chapter 9 describes audit and control practices governing the computer-based information system development process. Findings are presented, categorized in seven areas: user requirements, development standards and guidelines, project management, documentation, acceptance testing, post-installation review, and program change control. The relationship between these controls and data processing accuracy and completeness is also described. Important findings and conclusions include the increasing internal audit interest in the controls governing systems development, particularly those controls relating to acceptance testing, documention, postinstallation reviews, and program maintenance control.

Chapter 6

DATA PROCESSING AUDIT METHODS, TOOLS, AND TECHNIQUES

Changes in the data processing environment are resulting in the changes in the role of the internal auditor described in earlier chapters of this report. With greater emphasis being placed on computer application system and program controls, EDP auditors are developing new audit methods, tools, and techniques. The development of such tools and techniques is still in its early stages and many are adaptations of existing data processing techniques. Others, such as the generalized audit software packages now available, have been developed specifically to meet audit needs. Although computer audit tools and techniques are becoming widely used, much of the internal auditor's work still involves manual tracing, examination, and verification of transactions, records, and reports.

The transition from traditional record keeping to today's data processing application systems has been a progressive phenomenon. During the early stages of the application of computer systems to the business environment, little change in internal audit method was required. The application systems paralleled the manual systems they replaced. Transaction registers, ledgers, and reports were usually converted to data processing as an exact image of the corresponding manual procedures. Existing manual control procedures were carried forward in ways that made data processing operations almost transparent to the internal auditor. As a result, internal auditors could generally ignore data processing and leave their audit procedures basically unchanged. Thus, they continued their traditional work and audited around the computer. As more business systems have been automated and tied together, control procedures have changed and no longer parallel traditional manual procedures. For example:

- As the number of records on masterfiles has increased, application systems have been designed to display masterfile data on an exception basis using report generator programs or terminal access procedures. Several firms interviewed by SRI have masterfiles that are seldom printed in their entirety.
- As computer application systems have been tied together, transactions entering one application system can eventually affect other application systems without intermediate manual intervention, e.g., order entry often successively feeds transactions into inventory billing and accounts receivable applications. In addition, exception conditions may trigger internally generated transactions that have no analogy in record keeping.
- Transaction processing has been adopted by organizations using data communications and remote terminal entry facilities. Individual transactions can be entered by users directly into data files without intermediate batch checking, balancing, or subsequent batch reconciliation. Transactions may also be accepted and posted from several locations rather than from a single batch entry point.

Data processing applications that incorporate design concepts such as these rely heavily on application controls to identify errors and omissions and report them for subsequent manual resolution. In these situations, some of the traditional manual control procedures have been restructured and greater reliance is placed on application program controls. To this extent, the accuracy and reliability of computer application processing is more dependent upon application controls built into computer application systems than in the past. For this reason, many internal auditors feel it necessary to evaluate and verify these controls in order to judge the accuracy and reliability of computer application systems.

DATA PROCESSING AUDIT APPROACH

Considerable variations exist in the way internal auditors approach their work, depending upon experience levels in both audit and data processing, and the level of sophistication of the data processing environment. SRI field interviews indicated that, in addition, relatively few organizations have formalized procedures to guide the internal auditor in application reviews. Many organizations still rely on the ingenuity of internal auditors and the basic discipline inherent in the general approach to auditing. Most of the internal auditors interviewed followed some variation of a three-phase approach, which includes:

- Initial review and evaluation of the area to be audited and audit plan preparation

■ Detailed review and evaluation of processing logic and controls
■ Tests to verify compliance with established controls, and verification of selected data records.

Each of these phases is further discussed as follows:

Initial Review — The initial review is conducted by the internal auditor to familiarize himself with the application area to be audited. It usually includes a review of the job description, organization charts, procedural documentation, and the basic control structure of the application to be audited. The internal auditor also reviews transaction flow and may even trace selected transactions in order to understand processing sequences and identify controls and data elements important to the objectives of the audit. The initial review results in a specific audit plan that includes only those processing and control functions germane to the purpose of the audit. If control deficiencies or data errors, or both, are identified during subsequent phases of the audit, the scope of the audit plan may be extended to include compensating audit procedures.

Detailed Review and Evaluation — The second phase of the internal auditor's work focuses on fact-finding in the area selected for audit examination. The detailed review and evaluation includes internal controls, processing procedures, and data processing masterfiles. This activity includes observing procedures in user areas and data processing, tracing transactions, and analyzing control logs and records. In performing this detailed review and evaluation, the auditor is able to assess the adequacy of the control structure and secure detailed information needed for subsequent testing. The latter may require a review of computer application system and program documentation to secure record layouts from computer processing flowcharts. The results of this detailed evaluation are used to confirm the scope of the audit and to design the test procedures to be subsequently used.

Tests — The testing phase of the audit produces evidence of procedural compliance, and data accuracy and completeness. These tests may be performed manually by the auditor by tracing transactions, verifying authorizations, checking manual extensions, and balancing and reconciling accounts to transaction journals. Even when applications use the computer, much manual testing can be performed using regularly prepared input balancing reports, error exception reports, and account balance reports. An adequate audit trail should allow such a review to be performed by users as a matter of routine. Data verification can also be performed manually by reviewing masterfile listings and tracing account balances to control totals external to data processing. Generalized audit software packages are widely used to extract data from masterfiles and prepare customer account confirmations and other reports needed to verify balances.

Internal auditors use specialized audit software to monitor transaction amounts, account balances, and error aids within important computer application systems on a daily basis. If conditions are encountered during application processing that are at variance with audit control parameters, audit reports are prepared automatically to identify the variance conditions. Internal auditors can then investigate the conditions more closely. Audit subroutines to monitor computer application systems are used in conjunction with continuous audit projects.

Test procedures may be used by auditors to verify computer application program controls. For example, test decks are used to verify specific computations in the payroll or inventory application programs. Test procedures are described later in this chapter. Their objective is to verify application program controls.

In general the computer is an important aid to the internal auditor and its growing use as an audit tool is, in part, the subject of this study. With the computer, internal auditors can effectively and efficiently perform tests directly involving application program logic and data processing mastefile content. The computer can provide audit evidence faster than manual methods. However, care is required to ensure that evidence is produced in a form and quantity consistent with specific internal audit objectives. Despite the growing use of computer aids in auditing, internal auditors still perform extensive manual tracing and verifying after computer-prepared results are available to them.

The following sections describe data processing audit tools and techniques used in computer application control evaluation and verification, and data verification. Also presented are tools and techniques used in auditing computer service center operations and the computer application systems development process.

DATA PROCESSING AUDIT TOOLS AND TECHNIQUES

Internal auditors have adopted various data processing methods for use in auditing computer application systems, computer service center operations and application systems development. Development of these audit tools and techniques has been an evolutionary process that has grown in intensity during the last six to eight years, as auditors have sought more effective and efficient methods to audit the data processing environment. This development process is expected to continue unabated during the next few years as internal auditors seek to keep pace with the implementation of advanced data processing technology.

SRI has identified 28 EDP audit tools and techniques as a result of field interviews with internal auditors. Table 6-1 provides a summary of these tools and techniques. Usage information is available for many of these as a result of the SRI mail survey (see Table 6-2 at the end of this chapter). Each tool or technique presented has been classified according to the primary audit area it addresses. More detailed descriptions of most of these 28 appear in later chapters. (See footnote to Table 6-1 for an explanation of why all 28 tools or techniques were not completely documented.)

Techniques for Audit Planning and Management

This category includes two kinds of internal audit tools and techniques: first, techniques used to evaluate application systems for inclusion in current internal audit plans; second, techniques to provide internal audit staffs with specialized EDP audit capabilities.

Audit Area Selection — This is a procedure to collect and evaluate selected operating statistics to

Table 6-1
DATA PROCESSING AUDIT TOOLS AND TECHNIQUES

Tools and Techniques	Chapter Reference
Audit Planning and Management	
Audit Area Selection	10
Simulation/Modeling*	—
Scoring	11
Multisite Audit Software	12
Competency Center	13
Testing Computer Application Program Controls	
Test Data Method	14
Base Case System Evaluation	15
Parallel Operation	—
Integrated Test Facility	16
Parallel Simulation	17
Selection and Monitoring of Data Processing Transactions	
Transaction Selection	18
Embedded Audit Data Collection	19
Extended Records	20
Verification	
Generalized Audit Software	21
Terminal Audit Software	21
Special-Purpose Audit Programs*	—
Analysis of Computer Programs	
Snapshot	22
Manual Tracing and Mapping*	—
Computer-Aided Tracing and Mapping	23/24
Control Flowcharting	25
Computer Service Center	
Job Accounting Data Analysis	26
Audit Guide	27
Disaster Testing	28
Application System Development	
Postinstallation Audit	29
Control Guidelines for Use During System Development	30
System Development Life Cycle	31
System Acceptance and Control Group	32
Code Comparison	33

*Schedule constraints of the field interviews did not allow for complete documentation of the simulation/modeling technique. No organization visited was effectively using the technique. Parallel operation and manual tracing and mapping are traditional techniques that are already well documented. Special-purpose audit programs, by their very nature, are not transferable and consequently it was decided to present only the concept in Chapter 6.

identify unexpected variations, such as a high level of uncollected receivables. This technique uses computer programs to compare estimates of expected values with actual values to identify potentially important differences. This technique has the advantage of allowing internal auditors to screen many transactions or account balances for a number of operating locations and identify areas that warrant closer examination. A disadvantage of this technique is that models must be kept current in terms of changing characteristics of, or relationships between, variables used in estimating. Building and maintaining models can be time consuming, costly, and require specialized knowledge in their design and the use of modeling or programming languages. For more detailed information see Chapter 10.

Simulation/Modeling — This procedure compares estimates of expected values with actual values to identify potentially important differences between logically related account balances. Such modeling is an extension of ratios used to evaluate financial results, between both accounts and periods. The use of the computer allows more variables to be included in preparing estimates on a pro forma basis. This technique is similar to the audit area selection technique mentioned above, except that it is used only periodically to evaluate financial performance. In contrast, the audit area selection technique is used to monitor selected account balances on a continuing basis. The simulation/modeling technique has the advantage of allowing internal auditors to evaluate account balances and thereby identify unexpected differences that may warrant closer examination. A disadvantage of this technique is that models must be kept current in terms of changing characteristics of, or relationships between, variables used. Such modeling can be time consuming, costly, and requires specialized knowledge.

Scoring — This manual procedure is used to evaluate computer application systems to determine their relative importance to internal auditors from a risk viewpoint. Numeric values are assigned to selected characteristics, such as value of assets controlled, vulnerability to fraud, level of system or program modification, regulatory or management reporting prepared. Each factor is weighted according to its importance. Once application sysems are scored using this method, internal audit management is in a good position to effectively allocate internal audit resources in the areas of greatest risk. For more detailed information see Chapter 11.

Multisite Audit Software — This is a procedure for the centralized preparation and distribution of EDP audit software for use by decentralized EDP audit groups within a single organization. A single set of audit software is developed for use in several computer service centers by internal auditors assigned to those facilities. For example, a large business maintains regional data processing facilities to handle its nationwide retail accounts receivable. A standard accounts receivable auditing system is developed centrally and distributed to auditors at all data processing locations to aid the auditor during conduct of the audit. Such an EDP audit approach has the advantage of concentrating internal audit development skill and eliminating the resulting cost for decentralized, independent development efforts. It also encourages consistent internal audit practice throughout the firm's various data processing locations. This approach has little applicability in situations where different locations use different computer application systems. For more detailed information see Chapter 12.

Competency Center — This EDP audit capability is established at a central data processing location that is responsible for the execution of audit software programs. The competency center receives data files from other locations, executes the necessary audit software programs, and distributes the resultant reports to the originating internal auditor. This approach is primarily applicable to large multilocation organizations. It centralizes the execution of audit software programs and associated expertise, thus eliminating the distribution of software and training of EDP auditors in its use. For more detailed information see Chapter 13.

Techniques to Test Computer Application Program Controls

This category of EDP audit tools and techniques is used to test computational routines, programs, or whole applications in order to evaluate controls or verify processing accuracy and continued compliance with specified processing procedures. Such techniques are used for both the evaluation of application systems controls and for compliance testing.

Test Data Method — This procedure executes computer application programs or systems using test data sets, or test decks, and verifies processing accuracy by comparing processing results with predetermined test results. Internal auditors use this technique to test selected processing logic, computations, and control features within computer application programs. Such testing may include gross pay computations, interest computations, or input transaction validation. One of the advantages of test decks is that their initial use can be limited to specific program functions, thus minimizing the scope of testing and thereby its complexity. This technique is a good learning tool for internal auditors because initial use requires minimum EDP knowledge. Care must be taken to ensure that the scope of testing is broad enough to provide meaningful evidence consistent with audit objectives. For more detailed information see Chapter 14.

Base Case System Evaluation — This procedure executes computer application system programs using test data sets developed as a part of a comprehensive testing program, and verifies processing accuracy by comparing processing results with predetermined test data results. This technique uses test data developed by auditors and computer applications users in cooperation with data processing systems development personnel to provide comprehensive application program testing. The base case data set is intended to be used to verify correct system operations before production acceptance as well as to periodically verify the integrity of processing after production acceptance. Base case system test data sets are, by definition, comprehensive in that they are developed to provide selective testing of all features and functions within a computer application system. Although this technique provides the advantage of comprehensive systems verification and compliance testing, the effort required to maintain extensive data sets after initial installation is not inconsequential and close cooperation is required between users, auditors, and EDP personnel preparing test data and validating results. For more detailed information see Chapter 15.

Parallel Operation — This is a procedure to verify the accuracy of new or revised application system programs by processing production data and files using both the existing and the newly developed procedures, and comparing processing results to identify unexpected differences. This procedure is widely used by data processing personnel to verify new or revised application system programs prior to replacing existing procedures. It has the advantage of verifying new application system programs before existing ones are discontinued. This procedure may identify previously undetected problems, and builds user confidence in new application systems. Extended periods of parallel operations can, however, have the disadvantage of added processing costs resulting from duplicate processing.

Integrated Test Facility (ITF) — This is a procedure to process test data sets through computer application systems concurrent with production processing, and subsequently compare the test results with predetermined test data results. Procedures used in implementing an ITF must be carefully planned to ensure that production results and production data files are not affected by test data. The scope of an ITF may be limited to testing specific processing functions or computations, or may be designed to test all the logic within an application. The essential feature of an ITF is that testing occurs with the processing of production data. This technique has the advantage of allowing periodic testing without the need to set up separate test processes. Care must be taken, however, to ensure that test data are isolated from production data or that reversing entries are made to eliminate test data from production files. For more detailed information see Chapter 16.

Parallel Simulation — In this procedure, production transactions and files are processed using computer programs that simulate application program logic; selected processing functions can then be verified by comparing simulation results with production processing results. This test technique has the advantage of verifying selected processing procedures using production data and thereby obviates time-consuming test data preparation. Internal auditors using this technique, however, must prepare computer programs that simulate the production functions to be verified. Either specially prepared audit programs or generalized audit software can be used for this purpose. The use of generalized audit software has simplified the preparation of parallel simulation programs. For more detailed information see Chapter 17.

Techniques to Select and Monitor Data Processing Transactions

Data processing audit tools and techniques used to select and capture production data for subsequent manual audit and verification are included in this classification. These techniques are typically used to monitor production activity and select samples as part of a continuous auditing activity within the normal production process. Selection criteria are usually parameter controlled and use range tests, sampling techniques, or error conditions to trigger the selection of records for subsequent evaluation by internal auditors. Such techniques are used in compliance testing to monitor transaction processing and to select data for verification. This category includes input transaction selection programs, which are independent of application system programs, audit modules embedded within application systems, and the extended record technique.

Transaction Selection — This procedure uses audit software to screen and select transactions that are input to computer application systems as a part of the regular production processing cycle. Capabilities include monitoring activity levels and error rates by transaction, systematically selecting transaction samples for subsequent manual verification, and identifying and selecting exception conditions specified by internal auditors. The software is parameter controlled and totally independent of its corresponding production application system software. As a result, it is independently controlled by the auditor and can be installed without requiring modification to application system software. The cost of development and maintenance is the primary disadvantage associated with this technique. For more detailed information see Chapter 18.

Embedded Audit Data Collection — This procedure uses audit software to screen and select input transactions and transactions generated within computer application systems during production processing. Such audit subroutines are embedded within host computer applications. Activity monitoring, sampling, and exception reporting are all controlled by parameters. The design and implementation of such modules are highly application dependent and are usually performed as an integral part of the application-development process. This method is often referred to as SCARF—System Control Audit Review File. It has the advantage of providing sampling and production statistics, including both input and internally generated transactions. The primary disadvantages are the high cost of development and maintenance and the difficulties associated with auditor independence. For more detailed information see Chapter 19.

Extended Records — This technique gathers together by means of a special program or programs all the significant data that have affected the processing of an individual transaction. This includes the accumulation into a single record of results of processing over the time period that the transaction required to complete processing. The extended record includes data from all the computer application systems that contributed to the processing of a transaction. Such extended records are compiled into files that provide a conveniently accessible source for transaction data. It has the disadvantage of potentially increasing data storage requirements and costs, and adding to systems development costs (see Chapter 20).

Techniques for Data Verification

Data processing audit tools and techniques, such as generalized audit software, are included in this category. These techniques are used subsequent to production processing to select data from files based on logical or statistical sampling requirements, to foot and balance files or logical sections of files, such as divisional organizations or classes of accounts, to screen files for exception values, missing data, or duplicate entries, or to format reports for audit use. Also included is a modeling technique used to evaluate account balances.

Generalized Audit Software — General-purpose software accesses, extracts, manipulates, and presents data and test results in a format appropriate to internal audit objectives. Such generalized file handling software is usually controlled by parameters or simplified procedural statements that require a minimum of data processing knowledge. Generalized audit software has the advantage of allowing internal auditors to manipulate data processing masterfiles without preparing computer programs. A disadvantage associated with this technique is that, since evidence is limited to the data files, its usefulness in testing procedural compliance is limited. For more detailed information see Chapter 21.

Terminal Audit Software — This general-purpose software accesses, extracts, manipulates, and displays data from on-line data bases using remote terminal inquiry commands. This technique provides the same basic functional capability as the more widely used batch-oriented, generalized audit software. It has the advantage of quicker turnaround and interactive investigation, and it provides direct access to data files, allowing periodic internal audit examination of files without excessive setup or separate processing. It is, however, only useful in situations where on-line data bases have been established and are already in use. The details of this technique have been included in Chapter 21, Generalized Audit Software.

Special-Purpose Audit Programs — These computer programs are specially tailored to extract and present data from a specific application system's files, usually in an invariable format. Disadvantages associated with the use of special-purpose audit programs are their limited applicability, inflexibility, preparation cost, and the high level of computer programming expertise required. Due to the specific nature of each special-purpose audit program, no detailed chapter exists for this technique.

Techniques to Analyze Computer Application Programs

Data processing audit tools and techniques used to evaluate processing logic and procedures internal to application programs, systems of programs, and JCL (Job Control Language) are included in this section. These techniques are used during application systems development as well as during periodic postimplementation compliance testing. Included are snapshot, tracing, mapping, and flowcharting aids.

Snapshot — These program instructions or subroutines recognize and record the flow of designated transactions through logic paths within computer application programs. This technique is used by internal auditors to trace specific transactions through computer programs and secure documentary evidence of logic paths, control conditions, and processing sequences. The technique has the advantage of verifying program logic flow and, consequently, aids internal auditors in understanding processing steps within application programs. It has the disadvantages of requiring extensive EDP and computer programming knowledge, and it is often a time-consuming procedure for internal auditors to use. For more detailed information see Chapter 22.

Manual Tracing and Mapping — These procedures identify the flow of transactions and associated application controls, including source document origination, approval, and processing, as well as data processing transaction entry, computer processing, and the distribution and use of data processing reports. Manual tracing and mapping may include the analysis of application program listings to identify and evaluate application program logic and control functions. However, emphasis is on the identification and evaluation of manual procedures and controls external to application programs. Computer-aided tracing and mapping techniques are used to analyze application programs, complementing manual methods.

Computer-Aided Tracing and Mapping — These computer program subroutines identify program segments and/or subroutines used in processing test transactions. Computer-assisted tracing provides documentary evidence of the program statements used to process specific transactions. Mapping is a technique that provides evidence of processing sequences used at the subroutine rather than the application program statement level. These audit tools and techniques are used to verify transaction processing logic and identify unused portions of computer programs. Two disadvantages are associated with their use by internal auditors; first, extensive EDP and application programming knowledge are required; second, they are time consuming and involve detailed analyses. For more detailed information see Chapters 23 and 24.

Control Flowcharting — This procedure uses computer program flowcharting techniques to identify and present logic paths and control points within computer application systems. Standard analytical auditing symbols and techniques are used to develop visual profiles of computer application systems. These profiles provide useful vehicles for discussions with users and data processing personnel concerning internal application system controls. In addition, the flowcharts serve as an excellent mechanism for training new EDP auditors. For more detailed information see Chapter 25.

Techniques to Audit the Computer Service Center

During field interviews SRI documented these internal audit techniques that are used to evaluate and verify general controls in the computer service center.

Job Accounting Data Analysis — Internal auditors use this procedure, which selects, extracts, and presents job accounting information, to verify that persons submitting work for computer processing are authorized to initiate such processing. They also use this technique to monitor access to sensitive data files and/or application programs. The unauthorized and improper use of production files in application program testing can be identified through this analysis. For more detailed information see Chapter 26.

Audit Guide — This procedure is used by internal auditors to guide their review, evaluation, and testing of specific areas, such as the computer service center or a computer application system. Such audit guidelines are established to help ensure that internal auditors examine all facets of an area in their review. Audit guidelines may be simple checklists, or may include more extensive background information on control and audit objectives and audit criteria. The use of audit guidelines in data processing is becoming increasingly common, particularly as an aid to less-qualified internal auditors. For more detailed information see Chapter 27.

Disaster Testing — This procedure, simulating a disaster in data processing, is used to evaluate the effectiveness of data processing disaster contingency plans. Such tests may include retrieving and executing backup application programs stored off-site, reconstructing designated masterfiles using data files stored off-site, testing standby electrical power sources, and executing application programs and data files at alternative computer processing facilities. Periodic testing is usually supplemented with interim audits of off-site storage procedures for both critical application programs and data files. Disaster testing is becoming more important as management's dependence on data processing increases (see Chapter 28).

Application System Development Techniques

In this category five audit techniques are presented that are useful to internal auditors reviewing the controls governing application system development.

Postinstallation Audit — These procedures review, evaluate, and test new or revised computer application systems and associated controls, records and reports shortly after their installation. The purpose of conducting a postinstallation review is to determine if newly developed or modified computer application systems are, in general, performing as specified and desired by users, and to verify the accuracy and completeness of processing. A postinstallation audit serves to verify that application systems development has been properly performed and ensures that the results of subsequent processing are reliable. For more detailed information see Chapter 29.

Control Guidelines for Use During System Development — Procedures are developed jointly by internal auditors and data processing personnel to guide the evaluation and selection of appropriate computer application system controls and audit features. Such guidelines typically include two parts: first, a general statement of control objectives to guide the system designer in establishing processing procedures, both manual and automated, and associated control techniques; second, reference lists of control techniques found to be of value in successful computer application systems. Such guidelines provide structure in the process of evaluating and selecting appropriate application controls. For more detailed information see Chapter 30.

System Development Life Cycle (SDLC) — This is a method to structure the application system development process and subsequent maintenance activities associated with computer application systems. Use of the SDLC technique establishes a standard sequence of activities and checkpoints for the development of all computer application systems. The activities included within each successive phase of the development process are specified, with general criteria against which successful completion can be measured. The inclusion of checkpoints for internal audit participation is optional. However, when such internal audit steps are included at appropriate points in the development process, development work can be scheduled so as to allow adequate provision for internal audit participation. Thus, internal audit effort can be planned and scheduled within the context of overall systems development project plans, facilitating internal audit participation and proper evaluation of audit and control features. For more detailed information see Chapter 31.

System Acceptance and Control Group — This organization within data processing monitors application system development on a continuing basis to ensure that appropriate control techniques are incorporated for processing integrity. A System Acceptance and Control group reviews the adequacy of internal controls from a total system viewpoint, including manual and automated phases of processing. It also participates with other data processing personnel in establishing system development standards relating to internal control and auditablity. Although the Systems Acceptance and Control group resides within the data processing organization, its function is independent of application system development and maintenance activities. It is used in lieu of internal auditor participation in application system development to overcome two difficulties: first a lack of appropriate data processing knowledge and experience on the internal audit staff; second a desire of the organization not to potentially compromise the independence of internal audit through their participation in system development. Note, that auditor independence in relation to application system development is discussed in Chapter 3, Internal Control in Organizations Using Electronic Data Processing. For more detailed information see Chapter 32.

Code Comparison — This procedure uses the computer to compare two versions of a computer application program to identify differences in coding. The internal auditor uses the output of the comparison process to identify changes that have occurred between application programs and subsequent revisions. He then locates and analyzes the documentation that was prepared to request and authorize the program changes that have been made. Two approaches to program change control were identified during the SRI study: one uses source code as the basis for the comparison between two versions of a program; the second uses object code as the basis for comparisons. For more detailed information see Chapter 33.

TOOLS AND TECHNIQUES USAGE

One of the objectives of the study was to determine the relative frequency of use among a number of internal audit tools and techniques. Table 6-2 shows usage information based on the results of the Primary U.S. Mail Survey. Because the mail survey was initiated before field interviews with internal auditors, it did not include all tools and techniques. Usage information is, however, presented for the most important tools and techniques identified during the field interview phase of the research. Survey respondents were asked to report use in each of two classifications, system development and production.

Table 6-2 shows that generalized audit software and manual tracing and mapping are the two most frequently reported tools and techniques used in auditing production application systems. The test data method, i.e., test decks, was the third most frequently reported tool or technique used.

The three tools and techniques most frequently reported as being used by internal auditors during systems development were parallel operations, the test data method, and manual tracing and mapping.

The reported use of systems performance monitoring techniques, such as SMF (System Management Facilities), seemed high in light of field interview findings that failed to identify any internal auditors doing performance monitoring work. Telephone calls were therefore made to approximately 30 mail survey respondents who reported using these techniques. The results of this telephone follow-up indicate that although most of these organizations had performance monitoring programs, internal auditors were only indirectly involved, if they were involved at all. Internal auditors in organizations visited by SRI use SMF data, but not to evaluate computer system performance. Rather, they are using SMF data to determine who is using computer resources, computer application and utility programs, and data files. Based on this follow-up therefore, it appears that internal audit use of SMF data is limited to verifying that proper control is maintained over the use of computer resources.

AUDITING APPLICATION PROGRAM CONTROLS

A difference of opinion exists among internal auditors interviewed by SRI as to the most cost-effective approach to verifying computer application controls. Some auditors have ignored the controls within application programs, believing that if processing results are verified one can infer that application program controls are adequate and working effectively. The internal auditors who report this viewpoint spend little, if any, time examining application programs and controls and, accordingly, are not in a good position to judge the effectiveness of application system controls. This viewpoint overlooks the possibility that particular conditions not present during a processing period could occur in the future and produce unpredictable results.

Other internal auditors interviewed report they are involved in evaluating and verifying application program controls using techniques such as mapping and tracing at the application program level. They have immersed themselves in the data processing technology, including the evaluation of application program codes. When such activities complement the verification of processing results, the internal auditor is in a good position to judge the effectiveness of controls. However, such approaches involve much time and detail, and require a high level of data processing competency.

A compromise approach has been taken successfully by several firms interviewed. It includes thorough data verification procedures complemented by selective functional testing to verify application program controls, such as important computations and/or error detection and reporting routines. Audit tools and techniques used to perform such tests include test decks, ITFs, and parallel simulations. Proponents of this EDP audit approach report that it has two advantages:

- Specific application program controls, processing functions, and computations are verified, albeit selectively. Specific functions are selected for evaluation based upon their relative importance to audit objectives.
- Tests are performed without the auditor becoming involved with detailed application program logic; test data are constructed based on an understanding of the application program function performed, rather than on how it is coded in a particular application program.

When the internal auditor is involved at the functional level rather than at an application program logic level, audit work is less technologically complex and time consuming. Because EDP audit capability is a scarce resource, internal auditors supporting this approach report that they feel that consuming EDP audit resources in detailed evaluations at the application program logic level is not cost effective. They report that when functional testing is used in conjunction with data verification, both controls and processing results can be verified.

SUMMARY

SRI concludes that few present internal audit tools and techniques are adequate for verifying the accuracy and completeness of controls being used in computer application systems.

With the greater emphasis now being placed on computer application systems and data processing, new internal audit approaches, methods, tools, and techniques are needed. Internal auditors have recognized this need and adopted various data processing methods to audit computer application systems and other phases of data processing. The resulting tools and techniques have been used with some success. Such an adaptation is often the best available alternative, but may not effectively or efficiently meet all the internal auditor's requirements. The search for and development of new internal audit tools and techniques has been an evolutionary process that has grown in intensity during the last few years. Although development efforts can be expected to continue during the period ahead, they are not expected to keep pace with the general growth of data processing.

SRI has identified 28 EDP audit tools and techniques used by internal auditors in auditing application systems, computer service center operations, and the controls governing the application systems development process. These tools and techniques aid EDP auditors in evaluating and verifying application system controls and processing results, such as data files and reports. The number and variety of tools and techniques reflect the desire of internal auditors to find effective and efficient methods appropriate to the new data processing environment. The tools and techniques most frequently reported as being used, based on mail survey results, are generalized audit software, manual tracing and mapping, and test decks.

Although an increasing number of internal auditors are using the computer, many are still only auditing around data processing. These internal auditors are ignoring the controls within application programs, believing that if processing results are verified, application controls must be effective. Although such an approach does verify historical results, it overlooks the possibility that conditions not previously present could occur in the future with unpredictable results. Even though the internal auditor may use the computer to perform data validation in this manner, two important audit objectives are not realized. These are the evaluation of application program controls and the verification of application program controls.

Other internal auditors interviewed approached these latter two audit objectives (evaluation and verification of controls) by performing a detailed examination of application program logic and coding. Thus, all three audit objectives are satisfied by combining data verification with such an evaluation and verification of controls. However, such a detailed examination of application program logic and coding is costly, time consuming, and requires extensive data processing knowledge and skill. As a result, such an approach is often not cost-effective, even though computer-aided tools are available to assist internal auditors in their examination.

A third approach is successfully used by many organizations. It includes a thorough data verification, complemented with selective functional testing, to evaluate and verify application system and program controls, such as important computations or error detection and reporting procedures. These functional tests are performed without the internal auditor becoming involved in detailed programming logic; test data are prepared based on functional specifications, often provided by data processing users rather than data processing personnel. Thus, the internal auditor's work is less complex and less time consuming than if audit work is conducted at the program logic level. The combination of generalized audit software for data verification and functional testing methods, such as test decks or ITFs, offers a cost-effective approach to EDP audit that satisfies all three basic audit objectives. This combination of EDP audit techniques is not, however, widely used.

EVALUATION AND OUTLOOK

Although data processing verification and functional testing represent a satisfactory approach to EDP audit, the efforts of internal auditors to develop new and more effective EDP audit tools and techniques can be expected to continue through the period ahead as the scope and content of internal audit work expand, and new technology and application system concepts are introduced. Most of the development work in the past has been conducted on an uncoordinated and isolated basis. The exchange of information regarding alternatives, EDP audit tools and techniques, and approaches has occurred rather informally through professional contacts and professional associations. Public accounting firms have done much to facilitate the exchange of successful experience with specific audit tools and techniques. Their notable contribution in this regard has been in encouraging internal auditors to use generalized audit software.

Efforts to develop more effective EDP audit tools and techniques can be accelerated two ways. First, development programs within organizations should be based on cooperation between internal audit and data processing personnel. The participation of representatives from the organization's public accounting firm may also be appropriate and may provide an opportunity to evaluate their experience in developing similar EDP audit approaches, tools, and techniques. Close cooperation between internal audit and data processing, however, is critical to success in developing effective tools and techniques. Relatively little cooperation has occurred in the past within most organizations. This is because there is a lack of understanding between internal audit and data processing personnel of internal audit's responsibilities, goals and approach to auditing in the data processing environment.

Close cooperation during application system development is particularly important so that audit features can be built into new applications. Audit techniques that are integrated into application systems, such as ITFs and terminal audit software capabilities, are far more effective than elaborate audit techniques developed independently by internal auditors after the fact. The development of audit tools and techniques as an integral part of the design of application systems seems to hold the most promise for effective EDP audit in the future.

Second, the development work that takes place within individual organizations needs to be complemented by coordinated, industry-wide efforts involving groups such as data processing users, professionals such as The Institute of Internal Auditors, the American Institute of Certified Public Accountants, and equipment and software suppliers. Although useful tools and techniques can be developed within individual organizations, it seems unlikely that improvements on a broad scale can be achieved without bringing together interest groups that broadly represent the accounting and auditing professions, the data processing profession, and equipment and software designers. Such a cooperative effort will allow audit requirements to be viewed in the broadest possible information system context. Representatives of these interest groups contacted by SRI during the course of this research all indicate a great deal of interest in better understanding system auditability and control requirements in a data processing environment, particularly as new technology and application system concepts are introduced.

Internal audit management, data processing management, and top management can all encourage progress in both of these areas. A first step is to clarify the role of internal audit in data processing. A second step is to identify and define audit objectives relating to the data processing environment. Once these steps are taken and the role of the auditor in the data processing environment is clarified, serious efforts can get under way to close the gap between EDP audit capability and rapidly advancing data processing technology.

Table 6-2

USE OF EDP AUDIT TOOLS AND TECHNIQUES

Which of the following tools and techniques are used in auditing EDP application systems in your organization?

EDP Audit Tool/Technique	Percentage Used in Auditing Developments and Modifications*	Percentage Used in Auditing Production Systems*
Generalized audit software	12.5%	32.6%
Manual tracing and mapping routines	22.9	31.2
Test data method (e.g., test-decking)	27.1	26.6
Parallel operation	32.2	23.1
Tagged transactions (flagging transactions in "live" operations for later review)	12.0	20.9
Snapshot (picture-taking of selected transactions through the flow of transactions	10.0	18.4
Systems performance monitoring and analysis (e.g., SMF, SCERT)	8.2	15.8
Program source code comparison	9.6	14.5
Control flowcharting	8.3	9.0
Program object code comparison	4.7	8.9
Integrated test facility (mini- or dummy company)	4.2	5.0
Modeling (simulation)	9.5	7.6
Automatic tracing and mapping routines (analysis of source language and logic to determine if any program segments are not being utilized)	3.6	3.9
Other	6.5	10.5

*Percentages are based on actual responses weighted to reflect the probable response distribution of all organizations in the sampling frame. See the apendix for further description of weighted procedures.

Chapter 7

AUDITING COMPUTER APPLICATION SYSTEMS

Computer application systems are important to internal auditors because they are one of the three areas within data processing that affect the accuracy and completeness of data processing results. The other two areas, computer service center operations and application systems development, are discussed in subsequent chapters. The tools and techniques EDP auditors use to audit computer application systems have been classified under six separate application system phases of operation, which are described in this chapter. The two most important phases, according to the internal auditors interviewed, are transaction entry controls and data processing output controls. These controls represent the interface between data processing and user departments. Two other phases of increasing importance to internal auditors are data communication controls and data storage and retrieval controls, because these controls involve new system design concepts and data processing technology. The increasing development and implementation of application systems incorporating these new design concepts are resulting in the need for internal auditors to develop new audit techniques. Each of these phases of computer application control is described in this chapter, along with the EDP audit tools and techniques currently in use.

The accuracy and completeness of data processing are primarily dependent upon computer application control. This chapter provides an overview of such controls that govern the flow and processing of transactions, the maintenance of data processing records and files, and the preparation and handling of output reports. Such controls are built into computer application systems based on the specific requirements of their users. Although similar control techniques may be used in many computer applications, they are arranged to satisfy different functional control requirements. Control techniques are often similar, but their applications vary widely.

This chapter also presents an overview of the internal auditor's tools and techniques used to evaluate and verify application systems processing. Application controls and related audit tools and techniques are presented in six separate phases in the sequence of application processing. These include transaction origination, data processing transaction entry, data communications, computer processing, data storage and retrieval, and output processing (see Figure 7-1). This segregation of application controls and associated internal audit tools and techniques groups together control techniques that perform similar or related functions. It is based on the more detailed presentation found in the companion volume of this series, The Control Practices Report, Part II, Computer Application System Controls.

In this chapter, each phase of application system processing contains, first, a summary of more detailed material presented in The Control Practices Report, then a description of applicable internal audit approaches, tools, and techniques. The individual EDP audit tools and techniques are the subjects of later chapters. An attempt was made in preparing this presentation to show the relationship between individual controls and the relevant application system audit tools and techniques, but such a presentation was found to be impractical because a single audit technique is typically used to test or verify a series of controls rather than individual controls. As a result, control and audit techniques are presented separately for each phase of the application system process. Individual audit tools and techniques are often used in several different phases of the application system process. In such situations, they are presented in each section of the chapter that discusses a phase of application system processing in which they are found to be in use.

Organizing the material in this manner allows the internal auditor to consider control objectives and alternative techniques at various stages of processing. (However, it is necessary not to focus on individual phases or control techniques to the exclusion of overall control and/or internal audit objectives.) Audit and control objectives and techniques can only be effectively evaluated within the context of the total information handling process.

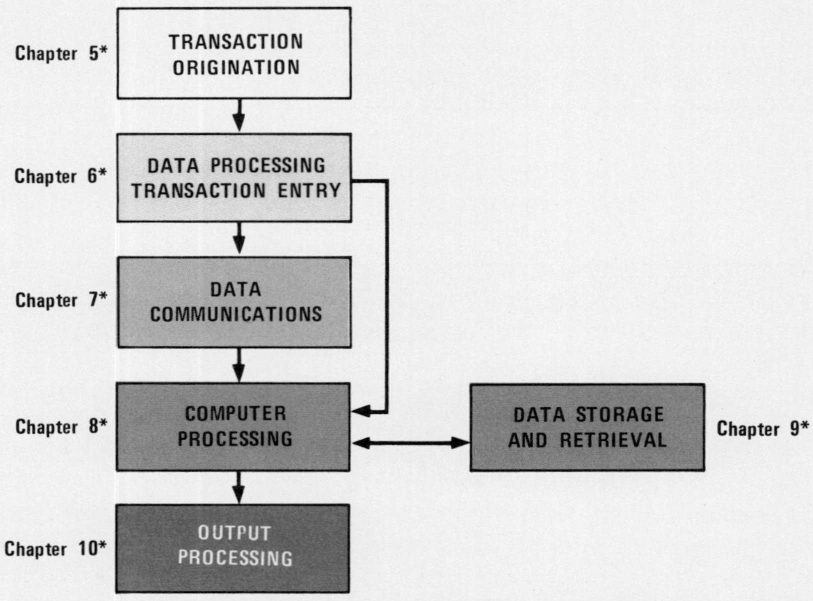

FIGURE 7-1 CLASSIFICATION OF APPLICATION SYSTEM CONTROLS

TRANSACTION ORIGINATION

Transaction origination controls govern the manual preparation and processing of transactions prior to their entry into data processing. They are, by definition, manual rather than automated and exclude user terminal data entry, which is described in the following section. This first phase includes the origination and processing of business transactions external to data processing. These transactions may eventually flow into data processing or be used to prepare other documents that, in turn, flow into data processing. For example, vendor invoices may be batched and sent directly to data processing for key punching, key verification, and subsequent data processing. As an alternative, a transaction register may be prepared by abstracting necessary data from vendor invoices. Invoices can then be retained in the accounts payable department with only a transaction log forwarded to data processing. The merits of these alternatives can be properly evaluated only within the context of specific computer application system requirements. They are included only to illustrate that the internal auditor is concerned with source transactions and controlling procedures even if they are not the actual documents that eventually flow into data processing. Both source documents and data processing transmittal forms are important in reviewing the application controls governing transaction origination.

Important transaction origination control areas can be seen in Figure 7-2 which shows the relationship of these five control areas. Three are in the direct flow of transaction processing. Source document retention is an off-shoot from this flow, and source document error handling is part of a feedback loop to source document origination. The transaction entry phase follows this phase. The five transaction origination control areas are:

■ *Source Document Origination* — These application controls include written procedures governing document origination and processing, as well as the design of source documents to minimize errors and omissions. They ensure proper storage, preparation, and manual processing of source documents.

■ *Authorization* — These application controls ensure that only properly authorized source documents are accepted for subsequent data processing entry.

■ *Data Processing Input Preparation* — These application controls include the accumulation of data processing input transactions, manual error checking, input batch preparation for subsequent transmittal to data processing, logging transactions and batches to be sent to data processing, and preparation of batch control totals for subsequent batch balancing during receipt and processing within the data processing function.

■ *Source Document Retention* — These application controls include the interim retention of source documents during processing, long-term retention of designated source documents, and removal and destruction of source documents at the termination of their retention.

■ *Source Document Error Handling* — These application controls govern the disposition of

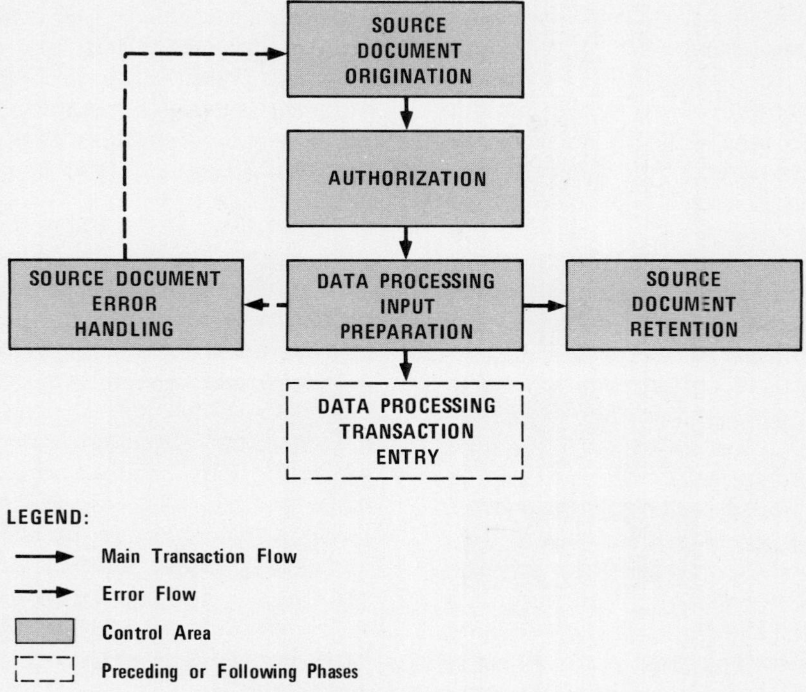

FIGURE 7-2 TRANSACTION ORIGINATION

incorrect source documents, i.e., error identification, logging, reporting, and correction.

Methods used by internal auditors to review the adequacy of such controls and perform tests of compliance include procedural reviews, observations in user areas, manual tracing of transactions and review of associated transmittal documents and logs, and a review of input error reports prepared by the computer. Manual tracing and source document verification are used to evaluate and verify compliance with input preparation procedures.

Internal auditors place emphasis on two areas of transaction origination. The first is transaction authorization. In verifying proper transaction authorization, internal auditors select data processing transactions and manually trace them back to their authorizing source document(s). In performing this examination, the auditors check to determine that the data processing transactions accurately reflect the data appearing on source documents. Source documents are also examined for proper authorizing signatures, as may be required.

The second area of emphasis is the preparation of transaction batches and associated control totals, transmittal documents, and control logs. In reviewing this area, internal auditors typically select a batch and trace it through the various manual processing steps, both in user areas and within data processing. Generalized audit software can be used to select transactions and batches from data processing files for subsequent manual tracing to verify proper transaction preparation and approval. Internal auditors also report the use of special subroutines embedded in computer application programs. Such audit subroutines regularly select transactions for verification as part of continuing internal audit programs. The selected transactions are subsequently traced and verified in user areas.

DATA PROCESSING TRANSACTION ENTRY

Application controls governing the entry of transactions into data processing can take two forms; batch data entry and terminal data entry.

The scope of the transaction entry phase of computer application system processing may include keypunch, key verification, terminal data entry, computer input validation, transaction error identification and reporting, and error reentry procedures. These functions are included within this phase of computer application system processing, whether performed in user areas or within data processing. As a result, internal auditors are interested in examining both automated and manual data entry procedures within data processing and user departments. Transaction entry encompasses both sides of the important interface between data processing and its users. Several internal auditors interviewed said that they believe this man/machine interface is the weakest, most error-prone link in the computer application system cycle.

These application controls include terminal transaction and batch transaction validation as well as associated manual balancing and transaction error handling. They exclude controls governing computer processing subsequent to transaction validation, which are presented in a subsequent section of this chapter. This segregation may seem to be arbitrary, particularly for computer application systems that have been designed on the basis of transaction processing concepts. However, it serves to segregate interactive application controls governing terminal data entry as well as traditional batch data entry controls still widely used from those controls governing subsequent phases of computer processing. Controls governing data communication facilities are included in the next section. Four important control areas governing transaction entry can be seen in Figure 7-3, which shows the relationship between these four control areas. From the transaction origination phase, the main line of flow passes through terminal or batch data entry, through transaction data validation, and on to either the data communications phase or the computer processing phase. The transaction error handling control area is part of a feedback loop to either transaction data entry or transaction origination, depending on the nature of the errors.

The four control areas in the transaction entry phase are:

■ *Terminal Data Entry* — Application controls to govern terminal functions such as data entry, data retrieval, transaction formatting and operating dialogues, and logging of terminal use and errors.

■ *Batch Data Entry* — Application controls to include the manual receipting, logging, and recording of input transaction batches, media conversions such as keypunch and key verification, and job setup.

■ *Transaction Data Validation* — Application program controls to ensure the accuracy and completeness of transactions entering the computer. These controls include tests to validate transaction type, data elements within transactions, processing dates and/or sequence numbers, as well as batch control totals.

■ *Transaction Error Handling* — Application system controls, both manual and computer application program controls, to identify, report, or divert transaction errors or omissions from subsequent processing. These controls include edit error reports, error logs, and procedures governing transaction error correction and reentry. Such application controls may be interactive in a terminal data entry environment.

Although the transaction origination and entry phases of application system processing involve different kinds of controls and control areas, they are complementary. As a result, internal audit programs usually encompass both areas and use similar audit tools and techniques.

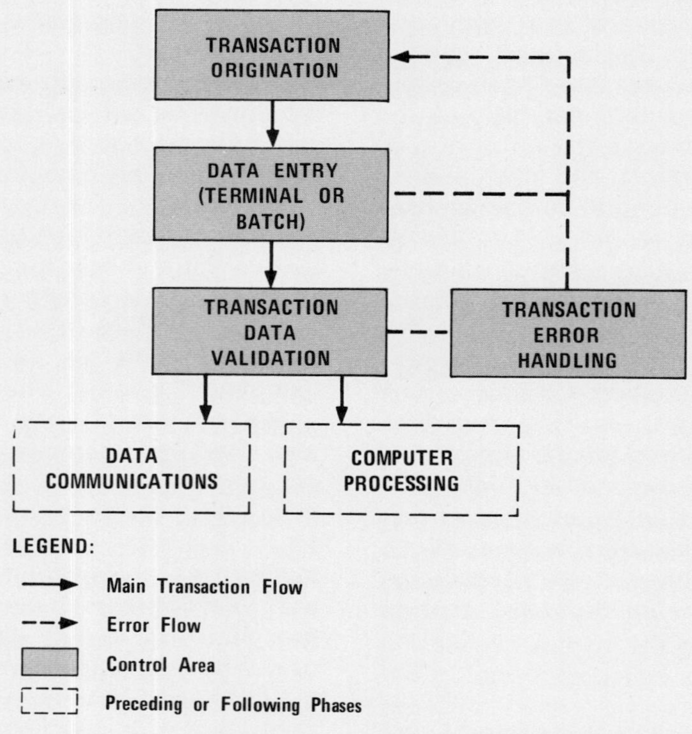

FIGURE 7-3 DATA PROCESSING TRANSACTION ENTRY

A method used by internal auditors to audit transaction entry controls is to review and evaluate written procedures governing transaction entry operations. Procedures in both data processing and user areas are included. Manual tracing of the flow of transaction and/or data processing input batches is used to evaluate manual control procedures and verify compliance. Observations and reviews are usually performed on such documents as batch tickets, routing slips, and logs and records used in balancing and reconciling data processing input.

Computer-aided audit techniques used by internal auditors include generalized audit software that is used to select transaction and/or batches from data processing files for subsequent manual tracing to verify proper transaction or batch data entry. Internal auditors also report the use of audit subroutines embedded in computer application programs to select transactions as part of continuous audit programs to verify transaction or batch data entry. These audit subroutines select transactions for audit purposes during normal input transaction processing. Internal auditors subsequently use these transactions to verify compliance with input processing procedures and transaction preparation, as described in the previous section. Smaller organizations perform these same functions manually by periodically selecting transactions from input batch balance listings or transaction registers. Transactions selected for audit in this manner are subsequently traced and verified manually.

Some of the auditors interviewed by SRI report using test data to both evaluate and verify the controls governing the entry of transactions into data processing. Test data procedures have been developed by auditors to verify terminal data entry controls. Such procedures involve the entry of test transactions by internal auditors and their subsequent reversal to prevent affecting the organization's data processing records and reporting. The use of traditional test data decks is also reported, particularly in organizations using batch entry procedures. In these situations, internal auditors are preparing test data sets, executing relevant application programs separate from production processing, and analyzing processing results to evaluate computer application controls. Other organizations interviewed have developed ITFs that allow internal auditors to enter transactions from terminal locations and test controls throughout computer application systems. These ITFs are designed to prevent test transactions from being included in the records and reports maintained for the organization.

DATA COMMUNICATIONS

Communication controls ensure that the flow of data between remote terminal locations and processing centers is complete and accurate, and that adequate message accountability, data protection, and error reporting are provided. Controls in this area also ensure the continuing security of information. During the early years of data communication development, controls were built into specific application programs and, until recently, data communication controls were thought of as being part of a particular application system. Now, however, data communication controls are becoming general controls rather than application system controls and more recent data communication hardware and software capabilities are, in fact, generalized. Data communication facilities are becoming transparent to terminal users and to the application system programs used to process their data. These controls are, however, presented in this application system controls chapter because they are not as yet widely viewed as general controls.

Three important data communication control areas are:

- *Message Input* — Controls in terminal equipment, such as terminal identification codes, and terminal functions directed by software, such as terminal polling, message identification, and security tables.
- *Message Transmission* — Controls governing message transmission between terminal equipment and receiving hardware and software. These controls typically govern message flow over common carrier facilities and include hardware controls such as line conditioning, forward error correction, validity checks, and scrambling and cryptographic techniques. A related software control is transmission batch control.
- *Message Reception and Accounting* — Controls at the computer service center location that govern the receipt and accounting for message traffic. Hardware controls include detection with retransmission, and backup power. Software controls, for example, include message validation techniques, sequence numbering and number checking, message logging, and error re-recording procedures.

More complete descriptions of these and other related controls are included in Chapter 7 of the companion volume, The Control Practices Report.

Methods used by the internal auditor to evaluate and perform compliance testing in the data communication environment are somewhat limited because of the highly specialized technical knowledge required. One approach used by internal auditors is to review the adequacy of and compliance with preventive maintenance and failure reporting procedures governing data communication network operations. A review of error reports and error logs provides an indication of the magnitude of problems associated with data communication network operations. The internal auditor may trace a number of failure reports to determine corrective action taken and the elapsed time necessary to resolve the reported problems. Interviews with network users invariably identify problems as perceived by them. In many instances, however, such problems are more imagined than real.

Internal auditors also use transaction testing procedures at remote terminal locations. In using such procedures, test transactions are entered directly into the data communication system in order to verify correct processing of error identification and reporting. If such transactions are processed against a production base, which is usually the case, provision must be made to reverse or nullify their effect. Integrated test facilities are being used effectively in the data communication environment, where test transactions and resulting reports can be prepared for fictitious entities concurrent with normal production without affecting production data files. Such testing procedures provide direct evidence of compliance with established data communication and processing controls.

In some instances, generalized audit software is used to provide evidence of compliance with established data communication controls. For example, selected transactions can be extracted from the data base to verify that required controls were in force at the time those transactions were processed.

COMPUTER PROCESSING

These controls govern processing subsequent to transaction validation. Controls in this area are treated separately from the controls governing data storage and retrieval. This separation reflects the trend toward generalized data storage and retrieval procedures and software that are becoming more independent of computer application procedures. It is also a useful separation for internal auditors because they often separate the audit applications along the same lines. For example, masterfiles are often examined independent of the processing logic and controls that govern their updating. Figure 7-4 shows the relationship between processing controls and other related phases of application system processing. Controls in this phase include manual procedures, such as console/operator interaction under certain conditions. Most processing controls, however, reside within the computer application programs that have been developed to perform specific processing functions, such as inventory accounting, accounts payable, or payroll. Such controls ensure the integrity of the application process and include the following control areas:

- *Processing Integrity* — Controls to prevent errors and omissions in the flow of data within and between computer programs and systems.
- *Restart and Recovery* — Controls to ensure that processing can be restarted in the event of an

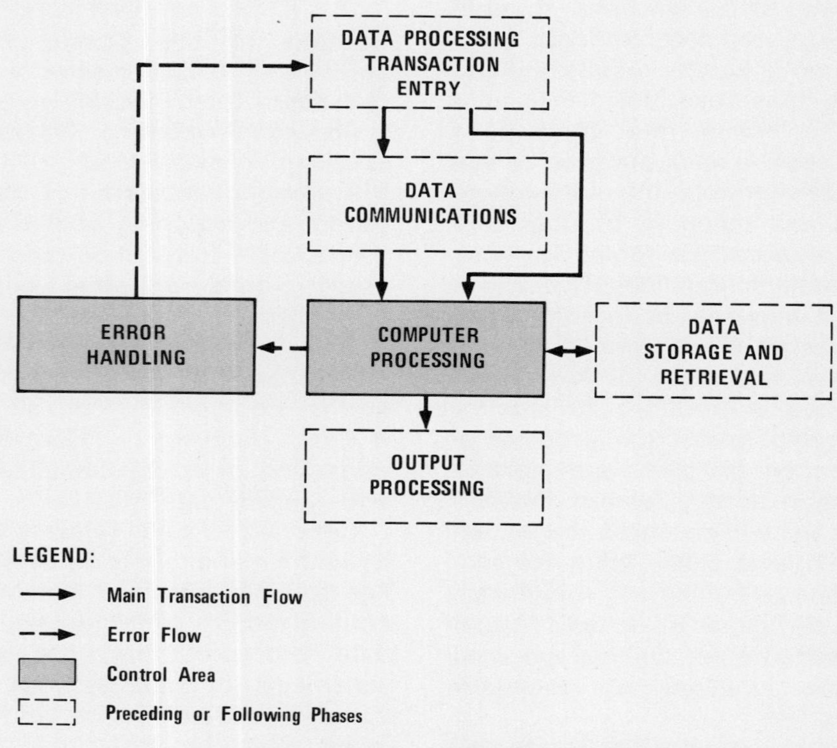

FIGURE 7-4 COMPUTER PROCESSING

unintentional interruption or error conditions that prevent further processing.

- *Processing Accuracy* — Controls within application programs to ensure the accuracy and reasonableness of the results of computations.
- *Operator Invention* — Controls to govern operator intervention through the computer console.
- *Security and Privacy* — Controls to ensure that data are not subject to compromise during processing by accident or through unauthorized, willful attempt to use application programs.
- *Error Handling* — Controls to ensure that erroneous transactions, both input transactions and those generated during the processing cycle, are identified and reported, subsequently corrected, and entered on a timely basis.

Internal audit techniques used in reviewing processing controls governing operator intervention include observations of computer operations areas and reviews of computer console log sheets. Test data methods are used by internal auditors to test for the adequacy of and compliance with processing controls designed to ensure processing integrity, accuracy, security and privacy, and error handling. Similarly, base case testing procedures and ITFs are used by internal auditors to verify processing controls.

Internal auditors also make use of computer program analysis methods, including transaction tagging, to develop objective evidence about processing logic. Tracing and mapping are also used to document the flow of transactions through programs, and identify unused program logic. Such techniques help the internal auditor understand and evaluate the controls that have been built into computer programs to ensure the integrity of processing. They also provide an opportunity to test the effectiveness of such controls. Internal auditors use tagging, tracing, and mapping to document processing logic at a particular point in time. Subsequent auditing examinations identify changes in processing logic, and allow the auditor to evaluate the impact of such changes on processing control.

Internal auditors also make use of specialized computer programs and subroutines to monitor transaction activity during production processing. Input transaction selection programs are used to monitor input transaction activity, screen transactions for accuracy and completeness based on auditor-provided criteria, and select input transactions for subsequent manual tracing and compliance testing. Although this technique is limited to input transaction files, embedded audit routines are used to perform the same functions for internally generated transactions.

Data verification techniques are used by internal auditors for two purposes. First, generalized audit software can be used to examine files to secure evidence of deficiencies or noncompliance with processing controls. Second, generalized audit software is used to verify the accuracy and completeness of accounting records and masterfiles maintained by data processing. Many auditors use these techniques to audit around the computer and rely on correct output as evidence of adequate and effective control procedures. This tends to be a shortcut approach that simplifies the auditor's task by eliminating an examination of the computer application program controls.

Generalized audit software is used as a tool in parallel simulation to verify the accuracy and completeness of selected processing functions. The parallel simulation technique processes production transactions against a copy of a production masterfile. The masterfile resulting from the simulation is compared to the corresponding production masterfile to identify differences. Generalized audit software is used to simulate the processing functions to be verified, which are usually limited to a few specific computations and operating procedures. The inclusion of too many simulated procedures can make final reconciliation or results difficult. Generalized audit software is also used to compare the simulated output masterfile to the actual production output master. The result of this comparison is a computer listing identifying differences that are then analyzed and reconciled by the internal auditor.

DATA STORAGE AND RETRIEVAL

Controls in this phase of application system processing ensure masterfile accuracy and completeness. They include:

- *Masterfile Updating* — Controls governing the updating of masterfiles.
- *Transaction/Masterfile Cutoff* — Controls that govern the matching of masterfile processing with proper input transaction cutoff dates to ensure that fiscal cutoffs or other important input cutoff schedules are maintained.
- *Data Security and Privacy* — Logical and physical control over access to the files during processing and in storage.
- *Error Handling* — Controls to ensure proper correction of errors identified during file maintenance and/or data retrieval.

Generalized audit software is a primary tool used by internal auditors to verify controls in these areas. For example, it is used to extract master records for confirmation to control totals maintained external to data processing, and to prepare confirmation statements of various types. It is also used to compare master records before and after updating takes place to verify that all transactions were properly posted. Transactions are selected and traced forward from origination to masterfile updating, and backward from masterfiles to source transaction documents. This type of tracing is used to verify that all transactions are properly processed and accounted for, and that cut-off dates or schedules are maintained. Generalized audit software is used for parallel simulation, as described in the preceding section.

Internal auditors also use reports produced during normal processing to verify processing accuracy by manually reconciling masterfile balances after updating to beginning balances and transaction totals. Well-designed application systems provide such control features so that data processing users are able to reconcile periodically for on-line applications and after each cycle for batch-oriented applications. Internal auditors can use these same facilities in many instances.

Test data methods are used to evaluate and verify controls to ensure that errors or omissions that occur during updating are properly identified, recorded, and reported. This is important because certain transaction errors may not be identified until transactions are matched to their corresponding master records. Such controls and associated audit techniques could be classified as computer processing controls. However, since they are dependent upon and directly impact master records, they are included in this application processing phase. Internal auditors interviewed report using test decks and integrated test facilities to evaluate and verify masterfile updating logic and error handling. These techniques are also used to verify logical controls governing logical access to on-line data files.

Physical controls governing data files involve both application controls and general controls governing the media library within the computer service center. Chapter 8 describes general controls governing the handling and storage of magnetic tapes and disk packs in the media library. Related application controls are security classificiations and retention schedules unique to individual application systems. Internal auditors verify compliance with these application control requirements by reviewing media library records and logs. Job accounting (SMF) data are also used to verify compliance with restrictions on access to sensitive masterfiles. See Chapter 26 for more information on this technique.

OUTPUT PROCESSING

Output controls are used to verify the completeness and accuracy of all phases of processing on a routine basis. They include balancing and reconciling input transactions to output reports and masterfiles control totals.

They also include controls governing the distribution, storage, records retention, and ultimate destruction of data processing reports in user areas. Output control procedures are used both in the data processing input/output control section and in user areas. Figure 7-5 shows the relationship among the six control areas of this phase. Balancing and reconciliation in data processing and the user department, output distribution, and records retention lie in the main flow of processing. Accountable document control has aspects that affect the first three of these areas. Error handling is part of a feedback loop to computer processing, the prior phase.

The six output control areas include:

- *Balancing and Reconciliation* — Control over procedures to balance and reconcile output to input and thereby ensure that all items had been processed accurately and completely. Balancing and reconciliation occurs in both data processing and user departments..
- *Output Distribution* — Controls to ensure that computer output is delivered in its entirety to the proper user at the required time.
- *Accountable Document Control* — Controls to ensure that the usage of output forms is regulated to prevent their unintentional or accidental misuse. Forms control includes negotiable documents used in computer processing, such as blank checks or warrants.
- *Retention* — Controls to ensure that output products are retained in accordance with legal, accounting, and other managerial requirements.
- *Error Handling* — Controls to ensure that the manual and automated handling of errors and their correction and reentry occurs on a timely basis.

Internal audit techniques used to evaluate output controls and test for compliance include observations in the data processing input/output area, the forms storage area, and user areas that receive the outputs from data processing. Internal auditors also trace output report handling to verify compliance with balancing and reconciliation procedures. Manual tracing and evaluation are in the examination of error reporting and error reentry procedures. The internal auditor's review includes the examination of output control logs, report distribution lists, and records retention documentation. This includes an examination of procedures governing the purchase, inventory control, and issuance of negotiable instruments. Logs and records are examined to verify that proper accountability is maintained. Associated procedures governing the handling, processing, signing, and distribution of negotiable instruments are traced and evaluated by internal auditors. Separation of duties is a particularly important part of this phase of an audit. Computer aids are used by the internal auditor in evaluations and examinations, in addition to the manual methods outlined above.

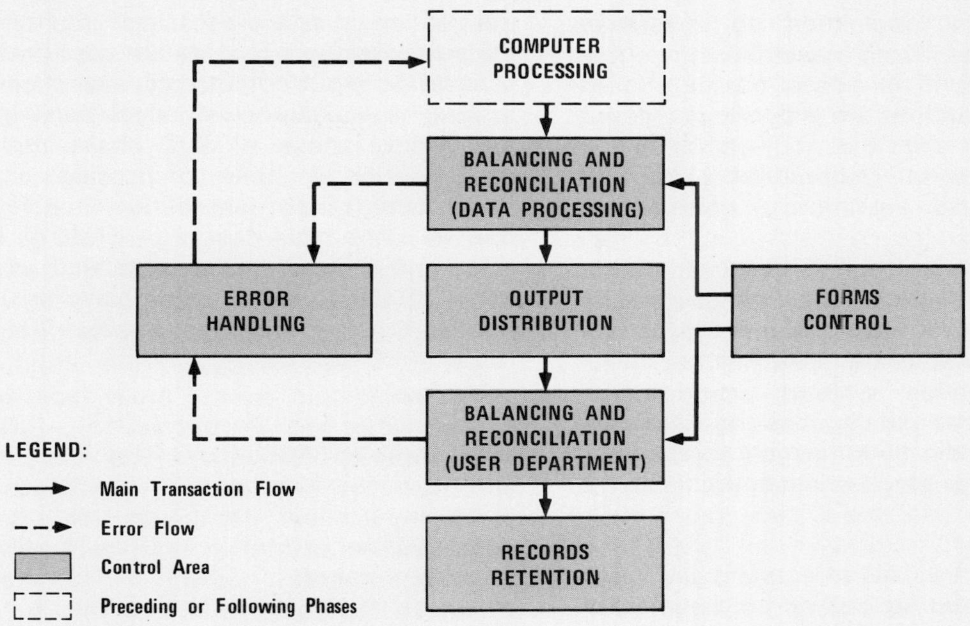

FIGURE 7-5 OUTPUT PROCESSING

Generalized audit software is widely used by internal auditors in compliance testing to verify the accuracy and completeness of the output and control reports. Using this technique, production control totals from output reports are balanced and reconciled to totals from their associated masterfiles. Integrated test facilities are used to monitor the accuracy and timeliness of the entire processing cycle, including the availability of production output. Manual reconciliation and balancing is still, however, widely used to verify reports and records to control figures maintained external to the data processing function.

SUMMARY

Six phases of computer application processing are discussed in this chapter with applicable audit and control techniques. The application system flow has been broken into these six phases in order to group similar controls or controls with similar objectives. This organization and presentation illustrate the variety of control objectives and techniques that may require internal audit attention. The companion volume in this series, The Control Practices Report, includes more detailed lists of control techniques applicable to each of the six phases. This chapter also provides information on the usage of audit tools and techniques applicable to the various phases of application and system processing. This presentation is designed to provide the internal auditor with an overview of audit and control techniques. Later chapters in this report provide detailed descriptions of specific audit tools and techniques.

Four phases of the application system process are becoming increasingly important to internal auditors: transaction entry, data communications, data storage and retrieval, and data processing output controls.

Transaction entry is becoming increasingly important because more complex manual procedures are required to complete application system program procedures that ensure the accuracy, completeness, and timeliness of transaction entry. This is particularly important in applications making use of terminals located in user areas, because such users may have direct access to masterfiles and may have an ability to freely add or delete information. Administrative controls in user areas are needed, as well as application program controls to guard against accidental or unauthorized entry and retrieval of information. Without adequate controls governing transaction entry and associated error detection, undetected errors can be inadvertently introduced into applications by user terminal operators. Since terminal systems may lack the explicit audit trails typically found in traditional batch processing systems, such errors can be difficult to correct, even if they are detected during subsequent steps in computer processing.

As terminal transaction entry facilities are introduced into user areas, both system designers and internal auditors must carefully evaluate requirements for and the effectiveness of manual controls governing data processing user personnel in their use of terminal facilities, and complementary computer program controls designed to prevent undetected errors and security violations.

Data communications is a second area of increasing importance to internal auditors. Communication controls as described in this chapter are, in general, transparent to internal auditors. That is to say, few internal auditors are concerned with or have specific tests to verify the controls governing data communications. The appropriate level of internal auditor involvement in verifying data communication controls is not clear. However, in the almost total absence of involvement in this area, it is concluded that internal auditors need to become more familiar with data communication controls as they affect the integrity of the total information handling process in order to determine appropriate audit approaches and techniques.

Data storage and retrieval is a third area increasingly important to internal auditors. This is because of the increasing number of application systems being designed around shared data bases using generalized data storage and retrieval software. The procedures and controls governing application programs are becoming independent of generalized software for data storage and retrieval. Thus, greater internal audit attention is needed to ensure the adequacy and effectiveness of separate controls governing generalized data storage and retrieval procedures.

Data processing output controls are a fourth area important to internal auditors because these controls govern the interface of output documents between data processing and the user departments. Internal auditors, users, and data processing personnel must ensure that adequate controls exist in the output processing phase to verify the completeness and accuracy of all phases of processing.

As internal auditors become more involved in auditing application systems, it will be necessary to acquire technical knowledge relating to the development in these areas. Close cooperation with data processing is needed to monitor trends in these areas and develop appropriate audit and control techniques.

EVALUATION AND OUTLOOK

With the increasing trend of top management to rely more and more on large complex computer applications systems, internal auditors will be required to audit all phases of data processing in a much more detailed manner than at present. Data communication audits will become increasingly important as more organizations develop on-line application systems to meet their requirements. Internal auditors will require more technically oriented tools and techniques to audit data communication systems and other areas of new technology. However, it is anticipated that the transaction entry and data processing output areas will remain the more important areas to audit due to the fact that they represent the interface between data processing and the user department.

Chapter 8

AUDITING COMPUTER SERVICE CENTERS

Computer service center procedures and controls are important to internal auditors because they directly affect the accuracy, completeness, and timeliness of data processing results. They complement application system controls; adequate controls are necessary within both computer application systems and the computer service center to ensure processing integrity. Increasing internal auditor emphasis on computer service center controls is a logical extension of the audit activity in evaluating and verifying application system controls. As internal auditors have gained data processing knowledge and experience, the scope of internal audit programs has been expanded to include periodic audits in areas such as input/output scheduling and control, media library, and physical security. Some organizations have comprehensive computer service center audit programs that include additional functions, such as separation of duties, computer environmental controls, malfunction reporting and preventive maintenance, resource planning, and user billing/charge-out procedures. However, organizations with smaller data processing operations continue to rely on consultants, external auditors and their data processing management to evaluate the adequacy of these controls.

The accuracy and completeness of records and reports produced by data processing are as much dependent upon general controls governing the computer service center as upon the application controls built into computer application systems. Accordingly, the traditional scope of internal audit is increasing to include computer service center operations. The general controls that govern computer service center operations complement application controls that are developed to meet the requirements of individual computer application systems. Application systems are usually designed to conform with prevailing computer service center development and operations standards. Because of this complementary relationship, internal auditors are becoming more involved in evaluating and verifying computer service center controls, just as they are becoming more involved in evaluating, testing, and verifying application controls internal to computer application systems and programs.

Field interview results indicate that the internal auditor's interest in procedures and controls within the computer service center is unclear to many data processing managers who indicate that:

- Internal auditors do not have the knowledge of data processing necessary to either evaluate or verify computer service center controls.
- Computer service center controls are evolving as new technology is adopted. Controls appropriate to new technology are innovative and often imperfect. They are, therefore, not subject to traditional internal audit approaches.

Many data processing managers interviewed do not understand why internal auditors cannot continue the practice of auditing around the computer. Data processing management does not realize the increasing importance of computer service center audits.

Because of the limited data processing knowledge available on many internal audit staffs and the failure of many data processing managers to understand and embrace an expanding internal audit role in data processing, internal audit activities within the computer service center are still in an early stage of development. Field interviews conducted by SRI indicate that involvement in auditing computer service center activities is increasing in large organizations. Eight areas of concentration have been identified. Three of these are closely related to application controls:

- Input/output control — Production scheduling, input/out controls procedures, set-up and production controls, error handling, report distribution.
- Media library—Physical security, inventory control, backup and off-site storage, retention, media cleaning and recycling.
- Separation of duties — Computer operations, equipment operations, media library, transaction origination, computer systems development.

Five additional areas are less directly related to application controls. They help to ensure the uninterrupted availability of data processing resources:

■ Environmental controls and physical security—Temperature and humidity, stable power source, alternative power source, fire protection, controlled physical access, release of data, reports and computer programs, casualty insurance, business interruption insurance.

■ Disaster recovery — Management responsibility statements, emergency action plans, facilities and data backup plans, and recovery process controls.

■ Malfunction reporting and preventive maintenance — Failure reporting and logging, preventive maintenance scheduling, malfunction correction.

■ Resource planning—Equipment load and utilization projections, staffing projections, documented planning, periodic reevaluation of plans and projections.

■ Job accounting verifies user billing/charge-out procedures, job accounting, billing algorithms, billing reconciliation, and periodic user billing statements.

AUDIT AREAS

The following sections present findings based primarily on interviews with large organizations in Canada and the United States.

Input/Output Control

Input/output control functions are maintained by data processing organizations to ensure the accuracy and completeness of data received and distributed. Effective scheduling is important because of the interdependence between manual and automated financial record-keeping processes. Application processing schedules are established by data processing and users, which recognize input availability, and the time required for data preparation (such as keypunch and key verification), and for processing. Timing of the flow of data among computer applications is also important to ensure the accuracy and completeness of data files. Essential characteristics of input/output scheduling and control of interest to internal auditors include the following:

■ A formal method of scheduling production applications and sequences of related applications. Input cut-off schedules and procedures should be documented and understood by affected users.

■ Written procedures governing the receipt of input from users, communication of job status, and the return of output to users. A single channel should exist for data processing batch input and output through a data processing input/output control group.

■ Input receiving procedures that include the logging of information such as batch numbers, time received, and batch control totals.

■ Verification of input authorization in accordance with applicable application control instructions.

■ Checks input batch control totals against control totals appearing on input edit reports produced by the computer.

■ Balance and reconciliation of output report totals and input control totals to prove the accuracy and completeness of data processed. Such checking, balancing, and reconciling is performed by data processing personnel in accordance with relevant application control instructions.

■ A record of processing errors and unusual conditions encountered during processing, for subsequent investigation.

■ The distribution of reports in accordance with relevant application control instructions.

The internal auditor's review of the input/output control function includes an analysis of established procedures, an examination of logs and records maintained, and observation to determine the extent of compliance with existing procedures. The adequacy of input/output control and scheduling procedures is evaluated by tracing the flow of data through the input/output control function. Interviews with internal auditors of major data processing user personnel identify deficiencies and recurring problems that affect the accuracy and completeness of data processing results.

Media Library Controls

Internal auditors are interested in the procedures governing data stored on processing media, such as magnetic tape and disk. Control over the access to sensitive or confidential data is also of interest to internal auditors. Elements in the control of the media library include:

■ Physical security and controlled access.

■ Separation of the media library from computer operations.

■ Inventory control records and procedures that account for physical location and contents of media files.

■ Off-premises storage provisions for important data files.

■ Retention procedures for data files to assure regulatory requirements are satisfied.

■ Procedures and systems controlling the release or issuance of data from the media library.

■ Quality control procedures for the cleaning and recertification of magnetic storage media.

Internal auditors interviewed by SRI used media library control guidelines taken from audit and data processing literature to evaluate the adequacy of existing media library procedures and controls. Compliance testing involves observation, a review of inventory records and logs, and the tracing of file backup and retention for one or more specific application systems. Large installations use automated inventory systems that provide lists useful in such tracing. Systems governing large tape-library inventories usually control by reel serial number and provide cross-reference indices by file contents. Such indices are useful to internal auditors in tracing and verifying library procedures. Job accounting records are also used by internal auditors to trace file usage by application and identify persons requesting computer services. This technique is used by internal auditors to detect, for example, the use of production files for program testing, a practice that can result in the loss or exposure of confidential data.

Separation of Duties

Internal auditors are concerned that an adequate separation of duties exists to prevent fraudulent use or misuse of computers, data files, or supplies such as negotiable instruments. The scope of internal audit interest in this area includes a proper separation of duties within the data processing organization, as well as among data processing and its users. For example, the separation of systems and programming personnel from computer operations prevents the programmers, who have the knowledge to manipulate programs and data files, from:

- Having access to the computer operations area
- Operating computer equipment
- Having access to data files maintained in media libraries

A further example of the separation of duties within data processing is the control of access to inventories of negotiable instruments such as checks and warrants. The responsibility for negotiable instruments inventory control should not reside with personnel who operate the computer equipment.

To maintain a proper separation of duties between data processing and its users, one organization interviewed by SRI has designed its application systems so that users have the means to maintain overall control of data completeness, accuracy, and transaction of origination. Such control is independent of controls maintained within data processing. In addition, data processing personnel are not to initiate input transactions or post changes to records. Internal auditors interviewed report that this emphasis on total user control has been effective in increasing user confidence in processing results.

Internal auditors evaluate the adequacy of the separation of duties in both data processing and user areas. This is done by reviewing organization charts, conducting interviews, making observations, and tracing the flow of selected transactions. Compliance testing also involves both data processing and user areas. Transactions are selected and traced to verify proper origination and authorization. Logs and records are examined to determine that controls have not been circumvented. Job accounting statistics accumulated by the computer's operating system software are analyzed to identify persons who have submitted work for processing, the programs used, and whether the processing was performed as a regular production job or as a test. Such tests verify that proper procedures have been followed in submitting data and initiating processes, and that controls governing the separation of duties are not bypassed.

Environmental Controls and Physical Security

Internal auditors are concerned with the uninterrupted availability of computing equipment, which in turn depends upon the adequacy of environmental conditions such as a stable power source, regulated temperature, and regulated humidity. The availability of standby power for use in an emergency and of suitable fire protection are also important environmental factors. These environmental controls not only apply to the computer operations area but also to the media library.

The adequacy of such environmental controls can usually be determined quickly through interviews with vendor service personnel who can provide written specifications for the complement of equipment installed. Objective evidence of compliance can be secured by using:

- Recording thermometers located for representative readings.
- Recording humidity indicators.
- Recording voltage indicators.
- Reviews of periodic start-up and checkout procedures relating to standby power equipment.
- Reviews of certification logs accompanying fire protection systems and equipment.

Internal auditors are also interested in two aspects of physical security: first, the adequate protection of computer equipment, software, and data files; second, the prevention of unauthorized access to sensitive or confidential information or computer programs. The general controls relating to physical security include:

- Access controls to prevent unauthorized entry into the computer operations area, media library, and locations where negotiable instruments are stored or processed.
- Authorization procedures and criteria governing the entry of personnel into restricted areas.
- Authorization procedures and criteria for the release or issuance of media library contents.
- On-line access to data.

In evaluating the adequacy of controls governing physical security, internal auditors often use guidelines available from audit and data processing literature. Several of the organizations interviewed by SRI used these sources to develop their own internal audit guidelines. Others interviewed had used consultants to establish appropriate guidelines. An evaluation of the adequacy of physical security usually involves a review of computer service center layout in terms of access from the outside. Such a review may involve facilities engineering personnel as well as data processing management. Compliance testing performed by internal auditors includes observations within the computer service center, and an examination of logs and records.

Disaster Recovery

Formal plans describing appropriate operational steps to take in case of emergency or disaster are required in order to ensure continued operation of the computer service centers during abnormal operational times. Many data processing organizations fail to maintain the appropriate level of control when faced with the change in operations resulting from an emergency situation. There must be well-thought-out plans for meeting most emergency problems that are likely to arise. In addition to protecting and backing up computer data files, programs, and run documents, the organization must keep all critical files, programs, and run documents in duplicate and store them in separate locations. There must also be well-controlled procedures for reestablishing the data processing functions once the emergency is over. These procedures must be fully developed and tested prior to their application. The procedures should include:

- Identification of responsible management and how to contact them.
- Use of backup facilities, if any, and how to use them.
- Methods for transporting backup data, programs, and documentation from the backup storage site to the computer service center.
- Control points and techniques to ensure data and program integrity during the transition.

In developing the procedures that govern the reestablishment of computer service center operations, it is wise to involve the user department as well as facilities management personnel. These people are useful in developing priorities and time schedules that will meet organizational needs. In addition, it is wise to review the contingency plan periodically to ensure it is still accurate and complete.

The major benefit of a thorough contingency plan comes from the ability of an organization to respond rapidly to disaster or exceptional situations that might otherwise cause considerable loss to, or total disruption of the organization. With the increasing reliance on data processing resources, particularly in centralized operations with major on-line requirements, the need for contingency planning cannot be overemphasized.

Malfunction Reporting and Preventive Maintenance

Formal procedures to report the occurrence or apparent occurrence of hardware and operating system malfunctions or failures are part of an effective preventive maintenance plan. Malfunction reporting provides a measure of the adequacy of preventive maintenance, the level of vendor maintenance service provided, and the rate of failure associated with the computer system. Because failures from the computer system can result in errors and omissions in financial and statistical records maintained by data processing, malfunction reporting is of interest to the internal auditor. Control elements associated with effective malfunction reporting include:

- Logging of equipment and operating system software malfunctions and failures, or suspected incidents of failure at the time of their occurrence.
- Reporting of instances of malfunction occurrence to responsible vendor service personnel.
- Follow-up procedures to ensure that each reported malfunction is investigated and effective corrective action for repair is initiated.
- Identification and tracing of intermittent malfunctions until they are resolved, and identification of recurring vendor problems.

Adequate preventive maintenance is of interest to the internal auditor because it ensures the continuing and uninterrupted availability or processing capability, and of the financial and statistical information maintained by data processing. Preventive maintenance programs vary from installation to installation depending upon the complement of equipment being used. Computer system vendors provide preventive maintenance programs and schedules for each device installed. These are based upon inherent design characteristics and statistical experience from all the vendors' installations regarding failures, causes of failures, and wear-out rates. Diagnostic routines run by vendor personnel during preventive maintenance ensure that hardware controls are functioning properly.

Operating system software also requires periodic maintenance, in the sense that modifications or new releases of software must be prepared, incorporated into the operating system, and tested. This software maintenance is often performed by data processing personnel with assistance or guidance from vendor software specialists.

Preventive maintenance control elements include:

- A written schedule for recurring equipment diagnostic and preventive maintenance procedures.
- A contractual maintenance agreement with the computer vendor or other qualified computer maintenance organization.

Internal auditors determine the adequacy of preventive maintenance and repair programs by interviewing data processing management, and vendor marketing and service personnel. In preparation for such interviews, some internal auditors have reviewed records of unscheduled computer system downtime and the time required to place the computer system back in operation. Although system reliability figures can be provided by most vendors, internal auditors seldom use such data as a basis for evaluating preventive maintenance programs. Rather, internal auditors are most often concerned with whether or not malfunctions are reported, logged, and repaired promptly, and that recurring malfunctions are identified and resolved by the vendor. The adequacy of failure reporting procedures is determined by an analysis of the procedures in use.

Compliance with established preventive maintenance schedules can be determined through interviews with data processing and vendor service personnel. Maintenance logs prepared by the vendor and computer console log sheets can be used to confirm that vendor maintenance schedules are maintained.

Compliance tests performed by internal auditors include a review of failure reporting procedures, documents, and logs, both those of the organization and of the vendor on-site. The examination and tracing of failure reports and logs indicate the type of malfunctions occurring, their frequency, and vendor corrective action.

Resource Planning

Resource planning is necessary within data processing to ensure that adequate computing and human resources are available to provide continuity in the processing of existing applications and to develop new applications as the organization's data processing needs grow. Data processing resource planning includes facilities, equipment, software, and personnel. Internal auditors are interested in the adequacy of and compliance with planning procedures, which encompass:

- Equipment load and utilization projections
- Staffing level projections
- Sources of information used for planning
- Techniques used to monitor plans
- Feedback to reevaluate plans.

In addition, internal auditors are concerned with consistency between data processing planning and the administrative controls that govern planning throughout the organization.

Internal audit approaches for evaluating the adequacy of planning procedures and for compliance testing include procedure reviews and examinations of annual planning documents that have been prepared and approved by data processing management. Supporting plans or pending decisions that would affect the asset value of existing equipment, require new capital investment, or result in long-term lease liability are also examined to ensure compliance with governing administrative controls established by the parent organization.

User Billing/Charge-Out Procedures

An evaluation of the administrative controls governing the billing or charge-out of data processing costs to users is of concern to internal auditors in some organizations to ensure there is an equitable basis for such charges and that billing is made in accordance with the prevailing policy, procedures, and documented user agreements, if any. Elements of this control procedure include:

- The use of automated job accounting methods within data processing.
- A billing algorithm that recognizes different billing rates for different resources and levels of processing priority.
- Reconciliation of user charges of total data processing department costs against budgeted costs.
- Identification and reporting of data processing department cost variances.
- Rerun cost allocation.
- Periodic user billing statements with application cost detail.

Internal auditors evaluate billing controls by reviewing governing procedures and records and by tracing billing information generated by job accounting software. Computer billing algorithms can be highly complex. Technical assistance is usually required if the scope of audit work is to include an evaluation of the billing algorithm in use. Compliance testing includes an evaluation of rate tables in use, tracing of billing statement detail back to job cost-accounting records, a reconciliation of monthly billing totals and total data processing costs, and a review of billing trends for selected computer applications.

SUMMARY

Internal auditors are becoming increasingly concerned about the control procedures used within the computer service center to ensure the accuracy and completeness of processing. This concern and increasing computer service center audit activity is an extension of the increasing emphasis being placed upon the evaluation and verification of controls governing all phases of data processing. The trend of greater internal audit involvement in auditing computer service center operations is expected to continue as internal auditors acquire more knowledge of data processing in general, and computer service center operations in particular.

The four computer service center control areas most important to internal auditors interviewed are:

- Input/output control, the important interface between data processing and its users.

- Media library controls, which ensure the safety of magnetic tape and disks while not in use and help ensure that correct data files are used in application processing.
- Separation of duties, which helps ensure the accuracy and completeness at successive stages of processing, discourage the circumvention of controls, and discourage fraudulent or unauthorized use of data, application programs, and processing resources.
- Computer environmental controls, particularly computer physical security.

These control areas are of primary importance because they most directly affect application processing results.

Other important control areas reported by internal auditors interviewed include computer malfunction reporting and preventive maintenance, and resource planning for facilities, equipment, software, and staff. The internal auditor's objective in examining these areas is to verify that controls are adequate to ensure continuing and uninterrupted availability of processing capacity upon which management information systems depend. A few of the large organizations interviewed report internal auditors are also examining data processing user billing or charge-out procedures used to allocate data processing expenses among users. Internal auditors provide an independent evaluation of the equity and correctness of data processing costs allocated to user departments.

Some organizations with large data processing facilities have established comprehensive programs for the periodic audit of computer service center operations. However, most of the organizations that have computer service center audit programs have limited programs which focus on individual control areas such as input/output control, media library control and physical security. As experience is gained, the scope of computer service center audits can be expected to expand. However, until more comprehensive audit plans are established and integrated with complementary audit plans for application systems and systems development, EDP audit programs cannot be totally effective. The various control areas within data processing must be viewed within the context of the total information processing process, rather than as just individual elements.

Two factors limit the effectiveness of internal auditors in the computer service center. First, they need more knowledge of and experience with data processing technology and control practice. This is being acquired in many organizations through closer cooperation between internal auditors and data processing personnel. Second, acceptance by data processing personnel of the internal auditor's proper role in auditing computer service center operations must be improved. Too often, neither top management nor data processing management understand the need to audit in this important area. These attitudes are changing as the importance of computer service center controls is better understood in the context of the total information process. Progress, although often slow, is being made in both of these areas.

Smaller organizations interviewed report continuing reliance on consultants, their external auditors, and data processing management to ensure that adequate computer service center controls are established and maintained. Their audit objectives are usually limited. Media library and physical security are most frequently mentioned as important control areas in the small organizations contacted by SRI.

EVALUATION AND OUTLOOK

In order to ensure the accuracy and completeness of computer-based information systems, internal auditors are being required to take part in computer application system development as well as to audit computer service centers and computer application systems. While internal auditors have been auditing computer service centers to some degree in the past, they will be required to develop more data processing knowledge and intensify their efforts in this area. The type of data processing knowledge to be developed includes an appreciation of data processing management problems, technical characteristics of data storage media and equipment, and data input/output problems experienced by users interfacing with data processing. Internal auditors will be required to work with data processing management to develop a comprehensive computer service center audit plan.

Chapter 9

AUDITING CONTROLS GOVERNING APPLICATION SYSTEM DEVELOPMENT

The traditional scope of internal audit is increasing to encompass application system development and the controls governing the development process. The development, testing, and installation of sophisticated computer application systems using advanced technology such as data communications and data base facilities require a disciplined and controlled development environment. Internal auditors recognize that the controls governing the system development process directly affect application system functional characteristics and the controls that ensure processing accuracy and reliability. Important controls frequently mentioned include application system acceptance testing and program change control. The increasing attention internal auditors are giving to the controls governing the development process is an extension of their greater involvement in evaluating and verifying application system controls. The application system development process is a relatively new area of internal audit involvement.

Auditors often review the general controls governing the application system development process as an extension of their participation in application system development. The accuracy and completeness of records and reports produced by data processing are, to some extent, dependent upon the controls governing the computer application system development process. As internal auditors have become increasingly involved in evaluating computer application systems and controls subsequent to initial implementation, they have also become interested in the general controls governing the development process. Internal auditors report they are concerned with application system development controls because they help ensure that:

- User requirements are properly satisfied.
- Adequate application controls are installed and maintained.
- Anticipated cost benefits or procedural improvements are realized.
- Adequate acceptance testing occurs.
- Projects are completed as scheduled and within cost budgets.

Internal audit involvement in the controls governing the application system development process stems from three audit concerns. These are to ensure that:

- Adequate administrative controls are maintained for a methodical and disciplined development process. Experience shows that unstructured and hurried development results in inadequate design and testing, which in turn results in undetected errors and omissions during subsequent production operations and generally unreliable processing results.
- Adequate application controls are incorporated into new or revised application systems to prevent undetected errors and omissions.
- Predictability is improved in system development, in both cost and schedule, by establishing a development sequence common to all system development project work.

In relatively few organizations, internal auditors are reviewing the controls governing the application systems development process. Internal auditors active in this area who were interviewed explain that to ensure the accuracy and reliability of computer application systems, they must examine the controls that govern the construction of the systems. This examination is in addition to their participation in the actual development of individual application systems.

The degree of internal audit involvement in the application system development process, as indicated in the questionnaire responses, was presented in Chapter 4. No statistical information was developed during this study to indicate the breadth and/or depth of internal audit involvement in evaluating application system development controls. Involvement in this area is occurring in relatively few organizations, which report that they expect their programs to expand as they acquire more knowledge and experience. They note, however, that to use such internal audit programs requires a good knowledge of data processing.

Data processing managers are not certain of the internal auditor's role in reviewing application system development goals. The rationale behind this audit work is not widely understood and the qualifications of internal auditors to perform such evaluations are not often accepted. As a result, few data processing managers relish internal audit participation in this area.

SRI field interviews have identified seven kinds of controls that govern the process of application system development. These are presented in the sequence that generally corresponds to that of the application system development process.

- User requirements—Data processing master plan, systems and programming authorization procedures, feasibility studies, user participation.
- Development standards and guidelines—Control guidelines, audit trails, programming standards, computer operations standards, application system testing standards.
- Project management—The system development life cycle (SDLC), project status reporting, project management.
- Documentation — System documentation, programming documentation, operations documentation, media library instructions, user's procedures and documentation.
- Acceptance testing — Test data preparation, test results verification, user test acceptance.
- Postinstallation review — Verification of compliance with original user specifications, evaluation of adequacy of application controls, cost benefits verification.
- Program change control — Change authorization, source program media library controls, change testing and test verification, reentry of modified programs into the production library.

Based on SRI field interviews, internal auditors report audit activities in all these areas to some extent, but they place emphasis on the latter four. They are concerned about the immediate effects of deficient program change control procedures, and, as a result, mention program change control most frequently, followed by acceptance testing and documentation. Of these, documentation is important to internal auditors because they depend upon it in reviewing application systems. Complete and accurate documentation allows a knowledgeable internal auditor to proceed with his work with a greater freedom from data processing personnel than is otherwise possible.

Internal auditors report two factors that have prevented greater emphasis from being placed upon auditing the controls governing the application system development process. First, many internal auditors still lack the data processing knowledge and experience needed to effectively audit controls within the data processing function. They lack relevant technical knowledge and, as a result, do not feel confident in this role and are often not readily accepted by data processing personnel. Second, auditing in this area is not given as high a priority as auditing programs that relate more immediately to financial and statistical information used by management. Some organizations audit acceptance testing, documentation, and change control in conjunction with application system and/or computer service center audits. Only the larger organizations interviewed recognized the controls governing the application system development process as a separate audit area.

The following sections present individual discussions of the seven control categories, based primarily on interviews with large organizations in Canada and the U.S.

USER REQUIREMENTS

The definition and documentation of user requirements are important to ensure that understanding is reached early in the relationship between data processing and user groups. Such documentation is also important to auditors because it provides a baseline from which to evaluate subsequent project activities. A formalized relationship between data processing and the users it serves typically includes:

- A formal procedure for requesting system and programming assistance from data processing. Most organizations use a printed form for this purpose.
- A data processing master plan that includes all approved development projects. Such a plan is needed to assist management to evaluate and resolve conflicting demands for data processing and development resources.
- A feasibility study for the particular application under consideration for development. The purpose of this study is to define the user's needs and prepare a sound cost-benefits analysis.
- Active user participation in system definition and design, and user approval of the design.

In reviewing these control areas, the internal auditor typically examines data processing project files for initiation and approval forms and cost-benefit analysis documentation. User participation is evaluated through interviews with users and data processing project personnel, as well as through an examination of project files for indications of user approval of various design documents.

DEVELOPMENT STANDARDS AND GUIDELINES

Standards and guidelines governing the design, development, and implementation of computer applications are important because they ensure that:

- Appropriate application controls are considered, selected, and installed during the development process.
- Adequate audit trails are provided to allow all transactions to be traced both forward and backward between their source and final reports and totals.

■ Suitable levels of operability and maintainability are achieved after implementation.

■ Adequate testing is performed to verify all processing logic, computations, and control procedures.

The approach auditors use in reviewing development standards typically includes an initial survey that results in preliminary conclusions on their adequacy. A second step is to compare existing development controls standards to standards and guidelines available in data processing literature. To perform this function the internal auditor may call upon knowledgeable data processing personnel who can explain the applicability of existing development standards. The final step is to determine compliance with existing standards and procedures. This is done by reviewing application documentation. The internal auditor may want to interview the user to help identify problems traceable to a lack of development standards or compliance with existing standards.

PROJECT MANAGEMENT

Project management controls provide a means to measure progress during applications development, and involve three elements.

■ A formalized structure for the development process with intermediate work products that can be approved by users participating in the development project. Many organizations refer to this as an SDLC, and use it as a standardized method of structuring all development projects.

■ Project status reporting that shows expenditures versus budget as work progresses. When the SDLC concept is used, project status reporting can be by phase of development.

■ Periodic management status reports.

Auditors can evaluate the adequacy of existing procedures based on project management criteria available in data processing literature. Compliance tests are performed by reviewing project planning documentation and holding interviews with users and data processing management. Continuing failure to realize schedules and budgetary targets strongly suggests project management deficiencies.

DOCUMENTATION

Adequate documentation is important for three reasons. It helps to ensure correct and efficient processing within both data processing and user areas by explaining how to use the computer application system; it increases the ease and accuracy of computer program maintenance; and it provides internal auditors and management with an important basis for independently evaluating application controls and compliance testing.

Control elements provided by a comprehensive documentation program include:

■ System documentation, including a clear statement of the system objectives; a flowchart showing the flow of information through the system and the interrelationship between manual and computer processing steps; system specifications that governed design and development; input forms and procedures; record formats and descriptions; descriptions of audit trails; and balancing and control procedures.

■ Program documentation, including descriptions and flowcharts necessary to allow efficient and accurate maintenance subsequent to initial installation. Such documentation normally includes control cards, Job Control Language (JCL), program listings, program test data, a testing log, input/output distribution instructions, data retention instructions, console operator instructions, and copies of program change request forms.

■ Operations documentation, including instructions that enable the computer operations function to accurately and efficiently run a computer application, balance inputs and outputs, and distribute reports. Restart and recovery procedures are also included. The requirements for operations instructions vary greatly from installation to installation, depending upon the operating systems, library procedures, and input/output controls that have been adopted.

■ Library documentation, including procedures for backup, retention, restrictions on access to sensitive data, and inventory record keeping.

■ User documentation, including a narrative description of the system's operation accompanied by a general flow diagram. This basic user documentation is supplemented by specific instructions governing the proper completion of input forms and transactions. Control procedures provide users with instructions they need to balance, reconcile, and maintain overall control transactions, masterfiles, and the results of computer processing.

■ Control documentation, including a narrative of specific points in application systems where the user, internal auditor, or data processing personnel can expect to find controls and methods for verifying their presence and adequacy.

Documentation controls should ensure that the responsibility for each step in a procedure is clearly established. The control elements that are described above are not intended as guidelines, but as illustrations of the kinds of documentation controls auditors look for during reviews.

In auditing documentation, the internal auditor's approach is to review existing procedures that govern documentation preparation. Compliance testing typically involves a review of program documentation, system documentation, operations documentation, and user procedures documentation. Finally, a review of documentation change control procedures and the distribution of documentation is an important step in the internal review of documentation controls.

ACCEPTANCE TESTING

Adequate testing is important to verify that specified processing logic has been properly developed and that application controls are properly installed. Acceptance testing involves extensive user participation to verify the adequacy of test data sets and the results of testing. Testing includes verification that specified inputs produce predetermined results, including error detection reporting, masterfile updating, and specified user output reports. The general controls governing acceptance testing include:

- Testing standards.
- Formalized guidelines or procedures for test data preparation and test execution.
- User participation in reviewing test results.
- User approval before production processing commences.

User involvement and approval are necessary to ensure that operation of the applications system conforms with original design specifications. User management approval is also important to ensure that user personnel are adequately trained in the use of the system and the control functions necessary to verify processing, accuracy, and completeness on a continuing basis.

Internal auditors verify the adequacy of these general controls by reviewing the testing plans established by data processing and the users. User interviews regarding test results identify preinstallation and postinstallation problems resulting from inadequate application system design and controls.

POSTINSTALLATION REVIEW

Postinstallation review is an important control used to determine that the computer application that has been developed and implemented satisfies the functional and internal control characteristics originally sought and specified. It is also an opportunity to determine that the cost benefits originally anticipated have been realized. The postinstallation review is the final test of whether users and data processing have successfully worked together to accomplish the development objectives approved by management. Such reviews often include internal auditors in the evaluation of application controls.

The existence of a postinstallation review policy and associated procedures can be determined through interviews with data processing management. An evaluation of such procedures typically includes observations of postinstallation review teams at work and a review of their working papers and final reports. Working papers and final reports can be used to determine compliance with existing procedures.

PROGRAM CHANGE CONTROL

Program change controls prevent unauthorized and potentially fraudulent changes from being introduced into previously tested and accepted computer programs. Elements of control include:

- A formal change request and authorization form and procedure.
- Approval procedures for programmers to gain access to source coding maintained in a source program library.
- Testing and certification of test results.
- Procedures for reentry of a modified program into the production library.

Because the entry of unauthorized changes into production programs represents a major exposure in terms of both fraud and access to sensitive programs and data, tight program change control is needed.

Compliance testing includes the use of job accounting information such as systems management facilities (SMF) data previously mentioned to check program revisions currently in production use. Source and object code comparison techniques are also used to identify changes that have been made to production programs. Internal auditors then can trace such changes back to authorizing documentation. These techniques assist the internal auditor in testing for compliance with existing procedures. Careful procedural review and analysis of change controls are needed to complete the audit in this area. These techniques will be of limited value unless a change control audit trail is required that allows program changes to be traced back to change authorization documents.

SUMMARY

Internal auditors, particularly in larger organizations, are beginning to review controls governing the application system development process because these controls can directly affect the accuracy and reliability of resulting computer application systems. Internal audit involvement in this area is a relatively recent trend that seems to be growing. Auditing the controls governing application system development is not the same as participating in the development of a particular computer application, although the activities are complementary and can be performed concurrently.

Internal auditors interviewed report four controls governing the system development process that can directly affect the accuracy and reliability of computer application systems:

- Documentation, which provides the manual procedures that must be followed to properly use an application system. Documentation also includes the logic, computations, and controls incorporated into the computer application programs and is an important aid to the EDP auditor.

- Acceptance testing prior to placing a new or revised application system into a production status; this is necessary to verify and confirm its proper operation.
- Postinstallation reviews to verify that installed applications are performing reliably and in a manner consistent with user requirements and expectations.
- Program change control procedures, which ensure that only authorized changes are properly made, tested, and placed into a production status.

Program change control is the concern most frequently mentioned in interviews with internal auditors. Documentation is, however, also frequently mentioned by internal auditors because it minimizes their dependence upon data processing personnel in performing audits and provides objective criteria for compliance testing.

Two factors that limit internal audit effectiveness in auditing the controls governing the system development process are the need for improved data processing knowledge and experience, and greater acceptance by data processing management. Some progress is being made as data processing experience is added to internal audit staffs.

Smaller organizations tend not to have separate audit program objectives to evaluate and verify the general controls governing application system development. Rather, these controls are audited in conjunction with computer service center or application system audits.

EVALUATION AND OUTLOOK

Internal auditors will increase their audit of the controls governing application system development. One of the primary results of this increased involvement will be a requirement for more and better documentation of all aspects of computer application system development as well as better documentation of the application system itself. Internal auditors will use this documentation to ensure that disciplined and structured approaches are being used by data processing project managers during the application system development process. In addition, internal auditors will report to top management on the adequacy of project management. Verifying that application systems being developed comply with development and operational standards will require internal auditors to work closely with data processing management and application system development project managers throughout the development process.

Part III

AUDIT MANAGEMENT TOOLS AND TECHNIQUES

Chapter 10

AUDIT AREA SELECTION

Audit area selection is a computerized technique, applicable to multilocation organizations, to assist the internal auditor to determine which locations to audit. The objective of the technique is to optimize the use of limited internal audit resources by pinpointing potential problem areas, thus directing the attention of internal audit to those areas of greatest concern. The technique entails the development of a location profile matrix that provides key indicator information for each location. Key indicators are financial or control information that can be used to evaluate location status and performance. Audit area selection, as used by the companies participating in this study, is applicable to large organizations with many locations and with highly integrated computer application systems. There are no conceptual limitations, however, on the applicability of this technique to other types and sizes of organizations.

TECHNIQUE OVERVIEW

Audit area selection is an audit technique that extracts key financial and operational information pertaining to each location of a multilocation organization, and presents this information for analysis and evaluation. The internal audit staff examines the reports produced and selects areas to be audited, based on absolute or comparative criteria. This information is presented in matrix form, enabling easy comparisons of actual to expected data for a particular location, and from location to location. Key indicators at the companies interviewed include past due accounts receivable, percentage of overdue shipments to customers, error rates on specific types of transactions, and processing time for cash application. Selection of the key indicators is critical to the successful use of this technique, as the objective is to minimize internal audit time by pinpointing potential problem areas and presenting the data as a profile of a set of company locations.

The technique is best applied to organizations with similar operations at the multiple locations, as the key indicators selected will in many cases be pertinent principally to the particular type of activity at most locations. Key indicators can be compared to preestablished criteria and historical performance at other locations, and appropriate variances, or "scores," calculated. Key indicators cannot be developed for all areas of interest to internal auditors, and the internal audit staff must recognize this limitation of the audit area selection technique.

This technique has potential value in improving the efficiency of internal audit operations. The location matrix, by presenting key indicator data in a consistent and concise format, enables the internal auditor to focus resources on those functional areas and computer application systems at specific locations with the highest potential for problems. In addition, reports produced by use of this audit technique can be used by management as an aid in controlling their various locations.

TYPICAL PROCEDURES

Organizations using this audit technique report the following steps in implementing and using audit area selection.

Step 1 — Indicator Selection — Identify the key indicators that will be used to evaluate a location's performance. Internal auditors at one firm report that the principal factor in indicator selection is the degree of exposure in the particular functional area. This firm also limits its indicator selection to operational, rather than performance factors; the emphasis is placed on internal control in the functional area rather than on the degree of success in achieving business objectives.

Step 2 — Assignment of Weighted Value to Indicator — A weighted value is assigned to each key indicator according to its relative importance. For example, uncollected and overdue accounts receivable have a higher importance to both the organization and its internal audit staff than the error rates on sales call transactions.

Step 3 — Development of the Computer Audit Area Selection Program — The impact of this step, which provides the audit area selection reports, and indeed of the technique itself, depends directly on the accessibility of the requisite data. Organizations using this method with the greatest success are those with highly integrated computer application systems installed in most major functional areas.

APPLICATION EXAMPLE

A major manufacturing organization has implemented this technique. At this firm, the technique is called the "branch office audit matrix." The branch office audit matrix is a profile of major functions of every branch office within the major corporate divisions. The system operates by extracting data on key indicators from the on-line business systems of the company. These indicators are applied against a matrix of established parameters to create an audit profile of every office by region within a division. The present audit profile consists of 24 key indicators, grouped under their major business functions. Some of these indicators are asset and billing control totals, customer order control, cash application, and accounts receivable uncollected. The completed matrix enables the internal auditors to assess the control posture of an entire region at one time, and to then audit those branch offices that appear to have operational deficiencies.

As a result of careful application of judgments derived from the matrix, internal audit resources are optimized and valuable audit time is saved. The matrix highlights unfavorable trends in a functional area (i.e., collections, cash applications, order control) across all branch offices. This enables headquarters' functional management to address weaknesses before they become major problems.

Four major reports are produced by this branch office audit matrix system:

- Report One shows grades for each key indicator for each office, measuring whether the office has met preestablished standards of performance. Grades are given as pass, fail, or data not available. Offices are not graded relative to each other.
- Report Two is a more detailed version of Report One and shows the actual application area scores and their weighting factors for all indicators. An office can pass in some application areas and fail in others and still have an overall passing score due to the relative weights assigned to each area.
- Report Three shows the actual data for each indicator for each office for the particular time period. This report is the most widely used of the four.
- Report Four shows 12 months of history for each indicator for each office. Data shown include percent of goal achieved by function, application score (which ties back to Reports Two and Three), and the number of months goals were achieved.

LIMITATIONS AND CONSTRAINTS

To effectively use audit area selection for a multilocation organization, it is desirable that the organization have integrated computer application systems installed in major functional areas, and that the information produced by these systems be accessible on a timely basis. This is a sophisticated audit technique if applied via integrated on-line computer application systems; consequently, highly capable internal audit and data processing personnel are required for the development process. From the internal audit veiwpoint at the firm in the application example, the matrix is not suitable for audit area selection in those areas of the branch that require physical audit analysis because of their fraud sensitivity, such as accounts payable, cash and bank accounts, or application of customer receivables, due to the automation of the audit tool. Their rationale is that fraud committed via the computer application system could be extended to include the audit tool as well, and that, to guard against this exposure, independent auditing is desirable.

IMPLEMENTATION CONSIDERATIONS

To implement the audit area selection technique, the requisite computer application systems to supply key indicator data must be in place. While no prohibition exists against preparing these data manually, manual preparation tends to reduce the savings in internal audit time. The key indicator data can be supplied to the audit area selection program in a number of ways. The organization using this method already had a computer application system installed to gather many and diverse data from its multiple application systems. The key indicators were selected from this application system. In other situations, key indicators could be supplied individually from a company's pertinent "source" application systems on a periodic basis, via telecommunications facilities, various magnetic media, or printed reports. The objective is to collate all key indicator data for internal audit management review, by whatever particular means appropriate to the organization.

The key indicators must be selected so as to enable internal audit management to allocate internal audit resources to potential problems in their areas of concern. These areas of concern are specific to the particular organization, its structure, and its characteristics. Key indicators, which are measures of performance of those areas of concern, are also specific to the organization. Generally, factors to be considered in key indicator selection are:

- Exposure to risk of fraud
- Exposure to loss of control
- Deviations of actual from planned schedule
- Unusual rates of change
- Variations of actual from budget.

These factors are necessarily as broad as the charter of internal audit. Cash receipt and cash disbursement areas are of particular interest to most, if not all, organizations, as are other areas involving asset control, profitability, and expense management. The firm using audit area selection, for example, selected cash management, billing, shipments to customers, and asset management as its areas of concern. For any organization considering audit area selection, the key question is, "From an audit standpoint, what is most important to us?" Limitations will frequently exist in the availability of management data, but within this constraint, key indicators can be selected to help internal audit management effectively plan audit programs.

TRAINING REQUIREMENTS

Little internal auditor training is required to use the audit area selection technique. As indicated in Table 10-1, a basic knowledge of data processing principles and concepts is desirable, as is a knowledge of application system development controls. Training requirements to develop and install an automated audit area selection program are more comprehensive. An advanced knowledge of data processing principles and concepts is required, as is a basic knowledge of computer application system structure. Most important, however, is the capability to select and develop the key indicators from the body of data available from the various computer application systems in use in the organization. This capability is a function principally of a comprehensive knowledge of these application systems coupled with an extensive knowledge of auditing.

COST FACTORS

The company discussed in the application example had an on-line data base system for collecting the various data required to calculate its key indicators. Therefore, it was not necessary to develop the data collection system in order to make the automated branch office audit matrix operational. At this organization, four to six man-months were required to determine which indicators would be used and to specify the reports needed. This did not include programming effort. The cost to run the system is minimal because the branch office audit matrix system was installed as part of the company's on-line data base system. The maintenance time for the system is directly proportional to how well the original indicators were chosen and how often the indicators are modified to meet changing internal audit requirements.

EVALUATION OF EFFECTIVENESS

Audit area selection can be of significant benefit to internal audit management in establishing an internal audit plan. Through the use of this technique, internal audit resources can be efficiently allocated to those areas of potentially high audit concern and to those areas with apparently high exposure to loss of control. However, the requirement of a comprehensive set of computer application systems places this technique beyond the scope of many organizations. For those organizations having such systems in operation or being planned, the technique should be considered. The outlook for the continuing use of this technique is good, as greater numbers of organizations continue to implement more of the integrated systems required to support audit area selection.

Table 10-1

AUDIT AREA SELECTION TRAINING REQUIREMENTS

Knowledge Area	Level* Development	Use
Data processing principles and concepts	XX	X
Computer application system structure	XX	—
Computer application system controls and procedures	X	—
Data management	X	—
Computer service center controls	—	—
Application system development controls	X	X
Computer application programming	X	—

* XX = Advanced; X = Basic; — = Not required.

Chapter 11

SCORING

Scoring is a planning technique that helps an auditor systematically select a computer application system for audit to maximize audit effectiveness. The technique identifies quantifiable characteristics of a computer application system that are significant from a risk analysis viewpoint. The characteristics are weighted and combined to obtain a system score. Several computer application systems may be scored in this way and the potential benefits obtainable from auditing the systems may be compared.

TECHNIQUE OVERVIEW

Scoring is a technique to assign a numeric value to a computer application system. This numeric value permits the auditor to classify computer application systems in order of their auditability needs. Under such a system the audit need is objectively determined rather than intuitively assessed.

From a study of the computer application system, the auditor identifies key characteristics. These will vary from organization to organization. Among the characteristics that may be considered are:

- Financial or nonfinancial system.
- Amount of assets controlled.
- Batch or on-line system.
- Number of major data files updated.
- Computer resources used.
- Software systems utilized (e.g., telecommunications, operating systems, HASP).
- Statutory requirements imposed.
- Number of major management reports produced.
- Vulnerability to fraud.
- Number of other key systems associated.
- Maintenance efforts expended.
- Experience of system personnel.
- Involvement of users in system design.
- Involvement of auditors in system design.
- Number of programs involved.

Each of the selected characteristics needs to be evaluated individually. All will not be of equal importance in determining the potential risk or exposure from a specific system. The auditors must devise a scoring algorithm that takes into account the characteristics important to their organization plus a method of weighting the importance of each of the selected characteristics.

With the scoring method, system selection for audit is done methodically, and the benefits of the system auditing can be more clearly perceived in advance. Such an evaluation of systems can help the audit planner to distribute and audit effort effectively and can provide a sound basis for assessing the relative audit benefits. However, the scoring method should not be used without careful interpretation of the results of scoring. Scoring provides a basis that objectively ranks computer application systems in terms of their relative risk potential. The first time the scoring system is applied, flaws in the algorithm are bound to be discovered. Intuition, management desires, and the results of previous audits of the area involved in the system may tend to override the scoring algorithm. For example, the first attempts at applying the algorithm may yield results that defy intuition or run counter to the expressed desires of management. This is a signal to review the list of factors and their weights. Thus it is necessary to repeatedly refine the algorithm to make it more effective.

TYPICAL PROCEDURES

Scoring of computer applications should be done on a periodic basis (e.g., semiannual, annual). The steps involved in using the scoring technique are:

- Step 1 — Develop a listing of computer application systems to be considered for audit.
- Step 2 — Gather the factual data as needed to implement the scoring technique.
- Step 3 — Create a score for each system under consideration.
- Step 4 — Rank the systems according to need for audit based on the scoring.
- Step 5 — From that ranking, apply audit judgment in developing a final audit plan.

APPLICATION EXAMPLE

The application example examined by SRI was that of an insurance company. At this company a factor matrix is developed for each system under consideration. Nine specific factors have been identified as being descriptive of a computer application system:

1. The amount of corporate assets controlled.
2. The number of major data bases updated.
3. The computer resources used.

4. Statutory requirements imposed.
5. The number of major management reports produced.
6. The number of other key systems associated.
7. The operations control role played.
8. Maintenance effort expended.
9. Number of programs involved.

Each of the nine factors is evaluated differently. For the first factor, system totals are computed on an annual basis for such things as premium dollars, total claims paid, reserves, assets, values, policy loans expenses, etc. These values are accumulated without regard to numeric sign and provide the base value for system evaluation. While financial impact may be the principal measure of system criticality and hence of audit need, other system factors modify this ranking. The next six factors are used to further the system rating.

Factor 2 has a value of 1.25 for systems that update major corporate data bases. Systems that do not are assigned a factor value of 1. A major data base is defined to be any masterfile that is either a comprehensive file in one particular insurance area or is one of several masterfiles maintained in a single system.

Factor 3 is determined from annual computer run time. A value of 1 is given to any system using fewer than 10 computer hours annually. A value of 1.1 is assigned to a system using from 10 to 100 hours, 1.2 to a system using from 100 to 500 hours, 1.3 to a system using 500 to 1,000 hours, 1.4 to a system using 1,000 to 10,000 hours, and 1.5 to a system using more than 10,000 hours.

Factor 4 is assigned a value of 1 for a system for which there is no statutory requirement, a value of 1.25 when one statutory body requires system outputs, a value of 1.5 if two statutory bodies require system outputs, and a value of 1.75 if three or more statutory bodies require system output.

Factor 5 is assigned a value of 1 if no major management reports result from the system and a value of 1.5 otherwise. A major management report is defined to have one or more of the following traits: It provides analytic data on performance results, it shows results of financial transactions, its reports relate to the complete life of the business, or it shows data that control the daily process cycle.

Factor 6 is assigned a value of 1 if the system is not a key link to other systems and a value of 1.25 otherwise.

Factor 7 is assigned a value of 1 if the system contains no vital control elements, a value of 1.5 if it has some control importance, and a value of 2 if it is vital to operational control. Vital control elements are those that detect errors or provide audit trails or update masterfiles.

A value for system criticality is determined by multiplying together the values assigned to Factors 1 through 7. System criticality is not the only factor in audit planning. In addition, one must have an estimate of the audit effort needed to perform a system audit. The last two factors are used for this purpose.

Factor 8 is assigned a value based on the man-months of maintenance that have gone into the system annually — the value of 1 if less than one man-month, 1.2 if between 1 and 5 man-months, 1.4 if between 5 and 10 man-months, 1.6 if between 10 and 20 man-months, 1.8 if between 20 and 100 man-months, and 2 if over 100 man-months. There is strong evidence that this factor may be as important as any. Experience has shown that audit effort is proportional to system maintenance effort.

Factor 9 is assigned a value according to the number of programs in the system. This factor relates to system size and complexity, which also are indicative of audit effort required. The value assigned is 1 if there are 1 to 5 programs, 1.2 if there are 6 to 10 programs, 1.4 if there are 11 to 20 programs, 1.6 if there are 21 to 35 programs, 1.8 if there are 36 to 60 programs, and 2 if there are more than 60 programs in the system.

The values assigned to the last two factors (numbers 8 and 9) are multiplied together with the product of the first 7 to form the final system score for audit planning purposes.*

Table 11-1 is a worksheet to be used to develop the final score for a computer application system using the nine indicated factors. For each system scored, the final score and the factors making up that score are transcribed to a comparison worksheet (see Table 11-2). The systems listed on Table 11-2 are then ranked according to high score. The highest score is the number one candidate for audit followed by the second highest score, etc.

LIMITATIONS AND CONSTRAINTS

The main limitation to this technique lies in identifying the correct factors and choosing the proper weightings for those factors. The scoring technique is also limited by the necessity for

*Note that this company has chosen to represent criticality by the product of factors 1 through 7 and audit effort by 8 × 9, and then assumes that:

Audit need = Criticality × Effort

It can easily be argued that a more rational definition of audit need is simply criticality, without consideration of audit effort at all. On the other hand, if a measure of audit cost-benefit is sought, a more reasonable formulation might be:

Audit cost-benefit = Criticality ÷ Effort

The fact that these considerations can produce three different formulations of measures in this area is an indication of the need for careful examination of both objectives and procedures when using this technique.

Table 11-1

FINAL SCORING ALGORITHM WORKSHEET

Factor	Criteria		Score
1	Assets controlled:		
	Type A ________		
	Type B ________		
	Type C ________		
	Total Assets		= _____
2	( ) Update major data bases		× 1.25
	( ) Does not update major data base		× 1.00 _____
		Results =	
3	( ) Uses 10 computer hours annually		× 1.0
	( ) Uses 10-100 computer hours annually		× 1.1
	( ) Uses 100-500 computer hours annually		× 1.2
	( ) Uses 500-1,000 computer hours annually		× 1.3
	( ) Uses 1,000-10,000 computer hours annually		× 1.4
	( ) Uses over 10,000 computer hours annually		× 1.5 _____
		Results =	
4	( ) No statutory requirement		× 1.0
	( ) One statutory body requires output		× 1.25
	( ) Two statutory bodies require output		× 1.50
	( ) Over two statutory bodies require output		× 1.75 _____
		Results =	
5	( ) No major management report required		× 1.0
	( ) Major management reported required		× 1.5 _____
		Results =	
6	( ) Not a key link to other systems		× 1.0
	( ) A key link to other systems		× 1.25 _____
		Results =	
7	( ) No vital control elements		× 1.0
	( ) Some control importance		× 1.5
	( ) Vital to operational control		× 2.0 _____
		Results =	
8	( ) One man-month of maintenance annually		= 1
	( ) 1-5 man-months of maintenance annually		= 1.2
	( ) 5-10 man-months of maintenance annually		= 1.4
	( ) 10-20 man-months of maintenance annually		= 1.6
	( ) 20-100 man-months of maintenance annually		= 1.8
	( ) Over 100 man-months of maintenance annually		= 2.0
9	( ) 1-5 programs in the system		= 1
	( ) 6-10 programs in the system		= 1.2
	( ) 11-20 programs in the system		= 1.4
	( ) 21-35 programs in the system		= 1.6
	( ) 36-60 programs in the system		= 1.8
	( ) Over 60 programs in the system		= 2.0

Results after Calculation of Multiplication of Factors 1 Through 7 _____ × Factor 8 _____ × Factor 9 _____ = Final Score_____

Table 11-2

COMPARISON WORKSHEET

System Under Consideration	Factors									Final System Scoring	Ranking
	1	2	3	4	5	6	7	8	9		

arbitrary judgments built into the factors (e.g., What is a management report?). The more judgmental the factors become the less reliable the results are when the total score is calculated. Also, it is more difficult to apply the scoring technique illustrated to newly developed systems because some factors used require information based on experience. For example, the factor relating to systems maintenance will be unknown until the system has been operational for some period of time. However, system test experience could be used as a predictor in this case, if such information is readily available.

IMPLEMENTATION CONSIDERATIONS

This technique deals directly with the allocation of internal audit effort. As such, an effort to apply the technique within an organization should invoke searching examination of the character of the organization's activities, goals, and particularly its posture toward loss exposure. These factors bear directly on allocation of internal audit effort, and therefore must be reflected in the scoring algorithm.

The formulation of the algorithms must also meet certain other pragmatic requirements. First, it must be based on the use of data that are readily available, defined for all systems to be scored, and have some historical consistency. Second, the algorithm must truly measure what the auditor wants it to measure. The application example points to the potential ambiguity in this regard. Finally, the algorithm must produce reasonable results. This obvious requirement should be empirically verified before the algorithm is used in practice. In particular, the relative scores of two systems should not be seriously different than the auditor's intuition dictates. Pairwise score comparison against intuition is a valid means of testing the algorithm. The algorithm should also be verified by assessing the reasonableness of the algebraic change in score when each input factor is changed.

Finally, the scoring process should be repeated periodically as a part of the planning of the internal audit department to take account of systems changes.

TRAINING REQUIREMENTS

For the experienced internal auditor, as noted in Table 11-3 there are no particular additional training requirements for using the technique. However, experience in the data processing environment is often valuable in the selection and weighting of factors used.

COST FACTORS

The cost to develop a system scoring method and to apply it is only the cost of the auditor's time. While development of the method can occupy several man-weeks, the time to apply it might be expected to be two days per application system. In the installation visited by SRI, scoring was experimental. The organization SRI visited had no present reliable cost factors available associated with using the scoring technique.

Table 11-3

SCORING TRAINING REQUIREMENTS

Knowledge Area	Level*
Data processing principles and concepts	X
Computer application system structure	—
Computer application system controls and procedures	—
Data management	—
Computer service center controls	—
Application system development controls	—
Computer appliction programming	—

* X = Basic; — = Not required.

EVALUATION OF EFFECTIVENESS

The technique is still considered experimental at the installation visited, and the staff's experience with it has not yet been extensive enough to permit a thorough evaluation. The use of a scoring technique increases the tendency to quantify audit benefit. There is a strong belief that real measures of audit quality are not quantifiable. In many situations, auditors believe that a more quantitative cost benefit analysis and justification of an audit plan would be welcome.

It is clear, however, that the determination of system characteristics to be used, their weighting, and their combination are critical to the utility of this method. The logical ambiguities of the method as applied in the example point to the pitfalls of casual use. The auditor must, in the use of this technique as with any other, know clearly what he is trying to measure and what results he is trying to achieve.

The outlook for this technique is uncertain. It has many intrinsic good points, but requires further development of more general methods and much field experience before it will gain wide acceptance as a tool of the internal auditor.

Chapter 12

MULTISITE AUDIT SOFTWARE

This audit technique can best be used by organizations having regional computer data centers and a centralized system development and programming staff. Application of multisite audit software entails the development of one set of computer audit programs to be used to test a computer application system being run at multiple locations. Effective use of this technique requires that the computer application systems be relatively similar. Two firms visited in the survey have applied the technique successfully; one to a 7-site complex for auditing accounts receivable, billing, and payroll computer application systems, and the other to a 17-site complex for auditing 22 computer application systems. Use of multisite audit software is generally more cost-effective than the use of multiple audit packages at multiple locations.

TECHNIQUE OVERVIEW

Multisite audit software is a set of computer audit programs used by organizations having several data processing centers. These audit programs are developed at a central location and are installed at the outlying data centers. The outlying data centers run the audit software under the control of the local internal auditors. There is no functional difference between multisite audit software and other types of audit software. One primary difference and advantage is that the development of one audit software package for use at multiple locations is generally more cost-effective than the development of multiple audit packages that are functionally similar. Also, the standardization that is inherent in the use of one audit procedure reduces training requirements, increases control, and enables more efficient use of the internal auditor's time.

To effectively use multisite audit software, the regional data centers must have similar computer application systems. The greater the similarity, the greater the success of this technique. Desirable areas of similarity are computer hardware and operating systems, functional computer application system design, file content and record formats, and the computer application system code structure. Slight dissimilarities, if well documented, will not reduce the effectiveness of this technique.

Multisite audit software provides a solution to two problems facing internal auditors. First, this technique, due to its standardizing influence, tends to minimize the effect of a lack of experience and training on the part of internal audit personnel. Inexperienced auditors can "follow the book" and perform an effective audit. Second, the repetitive use of multisite audit software by different internal auditors in different locations will tend to "get the bugs out" and will result in a more reliable computer audit program sooner than would be expected of a one-location program. In addition, the multisite audit software can be more sophisticated and probing due to its cost-effective characteristic; development costs are applied to auditing multiple locations. Also, suggestions from the many internal auditors using the software can result in the incorporation of functional improvements. The principal disadvantage of the technique is its lack of applicability to diverse operations; special procedures followed at particular locations are usually beyond the scope of the audit software.

TYPICAL PROCEDURES

The steps in developing this technique are described in the following paragraphs.

Step 1 — Identify the Areas to Audit — Select the computer application system to be audited by multisite audit software. This is a major step requiring a thorough analysis of multisite similarities and differences.

Step 2 — Set the Audit Objectives — Determine which factors are to be tested.

Step 3 — Analyze the System to Be Audited — Acquire a thorough understanding of the application system by reviewing the system documentation as it exists at all locations. Differences particular to each location are noted for inclusion in the specifications for the multisite audit software.

Step 4 — Develop Audit Procedures — Determine the methods to be used to audit the operation of the system, and document them.

Step 5 — Write and Test the Audit Software — Program the audit software package according to proper system development standards. Computer audit programs must be designed and written to run on the computers at the multiple locations. This can be a significant factor if the computers or their operating systems and other software are dissimilar.

Step 6 — Prepare the Operating Documentation — The operating documentation will contain instructions for the internal auditor using the audit software, and operating instructions for the regional data center, as well as proper application system documentation. Documentation for field internal auditors and regional data center personnel must consider that audits will be performed without benefit of headquarters assistance, and must also describe procedures to allow for location differences.

Step 7 — Distribute the Software — Distribute the software and the documentation for initial usage.

Step 8 — Solicit and Analyze Feedback from the Field — Incorporate changes to improve the audit technique based on actual experience in use.

Step 9 — Update — Update software and documentation.

At the firms visited, the audit software is developed by a computer audit specialist who has participated in one or more audits of the application area. His design objective is the development of a computer audit program that will require as little manual interface as possible by the internal auditors using the system. These audit programs contain such features as range, edit, batch, hash, and run-to-run totals, control totals, and footing totals, so that it is unnecessary for the on-site internal auditor to perform many of these routine tests.

Because the audit software is intended to be run at remote sites, documentation is very important; one organization uses the following format in preparing its audit software documentation:

- A narrative description of the purpose of the audit package, the objectives to be realized, and an index of the content of the package.
- The program names for the various programs to be audited and a descriptive paragraph outlining the function of each program.
- A complete set of job control language (JCL) cards.
- A detailed description of the purpose of the audit software.
- Detailed step-by-step instructions for the use of the audit software.
- A listing of the JCL.
- Sample listings of all the outputs that the internal auditor will receive from the program.
- Complete operating instructions for the computer operator at the data processing center.
- Keypunch instruction sheets, should any keypunching be required.
- Flowcharts of the audit software package.

The documentation manual is designed to be an independent document that can be used by a local internal auditor who has no programming experience, and a computer operator at the local computer center who will be responsible for running the package.

APPLICATION EXAMPLES

An international industrial firm has written audit packages at company headquarters to audit 22 systems being run at 17 international computer centers. To date, it has developed audit packages to:

- Calculate gross profit by product line.
- Compare customer master credit limit with the customer account balance. This program also matches customer detail against the summary record.
- Extract open items from the order invoice file by any general retrieval criterion, such as age.

Through the use of multisite audit software, this company has noted a decrease in the auditor's time required to perform an audit. In addition, local management can use the software to monitor its own operations during the year. The company cites one disadvantage; there is not enough user feedback to enable the internal audit staff to develop any custom packages for the local management, or to understand idiosyncracies that may be in the foreign systems. It is felt that this is primarily due to distance and language problems. These packages are distributed in object code and include the JCL that is required to run the package.

A nationwide retailer uses this technique to develop standardized audit packages for its regional internal audit staff. These packages are used when auditing a regional center, or when auditing local computer application systems. This technique enables this organization to apply company-standard auditing procedures throughout the country at a minimum cost. The computer system used to develop these specialized packages is a generalized audit software package available from a large firm of external auditors. To date, about 60 multisite audit software packages have been developed for regional use. This company feels that the technique has been beneficial in many ways:

- It offers improved efficiency of operations and control at a reduced cost.
- It offers increased audit efficiency and can aid in improving application efficiency because of ongoing monitoring of the application.
- There is an improvement in applications control at a low dollar cost.
- The regional internal auditors do not have to learn programming to use the packages. Whenever an internal auditor encounters a problem or a serious

instance of noncompliance, he can call on the headquarters internal audit department.

- There is also a possibility of improved detection of fraud, defalcation, error, or omissions because regional internal audit staff will be using a more sophisticated audit software program than might be possible if programmed regionally.

LIMITATIONS AND CONSTRAINTS

The following characteristics must be present in an organization for it to successfully use this technique:

- Reasonably common computer applications used in several data processing centers.
- An internal audit staff experienced in using computer audit software or equivalent packages.
- A central internal audit staff having sufficient knowledge of the local environments to develop applicable packages.

Packages must be both flexible and comprehensive if they are to meet audit objectives in different environments.

IMPLEMENTATION CONSIDERATIONS

The primary consideration in the analysis of the applicability of this technique is whether one multisite audit software package can fulfill audit requirements at diverse locations. Factors entering into this decision are the similarities and dissimilarities of the particular computer application systems and the hardware and software at the locations. Within each application system under consideration, the file structure and content, the processing logic, and the aggregate system structure must be examined. Hardware and software characteristics need to be examined to determine if a multisite audit software package can run on each system. Functional analysis of audit requirements is the responsibility of internal audit. Computer application system analysis and hardware and software analysis require extensive data processing knowledge, which are usually beyond the capabilities of internal auditors. In addition, ongoing audit program maintenance and maintenance change control must be considered to ensure that all locations use the current versions of the audit software.

Use of a generalized audit software package, rather than development of a custom audit program, usually will result in a cost savings and a smoother and quicker implementation. An analysis of available generalized audit software packages should be made to determine if such a package can fulfill audit objectives and if the package can run at the various locations.

TRAINING REQUIREMENTS

Internal auditor training requirements are minimal with this technique. Computer technical expertise is not required because the home office does the programming and the outlying data center runs the audit programs according to the instructions provided with the programs. At the firms in the application examples, the training requirements for an internal auditor vary from two to five days depending on the audit software package.

Regional audit personnel require no advance preparation other than training in the use of multisite audit software, in that the package is sent from the home office. The home office staff have complete control over the use of this technique as they are the only ones with the knowledge or the authority to change the package. Training requirements in the use of this technique by regional internal auditors are summarized in Table 12-1, and include a basic knowledge of data processing principles and concepts, computer application system controls and procedures, and computer service center controls. Training requirements to develop a custom audit package for a multisite environment include an advanced knowledge of data processing principles and concepts, computer application system structure, computer application programming, a basic knowledge of computer application system controls and procedures, computer service center controls, and application system development controls.

COST FACTORS

In the opinion of the firms cited above, specialized packages based on a generalized audit software

Table 12-1

MULTISITE AUDIT SOFTWARE TRAINING REQUIREMENTS

Knowledge Area	Level* Development†	Use
Data processing principles and concepts	XX	X
Computer application system structure	XX	—
Computer application system controls and procedures	X	X
Data management	—	—
Computer service center controls	X	X
Application system development controls	X	—
Computer application programming	XX	—

* XX = Advanced; X = Basic; — = Not required.

† Development training applies to the development of custom audit software rather than to the use of packages such as generalized audit software.

package are not very expensive either to develop or to use. At the retail firm in the example, the development time for a single application varies from one to four weeks. This firm has had one person, on average, working in the area for the last four years and has developed approximately 60 applications. The computer operation time per application is highly variable and depends on how much extraction or report printing time is required for the package. The development of a customized package not based on a generalized audit software package is more expensive. Costs of such a development effort are dependent on the scope and complexity of the projected multisite audit software.

EVALUATION OF EFFECTIVENESS

Multisite audit software offers the advantage of standardizing computer audit programs to the large organization with multiple computer sites. Functionally, there is little difference between the use of multisite audit software and a competency center. Each method uses standard audit programs to test computer application systems; the former running the audit programs at the local or regional computer site, the latter running the programs at a central site. As such, the use of multisite audit software tends to give more operational audit control to regional internal auditors, while retaining the cost advantages and standardization advantages of centralized audit systems development. The use of a generalized audit software package for the multisite environment should be considered, due to increased systems reliability, comprehensive documentation, and lower cost when compared to the development and use of custom audit programs. The outlook for multisite audit software is for increased use, especially if the trend toward decentralization, or "distributed processing" continues.

Chapter 13

COMPETENCY CENTER

A competency center is a computer center, established at a central location, that is responsible for the execution of audit software programs. The competency center receives data files from other locations, executes the audit software programs, and distributes the resultant reports to the internal auditor. The competency center approach to the execution of audit software is primarily applicable to large multilocation organizations. Through the competency center, the execution of audit software programs is centralized, thus eliminating many of the problems that might be encountered by executing audit software at multiple locations.

TECHNIQUE OVERVIEW

Use of this audit technique entails the identification or establishment of a computer center location to run computer programs for audit purposes. Internal auditors at remote locations transmit data files and processing specifications to the competency center, where the audit tests are run.

The internal auditor at the remote location prepares his processing specifications according to operating procedures and guides supplied by the competency center. Internal audit personnel at the competency center are responsible for the receipt of material from the field internal auditor, the development of the application, the running of the audit software, and the timely distribution of the output reports. In addition, competency center personnel are responsible for the preparation of operating procedures for use of the center, and for other training materials for the field internal auditors. Results of the test runs are returned to the internal auditor for analysis and evaluation.

Benefits cited by organizations using the competency center approach are as follows:

- The need to train and maintain the proficiency of many internal auditors in the use of audit software programs is eliminated.
- The scheduling difficulties of running audit programs at multiple production computer service centers is eliminated; the competency center location is solely responsible for running audit programs.
- A higher level of proficiency and consistency of computer service center performance is obtained in the execution of audit software programs, while eliminating duplication of effort (e.g., two auditors installing same programs at different locations).
- Centralized control of all proprietary files maintained by the audit staff is obtained.
- There is increased utilization of audit software tools due to convenience of use.
- A higher degree of independence is maintained by eliminating the internal auditor's need to rely on local data-processing support for programming and processing.

The principal disadvantage of the use of a competency center is the cost and the increased time required to transmit data to and from the center. The factors are discussed in subsequent sections.

TYPICAL PROCEDURES

The specific responsibilities of the competency center at the firms visited are as follows:

- Install and execute general-purpose audit software programs, and distribute the output to the internal auditor on a timely basis.
- Write programs to honor special requests that cannot be fulfilled by the execution of general audit software, and distribute the output to the internal auditors on a timely basis.
- Establish and maintain a central library of sensitive programs and data files from company locations, as required, to conduct future audits.
- Establish requirements, and monitor the timely and accurate receipt of required data.
- Establish and maintain accurate inventory records of data received, and provide for the security of this information from the time it is received until it is properly destroyed.
- Maintain adequate backup files and recovery procedures.
- Assist in the design, development, and testing of new audit software tools.
- Provide advice and counsel to all internal auditors regarding the use of computer audit tools.
- Establish and maintain accurate and comprehensive operating procedures regarding the receipt, transmission, storage, destruction, and security of data files and hardcopy information.

- Obtain necessary hardware and software support to accomplish the above.

LIMITATIONS AND CONSTRAINTS

The major potential limitation of a competency center, other than the identified cost factors, is the possible increase in turnaround time due to the additional time required to transmit data to, and receive reports from, the competency center. Thus, advanced planning is important to ensure that required data are available when needed, as is the scheduling of the internal auditor's time while awaiting output reports. The use of data transmission facilities, as opposed to delivery services, can substantially reduce the turnaround time. The use of competency centers becomes more complex when large data-base systems are in use in the organization. Such data bases, due to their size, cannot be copied and transmitted. The necessary data must be extracted at the remote location and then transmitted.

The competency center is an audit technique normally suitable for a very large organization, generally with a sophisticated internal audit staff. While there is no requirement that only audit software be run at the competency center, the control and independent aspects of internal audit responsibilities make the separation of processing responsibilities within the center a desirable factor of the concept.

IMPLEMENTATION CONSIDERATIONS

The use of the competency center is of primary interest to the internal audit staff, and consequently accurate and comprehensive documentation is essential. Operating procedures and training guides are the major methods by which internal auditors are trained in the use of the center and its audit programs. These procedures and guides are especially important to internal auditors in remote locations.

TRAINING REQUIREMENTS

Internal audit personnel manning the competency center must have a basic knowledge of data processing principles and concepts, computer application system structure, computer application system controls and procedures, and computer application programming. In addition, an advanced knowledge of computer service center controls is required. These knowledge areas are shown in Table 13-1. Competency center personnel must have a detailed and specific knowledge of the audit software in use at the center, as well as a knowledge of general utility programs. Their programming knowledge and experience will enable them to write programs to fulfill special requests that cannot be satisfied by the execution of generalized audit software tools in use at the center. Field internal audit personnel must have a basic knowledge of data processing principles and concepts, and computer application system controls and procedures. In addition, field internal auditors must be trained in the use of the competency center.

COST FACTORS

The cost of training and maintaining the proficiency of many internal auditors is significantly reduced through the use of a competency center. The cost of the audit software tools is the same as if those tools were used in a multisite audit software mode of operation. The most significant expense is the establishment of the competency center computer site, and the cost of the implementation and operation of the computer and its supporting devices and staff. The operating cost of the competency center is the same as the operating cost of performing audit functions elsewhere, provided all costs are allocated and machine utilization factors are equal. Frequently, this is not the case, and the competency center is an additional computer site with additional expenses.

EVALUATION OF EFFECTIVENESS

A competency center and multisite audit software have many functional characteristics in common. The use of each of these audit methods entails the application of a standardized computer audit method to a computer application system. The competency center approach is to run these audit programs at a central site, whereas multisite audit software is run at remote locations. There is nothing inherent in the establishment and use of a competency center that requires standardized audit programs; unique test programs could be developed and used for each computer application system run at each location, although this situation is infrequently encountered. Organizations using competency centers tend toward standardization and, therefore, toward the use of common computer audit programs to test their common computer application systems. The organizations using competency centers that participated in this survey find that the use of audit software tools during normal financial and operational audits increases significantly with the installation of a competency center. Prior to the establishment of the center, the incovenience of use and the problems associated with having many internal auditors install and execute audit software at multiple locations resulted in more limited use of computer audit software.

A competency center is an audit technique with applicability primarily to organizations with a centralized audit control policy. The decentralized structure of many organizations runs counter to the use of this technique, and as such, this audit technique has limited applicability.

Table 13-1

COMPETENCY CENTER TRAINING REQUIREMENTS*

Knowledge Area	Level† Internal Audit	Computer Operations	Programming
Data processing principles and concepts	X	X	XX
Computer application system structure	X	X	X
Computer application system controls and procedures	X	—	XX
Data management	—	—	XX
Computer service center controls	X	XX	X
Application system development controls	—	—	—
Computer application programming	X	—	XX

*Training requirements are included for computer operations and programming personnel manning the competency center.

†XX = Advanced; X = Basic; — = Not required.

Part IV

COMPUTER APPLICATION AUDIT TOOLS AND TECHNIQUES

Chapter 14

TEST DATA METHOD

The test data method verifies processing accuracy of computer application systems by executing these systems using specially prepared sets of input data that produce preestablished results. The method provides internal auditors with a procedure for verification of computer programs and applications. It is a method that can be used by internal auditors with only a modest data processing background when testing specific and limited program functions. It is a good technique to use initially in program verification because tests can be expanded incrementally, providing a learning situation for less experienced internal auditors. Special procedures are not usually required. The test data method is limited to computer processing verification and evaluation and is not an appropriate technique for verification of production data. No evidence is provided concerning the completeness or accuracy of production input data or masterfiles.

TECHNIQUE OVERVIEW

The test data method is one of the techniques more widely used by internal auditors to test and verify selected processing logic, computations, and controls in computer application systems. The test data method is used to test and verify:

- Input transaction validation routines, error detection and application system controls.
- Processing logic, and controls associated with the creation and maintenance of data processing master records.
- Computational routines such as interest, gross pay, or asset depreciation.
- Incorporation of program changes.

In addition, if transactions are prepared according to established user procedures, the method helps to evaluate the procedures as well as the computer programs tested.

The use of the test data method is usually limited to auditing a few features and functions of an application rather than to comprehensive auditing, such as would be provided by the Base Case System Test or Integrated Test Facility (ITF) methods. The use of this method for more limited testing and verification is a practical rather than technical limitation, i.e., the scope of audit is limited by the number of transactions and combinations of transactions the internal auditor is able to prepare and verify. This limit becomes increasingly important as the size and complexity of the application program increases.

This audit method, in its simplest form, is one of the least difficult methods used to verify computer programs. The major advantages of the method include the following:

- Objective evidence is provided illustrating the compliance of computer programs with established policies, specifications, and user procedures.
- Repeated tests can be run using established test data sets and verification to predetermined results.
- Minimum data processing assistance is needed to prepare test data and predefined results.
- Special programming is not usually required, and the internal auditor requires only a rudimentary knowledge of data processing.

The test data method is a good starting point in expanding an internal audit program to include compliance testing involving computer application programs. This is because useful tests can be planned and executed based almost exclusively on user procedures and input forms. Such an approach can be beneficial for internal auditors with limited data processing experience; however, complete user documentation must be available. As the internal auditors establish and execute tests to verify specific elements of a computer application, their knowledge of both the specific application and data processing in general is increased. Thus, this audit method can provide internal auditors with progressive practical experience and an opportunity to become better acquainted with the data processing functions in use within their organization.

TYPICAL PROCEDURES

The test data method is applicable to acceptance testing prior to the production use of a new application or changes to an existing application, and to periodic compliance testing after cutover to production status. Compliance testing is typically planned and controlled by the internal auditor. The material presented in this chapter is based on the experience of a large midwestern electronics manufacturing firm that is using the technique to audit established computer applications.

Successful use of the test data method at the firm visited by SRI is based upon a systematic approach that consists of an application review, test planning, test data creation, and testing and evaluation. This approach is described in the following paragraphs.

Application Review

This review or survey of the computer application to be audited has two objectives: to acquire an overall familiarity with the system procedures and general functions performed by users and data processing; and to determine the availability and adequacy of procedures and documentation relating to the application, both in user areas and in the computer service center. Steps in the applications review include:

Step 1 — Coordinate Audit Approach — User personnel and computer service center personnel are consulted. General audit objectives are discussed and cooperation is secured. This step is especially important for the first audit of a particular computer application system.

Step 2 — Review Available Documentation — User documentation includes forms, control logs, written procedures, and processing schedules. Computer service center documentation of interest to the internal auditors includes record formats, balancing and control procedures, control logs, system flowcharts, processing schedules, and record retention schedules. The review of this documentation is focused at the system level; review of individual programs and program logic is not necessary except in situations where little or no documentation is available. However, where the program contains specific data embedded within program logic routines the need to review the program is imperative (for example, tax rate, state, city or government codes, or depreciation rate may be written into the program). The internal auditor must acquire a good understanding of overall functions of the application and the various transaction types used.

Step 3 — Observe Input Preparation — The internal auditor visits each user area where input documents are prepared. During this visit, the auditor observes input preparation procedures and control procedures. A review of procedural compliance and a preliminary evaluation of the adequacy of input controls are performed. Particular attention is directed to input balancing, and the correction and reentry of transactions previously rejected during computer processing.

Step 4 — Observe Transaction Flow — The flow of transactions between user areas and the computer service center is important primarily from a control point of view. The internal auditor determines if adequate controls exist and are in use within the center to ensure that data are complete when received for processing. Input controls within the computer service center are a combination of manual control-desk procedures and automated input error detection routines. Transaction flows are in the form of batched documents with a transmittal slip having user-prepared control balances.

Step 5 — Observe Output Processing — Output processing is reviewed for both adequacy and compliance with established procedures. Output balancing, error correction and reentry, and the logging of control totals are of particular importance. Existence and use of audit trails by users in tracing errors and reconciling out-of-balance situations are also important areas to review.

Test Planning

Audit objectives and the scope of computer application testing are established once the application review is completed. The following two steps are taken during the planning phase:

Step 6 — Document Test Plan — The internal auditor develops a list of transaction types and conditions to be tested, and identifies the various types of errors and error conditions to be tested. He identifies the input validation routines to be tested and the input media to be used, i.e., user forms, card formats, or terminal entry. He determines whether live data or test data are more suitable for purposes of the audit. He identifies the master data files to be used, and the approximate test data volumes. The internal auditor determines the areas in which computer service center assistance may be required, and prepares a written work plan to aid user and computer service center personnel in understanding audit objectives, the scope of testing, and impact on their normal operations.

Step 7 — Coordinate Test Plan — The internal auditor meets with user and computer service center personnel involved with the application to explain the planned test, and secure their advice and cooperation. The cooperation of data processing personnel is essential because they must provide production computer programs and copies of masterfiles to be used in the test, and they must schedule computer time to execute the tests. In addition, provisions must be made to ensure that test data and files do not become mixed with production data and, thereby, introduce erroneous data into the organization's data processing records.

Test Execution

The final two steps encompass the testing activities themselves.

Step 8 — Test Data Creation — The creation of test data can be accomplished using a number of approaches. One of the simplest is to secure copies of all input forms and complete them so that each condition specified in the test plan is satisfied. This approach can involve preparing input forms to create a number of master records and then preparing transactions to test the various computations, controls, and processing logic to be verified. This approach can be modified by copying existing masterfile records on to a test master, and then preparing the desired test transactions. This avoids the often tedious and error-prone task of hand-coding input to create the master records needed for testing.

The most precise test data are test data sets that are prepared to verify specific program functions. This alternative offers three advantages: assurance that desired program functions are tested with known variables; test results can be predetermined to ease the test results evaluation process; and test volumes tend to be smaller and, therefore, testing requires less computer time. The disadvantage is the amount of time required to prepare test data sets to verify all the program functions of concern to the internal auditor, and the likelihood of human error in preparing the data.

It is less time consuming to select actual transactions as a test data set, but the disadvantages of this approach are twofold: transactions must be carefully chosen to test the phases of the computer application to be verified — it is easy to have a large number of transactions but overlook important program routines — and it is time consuming to trace the execution of the transactions. Predetermined test results can be prepared, but often tend to offset the time saved by using actual data.

Special computer programs called test data generators are available, and are in limited use by internal auditors. In most instances audit requirements would not justify the cost of such programs unless the generators were also used by computer application programming personnel for testing of systems in development. Test data generators provide a mechanized approach to the preparation of comprehensive data sets. Such programs generally provide the following capabilities:

- Ranges of values can be generated on separate transactions for a given data element. This capability can be used to more thoroughly test input validation routines, error detection routines, and computations.
- Simplified statements are used to generate data with multiple variations. This capability offers a direct time saving in input preparation.

Conversely, if voluminous output is generated, the internal auditor's verification task becomes more time-consuming. Test data generators can significantly reduce the clerical effort and errors that accompany manual test data preparation. Whether test data are manually or mechanically prepared, care must be taken to ensure that the test data developed will satisfy audit objectives.

Step 9 — Testing and Evaluation — After test data sets have been prepared, data processing schedules a test using the appropriate application programs from the production library. The production version of the programs should be used, rather than a recompiled version from the source program library. All test transactions and test files used must be segregated from normal production files to avoid introducing erroneous data. The results of processing should be held for the internal auditor rather than distributed in the normal manner. The internal auditor should satisfy himself that a proper test run is made; frequently, this is accomplished by his personal observation of the process.

Results of the test are then compared to precalculated expected results. Deviations, which require analysis, correction, and reentry, are frequently encountered. The test may have to be cycled several times to test all conditions and enable error correction and reentry. Test cycles should be minimized to avoid disruption of normal data processing production schedules. As with any audit procedure, unexpected results and deviations from established procedures should be documented.

APPLICATION EXAMPLE

A multidivision, multistate payroll application was audited using the test data method. The audit was accomplished by two internal auditors, supported by an experienced EDP auditor, and the audit procedure followed the approach previously described. The auditors had no prior detailed knowledge of the application. Two types of transactions were included in the audit.

1. File maintenance transactions such as the following, for which 25 existing payroll masterfile records were selected and copied onto a test masterfile for the audit:

- Addition of new employees, including the addition of an employee already on file.
- Termination, including termination of an employee not on file.
- Termination of an employee using an incorrect social security number.
- Placing an employee on leave-of-absence status.
- Changes in pay rates and job codes.
- Transfers of employees between locations.
- Various changes in employee-authorized deductions.

2. Time sheet transactions, for which 5 transactions of each of the following types were used to test approximately 20 different conditions:

- Pay-rate overrides, applicable to a single pay period.
- Pay-rate adjustments.
- Shift premium hours and rate adjustments.
- Overtime-rate hours.
- Sick-leave hours in excess of limits.
- Withholding computations, particularly state withholding.
- Gross and net pay computations.

Some employees' records on the test file were run correctly as a control. Transactions with invalid conditions were run to verify and evaluate error detecting and reporting routines. The elapsed time to perform the test and evaluation, including the application review and test plan preparation, was less than two weeks.

LIMITATIONS AND CONSTRAINTS

The test data method is intrinsically a program verification method. When input transactions are prepared using the standard user input forms and following the standard written user procedures, the scope of the verification is extended and the method can also identify inconsistencies, omissions, and errors in these aspects of the system under audit.

As with all effective auditing methods, use of this method requires a testing discipline that includes a test plan, carefully selected and prepared test data, and a thorough reconciliation. In addition, considerable manual effort by the internal auditor is generally required; the level of effort increases directly with the complexity of the system and the scope of the audit. Extensive data processing expertise on the part of the internal auditor is not required, but some knowledge of data processing is needed.

IMPLEMENTATION CONSIDERATIONS

When large, complex, or on-line applications are to be investigated, it may not be practical to use this method due, in part, to difficulties in setting computer resources and files aside for test purposes. The parallel simulation or ITF methods may be better suited for auditing such applications.

Implementation considerations other than auditor training, which is discussed in the next section, are limited to the scope of testing, the complexity of the application, and the effort to prepare test data. Internal auditors with limited data processing experience should limit their initial work with the test data method to less complex applications.

Transaction volumes should be held to a minimum to reduce the effort required to prepare test data sets, simplify evaluation of test results, and minimize computer usage. When testing involves a large number of variables, it may be desirable to run test data in subsets during two or more cycles. In general, it is desirable to segregate masterfile creation, masterfile change, and detailed transactions into separate processing cycles.

TRAINING REQUIREMENTS

The training requirements for the test data method are limited to the need to acquire a knowledge of data processing principles and concepts, and computer application system controls and procedures. These knowledge areas are summarized in Table 14-1. The internal auditor must have an understanding of the particular computer application system so that test data can be created to fulfill the auditor requirements. In addition, reports produced by the audit run of the system must be analyzed and evaluated by the internal auditor. A review of existing documentation of the computer application system will serve as an adequate training guide for the auditor, if such documentation is current, accurate, and complete.

COST FACTORS

Costs associated with the use of the test data method depend upon three factors:

- Size and complexity of the application to be tested.
- Scope of audit tests required.
- The experience and skill of the auditor in using the method, and his general knowledge of data processing.

Table 14-1

TEST DATA METHOD TRAINING REQUIREMENTS

Knowledge Area	Level*
Data processing principles and concepts	X
Computer application system structure	—
Computer application system controls and procedures	X
Data management	—
Computer service center controls	—
Application system development controls	—
Computer application programming	—

* X = Basic; — = Not required.

While no specific cost data are available to apply to these factors, Table 14-2 illustrates the effort associated with the payroll example discussed above. The payroll audit was performed in less than two weeks by two internal auditors, with part-time assistance from an experienced EDP auditor. The "Expected Time" column shows what might be expected if two internal auditors with limited data processing experience were to perform the same audit. In both columns, testing and results evaluation are combined because several test cycles were involved.

EVALUATION OF EFFECTIVENESS

The test data method can aid the internal auditor when program verification is an important part of evaluation and verification of controls. The method is applicable to both preproduction testing of new computer applications and audits subsequent to the installation of a computer application. Due to the nature of the method, testing is often limited to specific processing functions, computations, or controls, rather than to comprehensive testing of entire applications. Nonetheless, the modest cost and limited implementation requirements make the test data method attractive for program verification. It will continue to be an effective audit technique for testing and verification of computer application systems that are undergoing minimum change.

Table 14-2

TEST DATA METHOD EXPERIENCE, ELAPSED TIME

Phase of Activity	Actual Time	Expected Time
Application review	1 day	2 days
Test planning	½ day	2 days
Test data creation	2 days	3 days
Testing and evaluation	4 days	6 days

Chapter 15

BASE CASE SYSTEM EVALUATION

Base case system evaluation (BCSE) is a technique that applies a standardized body of data (input, parameters, and output) to the testing of a computer application system. This body of data, the base case, is established by user personnel, with internal audit concurrence, as the criterion for correct functioning of the computer application system. This testing process is most widely used as a technique for validation of production computer application systems. One major manufacturing company, however, utilizes the base case approach as a "means to test programs during their development, to demonstrate the successful operation of the system prior to its installation, and to verify its continuing accurate operation during its life." As such, this approach represents a total commitment by corporate management and each user department to the principles and disciplines of BCSE.

TECHNIQUE OVERVIEW

A base case is established when sufficient transaction data have been processed by a computer application system to ensure that all program functions have been exercised; when examples of all valid classes and many invalid classes of transactions have been introduced into the system and have been correctly processed; and when consistent and valid system output is achieved over repeated iterations of the processing cycle. If a change is introduced into any of the system components, the effect of that change can be evaluated by comparison of test results with the prior results of the base case.

BCSE is applicable to a highly structured organization that is committed to thorough and extensive testing of computer application systems during development and subsequent maintenance. The technique requires extremely heavy user involvement; BCSE is a system test technique in addition to being an audit technique.

A BCSE test package consists of:

- One or more files containing the information necessary to test those valid and invalid conditions established in the design of the system (and subsequent modifications). For example, if the system provides a masterfile against which updates are processed, a test masterfile must be provided to demonstrate the various update conditions.
- A predefined set of input transactions that are designed to test every reasonably anticipatable valid and invalid event in system processing.
- A precomputed output for each transaction tested, which could be provided by an independently prepared report or from terminal output samples.
- A manual or automated procedure for comparing all files and reports to identify changes.
- For on-line systems, the base case must include transactions that demonstrate those activities normally accomplished on terminals. In addition, the base case must demonstrate the operation of communications and other elements of the normal on-line operating environment.

Benefits of the BCSE approach, according to the organizations using the method, are described in the following paragraphs.

First, the user department participates in all phases of the development or modification process. This sustained involvement of the user enables a more thorough validation of the system during the design stage, rather than confining validation to postinstallation review. As a result, the computer application system more closely conforms to user requirements and the chance for subsequent surprises is minimized.

Second, due to the continual user involvement, the implementation of new computer application systems and the modification of older systems generally progresses far more smoothly than otherwise. A greater depth of planning is performed by each of the participants, and each is more aware of the other's schedules and responsibilities.

Third, system documentation is generally superior. The BCSE package, which augments the normal system documentation, is itself a full functional description of the system, and must be modified and updated as the system changes.

Fourth, the responsibility for establishing and maintaining the functional integrity of the system is placed within the user department. This reduces the opportunity for design errors caused when application requirements are interpreted by non-user analysts who are generally unfamiliar with specific applications.

Fifth, the establishment of a base case with its predefined results leads directly to the automation of a significant portion of the procedures for verification during the computer application system testing process. Utilization of such tools and techniques as file-to-file compare and code comparison programs can significantly reduce the time and effort usually expended in systems verification, and thereby produces greater accuracy.

The sixth area of significant improvement generated by BCSE is improved auditability of the computer application system. The body of standard test data provides the internal auditor with a proven and efficient means to test and verify the computer application system.

Disadvantages of the BCSE method include the additional expense of system development and the need for extensive user involvement. Without this extensive user participation and commitment, BCSE is not an effective audit method.

TYPICAL PROCEDURES

Application development at one firm using the BCSE technique follows the familiar system development life cycle of feasibility analysis through implementation and maintenance. After preliminary analysis and feasibility assessment and the preparation of a "Requirements Planning Package," the base case groups, composed of user department and systems personnel, begin their participation with the development of a functional test strategy and procedures appropriate to the specific application.

Upon approval of the package by the user and systems development management, and review by internal auditing and computer service center management, the Systems Analysis Department develops the general design specifications. Concurrently, the base case group commences development of the formats, layouts, and other data comprising the test package, including the coding of transaction data and required interim files.

As the programmers develop their code, they submit it to the data center for compilation and test. As the programs begin to be integrated as subsystems for testing, the computer service center executes the subsystems in a quasi-production environment, and the test results are returned to the base case group for validation, rather than to the programmer. During this period, there is an almost continual interaction between the systems, programming, and BCSE groups, with minimal participation from internal auditing.

Successful installation of a new or modified system is concluded with the review and acceptance of the "Installation Base Case" by internal auditing. Although they may review any project during any stage of development, internal auditing generally applies selection criteria to include those computer application systems that:

- Involve development costs projected in excess of $100,000
- Have direct impact on corporate financial or operational policy
- Are selected for review by corporate management.

The primary responsibility for the inclusion of auditability criteria lies with the manager of the user department authorizing the system implementation or modification. For those systems subject to audit concurrence and review, internal audit will include an assessment of the auditability of the system in its findings and will not concur if this auditability criterion is not met.

APPLICATION EXAMPLE

A major industrial corporation has implemented BCSE for billing, accounts receivable, commission accounting, equipment control, and other applications, and for the development of their new administrative teleprocessing network.

During the development of a new billing computer application system, their first project to use the BCSE approach, the Billing Department established a small staff to prepare a complete package of test transaction data concurrent with the development of programming specifications. Increasing interaction between the user group and the Systems Analysis and Design Department led to the exposure and correction of some significant design faults prior to the actual start of coding, which led, in turn, to greater participation in the design effort by the user department. The resultant system, although requiring somewhat longer to develop than anticipated, surpassed expectations in terms of reliability, accuracy, and overall integrity. Moreover, the effects of subsequent program modifications were anticipated with the same degree of reliability. The billing system produces over 600,000 invoices per month; 9 people are assigned to this application's BCSE group; up to 6 clock hours of computer time are required to run a complete test of the system using the full 7500 invoice transaction set, and 200 man-hours are required to validate the results.

The company's first step toward controlling the maintenance effort without relaxing test standards was to institute periodic "block cut-in" of enhancements and modifications. All application program changes are coded and tested at the program test level until a specific cut-off date, at which time new requests for changes are suspended and the coded changes enter BCSE as a block. Base case test results are analyzed and evaluated by data processing and user group personnel before the computer application system is placed into production with its enhancements. Internal audit will review "block cut-ins" that represent significant development costs or financial/operational exposure. The frequency of the periodic "cut-in" varies with the particular computer application system; for the billing system, changes occur three to four times per year. Accurate and comprehensive documentation is maintained regarding every modification to the computer application system during each "block cut-in" cycle.

LIMITATIONS AND CONSTRAINTS

This technique has no intrinsic technical limitations. It is, in fact, a formalization of the procedures used in any responsible, professional, and orderly validation of a computer application system. There is no practical way to prove, in the absolute and logical sense, that a system is correct. The only open avenue is to create a base case that is as exhaustive as possible and to apply it thoroughly. There are, however, operational and management factors germane to use of the technique. These are dealt with in the following sections.

IMPLEMENTATION CONSIDERATIONS

The following points regarding the implementation of BCSE are raised, not as limitations, but as factors that must be considered in determining its applicability to a given situation.

Time — BCSE generates greater interaction of the various departments over the cycle of system development, a higher degree of detailed documentation, and more rigorous testing. All these add to the time required to bring a computer application system to operational status or to implement changes.

Auditability — BCSE greatly improves the internal auditor's ability to detect unauthorized variations in application software, data files, and general transaction processing methodology. The area it cannot address, however, is the control over the validity of the data itself as they enter the system. For example, if a company pays an invoice for a product or service, BCSE can ensure that the transaction type is valid, the payment is properly applied, the proper reports are generated, and the correct data are "fed" to downstream processing systems. But BCSE cannot validate the amount of the payment or the legitimacy of the account to which it was posted. Consequently, while BCSE improves the auditability of systems, it does not obviate the need for complementary controls and security procedures.

Supporting Data — As the base case test is conducted for an application, any files produced by other applications that provide input to the computer application system under test must be available. Any files produced by the computer application system under test must be carried through the data entry level of the downstream computer application system to ensure compatibility.

TRAINING REQUIREMENTS

Within the user department, BCSE demands a staff with extensive experience in the functions of that department, coupled with some cross training in system analysis and design. This staff provides the interface between their application and computer system design and programming, and internal auditing, and is responsible for development of the base case input and output and for verification of each test. Specific knowledge requirements of BCSE personnel are summarized in Table 15-1; they include a knowledge of data processing principles and concepts, computer applications system structure, computer application system controls and procedures, data management (especially for on-line systems), computer service center controls, and application system development controls.

Table 15-1

BASE CASE SYSTEM EVALUATION TRAINING REQUIREMENTS

Knowledge Area	Level*
Data processing principles and concepts	X
Computer application system structure	X
Computer application system controls and procedures	X
Data management	X
Computer service center controls	X
Application system development controls	X
Computer application programming	—

* X = Basic; — = Not required.

COST FACTORS

The company included in the application example estimates annual cost in terms of salaries, computer time, and so on, attributable directly to BCSE at less than 1% of total data processing costs, with the major part of this cost being labor. Within the various user groups there are approximately 20 people, from analysts down to the clerical level, comprising the permanent base case test groups. Other personnel are called upon as required. The company estimates that 20% of the cost of a system is for base case testing. The incremental cost is estimated to be between 5% and 10%, e.g., even though 20% of the cost of a system is base case testing, some of the testing would have gone on even if there were not a base case system.

For this investment, the company feels it has obtained computer application systems of the highest integrity and accuracy, systems that are more easily audited and maintained and far more compliant to the requirements of the user groups. Further, it has the full intention of expanding the use of this method to cover all computer application systems.

EVALUATION OF EFFECTIVENESS

Base case system evaluation is a technique that applies a standardized body of data to a computer application system to verify processing logic. BCSE cannot provide evidence concerning data file content and integrity, procedure compliance, or input accuracy and thoroughness. BCSE is conceptually similar to the test data method in that both methods verify processing logic via test data; BCSE is a more comprehensive method and generally requires a greater degree of cooperation among user groups, internal audit and the system and programming staffs. This testing method is expensive to use and the outlook for its use in the future is limited.

Chapter 16

INTEGRATED TEST FACILITY

Integrated test facility (ITF) is a technique to review those functions of an automated application that are internal to the computer. Internal auditors' test data are used to compare ITF processing results to precalculated test results. The method is most frequently used to test and verify large computer application systems when it is not practical to separately cycle test data. The ITF technique is used for computer processing verification and evaluation and is of limited value for the verification of production data or data files. Limited evidence is provided concerning the completeness and accuracy of production input data or masterfiles.

TECHNIQUE OVERVIEW

An integrated test facility allows the internal auditor to examine the processing of a computer application in its normal operating environment. It is an audit technique that uses a fictitious or dummy entity (e.g., a false department or a dummy vendor) within the framework of the regular application processing cycle. The auditor can select the transactions or processing functions to be examined, and then apply the transactions to the fictitious entity during the normal processing cycle, along with regular transactions. Normal application processing produces the reports that the internal auditor uses to verify the completeness and accuracy of the functions being evaluated and/or verified.

The technique is described as "integrated" because the audit transactions are processed with production transactions, the audit master records reside on the same files as regular production and records (see Figure 16-1), and the fictitious entities are established as a part of the organizational structure. Accordingly, audit checks can be made as a part of the normal processing cycle. All transaction types, combinations of transaction types, logic paths, computations, and controls within a computer application that are pertinent to the ITF entity can be tested by this audit method.

Three factors differentiate ITF audit data and normal production data: all ITF data are keyed to a fictitious entity; special controls must be built into the application to prevent ITF data from being passed on to other computer applications; and controls, either manual or mechanized, are needed to exclude ITF data from being included in the organization's accounting records and reports. The three methods for separating ITF data and production data are:

- To modify programs to separate ITF data from production data.
- To reverse ITF data from production data by journal entry or other types of accounting entries at appropriate cutoff times.
- To design systems for automatically separating ITF data from production data. This results because the system provides for natural separation of data by some type of major class of entity on the masterfile. For example, if a system that performs a common process for multiple companies or divisions is *designed* to separate output by company or division, then the ITF could be a unique company or division and the system would automatically separate ITF data from production data for valid companies or divisions.

A number of important benefits are reported by organizations that use the ITF technique. Use of the ITF method by these organizations:

- Provides a means of comprehensive application testing for both internal auditors and system development personnel with virtually no special processing requirements.
- Enables audit checks on a regular basis with minimal operational difficulties.
- Enables audit checks on an unscheduled basis, and thereby provides a stronger deterrent to fraud.
- Incurs minimal operational cost; audit processing occurs during normal processing and adds only small incremental cost to the normal cost of processing.
- Provides objective evidence illustrating the compliance of the computer application system with established policies, specifications, and procedures.
- Benefits system development personnel during preproduction testing; and, once the controls are built into the system to isolate ITF data, enables the use of ITF by data processing personnel as a flexible and comprehensive test technique.
- Is also applicable as an acceptance testing procedure for system modifications being incorpor-

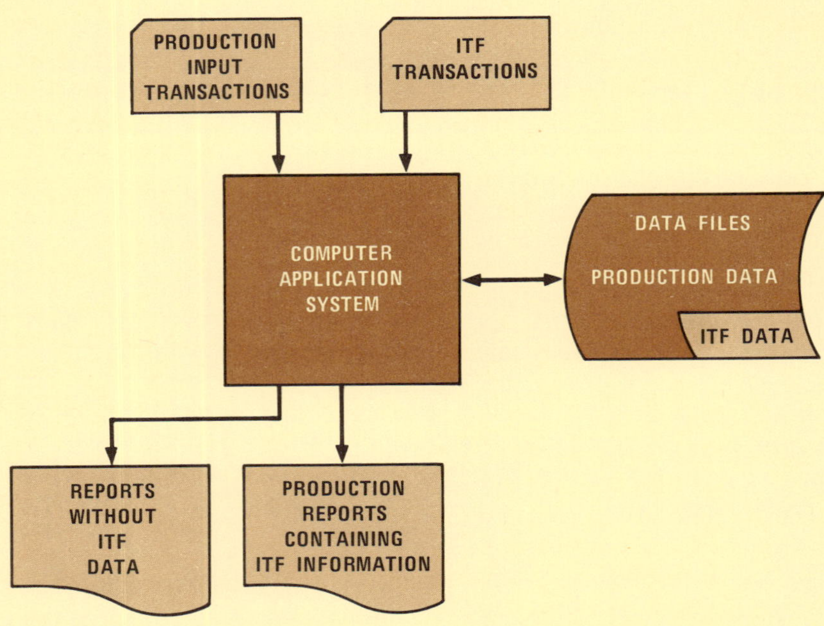

FIGURE 16-1 INTEGRATED TEST FACILITY

ated after the application becomes operational. After conventional testing, program modifications are incorporated into the production version of the application. Users, data processing, and internal audit personnel can then test the modified routines during normal processing by using the ITF data and records. When completely tested in this ITF mode, the new processing steps can be implemented with production data.

■ Aids an auditor's understanding of system evolution. This understanding becomes more important as systems become more complex.

TYPICAL PROCEDURES

The following steps in the use of ITF for internal audit are reported by an experienced EDP auditor:

Step 1 — Define Audit Objectives — The internal auditor develops an audit plan, defining those aspects of the computer application system to be tested. Transaction types, input validation routines, error conditions, and processing logic to be validated are selected and documented. A written audit work plan is prepared.

Step 2 — Create ITF Input Data — The creation of test data can be accomplished by preparing such data manually or by using a selected sample of actual data. Each method has its advantages and disadvantages. Manually prepared data, while time-consuming to prepare, can be more easily designed to test specific conditions of the particular computer application system. Actual data, while less time-consuming to prepare, must be analyzed and carefully selected to ensure that audit objectives are met.

Step 3 — Prepare Audit Control Worksheets — Results expected from the test run are manually precalculated and documented. These results can be in the form of printed output, visual display, data file contents, or other media specific to the computer application system.

Step 4 — Process ITF Input Data — Prepared test data are processed by the computer application system during the normal production cycle. No special computer time need be scheduled. The internal auditor should satisfy himself that a proper production run is made; frequently this is accomplished by his personal observation. Unscheduled audits can, however, require that the audit be made without the knowledge of the data processing department.

Step 5 — Review and Reconcile Test Results — Results of the test are compared to precalculated expected results. Unexpected results and errors are documented, evaluated, and reconciled. Frequently, more than one computer run will be required.

APPLICATION EXAMPLES

A large eastern university uses an ITF to audit its general ledger computer application system. The university is organized into various schools—law, medicine, business, and so on; each school is an independent entity within the general ledger. Consolidation techniques are used to prepare financial statements and reports for the university as a whole. The fictitious entity used in this situation is a school within the university's general ledger structure. Journals, general ledger reports, and statements for this fictitious school can be prepared, allowing auditors to verify general ledger processing. Auditors prepare and submit transactions that exercise various general ledger functions of concern to internal audit program objectives.

Processing logic and transactions are common to all schools within the general ledger, including the fictitious ITF school. Accordingly, transactions processed against the ITF are representative of those processed for the other schools.

Manual, rather than computer program, procedures are used to ensure that ITF data do not affect the university's consolidated financial reports and statements, because of the complexity of special programming in the school's general ledger programs. The manual procedures ensure that ITF transactions are limited to a value of $1, and that all transactions are reversed by manual journal entries after verifications are completed. It is possible for ITF data to be included in the consolidated financial reports if reversals are not properly entered. But in the opinion of the internal auditor, by limiting the value of ITF transactions to $1, their effect would not be material.

Audit management is, in general, satisfied with this ITF. They feel it is working well and provides improved auditability when compared with previous manual methods. The university plans to expand its use of the ITF method, beginning with its investment portfolio analysis application.

As a second example, ITF is used by a midwest utility in its customer billing application as part of a continuous audit program. The ITF encompasses customer billing and accounts receivable, including cash application and credit adjustments. The application is set up on a cycle billing basis with a month-end cutoff to prepare journals for the general ledger. Each month, 10 billing cycles are processed. Input is handled from three sources: mark sense cards prepared by operators; perforated paper tape from direct distance dialing equipment; and magnetic tape from direct distance dialing equipment.

Fictitious accounts have been established for the ITF with special billing addresses. Test data sets are introduced into each day's billing cycle by quality control personnel within the data computer service center. These data sets include mark sense cards, perforated tape, and magnetic tape. Computer processing results in customer invoices that are subsequently processed and mailed along with all other invoices prepared during the billing cycle. Bills received through the mail for the fictitious accounts at a designated post office box are returned to the computer service center quality control section, which then checks for completeness and accuracy of billing, legibility, and promptness. Note that test data and billing prepared are processed exactly as are other customer billings, including the mailing. The latter is primarily for convenience in order to avoid special manual separation of computer outputs, which would be time consuming, and to avoid special programming, which could provide an opportunity to defeat the purpose of the ITF.

Test data used have been prepared so that all combinations of accounts and service types are represented during a month's processing. Each fictitious billing prepared is compared to preestablished results so quality control clerks do not have any special calculations or reconciliations to perform. As each billing is received, the quality control clerk processes a credit adjustment to offset the effect of the test data on journal entries prepared for the general ledger at month end. Some credits may not be processed before closing; these present no real problem because their effect on the firm's $85 million operating revenues is miniscule. The total revenue generated for ITF purposes is less than $100.

Complete documentation of ITF input scheduling and preparation, expected billing results, and credit entry procedures were prepared by EDP audit personnel, and are administered by computer service center management under the surveillance of the internal audit department. Previously, internal audit personnel identified processing errors and omissions during their periodic audits of the customer billing application. As a result, computer service center management asked internal audit personnel to establish a program that would allow continuous quality control tests. The ITF was conceived and developed for this purpose. This ITF program has effectively pushed the audit process back into the computer service center, giving management an important measurement of processing integrity and control, and increasing the internal audit department's confidence that processing is being performed properly and is being effectively monitored. Present quality control section staffing totals six persons at three locations who have been trained in the use of this ITF.

The ITF has been operational since 1971 and took approximately one year of elapsed time to develop and install. No special programming was required, except to prepare test data in a perforated tape format, which is unique to the utility.

A third example of the use of an ITF is taken from the banking industry, where one bank has an ITF established in an on-line computer application. Ten fictitious banks have been set up on the computer files, each with individual branches and customer accounts. In addition, there is an ITF correspondent settlement bank. The system may be tested using either on-line terminal transactions or batched transactions. This ITF provides an opportunity to test and validate the entire range of transactions.

Application program controls have been implemented so that ITF data and totals are not included with production accounts on the file. In addition, this particular ITF has been established in such a way that all transactions are processed so that their net effect on the overall system's balancing is zero.

LIMITATIONS AND CONSTRAINTS

The ITF method is principally a program verification method. Use of the method requires a careful testing discipline on the part of the auditor; indeed, the same considerations that apply to the test data method also apply to the ITF method. In addition to those considerations, special care must be taken with ITF so that test data are not included in the organization's regular records. This can be accomplished through manual reversing entries, automated reversing entries, special programming, or even a decision on the part of the internal auditor as to immateriality, as was shown in the general ledger application example. The important point is the inclusion of this factor in the internal auditor's work plan.

IMPLEMENTATION CONSIDERATIONS

It is ideal to implement an ITF concurrent with the design and development of a new computer application. This is because the internal auditor can work with computer application system design personnel to understand and evaluate controls as they are being devised rather than having to rely on after-the-fact documentation. Also, the incremental cost of adding any necessary ITF controls is less when compared with making such modifications to existing systems.

Two important areas of concern to be addressed are that the operational integrity of the application should not be compromised by the ITF, and that the audit of the system through use of the ITF should be representative of normal processing results.

Close cooperation with the computer application system design staff is important for the successful development and installation of an ITF. Areas of particular importance include:

Application Review — The auditor must become familiar with transaction preparation procedures, controls, and the various reports prepared by the system.

ITF Requirements Definition — The internal auditor must establish the system's ITF requirements. These requirements should establish the ITF as an effective means of fulfilling internal audit requirements. The contribution and cooperation of EDP personnel are mandatory, especially if the internal auditor has little knowledge of data processing, but ITF's primary purpose is to serve the internal auditor's needs.

ITF System Testing — The auditor prepares test data that can be used to validate ITF controls and check the operation of the computer application system prior to system implementation.

TRAINING REQUIREMENTS

Little specialized training is required to use an operational ITF if the auditor has access to comprehensive and accurate system documentation and user documentation, and an ITF audit procedure. If such documentation is available, experience in general auditing and some experience in systems analysis will usually be sufficient for the use of an ITF. In the absence of well-documented procedures, considerable auditing and systems experience may be required to use an ITF as an effective audit tool.

Training requirements to develop an ITF demand that the internal auditor gain an understanding of the particular computer application system, and that he have extensive knowledge and experience in auditing computer applications. Computer programming experience is not usually required, although knowledge of program design principles is helpful in developing the necessary internal ITF controls. Training requirements are summarized in Table 16-1.

COST FACTORS

Cost factors for an ITF fall into one of two categories; the one-time cost of developing an ITF, and the continuing cost of ITF use.

Development

Costs of developing an ITF vary significantly, depending upon the size and complexity of the computer application, the nature of the business or organization, and the knowledge and experience of the auditor and the data processing staff. Table 16-2 summarizes the experience of some firms that participated in this study and have developed ITFs. The development effort includes both internal audit and data processing effort. The labor cost of ITF development for the organizations contacted is estimated to range from 3% to 10% of the total system development expense.

Continuing Use

The costs associated with the use of an ITF are relatively small. Cost factors include computer run time, which is minimal unless large volumes of test data are run, and test data preparation and results analysis. Test data preparation and results analysis are performed by the internal auditor; thus effort is dependent upon the scope of the audit and the complexity of the computer application system.

EVALUATION OF EFFECTIVENESS

The ITF technique provides the internal auditor with an effective and highly efficient method to evaluate

Table 16-1

INTEGRATED TEST FACILITY TRAINING REQUIREMENTS

Knowledge Area	Level* Development	Use
Data processing principles and concepts	X	X
Computer application system structure	X	X
Computer application system controls and procedures	X	X
Data management	X	
Computer service center controls	—	—
Application system development controls	X	
Computer application programming	—	—

* X = Basic; — = Not required.

and verify data processing programs and procedures. The major drawback to the use of the ITF technique is the time and effort required to define ITF requirements and develop the required ITF program controls. Although an ITF is an excellent tool to evaluate and verify computer program controls and processing, it provides limited evidence of the accuracy or completeness of input data or masterfile information. The outlook for continuing use of the ITF audit technique is good; ITF is an effective audit tool for complex systems and is applicable to auditing on-line systems. Expected development of more complex on-line systems will result in greater use of this method.

Table 16-2

GENERALIZED ITF DEVELOPMENT EXPERIENCE

	Development Time In Man-Months	
	Single Processing Unit*	Multiple Processing Unit*
Initial ITF	12	3-6
Second ITF	3-6	1-3

* The existence of "natural" separations, such as multiple companies or divisions, reduces the effort and cost expended to develop an ITF.

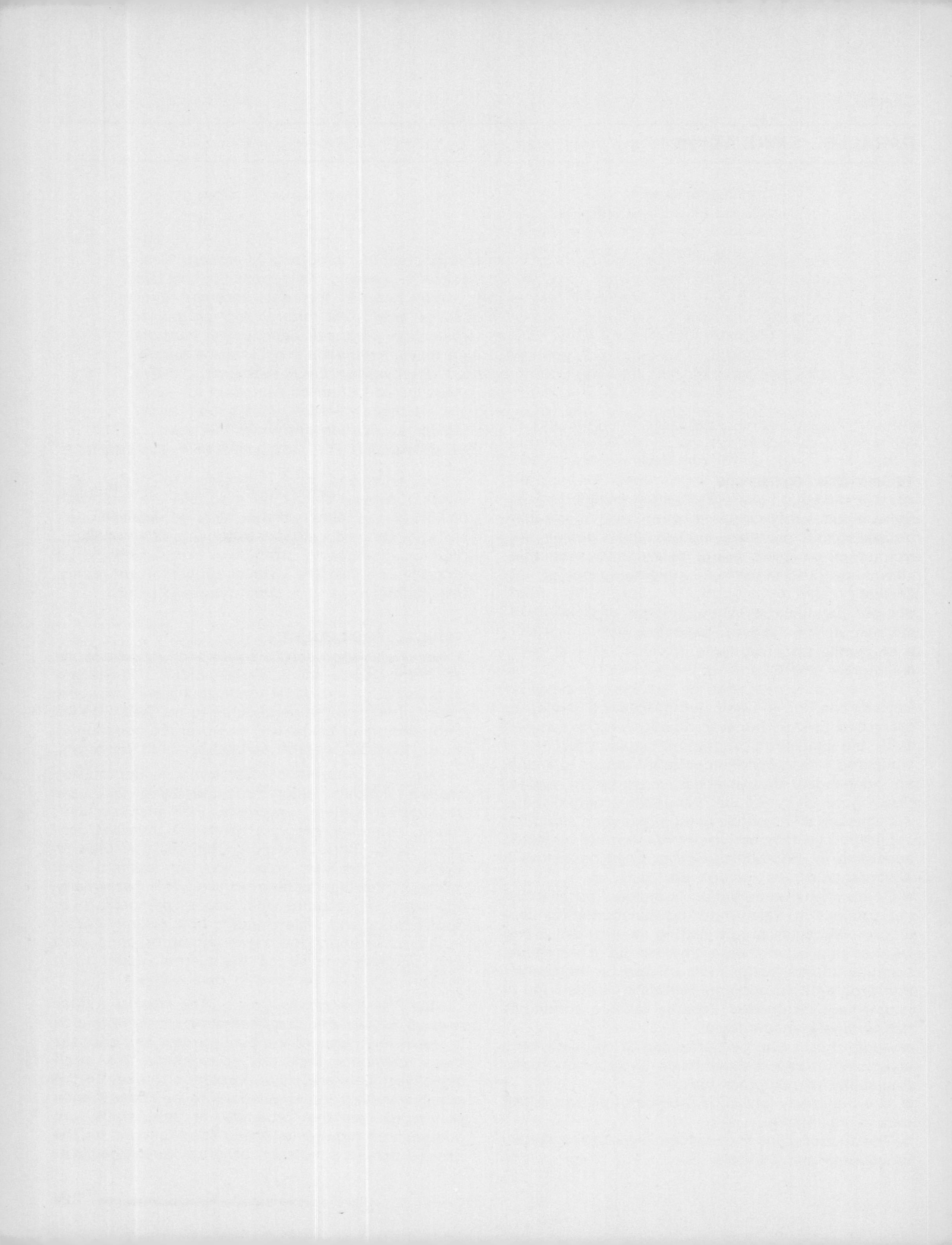

Chapter 17

PARALLEL SIMULATION

Parallel simulation is the use of one or more special computer programs to process "live" data files and simulate normal computer application processing. As opposed to the test data method and the integrated test facility, which process test data through "live" programs, the parallel simulation method processes "live" data through test programs. Parallel simulation programs include only the application logic, calculations, and controls that are relevant to specific audit objectives. As a result, simulation programs are usually much less complex than their application program counterparts. Large segments of major applications that consist of several computer programs can often be simulated for audit purposes with a single parallel simulation program. Parallel simulation permits the internal auditor to independently verify complex and critical application system procedures.

TECHNIQUE OVERVIEW

Parallel simulation programs accept and process the same input data as their corresponding application programs; they use the same masterfiles and attempt to produce the same results. This simulation process allows verification of computer applications for correct:

- Input data validation and control procedures
- Computations and processing logic
- Masterfile updating logic
- Controls and balancing procedures.

This method is described as "parallel" because all transactions for a particular processing cycle are processed by the normal application program as well as by the simulation program. Simulation results are compared with application program results to enable an independent and objective check by the auditor (see Figure 17-1). Parallel simulation programs need not simulate all functions of the production computer application system; only those functions to be tested according to the audit objectives need be included. Advantages of the method are that:

- Comprehensive validation is enabled by processing production data under normal operating conditions. More thorough testing is possible using parallel simulation than with a sampling technique, because all transactions are verified by the simulation programs. In addition, test data can be used to supplement production data to validate conditions not routinely encountered.
- Audit checks can be performed at any time, on a scheduled or unscheduled basis, subject only to the availability of computer time.
- The frequently laborious process of preparing test data is eliminated.
- The auditor gains knowledge of application system procedures and controls.

The time and cost necessary to design and develop parallel simulation programs are important disadvantages, although the use of generalized audit software can reduce these expenditures. In addition, ongoing changes to production programs must be incorporated into the parallel simulation programs; this maintenance is a continuing audit cost.

TYPICAL PROCEDURES

A systematic approach is required for success in the use of the parallel simulation technique. The size and complexity of individual applications will, to some extent, influence the procedures to be used. The six steps described below will, however, be common to most, if not all, parallel simulation audit programs.

Step 1 — Information Gathering — Information needed includes such documentation as user procedures, system flowcharts, EDP process flowcharts, computer program narratives, relevant program logic charts and computational formulae or algorithms, decision rules, and the content and format of the files to be processed. It is particularly important to acquire the user's perspective in documenting and understanding how the application works; accordingly, interviews should be conducted with user personnel so that the internal auditor is not limited to a data processing perspective.

Step 2 — System Analysis — The internal auditor reviews all available documentation for its relevance to the stated goals of the audit project and chooses those elements that are relevant to the audit objectives. This analytical process is the key to the effectiveness of the simulations to be subsequently performed, as the products of this study are documented requirements and specifications for the desired parallel simulation program. Such specifica-

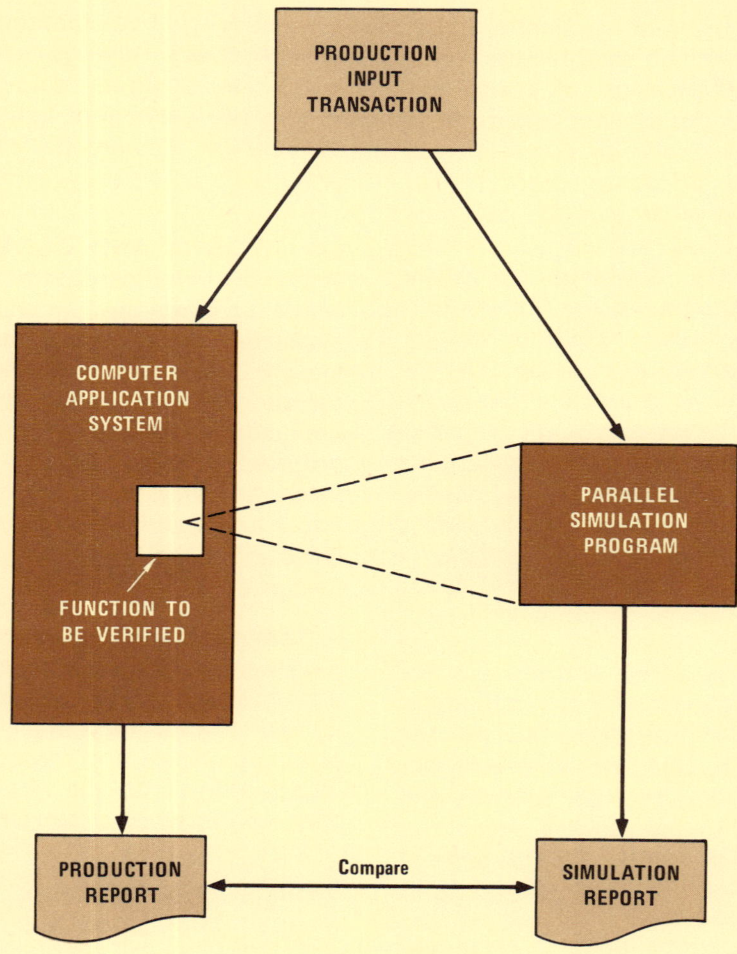

FIGURE 17-1 PARALLEL SIMULATION

tions need not be elaborate, but must be sufficiently complete to use as the basis for programming.

Step 3 — Program Development — Parallel simulation programs can be prepared by the EDP auditor, or by EDP staff personnel using the auditor's specifications. The key factors in determining who should actually prepare the programs are twofold. First, the degree of objectivity is important; it would be inappropriate for the programmer who is responsible for a mortgage loan application to prepare the mortgage loan parallel simulation programs. Second, the EDP auditor may not have the skills to prepare the parallel simulation programs. It is preferable for the parallel simulation programs to be written independent of the internal data processing department. This is not always possible or practical, but, to maintain objectivity, the auditor must either write the programs himself or devise adequate validation tests for the simulation programs to ensure that they perform according to desired audit objectives.

Parallel simulation programs are usually developed using a generalized audit software package or a high-level application language. Even with these powerful and flexible tools, considerable checkout and testing can be expected. The degree of effort to be expended and the time scheduled for program development and testing are extremely dependent on the knowledge and experience of the programmer.

Step 4 — Simulation Data Preparation — Input transactions, masterfiles, and relevant processing results are secured for the period or processing cycles to be simulated. Care must be taken to ensure that correct cutoff dates are maintained so that simulation results are comparable to the results of the normal processing. Copies of working papers, or records for any balancing, control-checking, or reconciliations performed during the regular processing cycle should also be secured.

Step 5 — Processing and Reconciliation — This step includes the actual simulation processing and reconciliation of these results to the results previously obtained from normal application processing. Differences between the results can occur because of the deliberate omission of conditions from the simulation program, or actual discrepancies between the processing procedures employed by the application system and the simulation programs. In either case, a reconciliation of processing results is necessary. It is usually not too difficult to reconcile differences due to simplified simulation program logic. Some of these conditions are not undesirable when considered in terms of the additional time it could take to develop necessary simulation program logic. Experience indicates it is usually easier to manually reconcile certain types of these differences rather than to create highly complex simulation logic, particularly if the areas of difference are not of great importance to the objectives of the audit. Some experimentation and rerun may be expected to reduce the differences due to program logic omissions. Once this manual reconciliation is complete, true processing discrepancies will be readily identifiable.

Step 6 — Evaluation of Exceptions — Exceptions, identified during simulation processing and reconciliation (Step 5), should be reviewed and analyzed by the internal auditor. The exception analysis will determine the specific conditions under which the exceptions occurred, identifying the erroneous processing procedures. The exceptions and their causes should be fully documented. Based on the audit findings, the auditor should recommend measures to correct the erroneous application procedures.

The first three of the above steps represent initial work required to develop the parallel simulation programs. Once these programs are developed, these steps need not be repeated, but it is necessary on a continuing basis to review documentation and identify changes relevant to the audit procedures that have occurred since the last audit, and to incorporate necessary parallel simulation program changes and perform associated validation testing.

Once the auditor has developed a parallel simulation package, he can reuse it with little maintenance, unless changes are made to the application being simulated in the specific area where the auditor is performing the simulation

APPLICATION EXAMPLE

A major bank uses parallel simulation to verify processing in a number of its financial computer applications. Savings interest calculations are simulated for all its passbook savings customers. The bank's EDP auditors find this technique preferable, from the standpoint of thoroughness and ease of use, to testing interest calculations by a sampling technique. The simulation program validates only the interest-accrual calculations and bypasses the rest of the passbook savings processing steps. Another simulation program calculates the unearned discounts on installment loans to verify that portion of the bank's installment loan computer application system.

LIMITATIONS AND CONSTRAINTS

The most significant constraint in parallel simulation is the time required to initially develop the parallel simulation program. This is discussed further under Cost Factors. Other notable limitations are learning the detailed logic of the computer application to be simulated, the technical skills required of the internal auditor in implementing this technique, and the training the internal auditor may have to undergo in basic computer concepts. In addition, the technique does not check noncomputerized portions of the system.

IMPLEMENTATION CONSIDERATIONS

The parallel simulation audit technique is suitable only for verifying specific computer application system processing logic. Careful consideration of the audit objectives and methodology is required, as the use of this technique requires the development and use of a wholly separate computer application system. The development effort for a customized system requires the commitment of internal audit and programming resources and an explicit set of design specifications. Changes to custom parallel simulation programs after implementation are more expensive than changes to a generalized audit software program. The use of generalized audit software should be considered as a means of reducing this development effort, if audit objectives can be satisfied by this means.

TRAINING REQUIREMENTS

Training to use this technique includes acquiring a knowledge of programming and of application system operation. The advanced preparation required is the most time-consuming part of the training, because the auditor must understand the system to be simulated and be able to select the specific functions within that system that are to be simulated. Internal auditor training requirements are summarized in Table 17-1, which shows that advanced knowledge in the principles of data processing, computer application system structure, and computer application programming are required, as well as basic knowledge in computer application system controls and procedures, data management, computer service center controls, and computer application system development controls. In short, extensive data processing knowledge is required to effectively use the parallel simulation technique. This technique should not be utilized unless the internal auditor is very familiar with the programming language to be used. The internal auditor of lesser skills should first consider use of a generalized audit software package to do simple file extractions, comparisons, and statistical sampling before attempting a parallel simulation.

Table 17-1

PARALLEL SIMULATION TRAINING REQUIREMENTS

Knowledge Area	Level*
Data processing principles and concepts	XX
Computer application system structure	XX
Computer application system controls and procedures	X
Data management	X
Computer service center controls	X
Application system development controls	X
Computer application programming	XX

* XX = Advanced; X = Basic.

COST FACTORS

The experience of one major user of parallel simulation was that two weeks were required to understand a typical current system, one week to design the simulation, one week to program the simulation using a generalized audit software package, and three weeks to test, check, and run the simulation. After the simulation was developed, it took approximately two hours of internal auditor time per run, plus the time required for the reconciliation of results.

Another organization's experience in preparing parallel simulations was that the time varied from 20 minutes to 100 hours to prepare a parallel simulation using generalized audit software. They reported that the average was probably less than one day. A third organization interviewed uses COBOL and reported that one-half hour to five weeks is required to prepare a simulation. The average for this COBOL user was about three days per simulation. The opinion of one simulation user was that use of generalized audit software will allow the preparation of tested code for parallel simulation in one-tenth to one one-hundredth of the time required to write a simulation in COBOL.

In the experience of these organizations, the key determinants of the time expended are the internal auditor's data processing experience, his knowledge of the system to be simulated, and the complexity of the parallel simulation programs.

EVALUATION OF EFFECTIVENESS

The parallel simulation technique provides the internal auditor with an efficient and effective method for validating specific application program functions. Limited evidence is provided on the accuracy or completeness of input data or computer files. For example, parallel simulation audit program design should include procedure (record count and/or dollar totals) to provide audit control of the data population under audit. Reconciliation of these controls (Step 5) is part of the audit process. The future use of this technique is promising as it is one of the most effective techniques for substantive testing.

Chapter 18

TRANSACTION SELECTION

The transaction selection audit technique uses an independent computer program to monitor and select transactions for internal audit review. The method enables the internal auditor to examine and analyze transaction volumes and error rates, and to statistically sample specified transactions. Transaction selection audit software is totally independent of the production computer application system and is generally parameter-controlled. No alteration to the production computer application system is required. This technique is especially suitable for noncontinuous monitoring and sampling of transactions in complex computer application systems.

TECHNIQUE OVERVIEW

Transaction selection uses software specified or developed by the internal auditor to screen and select transactions that have been input to the production computer application system. The transaction selection method is implemented as an independent computer application program, in which transaction files used as input to a production application are subsequently processed by the transaction selection program. The transaction selection program edits and validates input transactions according to criteria established by the internal auditor and can select specified transactions for subsequent analysis. Processing results are printed or otherwise displayed for review and evaluation. Transaction editing is performed to develop statistics for audit review. Information concerning errors, value ranges, counts by category, and the like can be provided. Transactions are selected according to parameters or preestablished criteria. The selection, or sampling, process can be designed to select by transaction content (all dollar amounts over $1000, for example), or by a statistical sampling method.

Transaction selection allows the internal auditor to monitor transaction activity; the internal auditor can regularly receive reports that identify changes in the level of activity for specific transactions. The auditor can also receive reports that detail transaction errors by cause and that calculate transaction error rates. This information is useful in identifying computer applications that merit additional audit attention and is an aid in planning internal audit work as well as identifying potential problems in user areas.

Using the computer for sample selection improves the completeness of audit work and therefore its quality. In this manner, the time required to manually select samples for audit programs can be reduced.

Disadvantages of the method include the cost of developing the transaction selection audit program and the increased cost of computer time to run the audit program. However, experience of organizations using this method indicates that, with an adequate volume of transactions, the increased computer time can be more than offset by the savings resulting from the reduction in the internal auditor's work load.

TYPICAL PROCEDURES

Transaction selection typically includes four basic steps, as described in the following paragraphs.

Step 1 — Develop the Transaction Selection Program — The format of transaction records is determined. The internal auditor defines the identity and value ranges of the parameters that may be used as selection criteria. The secondary functional characteristics of the program are determined and incorporated into the design. The detail design is completed, and the program is coded, tested, and documented.

Step 2 — Input Transaction Processing — Transaction files from the production processing cycle are read by the input module of the transaction selection software. Editing is performed and information is accumulated according to criteria supplied by the internal auditor. These criteria depend upon audit objectives but usually include error analysis and transaction counts by type, source, and dollar amount. Additional information pertinent to the particular organization and computer application system is accumulated. Information from the editing process can be retained on a data file, together with previously accumulated data to enable analysis of trends and history.

Step 3 — Transaction Sampling — Input transactions are selected according to criteria supplied by the internal auditor. Such selection criteria generally include all transactions with certain characteristics, or a sample of transactions. Further editing and other accumulations can be performed on the selected transactions, or the transactions can be printed for subsequent analysis. The selection method followed is usually every nth transaction (which results in selecting a certain percentage of all transactions), although any sampling technique can be applied.

Step 4 — Reporting — Reports are prepared for internal audit based on the selection of transactions during the processing cycle and on the statistics computed during the run. Reports contain such information as is required by internal audit to fulfill its audit objectives.

APPLICATION EXAMPLE

This illustration of the transaction selection technique is drawn from the experience of a large financial services firm that uses the technique to monitor the flow of input transactions into its life insurance and securities customer accounts. These customer accounts are audited on a continuous basis by the internal audit department. The overall effectiveness of this phase of the firm's internal audit program has been improved by the use of transaction selection because data on transaction activity and input error rates enable the internal audit department to direct its activities to those areas where potential problems exist, and the computer is used to select transaction samples more thoroughly and at less cost than if the same level of review was performed manually.

Transaction volumes for 1975 were between 4.5 million and 5 million transactions for the life insurance and security applications. Masterfile volumes are currently 350,000 records for the life insurance application and 900,000 records for the securities application. Both applications involve daily batch transaction processing and masterfile posting. The life insurance application includes approximately 400 valid combinations of user-originated transaction types, and the securities application includes 150 valid combinations of transaction types. In the opinion of the internal audit staff, the frequency of processing and the volumes involved create an environment well suited for continuous transaction selection, because of the firm's concern for accuracy in its records and statements of customers' insurance policies and securities holdings, and because the method ensures compliance with the extensive regulatory requirements in the industry.

The system design of the transaction selection program at this firm is based upon audit requirements and is generalized to the extent that, once the transactions are read, the auditor has complete flexibility as to the validation tests to be performed on various fields within the record, the criteria that are applied to the computer selection of records for further manual evaluation, and the organization and formatting of selected information for the auditor's reporting purposes. The decision to develop an independent transaction selection process was made so that the internal auditor would have control over all aspects of its processing. The internal auditor controls the transaction selection programs and their execution and is able to change selection criteria and reporting to fulfill his audit requirements.

LIMITATIONS AND CONSTRAINTS

This technique is useful for validating and sampling input transactions, but only inferences can be drawn concerning how well these transactions represent the entire body of input.

Input transactions are processed by the transaction selection program independent of the production computer application system. Consequently, all transactions must be processed twice, once for production purposes and again for audit purposes. The additional computer time required can be a significant limitation if the transaction selection programs are run frequently or if transaction volumes are large.

IMPLEMENTATION CONSIDERATIONS

The implementation steps associated with the development and installation of the transaction selection technique generally parallel those associated with the development of any business computer application. One major decision that has to be made in the process of designing and developing a transaction selection application is whether editing and selection criteria are to be preset or parameter-controlled. Preset criteria are generally less complex to design and code, but are less flexible in execution. Parameter-controlled criteria give the internal auditor more latitude; editing and selection can be set at the time the program is run and are better able to meet changing audit objectives. In addition, parameter-driven transaction selection programs can more readily be used to audit more than one computer application system. Since the transaction selection program is utilized in the production environment, the internal auditor should ensure that effective program change controls are implemented.

TRAINING REQUIREMENTS

Training for the use of this technique includes acquiring a thorough knowledge of the particular computer application and a knowledge of data processing principles and concepts. Training requirements to develop a transaction selection audit program include an advanced knowledge of data processing principles and concepts and a basic knowledge of computer application system structure, computer application system controls and procedures, and application system development controls. An advanced knowledge of computer application programming is required. Training requirements are summarized in Table 18-1.

COST FACTORS

Costs associated with the use of the transaction selection audit technique include development and use costs. Development costs vary with the complexity of the required programming, and to some degree with the complexity and characteristics of the particular application system. In addition, ongoing maintenance and alterations to the computer application system may require changes to be made to the transaction selection software. The cost of these changes depends upon their scope. Costs to use the transaction selection method are confined to the use of computer time to process the input transactions through the transaction selection programs.

EVALUATION OF EFFECTIVENESS

Transaction selection is an effective audit technique for selecting transaction samples for subsequent analysis. The technique provides no information regarding the computer application system processing logic, or data file accuracy, integrity, or completeness. The technique is especially useful if a moderate amount of transaction analysis is required to meet audit objectives. Embedded audit data collection is a better technique if continuous transaction monitoring is required or if transaction volumes are large. Use of generalized audit software should be considered if monitoring and selection requirements can be met by such a package. Transaction selection is not a preferred technique for on-line computer applications systems. The outlook for continuing use of this audit technique is limited. While the technique is useful and effective, audit objectives for many computer application systems can be better fulfilled by generalized audit software or embedded audit data collection.

Table 18-1

TRANSACTION SELECTION TRAINING REQUIREMENTS

	Level*	
Knowledge Area	**Development**	**Use**
Data processing principles and concepts	XX	X
Computer application system structure	X	—
Computer application system controls and procedures	X	—
Data management	—	
Computer service center controls	—	—
Application system development controls	X	—
Computer application programming	XX	—

* XX = Advanced; X = Basic; — = Not required.

Chapter 19

EMBEDDED AUDIT DATA COLLECTION

Embedded audit data collection uses one or more specially programmed data collection modules embedded in the computer application system to select and record data for subsequent analysis and evaluation. The data collection modules are inserted in the computer application system at points determined to be appropriate by the internal auditor. The internal auditor also determines the criteria for selection and recording. Subsequent to collection, other automated or manual methods may be used to analyze the collected data.

As distinct from other audit methods, this technique uses "in-line" code (i.e., the computer application program performs the audit data collection function at the same time it processes data for normal production purposes). This has two important consequences for the auditor: In-line code ensures the availability of a comprehensive or a very specialized sample of data (strategically placed modules have access to every data element being processed); retrofitting this technique to an existing system is more costly than implementing the audit programming during system development, hence it is preferable for the internal auditor to specify his requirements while the system is being designed.

TECHNIQUE OVERVIEW

This technique involves three elements:

- The embedded modules themselves.
- The collection criteria supplied by the internal auditor.
- Postcollection processes used by the internal auditor to analyze and evaluate the collected data.

The audit modules embedded in the computer application system (see Figure 19-1) act according to collection criteria supplied by the internal auditor. These criteria can be supplied either during system design or at the time of the audit, depending upon the version of the technique. In one version (called SCARF — System Control Audit Review File) the collection criteria are built into the modules themselves and are thus not easily alterable. This may suffice in those instances in which the auditor can fully specify his requirements during system design. A more flexible variation allows the internal auditor to specify the values of selected parameters at the time of the audit. The choice of which variation of the technique is used depends upon the need for flexibility required by the internal auditor, as well as the particular computer application system being audited.

In some instances the collected data may be in a format and order that can be used directly by the internal auditor. If not, additional utility programs or a generalized audit software package may be used to sort, reformat, or display the collected data in a form more suitable for the internal auditor's review and evaluation. Organizations using this technique stress its capability to monitor every datum for exception conditions as its most important advantage (an advantage it shares with the transaction selection technique). However, one firm using the technique found that the data being produced for audit purposes were too voluminous; the internal auditor must exercise care lest the sheer quantity of information destroys its utility.

TYPICAL PROCEDURES

Incorporation of an embedded audit data collection module during the development of a new system, or as a modification to an existing computer application system, generally consists of five steps. These are described in the following paragraphs.

Step 1 — Determination of Requirements — The internal auditor determines the audit requirements to be fulfilled. He identifies the data required, the frequency with which they are required, and the flexibility with which they are to be specified.

Step 2 — Functional Design — The internal auditor selects those points in the computer application system flow where the audit modules are to be embedded and identifies the criteria for triggering their action. In addition, he reviews the computer system design specifications to ensure that input and output formats and processing logic fulfill the audit requirements.

Step 3 — Detailed Design, Coding, and Unit Test — As the developing system proceeds through these activities, internal auditor participation is confined to review only, with the intent of ensuring that auditing

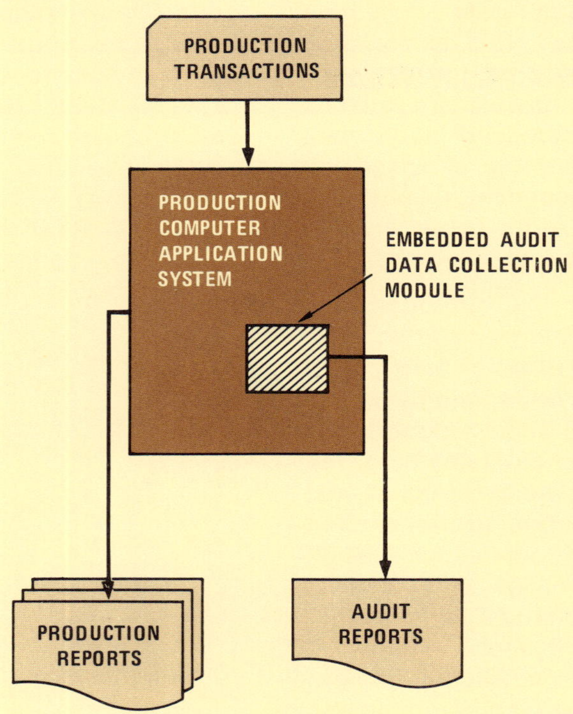

FIGURE 19-1 EMBEDDED AUDIT DATA COLLECTION

requirements are not compromised by lower level design decisions.

Step 4 — System Test — During this stage the internal auditor reviews test results to ensure that design requirements are being fulfilled by the system.

Step 5 — Maintenance of the Production System — The auditor reviews changes to the system to ensure the continuous satisfaction of audit requirements.

After development and implementation of the technique, the internal auditor is concerned with the recurring use of the technique in production running of the system. If the capability to vary selection criteria at audit-time is present, the internal auditor can select criteria that will cause the production of information to best meet the needs of the audit program he has developed. If the embedded audit data collection module is preset, no such capability exists, but, in either case, the process of review and evaluation of test results is the same. As with data generated by other audit techniques, test results are documented and reconciled according to the audit plan.

APPLICATION EXAMPLE

In the manufacturing firm visited by SRI, the accounts receivable data entry function is decentralized into regional offices throughout the western states. Each office manager receives an analytical report (not associated with the auditing technique) from the regular production run showing the various inputs from his office that have been processed by the accounts receivable computer application. This report, in addition to showing the current input, also shows several months' past data, thereby enabling trend analysis. If the office manager or an internal auditor notes a trend or condition that could indicate a problem, he advises the internal auditing department and they, in turn, select the necessary parameters to trigger the embedded audit data collection in the next scheduled processing of the accounts receivable system. The parameters that the internal auditor uses may select all transactions for a given office location or for another subset of the entire network. He also has the ability to "range" transactions, that is, to select those transactions with particular data elements with specified upper and lower limits. The auditor can specify Boolean (and/or/not) conditions for selection or various combinations of such conditions.

Use of this technique does not significantly affect the normal processing of the program, and produces a report of all transactions that meet the parameters and those data base records that were altered or referenced by the selected transactions. In addition, if the internal auditor has so indicated in the parameters, a file will be created for all of those selected transactions. This file can then be used by the internal auditor for subsequent computer analysis. The embedded audit data collection modules will continue to operate in this fashion until "turned off" by the removal of the parameter cards. The internal auditors at this organization are satisfied with the operation of the embedded audit data collection techniques. The capability of specifying test criteria at audit-time, depending upon the particular conditions to be audited, enables them to plan their audit programs flexibly to meet changing audit objectives and operating conditions.

LIMITATIONS AND CONSTRAINTS

The initial expenditures of time, effort, and resources necessary to effectively use this audit technique are generally more substantial than, for example, for the test data method. In order to ensure success, internal audit personnel must make a continuing commitment of their time to the computer application design process. In addition, the level of skill in data processing required of the internal auditor is higher than with most other audit techniques.

The comprehensiveness of transaction review, which is the chief advantage of this technique, can also cause the production of voluminous data for the internal auditor to examine. Because the technique will collect any and all kinds of data, each request for information must be carefully scrutinized. The firm that is using this technique in its accounts receivable system has established a procedure that requires the manager of internal auditing to approve each request for information, so as to control and supervise the operation of the process.

IMPLEMENTATION CONSIDERATIONS

The most significant implementation consideration is that this technique must be integrated into the production computer application system, since the implementation of the audit technique is tied to the development process of the computer application itself. The technique is most effectively implemented during the initial computer application system development process, rather than as a modification to an existing system. Close cooperation with the data processing staff is important for the successful implementation of the technique.

TRAINING REQUIREMENTS

The internal auditor participating in the development of an embedded audit data collection module must have a comprehensive knowledge of data processing and a thorough understanding of the specific application area. As indicated in Table 19-1, for the development of the technique, the internal auditor must have an advanced knowledge of data processing principles and concepts, and the structure of computer application systems. In addition, he must have a basic understanding of computer application system controls and procedures, data management, application system development controls, and, preferably, computer application programming. Training requirements in the use of the embedded audit data collection technique are not nearly as extensive and are limited to a knowledge of data processing principles, an understanding of the operation of the audit technique, and a thorough familiarity with the application area.

COST FACTORS

Developing and implementing this audit technique for the accounts receivable application example cost between $40,000 and $50,000 and required three months of effort. The development costs for other computer application systems will vary, of course. If the particular implementation of the technique is extremely limited in its capabilities, the cost could be much less, as would be the time required to develop and implement the necessary programming. The time and cost to develop a complex version of the technique will be considerable, and the internal

Table 19-1

EMBEDDED AUDIT DATA COLLECTION TRAINING REQUIREMENTS

Knowledge Area	Level* Development	Level* Use
Data processing principles and concepts	XX	X
Computer application system structure	XX	X
Computer application system controls and procedures	X	X
Data management	X	—
Computer service center controls	—	—
Application system development controls	X	—
Computer application programming	X	—

* XX = Advanced; X = Basic; — = Not required.

auditor must assess more closely the cost-effectiveness in this case. No quantitative estimates of the operating cost of the technique in the accounts receivable application were available, but the firm felt it was minimal.

EVALUATION OF EFFECTIVENESS

This technique provides the internal auditor and data processing control personnel with the capability to monitor the operation of a particular computer application system on a continual basis. The characteristics of the embedded audit data collection module determine the type of monitoring available to the internal auditor. At its most sophisticated level, this is an extremely flexible and comprehensive audit tool. Minimal additional computer running time is required and no special audit transactions need be prepared; the technique gives the auditor a "window" on the operation of the computer application system. At its least sophisticated level, the technique provides the auditor with few advantages over the use of generalized audit software, save for the use of computer time. Embedded audit data collection is not a suitable technique for the entry-level internal EDP auditor, but can be of significant benefit to the experienced internal auditor involved with complex and sophisticated computer application systems. The advent and expanding use of on-line computer application systems will result in increasing reliance on this audit method.

Chapter 20

EXTENDED RECORDS

The extended records technique gathers together by means of a special program or programs all the significant data that have affected the processing of an individual transaction. This includes the accumulation into a single record of results or processing over the time period that the transaction required to complete processing. The extended record includes data from all the computer application systems that contributed to the processing of a transaction. Such extended records are compiled into files that provide a conveniently accessible source for transaction data.

With this technique, the auditor no longer need review several files to determine how a specific transaction was processed. With extended records, data are consolidated from different accounting periods and different computer application systems so that a complete transaction audit trail is physically included in one computer record. This facilitates tests of compliance to organization policies and procedures.

TECHNIQUE OVERVIEW

The extended record technique provides a comprehensive audit trail for each transaction. From this audit trail data, transactions can be traced from inception to the final disposition of an organization's records, or backwards from consolidated totals to the individual transactions.

Most computer application systems are broken into modules to simplify programming logic and to contain the logic within the available computer memory. This segmentation often results in fairly small logic segments of a transaction cycle being processed within one program segment. The rules necessary to implement that segment of processing are contained only within the segment. The results of that processing are then forwarded to the next module, but frequently the criteria for arriving at decisions are not forwarded. The extended record technique requires that any significant data that affected the processing of that transaction be appended to the computer record.

The technique is applicable to all batch computer application systems, and indeed all application systems use the extended record concept to some degree. The question is the completeness of the extended record.

The audit trail provided by this means enables simplified retrievals of full transaction data from one computer record. Many times the data necessary to trace a transaction can be obtained, but must be gathered from several sources. For example, a payroll system may be broken into two segments, the first segment calculating gross payroll, and the second segment performing the gross to net payroll calculation. An auditor trying to substantiate a payroll amount would typically find that the input to the gross to net payroll segment contains only the gross pay amount. In this case, two audit searches would have to be performed to substantiate that the net pay amount was correct. The problem can be further complicated if more than two segments are involved.

Information affecting the processing of a transaction can be lost, discarded, or made inaccessible during the processing cycle. The primary reason for the loss of an audit trail is that, once the processing rules have been applied, only the results are carried forward (i.e., the data carried forward may be insufficient to reconstruct the transaction). In many cases, no hardcopy data are available for the internal auditor to substantiate how the results were calculated. This is especially true when one code or one field in a record is used for multiple functions. For example, if a field in the payroll record is used for a combination of pay corrections, suggestion awards, and special individual bonuses, an internal auditor checking that account cannot tell which of the items the amount represents. The extended record technique adds the necessary information to the transaction to substantiate the purpose of this special payment.

Implementation of the extended record concept involves analysis of the transaction audit trail needed for examination and reconstruction, and the time period over which processing data are to be accumulated. Decisions must be made as to what pieces of information are pertinent to processing decisions. Once these pieces of information have been isolated, they can be appended to the transaction record for examination and reconstruction purposes. The record content will continue to grow as the transaction moves through the processing cycle.

There are two main benefits to be derived from the use of the extended record technique. First, the auditors are involved in specifying audit trails; second, a complete audit trail on a transaction exists in a single, easily accessible place.

The major disadvantage to the extended record technique is the cost for building, processing, and maintaining more data on a transaction. First, extra cost is involved in designing and maintaining the extended records. Second, extra cost is occasioned by the programming to save the additional data. Third, additional execution time is expended to operate the extended record system. Fourth, extra cost is entailed in data storage media to hold the records. Last, additional costs are involved in retrieval and special-purpose programs to access and use the extra data.

TYPICAL PROCEDURES

An application of the extended record technique can be specified by auditors, but must be implemented by computer application programming personnel. It is valuable to have the auditor involved in the details of specifying and implementing the technique. A key part in implementing the technique is to list those pieces of information that will be needed for later analysis. It is in this area that the auditor can make the greatest contribution.

The best time to install this technique is during design of a new computer system. The technique will require planning for an extended record size and data base and program design. The general steps in implementing this technique are described in the following paragraphs.

Step 1 — Analyze the System — An important activity in implementing this technique is the analysis of the system from the audit trail viewpoint. An effective way to accomplish this is to analyze previous audit work papers and audit comments to determine what type of information was used and what type of information would have been helpful.

Step 2 — Analyze the Decision Process — Analysis should be made of the decision-making points in the data processing application. Key accounting decision points should be identified and a determination made of what data were used in arriving at each decision. If these data elements are not planned to be included in the historic records of the application, they are potential elements for the extended record concept.

Step 3 — Develop a List of Key Elements — From the above two steps, a list should be developed of key data elements to be included in the extended record. These are data elements currently either not included or not planned for inclusion in existing historic records. In many systems, the types of data needed for analysis are available at some time during the processing cycle, but are not retained for a sufficient period of time.

Step 4 — Determine Time Period — An important strength of the extended record concept is the consolidation of information from successive processing cycles into one record. The business factors affecting the time period of data accumulation for the application must be identified and accessed, and a suitable time period chosen.

Step 5 — Cost-Benefit Analysis — After a list of key elements has been developed, it is analyzed to determine the cost-benefit of adding these elements to records of the application. A suggested list of criteria for doing this is included in the Cost Factors section below.

Step 6 — Implement the System — When the additional elements have been agreed upon, the necessary system design and programming are undertaken. This includes the steps required to determine the most effective ways to gather and compile the data. Two ways are possible: The basic records of the system can be altered to accommodate the additional data, or a separate collection program or programs may be developed to extract the data periodically from the computer application system. It must be determined where in the system and at what point in time the data should be collected. In addition, the format and specification of data used in the extended record system must be determined.

APPLICATION EXAMPLES

SRI visited one organization that made extensive use of this technique in the billing application system area. The organization had four major billing systems for different lines of work. The systems contained basically the same types of information, but had different invoices due to the uniqueness of the line of business. Examinations by the corporate audit staff indicated problems in trying to substantiate the accuracy of the billed amounts. For example, the system permitted salesmen some leeway in pricing certain products. Thus, prices that did not conform to the organization's pricing manuals from an auditor's viewpoint could be either a pricing error, or a price override by a salesman. Records did not contain this type of decision information.

The corporate internal audit staff, working in conjunction with application system personnel, designed a system that would take data from the four billing systems and reformat them into a common billing history file. Each of the existing billing systems has been modified over a period of eight years to include all data elements on the billing history record.

The billing systems involved are daily billing systems. They are tape-oriented systems, which produce a daily file of transactions. Once per week, the records from the four billing systems are consolidated into an extended billing history record. Thus, for a year's billing for the organization, 52 tapes contain all the data necessary to reconstruct how a particular billed amount was developed.

One record is created for each line item on an invoice. The only exceptions are no-charge replacements and company use. Company use records and no-charge replacements are maintained on a special file for budgetary purposes.

The types of data that are contained on this extended billing history record that are not common to billing systems include:

- A reason code, which contains the reason for credits or adjustments.
- A special code to indicate whether it is a government contract price.
- A code to indicate whether it was a back-ordered item.
- A tax override code to indicate that sales tax is normally charged or not charged on this item because the rule was changed in this case.
- A pricing code to indicate whether the price was calculated from the standard computer rules, whether it was a special price, and who authorized the special price; several codes indicating how these special prices originated.
- A reentry code to indicate that the original record had been rejected from the system and was reentered. A series of codes includes the problem, as well as who reentered the data if authorizations are necessary.
- The date at which merchandise was priced, to obtain proper pricing for applying credits.
- The date merchandise was shipped.
- The date at which the computer record was created.
- A price adjustment code for determining why adjustments were made, for example, merchandise damaged in shipment.
- The taxing jurisdiction code.

While the internal auditors have made extensive use of this information for audit purposes, many other departments within the organization use the data. Some examples are sales analysis reports based on extended record data, product pricing reports indicating the authorizer and the amount involved in the use of price override codes, and listing to support sales tax withholding returns.

LIMITATIONS AND CONSTRAINTS

The concept of extended records is readily understandable and provides a complete audit trail. It is limited only by cost-benefit constraints. Ideally, each system would contain history records that provide a complete audit trail so that any interested individual could reconstruct the results of the processing cycle. Retention of information on which decisions are made increases control because it is more difficult to conceal processing exceptions. Therefore, the amount and types of data retained must be subject to cost-benefit analysis. Suggested criteria for cost-benefit analysis are contained in the Cost Factors section below.

The extended record concept is most suitable to high-risk financial systems, specifically those involving cash and readily merchandisable inventory. It is these types of systems that have traditionally caused the most control problems for organizations. While the concept has potential value in all systems, the cost-benefit for extending the records should be evaluated prior to its use.

IMPLEMENTATION CONSIDERATIONS

Extended records is a technique that internal auditors cannot install themselves. The technique is embedded into computer application systems. The inclusion of the extended records becomes an integral part of the computer application system. The necessary changes to the system, the extension of the record formats, the change in program coding, and changes to system documentation must be executed by the system analysts and programmers. The extent of these changes makes it desirable to wait until systems are redesigned or to use the technique on new systems.

The internal auditor can specify the elements that are to be added to the application system records. In the application example described above, the auditors reviewed these records on an annual basis and made recommendations to the system programmers for additional data fields to be included in the records. It is very difficult to initially develop a comprehensive list of all types of data that will ever be needed. The list provided by the auditors in this example had data to be added, as well as data that was no longer needed.

TRAINING REQUIREMENTS

Auditors specifying the extended record data need to have a thorough understanding of the application. Internal auditors making recommendations for extended data should be as knowledgeable about the objectives and goals of the application as senior system analysts in charge of the application. If data needed are not currently available in the system, the internal auditor must understand how the additional data can be collected and recorded. The cost for obtaining data not currently available in a system is far greater than for the data that currently exist in the system.

Internal auditors using extended records for analysis need to know basic data processing concepts as well as what data are contained in the records. Extracting data from computer records assumes the auditor's knowledge of basic data processing principles. While the auditors may not personally code the extract programs, they must be able to specify the fields wanted and format of reports. Also, they need to specify the logic that is required to transpose those data into the desired report format. Understanding the data records requires a knowledge of the system, including an understanding of the system's objectives and goals, the meaning of the data elements, including codes, and a general understanding of the processing rules that resulted in those data. If extracts are to be made by using generalized audit software, the auditor will have to be knowledgeable in that technique. Training requirements for use of the technique are summarized in Table 20-1.

Table 20-1

EXTENDED RECORDS TRAINING REQUIREMENTS

Knowledge Area	Level*
Data processing principles and concepts	X
Computer application system structure	X
Computer application system controls and procedures	X
Data management	X
Computer service center controls	—
Application system development controls	—
Computer application programming	—

* X = Basic; — = Not required.

COST FACTORS

The cost of the extended record technique is strongly dependent upon the system in which it is implemented. The amount of data currently contained in application system history records has a direct bearing on the cost of implementing this technique. The more data currently contained, the less the cost to extend the records to make them complete. The general complexity of the system, as well as of auditor requirements, also has a bearing on the cost.

The factors to be considered in evaluating the cost are:

- The additional data elements to be added to the application records.
- Whether the data are currently available in the system.
- The cost to modify the programs to provide those data.
- The cost to operate the system with the extended records.
- The storage media costs for the extended records.
- The cost to utilize the additional data.

Some of the benefits that can be applied against these costs in making a cost-benefit analysis are:

- Improved auditing and quality of control within the system.
- Value of conformance to organization requirements and regulations for complete audit trail data.
- Reduced cost in isolating causes of errors in the system.
- Reduced cost to perform special analyses.

The cost of the technique in the application example listed above was approximately 5% of the total cost of the billing systems. The user believes that this expenditure was worthwhile.

EVALUATION OF EFFECTIVENESS

Three main benefits were derived from the use of the extended record technique.

- The auditors are involved in specifying audit trails, which brings their expertise into ensuring comprehensive audit trails.
- A complete audit trail exists in one extended record.
- Complete historic data covering different accounting periods are available for analysis by various departments within an organization.

In the application example, the auditors were engaged in the initial specification of the data elements to be included in the audit trail. On an annual basis, they also had the opportunity to extend or contract the number of elements included in the extended record. This continual involvement by the internal auditors created an awareness of the need for audit trails and controls by the system application personnel.

The extended record technique provides in one record all the pertinent data relating to a transaction. Because of this, it is both economical and convenient to make specific extracts for analysis. Without this technique, frequently desirable analyses are not performed because of the complexity or cost of obtaining data. Also, data tend to become inaccessible during the processing cycle and, without such a technique as this, are not economically available for analysis.

The extended record technique consolidates processing from several accounting periods into one historical record. This permits both the auditors and other interested parties to review the results of time in a single place. Analysis that was time-consuming becomes practical because multiple files do not need to be accessed to ascertain when or how certain processing occurred.

The cost of obtaining these benefits may be high, however, especially on highly developed, complex systems. The concept of data-base-oriented systems, especially such systems in an on-line environment, largely avoids the necessity for the application of this technique. Thus, the outlook for future application of this technique is limited.

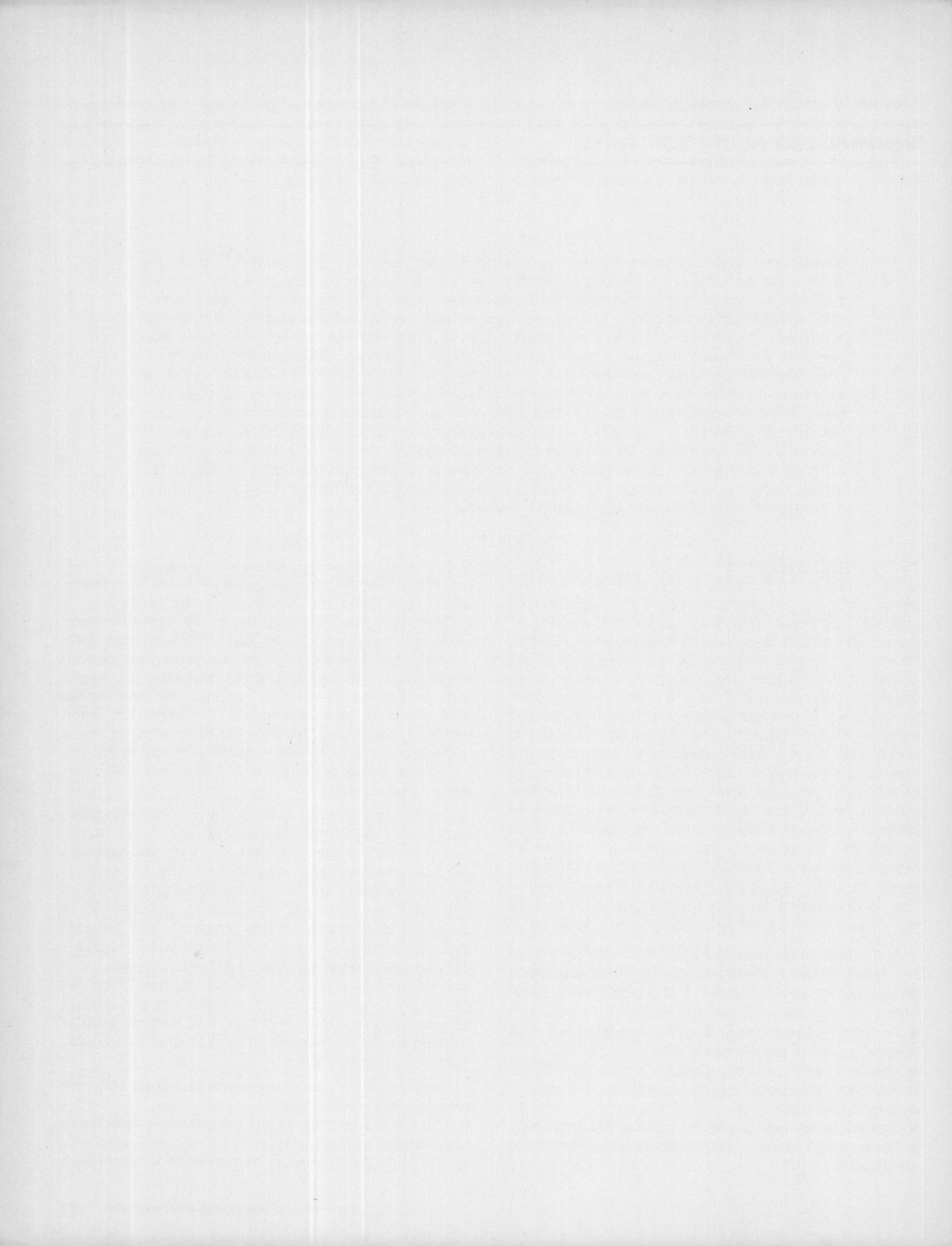

Chapter 21

GENERALIZED AUDIT SOFTWARE

Generalized audit software is the most widely used technique for auditing computer application systems. This technique permits the internal auditor to independently analyze a computer application system file. Most generalized audit software packages, because of their widespread use and long history, are ultra-reliable, highly flexible, and extensively and accurately documented. Generalized audit software programs are currently available that can foot, cross-foot, balance, stratify, select a statistical sample, select transactions, total, compare, and perform calculations upon diverse data elements contained within various data files. These extensive capabilities are available to the internal auditor to substantively test computer application systems. Generally, this audit method is used to test computer file data; little facility is present to test system logic, other than implicitly by the results that appear in the data files. No explicit compliance testing facility is contained in these programs. Historically, generalized audit software programs operated only in the batch mode. Recently, with the rapid expansion of on-line computer application systems, on-line generalized audit software has become available.

TECHNIQUE OVERVIEW

Generalized audit software is the term applied to a set of computer programs that have the capability to process computer data files under the control of input parameters supplied by the internal auditor. The computer data files can be in a number of forms (cards, magnetic tape, disk) and in a number of file organizations (sequential, or one of the direct-access techniques). The input parameters supplied by the internal auditor specify the types of files being processed, the processing logic to be applied to the files by the generalized audit software, and the types of reporting required. Thus, the auditor can use this method to test the same computer application in different ways at different times to meet his audit objectives. In addition, the generalized nature of these computer programs enables their use in testing many computer application systems, thus saving the cost of developing separate test programs for each of the organization's computer application systems.

A number of generalized audit software packages are available from reliable suppliers. These packages generally provide the same basic processing functions:

- Footing, cross-footing, and balancing entire files and/or selected data from a file.
- Selecting and presenting detailed data from a file.
- Performing various logical operations on data.
- Stratifying data.
- Statistical sampling and extracting information.
- Formatting reports and preparing confirmation statements.
- Screening specific data elements on a file, including checking for duplicate information, missing information, and the range of values present.
- Comparing two generations of the same file from different time periods, or two different files, with common data elements, from the same time period.

While most generalized audit software packages provide these capabilities, specific methodologies and features are somewhat different for each vendor's package. The internal auditor selecting a generalized audit software package must select the particular package that best meets his particular audit requirements.

On-line generalized audit software packages have essentially the same features as the batch mode versions. Differences are that fewer on-line versions are currently available and that on-line generalized audit software is subject to the same constraints as any on-line computer application system. It is expected that more on-line versions will become available in time. Constraints of such audit programs include the diverse aspects of data security in an on-line environment, period cutoff points, the difficulties of reconciling data being entered in a constant stream from multiple terminals, and internal auditor training in the techniques of using on-line computer application systems.

Benefits of the use of a generalized audit software package are as follows:

- The language used in the programs is familiar to the internal auditor.
- The audit package may be hardware independent.

- The audit package permits the internal auditor to independently analyze a computer application system file.
- The computer can be used effectively and efficiently in the execution of the audit procedure without the need for extensive training of internal audit personnel.
- The computer can be used as an audit tool with minimum dependence upon data processing personnel.
- Audit procedures can be easily changed to accommodate to changing operating conditions without time-consuming and costly computer program modifications.
- Changes in data processing applications and file structures are easily accommodated without extensive computer program modifications.
- Complex statistical and mathematical routines are available that are thoroughly tested and proved to be accurate.
- One generalized audit software package can be used for many computer application systems. This eliminates the need to use customized and dissimilar audit software packages developed for individual computer application systems.

The disadvantages of generalized audit software are its:

- Present nominal applicability to on-line systems
- Possible incompatibility with file structures used
- Limited logical and mathematical capabilities
- Operational inefficiencies.

TYPICAL PROCEDURES

Steps in the use of generalized audit software packages are described in the following paragraphs.

Step 1 — Define Audit Objectives — This step is a review of the computer application system to be audited and the development of a plan that identifies the specific test procedures to be used. The internal auditor reviews available documentation, such as system narratives, system flowcharts, record formats, and retention schedules. The internal auditor should acquire a good understanding of the overall function of the application and the various files used. Once the application review is completed, the internal auditor documents his test plan, identifying the specific data elements to be tested and the criteria to be used.

Step 2 — Prepare Input Data Specifications — Input specification forms are completed by the internal auditor. Each audit software supplier has a somewhat different form for this purpose, but all perform the same function. They describe the files, records, and data elements to be processed by the audit software package and the location of each needed data element within the record. Each data element is named and its size is specified, along with other pertinent characteristics, such as whether it is in an alphabetic, numeric, or binary form. The information needed to prepare input data specifications, such as file organization and record layouts, is usually secured during the system study.

Step 3 — Prepare Processing Specifications — The internal auditor prepares a processing specification form that defines the processing steps to be performed by the audit software in manipulating input data files and preparing desired audit reports. An extensive repertoire of processing instructions is provided by most vendors.

Step 4 — Prepare Output and Report Specifications — Output can typically take one of three forms: printed tabulations and listings, printed confirmation statements, and information on tabulating cards, magnetic tape, and/or disk. Printed reports usually provide three levels of totals and allow several reports to be prepared during a single processing cycle. Most, if not all, audit reporting requirements can be satisfied with the preprogrammed features provided by the audit software. COBOL-type language statements can be used with some of the software packages if complex requirements cannot be satisfied by available software capabilities.

Step 5 — Process Files Using Generalized Audit Software — The generalized audit software programs are run on the computer using the pertinent data files and the input parameters prepared by the internal auditor. The internal auditor should ascertain that the correct version of the file is being used and that all input parameters are being properly processed. Most generalized audit software packages contain an edit module to validate input parameters; this validation step should be monitored by the internal auditor. Frequently, the presence of the auditor will be required during the audit test.

Step 6 — Review and Evaluate Test Results — Test results are reviewed and evaluated by the internal auditor. Results are compared with expected values and all deviations noted and reconciled. Frequently, additional computer runs will be required. All test results, deviations, and reconcilements are documented.

APPLICATION EXAMPLES

This example entails a review of the allocation of customer payments on company accounting records for compliance with industry requirements. Allocation ratios based on the previous year's experience initially indicated a potential problem. Further review disclosed a program problem that had resulted in allocating payments incorrectly between two classifications of income accounts. The accounting department manually adjusted these allocations for report purposes. Audit software was used to verify the manual adjustments for reasonableness. Appropriate data were extracted from masterfiles for each customer account, and parameters were included in software logic to allocate income according to industry requirements. This example shows that, with audit software, manual adjustments for reasonableness could be verified in less time than it would have taken to write a program to analyze all payments made during the time that the program problem existed.

Another example of the use of generalized audit software from the same company is the identification and tracing of selected changes that have been made to the policy masterfile during a fiscal year. This examination supports the following audit objectives: to verify policies that have become inactive during the period (i.e., lapses and death claims); to test for unauthorized changes in certain key data (e.g., issue date, policy date, gross annual premium, face value); to select and list high-value policies; to test new business activity. The purpose of this examination is to verify compliance with administrative procedures governing policy master maintenance and policy change authorization and processing. It is also a test for the occurrence of unauthorized changes and provides an independent check on the controls routinely maintained to ensure the integrity of the policy masterfile.

The policy masterfile tests are accomplished by comparing masterfiles created at two different times. The masterfile includes approximately 350,000 policy records maintained on magnetic tape. Before comparison processing, this file is condensed to a file that contains a record of approximately 200 bytes in length for each policy master record. All audit reports are prepared from a single pass of the condensed masterfile.

LIMITATIONS AND CONSTRAINTS

Limited potential exists for incompatibilities to arise when one generalized audit software package is used for a wide range of computer application systems. Each supplier's generalized audit software package has its own limitations and design constraints. Suitability can be determined only through an evaluation of audit requirements, existing and planned computer application systems, and the specifications of each package under consideration. Most of the available software packages are extremely flexible, however, and this limitation should not be overemphasized, as generalized audit software is being widely used with excellent results.

As with the embedded audit data collection method, care must be exercised lest the test run produce voluminous output reports. Some software packages provide capability to limit and control the amount of output that will be generated by a request. Audit objectives need to be carefully planned and the audit work plan carefully administered so that test results can be efficiently and effectively reviewed and evaluated.

Last, and perhaps most important, generalized audit software is principally an audit method to test computer data files. As with many generalized programs, additional features exist to extend these capabilities, and generalized audit software is no exception. Mathematical subroutines can be used to test some aspects of system logic, sampling routines can extract data sets for more extensive analysis, and various generations of data files can be compared to test control procedures. Many other additional features exist in various generalized audit software packages to assist the internal auditor in different ways. These capabilities can be powerful tools in an audit program, but the internal auditor must be careful to consider that the computer-produced data file is the principal input and is itself potentially in error.

IMPLEMENTATION CONSIDERATIONS

Important factors for the successful installation and use of generalized audit software include:

- Software selection consistent with the organization's audit needs.
- Data processing department support.
- Audit staff training.
- Cost.

Cost and auditor training are discussed in following sections. Software selection and data processing department support are discussed below.

Software Selection — The selection of generalized audit software is often a matter of limited alternatives. Primary considerations in the selection process are to determine the use to which the software will be put and to ensure that the packages being considered can access the types of files that will be needed for analysis. The organization's external auditors may have their own package and may make it available to the internal audit staff. The data processing department may have a general-purpose file handler and report generator. In a large organization, both of these conditions may exist so that the internal auditor has two alternatives without looking outside. Economic and practical considerations may argue against securing another package if one has been installed on a firm's own computer. Such factors include:

- Software lease or purchase costs
- Installation costs for the second package
- Training costs for the second package.

A single generalized audit software package will usually meet the needs of most organizations. The practical problems of keeping internal auditors current in the use of more than one package tend to outweigh other benefits.

Data Processing Department Support — Cooperation between the internal audit staff and the data processing staff is desirable in the successful installation and use of audit software. Audit objectives can be achieved without such cooperation if technical expertise is available in the internal audit department; usually, this is not the case, and the cooperation of data processing personnel is needed in the following areas:

■ *Package Evaluation* — Internal auditors are concerned with the functional characteristics of available packages; data processing personnel are needed to evaluate technical consideration, file compatibility, and operating efficiency.

■ *Software Installation* — Installation is primarily a data processing department responsibility involving the preparation of JCL, availability of computer time, and adequacy of instructions governing proper operations.

■ *Production Scheduling* — The data processing department is responsible for providing the internal auditor with adequate computer time and minimal interference from normal production jobs.

TRAINING REQUIREMENTS

Training programs provided by generalized audit software vendors typically assume that internal auditors have a general knowledge of data processing. This would ideally include an ability to understand basic data processing documentation, such as application system flowcharts, logic flowcharts, and record layouts. Some knowledge of basic file organization techniques is also desirable.

It is not necessary for internal auditors to have computer application programming knowledge. However, system analysis experience in data processing systems is a great benefit. Training requirements are summarized in Table 21-1, and include an advanced knowledge of data processing principles and concepts, and a basic knowledge of computer application system structure and controls and procedures, and computer service center controls. A basic knowledge of data management is required; an advanced knowledge is highly desirable.

COST FACTORS

Cost factors associated with the use of generalized audit software fall into two categories, the one-time costs associated with procurement, installation, and initial training, and the continuing cost associated with using generalized audit software. The factors that affect time requirements to prepare and process requests are knowledge of the software package, knowledge of the system being worked with, and complexity of the audit request.

Table 21-1

GENERALIZED AUDIT SOFTWARE TRAINING REQUIREMENTS

Knowledge Area	Level*
Data processing principles and concepts	XX
Computer application system structure	X
Computer application system controls and procedures	X
Data management	X
Computer service center controls	X
Application system development controls	—
Computer application programming	—

* XX = Advanced; X = Basic; — = Not required.

One Time Costs — Acquisition costs of generalized audit software packages vary over a wide range. Some of the available packages are offered for sale by private vendors and public accounting firms. Other packages are leased on a per-run charge. Often, public accounting firms will make their package available to clients without charge.

Continuing Use Costs — The use of generalized audit software for audit of the insurance policy masterfile was discussed in the application examples. The time required to perform that audit work is summarized in Table 21-2. The elapsed times shown are for the first time that generalized audit software was used to audit the policy masterfile.

Table 21-2

INSURANCE POLICY MASTERFILE AUDIT

Activity	Elapsed Time
Definition of audit procedures and preparation of flowchart	2 weeks
Preparation of data, processing, and specification of report format	1 week
Validation testing	2 weeks
Computer processing (IBM 370/158)	2 hours

Because of overlaps in the above activities, the total elapsed time to complete this work was five weeks. Three man-weeks of effort were required. This was performed by an experienced internal EDP auditor who has prior experience with the specific audit software package used. He had no prior experience using the audit software on the policy master, but had a general knowledge of the insurance policy computer application system.

Future audits of the policy masterfile are expected to require no more than one week elapsed time and three man-days of the internal auditor's time.

EVALUATION OF EFFECTIVENESS

Generalized audit software is an audit technique that enjoys wide acceptance and usage by internal and external auditors. It is used primarily to test, examine, and balance automated records. The most important benefits of using this technique are the minimal training required of the internal auditor and the flexibility and rapid preparation time to perform basic audit tests. Care is required in preparation for an audit run if the generated reports are to adequately meet audit requirements, but this restriction applies to nearly all audit methods. Most available packages have advanced capabilities, in addition to basic test capabilities. Because of this, use of such packages provides an effective training vehicle. Internal auditors with minimal experience in auditing computer application systems can increase their level of skill by using the basic test capabilities initially and gradually incorporating more sophisticated tests into their audit programs. In addition, the wide use of generalized audit software has created a large population of auditors, both internal and external, who are experienced users, and consequently, advice and assistance are readily available. Versions of generalized audit software can perform many of the functions of parallel simulation and transaction selection. Consequently, generalized audit software should be considered as an option by internal auditors considering these methods. Generalized audit software will continue to be widely used. On-line versions of generalized audit software will come into more widespread use as more computer application systems are developed in the on-line mode.

Chapter 22

SNAPSHOT

Both internal auditors and data processing personnel periodically encounter difficulty in reconstructing the computer decision-making process. The cause is a failure to keep together all the data elements involved in that process. Snapshot is a technique that, in effect, takes a picture of the parts of computer memory that contain the data elements involved in a computerized decision-making process at the time the decision is made. The results of the snapshot are printed in report format for reconstructing the decision-making process.

The snapshot audit technique offers the capability of listing all the data that were involved in a specific decision-making process. The technique requires the logic to be preprogrammed in the system. A mechanism, usually a special code in the transaction record, is added for triggering the printing of the data in question for analysis.

The snapshot audit technique helps internal auditors answer questions as to why computer application systems produce questionable results. It provides information to explain why a particular decision was developed by the computer. Snapshot used in conjunction with other audit techniques (e.g., integrated test facility or tracing) provides the determination of what results would occur if a certain type of input entered the data processing system. The snapshot audit technique also can be an invaluable aid to systems and programming personnel in debugging the application system because it can provide snapshots of computer memory as a debugging aid.

TECHNIQUE OVERVIEW

Data processing personnel have a perpetual need for aids in analyzing why computer application programs perform in a particular manner. This aspect of programming has been, and continues to be, a difficult and time-consuming process. The number of paths through a computer program is far too great for any programmer to analyze every potential path in a complex program. The problem is magnified when series of programs are put together in a system. For this reason, computer applications continue to show systems flaws and produce unusual results years after they enter production status.

The objective of snapshot is to enable individuals to economically obtain the data they need to analyze either past or potential processing problems. One early solution to this problem was to stop a program at a selected point and take a core dump (i.e., complete memory printout). Complex operating systems and advanced programming languages now make this technique impractical. Snapshot is merely a means of selecting specific areas of computer memory for printout and analysis. The time of, or circumstances causing, the printout, and the particular data to be printed, must be predetermined. This involves writing specific instructions into the computer program to execute the snapshot printouts.

Snapshot offers the user the following advantages:

- Limited printouts concentrating on the needed data are available. Traditional computer lists and printouts often involve large amounts of data. In many cases these extensive data lists make it impractical, because of cost and time requirements, to isolate the problem. This forces many organizations to make manual corrections to erroneous transactions because the effort to isolate the computer problem is too costly.
- It enables problems to be isolated economically. Predetermined routines can quickly print out the data necessary for analysis purposes.
- It is a powerful debugging tool for computer programming and systems personnel. This advantage is the aspect that normally pays for the technique.

The disadvantages to the use of snapshot are:

- Its use must be predetermined. Snapshot is not able to react to other than predetermined conditions. It can, of course, be continually modified and expanded to be more powerful and effective. However, this does not solve the specific need for data when it has not been anticipated.
- Programming and systems effort are required to modify computer application programs to install the snapshot routines.
- A skilled data processing professional is required to effectively use the technique.

Organizations using snapshot indicated that its implementation is limited to new computer system applications, because snapshot routines must be embedded into the regular code of the application. Alterations to existing applications for this purpose are normally prohibitively costly.

TYPICAL PROCEDURES

There are three stages in the implementation of the snapshot technique: First, criteria must be devised to determine when the snapshot will be executed; second, the programmed routines that provide the snapshot data must be incorporated into the computer application system; third, a report-writing facility must be developed to print out the snapshot information in a useful form. These three stages can be accomplished by performing the following eight steps.

Step 1 — Select Snapshot Points

Though this phase of the implementation process is time-consuming and difficult, it is also the key to success with the snapshot technique. The critical points in a computer application that would be helpful in analyzing a condition must be selected. Some of these points are:

- When transactions enter the computer system.
- When transactions leave a program or complex routine.
- A point where key decisions are determined.
- A point where records are either consolidated or broken into two or more individual records.

Step 2 — Develop Method to Identify Records for Examination

The snapshot routines can be initiated in one of three ways. First, all transactions of one type can trigger the routines. For example, one could snapshot all credit transactions. (This could be done even more selectively by opting to snapshot credit transactions over $1000.) Second, the snapshot routine can be triggered by having specified ranges of input parameters. For example, internal auditors might want to examine the payroll records of personnel having a specific set of employee numbers. When any of those employee numbers appeared, the information relating to a specific segment of the transaction cycle would be printed. Third, snapshots can be made of all transactions passing a specific point in the computer application. This is normally done for rarely used routines, or for an unusual combination of conditions. For example, the decision criterion could be a special supplemental pay amount, or membership in a specific department. Combinations of these approaches may also be used.

Step 3 — Develop Snapshot Files

Because there will normally be more than one snapshot point in a system, the most logical way to print out snapshot data is to have the application program write a snapshot record in a snapshot file. The data are then printed in a special report-writer program.

Step 4 — Develop Method to Identify Snapshot Data

Several printouts may be available on the snapshot file for the same transaction. This occurs when a selected transaction passes two or more snapshot points. To facilitate the analysis, one must have a way to identify the various transactions and data elements from each snapshot record. Snapshot data identifiers would accomplish this by including the following kinds of information:

- A transaction identifier. For example, in an inventory system this could be the product number.
- A program or program module identifier to locate the program from which the snapshot occurred.
- A subprogram identifier for instances in which more than one snapshot occurred in a specific program or program module.
- Date or program cycle number to identify the time, day, or specific computer run in which the snapshot occurred.

Before snapshot data are printed in a report format, the records on the snapshot file could be sorted in various ways using snapshot data identifiers.

Step 5 — Design Snapshot Reports

Snapshot data need to be put in an orderly format to facilitate the analysis process and lessen the technical capability required of the individual analyzing the data.

The report format should include, first, a report identification giving the name of the report, addressees, and the date, time, or production cycle of the information. Changes in date or production cycle of information would cause a new report heading to appear and begin a new page. Second, the format should contain individual print lines with column headings; the information printed should include snapshot criterion, program or module number, snapshot point identifier, and information collected at the snapshot point. Documentation of the snapshot point explaining what data have been collected should be available so that the user can understand the printed data.

Step 6 — Incorporate Snapshot Into Programs

The incorporation of the snapshot routines should be accomplished by the data processing application programmers. This includes computer file specification, insertion of snap points (i.e., the point in the program that, when executed, will cause the snapshot routine to be activated), and any change to computer records caused by the method of identifying transactions for snapshot purposes.

Step 7 — Develop Snapshot Report Writer
Either a utility report writer or a special report writer routine needs to be developed to take the snapshot file and print it in the agreed-upon report formats.

Step 8 — Document Use of Snapshot
Because of their brevity, the reports from snapshot may be somewhat cryptic and require some decoding before use. For example, computer records may be printed as a block of characters without spaces. The reports require sufficient documentation for the auditor to interpret what data are printed on each report line and where on that report line each field of data is located. The documentation should provide as a minimum:

- A brief explanation of the purpose of the snapshot point.
- A list of the record types that cause the snapshot point to be activated.
- A detailed explanation of the data printed at each snapshot point.

APPLICATION EXAMPLES

In the one organization that SRI visited that uses snapshot, the impetus behind its use came from the internal auditing department. In this instance, snapshot is used in a computer application system designed to collect, consolidate, and report on budget information.

Several different computer application systems provide input to the budget status reporting system. In addition, there are several manual inputs to the system, including journal entries. The initial system had evolved through unit record systems to small batch-type systems that themselves were a conversion of the unit record systems to computer. The new budget status system was a complete redesign.

The internal auditors became involved in the redesign of the budget status application for a large-scale computer system. One aspect of the system that was difficult from an audit viewpoint was the consolidation of source transactions into consolidated budget figures. In certain instances, it was difficult to reconstruct consolidated amounts, primarily because in some instances amounts were prorated across different department budget accounts by different algorithms.

As a means of checking some of these allocations and consolidations, the internal auditors recommended that snapshot points be inserted at the key logic points. In this particular example, the internal auditors explained the snapshot concept and its objectives to the computer application systems personnel. The systems personnel then worked with the internal auditors to select the key snapshot points. After the key points were decided, the computer systems personnel incorporated snapshot into the application system. The method of triggering snapshot for transactions in this example was to add a special code to the input.

Both the internal auditors and the application systems personnel use the snapshot routine as a means of verifying that the application system is performing as specified before they place it into production. Through the snapshot routine, the auditors are able to look at the input transaction, the allocation algorithm, and the amounts going into accumulation to the various departments. Based on that, they can determine whether the program is operating according to the specifications. In three instances in which the system produced incorrect results, the causes were uncovered using the snapshot technique. This occurred during the acceptance test phase of the budget status application.

When the system became operational, the prime users of snapshot were the computer systems personnel. The internal auditors examine the budgetary system on a periodic basis and during those examinations sometimes use snapshot, but they do not use it regularly as an analysis tool.

LIMITATIONS AND CONSTRAINTS

The snapshot audit technique requires detailed planning in both building snapshot routines into the computer application and identifying transactions that will activate the snapshot routines. This detailed planning is necessary because, to obtain the processing results of a desired transaction, it is necessary to identify that transaction before it enters the system, and to preselect snapshot points. Without this detailed planning, the snapshot routine will not be an effective audit tool.

The analysis required to interpret the results of snapshot necessitates an individual with a detailed knowledge of the application system. The type of information normally produced by snapshot contains data in coded format and uninterpreted tables from computer programs with all data fields printed in a contiguous format. The processing rules must be known by the individual using snapshot. Thus, while snapshot is extremely effective in providing the data needed to perform a detailed analysis, the technique requires a highly skilled individual in data processing who is familiar with the computer program from which the snapshot was produced. This analysis process can be extremely time consuming. This problem can be alleviated somewhat by expending more effort in the design and implementation of the report-writer programs, to produce a more understandable report format.

IMPLEMENTATION CONSIDERATIONS

The snapshot audit technique is most advantageous to the organization when it is used by both data processing and internal auditing personnel. The impetus for installing snapshot could come from either group. However, it should not be a technique used only by internal auditors. Because the technique provides detailed information on transaction processing, it is valuable as a testing technique for data processing personnel.

Snapshot routines are coded into the main line of instructions in a computer systems application program. For that reason the only practical time to install snapshot is during the developmental stages of a new computer application. The internal auditor, as part of a development team, can help specify what data are wanted and where snapshot points should be located.

TRAINING REQUIREMENTS

The implementation of snapshot requires a skilled EDP auditor, knowledgeable in the processing rules of the computer application. Snapshot is normally built into a system during developmental stages. If an internal auditor works as part of the systems development team during the implementation stage, that auditor is the one best qualified to use the snapshot audit technique. The main impediment to the incorporation of snapshot in new application systems is the lack of internal auditors with sufficient skill to use the technique effectively. Training requirements for the use of an existing snapshot facility are less stringent. Table 22-1 summarizes training requirements for development and use.

The specific tasks to be included in training an auditor are to:

- Explain the concept and goals to be achieved from a snapshot routine.
- Instill an understanding of the computer application.
- Review snap-point documentation procedures.
- Review snapshot printouts.

Rotation of internal auditors between applications has been cited by the organization visited by SRI as hampering the continuing use of snapshot.

COST FACTORS

The major effort in implementing snapshot is the determination of where snapshot points should be located and what data are to be printed from each snapshot point. The effort required to implement snapshot at the installation visited is summarized in Table 22-2.

The manual effort to analyze output is difficult to estimate because each snapshot printout requires varying, but extensive, analysis. However, it is reasonable to assume that the cost to analyze the snapshot points will be far greater than the cost to produce the printed report.

EVALUATION OF EFFECTIVENESS

Internal auditors are not regular users of snapshot. Organizations where snapshot has been installed indicated that data processing personnel are the prime users of snapshot, when it is used. Internal auditors use it on an intermittent basis for unusual audit investigations.

Snapshot appears to be most advantageous in the acceptance test phase of a new system or extensions to an existing system. At these times, internal auditors use snapshot most extensively. After the system becomes operational, internal auditors' tests

Table 22-1

SNAPSHOT TRAINING REQUIREMENTS

Knowledge Area	Level* Development	Use
Data processing principles and concepts	XX	X
Computer application system structure	X	X
Computer application system controls and procedures	XX	X
Data management	X	—
Computer service center controls	—	—
Application system development controls	X	—
Computer application programming	X	—

* XX = Advanced; X = Basic; — = Not required.

Table 22-2

SNAPSHOT IMPLEMENTATION EFFORT

Implementation Task	Effort
Select an identifier technique Select snapshot files Design snapshot files Design snapshot sort codes Design snapshot reports Implement snapshot into programs	1-2 weeks
Modify each program to accommodate the snapshot file Implement each snapshot point Write JCL/per program Debug each program	2-3 days per program
Develop snapshot report writer	1 week
Execute snapshot — cost/transaction	$1 - $5

concentrate on compliance testing of rules as opposed to analyzing unusual processing results. The tendency is to let data processing personnel obtain the details behind processing, then to let the internal auditors use those data.

Snapshot is effective in providing the information necessary to analyze unusual processing conditions. The skill level necessary to use snapshot effectively is highly relative to both data processing skills and knowledge of the computer application.

Except for unusual circumstances, the benefit for internal audit of the use of snapshot is questionable. Other techniques such as embedded audit data selection and the integrated test facility tend to meet the same audit objectives that snapshot meets, but with more effective utilization of internal auditor time.

Chapter 23

TRACING

A traditional audit technique in a manual environment is to follow the path of a transaction during processing. For example, an auditor picks up an order as it is received into an organization and follows the flow from work station to work station. The internal auditor inquires of the clerk involved what actions were taken at that particular step in the processing cycle. Since he understands the policies and procedures of the organization, the internal auditor can judge whether they are being adequately followed. By the time the internal auditor has walked through the processing cycle, he has a good appreciation of how work flows through the organization. In a data processing environment, it is not possible to follow the path of a transaction through its processing cycle solely by following the paperwork flow. Many of the functions performed by clerks and the movement of hardcopy documents are replaced by electronic processing of data.

Tracing is an audit technique that provides the internal auditor with the capability of performing an electronic walk-through of a data processing application system. The audit objective of tracing is to verify compliance with policies and procedures by substantiating, through examination of the path through a program that a transaction followed, how that transaction was processed. It can be used to verify omissions. Tracing shows what instructions have been executed in a computer program and in which sequence they have been executed. Since the instructions in a computer program represent the steps in processing, the processes that have been executed can be determined from the results of the tracing audit technique. Once an internal auditor knows what instructions in a program have been executed, we can perform an analysis to determine if the processing conformed to organization procedures.

TECHNIQUE OVERVIEW

Tracing shows the trail of instructions executed through an application. Tracing is normally executed by utilizing an option in a programming language. The audit trail provided by tracing is dependent upon the computer language and trace package utilized. For example, higher level languages, such as COBOL and FORTRAN, are traced at the statement level. Lower level languages, such as ASSEMBLER, are traced at a more detailed level. The objective of tracing is to show which instructions within specific programs are executed during the processing of the transaction. This enables the internal auditor to determine which routines (i.e., processing rules) have been applied to that specific transaction.

Tracing can best be explained by examining an example (see Figure 23-1). The example, which is representative of higher level computer languages, shows records from two payroll files, a transaction record showing hours worked, and two records from a masterfile showing pay rates. The program merely calculates a gross wage. The trace listing shows what program statements have been executed and in what order. The trace listing shows that the program began with Statement 0001. Then all the instructions between Statement 0001 through Statement 0005 were executed. At that point, a transfer was executed from Statement 0005 to Statement 0003. A look at the records and at Statement 0005 shows that the employee number of the first record of each file was not equal, thus causing the transfer. The rest of the trace listing is interpreted in the same manner.

The internal auditor can limit the number of transactions traced by tagging desired transactions to indicate which particular ones he desires to follow through the system.

Tracing offers the following advantages:

- It enables the user to definitively know which instructions of a computer application were executed during the processing of specific transactions. After analyzing which instructions were followed, the internal auditor can determine why specific results were obtained in the processing of a transaction. This can then be compared against organization policies and procedures for compliance, which will help determine why questionable results were achieved when a transaction was processed through a computer application.
- It can be effective with either a live transaction

INPUT RECORDS

PAYROLL TRANSACTION FILE

EMPLOYEE NUMBER	LAST NAME	FIRST NAME	PAY YEAR	PAY WEEK	HOURS WORKED	HOURS EXCUSED
12345	SMITH	J	76	30	400	000

PAYROLL MASTER FILE

	EMPLOYEE NUMBER	HOURLY RATE	DEPENDENTS	YTD EARNINGS	YTD WITHHOLDING	YTD FICA
# 1	12321	0300	02	0229000	026800	11450
# 2	12345	0450	03	0333300	048000	16565

COMPUTER PROGRAM

STATEMENT NUMBER	STATEMENT
0001	Read Payroll Transaction
0003	Read Payroll Master
0005	If (Payroll Master) – (Employee Number) ≠ (Payroll Transaction) – (Employee Number) Then Go to 0003
0007	Wage = (Hours Worked) X (Hourly Rate)
0009	Print Wage
0011	Go to 0001

TRACE LISTING:

0001-0005, 0005-0003, 0003-0011, 0011-0001, 0001-0011, 0011-0001, etc.

FIGURE 23-1 HYPOTHETICAL TRACING EXAMPLE

processed through a production run or a test transaction being used for compliance testing.

The tracing technique has three disadvantages:

- It uses extensive amounts of computer time during execution. For example, the internal processing time may increase by a factor of 10 to 20. Total throughput increases by a factor of 2 to 3.
- It calls for an intimate knowledge of the computer application program on the part of the user. The result of the trace is a listing of executed instructions. The user of the trace must then go back and analyze the intent of those instructions to determine what happened.
- It requires additional coding to execute the trace routines.

TYPICAL PROCEDURES

Generally, tracing is not a technique developed by an internal auditor but, rather, is one used by an internal auditor. Three general approaches to tracing are to use a computer vendor's trace option routine, create a special-purpose trace routine, or use tracing via multiple snapshot points (see Chapter 22).

The most common and practical way to trace is to use the trace option available in several of the high-level computer languages (e.g., PL/1). Although organizations can develop their own in-house trace packages, such an approach is difficult to justify economically. If the language involved in the system under internal audit does not have a trace option, another internal audit technique should be used.

Use of the trace option involves a special compilation of source code, preferably accomplished by the application programmer but possibly accomplished by the internal auditor. After the recompilation has taken place, the trace option incorporated in the test program is available for use. The trace option is normally used only in testing because of the degradation it causes to the system's performance.

Once operational, the trace option can be turned on and off by limiting it to tagging transactions. This will enable it to trace specific transactions, or to trace selected types of transactions. After the option has been activated, it provides a listing of the program statements that were executed during the processing of the transactions in question.

When the trace listing has been produced, the internal auditor has the necessary information to use the technique. The items needed are the trace listing, the source program listing, the input transaction that is being traced, and any table or masterfile data that are used in the processing of that transaction. Examples of tables and masterfile data are items such as discount percentages, sales tax tables, pay rates, and explanation of codes. If any of these data have been overlooked during the planning phase, need for them will become obvious during the analysis of the trace.

The user of the tracing technique, in effect, does a "paper" validation of the logic of the program. This requires that the internal auditor keep a running record of variables, such as account balances, so that he can simulate program results at each program step. From this procedure, the internal auditor then can determine how a particular transaction was processed. The final processing step is to compare the internal auditor's conclusions with the actual conclusions from the computer run. They should be the same. A discrepancy means that there was a computer malfunction (which is extremely rare), or that there is a logical error in the program. The internal auditor must resolve the discrepancy to his satisfaction.

APPLICATION EXAMPLE

Tracing can be used for acceptance testing of new systems and for compliance testing of an existing application program or system. However, the only cases that SRI found involved use of the tracing technique for acceptance testing. For instance, it was used by internal auditors performing an acceptance test on a complex billing routine. The billing through this particular system was significant in respect to the total organization income.

One program in the billing routine involved a complex billing algorithm. The internal auditors did not desire to look at static program listings but wanted to evaluate how those programs operated in a production environment. Several test examples were run through the one program containing the complex billing algorithm. For the test, the trace option was incorporated into the program and activated for the processing of those transactions. The internal auditors evaluated the results and satisfied themselves that the program was operating correctly.

LIMITATIONS AND CONSTRAINTS

The tracing audit routine is the one technique that shows how transactions are processed through a computer program. It is a strong audit technique; however, it is costly both from the standpoint of computer time utilized and individual time to execute the analysis of the trace. Its value is in analyzing critical programs or routines in programs that, in the opinion of the internal auditor, must operate correctly. In these instances, the time and effort required to trace the logic are justifiable.

Tracing remains a valuable data processing debugging technique. It enables data processing personnel to isolate computer bugs that are difficult to locate by any other means. When internal auditors use this particular technique, they may wish to work closely with data processing personnel. The help of data processing personnel in following instruction paths through a program can greatly speed up the analysis work, due to their familiarity with the programs. The assistance should be technical, however, and should not include analysis or the developing conclusions.

IMPLEMENTATION CONSIDERATIONS

Implementation of tracing is not difficult, assuming that a suitable trace option is available in the programming support software for the application system under consideration. In this instance, the steps involved in implementation are to:

- Determine which program or programs will be traced using the trace option.
- Determine the method of indicating which transactions are to be traced (e.g., tagging).
- Determine how the trace option can be activated for the tagged transactions.
- Prepare the necessary program statements, following the procedures recommended in the documentation of the support software.
- Perform any preliminary processing necessary on the programs before executing the trace.
- Execute the programs with trace option, using as input the specially chosen transactions.
- Follow the analysis procedures described in the example, after the trace listing has been provided.

The use of this technique should be restricted to those instances in which it is essential to know the exact processing logic.

The use of the trace option can result in thousands of output records. Caution must be exercised by users of tracing to limit the number of transactions traced to the minimum to avoid excessive output. For compliance testing, only one of each type of transaction should be traced.

TRAINING REQUIREMENTS

The internal auditor using tracing must be knowledgeable in both data processing and the application system being traced and must have programming experience. Tracing requires the user to comprehend the use of the instructions being traced, as well as the structure of computer records. Table 23-1 summarizes training requirements for this technique.

Table 23-1

TRACING TRAINING REQUIREMENTS

Knowledge Area	Level*
Data processing principles and concepts	XX
Computer application system structure	XX
Computer application system controls and procedures	XX
Data management	X
Computer service center controls	—
Application system development controls	X
Computer application programming	XX

* XX = Advanced; X = Basic; — = Not required.

COST FACTORS

The costs associated with tracing are primarily for computer time and internal auditor time. The steps involved to incorporate the trace option into a source program are not extensive. An individual familiar with how to incorporate the trace option should spend no more than 1 hour building it into the program.

Costs are incurred in the following areas:

- Altering the application program to use the trace option. The cost is dependent upon the programming language and support software and upon the amount of tracing data desired from the program.
- Executing the program utilizing the trace option. Internal computer time will run from 10 to 20 times normal, and total execution time will be about twice normal. The total cost is dependent upon the number of transactions executed using the trace option.
- Analyzing the results. It is not uncommon for an auditor to spend 4 to 8 hours tracing one transaction through a complex program.

EVALUATION OF EFFECTIVENESS

Tracing is an effective technique for the specific purpose of analyzing the logic paths in a critical and complex computer program. It is a costly technique in both computer time and auditor time. The technique should be reserved for the few instances in which the internal auditor believes it critical to ascertain that the logic in a particular program is correct.

The outlook for detailed computer program analysis techniques in general appears limited. Although in specific instances these techniques are valuable, other techniques such as the integrated test facility appear to make better use of the internal auditor's time.

Chapter 24

MAPPING

Mapping is a technique to assess the extent of system testing and to identify specific program logic that has not been tested. Mapping is performed by a software measurement tool that analyzes a computer program during execution to indicate whether program statements have been executed. The software measurement tool can also determine the amount of CPU time consumed by each program segment.

The original intent of the mapping concept was to help computer programmers ensure the quality of their programs. However, auditors can use these same software measurement tools to look for unexecuted code. This analysis can provide the auditor with insight into the efficiency of program operation and can reveal unauthorized program segments included for execution for unauthorized purposes.

TECHNIQUE OVERVIEW

Software measurement tools monitor the execution of a computer program by counting the exact number of times each program statement is executed. They also measure the CPU time of each statement by use of sampling techniques. The results of these software measurement tools are analytical reports that include any or all of the following information:

- A list of any program segments not executed.
- A list of the steps consuming the most CPU time.
- A list of the source program showing the total number of times that each statement was executed.

The EDP auditor can use these reports to evaluate the extent of system testing. Untested steps can be identified and discussed with systems and programming personnel to ascertain their importance. The number of executions for a particular step can also be compared to counts of input records to verify that programs are operating correctly.

The advantages of software measurement tools are increased efficiency of the computer operation through identification of unused code, assessment of the adequacy of the programmer's debugging procedures, and isolation of the unexecuted code that may have been inserted for unauthorized purposes. There are no major disadvantages other than the cost of obtaining the necessary software measurement tools, plus the time associated with the use of those tools.

TYPICAL PROCEDURES

The typical procedures in executing the mapping technique are:

Step 1 — Obtain a suitable software measurement tool if the organization does not already have one.

Step 2 — Select the program or programs to be analyzed.

Step 3 — Execute the mapping of the selected program.

Step 4 — Analyze the results for the impact on the organization.

APPLICATION EXAMPLE

The organization visted by SRI used a proprietary software measurement tool. This software analyzes source program statements and shows whether program statements have been executed and where CPU time is consumed.

The preprocessor portion of this program reads a program and produces a modified source program containing measurement statements and information. The modified program is then prepared for execution and is executed. The executed program produces results identical to the user's original program. In addition, execution analysis data are accumulated during program execution and are written to a file. The postprocessor portion of the program then analyzes the data and correlates them with the original source program to produce the analysis reports.

This software has been used to evaluate the test of a batch-oriented system as part of a systems postaudit. The system consited of 12 programs, of which 3 — an edit program, a masterfile update program, and a report program — were selected for testing.

During the execution of the three programs, this software provided the following detail:

- A list of source statements that contains the number of times each statement was executed.

■ A histogram that shows the percentage of CPU time spent in each source statement.
■ A list of statements not executed.

A review of this information showed that the testing had been incomplete. The information was also used to validate the proper operation of the masterfile update program.

Such software may also be used to verify that the program instruction executions were consistent with output data. Consider, for example, a job in which a given number of orders were processed in five batches. Review of output batch reports verified that the given number of executions for the orders were accounted for in the output report.

By comparing output report counts to internal COBOL execution counts, the validity of the system was established. Thus, the auditor can place credence in the operation of the system.

LIMITATIONS AND CONSTRAINTS

In testing large systems, it is undesirable to use software measurement tools for every program in the audit because the time necessary to develop the test data, and then execute the tests, can prove excessive. Under these circumstances, it may be necessary to select key programs within a system for testing. These key programs might be an edit and validation, masterfile update, and report programs.

Although software measurement tools can be used to ensure that program steps have been executed, they do not ensure that execution was performed in the proper sequence. Software measurement tools do not ensure that the program executes in accordance with the intent of the programmer (i.e., that the program does the right thing).

TRAINING REQUIREMENTS

EDP auditors require training in how to use software measurement tools. This training includes how to analyze the results produced by such tools. In addition, systems programming assistance is generally necessary the first time an EDP auditor uses a software measurement tool. The tool must be loaded to the system, and job control language must be prepared to execute the test. Once the appropriate test data and program are selected, it is relatively easy to execute the package. EDP auditors can be trained to use this technique in about one day. The experience requirements prerequisite to training in the use of the technique are shown in Table 24-1.

COST FACTORS

Several software measurement tools are available on the market. The proprietary package discussed earlier had an initial cost of approximately $6500 to purchase or $350/month to lease. Costs can probably be recovered faster if programmers and auditors share the use of the package to improve the efficiency and quality of programs. The ongoing costs are in preparing the program for use and executing it, and are generally nominal. The cost of the auditor's time varies, depending on the audit objective to be accomplished.

Table 24-1

MAPPING TRAINING REQUIREMENTS

Knowledge Area	Level*
Data processing principles and concepts	X
Computer application system structure	X
Computer application system controls and procedures	—
Data management	—
Computer service center controls	—
Application system development controls	—
Computer application programming	X

*X = Basic; — = Not required.

EVALUATION OF EFFECTIVENESS

Software measurement tools offer the internal auditor an effective means for analyzing computer program code. They focus analysis at the instruction level. These tools are detailed in application, requiring the internal auditor to comprehend the computer program logic. These tools will not prove that the program performs in accordance with the intent of the system analyst. The tool shows only what portions of the program have been executed.

Internal auditor use of software measurement tools is restricted to the accomplishment of specific audit purposes. The future use of such tools by auditors will most likely remain limited.

Chapter 25

CONTROL FLOWCHARTING

In a complex business environment, it is difficult to thoroughly understand the total system of control of an organization within its total business and operational context. A graphic technique, or flowchart, for simplifying the identification and interrelationships of controls can be a great help in evaluating the adequacy of those controls and in assessing the impact of system changes on the overall control profile. Flowcharts facilitate the explanation of controls to a system analyst or external auditor, or to personnel unfamiliar with specific operational systems; they also aid in ascertaining that controls are operating as originally intended.

The audit area control flowchart technique provides the documentation necessary to explain the system of control. Often an organization's information about controls is fragmented. This makes it difficult to obtain a clear picture of the controls operating within the organization. The availability of an overall picture of controls, using several levels of flowcharts, facilitates understanding.

TECHNIQUE OVERVIEW

This technique entails the use of a combination of flowcharting symbols and narrative description to define all the controls relating to a system in the total business context of that system. The flowchart defines all control points within the system at multiple levels. The highest level of flowchart defines the major processing interrelationships and their controls in the overall business environment. The next, or major application level, further breaks out these areas of control; they can be, if necessary, carried to process and job step levels if details are required.

Data processing, audit, and user personnel perceive control requirements from slightly different perspectives. The flowchart technique addresses this problem by providing a graphic meeting ground from which variations in perspective can be identified, rationally discussed, and resolved. In this sense it is a communications and training aid.

The technique of outlining control of the systems within the overall operating environment is an almost universally applicable technique. The technique can be used in both existing and new application systems. However, in very large organizations, the task may be too great to permit effective use of the technique.

In the application of the technique to a new system, controls are developed at the process and job step levels during the system specification phase. The interface of the new application system with the controls of the existing application can be compared using flowcharts. The new application system should be incorporated into the overall control plan of the organization without reducing the level of systems auditability and control.

The overall flowchart that provides the basic reference for this technique uses the standard analytical auditing symbols.* These symbols are organized with job step sequence going down the page from top to bottom, and with the individual departments performing functions going across the top of the page from left to right, so the processing flow of the controls using these symbols is linked, using the combination of job step and the area or department in which the function is performed. Figure 25-1, adapted from *Analytical Auditing** provides a good example of the process documented during field interviews.

This flowchart approach to developing overall control profiles has the advantage of providing a serviceable tool for EDP auditors when training other auditors and systems personnel in proper control and auditability feature implementation. An additional advantage of this technique has been in the operational auditing of systems to identify lack of control in key areas. In one recent system reviewed by SRI, a number of such variances in control were quickly determined through the use of this technique.

The sole disadvantage is the cost to develop and maintain the flowcharts.

---

*These symbols are described by R. M. Skinner, F.C.A., and R. J. Anderson, C.A., *Analytical Auditing* (Pitman Publishing Corp., 1966).

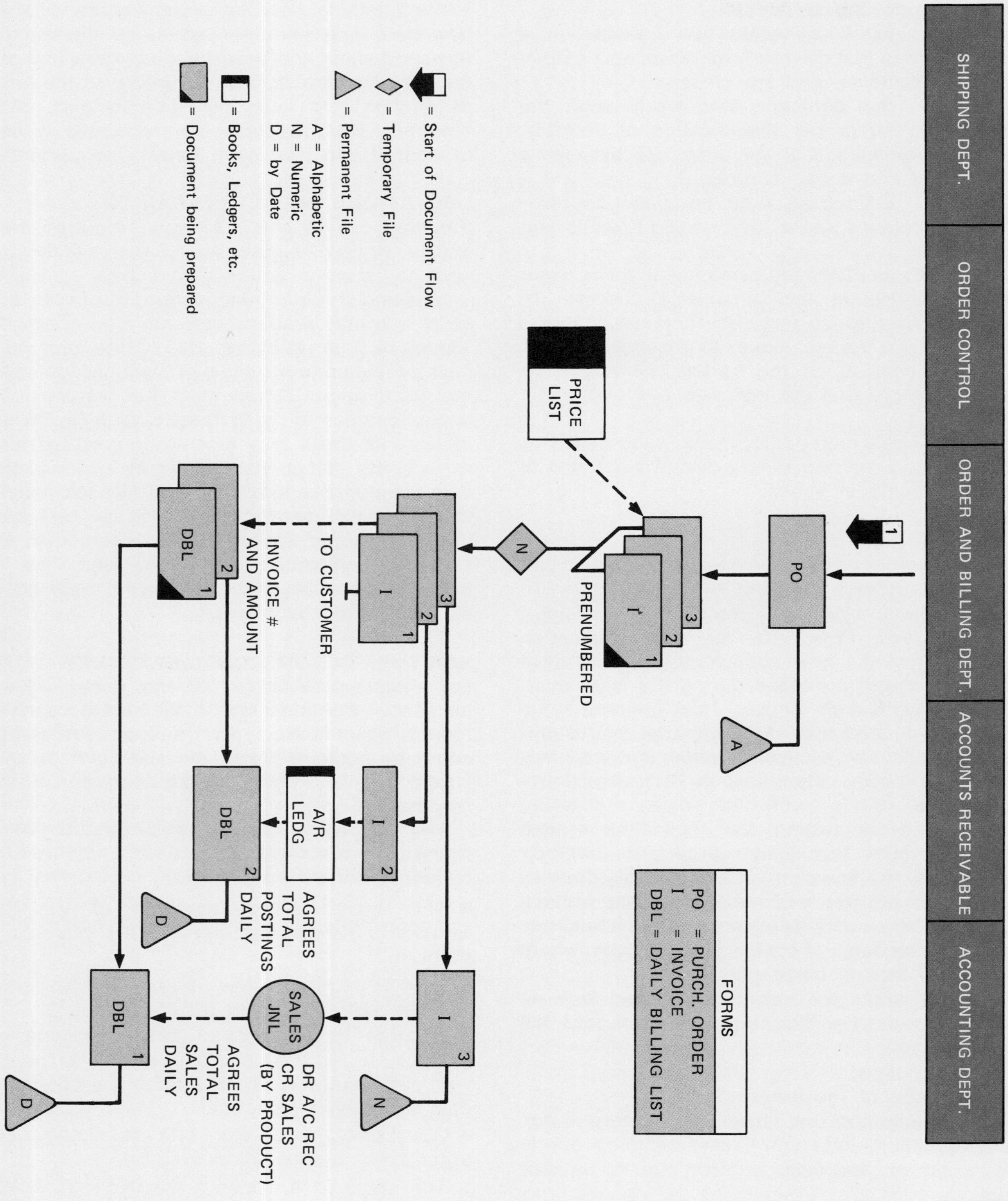

SHIPPING DEPT. | ORDER CONTROL | ORDER AND BILLING DEPT. | ACCOUNTS RECEIVABLE | ACCOUNTING DEPT.

1

PO

A

FORMS

PO = PURCH. ORDER
I = INVOICE
DBL = DAILY BILLING LIST

3
2
1
I

PRICE LIST

PRENUMBERED

N

3
2
1
I

TO CUSTOMER

INVOICE #
AND AMOUNT

2
1
DBL

I 2

A/R LEDG

DBL 2

AGREES
TOTAL
POSTINGS
DAILY

D

I 3

N

SALES JNL

DR A/C REC
CR SALES
(BY PRODUCT)

AGREES
TOTAL
SALES
DAILY

DBL 1

D

= Start of Document Flow

= Temporary File

= Permanent File

A = Alphabetic
N = Numeric
D = by Date

= Books, Ledgers, etc.

= Document being prepared

FIGURE 25-1 FLOWCHARTING EXAMPLE

TYPICAL PROCEDURES

The approach used in implementing the technique entails the following six steps:

Step 1 — Establish within the organization a coding structure that discretely identifies application, processes, elements, and job steps.

Step 2 — Train personnel who are to apply the technique in the proper identification of controls, including a knowledge of the difference between a good control and a bad control.

Step 3 — Train EDP audit personnel in flowcharting techniques, using the selected flowcharting symbols.

Step 4 — Train EDP audit personnel in the relevant narrative description and provide a checklist of important points to be included in these data.

Step 5 — Use the techniques in documentation of the overall controls of the system. Compare the results to ensure that the staff has been uniformly trained.

Step 6 — Apply methodology both in new systems development at the preliminary design stage and in ongoing operational audits.

APPLICATION EXAMPLE

Although it would be highly desirable to develop first the overall high-level flowchart, the organization SRI visited decided to emphasize first the development of the lower level flowcharts for new application systems. All major new application systems have control flowcharts produced during the application system's specification phase. This preparation is usually coordinated with the project leader responsible for application systems development, and at a minimum includes identification of all control requirements, along with the data processing auditor's plan for testing the application system during and after the design cycle. As currently implemented, the flowchart of the controls goes all the way to the job step level (i.e., the job step within a process, within an application area, within a business area). Thus the detail of control is at the point where a single job step is being performed.

These job steps are individually coded with an identification number that is broken out into the following units:

- Application level.
- Identification of the process.
- Element definition (e.g., user input, control input, data preparation, data entry, card-handling operations, burst or decollate, control output, or user output).
- The job step itself.

Accompanying this flowchart, using the symbols as previously described, is a narrative cross-referenced to each of the functional symbols, indicating additional information regarding the steps. For ease of reference, a sequential number is used to reference the symbol as opposed to repeating the entire functional notation in some cases. In using the flowchart, one merely need go to the top of the flowchart sheet and view the input arrow that goes to the first function or box. By going to the narrative description and following the flowchart, one can determine what functions are performed in the area of control and how each function is performed.

LIMITATIONS AND CONSTRAINTS

Effective use of this technique requires that the analyst or EDP auditor applying the technique be able to identify controls and have the skill to understand the interrelationship of controls, so that he or she may properly evaluate their effectiveness. Therefore, the effectiveness of the technique is directly related to the skills of the individual applying the technique. Caution must be exercised in the implementation of the technique, as the mistaken use of extreme detail may tend to conceal, rather than expose, key points. This detail may also increase the data maintenance effort of these data so dramatically that they will soon fall into disuse and become obsolete. Larger organizations, in particular, should consider limiting the control flowchart. This limitation can be overcome by suitably breaking down flowcharts into segments.

IMPLEMENTATION CONSIDERATIONS

For effective utilization of the control flowchart technique, the audit staff must have a capability in control identification and a basic knowledge of computer systems. Also, the audit staff must have cooperation and support from users and from data processors.

The following characteristics should be considered when evaluating the appropriateness of this technique for an organization:

- The impact of development of the control flowcharts (initial start-up) on the planned audit program.
- Cost of training and/or upgrading audit personnel to effectively implement the technique.
- Benefits to be derived from flowcharting; for example, as a communications device for interaction with users, auditors who are not data processors, and data processing personnel.
- Complexity, size, and rate of change of the organization's application systems.
- The stage in a system's life cycle at which the system is operating. If major resystemization is under way, the control flowchart technique might be appropriate for new, but not old, systems.

Some of the operation requirements imposed by this technique are:

- The corporate audit staff expertise in identification of controls must be applied to the creation of the initial control flow.
- User involvement will be required in order to establish the actual control structure.
- System analyst participation in validation of computer-based controls will be highly desirable to ensure adequate coverage of the control flow.
- Exception controls, as well as "main line" operations, must be clearly defined when developing the full control profile.

Control over the use of the technique is readily accomplished through the review of the documents and the evaluation of the quality of the work performed. Maintenance of the technique requires considerable effort and ongoing attention to ensure that changes in systems that affect controls are reflected in the documentation.

TRAINING REQUIREMENTS

Since a general knowledge of computer control techniques is required, the audit staff may require supplementary computer training. Training requirements in the specific flowcharting technique are required. This training can normally be accomplished in one or two days. The facility for auditor recognition of control points is mandatory, but this is a continuing requirement for effective audit in any case. Experience requirements for effective use of this technique are listed in Table 25-1.

Table 25-1

CONTROL FLOWCHART TRAINING REQUIREMENTS

Knowledge Area	Level*
Data processing principles and concepts	XX
Computer application system structure	X
Computer application system controls and procedures	XX
Data management	X
Computer service center controls	—
Application system development controls	XX
Computer application programming	—

* XX = Advanced; X = Basic; — = Not required.

COST FACTORS

The organization visited found it difficult to be specific in regard to the time and cost of implementing this technique because of the large differences in complexity of application systems and the relative knowledge and training of the EDP auditors who would be applying these techniques. However, it was estimated that the average development time would not be more than two man-days for a medium-sized application. Of course, maintenance time is determined by the requirement to ensure that the change does not impact the overall control structure of the system.

Additional factors that affect the range of time or cost certainly include the complexity of the system, the interfaces between varying systems or job steps, and the skill and discrimination of the analyst in properly and succinctly recording the functions.

EVALUATION OF EFFECTIVENESS

The technique as described and defined is a very useful technique, which has broad applicability in the systems design process. It is valuable for existing systems, but is primarily suggested for new systems. The organization visited endorsed its use by a properly trained and properly motivated staff.

There was found to be considerable improvement in the efficiency of operations through the use of this technique because of better controls. The analysis associated with developing the control flowcharts first caused greater understanding of controls on the part of the system analyst. Second, it provided a documented base for analysis for other individuals wishing to become aware of the controls in place and the relationship of one system to another at control interfaces. This organization felt that, although the technique is potentially highly valuable, the implementation in the organization had not adequately reflected its true value. Additional benefits found by SRI were as follows:

- Improved application efficiency resulted from the analysis of controls in an orderly fashion.
- Improved application control resulted because inadequacies in control were discovered.
- Improved auditor detection of noncompliance with application control procedures resulted.
- Improved evaluation of quality or correctness of processing was effected.
- Improved communications resulted among data processing personnel, the EDP auditor, and other auditors.

Part V

COMPUTER SERVICE CENTER AUDIT TOOLS AND TECHNIQUES

Chapter 26

JOB ACCOUNTING DATA ANALYSIS

Job accounting facilities are available through most computer vendors as an adjunct to their operating systems. The job accounting facility is a feature of the computer operating system software that provides the means for gathering and recording information to be used for billing customers or evaluating systems usage. Examples of information collected by a job accounting facility are job start and completion times, usage of data sets, and usage of hardware facilities. These job accounting systems were designed by the vendors to serve the operating needs of the data processing department. However, much of the information provided by these facilities is of interest to internal auditors.

Two types of job accounting data, the accounting records and the data set activity records, are of interest to the internal auditor. Accounting records consist of records that show which user used which programs, how often, and for how long. They include an identification of the user, the hardware features required by the job, the time it took to perform the job, and how the job was completed. Data set activity records provide information about which data files were used during processing and who requested the use of the data sets. Within the information contained in these records are the data set name, record length, serial number of the volumes, and the user of the data set.

The internal auditor can use data from the accounting records to verify charges for use of the computer resources. They also enable the auditor to verify that only authorized individuals use the computer. Data set activity records provide the auditor with a means to verify that data are being used by authorized individuals.

TECHNIQUE OVERVIEW

Most computer main frame manufacturers provide the customer with a job accounting facility. Two of these facilities are IBM's System Management Facility (SMF) and Burroughs EDP-TABS. Facilities such as these are used to collect and record operating statistics that are needed in calculating charges billed to computer system users. They are also helpful in providing basic data that can be used to evaluate the performance of the computer system. These data would be impractical for an auditor to obtain exclusively for audit purposes, due to the complexity in collecting the data as well as the extensive job processing activity on which data must be collected.

To use job accounting data, the auditor must specify a data reduction program to extract the data that are needed for audit purposes from the job accounting data file. This information then becomes the basis for audit analysis or audit investigation of who is using computer resources, which resources are being utilized, and how extensive is that use.

Use of job accounting data offers the following advantages to an internal auditor:

- It provides data on the use of the data processing resources.
- It is the most economical source of these types of data.
- It provides the auditor with background information on how the data processing operation functions.

Job accounting systems have certain disadvantages for auditors:

- These systems can involve hundreds of thousands of records per month.
- An auditor must be skilled in data processing to use job accounting data effectively.
- The auditor is unable to control the source of data through job accounting facilities, because the facilities operate in the data processing environment and as such are subject to manipulation through the computer operating system software.

Job accounting facilities are applicable to audits whose objectives relate to accountability of computer resources or security of computer data. Comprehensive information is provided by these facilities concerning who used what program, hardware device, or data file.

TYPICAL PROCEDURES

The procedures for using job accounting data in a data processing audit are basically the same as when undertaking a data processing audit using audit software (see Chapter 21). Both involve extracting data from a file of records. The methods for transforming job accounting data into a useful audit report are more complex than most audit software applications, due to both the complexity and quantity of data available.

The steps that an auditor takes in an audit involving job accounting data are:

Step 1 — Define the objectives of the audit.

Step 2 — Determine if the job accounting facility can provide the data necessary to meet those objectives; if so,

Step 3 — Specify the procedures and programs required to gather the data needed to meet the objectives. This will require selecting the record types needed from those available, determining which fields in those records are to be extracted, determining which field or fields are to be used as the sort key, defining the report format wanted, and writing an extract program to obtain the wanted data from the job accounting file.

Step 4 — Execute the extract program.

Step 5 — Perform the audit using the data, including documenting findings and developing conclusions.

The two most difficult steps are determining whether job accounting facilities can provide the data to meet the audit objectives and specifying the procedures and programs needed to obtain those data. To determine whether the job accounting data can provide the type of information needed by the internal auditor, the auditor must become thoroughly familiar with the outputs and file contents of the job accounting system providing those data. Computer vendors provide detailed manuals explaining the type of information available from the job accounting systems. Auditors should study these manuals to familiarize themselves with what is available.

A common mistake of internal auditors using job accounting systems is building the audit around the capabilities of the job accounting system rather than determining first the audit objectives.

Auditors can use generalized audit software to extract data from job accounting data files. This provides the auditor more independence in the extraction of data than when the data are obtained for him by data processing personnel.

APPLICATION EXAMPLES

SRI found internal auditors interested in using job accounting data, but found few internal auditing groups actually doing so. Staff at organizations visited explained that the limited use of these facilities is due to the fact that systems like SMF are generally considered to be tools of the data processing department and have not been, until recently, considered sources of information for audit purposes.

Two examples in which SMF has been used effectively by internal auditors are described below. The first example deals with verifying that only authorized individuals are using data sets, the second with analyzing performance of computer systems.

Example One — Authorized Users of Data Sets — The objective of this audit was to determine that data sets were being utilized only by properly authorized users. In this organization, the control of the data sets belongs to the user. The operating procedures require user permission prior to having a data set used by a job.

The internal auditors wanted to determine if that standard was being enforced. The method that they selected was to obtain from SMF a listing of all users of financial data sets. The auditors reviewed the applications in production in the data center. From that, they selected a sample of financial applications and, from those applications, the data sets they considered to be most desirable for unauthorized use. This list of data sets (approximately 250) was the basis of selecting data from SMF.

The audit method was to produce, from SMF data, confirmations to go to the user. The confirmation contained the name of the data set, together with a listing of who used the data, when it was used, and how often. The internal auditors investigated those individuals that the user indicated on the confirmation should not have had access to the data.

The method using SMF in the audit was as follows:

1. All records pertaining to data use for the period under audit were selected from SMF. In this example, the auditors selected a period of one week. The SMF records were selected for the data files previously identified by the internal auditors.
2. From the selected record, the following data were extracted:
   a. Date the data set was used
   b. Job name
   c. The user identification code
   d. Data set name.
3. The file of records developed as a result of Steps 1 and 2 was sorted as follows:
   a. Primary sort field is the data set name
   b. Secondary sort field is the user identification name
   c. Final sort field is date of use.
4. From the sorted file, a special program written in the organization's audit software language developed the audit confirmations. The user was provided with a list of each use of the data set. The report is in sequence by data set use so all users are listed together by date of use.

5. The internal audit group forwarded the confirmation letter directly to the user, and responses from the user are sent directly to the internal audit department.

The results of the audit found inconsistent compliance to the standard under review. Numerous violations were uncovered, although none was judged to be serious. The result of the audit was a tightening of the procedures on obtaining access to data sets.

Example Two — Performance Evaluation of Programs — Discussions between the data processing manager and the internal auditor revealed that there was a wide range of performance by individual programming groups. Programs of approximately the same size and function varied widely in execution times. The data processing manager felt that, if some measures of performance could be obtained, the good programming concepts and practices of one group that resulted in efficient programming could be transferred to other groups. The internal auditor was given the challenge of trying to obtain such statistics.

The approach the internal auditor took was to use data from SMF as a means for evaluating performance. In this instance, the internal auditor decided to give the data processing manager statistics on the amount of CPU time required to process one input transaction by various applications. The hypotheses behind this approach were as follows:

- While commercial applications vary greatly in objectives, the general flow of processing remained consistent. For example, the programs all perform edits of input transactions, update masterfiles, sort records and prepare output reports.
- The systems all use the same programming language.
- Most of the programming logic is involved in reading, writing, sorting, auditing, updating, and reporting on input transactions. Complex computer processing is only a minor segment of the total computer time.

The steps undertaken using SMF are as follows:

1. Determine the applications to be analyzed. From that list, determine which program reads in the initial transaction data. Each input record is considered the equivalent of one transaction. This may not be the first program in the system because several cards may have to be edited and then put together into one input computer record.
2. Select the SMF records written at the completion of a job and the records written whenever an input data set is opened for processing by a user program.
3. For each application, one completion record and one input data set record type are extracted from the SMF file. Only one completion record exists, but the specific input data set record that has the input transaction count must be selected.
4. For the completion record, the following data are selected:
   a. Job name
   b. Amount of CPU time utilized
   c. Record type indicator
   d. Date
5. From the data set record, the following data are extracted:
   a. Job name
   b. Number of records processed
   c. Record type indicator
   d. Date
6. The two record types should be sorted as follows:
   a. By job name field as a primary sort
   b. By record type field as a secondary sort
   c. By date field as a final sort
7. A special report was prepared showing one line for each job. The line in the report included the date, job name, the CPU time utilized by the job, the number of records processed, and then a calculation performed that showed the CPU time per input transaction record.

Steps 4, 5, and 6 include the date field, so that when jobs are run more than once in the period under audit they will be segregated. If jobs are run more than once per day, a time field must also be added.

Internal auditors do not normally get involved in audits of this type. The example is given to show the wide range of audits that can be performed with SMF rather than as a suggestion of an audit to be undertaken by internal auditors using SMF.

LIMITATIONS AND CONSTRAINTS

Two technical aspects of using job accounting information cause concern to internal auditors regarding its use as an audit technique. Fortunately, procedures can be implemented that overcome most of the limitations caused by these constraints (see the following section). Both constraints relate to the fact that the auditors themselves do not have control over the collection of the data. The first constraint is that a job accounting facility runs in conjunction with the vendor's operating system. This means that the job accounting facility is subject to any manipulation to which the operating system is subject. The second constraint is that job accounting facilities do not have an overall control mechanism, such as sequence numbering occurrences or controlling total number of records in some manner. This means that when the auditor begins using the data files there are no controls to determine whether or not that file itself has been manipulated.

Job accounting systems contain large numbers of records of technical data, often packed in cryptic format. The use of these systems, therefore, requires an auditor knowledgeable in both data processing and the job accounting system.

IMPLEMENTATION CONSIDERATIONS

It is not uncommon in a medium to large-sized computer operation to produce several hundred thousand SMF records a month. While these data are exhaustive and provide a very extensive audit trail of activities in the computer center, a high degree of technical competence in data processing principles is also required for their use.

Preplanning of audits involving job accounting data is a necessity. The amount of data to be examined and the potential size of audit reports necessitate complete definition of audit objectives. It is feasible using job accounting data to produce more leads for audit investigation than could possibly be investigated. This preplanning should include what the final reports should be, plus a good estimate of the number of report lines.

Because of the large number of records produced by job accounting facilities, sorted and consolidated reports represent the most practical use of these data. Each time a data set is accessed, a record is generated. This may happen hundreds of times a day. Auditors should consider consolidating all activity common to an entity so they can first look at total activity. For example, when analyzing job accounting data, auditors should look at data consolidated by job, by program, by user, or other common denominator and then determine which of those appear to warrant more investigation. Frequently, the same programs can be run that were used to consolidate the detailed data. This can be done by eliminating the consolidating routine.

Job accounting systems are mainly beneficial to the data processing department. Auditors are secondary users of these data and do not normally have the data collected specifically for audit purposes. Knowledge of data processing operations is essential to analysis of performance, data use, and method of charging for use of the computer facilities using SMF data. However, determining whether SMF can be effectively used in an audit is a judgment to be made by a skilled EDP auditor.

A number of measures can be taken to ensure the completeness and accuracy of job accounting data if they are to be used for audit purposes. Among these measures are:

- Segregation of duties between computer operations personnel and systems and programming personnel should be enforced.
- User and systems and programming personnel should be excluded from the operations area. This limits their opportunity to manipulate job accounting data during the operating stages.
- System programmers should be organizationally separate from the application programmers.
- A separate library function should maintain control over job accounting data files after they have been dumped from the on-line system.
- An external numbering system should be used for job accounting data files to determine that all files are present for audit purposes.
- Options permitting user-coded routines should be precluded except for unusual circumstances. However, these user-coded routines offer a good analytical tool for auditors. It is quite easy, through user-coded routines, to include, modify, or exclude specific records.
- There should be adequate logs that show what files were created so that an audit trail exists.

These steps will not provide a foolproof control over manipulation of data, but the steps will give a reasonable degree of assurance that the internal auditors are looking at complete and accurate job accounting data.

TRAINING REQUIREMENTS

Internal auditors using job accounting systems for audit purposes should have a minimum of one year of data processing experience with operating system software. These individuals can be trained to use these facilities in three ways: Attendance at vendor schools; on-the-job training in the data processing department by individuals knowledgeable in job accounting operations; and, study of manuals, periodicals, and other written information on the use of job accounting facilities.

From an independence viewpoint, the auditor should attend a vendor school so that he is completely familiar with the features. Practical considerations and installation conventions can be learned through on-the-job training at the installation. However, since job accounting facilities are not designed as an audit tool, the audit approaches and concepts must be auditor developed.

The training time for a skilled EDP auditor to become effective in the use of these facilities is two to four weeks. Because many reports are user written, the auditor should also be familiar with either an audit software language or computer language that can take the data file and consolidate, sort, and print the necessary reports. General training levels are summarized in Table 26-1.

COST FACTORS

The organization visited did not accumulate the cost of an audit using job accounting data costs. Among the reasons for not doing so are the following:

- The cost of the job accounting facility itself, if a rental item. If obtained for data processing department usage, this aspect of cost may not be charged to other users.

- The cost of specifying and coding the programs necessary to extract the specific records desired.
- The cost to specify, code, and execute the programs that produce the reports from the extracted data file.
- Costs associated with internal auditor time. These include, first, the cost to determine the types of data needed in the audit reports; and, second, the cost for audit analysis and follow-up of the data provided by the reports.

Table 26-1

JOB ACCOUNTING TRAINING REQUIREMENTS

Knowledge Area	Level*
Data processing principles and concepts	XX
Computer application system structure	X
Computer application system controls and procedures	X
Data management	X
Computer service center controls	X
Application system development controls	—
Computer application programming	X

* XX = Advanced; X = Basic; — = Not required.

The installation visited indicated the cost to use SMF data was roughly equivalent to the cost of performing an audit on a computer system application requiring the development of a complex program using computer audit software.

EVALUATION OF EFFECTIVENESS

The main benefit to be derived from using job accounting data for audit purposes is that such data enable auditors to examine in detail the use of the resources of an organization's computer facilities. Data are available from a job accounting facility concerning who uses the data processing resources, how much of the resources they use, and what data they use, as well as whether or not procedures such as password usage are being followed. As internal auditors become successful in using job accounting data, the use of these facilities increases.

It is necessary to have a skilled EDP auditor to use job accounting data effectively. Both the data and the operations being audited are complex. Without the specialized knowledge on the part of the auditor using these data, there is little probability of the audit being effective.

Job accounting data used for audit purposes can be a costly audit method if misused. Therefore, it is essential that the use of these data be planned in detail. This planning will be a significant part of any audit using job accounting data.

Chapter 27

AUDIT GUIDE

An audit guide provides guidance to an internal auditor on how to accomplish an audit of an area (e.g., computer service center) or a system (computer application system) by means of questions, follow-up actions, and steps to perform. Audit guides for auditors have proved their value over years of usage. The use of audit guides in the computer area is a natural extension from the audit of manual systems. The prime difference between audit guides for manual systems and audit guides for computer systems is the data processing background necessary to effectively use the data processing auditing guide. Without this data processing background, the auditor will be unable to comprehend the importance or meaning behind some of the questions in the guide.

Audit guides are used by internal auditors to evaluate performance with regard to use of resources (efficiency) as well as in terms of the satisfaction achieved by the users (effectiveness) of computer application systems. The use of audit guides reduces preparation time by taking advantage of past experience and provides uniformity for the evaluation process.

TECHNIQUE OVERVIEW

Audit guides provide assistance to the internal auditor in performing an audit. They include an audit approach, a series of questions to ask, actions to take based on the answers, and suggested analysis criteria. The use of an audit guide may be the basis for a complete audit, or it may just provide the information that narrows down the scope of audits to areas prone to loss exposure.

Audit guides offer the following advantages:

- Extensive, complete checklists based on years of experience.
- Reduced audit preparation time.
- Availability to the auditor of the combined experience of the compilers of the guide.
- Uniformity in auditing similar installations.

Some of the disadvantages associated with audit guides are that:

- Overreliance on audit guides may cause some obvious audit findings to be missed.
- Reasons for questions in an audit guide may not be fully comprehended by the auditors using the guide.
- Questions in the audit guide may not be applicable to the organization under audit.

Audit guides in the data processing area are becoming more sophisticated in both method of use and content. While these guides still require the auditor to have a data processing background, they do provide guidance for actions to be taken based on the answer to a question. While some organizations develop their own audit guides, most start with standard audit guides available from a variety of sources and then modify them for local needs.

TYPICAL PROCEDURE

Audits based on an audit guide are similar in approach to other audits. The main difference is that the audits based on the guide rely on the predetermined questioning and approach for the basis of collecting and analyzing data. In performing an audit using an audit guide, the internal auditor should proceed as follows:

Step 1 — Establish clearly the purpose and scope of the audit.

Step 2 — Select an appropriate audit guide and make necessary modifications based on the particular audit objectives.

Step 3 — Prepare a plan for the staffing and time required to make the audit, the skills required of the auditors, and additional technical support needed.

Step 4 — Utilizing the first part of the audit guide, perform an initial survey, interviewing auditee management to obtain background information, to gather documents describing the organization under audit, their equipment, and applicable standards, and to gain an understanding of organizational policies and standards.

Step 5 — Utilizing the remainder of the audit guide, interview and gather data from users and auditee employees.

Step 6 — Analyze the data, making additional audit analyses as required.

Step 7 — Write a final report indicating the conclusions drawn from the audit and supporting each conclusion by the finding upon which it is based.

APPLICATION EXAMPLE

At the installation SRI visited, the broadly stated objective for auditing computer centers was to appraise how effectively the multiple computer service centers carry out their responsibilities for providing efficient and economic data processing services to their users. This objective is accomplished by reviewing the center's management functions of planning, organizing, directing, controlling, and evaluating services. The internal auditor does perform regularly scheduled audits of the centers as well as specific audits of limited areas as the situation demands.

The computer service center audit focuses on the quality of the services provided by the center. It also focuses on the assets that are entrusted to the center and on the proficiency of various levels of management in effectively applying these assets.

Since the computer centers operate largely as computer utilities, with users retaining responsibilities for preparing and submitting the jobs, this audit does not evaluate the jobs and their quality, nor does it audit financial performance and record keeping.

The internal auditors used detailed checklists in the performance of their audit of the computer center. These checklists were developed to meet their specific audit needs. The checklists were broken into segments that represented the various functions of the computer center. The main sections of the audit guide used by the organization SRI visited included:

1. Introduction
   a. Organization and responsibilities for computing activities
   b. Role of the auditor and purpose of computer center audits
   c. Conduct of a computer center audit
   d. Purpose and organization of the computer center audit guide
2. Initial survey
   a. Introduction
   b. Information to be gathered
3. User relations and services
4. Computer resource management
   a. Introduction
   b. Organization and facilities
   c. Machine room operations and closely related activities
   d. Production control
   e. Systems programming
5. Service resource management
6. Center management
   a. Organization and responsibilities
   b. Administration
   c. Planning
7. Measurement and evaluation of computer utilization
   a. Introduction
   b. Availability
   c. Usage
   d. System balancing
   e. Long-range planning
8. Media library operations

The approach used in this particular audit guide can best be illustrated by three excerpts from it, presented in Exhibits 27-1 through 27-3. Exhibit 27-1, which shows the purpose and organization of the computer center audit guide, is from 1.d in the list above.

All sections of the guide follow a fairly standard format. An overall introduction (2.a above) describes the activities that must be carried out in the utility-type computer center environment. An example of this part of the audit guide is shown in Exhibit 27-2. Following the overall description of each kind of activity to be audited, a "Fact Finding Guide" is provided, in two parts. Part A is a tabular listing of questions for which "yes" or "no" answers are desired. Opposite each answer is a box in which the appropriate answer to each question can be checked. The answers to these questions indicate the current situation. Keyed to each answer is a number that refers to a specific follow-up action to be performed by the auditor. These follow-up actions are described in Part B of the "Fact Finding Guide." Exhibit 27-3 is an example of the questions and follow-up actions.

LIMITATIONS AND CONSTRAINTS

When audit guides are used by internal auditors in performing an audit, they should be used as guides and not accepted as the only specific steps necessary to do the audit. They are intended to help organize the fact-gathering part of the audit. They serve to jog the mind of the auditor so that important aspects of the audit are not overlooked. If this general approach is followed, audit guides can work extremely well in improving audit performance.

There are three general limitations to the use of audit guides. First, guides may not be applicable to the organization under audit; second, auditors can place too much reliance on a guide's content, thus limiting performance of their audit; and third, without proper indoctrination of the auditor in the use of a guide, the user may misunderstand the intent of a question or follow-up action. These limitations can lead to improperly performed audits. If audit guides are used by junior auditors, the answers to questions and the data gathered should be reviewed in detail by senior auditing personnel.

Purpose and Organization of the Computer Center Audit Guide

This document is a guide to assist personnel in auditing the computer centers. It has been prepared to aid the auditors in reviewing and evaluating the effectiveness of the management and operation of each center. It is not intended to be used to review the computer center manager's equipment purchasing or financing practices, nor is it designed to help users audit the effectiveness of automated data processing systems that may use the computer centers.

This guide has been organized to assist the auditors in reviewing each center's activities either as a whole or in specific segments only. Therefore, the information is divided into eight discrete sections.

- Section 1 — Background and introductory material about the organization of the guide.
- Section 2 — Guidelines for the initial survey that is to provide the auditors with a first impression of the situation at the center by obtaining background information and documentation on policies, procedures, standards, and management reports.
- Section 3 — Helps auditors review the user relations and services provided by the center. In essence, this aspect of auditing a center is primarily concerned with reviewing with users the extent to which they feel the center is responsive to their demands.
- Section 4 — Concerned with computer resource management. Its emphasis is on how well the various computing facilities are operated. It covers issues such as effectiveness of work flow through the machine room.
- Section 5 — Concerned with review of services resource management. In this section, the effectiveness of managing activities such as system analysis and programming efforts for users is reviewed.
- Section 6 — Provides the guidelines for auditing the overall management of the center, including its organizational responsibilities, administration, and planning functions.
- Section 7 — Provides information on how to perform an audit of the effectiveness of the computer utilization.
- Section 8 — Relates to a specific function (media library).

EXHIBIT 27-1 EXCERPT FROM AN AUDIT GUIDE

II. INITIAL SURVEY

A. INTRODUCTION

The purpose of the initial survey is to provide the first set of information about the center, information needed to direct and execute an audit efficiently. Through a set of interviews on the management level, the auditor/s should obtain background information on the development of the center, its organizational ties, its purpose, the types of services it provides, the resources available to it, how they are applied, who its customers are, and the bases for its service charges.

As much documentation as possible should be obtained, since documentation on policies, procedures, plans, and management reports can indicate the effectiveness of center management.

The background information obtained through the interviews and the availability of documentation — or the lack of same — will allow the auditor/s to prepare an audit plan that properly addresses itself to the areas that seem to need special attention.

B. INFORMATION TO BE GATHERED

In this intial survey, the auditor/s should attempt to gather as much of the following information as possible.

Obtain from the computer center management an overview of the historical development of the center from its founding to the present. Determine whether a charter statement for the center exists and whether policy statements reflecting the charter have been prepared and issued by the center.

Obtain documentation of the structure and organization of the center, such as organization charts, policy statements, job descriptions, personnel listings, descriptions of services. Indications of the established delegation of responsibilities should be obtained, as well as of the separation of authority, how these are defined, and the controls in force to assure proper adherence.

Lists of all assets of the center, reflecting the entire complement of facilities and hardware, as well as software, should be obtained, together with supporting layout plans. Supplementing documents for the various functional areas (e.g., standards manuals, operator manuals, user manuals, equipment lists and layouts, facilities plans, user lists) should also be gathered.

If performance reporting systems have been established, analysis of management's use of them to determine whether objectives are being met or what corrective actions need to be taken will indicate potential center problems.

Documentation of planning done for the center, operational as well as financial, for the short term and the long term, should also be requested.

For an overview of the administration of the center, a set of procedures or directives pertaining to internal as well as external functions should be obtained. Samples of departmental and overall budget sheets, monthly income and expense statements, procurement policies, vendor billing, and reconciliation and payment procedures will permit additional insight into the proficiency of administrative operations.

Personnel management will be reflected in the available hiring policies, functional descriptions, personnel development plans and training programs, and career path and promotion plans.

EXHIBIT 27-2 EXAMPLE OF INTRODUCTORY SECTION TO CHECKLIST

TABLE 1

FACT FINDING GUIDE: INITIAL SURVEY

A. SITUATION

	Yes Action Step	No Action Step
Is the development of the center described and has its purpose been officially defined?	B-1	B-2
Is the organization of the center documented and are policy statements available?	B-3	B-4
Is a description of user services and how to use the center available?	B-5	B-6
Is formal documentation of functions, assets, and controls established and in use?	B-7	B-8
Is proper documentation of center planning functions available?	B-9	B-10
Are administrative procedures formally documented and distributed?	B-11	B12
Is documentation of personnel management plans and procedures available?	B-13	B-14
Have performance reporting systems been implemented?	B-15	B-16

B. FOLLOW-UP ACTION

1.a Obtain a copy of the description of the historical development of the center.

1.b Obtain a copy of the charter statement describing the purpose of the center.

2. Obtain an oral description of the historical development of the center and its purpose and an indication of who defines its purpose.

3. Obtain the organization plan, policy statements, job descriptions, and personnel listings. Determine whether they have been updated to reflect current status.

4. Obtain management's explanation for the reasons behind the lack of proper documentation of the center structure and policies. Obtain and record an informal description of the existing situation.

5. Determine why no user manuals, etc., are available. Prepare with management a list of services.

6. Obtain copies of the user manuals and learn how to use the center.

EXHIBIT 27-3 EXAMPLE OF CHECKLIST AND FOLLOW-UP ACTION

7. Obtain a description of all job functions, internal procedures, controls installed, and measures taken to assure adherence to them.

8. Obtain explanation of the absence of formal documentation of assets. Record management's description of the manner in which it keeps track of the center assets.

9. Obtain available documentation of all center planning functions with supporting input data as used in operational and financial planning, both for the short term and the long term.

10. Obtain management's explanation for the absence of formal planning documentation. Get indication of how planning is done and factors that influence it.

11. Obtain copy of inventory records, overall and departmental budget sheets, monthly income and expense statements, variance indicators, procurement policies, vendor billing, and reconciliation and payment procedures.

12. Obtain management's explanation for absence of formal description of how these functions are executed and supervised.

13. Obtain copy of hiring policies, functional descriptions of individual jobs, personnel development plans, training programs, career path and promotion plans, and any other personnel management documentation.

14. Obtain indication from management as to the extent to which personnel plans have been established and how they are formulated, communicated, and executed.

15. Obtain copies of documentation prepared, approved, and issued by management and the expressions of philosophies and policies that govern them. Also obtain copies of performance reports as received by management, as well as documentation on corrective action steps taken and the follow-up reporting on their effect. Determine what performance monitoring facilities are being used by the center.

16. Obtain management's explanation of how it monitors performance of the various center functions, and corrective actions to remedy shortcomings.

EXHIBIT 27-3 EXAMPLE OF CHECKLIST AND FOLLOW-UP ACTION (CONTINUED)

IMPLEMENTATION CONSIDERATIONS

When audit guides are used by an organization, they need to be reviewed to ascertain the questions that are applicable to the organization under audit. In addition, the audit guide should be reviewed from a completeness viewpoint. Audit management should determine that all the proper questions are being asked in the audit guide.

Organizations have taken generalized audit guides and reworked them to meet their specific needs. Several organizations that SRI visited have their own internal audit manual. These manuals included audit guides for auditing specific functions in the organization. Many of these audit manuals were the result of taking others' audit guides and adapting them.

Internal auditors can obtain guides in the following ways.

- From associations such as: American Institute of Certified Public Accountants, The Institute of Internal Auditors, Bank Administration Institute, Canadian Institute of Chartered Accountants.
- From major certified public accounting firms and chartered accounting firms.
- From organizations supplying manuals and an updating service such as: Auerbach, Datapro, FAIM.
- From publications such as: *Security, Accuracy, and Privacy in Computer Systems* by James Martin (Prentice-Hall, 1973); *AFIPS System Review Manual on Security, AFIPS, Montvale, N.J. (1974); Computer Security,* National Computing Centre (Manchester, U.K.); *Guidelines for Automatic Data Processing, Physical Security, and Risk Management,* National Bureau of Standards (1974).

Audit guides obtained from the above sources can be modified to meet the specific needs of an organization. It is recommended that two or more audit guides for one area be obtained. At that time, the senior auditing personnel can combine the questions and approaches on the audit guides with their own knowledge of the organization in that area. This would result in an audit guide meeting the specific needs of the organization.

TRAINING REQUIREMENTS

Audit guides should have training material associated with them. In order to use audit guides effectively, it is necessary to know the intent behind the questions and to know the requisite follow-up action if a negative answer is obtained. It is desirable to have junior auditing personnel work closely with senior auditing personnel as they begin to use audit guides.

The knowledge prerequisites for use of audit guides in the data processing area are summarized in Table 27-1. The training required for the use of an audit guide is normally obtained from two sources — first, the training material associated with the audit guide, and, second, on-the-job training with a senior auditing person using that audit guide.

Table 27-1

AUDIT GUIDE TRAINING REQUIREMENTS

Knowledge Area	Level*
Data processing principles and concepts	X
Computer application system structure	—
Computer application system controls and procedures	X
Data management	—
Computer service center controls	X
Application system development controls	—
Computer application programming	—

* X = Basic; — = Not required.

COST FACTORS

Audit guides used properly should reduce the cost of undertaking an audit through substantial reduction in the audit preparation time. The amount of savings depends both on the scope of the audit (i.e., larger jobs require a longer preparation time) and on the steps in a specific audit provided by the guide itself (i.e., the percentage of the audit that can be implemented using the audit guide).

The cost of using the audit guide includes purchase cost, if any, and the cost of modifying those checklists that must be modified for the organization under audit. The cost of obtaining the audit guides can range from zero to several hundred dollars when purchased from updating services.

EVALUATION OF EFFECTIVENESS

Audit guides are a means of providing internal auditors with standardized audit approaches for a specific function. The name "guide" implies that they are to guide the auditor during the audit process, and not to direct every step of the audit. The auditor must still rely on experience, intuition, and preliminary results of the audit in determining the full scope and test to be performed during the audit. The objectives of an audit guide are to organize the audit approach for an auditor, reduce preparation time, and ensure a level of completeness on the audit.

Organizations have found audit guides in the data processing area to vary in their usefulness. However, audit guides for computer service centers have been proven over a period of time and are effective in reducing the amount of effort required to undertake an audit. In addition, they tend to improve the scope and quality of the audit.

Chapter 28

DISASTER TESTING

Most computer service centers develop plans for dealing with disaster. The disaster testing technique tests the validity of these plans by exercising the methods that would be used in such an event. The disasters provided for range up to complete destruction of the computer service center itself.

The objective of a disaster plan is to ensure effective protection against loss of corporate information. The auditor, on an unannounced basis, simulates a disaster in the computer service center to test the adequacy of the center's contingency plans. The test is performed periodically.

TECHNIQUE OVERVIEW

Disaster testing cannot be attempted unless the computer service center has done an adequate job in disaster planning. If adequate planning has not been done, it may be necessary for the auditor to assist the center manager in the preparation of a plan. An adequate plan requires the identification of all high-priority application systems, storage site locations, and alternative processing sites. The plan must also address alternative site organization, file-cycling technique, transportation, and procedures for security, control, and recovery.

Disaster testing is a technique applicable to computer service centers of all sizes. The major advantage offered by the technique is the assurance to management that the disaster procedures developed by the data processing department do, in effect, protect the organization against loss of information. Two additional advantages are offered. First, a test will disclose potential weaknesses resulting from inadequate procedures or failure of employees to follow procedures adequately; second, periodic tests remind employees that such procedures might actually be used. The main disadvantages are the disruption of the computer center production schedule and the expenditure of computer resources for the performance of the test.

TYPICAL PROCEDURES

After the auditor has determined that the computer service center has an adequate disaster plan, he can test it by choosing a system and determining the point and time of the simulated disaster. The center manager and others, such as the tape librarian and the data control and operational software supervisors, are notified that a simulated disaster has occurred and the disaster plan must be put into effect. The manager then designates an individual to go to the contingency site to obtain all the necessary procedures, data files, and software systems. It is important that the internal auditor accompany this individual to ensure that the data to recover the system are retrieved only from the contingency site. Using the data processing disaster plan checklist for each system, the individual retrieves the appropriate operations run-books, job tickets, monitor-control cards, object decks, data control procedures, most current tape reel numbers, and balance control totals for the system to be recovered.

When the material is collected, data control personnel prepare the job tickets and forward the job to computer operations, where the computer operator runs the recovery test to completion. The auditor must observe the handling and preparation of data throughout the recovery and compare completed output reports to the original reports to ensure that the data are accurate and complete.

APPLICATION EXAMPLE

The organization visited by SRI felt that the procedures must be periodically tested under conditions as realistic as possible. The computer to be used for the test must be totally cleared of all files, operating systems, etc., insofar as is practical, to simulate a foreign site. The organization visited had a large-scale computer. Before starting the disaster test, the system was cleared and powered down. The following steps were executed by the internal auditors in the disaster test:

1. Go to the data center recovery storage area and pick up the following tapes:

- Stand-alone utility tape — included in the canister is a list of sample JCL cards that will have to be punched.
- Latest masterfile tape.
- Operating system (OS) tape.
- Program library tape.
- Input data tape.

2. Perform the following steps on the cleared computer:

- Power up the computer system.
- Restore the latest masterfile tape by a utility program.
- After copying the latest masterfile tape, use a utility program to resore the operating system tape to disk.
- Reload the system after this operating system disk has been successfully restored and the System/Residence is back in existence.
- Punch the necessary JCL decks and use them to load all system packs.
- Punch JCL decks to load masterfiles.
- Upon completion of file loads, check control totals against file dump summary and user control registers for balance. If unequal, note variance for analysis.

The system is now ready for production. Total estimated time to reach this is two hours.

3. Obtain the data, programs, job control cards, operator instructions, and other information necessary to rerun the job; rerun the system. (Before performing Steps 1 and 2, the auditors had randomly chosen a system for rerun.)

4. Compare the results from the rerun with the results from the actual run and note the differences.

LIMITATIONS AND CONSTRAINTS

The technique has the disadvantage of being disruptive of computer service center operations for the duration of the test. Although the test selected should not exceed one to two computer processing hours, the elapsed time is generally four to six hours to complete the exercise successfully.

IMPLEMENTATION

Before any disaster plan can be tested, recovery procedures must be formally documented, clearly understandable, and updated for any changes in the environment. These procedures must be kept in disaster storage along with other protected documents, and responsible personnel assigned by computer service center management must be capable of executing the recovery procedure.

All input to the test must come *only* from the contingency site. A written report of the test, on a step-by-step historical basis, must be prepared and retained for audit purposes.

TRAINING REQUIREMENTS

Internal auditors using the disaster testing technique must have an understanding of both the operating procedures of the organization and the system to be tested. No special training is associated with the disaster testing technique. The training needed is the data processing training that enables the EDP auditor to understand methods of operation in the computer service center (Table 28-1). If an auditor does not have this type of training, it may be desirable to have that auditor cross-trained for a week in the computer service center before undertaking the disaster testing technique.

COST FACTORS

Each type of disaster has a level of risk resulting from local environmental conditions and the consequences to the company operations. The costs of developing plans and procedures, maintaining disaster storage files, and procuring protective devices must be weighed against those risks and consequences. Since the relative impact of these two factors may be different in various environments, decisions involving the extent and capabilities provided by a given contingency plan must be approved by the level of management directly responsible for the functions being accomplished at a given computer service center. This level of management must also identify the priority of precedence assigned to each

Table 28-1

DISASTER TESTING TRAINING REQUIREMENTS

Knowledge Area	Level*
Data processing principles and concepts	X
Computer application system structure	X
Computer application system controls and procedures	—
Data management	X
Computer service center controls	XX
Application system development controls	—
Computer application programming	—

* XX = Advanced; X = Basic; — = Not required.

system so that, if only a few systems can be operated, those most important to continued company business operations are identified in advance.

It is incumbent upon computer service center management, in coordination with the insurance department, to determine the element of risk, the level of exposure in dollar costs, and the ultimate requirement for additional insurance. Since the system auditor can easily assess the ability of the center to recover, he can contribute to evaluating the company's potential exposure to loss.

EVALUATION OF EFFECTIVENESS

The organizations that SRI visited have found this technique to be extremely effective. An empirical test of paper procedures is always revealing, and, in an area that is so essential to the viability of an organization, use of this technique can provide realistic data and foster management confidence in the capability of the data processing function to survive a disaster situation. The technique will continue to grow in application in the future and will be an important part of the resources of the internal auditor.

Part VI

APPLICATION SYSTEM DEVELOPMENT AUDIT TOOLS AND TECHNIQUES

Chapter 29

POSTINSTALLATION AUDIT

The postinstallation audit technique prescribes the formal, standardized procedures to be followed by internal auditors in examining computer application systems after they are placed in a production environment. That controls are built into the system does not guarantee that they will function properly once the system is operational. This formal approach to postinstallation audit provides an orderly, systematic method for the auditors to examine the effectiveness of these controls in an operating environment.

Postinstallation audits are performed periodically; however, the most beneficial time to undertake a postinstallation audit is three to six months after the system is in a production environment. At this point, start-up problems are usually corrected and operating personnel are accustomed to the use of the system.

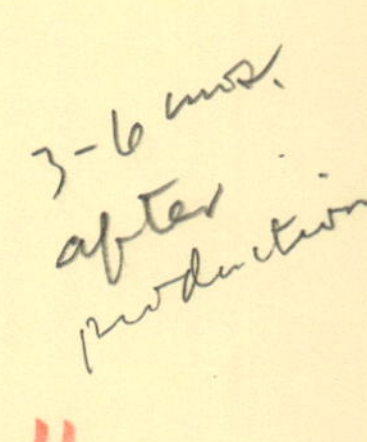

The objective of a postinstallation audit is to verify compliance to organization policies and procedures and to determine if the system is achieving the results for which it was developed.

TECHNIQUE OVERVIEW

Postinstallation auditing of a computer application system entails not only the computer programs but the manual interfaces throughout the computer application system. The postinstallation audit covers all operations, from the preparation of the original source document through the use of the final output reports. Consequently, manual user functions related to the system are included as part of any postinstallation audit.

The scope of the postinstallation audit can be very extensive, or limited, depending upon the specific audit objectives. In either case, applicable postinstallation audit procedures are identified and followed. As with any audit, the objectives need to be clearly defined before commencing the audit. The following control areas may be included in a postinstallation audit:

- Input control
- Processing control
- Output control
- Error correction
- System change control
- User comment
- Audit trails
- Disaster recovery
- Retention
- Documentation.

These control areas are not all-inclusive and, in a given audit, not all areas will be covered. Each application system under audit requires the development of a specific audit program. The scope of the audit and the techniques involved in performing the audit will be determined by the audit objectives. For example, if those objectives require extensive extracts from data files, additional time will be needed to plan, prepare, and execute those extract programs.

The advantages of performing a formal postinstallation audit are fourfold:

- Verification that the data are accurate and complete.
- Verification that the system complies with organization policies and procedures.
- Verification that the system satisfies its objectives.
- Independent evaluation of the adequacy of the application system controls.

Control weaknesses discovered after system installation are usually difficult and costly to correct. This technique focuses attention on such weaknesses and can contribute to informed decisions in dealing with them.

TYPICAL PROCEDURES

The postinstallation audit technique is an organized approach to auditing a computer application system. The technique presented is a restructuring of well-established manual procedures to take account of the characteristics of computer application systems.

Postinstallation audit can cover all aspects of a data processing application. However, any particular audit may elect to cover only a segment of those aspects. The aspects that are covered by one organization visited by SRI are listed in Exhibit 29-1, the outline of that organization's postinstallation audit procedure.

To fulfill the objectives of the postinstallation audit, the internal auditor will need a thorough knowledge of the application system and its objectives. This will require a study of user manuals and system flows. This information, along with the data processing documentation, will give the auditor a sound basis for the review.

The steps followed by an audit group in planning and conducting postinstallation audit are the following:

Step 1 — Determine Which Step Is to Be Audited — This might be accomplished by the scoring audit technique (see Chapter 11).

Step 2 — Set Audit Objectives — This is the responsibility of the internal audit department, but may be done in conjunction with the external auditors, general management, data processing management, and/or user management.

Step 3 — Gain a Thorough Knowledge of the System and Its Objectives — This entails reading user manuals and data processing manuals and gaining familiarity with organizational policies and procedures relating to the application system under audit.

Step 4 — Develop a Detailed, Formal Audit Procedure — (Exhibits 29-2 and 29-3 are excerpts from such a procedure used by an organization visited by SRI).

Step 5 — Prepare and Execute Any Audit Extract Program Necessary to Provide Audit Information — Generalized audit software may be applicable (see Chapter 21).

Step 6 — Complete the Data Gathering Phase — This can entail interviewing various organization employees and obtaining data in addition to those gathered from audit software extracts.

Step 7 — Analyze the Data Gathered — This will provide the audit findings or will create a need to gather more data to satisfy incomplete conclusions.

Step 8 — Prepare an Audit Report

Step 9 — Prepare Recommendations for Improvements (if any) in the Formal Procedures

APPLICATION EXAMPLE

Postinstallation audits at organizations visited by SRI cover a wide variety of topics. When approaches are standardized, the method is a general procedure that will cover a wide range of situations. It can then be adapted by the auditor for each specific situation encountered.

Among the objectives of a postinstallation audit at one organization visited are:

- To determine if the system meets the user's objectives.
- To ascertain if the system is adequately controlled.
- To determine if the system documentation meets the organization's documentation standards.
- To determine if the data handled by the system are complete and valid.

The organization's method of achieving these objectives is to provide the internal auditor with an all-inclusive list of audit procedures. The internal auditor then sets the objective for that specific audit and uses the appropriate audit procedures.

The given procedures are used as a guide by the internal auditors and are modified where appropriate. The standardized procedures provide the auditor with a unified approach to the audit of operational computer system applications. At the conclusion of the audit, the auditors also evaluate the effectiveness of the procedures and recommend specific modifications.

LIMITATIONS AND CONSTRAINTS

Formalized approaches to audits of installed computer system applications cannot encompass the variety of situations posed by different applications. Thus, such an approach should not be considered to be the final and complete procedure to be followed. Overreliance on procedures can unduly limit auditor initiative. Also, if the procedures are allowed to become static, their usefulness degrades.

IMPLEMENTATION CONSIDERATIONS

The application of formalized procedures for postinstallation audit is, in the main, a straightforward process, similar in concept to the use of any audit guide. Because of the complexity of many computer application systems, however, the proper use of postinstallation audit procedures requires that the internal auditors participating:

- Have a high level of data processing technical knowledge.
- Be competent and current in data processing practice.
- Have not participated in the design phase of the system under audit.

TRAINING REQUIREMENTS

Postinstallation audits of computer application systems should be performed by experienced EDP auditors. Some organizations are more rigid in their requirements than others, but most do require auditors knowledgeable in data processing concepts and terminology. The background of the auditor performing postimplementation audits normally includes:

- An understanding of how computer systems are developed.
- Experience in data processing to the level of being able to understand the steps in writing a computer program.
- An understanding of audit approaches and audit methodology.

Knowledge and training prerequisites are summarized in Table 29-1.

Table 29-1

POSTINSTALLATION AUDIT TRAINING REQUIREMENTS

Knowledge Area	Level*
Data processing principles and concepts	XX
Computer application system structure	X
Computer application system controls and procedures	XX
Data management	X
Computer service center controls	—
Application system development controls	—
Computer application programming	—

* XX = Advanced; X = Basic; — = Not Required.

COST FACTORS

Developing a postinstallation audit program requires auditor time to formulate and compile the procedures.

The cost to utilize this technique is the auditor time associated with performing the audit. With this technique, the auditor should be more effective in the available audit time. The net result is a cost savings, in that auditor productivity is increased.

EVALUATION OF EFFECTIVENESS

A formal procedure for postinstallation audits of computerized applications standardizes the audit approach. Without this standardized approach, the possibility exists for inconsistent audits. The goal of most data processing departments is to operate under standards and guidelines. These guidelines and standards attempt to promote consistency between computer application systems. A standardized approach to auditing computer application systems aids in accomplishing organizational objectivies.

The audit procedures illustrated in the exhibits were used by one organization as guidelines for audit. As guidelines, postinstallation audit procedures build the base for experienced auditors to isolate potential system problems; if the procedures can do this, they have served their purpose. At this point, the auditor can investigate those problems using traditional audit procedures.

It is essential for organizations to audit their computer application systems. As a minimum, audits should occur shortly after the system becomes operational and then on a periodic basis.

The organization visited found the standardized audit approach to be much more effective than having EDP auditors undertake audits based on their individual experiences. The formalized approach offers the ability to respond continually to changed conditions, and it can be improved by drawing on the collective experience of many auditors doing postinstallation audits.

I. EDP/USER PROCEDURES AND STANDARDS

   A. Planning, Development, and Control
   B. Organization and Personnel
   C. User Interface
   D. Expense Control
   E. Equipment Configuration for System

II. CONTROLS

   A. Input Controls
   B. Process Controls
   C. Error Controls
   D. Output Controls
   E. Audit Trail
   F. User Controls
   G. Operating Controls
   H. Data Control Function

III. SYSTEMS REPORTS

IV. DOCUMENTATION

   A. System Documentation
   B. Program Documentation
   C. Program Revisions
   D. Operators' Instructions

V. DATA FILE MANAGEMENT AND STORAGE

   A. Data Processing Library
   B. Backup Files
   C. File Retention
   D. Backup Facilities

VI. UTILIZATION REPORTING

VII. SUPPLIES AND FORMS

EXHIBIT 29-1 OUTLINE OF POSTINSTALLATION AUDIT PROCEDURE

I. EDP/USER PROCEDURES AND STANDARDS

A. Planning, Development, and Control

1. Gain an understanding of user needs through interviews, inquiry, special-interest publications, and other sources.

2. Assess whether or not the user's needs, as documented in Step 1, are "in fact" met by the system under review, including frequency, proper distribution, timing, and accuracy.

3. Document any problems facing the user; where possible, recommend feasible enhancements to suit his needs.

4. Do information flows exist which adequately support system decision-making activities (e.g., report sent to management)?

5. Determine whether formal requests for new or revised data processing applications were prepared, and submitted with proper authorization signatures.

6. Determine whether approval for each major application change is supported by a study of costs and benefits.

7. Determine if the system violates organizational procedures.

B. Organization and Personnel

1. Obtain and review an organization chart of the user activity. Evaluate organization structure as to whether it is causing any system control weakness.

2. During the interview, keep a record of your evaluation of the user staff, in respect to technical abilities, interest, and responsibility. Document and report any significant weaknesses affecting user operations.

C. User Interface

1. By review of documentation, correspondence, and discussions with the user departments on newly implemented systems, determine the extent to which the operating departments participate in system design. Was it effective?

2. Check data processing records that indicate the average time:

   - Between user input and starting of the system.

   - Between system output and return to data control for user pickup. (Lengthy delays could be indicative of programming problems, operator error, input error, system problems, poor scheduling, or inefficient handling of jobs by data control.)

   - Between receipt by data control and return to the user.

EXHIBIT 29-2 EXCERPT FROM POSTINSTALLATION AUDIT PROCEDURE

II. CONTROLS

E. **Audit Trail**

Identification Controls

1. Ensure that there is some method of identifying and locating the component file records and input/output source documents involved in the processing of a given transaction or in the accumulation of a given total.

2. Ensure that each document and machine-sensible file record has some unique identifier.

3. Verify that each document and machine-sensible file record is filed in a significant and planned sequence to facilitate accessibility.

4. For on-line systems using destructive updating of random access files, ensure that there is a tape file of the status of a masterfile record prior to updating, the change causing the update, and the status of the masterfile record after updating.

5. Ensure that, for all transactions and accounts drawing a large number of inquiries, regular provisions are made to supply the records necessary for answering any inquiries. Ensure that there is a means for tracing the summary amount back to the individual transaction elements.

6. Where a system that the auditor is reviewing contains substantial gaps in the audit trail —

   a. Evaluate the adequacy of test data used to prove out the system.

   b. Outline the input and output elements of the program and evaluate the error-checking and control routines for input validity. Determine what type of editing the programs are doing for sequencing batch totals, transaction completeness, and record counts.

   c. Determine whether the programs contain the following types of validity checks:

      - Reasonableness

      - Minimum and maximum values

      - Transaction code validity

EXHIBIT 29-3 EXCERPT FROM POSTINSTALLATION AUDIT PROCEDURE

Chapter 30

CONTROL GUIDELINES FOR USE DURING SYSTEM DEVELOPMENT

The best opportunity for internal auditors to affect the system of internal controls in a computer application system is during the system development phase. During the developmental phase, changes and extensions to the system of internal control can be accomplished with considerably less cost and effort than after the system becomes operational, when it may not be practical to make modifications.

Internal auditors are becoming involved in the design phase of new computer application systems. Their participation during the design phase is intended to ensure that the system controls specified by the system analyst provide confidence in the integrity of the system.

Several organizations visited by SRI believe that it is important for the internal auditor to retain independence during the system design phase. To ensure this, the internal auditor is not under the direct organizational control of the project leader and does not specify controls but, rather, reviews and makes recommendations for improvement of the planned level of control. To aid in carrying out this function, two organizations provide their internal auditors with control guidelines. These guidelines are not intended to constrain the development of additional controls but, rather, to provide a general framework for the satisfaction of the organization's control objectives. The auditor, working with these guidelines supplementing his own experience in control and audit, works with system analysis and development personnel to ensure the integrity of the system.

TECHNIQUE OVERVIEW

The responsibility for the specification of application system controls for new systems rests with the user departments, while responsibility for the realization of the specifications lies with the system designers and implementers. Controls are an important element of all systems, whether they are manual or computer-oriented, and they encompass the total system — both external and internal to the computer environment. Application system controls are identified and documented by the project team, and there should be agreement between the system area and users that the controls are adequate. Administrative responsibilities for the balancing and other control features of the system are assigned prior to installation of the system. It is important to remember that even the best system controls are worthless without adequate administration and enforcement.

The internal auditor, by reviewing system controls during the developmental stages, has the opportunity to interact with the system designers when it is least expensive to make changes. Traditional auditing would call for the review to occur after the system had been placed into production. Unfortunately, in data processing this has proved to be a costly time to make changes in application systems.

The internal auditor working with system application development personnel works as if he were a member of the development team. However, the working relationship is such that, while the internal auditors work with the team, they are not team members in the sense that they take direction from the team leader. Any specific tasks assumed by the internal auditors are voluntarily accepted in an effort to improve audit and control. This enables the internal auditor to maintain objectivity and independence. The internal auditor receives copies of system documentation, is invited to status and working meetings of the developmental team, and has the opportunity to input comments on controls to the team. The relationship was found to be most successful when handled informally, although any such relationship must be backed up by a clear management mandate for auditor participation.

Control guidelines of this type offer two advantages:

- They help ensure consideration by the developers of controls deemed important by the internal auditors.
- They help avoid the disruption and expense of postinstallation system modifications.

The potential disadvantage is the threat to the internal auditor's objectivity that is posed if he steps beyond the exercise of the guidelines and assumes too integrated a role in the development.

TYPICAL PROCEDURES

During the system design phase, the internal auditor

performs the following 10 steps. Note that the first 7 steps are fact-gathering steps and are executed over most of the development time during which the system specifications are being prepared. Steps 8 through 10 involve documenting what the internal auditor has uncovered. The documentation is then reviewed with the user and data processing personnel.

Fact Gathering
Step 1 — Determine system control requirements
a. Define input controls
b. Define processing and output controls
Step 2 — Determine file security controls
Step 3 — Determine audit trail requirements
Step 4 — Determine data retention requirements
Step 5 — Determine error control procedures
Step 6 — Describe any changes in accounting method
Step 7 — Review controls to ensure all objectives have been accomplished
Documenting
Step 8 — Prepare a controls memorandum stating audit findings
Step 9 — Review control reports
Step 10 — Review controls memorandum, controls checklist, and control reports with user and operations personel

APPLICATION EXAMPLES

In two organizations visited by SRI, the internal auditors had a close working relationship with the data processing department. Data processing told the internal auditors what new systems were being developed and the time schedule associated with the application system. The internal auditors then determined in which application systems they desired to participate as part of the system development effort.

The time of greatest internal auditor involvement in system development is between the feasibility study and the actual coding of programs. During this system specification and design stage, the auditor reviews the application system controls being proposed by the system analyst. He also acts as a consultant to the system analyst in considering alternative means of control.

In the two organizations visited, the internal auditors had developed control guidelines for new systems. The internal auditors used these guidelines as a basis for their review of computer application controls and not as a list of controls that had to be installed, or as a comprehensive list of controls. Excerpts from one of these guidelines appear in Exhibit 30-1.

LIMITATIONS AND CONSTRAINTS

The use of internal auditors during the system design phase of computer application systems can be a lengthy and time-consuming process. The success of this involvement is often dependent upon the caliber of the individual who participates with the development team. It has been the experience of the organizations whose internal auditors are involved in this phase that most success has been obtained from using EDP auditors who have had experience in system design.

Because the system development phase is an extensive one, these organizations have found that continuity of internal auditing personnel is important. When an individual is participating with a development team from the internal auditing department, it should be a long-term commitment. The internal auditor participating with a development team should be committed to that project for the duration of the development phase. The internal auditor participating with the development team should not be the same auditor who does the postinstallation audit.

Reporting of progress by the internal auditor on the system development team is a potential problem area because of separate reporting relationships for developer and auditor. Therefore, interim reports by internal auditors have been handled on an oral basis with internal audit management unless serious problems exist that cannot be resolved at the development team level.

IMPLEMENTATION CONSIDERATIONS

The successful use of internal auditors in the development phase of computer application systems is highly dependent on good interpersonal relations among team members. Because the application system is somewhat abstract at this phase of development, it is difficult to apply strict procedures to the process. Factors for consideration for this aspect of auditing are:

- Obtain strong top management support for internal audit participation in system development efforts.
- Assigh an EDP auditor with experience in system design.
- Make the assignment for the duration of the development phase.
- Allocate a specific number of hours to the task as a limitation to involvement.
- Use standard control guidelines to be sure the basic control objectives have been satisfied.
- Ensure that the internal auditor assigned to the developmental team has access to all data available to the system analyst.

The auditor is not an official member of the system development team. Rather, he retains independence and performs a traditional review function to

1. **Input Controls**

a. Responsibilities for the initiation, review, and/or proper authorization of transactions should be clearly established.

b. There must be adequate procedures to ensure that all transactions are received for processing (e.g., batch controls, prenumbered documents).

c. There must be adequate procedures to ensure the correct recording of all critical fields of original input data on cards, magnetic tape, or disk (e.g., key verification, self-checking digits, control totals, hash totals).

d. If on-line data transmission is used for input there must be adequate controls to ensure that transmission is correct and no messages are lost (e.g., message counts, character counts, dual transmission).

There must be adequate procedures to ensure security over the use of terminals (e.g., passwords, terminal identification, message recap at end of day).

e. Adequate use must be made of the computer's ability to make logical data validity tests on critical fields of information (e.g., tables of valid codes, check digits, limit tests, reasonableness tests, missing data, editing, invalid combinations of data).

2. **Processing and Output Controls**

a. There must be adequate control to ensure all transactions received are processed through the entire system (e.g., externally determined batch control totals passed from run to run).

b. There must be adequate controls to provide assurance regarding the integrity of the processing and the output produced. This type of control can take a variety of forms and will depend on the equipment, application, design characteristics, imagination of the analysts, etc.; however, the quality of these controls will profoundly affect the reliability of a system. The overall processing controls should be developed as close to the source of the transaction as possible and carried through the entire system. Ideally, they should be developed by the users (e.g., input totals and predicted masterfile totals), but where this is not practical they should be developed in the input run. The user should be involved in the ongoing administration of the control process to the fullest extent possible.

c. If the system must balance to general ledger accounts or other overall system control, it must be designed with a practical means of identifying individual differences on a regular basis and the timely correction of these differences.

EXHIBIT 30-1 EXCERPTS FROM SYSTEM DEVELOPMENT CONTROL GUIDELINES

ascertain that the system of internal controls is adequate. The auditor advises top management of the adequacy of internal controls before the application becomes operational.

TRAINING REQUIREMENTS

The training required prior to an internal auditor's being assigned to a system development team includes experience in both auditing and computer application system design.

For example, one organization visited by SRI requires its internal auditors on system development teams to have at least one year's experience in programming and system analysis and design. In addition, they undergo a four-day basic system control course, the objectives of which are to:

- Recognize the necessity for controls in application systems in general.
- Design a system control plan for a sequential magnetic tape application system, given predetermined control objectives and a basic system design.
- Evaluate control techniques to determine that given control objectives have been accomplished in a sequential, magnetic tape, application system.
- Encourage imaginative thinking and "sound judgment" in designing and evaluating system controls for sequential magnetic tape systems.

Knowledge and training prerequisites are summarized in Table 30-1.

COST FACTORS

None of the organizations visited by SRI had developed a cost-benefit ratio for internal auditors on system development teams. The costs involved were determined to be those of the internal auditor's time and the associated costs of being a member of the development team. Commitments varied widely between systems.

Table 30-1
SYSTEM DEVELOPMENT CONTROL TRAINING REQUIREMENTS

Knowledge Area	Level*
Data processing principles and concepts	XX
Computer application system structure	XX
Computer application system controls and procedures	XX
Data management	X
Computer service center controls	XX
Application system development controls	XX
Computer application programming	X

* XX = Advanced; X = Basic.

EVALUATION OF EFFECTIVENESS

The organizations visited by SRI felt it was important to have internal auditors involved in the developmental phase of key application systems.

Experience at these organizations showed the data processing department system analysts were reluctant to make major changes to operational systems. Good control recommendations by internal auditors were often not being implemented because of the cost to install that control in an operational application. Changes can also cause new application problems.

The addition of an internal auditor to a system development team provides an input into the project specifications from a control specialist. It does not ensure that the system will be well controlled, but does ensure that the control aspect of the system will be given attention. It appears to be an effective technique for directing attention toward the development of controls in new systems. In SRI's opinion, the area of system development is the most fruitful for application of increased internal audit attention.

Chapter 31

SYSTEM DEVELOPMENT LIFE CYCLE

In computer application programs, careful development can prevent expensive after-the-fact changes. Data processing professionals are increasingly devoting time to reviewing and checking computer application systems during development to minimize costly modifications after installation. EDP auditors, such as those in one large government organization visited by SRI, are taking advantage of this approach on the part of data processing to strengthen their own review of the development process. In so doing, the auditor and the data processor are assured that their computer application system objectives are fully met.

TECHNIQUE OVERVIEW

This technique codifies the intrinsic structure of the system development process into phases and identifies quality control checkpoints at the end of critical tasks in the phases. At these points, auditors observe and evaluate status and products to ensure that system auditability and control provisions are suitable and are being suitably executed.

APPLICATION EXAMPLE

Large computer application systems are developed in a series of phases. At one organization visited by SRI, the development phases are:

- Project definition
- System design
- Detailed design and programming
- System test
- Conversion.

Each phase is further divided into tasks. At the end of critical tasks in each phase, and at the end of each phase, a detailed review is made to determine whether the system objectives are still being met. While these reviews encompass all aspects of the computer application system, those that are of immediate concern to the EDP auditor are emphasized here. For his review, the EDP auditor designates the completion of certain tasks in each phase as quality control checkpoints.

The project definition phase consists of eight tasks:

1. Organize the project (Checkpoint 1)
2. Analyze the present system
3. Summarize cost of present system
4. Determine new information requirements (Checkpoint 2)
5. Prepare conceptual system design
6. Estimate user costs and benefits
7. Estimate data processing costs and benefits (Checkpoint 3)
8. Approve/disapprove recommendations

The three checkpoints, Tasks 1, 4, and 7, are reviewed, upon completion, by the EDP auditor. At these checkpoints, he makes the following checks:

- Checkpoint 1 — Review the project organization, review the arrangements the user has made with the system development department, and review the plans and work program for the design.
- Checkpoint 2 — Review the analysis of the present system, review the cost of the present system, develop conclusions, and review the project control.
- Checkpoint 3 — Review the conceptual design documentation, discuss practical considerations of the conceptual design, review new system requirements, review cost-benefits, and make a presentation to management on the audit department findings.

The system design phase is made up of 10 tasks as follows:

1. Organize the project (Checkpoint 4)
2. Design output reports (Checkpoint 5)
3. Design computer processing
4. Design file requirements
5. Design input requirements (Checkpoint 6)
6. Establish equipment requirements
7. Determine installation approach (Checkpoint 7)
8. Estimate user costs and benefits
9. Estimate data processing costs and benefits (Checkpoint 8)
10. Approve/disapprove recommendations

At the checkpoints — the completion of Tasks 1, 2, 5, 7, and 9 — the EDP auditor does the following:

- Checkpoint 4 — Review the organization of the project at the system design phase, commence monitoring that performance, review the communications between the project team and management, and review the project definition and other miscellaneous considerations, such as detail work programs.
- Checkpoint 5 — Review detailed design output reports, the method of developing these reports, the

documentation of the reports, and the project management.

■ Checkpoint 6 — Review the design of the computer process, the design file requirements, the design input requirements, and generally review the project management.

■ Checkpoint 7 — Review the equipment requirements and determine the installation approach and the adherence to the data processing departmental standards.

■ Checkpoint 8 — Review the cost-benefits, the adherence to the data processing departmental standards, and the general project management to date.

The detailed design and programming phase is made up of 10 tasks:

1. Organize the project (Checkpoint 9)
2. Document data base files
3. Design source documents in detail
4. Prepare program run write-ups (Checkpoint 10)
5. Flowchart, code, test, debug, and document programs
6. Plan the system test
7. Plan the conversion
8. Develop control procedures
9. Develop clerical procedures (Checkpoint 11)
10. Obtain management approval

At the quality control checkpoints of this phase, EDP audit review is concerned with the following:

■ Checkpoint 9 — Review the organization of the project, the equipment considerations, planning considerations, and any other miscellaneous considerations, such as specialized competence or steering committee participation. Generally monitor the performance of the project team and review their communications with management.

■ Checkpoint 10 — Review the documentation of the data base files, the design source documents, and the program run write-ups.

■ Checkpoint 11 — Review the detailed system design, the programming and debugging, the plan of the system test, the plan for conversion, and the development of the clerical procedures that may accompany any of these plans.

The system test phase is made up of eight tasks:

1. Organize the project (Checkpoint 12)
2. Review system for adherence to standards
3. Create test data
4. Perform system test
5. Evaluate test results
6. Train users and data processing personnel
7. Build masterfiles (Checkpoint 13)
8. Approve/disapprove test results

At the checkpoints, the EDP auditor will perform the following actions:

■ Checkpoint 12 — Work continuously with the system development people throughout this phase to ensure that the system runs according to specifications. This is the beginning of the system test. In this phase, the auditor reviews the organization of the project in this area, the equipment considerations, the planning, monitors the performance, and takes care of any other miscellaneous considerations that may arise.

■ Checkpoint 13 — This checkpoint, too, requires continuous monitoring during Tasks 2 through 7 of this phase. The auditors are working hand in hand with the system and programming personnel to review the system for adherence to standards, create test data, build masterfiles, and take any other necessary actions to test the system. This phase requires the most time of any of the 15 checkpoints. Unlike the previous checkpoint activities of the EDP auditor, these require more continuous involvement on his part. The audit effort spent on the previous checkpoints will have prepared him for these two important efforts that lead to the thorough test of the computer application system for adherence to user needs and audit requirements.

The conversion phase is made up of four tasks:

1. Organize the project (Checkpoint 14)
2. Conversion
3. Monitor system performance (Checkpoint 15)
4. Final acceptance of system

At the last two checkpoints, the EDP auditor makes his final assessment of the computer application system.

■ Checkpoint 14 — Review the project organization and planning, monitor the performance during this phase, review the communications with management, and take care of any other miscellaneous considerations.

■ Checkpoint 15 — Review the system functions, the user capability, the computer operations, the system organization, the completion of assignments, documentation, and any other miscellaneous factors.

Finally, the auditors in this organization found it useful to perform an additional checkpoint activity. This is a postimplementation review, designed not only to examine the computer application system in operation, but also to evaluate the effectiveness of the checkpoint procedures themselves. As data processing technology changes, so also must the EDP auditors' procedures change to reflect the new technology, particularly that being increasingly used to support computer application system development.

IMPLEMENTATION CONSIDERATIONS

The major conditions for implementing the quality control checkpoints are:

■ The data processing department must have developed data processing standards and procedures that the EDP auditor can check for compliance during the computer application system development.

- The data processing department must have developed a formal phased development procedure, similar to that illustrated.
- The EDP auditor can then identify the quality control checkpoints at which he can perform his audit review.

When these conditions have been established, the EDP auditor can become part of the review team that monitors the creation of new computer application systems. When his role is clearly specified in this way, and carefully integrated with the various data processing steps, the EDP auditor's contribution can be effective not only in assuring that audit control objectives are met by the new system, but also in ensuring the cost-effective completion of the computer application system development.

As we have seen, much documentation is required for the technique to be effective. First, data processing standards and development procedures must be documented. Auditing department quality control checkpoints must likewise be documented so that each quality control checkpoint is associated with a development task and so that the operations the auditor will perform are clear. When this is done, the EDP auditor can review the development with regard to data processing standards and predetermined EDP audit quality control checkpoint procedures, and can make commonsense evaluations.

This technique requires little maintenance beyond that needed to update audit procedures to conform to changes in data processing standards and development procedures. However, the internal audit department should constantly reevaluate its own quality control checkpoint procedures to institute any changes found effective in practice.

TRAINING REQUIREMENTS

The EDP audit training requirements are summarized in Table 31-1. To be fully effective, however, the EDP auditor should have a thorough grounding in data processing concepts and development techniques. This need not be an in-depth knowledge of particular technical details, but should be a broad knowledge of data processing. Some computer technical expertise is required during testing — Checkpoints 12 and 13.

Non-data-processing personnel can become familiar with the technique in about two months, but they generally require four to six months additional specialized data processing training in order to interface effectively with data processing designers and programmers. Considerable advance preparation is required since the auditor should review current data processing departmental standards in detail prior to performing the quality control checkpoint reviews.

Table 31-1

SYSTEM DEVELOPMENT LIFE CYCLE TRAINING REQUIREMENTS

Knowledge Area	Level*
Data processing principles and concepts	XX
Computer application system structure	X
Computer application system controls and procedures	XX
Data management	X
Computer service center controls	X
Application system development controls	XX
Computer application programming	X

* XX = Advanced; X = Basic.

COST FACTORS

This is an extensive technique and can take considerable time to develop. The initial development cost of the technique can, therefore, be substantial in organizations where no formal data processing standards currently exist. For most organizations that will not prove to be the case. Where such standards exist, EDP audit review of the standards and procedures, taken together with the plan illustrated here, should lead quickly to an effective plan for quality control checkpoint review.

The effort required to perform audit reviews according to the checkpoint will, of course, depend on the magnitude of the development. Experience indicates that the EDP auditor can expect to take from two to six man-days to effect a working arrangement with a data processing development team, and from two to six additional days performing the reviews at each checkpoint, except for Checkpoint 13. As we saw previously, the EDP auditor is continuously involved here and, in consequence, may require from 10 to 60 man-days to make the reviews needed.

As a further guide, the approximate percentage of total EDP audit time required in each checkpoint is shown in Table 31-2. For best results, the technique requires substantial audit effort. As the size and importance of the development increases, the audit effort increases proportionately. The cost of its application also means that its use, in full detail, should probably be limited to sizable data processing developments. For lesser developments, the technique can be abbreviated or replaced by less stringent reviews.

Table 31-2

TIME REQUIRED FOR EDP AUDIT OF CHECKPOINTS

Quality Control Checkpoint		Percentage of EDP Audit Time	
Project definition phase	1	5%	15%
	2	5	
	3	5	
System design phase	4	5%	33%
	5	5	
	6	10	
	7	3	
	8	10	
Detailed design and programming phase	9	5%	22%
	10	8	
	11	9	
System test phase	12	5%	20%
	13	15	
Conversion phase	14	3%	10%
	15	7	

EVALUATION OF EFFECTIVENESS

The performance of EDP audit reviews of data processing developments using the quality control checkpoint technique is effective in ensuring the development of computer application systems that are effective in meeting user needs, more auditable, less prone to error, and more easily modified. These attributes are of benefit to data processing internal auditors and to users.

Experience with data processing computer programs is that the time spent to prevent errors is more than compensated for in decreased maintenance costs. Further, by making early reviews more formally and more carefully, one can substantially reduce the costs associated with eliminating discovered errors — often by a factor of two or more. Thus, carefully conducted development reviews, such as those done following the quality control checkpoint technique, are well worthwhile.

Chapter 32

SYSTEM ACCEPTANCE AND CONTROL GROUP

When the EDP auditor determines to monitor and review the computer application development process, he faces the choice of how best to perform the review. Although the substance of the review is unchanged, the EDP auditor may choose to perform the review himself or to rely on the efforts of another group. To perform the review himself is the choice made by many EDP auditors, even though substantial effort and training may be required to do an effective job. The fact that much of the training required has to do with data processing rather than with EDP auditing has, among other factors, caused the auditors at a large insurance company to decide upon another approach. The company has established, in the data processing department, a Systems Acceptance and Control group to perform systematic reviews of computer application system developments and to create and maintain effective computer application system standards, particularly in the area of auditability.

TECHNIQUE OVERVIEW

A Systems Acceptance and Control group is part of the data processing department. Its function is to provide a focus for the continual review and monitoring of significant computer application developments. In an organization such as the insurance company visited by SRI where internal audit emphasizes operational audit, the use of a surrogate to audit development activities is a valuable technique. Furthermore, since the auditor is never directly involved with the application development, there can be no possibility of a loss of independence on the part of the internal auditor.

Besides its review function, the Systems Acceptance Control group must promote and maintain computer application standards regarding auditability and user control. These standards are complementary to those established in data processing. Where the latter emphasize the standards and procedures that promote effective and cost-beneficial application development and computer operations, the standards developed by the System Acceptance and Control group stress those procedures that should be incorporated in new computer applications to ensure the fidelity of their operations, not only within the data processing department, but also in the interface to user areas.

APPLICATION EXAMPLE

A Systems Acceptance and Control group need not limit its activities to any particular control area. At the organization visited by SRI, the Systems Acceptance Control group has limited itself to ensuring that proper controls are instituted in data processing. It is concerned with proper handling of user input documents, with proper machine processing, with good program controls, with output correctness, with user output distribution controls, and with restart and recovery processes. It does not consider those complementary controls that might be established in data processing user organizations to ensure that their use of the data processing facilities is correct. In this organization this latter is still the province of the internal auditor.

The advantage of a Systems Acceptance and Control group is that it ensures that new computer application system developments result in properly controlled computer application systems that meet those standards against which subsequent EDP audit will assess the operational system. Thus, a Systems Acceptance and Control group reduces the cost of performing an operational audit because there is greater assurance that proper controls are in place. The audit effort needs to concern itself not so much with the existence of controls as with their effective operation.

LIMITATIONS AND CONSTRAINTS

There seem to be no essential limitations to the use of a Systems Acceptance and Control group in any organization of sufficient size. Once the view is taken that new computer application developments should be subject to thorough and continual audit review, the decision has been made to expend the necessary resources to accomplish such reviews effectively. Here, the only choice was whether to bear such costs in the internal audit department or to create a new group to effect the reviews. The choice of the latter course was determined by many factors. Important among them was the desire of internal audit to concentrate on operational audits and a feeling that too close association with a computer application could compromise the audit of that system in an operational audit.

IMPLEMENTATION CONSIDERATIONS

To implement a Systems Acceptance and Control group, an organization should consider the following steps. Before installing a Systems Acceptance and Control group, an informal committee composed of data processing and internal audit staff should determine the best group structure and develop a charter for the Systems Acceptance and Control group. This experimental period may last from one to two years and should encompass the development of at least one major computer application system. Following such an experimental period, it will be possible for an organization to determine the proper place for the Systems Acceptance and Control group and determine its charter.

In the company under discussion, the Systems Acceptance and Control group has been placed in the data processing department at the same level as the data control group, the machine operations group, and the systems development group. All report to the vice-president of data processing. Although the Systems Acceptance and Control group is in the data processing organization, it is independent of the other groups and can therefore perform its function appropriately. Currently, the Systems Acceptance and Control group is staffed with data processing people who have had some audit training. The internal EDP auditor, who participated in the Systems Acceptance and Control experimental committee prior to the formal establishment of the Systems Acceptance and Control group, no longer takes an active role in the Systems Acceptance and Control group. Rather, its operations are subject to operational audit, as are those of any other groups in the organization. Training for the Systems Acceptance and Control staff encompasses techniques of systems development, techniques of systems controls, and knowledge of the audit function. The cost of a Systems Acceptance and Control group depends on its size. The cost of its operation is roughly proportional to the number of members in the group itself. The example Systems Acceptance and Control group has a staff of 5 in a total data processing staff of some 600. Whether that ratio is appropriate for a Systems Acceptance and Control group is not known but it may be taken as an initial guide.

TRAINING REQUIREMENTS

Since the EDP auditor is not directly involved with the Systems Acceptance and Control group once it is established, the training requirements should not be directed to the auditor, but rather to a member of the Systems Acceptance and Control group. Since the group is part of the data processing department, the training can be expected to be more deeply rooted in data processing concepts and techniques. In this company, the members of the Systems Acceptance and Control group have a deep knowledge of the procedures of data processing and of computer application development practices, supplemented with training in audit techniques.

This is in contrast to the training required to develop an EDP auditor, in which case the usual process is to train an auditor in data processing skills. In this organization, however, it is felt that the kind of detailed knowledge of application testing and application development procedures required for monitoring a development is such that it is more effective to train a professional data processor in those audit techniques needed, than to train an auditor to the depth required in data processing.

Table 32-1 summarizes the training levels required for effective performance in the Systems Acceptance and Control group.

COST FACTORS

The costs of a Systems Acceptance and Control group are directly dependent on the size of the group in relation to the total data processing budget. In this company, they are about 1% of the personnel costs. The time and effort to develop the group concept and to create its charter were considerable. A committee composed of representatives of data processing and internal audit met regularly for two years and spent some three to four man-years in all.

Table 32-1

SYSTEM ACCEPTANCE AND CONTROL TRAINING REQUIREMENTS

Knowledge Area	Level*
Data processing principles and concepts	XX
Computer application system structure	XX
Computer application system controls and procedures	XX
Data management	XX
Computer service center controls	XX
Application system development controls	X
Computer application programming	X

*XX = Advanced; X = Basic.

Yet the direct cost of the group is perhaps better understood when the group is specifically identified and is not simply part of the budget of another organization. By identifying such review costs explicitly, one can obtain a clearer idea of their magnitude and the corresponding benefits.

However, the existence of the Systems Acceptance and Control group does not automatically mean that the level of costs is held at the percentage indicated. Some part of the data processing development effort will also be devoted to the activities of control and application system testing. In addition, some internal audit effort will need to be expended in the same area. However, here it is felt that the clear identification of the role is a benefit not readily obtained by any other technique.

EVALUATION OF EFFECTIVENESS

By establishing the Systems Acceptance and Control group, this organization created a continuing unit responsible for controls in computer application systems. The existence of such a standards organization and monitoring group for auditability and control considerations emphasizes their requirements for proper controls and provides a strong mechanism to ensure their presence in new application systems. Whatever the controls are, the Systems Acceptance and Control group made it easier to install, maintain, and ensure their effectiveness in meeting this company's control objectives.

The effectiveness of the Systems Acceptance and Control group is measured, in the long term, by the effectiveness of the application system controls and the audit recommendations following an operational audit. The existence of a Systems Acceptance and Control group falls in the "ounce-of-prevention-pound-of-cure" category, in that it should prevent the development of ill-controlled systems and lead to positive operational audits.

The Systems Acceptance and Control group has been effective. As the internal EDP auditor has become concerned more with the prevention of computer abuses than with their detection, the establishment of an ongoing group tasked to inhibit the growth of badly controlled systems has been valuable. In this well-controlled organization with a strong Systems Acceptance and Control group, operational audit has reduced the cost of auditing the data processing area and has enabled the internal auditors to concentrate on examining controls in user areas.

Chapter 33

CODE COMPARISON

Code comparison entails comparison of two copies, made at different times, of the program coding for a particular application. The objective of this technique is to verify that program change and maintenance procedures and program library procedures are being followed correctly. The auditor uses the output of the comparison to identify changes that have occurred between the making of the two copies. He then locates and analyzes the documentation that was prepared to authorize and execute the changes. This technique supports compliance testing rather than substantive testing. Code comparison is especially useful for auditing programs that perform critical business functions and are subject to continuing change.

TECHNIQUE OVERVIEW

Two approaches to code comparison are possible: comparison of source code and comparison of object code. Source code is the program code expressed in the form used by the programmer (e.g., coding in COBOL, FORTRAN, PL/1). Object code is code in the form executable by the computer. Before a program can be executed by a computer, the source code must be processed (compiled) by a program called a compiler to convert source code to object code. While source code is easily interpreted by a skilled programmer, object code is quite time consuming to interpret, even by a very skilled programmer. Thus, when the auditor compares two versions of a program in source code form he is not actually comparing the forms of the code that are directly executable by the computer. He is, however, comparing two versions of the code that are much more understandable than the object versions. Experience has shown this technique is most appropriate when used on key or sensitive programs.

Figure 33-1 schematically depicts the alternative approaches to code comparison. The figure shows four possibilities for code comparison. The first of these is the comparison between two versions of source code taken at different times (Time 1, Time 2). The second possible comparison is between the object code forms derived from the source codes taken at Time 1 and Time 2. The other two possibilities are both object code comparisons that are derived from comparing the object code taken at an earlier time (Time 1 or Time 2) with the object code derived from a compilation of the source code conducted under control of the audit staff. The third and fourth cases, although they also test conformance to the procedures, focus on conformance to the compilation and library procedures within the data processing department.

It should be recognized that a comparison made between two object code versions of a program is at least as valid as between two source code versions, but it is more difficult to utilize in a constructive way. This is because any discrepancies found between two object code versions will be very time-consuming to translate backwards into the more easily understood source form. Therefore, the auditor is handicapped in testing procedure compliance based solely on discrepancies in object code versions. For this reason, source code comparison offers the most convenient avenue for the testing of program change procedure compliance. On the other hand, the most effective of these two techniques for auditing media library procedures is object code comparison.

The main advantage of this technique is the thoroughness and relative ease with which program changes can be specifically identified to satisfy the need for compliance auditing of change and library procedures. Programs to implement the code comparison are relatively simple and run with only a modest expenditure of machine time. Therefore, costs attendant on the use of this technique are relatively low. The technique is most successfully used when regularly scheduled copying of programs is undertaken. In this case, the copy of each program is compared with the prior generation and is then set aside for comparison in the next cycle.

The programs that compare the two versions of the code typically sequence the two versions in a side-by-side fashion, assigning a common series of line numbers and identifying inconsistencies between the two versions. One such program currently available from a computer manufacturer provides two separate listings, one for each version, each citing the differences in the opposing version and

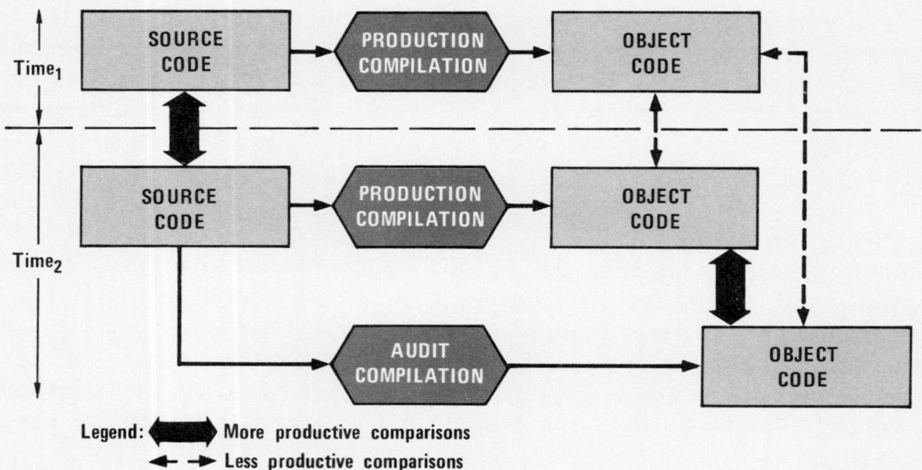

FIGURE 33-1 ALTERNATIVE MODES OF CODE COMPARISON

using the common line number as a reference. Other programs provide similar facilities.

TYPICAL PROCEDURES

Internal audit procedures for using the code comparison technique, after the computer programs are available for use, are as described in the following paragraphs.

Step 1 — Selection of Computer Application Programs to Be Audited — The internal auditor determines which computer application programs are to be verified by the code comparison technique. Selection criteria applied by the organizations participating in this study are the degree of risk incurred through program misuse (such as would be encountered in payroll, accounts payable, and negotiable securities systems) or selected spot-checking.

Step 2 — Planning of Procedure — The internal auditor verifies that the correct copies of the computer programs to be verified are available. He secures the cooperation of the data processing department in scheduling the computer run. He ensures the availability of the pertinent program change authorizations.

Step 3 — Supervision of Code Comparison Program — The internal auditor ensures that the correct versions of the application programs are processed by code comparison. Frequently, this is accomplished by the auditor being present while the computer run is in progress.

Step 4 — Examination and Reconciliation of Test Results — The internal auditor examines all differences produced by the code comparison procedure and reconciles each difference to the program change authorizations. All differences and their resolutions are documented.

APPLICATION EXAMPLES

A manufacturer of business equipment has defined a category of "sensitive programs" that are subjected to code comparison of source programs. A sensitive program is one in which unauthorized program changes could result in substantial fraud losses to the firm. This criterion applies to 15 or 20 programs, all of which are in the payroll and accounts payable area, out of a total of 600 to 700. Half of these sensitive programs are code-compared each year by the internal audit group, while the other half are audited by the external auditor. In the following year, the roles are interchanged.

Source code comparison has been in large-scale use for over a year by the internal audit staff of this firm. The director of internal auditing feels that this audit method has been very successful. No fraud has been uncovered but several gaps in the control procedures were found. A new change control procedure has been formulated to correct these deficiencies.

The source code comparison programs are utilized only for auditing of change control procedures. Although some consideration is given to the functional content of the application program changes, the primary audit objective is to establish a system in which no person who has access to the programs can accomplish a fraud alone.

A major oil company wrote its own code comparison test program. Application programs selected for audit by a code comparison are routinely copied on a periodic basis. At audit time, the current version of the application program is source code compared to the latest copy. Differences are reconciled by the internal auditor by tracing back to the program change authorization file. The current version of the source code is then compiled and the resulting object code is compared with the latest copy. Differences are again reconciled by the internal auditor. In the opinion of this particular organization, object code comparison does not work well due to different versions of the compilers and operating systems. Source code comparison has worked well.

LIMITATIONS AND CONSTRAINTS

The use of the source code comparison technique and the computer programs available to perform code comparison impose no substantial limitations in and of themselves; their use is straightforward and uncomplicated. Perhaps the major concern of the internal auditor should be to understand what the test programs do not do, because the test programs cannot address directly the legitimacy of the functions of the computer application programs. Thus, the internal auditor should not be lulled into a false sense of security about the functional integrity of the computer code, even though the code comparison technique can fully prove the integrity of the code from a change procedure standpoint. The analysis by an internal auditor to determine if the source code changes are appropriate can be time-consuming and difficult.

IMPLEMENTATION CONSIDERATIONS

The implementation of a code comparison program requires careful planning if audit objectives are to be met. The code comparison program, whether purchased or written, must functionally and operationally fulfill audit objectives. Procedures must be instituted to ensure that application programs to be audited are copied and retained under adequate control and security. These procedures and their effective adherence are especially important in the use of this audit technique, as the audit objective of code comparison is the evaluation of normal program change and library procedures.

TRAINING REQUIREMENTS

Training requirements for internal audit personnel in the use of the code comparison method are significant. Familiarity with computer program listings is required, as the code comparison software typically prints such a listing as a means to indicate discrepancies. Knowledge of computer programming is highly desirable if the internal auditor is to be able to reconcile particular sections of program coding to particular program change authorizations. Assistance of the data processing staff can be solicited, although this is somewhat self-defeating; the code comparison technique is primarily intended to disclose unauthorized program changes by the data processing staff.

Training requirements to implement a code comparison program depend on the type of program secured. A program procured from a vendor requires little programming knowledge and only a knowledge of the required functions. A code comparison program written "in house" requires programming skill — either on the part of the internal audit staff or the data processing staff. Specific knowledge areas are summarized in Table 33-1.

Table 33-1

CODE CONVERSION TRAINING REQUIREMENTS

Knowledge Area	Level*
Data processing principles and concepts	XX
Computer application system structure	—
Computer application system controls and procedures	XX
Data management	—
Computer service center controls	X
Application system development controls	—
Computer application programming	XX

* XX = Advanced; X = Basic; — = Not required.

COST FACTORS

Cost factors of the code comparison technique are twofold: program acquisition and program use. Acquisition cost of one source code comparison program available from a vendor is approximately $1000; costs to develop such a program would probably exceed that amount, although features tailored to the organization's particular audit objectives could be included. Cost factors in use are almost entirely computer time charges. These are relatively "fast" programs requiring relatively little computer time. Specific costs depend upon the computer being used and the size of the application programs being audited.

EVALUATION OF EFFECTIVENESS

The code comparison audit technique is effective in the evaluation of program change procedures and of program library procedures. No evidence whatsoever is provided on application program efficiency, or on data reliability. The experience of organizations using the technique indicates that code comparison is best utilized to verify that proper procedures are being followed in "sensitive" applications (i.e., those where the risk of loss is high, though nothing inherent to the technique itself precludes its use elsewhere). This technique has a limited usefulness, but will continue to be an effective technique for the specific audit purposes described above.

APPENDIX

RESEARCH METHODOLOGY

RESEARCH METHODOLOGY APPENDIX

INTRODUCTION

Research methodology was established by SRI in consultation with the Steering Committee and the Advisory Committee of The Institute of Internal Auditors (IIA). Two complementary objectives guided the formulation of the research methodology. First, specific audit and control techniques were to be identified, documented, and included in the final SRI reports based on visits to leading businesses and government organizations. The results of this phase of the research were intended to be the documentation of specific audit and control techniques of proven value. In addition, SRI field interviews were intended to obtain management perspectives relating to trends and expertise in EDP audit and data processing control.

Second, a mail survey was designed to identify practices and trends in internal audit and in data processing for broad segments of business and government, both domestic and international. The mail survey also was utilized to further identify management perspectives relating to trends and expertise in EDP audit and data processing control. The procedures used in both phases of this SRI research were coordinated with and approved by The Institute of Internal Auditors.

FIELD INTERVIEW METHODOLOGY

Field interviews were conducted at over 40 selected businesses and government organizations in the United States, Canada, Europe, and Japan. These companies were believed to be leaders in their approaches to data processing and/or internal auditing in the data processing environment. The two objectives of these field interviews were first, to document audit and control techniques proved to be of value in the experience of the company interviewed. The documentation of these findings was intended to be the basis for the knowledge transfer among practitioners in data processing and EDP audit. The second objective was to obtain a knowledge of management's perspective on data processing and internal audit through interviews with top management, data processing management, and internal audit management. Such information was intended to supplement that collected through the SRI mail surveys, and to provide insight to aid in analyzing and evaluating the results of the mail survey.

FIELD INTERVIEW DEVELOPMENT

Before designing the structured interview guidelines for the field interviews, SRI developed a general outline of the final reports. These final report outlines were reviewed and tentatively approved by members of the Steering Committee of The Institute of Internal Auditors. Utilizing these draft report outlines, SRI then identified all the data elements that would need to be collected to answer the appropriate questions and write the final reports. The data elements were also reviewed and tentatively approved by members of the IIA Steering Committee. The next step was to design a structured interview guide that would be used by all the interviewers during the on-site visits. This interview guide went through two iterations, after which members of both the IIA Steering Committee and SRI approved its final format. A pretest was conducted using the structured interview guide. The results of this pretest were reviewed with the IIA Advisory Committee. Comments and recommended improvements agreed upon between the IIA Steering Committee and SRI were then incorporated. This second draft of the structured interview guide was then fully field-tested at two independent and unrelated sites. After this test, the interview guide was slightly modified and put into its final format.

Company Selection and Interviews

A list of more than 175 organizations was selected jointly with The Institute of Internal Auditors from over 300 candidate organizations proposed by the Advisory Committee of The Institute of Internal Auditors. A subsequent telephone survey performed by SRI was used to qualify the audit techniques and controls in use at these candidate organizations. As a result of the telephone survey, the list was reduced to 75 organizations. Of these, 45 were ultimately visited by SRI (see Table A-1). In selecting the organizations to be visited, an effort was made to maintain a degree of representation in terms of industry groups and company size as well as not to duplicate the documentation of the same audit techniques and controls. Because only leaders in internal audit and data processing were sought, however, the companies visited tended to be large commercial, industrial, and governmental organizations. Company selection included organizations in Canada, Europe, and Japan as well as in the United States. Contact was also made with several small data processing users in an attempt to identify audit and control techniques that would achieve a degree of consistency in the information gathered and documented.

Early experience at conducting the field interviews indicated that the management-oriented questions in the interview guide were being answered repetitively e.g., management personnel from widely diversified industries and geographical areas were giving the same answers to the same questions. As a result of this, after the first 10 to 15 field interviews, the interview guide was simplified to the extent that less than one-half of the management-oriented questions were still used. This decision was made because it was felt that SRI had collected all the data that were necessary in this area. With regard to the portion of the interview guide that was used to document audit and control techniques, the interviewers found that it was difficult to secure information on cost factors, training requirements, and the effectiveness of audit techniques and controls.

Field interviews were scheduled not to exceed one week at each organization. When possible, a member of the organization's public accounting firm accompanied SRI during the interviews. This occurred in only about half of the interviews because of difficulties involved in scheduling or because some organizations requested that their public accountants not be present during the SRI interviews. In other cases, IIA personnel or Steering Committee personnel accompanied the SRI interviewer. Most of the interviews were conducted in two or three days, with an additional four to five days to document interview findings. Follow-up telephone calls were used to secure information to supplement that obtained during the on-site visits. In a few instances, a follow-up visit was made to secure supplementary information and to review documentation prepared as a result of the first visit. In many instances, documentation prepared by SRI as a result of the field visit was sent to the organization visited for its approval and/or revision.

Field Interview Data Analysis

The results of interviews with management were manually tabulated on cards for subsequent analysis and evaluation during the preparation of the final reports. This information was sorted into various topical areas for analysis in an attempt to identify management attitudes and concerns relative to internal audit and control in a data processing environment. Much of the information included in the final reports was based on a synthesis of these field interview data. Although one small data processing user, a midwestern municipality, was visited, most of the audit and control techniques that were documented and included in the final reports were secured from larger organizations with well-established internal audit and data processing programs.

Table A-1
ORGANIZATIONS VISITED DURING SRI FIELD INTERVIEWS

Aetna Life & Casualty
Arthur Andersen, Japan
Atlantic Richfield Company
Bell Canada
British Columbia Hydropower
Burlington Northern
Burroughs Corporation
City of Wyandotte, Michigan
Coopers & Lybrand, Tokyo
Del Monte Corporation
Eastman Kodak Company
Federal Home Loan Bank, Des Moines
Federal Reserve Bank, Kansas City
Fuji Bank, Japan
The B. F. Goodrich Company
Harris Trust and Savings Bank
The Hartford Insurance Group
IBM Corporation
Investors Diversified Services, Inc.
Lever Brothers, London
Lockheed Missiles and Space Division
Los Angeles County
3M Company
Manufacturers Hanover Corporation
Massachusetts Mutual Life Insurance Company
Mervyn's Department Stores
Michigan Bell
The Northern Trust Company
Pacific Gas and Electric Company
J. C. Penney Company, Inc.
N. V. Philips, Holland
Price Waterhouse, Japan
Shell Oil Company
Skandia Group, Sweden
Standard Oil Company (Indiana)
State Farm Insurance Companies
Tenneco, Inc.
Touche Ross & Co.
Twentieth Century-Fox
U.S. Department of Agriculture
United California Bank Association
United States Steel Corporation
Western States Bankcard
Xerox
Yale University

Interview Procedure

The interview procedure used included a preinterview questionnaire, a structured interview guide, and a specific format for the documentation of EDP audit tools and techniques. Before each field visit, the scheduled interviewer contacted the director of internal audit or the manager of data processing and explained the objectives of the research and the procedures to be used. A brief preinterview questionnaire was then sent to collect basic information about the organization and scope of the candidate's data processing and internal audit activities. Data processing and internal audit managers were asked to identify audit and control techniques they felt would be of interest for purposes of the research. When this questionnaire was returned to SRI, it was evaluated in terms of the tools and techniques in use at the specific organization and their applicability to the research. This usually led to another telephone conversation before the interview.

After receiving and analyzing the preinterview questionnaire, the SRI interviewer contacted the director of internal auditing or manager of EDP to establish a mutually convenient agenda and interview schedule. Interview agendas were subject to modification to avoid visits that would duplicate EDP audit or data processing controls documented during previous interviews.

Interview guides were established for visits with top management, data processing management, and internal audit management, respectively. Because a number of SRI staff members were involved in conducting field interviews, these guides were established to obtain a consistent and structured interview approach.

MAIL SURVEY METHODOLOGY

Questionnaire Development

Before designing the questionnaire, SRI developed general outlines of the final reports which were reviewed and tentatively approved by members of the IIA Steering Committee. These outlines were then used to develop both the structured interview guide and the mail questionnaires. SRI developed three separate questionnaires, one each for executive management, internal audit, and data processing respondents.

Using the tentative final report outlines, SRI identified all the data elements that would need to be collected to develop the appropriate questions and write the final reports. These data elements were also reviewed and tentatively approved by members of the IIA Steering Committee.

Next, SRI wrote the questions to be included in each of the three questionnaires. After these questions were assembled into their respective questionnaires, they were reviewed by the IIA Steering Committee and were substantially modified. Many of these modifications were suggested by the Advisory Committee to which the Steering Committee looked for guidance. After incorporating these modifications into the three questionnaires, SRI field-tested the questionnaire at four sites. SRI personnel hand-carried the questionnaires to selected sites and asked the appropriate management, auditing, and data processing personnel to complete the questionnaires. After this field test, the questionnaires were slightly modified again to improve clarity, brevity, and completeness.

These drafts were then reviewed by SRI and The Institute of Internal Auditors during a week of meetings held at Menlo Park, California. Substantial changes were made during these meetings. The drafts resulting from these meetings were submitted to The Institute of Internal Auditors and were reviewed one more time. This review resulted in final approval of the mail questionnaires. The final versions of the questionnaires were printed in three booklets (management, internal audit, and data processing), each of a different color.

Samples

The Institute of Internal Auditors and SRI chose seven different sampling frames from which to select organizations in the United States, Canada, Western Europe, and Japan. Four of these frames (lists) were used to select U.S. organizations, as follows:

1. A sample of 261 organizations in regulated industries (finance, insurance, utilities, and transportation) and 239 organizations in nonregulated industries (e.g., manufacturing, retail, education) was selected at random from Computer Intelligence, Inc.'s file of commercial, industrial, and institutional organizations that have computer installations with a monthly rental greater than $20,000. The organizations in this sample represent the approximately 3,000 largest (nongovernment) U.S. organizations with computer systems. This sample is referred to as the Primary U.S. Mail Survey.

2. A sample of 500 organizations was randomly selected from Dun and Bradstreet's Million Dollar Directory, which includes all (nongovernment) U.S. organizations with a net worth of $1 million or more. Organizations in this sample did not necessarily have computer installations. This sample is referred to as "smaller U.S. organizations."

3. The state auditor in each state was included in the survey. At a later date, questionnaires were readdressed to specific agencies (known to have computers) in 15 states from which a response had not been received.

4. A sample of 48 federal agencies was selected purposively (nonrandomly) on the basis of the likelihood that each would have information relevant to the study.

The Canadian sampling frame was defined as all organizations that were listed on International Data Corporation's file of Canadian computer installations and that had computer systems with a monthly rental value of at least $24,000. A random sample of 250 organizations was selected from this sampling frame.

The 150 Western European organizations selected comprise a systematic random sample of Europe's approximately 600 largest industrial firms. The following nations (and the number of organizations in each) were included in the survey: Austria (3), Belgium (6), Denmark (2), Finland (2), France (19), Germany (47), Great Britain (37), Italy (7), the Netherlands (8), Norway (1), Sweden (13), and Switzerland (5).

The Japanese sample consisted of the 73 largest industrial and commercial organizations in Japan, as listed in *Fortune* magazine, August 1975.

Of these samples, only the Primary U.S. Mail Survey was intended to provide statistically supportable generalizations. The other surveys were included to supplement this survey and to provide an international and governmental flavor to the study.

Survey Procedures

For all surveys of U.S. organizations, the following procedures took place: One week before the questionnaires were mailed, an "advance" letter was sent to the chief executive officer (CEO) of each organization in the samples. This letter informed the recipients that they were about to receive the questionnaires and told them of the nature of the study, its sponsors, and so on.

All three questionnaires (for management, data processing, and internal audit) were sent to the CEO in each organization. Included with each questionnaire was a cover letter from SRI, a brief study description, and a postage-paid preaddressed return envelope. The CEO was asked to complete and return the management questionnaire himself and to forward the other two questionnaires to the appropriate individuals in his organization. He was also requested to complete and return the enclosed postage-paid postcard asking for the names and titles of the individuals to whom he was forwarding the audit and data processing questionnaires.

Ten days after the questionnaires were mailed, reminder letters were sent to all CEOs, thanking them for their participation if they had already responded and urging them to respond if they had not yet done so. Ten days after this letter was sent, a second reminder was mailed to those who had not responded by that time. Reminders were also sent to persons whose names had been received on the returned postcards. In addition, thank-you letters were sent to each respondent.

Procedures for the Canadian, Japanese, and European surveys were similar to those described above, with the following exceptions: "Advance" letters were not sent to potential respondents in any of these surveys; Canadian CEOs received only one follow-up letter; some telephone reminders were made to CEOs in Japan. For the European survey, the cover letters were translated to each respondent's native language, but all questionnaires were in English. This fact almost certainly lowered the response rate from non-English-speaking countries.

Survey Response Rates

Table A-2 shows, for each survey, the number of organizations in the sample frame, the sample size, and the number of organizations from which at least one completed questionnaire was received.

Telephone Surveys of Nonrespondents

Two separate telephone surveys of nonrespondents were made. The first, a survey of nonrespondents in the smaller U.S. organizations sample, was prompted by a very low return rate and a high number of firms reporting having no EDP facilities. In this survey, 50 firms which had not responded to the mail survey were contacted to find out why the questionnaires had not been completed and returned to SRI. On the basis of the results of this survey, it was estimated that approximately 50% of the sampled organizations did not have EDP facilities.

The second telephone survey was of a sample of nonrespondents in the Primary U.S. Mail Survey sample. In this survey, 100 organizations were contacted to estimate the possible differences in response between mail survey respondents and nonrespondents. To this end, selected questionnaire items were asked of management, audit, and data processing representatives at each firm contacted. The telephone responses were then compared with the mail responses, and the results were reviewed by SRI in an effort to identify systematic differences between the two groups. Although some differences were found, it was concluded that they did not affect the conclusions presented in these reports.

Processing Survey Returns

All returned questionnaires were hand-edited for legibility and procedural mistakes and then were keypunched with 100% verification. Once entered onto the computer, the data were submitted to internal consistency and range checks.

Weighting Procedures

To make the returns from the Primary U.S. Mail Survey organizations as representative as possible of

Table A-2
SURVEY SAMPLE SIZES AND RESPONSE RATES

Survey	Size of Sample Frame	Size of Sample	Number of Organizations Responding	Percent of Organizations Responding
Primary U. S.	3,337	500	283	57%
Smaller U.S. Organizations	30,000	500	101	20
U.S. State Agencies	50	50	23	46
U.S. Federal Agencies	48	48	33	69
Canada	1,008	250	113	45
Europe	600	150	52	35
Japan	73	73	19	26

that sampling frame, two weighting procedures were performed:

1. As noted above, the sample for this survey consisted of 261 organizations in regulated industries and 239 organizations in nonregulated industries. These sample sizes represent an oversampling of regulated industries and a concurrent undersampling of nonregulated industries. (Approximately 25% of the regulated firms on the sampling frame were selected for the survey, while only about 10% of the listed nonregulated firms were selected.) Consequently, in order to combine the group's results in a meaningful way, it was necessary to weight the responses according to their original proportions in the sampling frame.
2. Early analysis of the returns of the Primary U.S. Mail Survey organizations indicated that larger companies were more likely to respond than were smaller companies, and that regulated companies were more likely to respond than nonregulated companies. To eliminate the unduly heavy effect of the larger companies and of those in regulated industries, the companies were grouped into categories on the basis of their size (gross sales and number of employees) and their regulatory status. Each category's responses were then weighted according to their proportions in the sample.

The computed weights are shown in Table A-3.

TABULATION OF SURVEY RESULTS

The results of each survey were tabulated by computer using the Statistical Package for the Social Sciences (SPSS). Response-frequency distributions were obtained for each question on each of the three questionnaires, and cross-tabulations of responses to each question by the seven surveys and the site visits were produced. For the Primary U.S. Mail Survey, cross-tabulations were also performed on selected questions within each questionnaire and between questionnaires. In addition, for selected questions, responses were tabulated separately for organizations in regulated industries and for those in nonregulated industries.

Table A-3
WEIGHTS ASSIGNED TO THE RESPONSES FROM THE SURVEY — PRIMARY U.S. MAIL SURVEY

Regulated Industries

Gross Sales (in millions)	Number of Employees 0-699	700-3999	4000+
Missing data	7 (n=11)*	5 (n=12)	6 (n=4)
$0-$49	7 (n=21)	6 (n=4)	———†
$50-$199	7 (n=15)	6 (n=46)	6 (n=3)
$200+	10 (n=2)	5 (n=27)	6 (n=32)

Nonregulated Industries

Gross Sales (in millions)	Number of Employees 0-699	700-3999	4000+
Missing data	28 (n=6)	33 (n=4)	13 (n=4)
$0-$49	37 (n=16)	24 (n=8)	9 (n=1)
$50-$199	———	20 (n=9)	18 (n=11)
$200+	———	17 (n=9)	14 (n=42)

*n = number of companies responding.
†A line indicates that no companies in that category appeared in the sample.

GLOSSARY

GLOSSARY

Every attempt has been made to avoid the use of technical terminology and jargon, either accounting, internal audit, or data processing. Some terms are, however, used that have a meaning that may not be clear to some readers. Accordingly, a brief glossary of selected terms is provided.

Auditability — Features and characteristics of an information system, either computer-based or manual, that allow verification of the adequacy and effectiveness of controls and verification of the accuracy and completeness of data processing results.

Audit Trail — Accounting control procedures that provide documentary evidence of processing so that original transactions can be traced forward to related records and reports, and records and reports can be traced back to their component source transactions.

Computer Application System — A computer-based information system that includes both manual and computerized procedures for source transaction origination, data processing and record keeping, and report preparation.

Data Base Management — A systematic approach to storing, updating, and retrieving information from central files, where many users or even remote locations have common access.

Data Communications — The movement of computer and coded information by means of electrical transmission systems.

Distributive Processing — An arrangement of computers within an organization that has several separate computer facility locations. The computers are interconnected to work in a cooperative manner rather than as conventional single-location facilities.

EDP Audit — A specialized phase of internal audit that pertains to the review, evaluation, and verification of the controls governing data processing, and the results of data processing, such as data files and reports.

Internal Controls — Procedures that ensure the accuracy and completeness of manual and automated transactions, origination and processing, record keeping and reporting, and the avoidance, detection, and correction of errors and omissions.